Pausanias

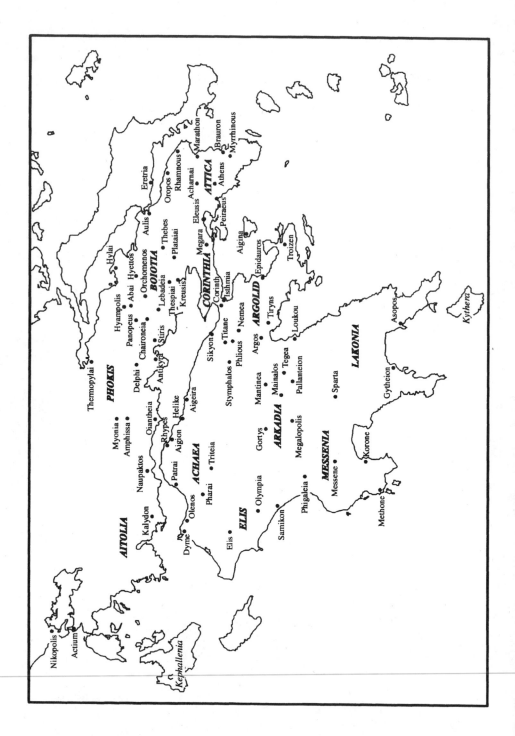

PAUSANIAS

Travel and Memory in Roman Greece

Edited by
SUSAN E. ALCOCK,
JOHN F. CHERRY, &
JAŚ ELSNER

OXFORD
UNIVERSITY PRESS
2001

OXFORD
UNIVERSITY PRESS

Oxford   New York
Athens   Auckland   Bangkok   Bogotá   Buenos Aires   Calcutta
Cape Town   Chennai   Dar es Salaam   Delhi   Florence   Hong Kong   Istanbul
Karachi   Kuala Lumpur   Madrid   Melbourne   Mexico City   Mumbai
Nairobi   Paris   Sâo Paulo   Shanghai   Singapore   Taipei   Tokyo   Warsaw

and associated companies in
Berlin   Ibadan

Copyright © 2001 by Oxford University Press

Published by Oxford University Press, Inc.
198 Madison Avenue, New York, New York 10016

Oxford is a registered trademark of Oxford University Press.

Library of Congress Cataloging-in-Publication Data
Pausanias : travel and memory in Roman Greece / edited by S.E. Alcock, J.F. Cherry & J. Elsner.
      p. cm.
   Includes bibliographical references and index.
   ISBN 0-19-512816-8 (cloth)
      1. Pausanias. Description of Greece.   2. Greece—Description and travel—Early works to
1800.   3. Greece—Antiquities.   4. Greece—Historiography.   I. Alcock, Susan E.   II. Cherry,
John F.   III. Elsner, Jaś.
DF27.P383 P38 2000
938'.09—dc21   00-022461

Frontispiece: Location of principal places mentioned in the book.

9 8 7 6 5 4 3 2 1
Printed in the United States of America
on acid-free paper

For Silvia, Britten, and Bax

Preface

This volume is dedicated to the principle that Pausanias deserves more—and more ambitious—treatment than he tends to receive. The editors independently discovered, early in their careers, what Konstan here calls "the joys of Pausanias": Elsner, for instance, through his interest in pilgrimage; Alcock with her exploration of landscapes in Roman Greece.[1] Part of the fascination of using him, we found, was that the *Periegesis* was infinitely richer, and more stimulating, than one would have expected from its conventional reputation. Over the centuries, Pausanias has, of course, been considered a happy survival, a marvelous cornucopia, an ancient Baedeker, and a sturdy resource to mine for names and places, fragments of history, and versions of myth. He has also been periodically decried as long-winded, tedious, inaccurate, and digressive. The idea that the *Periegesis* might have much more to offer than either an interesting factual bricolage or a way to generate checklists of civic cults was, at least until quite recently, rarely considered.

That situation is now changing drastically, and for once, a clear turning point can be identified. It is fair to say that this collection of essays would never have had its genesis without the revolutionary work of Christian Habicht and his 1982 Sather Classical Lectures, published in 1985 as *Pausanias' Guide to Ancient Greece* (rev. ed., 1998). Habicht not only offered a passionate and cogent defense of the Periegete's accuracy but also began to place the account in its own historical and social context and to push the edges of its interpretive envelope. His decision to take Pausanias seriously, coupled with a simultaneous growing curiosity about the world of the so-called Second Sophistic, has contributed to a florescence of "Pausaniacs" at the end of the millennium: books,[2] conference proceedings,[3] an *index verborum*,[4] a fast-growing assemblage of articles throughout the 1990s, and—not least—two new critical editions with extensive commentary book by book[5].

This outburst, as Henderson notes, parallels a similar surge of interest at the turn of the nineteenth century, which one might perhaps call the "First Pausanian Sophistic." Habicht provided a seminal impetus in late-twentieth-century studies, in part by uniting the best in German- and English-language scholarship and by combining historical and archeological approaches; likewise, the late nineteenth century left an extraordinarily erudite and interdisciplinary scholarly monument to tower over *its* Pausanias, in the form of the great six-volume translation and commentary made by Sir James George Frazer (1854–1941). At the center of Frazer's work throughout the 1880s and 1890s ("a work on which I have spent, well or ill, some of the best years of my life"),[6] his *Pausanias*'s *"Description of Greece"* not only is an authoritative summation of its field across all areas of contemporary study in all the European languages but was also a crucial opening and scholarly supplement to Frazer's more famous and influential interests, including the study of mythology, ritual, and anthropology.[7] Pausanias, it would seem, appears to intrigue people in a fin-de-siècle, transitional or commemorative mood, as well as scholars (like Frazer and the "Cambridge Ritualists") eager to transgress disciplinary boundaries, whether in the late twentieth century or the late nineteenth.

We decided to fan the flames of the modern Pausanian revival by assembling within a single volume a diverse cast of characters: classicists, ancient historians, archaeologists, art historians, historical geographers, intellectual historians, and cultural anthropologists. The intention was very much to expand both the appreciation and the scholarly exercise of Pausanias: in part by inviting some of the best people available in their respective fields to participate, in part through the sheer "shock value" of seeing such variant disciplines and such different investigations placed side by side.

The collection is divided into three roughly equal parts: "Pausanias and his *Periegesis,* the Traveler and the Text"; "Studies and comparisons"; and *"Nachleben."* The divisions reflect some of the main currents, realized or potential, in research on the *Periegesis*. Part I might be perceived as the more traditional in tone, dealing as it does with the individual author and the nature of the composition. In chapter 1 Jaś Elsner immediately establishes the case for seeing the *Description of Greece* as a literary construct and not as a farrago to be dismembered at will. Ewen Bowie, in chapter 2, responding to the work of Habicht, contributes an up-to-date review of central questions regarding the authorship, inspiration, date, and motivations lying behind the *Periegesis*. In chapters 3 and 4, C. P. Jones and Ian Rutherford each explore specific topics within this broader ambit: the former investigating and assessing the source for much of Pausanias's information (his guides), the latter reexamining the arguments over the heated question of whether or not his activities could be termed "pilgrimage."

Part II offers a selection of studies that spring from the text of the *Periegesis*. In two cases, these focus on specific sections of Pausanias: the Chest of Kypselos (5.17.5–19.10) in chapter 7, by A. M. Snodgrass, and the *Messeniaka* of Book IV in chapter 8, by Susan E. Alcock. Snodgrass uses the famous chest at Olympia, and Pausanias's lengthy exposition of it, to approach a body of issues: not only how Pausanias interpreted works of art but also just what types of challenges particularly attracted him. Pausanias's account of the "many sufferings of the Messenians" (4.29.13), for Alcock, offers one means to explore his strategies of narrative and what they reveal and conceal; their impact on later readings of Messenian history and archaeology is patent. In the two other chapters of Part II, Pausanias is drawn into a wider discourse. In chapter 6 Ada Cohen situates Pausanias in the realm of artistic innovations, with the unprecedented visual representation of travel in Hellenistic and Roman times. James I. Porter, also does something quite unusual, in chapter 5, by juxtaposing Pausanias with Longinus and Dio Chrysostom. By considering the *Periegesis* as something fit to be discussed in the context of other authors and their creations, entirely new fields of inquiry are opened up, be it Pausanias's relation to the "sublime" or his place in the wider literary landscape of the Second Sophistic.

Part III explores the *Nachleben*—the powerful, if much underestimated, aftershock of Pausanias's writings that followed his rediscovery and printing in the Renaissance. Because of his very matter-of-factness, his apparent transparency, Pausanias was long taken (equally matter-of-factly) at harmless face value. Only recently have the judgments and instincts he instilled in his innumerable later readers begun to be realized in their full efficacy. In chapter 10, J. M. Wagstaff's exegesis of the work of Colonel William Martin Leake (1777–1860)—and of Leake's reliance on Pausanias—demonstrates the interdependence of travelers' accounts through the ages. Susan Buck Sutton approaches this same dependence from a different angle in chapter 9, describing how one small section, a couple of sentences in Book II, has guided the viewing of a single Greek valley for nearly two millennia. Far from a blameless Baedeker, Pausanias emerges as a central shaping force in perceptions of just "what was important" (and what not important) about Greece—perceptions that are astonishingly pervasive still today. In chapters 11 and 12, John Henderson and Mary Beard explore this phenomenon in the late nineteenth century, through the figures of "feeble Farnell" and Jane Ellen Harrison and their very different readings of the *Periegesis*. The former bought completely and complacently into an elevated, Olympian version of the Pausanian vision, whereas the latter, exploring the cracks and "byways of Pausanias's synthesis," perceived that the Periegete actually "lets out quite unconsciously a good part of the secret"—a secret of loss and change and nostalgia.

In addition to the main commissioned essays, we invited a number of specialist commentators—some expert in Pausanian studies and others in adjacent fields such as the historiography of travel—to respond to the book with shorter pieces. These are placed at the end of their respective parts, where we thought they would best resonate with the other essays. Among the commentators, Stephen Bann and Paul Cartledge both examine Sparta: the former from the point of view of Enlightenment travel writing and the latter as an ancient historian inevitably indebted to Pausanias. Bettina Bergmann contrasts the visual inscription of the Roman landscape with Pausanias's textual inscription, while Mario Torelli casts a professional editor's eye once again on the complex interrelations of text and archaeology. David Konstan and John F. Cherry both weigh the *Periegesis* against later writing and travel: the first looking at the joys of nostalgic return to an ancestral homeland (not only in Pausanias but also in the somewhat later text of Athenaeus), the second exploring the *Description of Greece* within the specific genre of travel literature. Finally, in the book's coda,

Jaś Elsner explores some ways in which the Romantic vision of Joseph Michael Gandy's *The Persian Porch and Place of Consultation of the Lacedemonians* (reproduced on the book jacket and in figure 27) is itself a visual commentary on and transformation of the text of Pausanias.

It is worth mentioning explicitly that Pausanias's text has been known by various titles in English, and we have used these interchangeably throughout the volume. Indeed, we do not know what Pausanias himself called his work. The earliest name recorded (by Stephanus of Byzantium) is Περιήγησις Ἑλλάδος and the title *Periegesis* (literally meaning a "leading around") is perhaps the most technically correct.[8] The native English word that most closely approximates this is probably *description,* which explains the popularity of *Description of Greece* and *Descriptio Graeca,* respectively, as English and Latin translations of the title. Perhaps a little more culturally misleading is the title *Guide to Greece.* While not incorrect in itself (in that "guiding" usefully alludes to the "leading around" implicit in the word *periegesis*), that formulation nonetheless evokes modern guidebooks such as the *Blue Guide* or the *Baedeker,* works that represent a somewhat different genre of writing from a travel book.

The book began many years ago with a whispered conversation in the library of the Faculty of Classics at the University of Cambridge. Many people have since aided it along its subsequent course. The editors would like to thank, not least, all the contributors, who provided their chapters and commentaries in good time and (usually) good order. The smoothness with which the book came together, we suspect, is further confirmation that Pausanias has become a subject of wide interest, a "hot property." We also thank the Getty Research Institute for the Humanities, for allowing the use of Joseph Michael Gandy's *The Persian Porch and Place of Consultation of the Lacedemonians,* and in particular Claire Lyons for her help and advice in finding the image. Thanks also to our editors and their associates at Oxford University Press, New York. The Office for the Vice President of Research, the University of Michigan, provided funds to aid in the book's preparation.

February 2000

S. E. A.
J. F. C.
J. E.

Contents

PART I

PAUSANIAS AND HIS *PERIEGESIS*, THE TRAVELER AND THE TEXT

Structuring "Greece"

Pausanias's Periegesis *as a Literary Construct*

L ike Pausanias gazing from the sea at the promontory of Sounion (1.1.1), let us for a moment entertain a prospect simultaneously invigorating and humbling. Imagine that the travel book of Pausanias is more than a compendium of detailed observations and errant digressions to be cherry-picked by archaeologists or anthropologists or historians for its useful accounts of lost monuments, peculiar rituals, or unusual variations of standard histories or myths. Imagine that the text is a creative contribution to a particular genre of ancient travel literature, one that has not, alas, fared very well in the lottery of survivals from antiquity. Imagine that the *Periegesis of Greece* was written carefully—its every sentence and description deliberately placed according to a conscious pattern of selection that might reveal (if only we could but uncover its motivations and underpinnings!) the ways that Greek-speakers of the second century A.D. actually thought about their world. The book has, after all, a beginning, a middle, and an end, and it was structured, not to create a simple description of where a traveler happened to tread (coupled with his not particularly original prejudices about history and art), but rather to orchestrate an argument designed to influence its readers in ways as much ideological as factual.

Underlying this desire for the text of Pausanias to be taken as a wonderful text, which deserves to be read closely and carefully as a coherently conceived piece of writing, is the conviction that travel literature in general is more than a mine to be excavated by historians in search of facts. Classicists have shown some reticence in taking the literature of travel seriously as a genre with its own specific ideological concerns, generic preoccupations, and formal problems.[1] But in other disciplines—not least geography, anthropology, history, and literary studies—there has been a growing recognition of the significance of travel writing for such contemporarily popular themes as postcolonialism, imperialism, and Orientalism.[2] My aim here is not to ram Pausanias into the procrustean bed of modern cultural concerns, though whether we can ever entirely avoid doing this to an ancient author is perhaps a moot point. Rather, I want to take his writing seriously *as writing*. I shall attempt to identify, both on the large scale of the text as a whole and also on the more manageable scale of a particular case study (I shall focus on Olympia, in Books V and VI), how some of the text's various techniques for communication—from "descriptions" to "digressions"—may work to tell a particular and carefully selected set of stories and to structure an imaginative geography.[3]

The Question of Genre

Why, one might ask, is the *Periegesis of Greece* structured as it is? One answer might be that it broadly reflects the way Pausanias traveled and the order in which he wrote his diaries and subsequently revised them for publication. We are certainly offered ten books, which begin *in medias res,* rounding the heights of Sounion on the Attic coast by boat before disembarking and entering the Piraeus (1.1.1), and which end *in medias res* on the Locrian coast at Naupactus with a wonderful tale about a vision in a dream, an act of healing by Asclepius, and the votive dedication of a sanctuary that Pausanias finds in ruins (10.38.13).[4] Effectively, the text works as a kind of written map, encircling the Peloponnese (the subject of Books II–VIII), opening and closing to the north with Attica (Book I) and then Boeotia and Phocis (Books IX and X). Of course, the textual status of both the opening and the ending has been questioned—with Bowie (chap. 2, this volume) postulating the possibility of a missing preface, and others worrying about potential losses at the end.[5] As it stands, Pausanias's *Periegesis* eschews the portentous *proemia* of ancient geographies (such as the openings of Strabo and Pomponius Mela) for the practical bustle of more utilitarian handbooks (like the *Periploi,* in particular the *Periplus Maris Erythraei*).[6] The ten books do appear to have been written one after the other in the order in which they stand.[7] However, they are interconnected by over one hundred cross-references—about two-thirds referring the reader back to earlier parts of the narrative, while the rest anticipate matters still to come.[8] The ten books themselves, so far as we can tell, are roughly as Pausanias wrote and ordered them (at least the text is so divided in the manuscripts),[9] and the book titles (*Korinthiaka, Lakonika,* and so forth) are independently attested in the margins of a late thirteenth-century manuscript of excerpts from Strabo and Pausanias collected by the Palaeologan florilegist Maximus Planudes (ca. A.D. 1260–1310) in Constantinople.[10]

The text's structure, then, fulfills a double purpose. First, it takes the reader on a vicarious journey in the author's footsteps, following the roads he walked to the places he saw (even retelling the tales his guides told him).[11] And it does so in the order that he himself traveled—recapitulating, through the time spent reading, the passage of (a longer) time spent on the road. In other words, to appropriate the insights offered by Michel de Certeau's reading of Montaigne's famous essay on cannibals, the text is both a narrative of space (composing and distributing its places and monuments according to their positions along the roads of Greece) and a construction of how the reader is to relate to that space (the space called "Greece"—or rather at 1.26.4, *panta ta hellenika,* "all things Greek")[12] by being placed in the phenomenological position of traveler.[13] Like Herodotus's account of the Scythians in Book IV of the *History* (to which Pausanias is of course heavily indebted as both a historical and a historiographic model),[14] the *Periegesis* combines a representation of the Other (in this case of Greece by a Greek-speaking foreigner, a native of Asia Minor)[15] with the self-accreditation of the text as witness for the Other (in that authentically Greek histories and myths are made to "speak" through and for the Greek monuments that Pausanias and his readers encounter in the course of the description). Hence, like Herodotus's Book IV and Montaigne's *Of Cannibals,* Pausanias's *Periegesis* constructs itself within what de Certeau calls the "heterological tradition, in which the discourse about the other is a means of constructing a discourse authorized by the other."[16] If we believe Pausanias to be a pilgrim,[17] then the simultaneous act of recapitulating a sacred journey (through writing) and allowing others to partake in the pilgrim's original ritual of traveling (through the act of reading) is itself the final stage of the author's pilgrimage through Greece.[18] Pausanias's choice of structure—apparently so simple and unreflective—has the virtue of naturalizing, through the relentless "and next we come to this place" quality of the travel book, his text's subtle reflection on Greece as other (the Ionian ethnographer's exploration of the foreign through its own monuments, myths, and stories) and simultaneously as self in the Greek-speaking pilgrim's confrontation with all that is most essential and most sacred about the Greek tradition, just as Philostratus's Apollonius would confront the sites of Greece as both pilgrim and object of pilgrimage in a hagiography penned within half a century of Pausanias's *Description of Greece.*[19]

Second, the text's systematic signaling of cross-references somewhat denies the haphazardness one may feel in being put in the hands of this particular traveler on this particular set of journeys. When we pass the figures of Hermes that constitute the boundary between Argolis and Laconia (as well as the division of Books II and III: 2.38.7 and 3.1.1), for instance, we learn that the autochthonous founder and first king of Laconia, Lelex, had two sons, Myles and Polycaon, who was younger. "Polycaon," we are told, "retired into exile, the place of his retirement and the reason for it I will set forth elsewhere" (3.1.1). Only at 4.1.1, at the opening of the *Messeniaka,* do we learn that the exile was to Messene, which Polycaon conquered and named after Messene, his wife. At the very least, whatever plan originally impelled his route, by the time Pausanias came to revise and to publish his book, it had acquired an interconnectedness beyond the mere juncture of regions and roads on the terrain. From the reader's viewpoint, despite the apparent waywardness of wandering from village to village on the roads through the wastes of Roman Greece,[20] Pausanias's cross-references show a clear structure in mind: he knows at Sparta that he will shortly be off to Messene, as he knows in Messene (4.29.12) that he will later be in Arcadia (8.51.5–8), and so forth. His text has it both ways: it is simultaneously a spontaneous journey into the famous sites and unknown byways of Greece and, at the same time, it is a carefully structured compendium of chosen regions, fashioned and ordered through travel into a continuous narrative and rendered through "digressions" (historical, religious, mythological, art historical, ethnographic) into a careful portrait, a deliberate ideology, of "Greece."

The ten books begin with Attica and end in Phocis, the first and last books each focusing principally on one of the major tourist and religious sites in Roman Greece: namely, Athens (1.2.1–30.4) and Delphi (10.5.5–32.1).[21] In the center, straddling the middle pair of books, V and VI, is the site that all Greeks acknowledged as the very center of Greece: namely, Olympia, with the Olympic Games, which brought all the Greeks together in the Panhellenic festival par excellence.[22] Pausanias himself hails Olympia, along with Eleusis, as being at the apogee of the experience of Greece:

> Many are the sights to be seen in Greece, and many the wonders to be heard; but on nothing does heaven bestow more care than on the Eleusinian rites and the Olympic Games. (5.10.1)

Other ancient writers agree.[23] Interestingly, here it is not the places as such but the ritual activities attached by tradition to those sites that Pausanias singles out as of central importance. Is this literary patterning of "Greece" in a structure that emphasizes its most historic, sacred, and artistic sites and places the three principal cultural/cult centers (at least from a second-century A.D. perspective) at the beginning, middle, and end of the text to be understood as simply a matter of chance or as no more than a particular traveler's itinerary? Or can one be tempted to regard the choice of opening, close, and center as a deliberate kind of mapping—a marrying of the actual topography of Greece with a *"géographie imaginaire"* in which the very structure of Pausanias's space tells a story of myth-historical evocations *through* the bald accumulation of sites visited?[24]

In effect, despite the apparent structure, which moves the pace of the text (its reading and writing) along a set of roads (the appearance of an actual journey through real space), in fact each site is a cipher for something else. The places themselves, their material monuments and appearance, cannot be separated from the activities that take place there, whether in the present or in the deep past, or from the stories, myths just as much as histories, associated with them. Every footstep to a new site is equally a narrative movement to a new story or a new ritual. In a grand site, like Olympia, each new victor statue or sacred altar is an entrée to a further anecdote. Together, woven as a web of interconnected cross-references, the places and objects (that part of the Pausanian project which actually is a descriptive topography of Greece) constitute much more than a material account: they evoke, they *are* an imaginative geography in which each site and all the sites together are infused with the myth-historical essence of Greekness. To put this in the terms employed by Porter (chap. 5, this volume), every discrete item (every spot, every ruin) in Pausanias's text—and therefore in the landscape of Greece, out of which it has entered the text—evokes that ideal fantasy of "Greece" which might be called the "Pausanian sublime."

The different books themselves are quite deliberately varied as to the balance of monuments and associated myth-historical narratives. Books I and VI begin *in medias res;* Books II and IX have brief historical introductions (constituting 1 and 2½ Teubner pages, respectively);[25] Books V, VIII, and X have rather longer introductory sections (10, 10, and 6½ Teubner pages respectively);[26] while Books III, IV, and VII offer very long myth-historical narratives before Pausanias plunges us into any monuments (nearly 25, 69, and over 45 Teubner pages, respectively).[27] Despite modern readings, which focus on specific areas of modern concern and hence rupture the integrity of the text (so that we get an archaeological Pausanias, a religious Pausanias, Pausanias as historian, and so forth), the range of interests in the *Periegesis* cannot really be separated. Together (as a seamless whole) they constitute that peculiar imaginative entity which is Pausanias's Greece.

The monuments themselves are interspliced with myth-history in different ways in the different books. For example, in Book IV (the *Messeniaka*), the monuments are separated from, and subordinate to, the long and involved history of the Messenian people, their exile and their return (on which, see Alcock, chap. 8, this volume):[28]

> Hitherto my account has dealt with the many sufferings of the Messenians, how fate scattered them to the ends of the earth, far from the Peloponnese, and afterwards brought them safely home to their own country. Let us now turn to a description of the country and cities. (4.29.13)

Likewise, in Books VII and VIII, general histories of Achaea and Arcadia precede the description of noteworthy sites. By contrast, in Book IX, Pausanias gives relatively brief local histories before each stage of his visit, so that the description of Plataea (9.2.1–9.4.4) follows the short history of Plataea (9.1), while that of Thebes (9.7.6–9.17.7), including the long digression on Epaminondas (9.13.1–9.15.6), follows the history of Thebes at 9.5.1–9.7.6.

All this may seem to be rather peculiar by the standards of other, generally more rhetorical and high-flown works of the period (e.g., the writings of Lucian or Aelius Aristides) or of much less ambitious and more practical projects than that of Pausanias (like the *Periploi*). But I would argue that our preconceptions of Pausanias (which have in general tended toward seeing him as possessed of very little flair) are strongly influenced by his own structuring of the text, which is in itself far from innocent or naive. Nothing makes the *Periegesis of Greece* seem more like a Baedeker to the modern reader than the initial plunge *in medias res,* without so much as a word, let alone a generous chapter or two, of grandiloquent introduction on the pattern of a Pomponius Mela or a Strabo. The fact that the text's beginning, middle, and end collide with the principal sites of Greece works to lull the reader into the expectation that these sites are indeed its main topic.[29] There is even a certain literary delicacy in the chiastic structure whereby moments of significant pause for aesthetic description or contemplation in both Athens and Delphi (i.e., at the beginning and the end) coincide with fresco cycles by the famous fifth-century painter Polygnotus of Thasos (1.22.6–7 and 10.25.1–10.31.12), with both the mural programs described pursuing Homeric themes.

To my mind, these various considerations make it hard to resist the conclusion that the *Periegesis* not only is carefully structured but was so for a purpose. Its genre—which combines ancient periegetic traditions of local description with travel and pilgrimage accounts—owes much to the distant model of Herodotus,[30] to a deliberate contrast with the pattern of (nonphenomenological) ethnographic historiography best exemplified by Strabo, and to the Roman Imperial development of an official geographic tradition under Augustus and Agrippa (which itself had roots, to be sure, in the Hellenistic world).[31] The fact is that the choice of genre was a *choice*. This is not as obvious in the case of Pausanias, who wrote nothing other than his *Periegesis* (so far as we know), as in that of Lucian, who chose to write a pilgrim's travel narrative in Ionic Greek (*De dea Syria*), along with numerous works in other genres from fiction and rhetoric to dialogues and satire.[32] In the case of Lucian, the apparent sincerity, piety, and lack of satirical spin of the narrator's voice in *De dea Syria* has frequently led to an assumption of naiveté on the part of the writer and hence a denial of Lucian's authorship.[33] In the case of Pausanias, the same qualities have led to the author's dismissal as "a man made of common stuff and cast in a common mould," with "his intelligence and abilities . . . little above the average, his opinions not very different from those of his contemporaries."[34] In both cases, the dismissal is really a rejection of a genre of writing and the constraints on authorial freedom necessarily imposed by the choice of literary model. One may as well dismiss poetry for being in verse.

Centering Greece: Making a Text out of Olympia

At the opening of his paper in this volume (chap. 7), Snodgrass makes the interesting observation that Pausanias's descriptions may be read as his own (one might even say travel writing's own) version of what manifests as *ekphrasis* in more rhetorical texts. Such descriptions, like the other kinds of "digression" in the text, mark special moments for pause and appreciation, for reflection and commentary, within the pace of the narrative of sightseeing. They vary the pace—both that of the vicarious journey as we walk in the author's steps and that of the reader as he or she struggles through what Frazer called "the tedium of the topographic part" of Pausanias's work.[35] I would add that the extended passages—in particular, the descriptions—share with *ekphrasis* in the poets the quality of reflecting generally on aspects of the work as a whole, in the small and focused scale of a particular set of objects or monuments. Let us test this hypothesis by narrowing down this discussion to a case study of Pausanian Olympia (Books V and VI). By focusing not only on the site and its various remains but also on the text's "digressions" and especially its descriptions of chosen objects, perhaps we can unravel some of the text's meanings as they are contained in its structure. Apart from its intrinsic interest, Pausanias's Olympia has an unusual status within the whole text: one site (uniquely) straddling two books at the very center of his Greece.

The two books on Elis (V and VI) may be taken together (see fig. 1). After the introductory myth-historical section (5.1.1–5.5.2), Book V moves swiftly toward Olympia along the road north from Kyparissiai in Messenia (where Pausanias ends his *Messeniaka,* 4.36.7, at the river Neda).[36] After brief accounts of

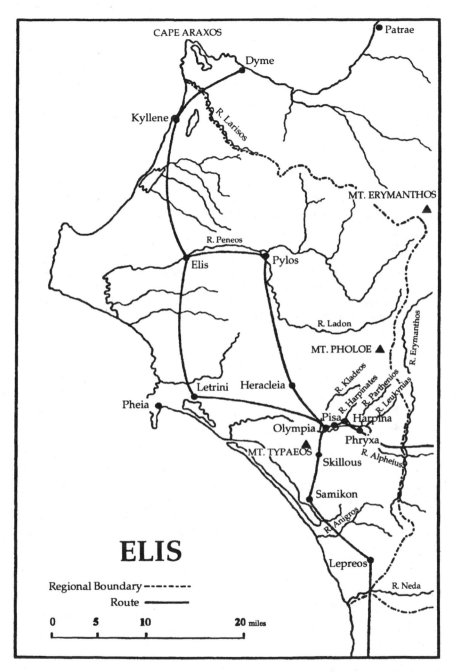

FIGURE I. Map showing Pausanias's route through Elis. (After R. E. Wycherley, *Pausanias, "Description of Greece": Companion Volume to the Loeb Edition*, vol. 5 [Cambridge, Mass., 1935; rev., ed. 1955].)

Lepreos and Samikon on this road (5.5.3–5.6.8), Pausanias offers a geographical and myth-historical introduction to Olympia itself and to the Games (5.7.1–5.9.6). He remains in or around Olympia for the bulk of and across Books V and VI, only leaving at 6.21.3. The rest of Book VI, like the opening of Book V, takes the reader along the main roads out of Olympia to see the sights eastward at Pisa and Phryxa (6.21.6–6.22.4), to Pylos and Heracleia, north of Olympia (6.22.4–7), and to Elis itself in the northwest (6.22.8–6.26.10). The book ends at the river Larisos, which constitutes the boundary of Elis and Achaea, the subject of Book VII.

The main discussion of Olympia itself is divided into eight substantial sections (see table 1).[37] Pausanias is very keen to distinguish and separate the three sets of sculptural monuments he describes in the Altis (i.e., images of Zeus, votive offerings, and victor statues, my numbers 4, 5, and 6 in table 1),[38] and he provides his readers with two programmatic statements of what he is doing:

> From this point my account will proceed to a description of the statues and votive offerings; but I think it would be wrong to mix up the accounts of them. For whereas on the Athenian Acropolis statues are votive offerings like everything else, in the Altis, some things only are dedicated in honor of the gods, and statues are merely part of the prizes awarded to the victors. The statues I will mention later; I will turn first to the votive offerings and go over the most noteworthy of them. (5.21.1)

> I have enumerated the images of Zeus within the Altis with the greatest accuracy. For the offering near the great temple, which is supposed to be a likeness of Zeus, is really Alexander, the son of Philip. . . . I shall also mention those offerings which are of a different kind, and not representations of Zeus. The statues which have been set up, not to honor a deity, but to reward mere men, I shall include in my account of the athletes. (5.25.1)

What is particularly interesting about these three sets of dedications and also the altars (number 2 in table 1) is that they all occupy the same relatively constrained space (of something less than 200 m[2]) within the boundaries of the Altis, or the grove sacred to Zeus (the word "Altis" is derived from *alsos,* "grove," 5.10.1),[39] in which the two temples of Zeus and Hera, as well as the treasuries, also stood. This means that almost the whole of Books V and VI (from 5.10.1 to 6.19.15, as well as the account of the Hippodameion, 6.20.7–

TABLE I. The Structure of Pausanias's Description of Olympia

1. The temple of Zeus, 5.10.1–5.12.8 (including the cult statue by Phidias, 5.11.1–9).
2. The enumeration of the sixty-nine altars in the Altis, 5.13.1–5.15.12.
3. The temple of Hera, 5.16.1–5.20.5 (including the Chest of Kypselos, 5.17.5–5.19.10).
4. The enumeration of the statues of Zeus in the Altis, 5.21.2–5.25.1.
5. The enumeration of votive offerings in the Altis (which are not statues of Zeus and which are not honors for men), 5.25.2–5.27.12.
6. The enumeration of victor statues in the Altis, 6.1.3–6.18.7.
7. The discussion of the treasuries, 6.19.1–15.
8. Mount Kronios to the north of the Altis and the racecourses to the east, 6.20.1–19.

9), takes place in the Altis.[40] This most sacred of Panhellenic spaces incorporates, "just as at Delphi" (6.19.1), buildings dedicated as treasuries by other cities (not only Greek ones)—Sicyon, Carthage, Epidamnos, Sybaris, Byzantium, Cyrene, Selinos, Metapontum, Megara, and Gela. Effectively, the experience of Olympia—which Pausanias describes as particularly blessed for its games (ἀγῶνι [5.10.1])—is distilled to the discussion of the sacred grove, into which the whole meaning and interest of the site are compressed. Instead of examining the contents of the Altis object by object as they stand, Pausanias chooses a series of thematic headings under which to group the key items. These he then proceeds to investigate in very different ways, each time effectively retracing his (and his readers') steps around the same sacred space with a different exploratory hat on (as it were). The deliberate comparison of the Altis with both Athens and Delphi—not just Greece's other most sacred sites but also Pausanias's own opening and close (at 5.21.1 and 6.19.1)—is significant in pointing to the place of the Altis within his conception of Greece.

The pilgrimage round the Altis is figured as a series of journeys, with objects grouped thematically. Two images that the sightseer would find next to each other on the site may thus appear in different sections, even in different books:

> Next to Pantarces is the chariot of Cleosthenes, a man of Epidamnus. This is
> the work of Ageladas, and it stands behind the Zeus dedicated by the Greeks
> from the spoil of the battle of Plataea. (6.10.6)

This Zeus is the subject of a lengthy description at 5.23.1–5, where the chariot of Cleosthenes is signaled as appearing later in the text. Effectively, this separation of items that are juxtaposed by topography and placement constitutes a kind of cataloguing by discrete categories in which the constituents of Pausanias's Greece belong in conceptual groupings that are neither simple nor haphazard. This taxonomy of objects (which may be the result of viewing the sites of Greece and thinking deeply about how best to structure them as a narrative or may precede the actual experience of visiting) certainly determines the representation of Pausanian Greece as discourse. The different categories of objects are separate not only in their places within the *Periegesis* but also by virtue of the kind of journey through which Pausanias sees fit to incorporate them in his account.

Altars

The account of the altars is entirely ritual centered, with Pausanias deliberately following the pattern of local liturgy in his enumeration and again feeling the need to say so programmatically (see fig. 2):[41]

> My narrative will follow the order in which the Eleans are accustomed to
> sacrifice on the altars. (5.14.4)
>   The reader must remember that the altars have not been enumerated in
> the order in which they stand, but the order followed by my discussion is that
> followed by the Eleans in their sacrifices. (5.14.10)

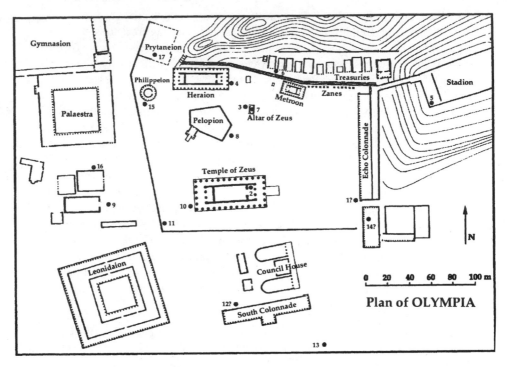

Gymnasion

Prytaneion
17

Philippeion
Heraion
15

Palaestra

Pelopion
Altar of Zeus
Metroon
Zanes
Treasuries

Stadion

Echo Colonnade

16

9

Temple of Zeus

10

11

1?

14?

N

Leonidaion

Council House

South Colonnade

Plan of OLYMPIA

0   20   40   60   80   100 m

12?

13

FIGURE 2. Plan of Olympia, with the likely positions of the altars numbered in the order of Pausanias's description. (After R. Etienne, "Autels et sacrifices," *Entretiens Hardt* 37 [1992]: 291–319.)

He explicitly eschews any kind of ordinary topographic logic, in order to take his readers on a vicarious sacrificial journey, whose temporal and spatial progress echoes the actual performance of sacrifice in a ritual that, we are told, takes place every month (5.15.10). After giving the layout of the altars and writing as if the sacrificial process were in progress ("they sacrifice to Hestia first, secondly to Olympic Zeus, going to the altar within the temple, third to ⟨ . . . ⟩, fourthly and fifthly they sacrifice to Artemis and to Athena," etc., 5.14.4–5),[42] Pausanias proceeds to explain the "ancient manner" of the Elean ritual, describing the details with his usual observant precision:[43]

> They burn on the altars incense with wheat that has been kneaded with honey, placing also on the altars twigs of olive, and using wine for a libation. Only to the Nymphs and the Mistresses do they not pour wine in libation, nor do they pour it on the altar common to all the gods. (5.15.10)

The nature of the trip round the altars (judged variously as "pedantic" and following a "very leisurely and erratic course")[44] requires Pausanias to retrace his steps more than once. Having begun at the altar of Olympic Zeus (5.13.8–5.14.3), he returns there twice—before the altar of the unknown gods (5.14.8) and when he comes to the altar of Zeus Kataibatos (5.14.10)—and finally for the third time at the end of his trip round the altars (5.15.9). It is at the second of these moments of return that Pausanias reminds us that he is structuring this part of his account according to the processional order of sacrifice rather than according to a pattern of topographic proximity. Before his final return to the altar of Olympic Zeus, Pausanias makes a brief excursus out of the Altis to the main altars in the surrounding buildings (5.15.1–6). Here he twice reminds us that he is "outside the Altis" ἐκτὸς τῆς Ἄλτεως [5.15.1, 4]),[45] before signaling his return to the Altis explicitly at 5.15.7. The very phenomenological nature of the description of the altars is a microcosm of one aspect of the pattern whereby Pausanias describes the whole of Greece. The altars figure as elements in a ritual experience which combines bodily movement with devotion, mythological and historical information, and religious detail. The constant return to a main center from which the different elements of the description branch out reflects the way all his books are structured as descriptions of the sites along the roads leading out from key local centers.[46]

Statues of Zeus

The account of the altars is sandwiched between the discussions of the two great temples in the Altis, dedicated to Zeus and Hera—very appropriately, since several of the altars must have occupied the space in between the two temples. On emerging from the Heraion (at 5.20.9–10), Pausanias mentions quickly the smaller temples known as the Metroon and the Philippeion, which flanked the temple of Hera to the east and west, respectively. He next embarks on his examination of the statues of Zeus (5.21.2–5.25.1). This time he follows a topographically motivated route circling the Altis clockwise from the Metroon via the foot of Mount Kronios to the northeast (where stands the platform displaying the set of statues known as Zanes, 5.21.1–18). Next, he moves southeastward toward the entrance to the stadium (5.22.1), south again to the Hippodameion (5.22.2), and further south to the entrance to the Bouleuterion near the southwest corner of the site (5.23.1). Finally, he returns northeast toward the temple of Zeus (5.24.3) and beyond it to the Pelopion (5.24.5). The statues provide the starting points for a series of discussions—most notably of the various crimes committed by Olympic competitors, for which they were fined and so provided the money to create the Zanes (5.21.2–18). By the time Pausanias has completed his list of images of Zeus and their dedicators, the reader is again impressed with the panhellenic nature of the sanctuary, since the statues' donors come from all over the Greek-speaking world. At the end of the list of images of Zeus, Pausanias briefly abandons the pattern of describing a class of objects according to their topographic proximity along a chosen route in order to jump back to the Bouleuterion (just south of the main site, apparently outside the Altis proper to judge by modern plans but explicitly defined as within the Altis at 5.15.8). This statue of Zeus is the one "most likely to strike terror into the unjust" (5.24.9). This is the image before which athletes, their fathers, brothers, and trainers, as well as the overseers of the races, take various oaths according to a specific ritual involving sliced boar's flesh (5.24.9–10).

The description of this category of images causes Pausanias to retrace his steps in the Altis, this time according to a different pattern from his journey round the altars. Just as his subject of interest is different (statues of Zeus rather than altars), so his mode of guiding the reader changes. Instead of a ritual-centered movement around the Altis, focusing on details of sacrificial action and divine mythology as he did with the altars, Pausanias here emphasizes dedicators, both private individuals and city-states (mentioning only a few artists), and myth-historical narratives of how the images came to be there. His account here, instead of evoking the simultaneously local and panhellenic nature of ritual at Olympia as with the altars, emphasizes the panhellenic constituency of those who came to worship at and adorn the site. Principally, this constituency comprises Greek-speaking states (the people of Cynaetha, 5.22.1; of Apollonia on the Ionian Sea, 5.22.2; of Leontini, 5.22.7; and so forth); but it also includes Romans in the person of Mummius (5.24.4). His pattern of movement is from one statue to the next according to their proximity in space, effectively circum-ambulating the site of the Altis clockwise before returning to the temples in the center.

Votive Offerings

The votive offerings follow the images of Zeus immediately (5.25.2–5.27.12). These too are enumerated according to a topographic pattern, which moves (with fewer signals to give us a precise sense of locations) from dedications on the periphery of the Altis by its walls (e.g., at 5.25.5 and 7) to a series "near the great temple" (5.25.8). The offerings of Mikythos, which are "numerous and not together" (5.26.2), and others near them (5.26.2–7) seem to be ranged close to the temple of Zeus to the north and east,[47] with a row of south-facing dedications adjoining the Pelopion standing opposite the north peristyle of the temple of Zeus (5.27.1–10). The section (and Book V itself) all but ends at the very center of the Altis (κατὰ μέσον μάλιστά που [5.27.11]) beneath the plane trees which presumably gave the Altis its name. Here there is a bronze trophy dedicated by the Eleans in celebration of a victory over the Spartans. Just as at the end of the description of the altars, so here Pausanias moves briefly outside his structure. The last dedication he mentions, the offering of the Mendeans (5.27.12), which he does not place and which therefore may not be under the plane trees in the center of the Altis, is one that he nearly mistook for a victor monument.[48] It thus bridges this section of the description with the account of victor statues at the opening of Book VI.[49]

The section on votive offerings takes the visitor around the site for the third time, giving the impression of a less linear topographic pattern than in the enumeration of statues of Zeus. Rather, it sketches areas of space and moves relentlessly inward—from the periphery, to a more central space (between the Pelopion and the temple of Zeus), and finally to the very center of the site itself. The monuments described are distinguished as usual by their dedicators and stories of origin or artists, emphasizing again both the panhellenic focus of the sanctuary and its venerable age (which reaches back beyond the extant offerings of Mikythos, 5.26.2–7, and their textual affirmation in Herodotus at 7.170, as Pausanias notes at 5.26.4, to the deep mythical past). These votive offerings include a monument whose impact is less aesthetic than magical: the remarkable bronze horse of Phormis, which is small and artistically inferior but the result of magical skills (ἀνδρός μάγου σοφίᾳ [5.27.3]). It contains the *hippomanes,* which sends stallions so mad with passion that they race into the Altis to make desperate love to the ugly, tail-less bronze (5.27.2–4). The horse of Phormis allows Pausanias to "digress" into "another marvel I know of, having seen it in Lydia" (5.27.5), and hence to bring the section to a climax with a series of stories about magical or divine intervention. The last offering discussed (before the two trophies at the end of Book V) is the bronze Corcyrean ox, which the god of Delphi specifically ordered should not be removed from the sanctuary but should be purified after a boy died when he hit his head against it (5.27.10).

Victor Statues

The first eighteen chapters of Book VI, an account of "the statues of racehorses and of men, whether those of athletes or ordinary men" (6.1.1), is Pausanias's fourth and last journey round the sanctuary space of the Altis (see fig. 3).[50] Not only is this by far the longest of the Altis descriptions, but it is also the place where Pausanias can dwell at length on the Olympic Games themselves, through the filter of the images of some of the most famous victors. He is careful at the opening to define the theme:

> My work . . . is not a list of athletes who have won Olympic victories, but an account of statues and votive offerings generally. I shall not even record all those whose statues have been set up . . . Those only will be mentioned who themselves gained some distinction, or whose statues happened to be better made than the others. (6.1.2)

Implicitly, and typically, the account of the victor statues stands simultaneously as an aesthetics of Classical statuary and a myth-history of the Olympic Games.

The journey round the victor statues is divided into two sections: the first discussing 168 statues between the Heraion in the northwest of the Altis and the Leonidaion in the southwest (6.1.3–6.16.9); and the second focusing on 19 statues between the Leonidaion and the main altar of Zeus near the center of the site (6.17.1–6.18.7) (fig. 3).[51] Although Pausanias offers very little topographical information here beyond saying that one statue is "beside," "near," or "next to" another, his route can be traced by relating the images he describes to the findspots of extant bases or other remains. Of the roughly two hundred victor monuments mentioned by Pausanias, some forty are known from recovered fragments.[52] His concentration on inscriptions would mean that any contemporary reader of his text would have had no problem following him. This last trip through the Altis is certainly the most museological. More even than the most conscientious of modern museum visitors, who may stop to read and

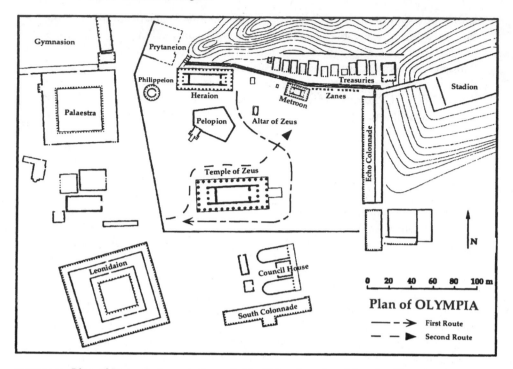

FIGURE 3. Plan of Pausanias's route through the Altis when describing the Olympic victor statues. (After H.-V. Herrmann, "Die Siegerstatuen von Olympia," *Nikephoros* I [1988]: 119–83.)

assess every label, Pausanias not only read but also took the trouble to transcribe—with remarkable care and precision—more than two hundred athletic inscriptions, usually attached to statue bases in the form of verse epigrams.[53]

The Altis as Text

This brief foray into Pausanias's Altis, which has assessed only his periegetic trips around the site in the open air—omitting both his account of the temple of Zeus and his discussion of the temple of Hera (with its remarkable collection of relics), as well as the treasuries—shows a topography being thought through and refashioned as text. Each journey is thematic in that it selects specific material objects at the site which Pausanias believes to be related in some way, and it combines them in a topographically meaningful trajectory (even if this turns out to be, in the case of the altars, a topography of ritual practice rather than spatial proximity). As a result, if the *Periegesis* were to be used as a guidebook on-site (something perfectly practicable, especially were it available in codex instead of scroll form),[54] the monuments discussed in each trip would be easily identifiable to a visitor. However, beyond the practical, these objects grouped as trips around the Altis (altars, images of Zeus, votive offerings, and victor statues) stand metonymically for the key aspects of Pausanian Olympia: its ritual primacy, its prime deity (cf. 5.13.1), the long history of panhellenic worship at the site (which is reiterated and hence emphasized incrementally in the various sections), and (at greatest length) the Olympic Games. To these themes may be added Libon's Doric temple containing Phidias's cult image, one of the wonders of the world:

> I know that the height and breadth of the Olympic Zeus have been measured and recorded; but I shall not praise those who have made the measurements, for even their records fall far short of the impression made by a sight of the image. Nay, the god himself according to legend bore witness to the artistic skill of Phidias. For when the image was quite finished Phidias prayed to the god to show by a sign whether the work was to his liking. Immediately, runs the legend, a thunderbolt fell on that part of the floor where down to the present day the bronze jar stood to cover the place. (5.11.9)[55]

In addition, the Altis boasts the Heraion, which is more densely crowded with antique treasures of various kinds than any other temple described by Pausanias, and perhaps served as the sanctuary museum (on something like the pattern of a cathedral treasury).[56]

Each of these segments of text is inseparable from sections of the site or from paths through it: the thematics of Pausanias's written version of Olympia effectively *are* its monuments, layout, and phenomenological experience in space and time. But at the same time, each of these themed sections or journeys, though quintessentially Olympian, nonetheless reflects the archetypal subjects of the *Periegesis of Greece* as a whole. Just as the objects within the Altis, once they have been refigured as text in Pausanias's discourse, become metonyms reaching toward the essence of Olympia, so Olympia itself—at the heart of Greece—stands as a grand metonym for the whole of Pausanias's Greece. Particular sections of the Olympic discourse—for example, the ritual pattern of visiting the altars or the scholarly museology of reading the inscriptions on the Chest of Kypselos and the victor statues—reflect Pausanias's general practice elsewhere. They stand almost as programmatic paradigms of method and substance in the way that ekphrastic passages in Greek poetry and fiction often serve as the writer's self-reflection on his own project.[57] Moreover, by incorporating narratives of all the *hellenika* (in the form of dedications, stories, and victors) in this most archetypally panhellenic of sites, Pausanias's Olympia is not just a metonym for the rest of Greece but actually contains and evokes the whole of Greece. Most poignantly, Pausanias's Messenians only truly return from their long exile when their luck at the Olympic Games returns (6.2.10). For a Greek on the Pausanian definition, to be at Olympia is to be back home.

When Pausanias tells us that measurement and recording fail to do justice to a monument as significant as Phidias's Zeus (5.11.9), he is not just signaling the uniqueness of a particular object. The inadequacy of description—and in particular of the kind of factual and pragmatic description (by contrast with high-flown rhetoric) of which Pausanias is a master—is a self-reflexive comment on the nature of his own writing. It says, like other signaled absences in his discourse, that the full desire of Pausanias's text—or, to put it in the terms of James Porter's description of that desire's goal, the sacred-historical "sublime" to which the text constantly moves (see chap. 5, this volume)—cannot in fact be fully encapsulated by the act of writing or reading.[58] Ultimately, as Pausanias puts it of Eleusis, the other supreme site in his Greece (see 5.10.1), "what the uninitiated are prevented from seeing, they cannot learn [by reading]" (1.38.7). His text is a spur to do what he did and see what he saw (including the necessary rituals and initiations); it can never be a replacement.

The highly cultural emphasis on the Altis as a supreme sacred museum should not blind us to the fact that it remains the *grove* sacred to Zeus at the center of Greece (see esp. 5.10.1). If we read Pausanias's trip through Greece as an account of nature as well as culture, in which the very land is enchanted by divinity no less than the antique deeds and creations of Greece's noblest men (which still dot the landscape in Roman times), then that path is above all measured in sacred groves, whose trees mark the shrines of heroes and gods.[59] Again, the Altis is the archetypal, as well as the exceptional, site in this pattern— the pinnacle of natural Greece as well as of cultural Greece, with plane trees at the center of this most central *also* (5.27.11), with white poplar wood from the Acheron prescribed as the only fuel to be used in the sacrifices of Zeus on the site (5.14.2), and with wild olive trees growing in abundance where they grew for the very first time back in the autochthonous past, on the banks of the nearby Alpheius (5.14.3).[60]

Greece as Discourse

This chapter has explored some aspects of the way Pausanias turned the landscape of Greece into a rhetorical discourse. His "Greece" is, of course, a fantasy. It consisted of an enchanted past, of living myths and rituals whose apparent antiquity guaranteed their modern meanings, of ruins and monuments executed by the hallowed hands of the great. In short, its nostalgia, its "sublime," makes the *Description of Greece* one of the first truly monumental Romantic texts, and it is not surprising that the *Periegesis* has particularly appealed to Victorian neo-Romantics (especially archaeologists and seekers of lost religions), such as those discussed elsewhere in this book. But what makes Pausanias's "Greece" so interesting as a rhetorical argument is the intimate closeness he contrives between the fantasy and its myriad of actual embodiments in all the stories, sites, and features of the landscape that are the material of his text. Olympia is in this sense no different from any other site (although the detail of its treatment makes it exceptional): every place Pausanias's narrative comes to, every ritual or story it relates, is ultimately a channel into his ideal of a "Greece" that once was and still is as it once was, despite the decline of modern times.[61] Every part of the discourse is potentially as programmatic, as self-reflexive, as Olympia.

At the same time, the mythical totality which the text attempts to purvey is always selective. Pausanias's Greece is inevitably a florilegium of what he most wished to collect, of those bits which would best evoke the sublime fantasy of the whole (which arguably had never existed as Pausanias imagines it and certainly never possessed the perfect plenitude with which he imbues it). The interesting aspect of this is that the writing of Pausanias's Greece (as florilegium) is parallel to the process of reading the text of his Greece. No reading of Pausanias has ever been anything but a selection of passages—not even that of Frazer, whose six volumes of introduction, translation, and commentary (not to speak of the supplementary volume of maps or the one-volume selection of choice items published twice under different titles)[62] represent a good many more words devoted to Pausanias than Pausanias ever wrote himself.[63] Every reader's selections are strung together in a manner that suits the reader's own desire, the reader's view of what the *Periegesis of Greece* is trying to accomplish. That is to say, the only way to approach Pausanias's text is as he himself approached his Greece: choosing what pleases us but tying those selections together according to an ulterior set of aims. Pausanias's own subject matter (all the items and stories he comes across) was not the only influence on the shaping of his book, however much its structure holds to the contours of a geography, just as what we make of his work encompasses the written text plus what we bring of ourselves to the reading.

The problem of asking what Pausanias himself brought to his project—or, in other words, penetrating his agenda—is complex. He was not only antiquity's supreme collector of myths and recondite histories but was also (like perhaps all the greatest collectors) one of the Classical tradition's finest mythographers in his own right. His collection of *hellenika* (from the general topographies of his individual books to the very specific enumerations of particular offerings from particular cities at sites like Olympia) assembles the materials of "Greece" as places, objects, buildings, and rituals. But it simultaneously makes every object or event, as Pausanias meets it in his time, into a direct channel to the myths and histories in which Greek identity is represented as inhering for all time. In stitching together these narratives (and never forgetting the vastly evocative cultural resonances for which they are made to stand), Pausanias formulates his own myth-history of Greece, which has, it turns out, been the foundation for many of our own most potent philhellenisms. This is a rhetorical enterprise of the highest order.

The very selectivity and the careful stringing together of items along the routes of Pausanias's text are in fact highly rhetorical in the ancient sense. There is a large recent literature (indebted fundamentally to Frances Yates's brilliant exploration of the ancient "art of memory") on Graeco-Roman techniques of visualizing the passage through space—real or imaginary—as a way of memorizing the structure of a speech or train of thought.[64] When Quintilian recommends "a house, . . . public buildings, a long journey, the ramparts of a city, or even pictures" (*Institutio oratoria* 11.2.21) as the kinds of spaces to be used for the retrieving and ordering of memorized information, he is effectively listing the key items subjected in Greco-Roman education to the ancient rhetorical techniques of *ekphrasis* or *periegesis*. Pausanias's *Periegesis* is precisely such "a long journey" (or set of journeys), with the sites and monuments along the paths he treads observantly noted and, in the words of the anonymous writer of the rhetorical treatise *Ad Herrenium* (3.18.31), "well studied in order that they can stick to us permanently."[65] Pausanias's Greece not only is an extraordinary exercise in cultural memory[66] but is also recorded and organized according to the patterns recommended by ancient theory about memory.

I am not suggesting that Pausanias's text is a grand mnemonic, but rather that some aspects of its structure and of the choices made in that structure are shared with much more overtly oratorical texts and practices. It is significant that the writers of the ancient rhetorical handbooks, known as the *Progymnasmata,* chose to define the richly complex rhetorical trope of *ekphrasis* as a form of *periegetic discourse* (ἔκφρασίς ἐστι λόγος περιηγηματικός, the opening words of the sections on *ekphrasis* in the works of Theon, Hermogenes, and Aphthonius).[67] Just as the authors of the *Progymnasmata* sought to explain *ekphrasis* to their readers by referring to the less high flown trope of *periegesis,* so Pausanias's text (apparently rather bald and bare of oratorical flights) borrowed from the rhetorically trained culture of its time. In fact, it would be truer to say that it was simply part of that culture and no less imbued in the discursive techniques of rhetorical education than any other work of the Second Sophistic. While Pausanias's book is exceptional among those that have survived from the second century, not only in form and purpose but also in its particular ways of constructing Greek identity,[68] it is nonetheless of its time in the very complexity of the ways in which its discourses are arranged.

What is perhaps most remarkable about the *Periegesis of Greece,* from the point of view of its writing, is the unusual care the author took in transforming landscape into discourse. Pausanias's work reflects a deep and ongoing process of wrestling with a transcription that would both evoke his Greece as a set of ideals in literary form and preserve the geographic particularity of the topography he walked through. Part of the difficulty lay in evoking the nature of journeying—both as a particular kind of movement from site to site and as an incremental process of learning through experience—despite the written form of the map he constructed. Pausanias draws on the rhetorical skills of Second Sophistic education in somewhat unexpected ways to accomplish this task, using not only the art of memory and the genre of *periegesis* but also the conventional forms of travel literature as inherited from the literary tradition of Herodotus, on the one hand, and the pragmatic traditions of mercantile and imperial travel catalogues, on the other. We cannot know, of course, if in doing this, Pausanias created a text that would always be exceptional among ancient writings. But I suspect that it was.

Inspiration and Aspiration

Date, Genre, and Readership

Date

I begin by considering some questions concerning Pausanias's date. The indications offered by passages in his work leave little room for doubt about the rough dates of its composition, and point chiefly to the reign of Marcus Aurelius.[1] Book I, on Attica, had been finished, Pausanias tells us explicitly (7.20.6), before Herodes Atticus's construction of his Odeion in Athens to commemorate his dead wife, Regilla. Regilla died very late in the 150s or in A.D. 160 or 161. We need not suppose the Odeion to have been begun, far less completed, immediately after her death, even if the poems commissioned by Herodes for Regilla's monument on the *via Appia* should fall soon after 160 (given that the career of their poet, Marcellus of Side, was chiefly under Hadrian and Pius).[2] A date of ca. A.D. 165 for the Odeion and as a terminus ante quem for the completion of Book I fits our other evidence. Book II (2.27.6) refers to building at Epidaurus by a senator Antoninus, undoubtedly Sextus Iulius Maior Antoninus Pythodorus, who was active in the 160s, and not the emperor Antoninus Pius.[3] An adjacent paragraph of Book II (2.26.9) cites as having been constructed (γέγονεν) in Pausanias's time an Asclepieion at Smyrna[4] which from other evidence we know was still being built in September of A.D. 147.[5] That Books I and II should be compositions of around A.D. 160 (rather than, say, around A.D. 150 or, as Habicht holds of Book I, not later than A.D. 155) is supported by firmer and more precise dates for Books V and VIII. The 217 years that had elapsed from the refounding of Corinth by Julius Caesar in 44 B.C. give A.D. 174 as the year of 5.1.2; reference at 8.43.6 to Marcus Aurelius's German victory puts that passage after summer or autumn of A.D. 175. Less helpfully for this question, the Costobocan invasion puts 10.34.5 later than the date of that incursion, that is, A.D. 170 or 171.

How many years of writing did Books V–X require? If Books I–IV took a decade (say, A.D. 165–74; it would be longer on Habicht's earlier dating of

Book I), can the last six books have been finished in the seven or so years before Marcus's death in A.D. 180? That is certainly possible: composition of early books could well have been slower because, while putting them together, Pausanias was still inspecting sites and consulting written works relating to his later books, as well as developing his method of writing. Habicht's suggestion that Pausanias was hardly writing later than A.D. 180 is one that I would endorse, but I would offer different arguments. Habicht notes that Pausanias mentions all emperors from A.D. 98 up to Marcus, but not Commodus.[6] Pausanias's references to emperors, however, are not systematic, but arise from their context. Hadrian is often mentioned (a point to which I shall return), but Pius and Marcus only once, in the long chapter at 8.43, where citation of Pius's benefactions to Arcadian Pallantium develops into a sustained and balanced laudation of the reign of Pius. That encomium ends with a much briefer section, on Marcus, five lines mentioning only his succession to Pius, his homonymity to him, and his own punitive victory over the Germans. I offer two reasons for holding that Marcus was still alive when this chapter was written. First, when Pausanias has just noted the succession of Pius by Marcus, it would be odd for him to say nothing of Commodus's sole rule after A.D. 180. Second, and more tentatively, I suggest that the difference in scale and tone between the section on Pius and that on Marcus is chosen by Pausanias as appropriate to a dead and to a living emperor, respectively. The achievement of Pius can be summed up and assessed, and enthusiastic praise of the dead need not seem like flattery. By contrast, a single deed—necessarily unrepresentative—suffices for an emperor whose life's contribution as a whole cannot yet be judged (a point that would readily occur to an admirer of Herodotus; see the section "Genre, Language, and Style," below).

Chapter 8.43 certainly antedates A.D. 180, but that helps us little with Books IX and X. We might argue that the resistance to the Costoboci, which Pausanias credits chiefly to the Olympic victor of A.D. 162, Mnesibulus,[7] would have given him a chance to offer a rounded appreciation of Marcus similar to that of Pius in 8.43, and hence that Marcus was still alive when Book X was reaching its conclusion. But the silence of Books IX and X concerning Commodus counts for little. Failure to mention Commodus in the context of Pius leaving the empire to Marcus, however, is a different matter. Indeed, I would like to press this evidence further. In A.D. 177 Commodus became joint emperor with Marcus. If this had happened by the time of writing of 8.43, is it not odd that the expansion of the *laudatio* of Pius by a brief note of Marcus's succession should not have been further updated by a comparable reference to Commodus? If both these suggestions are accepted, Book VIII antedates A.D. 177; Books V–VIII were composed within the span 174–177; and Books IX–X probably were written by 180, as Habicht argued.

Six books in six years from A.D. 174 to 180, yet only four in the nine years from ca. A.D. 165 to 174? As I have already said, reasons can be excogitated for the early books' reaching completion more slowly. But if this chronology for the later six books is accepted, and if we reflect on the pace of other contemporary writers, we shall hesitate to bring Book I much, if at all, before A.D.

165. Cassius Dio was to spend ten years in gathering material and only twelve more in writing up his eighty books.[8]

The production of a single literary work is a matter quite different from that of a whole career. We know nothing about Pausanias the person from any other source; we would be unwise to assume that the *Periegesis* was his only work. A reader of the *Anabasis* by his older contemporary Arrian of Nicomedia might form the impression that this was Arrian's only major work, certainly his *chef d'oeuvre*; yet we know of a string of other works, at least two of which were almost certainly bulkier than the *Anabasis,* and to one of which (as to the *Anabasis*) he professed lifelong commitment.[9] That the *Periegesis* exudes its author's total commitment to the task in hand should not lead us to exclude other writings at other stages in his career.

So where does its research and composition fall within Pausanias's life span? Somewhere toward its end. There is only one sign that it is unfinished: a promise, at 9.23.7, of a later treatment of Locris that is not redeemed. But there are no other rough edges, and only one remark (8.9.7) that might imply advanced years. How old, then, was Pausanias in the 160s when sections of the work began to reach completion? His expressions ἐπ' ἐμοῦ ("in my time"), κατ' ἐμέ ("contemporary with me"), ἐφ' ἡμῶν ("in our time"), and καθ' ἡμᾶς ("contemporary with us")[10] refer to events as early as the creation of the tribe Hadrianis in Athens, either in A.D. 121/2 or in 124/5. At the very latest, then, he was born by 124/5. But such expressions are often used to refer to a point within adult life, and that too is how I would suggest we should take his well-known reference to Antinous: "I did not see him when he was still among the living, but I have seen him in statues and paintings."[11] The remark seems to imply, as Habicht, for example, holds, that Pausanias would have been old enough to have seen Antinous before his death in the Nile on 30 October, A.D. 130, and even perhaps suggests that by then Pausanias had reached the years of discretion or, rather, aesthetic judgment. Perhaps, then, Pausanias was already in his teens by the 120s, having been born ca. A.D. 110 rather than ca. A.D. 115. Perhaps Pausanias was composing Book I of the *Periegesis* when he was already well into his fifties and was approaching seventy when he completed the work not later than A.D. 180.

Was this somewhat slight modification of Habicht's conclusions worth the argumentative ink? It does have some consequences, albeit modest. The earlier we make Pausanias's birth, the more exposure he has to the philhellenism of Hadrian, and the more he might be supposed to identify Hadrian's reign with his own youth. On my tentative chronology, Pausanias would have been thirteen or fourteen when Hadrian made his first extended tour of *provincia Asia* in A.D. 123/4, and perhaps already learning rhetoric and attending a sophist's lectures when Hadrian returned in A.D. 128/9. He would have been old enough to make a first visit to Athens by the time Hadrian dedicated the Olympieion in A.D. 131/2 (see 1.18.6), and to feel the shock waves in the eastern provinces when the Bar Kochva revolt in Judaea was suppressed (Magnesia, like so many cities of Asia Minor, had some sort of Jewish community).[12] The long reign of Pius—twenty-three staid and solid years of an emperor who reduced the public salary of Mesomedes, virtuoso exponent of the most fashionable form of contemporary Greek singing, *citharoedia*[13]—would have fallen in Pausanias's middle life, as he aged from twenty-eight to fifty-one. By A.D. 165 the reign of Hadrian is part of Pausanias's irrecoverable past. The degree whereby his enthusiasm for Hadrian's benefactions and buildings exceeds that for those of his Antonine successors no doubt partly reflects a real, quantitative difference in those benefactions. It also matches the uniquely high praise lavished on Hadrian by other Greek writers of the later second and early third centuries.[14] Hadrian's association with Pausanias's youth may have played a part in creating his personal perspective.

Origins

I shall say less about Pausanias's geographical and social origins. The case for his native city being Magnesia ad Sipylum seems to me overwhelming.[15] Elements in the mythological and historical traditions of Magnesia might be guessed to have stimulated Pausanias's interest or affected his attitudes. The legend of Tantalus and Pelops may have turned his eye to mainland Greece and contributed to his recurrent interest in the way that the inhabitants of Greek cities or territories articulated their location in terms of foundation myths.[16] The great battle in which Antiochus was defeated by Scipio might have focused his mind on the decisive impact of Rome on the development of the Greek world. The anti-Mithridatic stance taken by Magnesia, highlighted in Pausanias's brief mention of Mithridates's general Archelaus (1.20.5), may play some part in the balance Pausanias reached between condemnation and acceptance of Roman aggression. Magnesia's status as *civitas libera* may have given him a different perspective on the losses and reacquisitions of freedom by the cities or province of Achaea.

But all these are guesses. Many Greek cities of Asia Minor would have offered a similar stimulus. What may deserve more attention is the fact of its being a city of Asia Minor, and in particular of *provincia Asia,* not a city of mainland Greece. On the one hand, it was this area that saw the greatest concentration of literary activity in the Greek world of the second century. Its leading cities were especially prominent as centers of the display and teaching of sophistic rhetoric; the young came from other provinces to learn from epideictic stars in Pergamum, Ephesus, and Smyrna. It also produced writers of all sorts in greater number than mainland Greece. On the other hand, mainland Greece had the greater authority as a repository of Greek tradition and as a living monument to the Greek past. It was from mainland Greece that Greeks sailed to take Troy; it was from mainland Greece that colonists settled Asia Minor; it was in mainland Greece that Darius and Xerxes were resisted; it was the collapse of mainland Greek cities before Macedon that could be seen as the end of an era of Greek independence. Pausanias's Magnesian origins may have directed him to literary activity more firmly than would upbringing in any city of mainland Greece other than Athens; and they may have enhanced his fascination with the past of a mainland Greece to which he was a visitor and in no city of which he was a native.[17]

Genre, Language, and Style

Literary activity was undoubtedly prestigious among the Greek elites of the Antonine Age.[18] Some forms drew more acclaim than others. If one read only Philostratus, one might suppose that sophists were by far and away the most prestigious literary artists. Certainly their chief medium, public display, gave them a higher profile; and their public recognition (e.g., by emperors in the form of honors and privileges or by cities in the form of honorific statues and accompanying texts on stone) is better established than that of historians and poets, or even of the sophists' often look-alike rivals, philosophers. But men of the very highest rank in Greek society might be drawn to writing history, as they were to a sophistic career, in a way they would not be drawn to the composition of poetry or of scholarly monographs on earlier literature. Moreover, historians could also achieve public recognition: witness the honors at Argos to Pausanias's close contemporary P. Anteius Antiochus of Cilician Aegeae for his work on early Argive history (with diplomatic consequences).[19]

It is in the tradition of Herodotus that Pausanias clearly wishes to place himself. There is indeed a line of ancestry that goes back beyond Herodotus to Hecataeus, and perhaps one that passes through the second-century B.C. periegete Polemo of Ilium. But Hecataeus allocated genealogical mythography and periegetic geography and anthropology to two quite different works—the four-book *Genealogies* (Γενεαλογίαι) and the two-book *Journey round the World* (Περίοδος Γῆς)—and is not known to have said anything at all about monuments. Polemo of Ilium seems to have united different types of inquiry in single works but to have allocated separate works to different sites.[20] The decision to interweave mythology and history with discussion of monuments, and to do so in one large work, marks Herodotus as Pausanias's chief model, even if he is a model from whom Pausanias diverged in many ways, particularly in the relative proportions of description and narrative. To Herodotus can be traced Pausanias's scrupulous citation of conflicting sources, his somewhat ostentatious silence on some religious matters, and the fact that many of his modest total of personal comments relate to religion and to the gods' punishment of human wickedness. That Pausanias comes across as a more restrained commentator and a more austere communicator of detail may be partly attributable to some *imitatio* of Thucydides too,[21] but we must also allow that these traits might to some extent reflect his own personality.

My statement that Pausanias's chief models are Herodotus and, second, Thucydides is based in the first instance on his approach to his material and to the impressions I have formed when reading his text. These impressions are necessarily subjective, but they are supported by more systematic analyses performed by others. When I recently looked again at Ove Strid's study, I was encouraged to be reminded that its conclusion was the same: "Die Sprache und der Stil des Pausanias zeichnen sich durch ein grundsätzlichen Klassizismus aus, der hauptsächlich herodoteisch geprägt ist. Neben Herodot hat vor allem Thukydides als Vorbild gedient."[22]

It might reasonably be asked why, if Pausanias's chief model was Herodotus, he did not decide to write in Ionic Greek. It was indeed an option, but it was one taken up by very few of his contemporaries. Arrian used it for his *Indike* ('Ινδική), the ethnography of India that imitates both Ctesias and Herodotus and that was very probably in circulation by the time Pausanias began writing.[23] But Arrian, like Pausanias, was also strongly influenced by Herodotus as well as by Thucydides in the works he wrote in Attic.[24] Lucian used it for his work *On the Syrian Goddess* (περὶ τῆς Συρίης θεοῦ), an essay that deftly walks the tightrope between ethnography and parody but is hard to date within Lucian's writing career. His *How to Write History* also adduces or invents historians who wrote in Ionic and borrowed Herodotean phraseology to narrate Lucius Verus's Parthian wars.[25] This last work is the only one of these three for which we have a secure date, around A.D. 165/6, so it was almost certainly too late to have been a factor in deterring Pausanias from choosing Ionic. But Lucian's satire shows that the choice of Ionic could readily be perceived as quirky, and such a perception is reinforced by the fact that both Arrian and Lucian himself use Ionic only for a small fraction of their considerable output, and indeed for a particularly exotic brand of ethnography. For Pausanias, following up the side of Herodotus that commemorated the actions and monuments of Greeks, and not his ethnographic side, which earned him Plutarch's epithet "fond of non-Greeks" (φιλοβάρβαρος), the choice not of Ionic but of Attic Greek, standard in historiography, was virtually inescapable.

We hardly need to be reminded, after all, that by the years of Pausanias's rhetorical education (suggested above to be the later 130s), the modeling of educated written and even spoken Greek upon that of Classical Athens had long been the rule, and the following decades were to see even greater emphasis on restriction of acceptable vocabulary to what could be documented in canonical authors. A leading Atticist over these decades was Herodes Atticus, one of the very few contemporaries to be mentioned by Pausanias. Some degree of Atticism in vocabulary and syntax was undoubtedly the norm wherever Pausanias studied rhetoric—which might well have been at first in Magnesia, though it is likely that he moved on to (or even started in) a larger city with bigger stars. This would most probably have been Smyrna, which was both nearer Magnesia than Ephesus or Pergamum and a city with which Magnesia had some sort of connection.[26] A move to Athens even at this stage in his career is equally possible. But whether his training was in Asia Minor or Athens, the choice of Attic for a work whose spirit was to be chiefly Herodotean is no surprise.

There must, however, have been some temptation to mark himself off as different from both Herodotus and Thucydides, and it was once thought that he succumbed to this temptation to the extent that his style was in general "Asianic" and in particular owed much to Magnesia's greatest literary figure, the third-century B.C. orator and historian Hegesias. In an era in which Greeks were as proud as they had ever been of their native cities, it would be understandable that Pausanias should have admired Hegesias in the same way as Dionysius of Halicarnassus admired Herodotus; if he did indeed study rhetoric in Smyrna, understandable too that Pausanias should have exhibited some of the more irritating features of an Asianic style that we find in the extant declamations of Smyrna's sophistic doyen M. Antonius Polemon of Laodicea. It has been clear, however, since Strid's systematic study, that Hegesias can have had little influence on Pausanias's style, which yields few of the contrived images, short cola, and rhythmical clausulae that were bequeathed by Hegesias to what others branded as an Asian style. One of the chief grounds for the hypothesis was Pausanias's often unusual word order, but Strid showed that many of the *hyperbata* in Pausanias have Classical precedents, some in Herodotus and Thucydides; that there is no good reason to suppose that the point of the word order is to achieve rhythm; and that a regular feature of Asianic rhetoric, the avoidance of hiatus, is not sought by Pausanias.[27] Szelest had already shown that Pausanias's clausulae align him with Philo, Chariton, and Lucian, and so although some of these are indeed found in Asianic writing, they do not mark him as an Asianist.[28]

These points make some contribution to our location of Pausanias. Attached as he must have been to Magnesia and to its traditions,[29] he eschewed Hegesias's style in favor of one closer to that of fifth-century B.C. models. Pausanias may, of course, have seen that over ten books such a style would cloy disastrously, and indeed one motive for his variation in word order has reasonably been supposed to be avoidance of monotony. But more important, surely, was his perception that for celebrating the monuments and deeds of a past which entered a new and less distinguished era with the battle of Chaeronea a fifth-century style was more appropriate than a third-century style.

A Preface?

All the issues pursued in the preceding section—including the degree of Pausanias's attachment to Magnesia—would have been much easier to assess if his book had had a preface, even a brief one. I remain extremely puzzled by the abruptness of the direct and unmediated entry into the topography of Attica offered by the opening sentence of his text. It is unlike the openings of the two authors whom I and others take to be his chief models, both of whom offer a signature and a brief statement of purpose, as earlier did Hecataeus in his *Genealogies*.[30] It is unlike most extended prose works of the second and early third centuries A.D. of which we have the beginning or at least know something of it: for example, Amyntianus's work on Alexander, Appian's *Roman History,* Arrian's *Bithynica*,[31] the histories of Cassius Dio and Herodian, Philostratus's *Lives of the Sophists* and *Apollonius*. It is also unlike the novels of Chariton (ostentatiously adopting a Thucydidean pose) and Longus. For the earlier Imperial period, we have prefaces for the histories of Diodorus and Josephus (*Antiquities* and *War*), and for the later period, we have prefaces for those of Eusebius and Procopius. There are indeed works with similar openings: the

Library of Apollodorus, close to Pausanias in its subject matter, has no preface, though the abrupt opening of Pausanias comes closer to that of Achilles Tatius, whose sailor's-eye view of a coastline I have sometimes thought of as reflecting that of Pausanias. There is another possible parallel in Arrian's *Indike,* but that might be seen as a special case, since the work should be viewed as an appendix or adjunct to the *Anabasis.* The *Anabasis* itself is one of a group where a veiled signature comes not at the beginning but later in the work, in the "second preface" of 1.12; the extreme case is Heliodorus's *Aithiopika,* where the signature come right at the end of the tenth book.

I suggest that Pausanias's text is likely to have had a preface that we have lost: not a syntactically integral preface like those of Herodotus or Thucydides but a prefatory paragraph (or paragraphs). Alternatively, there could have been a dedicatory letter.[32] The opening sheets of a papyrus roll and opening pages of a codex are of course especially vulnerable to damage or loss in transmission, and there are comparable instances in both Greek and Latin literature. In Greek literature of this period, for example, the opening of Arrian's *Tactica* has been lost. But the closest parallel is perhaps the traditions of the *Controversiae* of the Elder Seneca. There are two traditions: one contains only abbreviated forms of the *controversiae* but does have a general preface, which must have stood before Book I, and other prefaces for Books II, III, IV, VII, and X; the other tradition preserves Books I, II, VII, IX, and X complete, but not the first preface or that to Book II, although it does have the prefaces to Books VII, IX, and X.[33] A similar missing preface may be conjectured for Suetonius's *Lives of the Caesars,* and the first *Life,* that of Julius Caesar, certainly lacks its beginning.[34] What I propose is that there may have been a nonintegral preface that stood before the text of Pausanias's Book I and that said something of Pausanias's identity and his work's purpose.

Aspirations

The absence of such a preface has helped some scholars to hold that Pausanias did not pursue literary fame, a comforting corollary to the view that he apparently attained none. The first of these hypotheses does not seem to me to follow from his failure to name himself in the text that we have. Even if a preface has not been lost, Pausanias must have assumed that rolls of his work would be identified by his name and that that name would be observed when these were purchased or borrowed by individuals, or when they were accessioned by libraries. The restraint that he displays in offering his own opinions should not be confused with modesty; indeed, these opinions are often offered with a firmness that betokens considerable self-confidence.[35] Again, the practice of Herodotus and Thucydides should be kept in mind. It would be hard to dissent from such conclusions as those of Habicht ("Pausanias was out to preserve as much for posterity as he could of the inheritance of the past") or of Ebeling, whom he quotes ("While there is a certain antagonism between his historical and his periegetic plans, both were united in his aim to connect the past with the present").[36] But pursuit of these aims was in no way incompatible with an attempt to put his own literary achievement on the cultural map, as historians before him had shown and as Herodian was to formulate explicitly a generation or so later.[37]

Once more his style must be thrown into the balance. Like his subject matter, it is clearly the product of much hard work, and an impressive product at that: "Was er literarisch leisten wollte—das Resultat mag uns, den Modernen, gefallen oder nicht—, ist ihm tatsächlich auch gelungen."[38] Nor is it reasonable to suppose that he would have distanced himself from the φιλοτιμία of sophists. His critical remarks on the captiousness (τὸ φιλαίτιον) of those who in his time enjoyed a professional authority on the issue of the composition of Homeric and Hesiodic epics surely refer not to sophists[39] but to γραμματικοί (teachers of language and literature), who were often also κριτικοί (critics). We simply do not know his view of sophists.[40]

Did he, then, succeed in attracting the notice or approbation of his contemporaries? We should concede that here too we cannot know to what extent he did or did not. We have far too small a sample of Greek writing from the decades following the 170s to judge whether or not the work was favorably received. Its absence from most of what we do have can tell us almost nothing—just as it was not, I believe, significant that no contemporary seemed to have mentioned Lucian until Strohmaier spotted a reference in an Arabic translation of a work of Galen; nor, I have argued, is almost total silence on Greek novels a safe index of their having had a low literary status.[41] I would imagine—but this must be speculation—that a man who put so much effort into gathering, sifting, and writing up his material also took steps to have parts of it heard and as much as possible read. Public readings from literary works (ἀκροάσεις) were still one way to achieve this, and we should not discount their possibility for Pausanias. Live oral performances were regular not only in the *odeia* and theaters of major and even minor cities but also at the great panhellenic *agones*.[42]

Pausanias's books on Olympia and Delphi could well have had an airing on-site. But texts in public and private libraries were manifestly a longer-lasting guarantee of fame. Preface or no, Pausanias is likely to have given copies to friends and may well have sent them to city libraries. His rough contemporary Heraclitus of Rhodiapolis, honored in his πατρίς as "the first in all history to be a doctor, a historian, and a poet of medical and philosophical works," gave copies of these works (in prose and in verse) to Alexandria, Rhodes, and Athens.[43] Pausanias might also have hoped that a major library might solicit his work: the epitaph on Marcellus of Side, presumably composed by himself, boasts that his works were "dedicated" in Rome by Hadrian and Pius, which means, I suppose, that the procurator in charge of the libraries in Rome had them acquired.[44]

The suggestion that Pausanias was read by nobody in succeeding centuries must, however, be questioned.[45] Our manuscripts of Aelian's *Historical Miscellany* (ποικίλη ἱστορία) 12.61 adduce Pausanias (8.36.6) as saying that Megalopolis resembles Thurii and Athens (about which Aelian is writing) in having a cult of Boreas: Παυσανίας δέ φησιν ὅτι καὶ Μεγαλοπολῖται (and Pausanias says that the people of Megalopolis also do so). The authenticity of this sentence was questioned in 1668 by Faber in his edition of Aelian, but for no compelling reason. Matthew Dickie has recently argued that Philostratus in his *Apollonius* either uses a source also used by Pausanias or, more probably given some close verbal echoes, draws on Pausanias himself.[46] I would like, very tentatively, to suggest a third ancient reader, Longus. In his vivid and numinous narrative of Pan's divine intervention to save Chloe from her Methymnan captors at 2.25.3–29.3, Longus begins with a brief account of miraculous sights and sounds perceived toward the end of the day of her capture:

> ἄρτι δὲ παυομένης ἡμέρας καὶ τῆς τέρψεως ἐς νύκτα ληγούσης, αἰφνίδιον μὲν ἡ γῆ πᾶσα ἐδόκει λάμπεσθαι πυρί, κτύπος δὲ ἠκούετο ῥόθιος κωπῶν ὡς ἐπιπλέοντος μεγάλου στόλου. ἐβόα τις ὁπλίζεσθαι, τὸν στρατηγὸν ἄλλος ἐκάλει, καὶ τετρῶσθαί τις ἐδόκει καὶ σχῆμά τις ἔκειτο νεκροῦ μιμούμενος. εἴκασεν ἄν τις ὁρᾶν νυκτομαχίαν οὐ παρόντων πολεμίων. (2.25.4)

> The day was just coming to a close, and the night was bringing their enjoyment to an end, when suddenly *the whole land* seemed to blaze with fire, and they heard a *noise* of splashing oars, as if a huge fleet was sailing against them. Someone shouted out that they should arm themselves; someone else called for the general; someone looked as if he had been wounded; and someone else lay there looking like a corpse. You would have thought you were seeing a night attack—but there was no enemy there.

Longus then winds up the tension by introducing the following day's events with the stage direction that "the day was much more terrifying than the night":

> τῆς δὲ νυκτὸς αὐτοῖς τοιαύτης γενομένης ἐπῆλθεν ἡμέρα πολὺ τῆς νυκτὸς φοβερώτερα. (2.26.1)

> After a night like that, the day came; and this was much more terrifying than the night.

The ensuing details include many spine-chilling miracles, some modeled on the Homeric hymn to Dionysus, and the wrathful appearance of Pan himself to the Methymnan commander Bryaxis in a dream.

The tone of the narrative and the very effectively created atmosphere of supernatural happenings seem to me to recall Pausanias's narrative of the miraculous divine defense of Delphi against Brennus and his Gaulish horde in 279 B.C. (10.23.1–7):

> (1) . . . καὶ τοῖς βαρβάροις ἀντεσήμαινε τὰ ἐκ τοῦ θεοῦ ταχύ τε καὶ ὧν ἴσμεν φανερώτατα. ἥ τε γὰρ γῆ πᾶσα, ὅσην ἐπεῖχεν ἡ τῶν Γαλατῶν στρατιά, βιαίως καὶ ἐπὶ πλεῖστον ἐσείετο τῆς ἡμέρας, βρονταί τε καὶ κεραυνοὶ συνεχεῖς ἐγίνοντο. (2) καὶ αἱ μὲν ἐξέπληττόν τετοὺς Κελτοὺς καὶ δέχεσθαι τοῖς ὠσὶ τὰ παραγγελλόμενα ἐκώλυον, τὰ δὲ ἐκ τοῦ οὐρανοῦ οὐκ ἐς ὅντινα κατασκήψαι μόνον, ἀλλὰ καὶ τοὺς πλησίον καὶ αὐτοὺς ὁμοίως καὶ τὰ ὅπλα ἐξῆπτε. . . . (4) τοιούτοις μὲν οἱ βάρβαροι παρὰ πᾶσαν τὴν ἡμέραν παθήμασί τε καὶ ἐκπλήξει συνείχοντο. τὰ δὲ (ἐν) τῇ νυκτὶ πολλῷ σφᾶς ἔμελλεν ἀλγεινότερα ἐπιλήψεσθαι. ῥῖγός τε γὰρ ἰσχυρὸν καὶ νιφετὸς ἦν ὁμοῦ τῷ ῥίγει. . . . (7) ἐν δὲ τῇ νυκτὶ φόβος σφίσιν ἐμπίπτει Πανικός. τὰ γὰρ ἀπὸ αἰτίας οὐδεμιᾶς δείματα ἐκ τούτου

φασὶ γίνεσθαι. ἐνέπεσε μὲν ἐς τὸ στράτευμα ἡ ταραχὴ περὶ βαθεῖαν τὴν ἑσπέραν,
καὶ ὀλίγοι τὸ κατ᾽ ἀρχὰς ἐγένοντο οἱ παραχθέντες ἐκ τοῦ νοῦ, ἐδόξαζόν τε οὗτοι
κτύπου τε ἐπελαυνομένων ἵππων καὶ ἐφόδου πολεμίων ⟨αἰσθάνεσθαι⟩. μετὰ δὲ
οὐ πολὺ καὶ ἐς ἅπαντας διέδρα ἡ ἄνοια.

(1) ... and the barbarians were sent contrary portents by the god, more swiftly
and more manifest than any others we know. *The whole land* occupied by the
Gauls shook violently for the greater part of the day, and there was continuous
thunder and lightning. (2) The thunder terrified the Gauls and prevented them
from hearing the orders being given, and the thunderbolts would set on fire not
only the man whom they struck but his neighbors and their weapons alike ...
(4) Such were the disasters and terror that afflicted the barbarians throughout
the day. But the events of the night were going to inflict even greater distress
on them. For there was an intense cold, and snow along with the cold. ... (7)
And during the night Panic fell upon them (for terrors without cause are said
to be brought about by Pan). The confusion fell upon the army late in the
evening, and to begin with, those who were driven out of their senses were
few, and these thought that they heard the *noise* of horses charging at them
and of the advance of enemies. But before long the madness swept through
them all.

The sequence "*x* was yet more terrible than *y*" may seem an obvious rhetorical move, but I have not found it elsewhere together with the contrast between day and night. The nearest phrase is one in Cassius Dio, used of the
problems faced by Alexander Severus, where the state of affairs in Parthia is
described as "even more frightening."[47] The presence of κτύπος and the phrase
ἡ γῆ πᾶσα/ἥ τε γὰρ γῆ πᾶσα in both passages might also be thought to support
some degree of dependence. There is, of course, a possibly significant difference
in the sequence of thought: in Pausanias the nocturnal events are even more
excruciating than those of the day, whereas Longus has his daytime events more
terrifying than those of the preceding night. This, however, is not a strong
counterindication in an author who is keen to reverse many of the stereotypes
of his predecessors. My hypothesis is that in constructing a scene of terrifying
miraculous manifestations of divine intervention, Longus drew on a narrative
that he happened to recall, whether working from memory or from consultation
of the text. That Pausanias had described the panic afflicting the Gauls as φόβος
Πανικός, although Apollo and perhaps Artemis were generally credited with the
supernatural interventions, may have been one factor that highlighted the passage's appropriateness as a quarry.

As I have said, my hypothesis is tentative. I may have missed a passage in
a well-known author that could demonstrate the trope to be commoner than I
have thought; and in any case it is open to the skeptic to propose that what
Longus knew was the text not of Pausanias but of his Hellenistic source (Timaeus?) for this celebrated event. But if use of Pausanias by Longus were the
correct explanation, two conclusions of interest would emerge. First, we have
another reader of Pausanias, very probably in the generation after his publication. Second, we have a terminus post quem for Longus's *Daphnis and Chloe*:
the novel cannot be composed earlier than the 180s.

The issue of how Pausanias expected his work to be read also deserves brief attention. Although I see Pausanias's work as primarily intended to be heard or read by literary connoisseurs, people with as traditional an education as Pausanias himself and Longus, Aelian, and Philostratus, I also accept that his systematic coverage of each area by routes radiating from a central place made it suitable for use as a guidebook on-site, like a Baedeker or *Blue Guide*. But I do not share Habicht's view that inclusion of this objective would have been miscalculation. I think he goes rather too far in conjuring up difficulties: "Imagine handling the stack of bookrolls in the heat of a summer day in Arcadia and trying to find the passage describing, let us say, the temple of Apollo at Bassae."[48] But the one book devoted to Arcadia will have been accommodated on a single roll; and for any reader that Pausanias could imagine, that roll will be carried and doubtless unrolled by a slave. The traveler likely to use his work is the same sort of πεπαιδευμένος who would savor literary descriptions of antique monuments and ancient deeds in a library or lecture hall, so the mythological and historical material becomes less obtrusive than Habicht suggests. Pausanias may after all have got it right; but, as I have said of the general issue of readership, we do not really know the answer to this question, and so we should not feel obliged to find reasons for hypothetical failure.

I close my discussion of this issue by noting that Pausanias's supposed lack of literary success should not be explained by saying "The tide of philhellenism was already ebbing."[49] Despite the problems of Marcus Aurelius on the northern frontiers, the unsatisfactory rule of Commodus, and the civil wars that followed his murder, nevertheless the half century from A.D. 180 to 230 showed no diminution of Greek cultural activity. Works in all genres continued to be written and, we should assume, heard or read; Philostratus's *Lives of the Sophists* registers no discernible break or change in the epideictic world. Even the half century after that, when our sources are significantly poorer, clearly saw a continuation of sophistic rhetoric and of historiography and equally of the elite education without which these genres would have withered.

Nothing in what I have argued offers a radically different view of Pausanias than that which has been built up over decades of modern studies. But I hope that if the arguments are accepted, we shall have a Pausanias who is less puzzling to us, and who emerges with greater clarity of purpose and a surer understanding of his potential readership, than Habicht's Pausanias.

Pausanias and His Guides

Who was Pausanias? And what was Pausanias? The first question, concerning Pausanias as a person, has become much clearer in recent years. He was from western Asia Minor, probably from Magnesia ad Sipylum, and was not a sophist from Cappadocia or a geographical writer from Damascus; he was independent and thoughtful, a reliable witness to the objects he described, and a keen connoisseur of Archaic and Classical Greek art.[1] What he was, as a question of social taxonomy, is not so clear. The customary epithet, "the Periegete," conveys little more than that he is the author of the extant work called by Stephanus of Byzantium, and perhaps by Pausanias himself, *Periēgēsis tēs Hellados* (Description of Greece). In recent years, he has also been classified as a "pilgrim," and a recent addition to the Entretiens Hardt under the title *Pausanias historien* avoids the term "periegete" altogether.[2]

The present study takes up the problem of placing Pausanias in his social context, but by an indirect route. Instead of analyzing his personality or opinions, subjects that have been discussed almost to exhaustion in recent years, I take up the question of his acquaintances, and in particular those who served him as sources of information. The current tendency is to emphasize Pausanias's isolation: his modesty in comparison with the sophists, who might appear to dominate the intellectual life of his period; the lack of contemporary references to him; the precarious survival of his work.[3] Yet it is only in his reluctance to provide information about himself as a person that he can be said to have "kept the lowest possible profile";[4] as an authorial voice, he holds his experiences and opinions before the reader on almost every page. As in Herodotus, his chief Classical exemplar, the subjects of Pausanias's discourse are filtered to us through an atmosphere of unceasing debate and commentary.

In an attempt to recover something of this atmosphere, I will discuss those persons whom Pausanias calls "expounders" (*exēgētai*) and their relation to the people called "guides" (*periēgētai*) by other authors. He mentions a number of acquaintances, usually without name: "a man from Mysia," "a man from Cyprus," and so on. Even more frequently, but with a similar reticence, he refers to "expounders," sometimes by a periphrasis such as "those who recall the antiquities." Of these expounders, four are qualified with an objective genitive as "the expounder of local matters" (*ho tōn epichōriōn exēgētēs*). More often, the genitive is a possessive, refering once to a region ("of the Lydians") and more usually to a city ("of the Megarians"); the home cities of a few expounders have to be inferred from the context. Elis, with its dependent shrine of Olympia, is a special case: besides referring twice to the "expounders of the Eleans," Pausanias refers simply to "the expounder at Olympia" and also to "the expounder" as participating in the monthly sacrifices of the Eleans. The variation is doubtless due to his thinking sometimes of a specific person, sometimes of a group.[5]

The verbs that he uses in connection with the singular or plural expounders are mostly in the imperfect tense, *elegen, ephasken, edeiknuon* ("*X* was saying," "*X* was alleging," "*XX* were showing"). This tense, which might be named "the imperfect of recollection," is very frequent in Pausanias, and he never seems to use it of sources who are known to have left written works.[6] It is also found in other writers when they recall things seen or heard on their travels. He sometimes uses a present tense or its equivalent—*pareitai*, "it is not said"; *lelēthen*, "it has escaped"; *homologeitai*, "it is agreed among"—and here he may refer either to oral or written sources or to both at once.[7]

These expounders raise a number of perplexing questions, not always confronted, which in their turn reflect on the author himself. Some are certainly written authorities, but can we tell which? Are they, as often supposed, identical with the people elsewhere called "guides"? If Pausanias's contemporaries, are they more or less well-informed guides similar to those encountered by the modern tourist, as again is often supposed, or are they rather local scholars? Finally, what is Pausanias's relationship with these people, and what can they tell about his own position in the republic of letters as it existed in his day?

Pausanias himself—it comes as a slight surprise—never uses the word *periēgētēs* or its cognates, but only *exēgētēs*. In normal Greek, the basic meaning of the uncompounded *hēgeomai* is "lead." *Exēgeomai* apparently derives its sense of "expound" from the idea of "setting out," "displaying," while *perēgeomai*, when used transitively, means "to show the way around something," "give guidance about."[8] Only once does Pausanias refer to an expounder's leading him to a specific site; this is "the expounder of local matters" at Megara, who took him to a place called *Rhous* outside the walls of the city.[9] Of his other expounders, one is certainly a writer, the epic poet Lykeas of Argos, known only from Pausanias's references.[10] In general, however, there can be little doubt that his expounders did in fact serve him as guides, and that his avoidance of the word *periēgētēs* is a stylistic choice, not a descriptive one.

The reason is surely his reverence for Herodotus and his general conservatism of language, for whereas *exēgētēs* is used by Herodotus and other Classical authors, the noun *periēgētēs* (unlike *perēgeomai* and *periēgēsis*) is first attested in the Roman period.[11] We may compare Pausanias's total avoidance of the usual word for "read," *anagignōskō*, in favor of the Herodotean *epilegomai*, a choice that might have struck his readers as eccentric.[12] Given these stylistic oddities, we might wonder why he did not take a further step, as did certain of his contemporaries, such as Lucian, and actually write in the Ionic dialect. Though there can be no certain answer, he might have felt that such a choice would have been stylistically flamboyant in his own day, a distraction from the air of studiousness and sincerity that he wished to convey.

Pausanias names three of his expounders, and one is an author of unknown date, the poet Lykeas of Argos mentioned above. Another has been taken to be an author, but this goes against the evidence of the imperfect tense. Discussing the celebrated Amphiaraion of Oropos, a shrine that flourished mainly in the Hellenistic period, Pausanias says, "Iophon of Knossos, one of the expounders (*tōn exēgētōn*), alleged oracles in hexameters (*chrēsmous en epesin pareicheto*), which he said were delivered by Amphiaraos to the Argives who made the expedition to Thebes. These verses were lavishly adapted to attract the many (*to es tous pollous epagōgon akratōs eiche),*" but Pausanias argues that they must be spurious, since ancient *manteis* did not give oracles. The imperfect tense of the verbs *pareicheto* and *eiche* would be odd if he were referring to a written source, and again he seems rather to be recalling something from his experience, not from his reading. Iophon could well have been a devotee of the hero Amphiaraos who had settled at the shrine, or in Athens, and become a local expert.[13] The last of Pausanias's named expounders is Aristarchos of Elis, who "told" him (*elegen,* again an imperfect) a story about a corpse, or rather a skeleton, found when the roof of the Heraion at Olympia was being repaired about a generation before. He is agreed to be one of the author's oral informants, and his name is found in the great family of Elean *manteis,* the Iamids.[14]

Pausanias's reflections on Iophon and his oracles are not the only occasion on which he links expounders with "the many." Discussing the bones of giants, he refers to his experience at Temenouthyrae in upper Lydia. When bones were discovered there of human shape but superhuman size, "a story got out among the many (*logos ēlthen es tous pollous*) that it was the corpse of Geryon, son of Chrysaos. . . . But when I spoke in contradiction and argued (*apephainon*) that Geryon was in Cadiz, . . . then the exegetes of the Lydians revealed the true explanation (*ton onta edeiknuon logon*), that the corpse belonged to Hyllos," a son of Gē (Earth) and not the better-known son of Heracles. This might suggest that the Lydian expounders concealed the truth until refuted by Pausanias, but he might only mean that, once he had contradicted the prevailing view, regional experts were consulted and came to a conclusion that corroborated his.[15]

A criticism that he makes on the expounders of the Argives is more clearly unfavorable. Arguing against the claim that Argos had the tombs of Deianira and Helenos, the son of Priam, and the Palladium as well, Pausanias observes, "The Argive expounders are aware that not everything they say is true, but they say it all the same, for getting the many to change their opinion is no easy task." This comment, however, reflects not only mendacity on the part of the expounders but also the persistence of local belief.[16]

Such reflections on expounders and "the many" do not in themselves show that such persons were of low social class. The Greek expression "the many" may mean other things than "the masses," "the vulgar." Pausanias often uses "the many" when disagreeing with widely held views; thus, "a story has penetrated the many that Theseus handed power to the people . . . In fact, other falsehoods too are repeated by the many because they are inattentive to research (*historias anēkooi*) and put their trust in whatever they hear from childhood in choruses and tragedies." It is not likely that, outside major centers such as Athens and Smyrna, ordinary citizens were able to hear "choruses and tragedies" from a tender age. Pausanias must refer to the educated classes, those whom other authors call "the educated" (*hoi pepaideumenoi*), the kind for whom Plutarch writes in his treatise *On How the Young Should Listen to the Poets*. Pausanias designates his preferred readers by the exact contrary of his reflections on "the many": "the studious" (*philēkooi*).[17]

In general, therefore, Pausanias treats his expounders much as he treats his other informants, "the man from Mysia," for example, sometimes agreeing with them, often not. So far nothing has emerged to suggest that these are people of an essentially different kind from others whom he met on his travels, except in being rooted in a single place and not itinerant. They are not "the man in the street" but rather the *gens moyen cultivés,* educated but not learned. Nonetheless, the fact that discussions about giants' bones and the mythic past of Athens prevailed even at this social level suggests the hubbub that Pausanias attempts to dominate by his own scholarship and sureness of judgment.

We can now move to the question of the "expounders" and "guides" known from other texts and from inscriptions and in particular confront a conception of them that goes back to the first systematic study, that of Preller in 1838.[18] He popularized a view that such local informants were similar to the *Ciceroni* known to nineteenth-century tourists, "very low people, induced by a small wage to undertake a rather demeaning trade, and only superficially acquainted with literature" (*homines infimos, mercedula ad quaestum ignobiliorem faciendum adductos, litterasque neglegenter doctos*); some were, however, above the average, for example, Aristarchos, Pausanias's informant at Olympia.[19] This idea was then taken up, and given vivid expression, by Sir James Frazer:

> We know from other ancient writers that in antiquity, as at the present day, towns of any note were infested by persons of this class who lay in wait for and pounced on the stranger as their natural prey, wrangled over his body, and having secured their victim led him about from place to place . . . until having exhausted their learning and his patience they pocketed their fee and took their leave.[20]

In fact, a brief survey of such guides, whether called *exēgētai* or *periēgētai,* in literature and inscriptions suggests that this view of them as simple *Ciceroni* is erroneous. To take *exēgētai* first, Strabo uses this word of those who showed the visitors of Heliopolis the local *hiera,* probably shrines rather than rites.[21] Closer to Pausanias in time, in Longus's *Daphnis and Chloe* the narrator recalls how when hunting on Lesbos he came to a cave adorned with an *eikōn,* presumably a painting rather than a sculptural relief, and was impelled to seek out an "expounder of the image" (*exēgētēn tēs eikonos*). Recast in the narrator's own words, the explanation occupies the rest of the work, and at the very end the circle is closed when Daphnis and Chloe (or perhaps their children: the text is uncertain) "adorned the cave, dedicated images (*eikonas*), and set up an altar of Love the Shepherd." While Longus might only mean the *nomen agentis* in the sense of "someone to explain" rather than a local antiquary, the latter seems the likelier meaning, and if so the whole novel can perhaps be regarded as the literary transformation of a guide's monologue, what Plutarch calls a *rhēsis*. By a coincidence, one of the very few epigraphic examples of such a guide, though he is designated a *periēgētēs* and not an *exēgētēs,* comes from Lesbos.[22]

In epigraphy,[23] the richest source for such people happens to be Olympia, the site at which Pausanias mentions them most often, and his testimony is in fact crucial for interpreting the pertinent inscriptions. Over sixty stones, some of them tiny fragments, contain what Dittenberger called "lists of cult personnel," and his discussion is still fundamental. These do not show all the personnel of the sanctuary, but only the participants in the monthly sacrifices described by Pausanias, and they cover a period from the 30s of the first century B.C. to the third quarter of the third century A.D. Up to the first half of the second century A.D., they list only one *exēgētēs,* but thereafter two. There is also a curious fluctuation in their titulature, since in four of the lists, widely separated in time, they appear as *periēgētai.* Dittenberger saw that this variation was due to the pressure of popular usage, with the newer coinage of *periēgētēs* displacing the traditional title. Their functions, it may be presumed, included both guiding the officiants around the altars and ensuring that the various sacrifices were correctly performed. Such officials could well have given information to a learned visitor from Lydia or Ionia.[24]

Elsewhere than in Olympia, epigraphic *periēgētai* are extremely rare.[25] At Hermione in the Argolid, at some time in the Imperial period, a certain Smyrnaia is commemorated as "daughter of Leontidas, the guide (*periēgētēs*) and physician-in-chief (*archiatros*)," clearly a member of the local aristocracy and no needy *Cicerone.*[26] At a site in the territory of Mytilene, the city honors a certain Besos, an archiatros not subject to liturgies (*aleitourgētos*); that is, he is exempted from public services by local decision and in accordance with imperial law. The text records his many civil and religious offices, ending with the enigmatic phrase "leading sacrificer (*prothytēs*) of the most sacred emperor and of the sanctuaries of the city, and guide (*periēgētēs*) for forty years now, and without salary or fee, unlike his predecessors" (*tou de theiotatou autokratoros kai tōn tās polios eirōn prothytan, kai <kai> periēgētan eteōn ēdē tessarakonta, kai pros aneu syntaxios kai misthou, ouch hōs oi pro autou*). The Greek is not perfectly clear, but the person must be of high local standing, involved in many of the traditional cults of the city as well as in the cult of the reigning emperor.[27]

In literature, the best evidence for the activity and standing of *periēgētai* comes from Plutarch. In his Delphic dialogue, *On the Oracles of the Pythia,* a young man from Pergamum called Diogenianus is visiting the sanctuary while Plutarch's friend Philinus and other learned men lead him around.[28] As narrator, Philinus begins his account at the point where "the guides (*periēgētai*) were going through their set pieces, paying no attention to us when we asked them to shorten their monologues (*rhēseis*) and most of the inscriptions." Later, after a discussion among the learned visitors, "a silence fell, and then the guides again began to offer their monologues." When the party gets involved in another erudite question, one of them observes, "We seem rather rudely to be depriving the guides of their proper job." Later still, when one of the party puts a question to the guides but gets no reply, another of the group jokes that they have been struck dumb by the learned conversation.[29] These guides appear to be well-meaning officials, eager to display their stock of knowledge and yet not concealing their ignorance. Just as Plutarch's guides resemble Pausanias's expounders, so Plutarch's Diogenianus, the learned and confident young visitor from Asia Minor, perhaps gives an impression of Pausanias as he toured the sights of old Greece.

Two of Plutarch's *Table Talks* involve a guide called Praxiteles. In the first, which depicts a dinner in Corinth during the Isthmian Games, he begins the discussion of the pine used for crowning the victors, a subject also of interest to Pausanias. The second is again set in Corinth during the Isthmia, and a certain Sospis is entertaining "his closest and most scholarly friends" (*tous malista philous kai philologous*). Here Praxiteles, called on by the local teacher of literature (*grammatikos*) to rebut two "rhetors," gives a learned discourse on the palm frond customarily given to victors in all contests.[30] He is thus in company with the most erudite persons at the festival, and once again we are in a world very similar to Pausanias's, in which visiting scholars mingle with local antiquaries as their social equals, now accepting their views and now disputing them.

As might be expected, Lucian's allusions to contemporary periegetes are more satirical. In the *Charon,* or *Observers* (*Contemplantes*), Charon gets a tour of the upper world from Hermes, who is portrayed as one acquaintance doing a favor for another, even if he anticipates "payment" in a beating from his habitual employer, Zeus. Aeacus gives Menippus a similar tour of the underworld in the *Dialogues of the Dead,* and guides led by the hero Nauplius do the same for the narrator in the *True Histories*. In the *Lover of Lies* (*Philopseudes*), the main speaker, Tychiades, deplores the way in which cities and nations tell lies about the gods. His interlocutor claims that Athens, Thebes, and other cities are only trying to make themselves more venerable, "and moreover, if you were to deprive Greeks of all these fables (*muthōdē*), nothing would save the guides from starvation, since no visitors would want to hear the facts even free of charge." The *Amores* is probably a work of the third century, attributed to Lucian because of the subject matter, though very different from him in style.[31] The main speaker, Lycinus, recalls a visit to Rhodes. "As I went round the colonnades in the Dionyseion, I was looking at the pictures, both enjoying the view of them and recalling heroic myths, for immediately two or three persons had rushed up to me, telling every story for a small fee." The inscription from Lesbos discussed above showed that some guides, though not the more high-minded ones, charged fees, but it does not follow, as Preller inferred, that guides were in general "people of the lowest class" or Frazer's "persons . . . who lay in wait for and pounced on the stranger."

As a contrast with Lucian, a passage of Christian literature, probably to be dated to the third century, gives a picture of such guides very similar to Pausanias's, though it escaped Preller and all those who have subsequently discussed the question. The author of the *Exhortation to the Greeks,* a work ascribed to

Justin Martyr, tells how he visited Cumae and there, in company with guides, saw the celebrated cave of the Sibyl, a "great basilica carved from a single stone," and the other places associated with her. "They also said, claiming to have heard it from their ancestors, that those who received the oracles in those times, being without education, often mistook the proper meter, and this, they said, was the reason for the faulty meter of some lines." These guides were therefore educated persons, eager to excuse the Sibyl's metrical errors, rather as Plutarch was eager to explain why the Pythia no longer used verse. It happens that Pausanias too had visited Cumae and seen many of the same sights.[32]

To conclude, despite Pausanias's old-fashioned use of *exēgētes* rather than *periēgētēs,* his picture of his local informants does not differ substantially from that of contemporary authors and documents. These are not Preller's "low people" but respectable local antiquarians, not always as knowledgeable as the learned visitors they accompanied but able to hold their own in the company of "the educated." The kind of society that Plutarch portrays in his Pythian dialogues and his *Table Talks,* with its mixture of sophists, professors of literature, philosophers, lawyers, doctors, and wealthy amateurs, may well reflect the circles in which Pausanias himself was to move some fifty years later. (By contrast, the dinner of Livius Larensis, which is the setting of Athenaeus's *Deipnosophists,* gives the impression of a literary fiction.) Pausanias belongs at that middle level of the Greek intelligentsia which is perhaps represented better by inscriptions than by literature. At the same level, or only slightly below, stood the local antiquarians who supplied him with information, the guides whom he calls with a quaint conservatism "expounders."

Tourism and the Sacred

Pausanias and the Traditions of
Greek Pilgrimage

A mong the places that Pausanias visits, and for which his *Periegesis* is meant as a guide for potential visitors, probably a majority are religious centers. Among visitors to religious centers, some at least deserve to be called pilgrims. Debate has raged recently over whether or not Pausanias is writing for an audience of potential pilgrims, and whether or not he himself deserves to be called a pilgrim. This chapter reconsiders these questions and supports the view that the intended audience of the *Periegesis* included pilgrims, situating it within the history of pilgrimage and the Greek world, and in particular within the "pilgrimage culture" of the Antonine Age.

Preliminary Issues

Definitions

Until recently, pilgrimage in the ancient Greek and Roman world was a neglected subject. We are now beginning to understand how central it was to the fabric of national and international politics at all periods of ancient history.[1] Principal forms include the great state pilgrimages (*theoriai*) of Classical Greece to the panhellenic sanctuaries for festivals and for other reasons; personal pilgrimage to healing sanctuaries, particularly important from the Hellenistic period onward; and pilgrimage within Greco-Roman Egypt, which is well attested from the periods of Ptolemaic and Roman rule.

Because of the comparatively recent development of academic interest in the subject, fundamental issues are only now being confronted. Along with the all-important question of what counts as evidence for pilgrimage, there is the crucial issue of how we define it. "Pilgrimage" is a useful word, as long as we divest it of any association with Christianity. In Christianity, pilgrimage can be a metaphor for the Christian life: "reaching the Holy Land" is an easy metaphor for achieving salvation after death, and if that is so, the journey there may stand for suffering in life and even for physical death. Pilgrimage is therefore a time of penance, and the pilgrim is encouraged to make the journey uncomfortable. These associations are not confined to Christianity: we find them to some extent also in Islam, and the idea of pilgrimage as a metaphor for the transition through death to a new birth goes back to Plato, and perhaps even to the ancient Egyptians.

However, it is important to recognize that these associations are not characteristic of all manifestations of pilgrimage. The modern concept of "pilgrimage" (as colloquially understood) tends to suggest—perhaps wrongly—a personal pilgrimage, whereas ancient pilgrimages were generally sponsored by the *polis* and a matter of group travel; to a modern reader, the word "pilgrimage" may suggest a penance, a period of self-denial and suffering, whereas ancient pilgrimage tended to be characterized by joy and celebration.

The borderline between what is and is not a pilgrimage is not always straightforward.[2] One problem is the relationship between pilgrimage and tourism. Conceptually, we contrast the two easily, the latter being a matter of visiting a sanctuary purely for the sake of the visit, whereas the motives for the former have to do with personal piety and religious celebration. But even the most scrupulous critic may have difficulty distinguishing the two in all cases, and it is by no means clear that the ancient Greeks distinguished them in the same way. The difficulty, even impossibility, of making this distinction forces us to redefine the relationship between pilgrimage and tourism. It may be that some activities which moderns would intuitively class as tourism would now turn out to be pilgrimage. And even if a more or less independent notion of tourism appears in the Hellenistic period, I would argue that tourism and pilgrimage cannot be easily distinguished in the Classical period.

Pausanias: Pilgrim, Tourist, Pepaideumenos?

Pausanias's *Periegesis* documents a journey round Greece, visiting primarily sacred locations. He moves from Athens to Delphi, via Olympia and the Peloponnese, following on land the route taken by seaborne Athenian sacred delegations. The difference is that Pausanias makes a huge number of detours en route, but even sacred delegates made stops on their journey.

Where do we site the *Periegesis* on the borderline between pilgrimage and sightseeing? Specifically:

(a) Are pilgrims Pausanias's intended audience—either (a_1) all of the intended audience or (a_2) at least part of it?
(b) Is Pausanias himself a pilgrim?

Point (b) is harder to prove than (a), and (a_2) is easier than (a_1).

Elsner has argued that Pausanias is a pilgrim and writes for pilgrims. He works with a broad definition of pilgrimage, stressing the issue of identity: working from the premise that Pausanias is interested in Greek cultural identity, specifically an identity rooted in the Greek past (hence he tends to ignore the Roman present), Elsner suggests that this interest in cultural identity links Pausanias with the attitudes and expectations of pilgrims in many different cultures. In addition, Pausanias shows religious sensibility, in respect of both overt sites and hidden doctrines; hence there is a contradiction between the overt strategy of the guide and the reticence of the initiate. Finally, Elsner shows that the circuitous route taken by Pausanias is compatible with pilgrimage in other cultures.[3]

This thesis has come in for criticism from authorities on Pausanias. Typical is Arafat, whose reasons for denying pilgrimage to Pausanias include:

(i) that Pausanias is interested in civic identity (Arafat presumes that a pilgrim would not be);

(ii) that Pausanias has no particular religious objective and is not a devotee of deities (whereas a pilgrim would be); and

(iii) that Pausanias is a *pepaideumenos* (man of education), which is a property inconsistent with being a pilgrim.[4]

Arafat's objections stand up as long as we work with modern notions of pilgrimage based on modern salvation-religions. But they lose their force if we work with a view of pilgrimage based in the Greek and Roman world.

Point (iii), the issue of Pausanias's *paideia*, I will address below. As to point (i), the issue of civic identity, since it is the *polis* that regulates religious behavior in Classical Greece, we would expect sacred visitation to be bound up with the *polis*.[5] And in fact one of the distinctive characteristics of pilgrimage in Classical Greece is that it was largely a matter of reciprocal communication between states and not a matter of private visitation. By the Antonine Age, we find an increasing frequency of pilgrimage by private individuals; Aelius Aristides is a good example here (see the final section, below). Nevertheless, the *polis* remains to a large extent the focus of ritual activity.

As to point (ii), the issue of being a devotee, adherence to a single deity is not part of Classical religion either, where worship of the whole pantheon of deities is more the norm, especially on the civic level.[6] But pilgrimage and polytheism are not incompatible; as the case of Hindu India shows, polytheism simply offers more opportunities for pilgrimage, and it can be argued that, in general, pilgrimage in polytheistic societies is typically rich and multifaceted.

But here a second point should be made: we need to distinguish Pausanias the pilgrim from Pausanias writing for pilgrims. We need not imagine that the typical pilgrim for whom Pausanias is writing visited all the sanctuaries that Pausanias himself visits. The scope of Pausanias's pilgrimage necessarily exceeds the likely dimensions of the pilgrimages of his audience. In including all likely pilgrimages within it, the *Periegesis* could be said to achieve the status of a sort of hyperpilgrimage.

Pausanias and *Theoria*

Pilgrimage and Vision

One of the chief problems in arguing that Pausanias is a pilgrim is the absence of ritual activity in his accounts of visiting religious sites (Arafat hints at this).

All Pausanias does at the sanctuary is look at the things there and report stories about the places. He sacrifices rarely (e.g., on Aegina). Surely, the argument goes, if he were a pilgrim, we would expect some sort of ritual activity to be described. As it is, he seems more like a tourist than a pilgrim.[7]

The point to make here is that one of the key ideas in Greek pilgrimage traditions is *theoria,* which combines vision and intellectual inquiry.[8] The word is particularly common for state pilgrimage, but it is occasionally used for pilgrimage by private individuals as well. A parallel can be drawn with the pilgrimage tradition of Hindu India, where an important role is played by the activity of *darshan,* which means "vision" or "contemplation" and the religious insight that accompanies this process, sometimes achieved as the end product of pilgrimage, sometimes achieved through seeing a famous or sacred person or persons.[9]

In Greek tradition, watching may be part of a more complex structure of ritual activities at the sanctuary, but it can also be important on its own.[10] The paradigm case is when spectators watch athletic competitions, a special type of sacred spectacle. But more broadly, the object of contemplation may include cult statues, temples, and artifacts. To take a literary example, in Euripides's *Andromache* (1086–88) a messenger reports that Neoptolemus and his companions devoted three days to contemplation (*thea*) of the sanctuary before offering sacrifice.[11] Here contemplation is represented as an activity typical of peaceful pilgrims, by implication contrasted with the hostile approach to the sanctuary that Neoptolemus makes in conventional versions of the myth.

Pausanias fits perfectly into this tradition of ritual contemplation. Every page of the *Periegesis* shows examples. One thinks of his disappointed excursion to see the statue of Demeter Melaine: "It was mainly to see this Demeter that I came to Phigalia" (8.42.11). Looking at the key sites in a shrine is exactly what religious visitors had always done.[12]

Pilgrimage and Tourism

Because of the visual emphasis of ancient Greek pilgrimage, making a distinction between pilgrimage and recreational sightseeing is usually difficult and may even be methodologically inappropriate.[13] The speaker of Isocrates's *Trapeziticus,* a young man from the Bosporus, says that he has been sent off by his father to Athens and the rest of Greece *kat' emporian kai kata theorian* (by way of trade and *theoria*). Again, in a fragment of the *Deliakos* of Hyperides (frag. 70 Blass), certain rich Aeolians—later to be murdered on Delos—are said to have left their home *kata theorian tes Hellados* (by way of *theoria* of Greece). In both cases, the expression seems to imply visiting a number of places rather than making a pilgrimage only to one. However, it is not unlikely that many of the places to be visited *kata theorian* were religious centers. Was this secular sightseeing? Or perhaps a form of sightseeing with a religious dimension, a sort of "sacred tourism"?

The practice of "sacred tourism" is also found in Egypt. In the temple of Seti I of Abydos (known to the Greeks as the *Memnonion*), three fifth-century visitors left a graffito which says that each of them *ethesato* ("watched"; the Ionic form of *theaomai*). Was the viewing referred to here merely recreational? Or was it motivated by a belief in the sacredness of the place? The latter might be thought unlikely at this period, but one should bear in mind that at least some Aramaic-speaking visitors to Abydos from this period seem to have been motivated by religious feeling.[14] So, too, in a documentary papyrus from the late second century B.C., an official in Alexandria asks that certain sites in the Fayyum, particularly the Labyrinth, be prepared for the visit of a Roman official called Memmius who was coming there *epi theorian* (for *theoria*). This sounds more like sightseeing than pilgrimage, particularly since one need not expect a Roman official to have a religious motivation for visiting Egyptian sites on the Nile. But a religious element seems to be present nevertheless, since sacrifice is referred to.[15]

What, then, of the relation between pilgrimage and tourism? Conceptually, we contrast the two easily, the latter being a matter of visiting a sanctuary purely for the sake of the visit, whereas the motives for the former have to do with personal piety and religious celebration. But even we may have difficulty distinguishing the two in all cases, and it is by no means clear that the ancient Greeks distinguished them in the same way.[16] Pilgrimage is often accompanied by sightseeing of sacred places that borders on tourism; and tourism, if it existed at all, would tend to focus on sights of religious interest and hence be difficult to distinguish from pilgrimage.

Theoria *and Identity*

For Elsner, as we have seen, the defining feature of Pausanias's pilgrimage is identity. In fact, if we look at the traditions of state pilgrimage in Greece, we find that self-definition is at the heart of the phenomenon. The pilgrims who attend a sanctuary are drawn from a definite catchment area. Some catchment areas are regional, drawing in members of an ethnic group or a small geographical zone. A good example is Delos, where the *panegyris* was an old Ionian meeting place; during the period of the Athenian empire, it was taken over by Athens. In the Hellenistic period, its catchment area broadened, and it developed a special link with powerful islands in the southwest Aegean, including Kos. A well-attested site from the Roman period is that of the oracle of Claros in Asia Minor, an oracle that does not seem to have become widely used until the second century A.D., when it started to rival that of Didyma. We have copious evidence at Claros in the form of inscriptions recording sacred delegations sent there, and inscriptions that record oracles are found in the cities from which the oracle's various consultants had come. Consultants come from a number of different parts of Asia Minor, as well as from the Black Sea and north Greece, but not from mainland Greece, and among cities of Asia probably from recently hellenized cities rather than from Greek ones.[17]

Other sanctuaries were panhellenic. Pilgrimage was typically a movement from the local to a panhellenic center. The panhellenic was a cultural value, incorporating ideas about the excellence of Greek art, athletic prowess, the great achievements of the past. Since a genuine political union never developed in Greece, the great sanctuaries were the principal focus for national identity.[18] Pilgrims had contact with the panhellenic in several ways: they saw artifacts from all over Greece in sanctuaries;[19] they made contact with pilgrims from other states and exchanged information;[20] and as for the political dimension,[21] diplomacy took place at the *panegyris,* where to take part was to be a member of the panhellenic community, to be excluded was a political snub (though only rarely did the panhellenic *panegyris* become the occasion for cohesive and unilateral political action).

As well as fostering a sense of local identity among members of individual *poleis,* pilgrimage would also have encouraged a feeling of connectedness among different groups attending a *panegyris.* This trend was particularly strong at the regional level, where to modern perception there may be ambiguity about whether an organization of states focused on a single sanctuary was political or religious in spirit.

At the panhellenic level also, sanctuaries and festivals that welcomed pilgrims from the whole Greek world were the focus for the development of a limited sense of the common ethnicity of all Greeks. That local allegiances remained strong seems to be indicated by patterns of dedications at major sanctuaries: dedications in the name of individual *poleis* were grander than those done in the name of the Panhellenes.[22] But there are also signs that panhellenic identity sometimes took precedence—for example, in the tone of Isocrates's *Panegyricus* of 380 B.C., which calls on all Greeks to make a concerted effort against Persia.

Hence, when we ask the question "Of what, exactly, was the contemplation implied in the word *theoria* a contemplation?" the answer is as much "shared traditions of cultural identity" as anything else. This is another respect, then, in which Pausanias's pilgrimage is traditional.

Periegesis and Pilgrimage

Another way into the problem is to consider the meaning of the genre term *Periegesis* in the title of Pausanias's work. A *periegesis* is usually understood to be a geographical catalogue, cast in the form of a tour, often of a local area but sometimes more extended in scope. The form is related to local history. Modern scholarship has established that there was a specifically periegetic form of historiography, stretching back at least to the third century B.C.; its origins might even be discerned as early as the *Epidemiai* of Ion of Chios in the fifth century B.C.[23]

The best-attested early manifestation of the genre is Polemo of Ilion, whose works are found in a large number of fragments collected by Preller. Polemo's interests were largely religious; and his religious credentials are guaranteed by the fact that he was a Delphic *proxenos.*[24] At Athens, he wrote about the dedications on the Acropolis and about the sacred way from Athens to Eleusis; for Sparta, he wrote about dedications; he wrote a book about Samothrace, which was at least partly concerned with religious issues; he wrote about the festivals of Heracles at Thebes; he wrote about Delphi (the dedication in the Sicyonian treasury of a book by Aristomache, a poetess from Erythrae, when she had won at the Isthmian Games).[25] And he wrote about Olympia too: the work *Helladikos* (perhaps the same as the *Periegesis kosmike*), whether or not it is rightly ascribed to him, described the temples of the Metapontians and the Byzantians and the temple of Hera at Olympia.[26] Lastly, Polemo wrote about his home town of Ilion; the fragments contain an aetiology of the cult of Apollo Smintheus.[27] Even that work could have a pilgrimage dimension, since the tombs of the fallen Greeks at Troy had been a bona fide destination for pilgrims at least since the time of Alexander the Great. The area's importance is most vividly illustrated by an account by Philostratus, writing in the third century A.D., of the yearly pilgrimage to the Troad of Thessalian youths.[28]

Polemo's religious interests are also clear in a work entitled *Peri tou diou kodiou* (On the Divine Fleece), an object apparently used for sacrifice:

> After these preliminaries, (the priest) proceeds to the celebration of the mystic rites; he takes out the contents of the shrine and distributes them to all who have brought round the tray. The latter is an earthenware vessel, holding within it a large number of small cups cemented together; and in them are sage, white poppy seeds, grains of wheat and barley, peas, vetches, okra seeds, lentils, beans, rice-wheat, oats, compressed fruit, honey, oil, wine, milk, and sheep's wool unwashed. The man who carries it, resembling the bearer of the sacred winnowing fan, tastes these articles.[29]

His work *Pros Neanthen antigraphai,* an attack on Neanthes of Cyzicus, who wrote *Peri teletes,* also contained a discussion of religious matters.[30]

We certainly cannot state that all periegetic writing is religious in purpose. The few surviving fragments of Diodorus the Black, another figure from the third century B.C., leave no such trace; nor do those of Heliodorus of Athens or the better-attested *periegesis* of Athens and Boeotia now ascribed to Herakleides.[31] However, we hear of a few other writers, not explicitly awarded the title *periegetes,* who might be thought to resemble Polemo. An example is Agaklytos, who wrote on the *kolossos* of Kypselos at Olympia; another is Anaxandrides of Delphi, who wrote about dedications there.[32]

Periegetic writing is not about pilgrimage only, but pilgrimage is one of the things that it included. Two examples of religious *periegesis* have been mentioned earlier: Isocrates's *Trapeziticus,* whose narrator says that he has been sent off by his father to Athens and the rest of Greece "by way of trade and *theoria*"; and Hyperides's *Deliakos,* which mentions rich Aeolians who left home "by way of *theoria* of Greece." Traveling "by way of sightseeing" (*kata theorian*) is the complement of periegetic writing. Most of the sights seen must have been sacred, and many travelers taking part in such trips must have been motivated by religious feeling, even if in other cases the motivation may have been closer to recreational curiosity. In both cases, the borderline between pilgrimage and sight-seeing is fluid.

A different way in which *periegesis* engages with the sacred is in the announcing of festivals. Officials (like tourists, travelers, and pilgrims, they too are called *theoroi*) sent out by states such as Delphi to announce festivals followed certain key routes, which can be reconstructed thanks to lists of official hosts (*theorodokoi*) preserved in the sanctuaries, which articulate panhellenic space. One of the routes followed by the Delphic *theoroi* did indeed wend its way round the Peloponnese, though in a different direction from that of Pausanias.[33] It has been suggested that the deep impression made on the Greek mentality by such lists is reflected already in the Homeric Catalogue of Ships.[34]

Interestingly, in late inscriptions, *periegetes* was a sacred term, alternating with *exegetes*. We find this usage at Olympia and at Athens, where a certain Licinius Firmus is described as a *periegetes kai hiereus* (*periegetes* and priest).[35] The editors of the Olympian inscriptions claim that this is popular language creeping in, there having been a popular confusion with *exegetes*. Maybe so, but what would such a confusion imply? Surely that *periegesis* was by then thought to be a religious concept, like *exegesis*. The *periegetes* has privileged knowledge of the site, analogous to, but somewhat superseding, the knowledge of the *exegetes,* with whom Pausanias the Periegete often competes.[36]

Pilgrimage and Intellectuals

Pausanias is interested in learning, not just about the details of sites and about epichoric religion, but also about more abstract religious and philosophical principles. Thus, in the temple of Asclepius at Aigion (7.23), he argued about the nature of Asclepius with the man from Sidon; both ended up accepting that Asclepius was air. And at 8.2.3, he tells us that when he started his journey, myths such as the myth of Cronos had seemed like foolishness, but when he reached Arcadia, he came to realize that they contained wise truths in the form of riddles.

This intellectual component in Pausanias's project has been seen as an obstacle to labeling him a pilgrim. Arafat simply thinks the two categories are incompatible. Swain argues that if Pausanias was really a pilgrim, one would expect his conversion to religious belief to have occurred before he set out.[37]

In fact, ancient pilgrimage easily accommodates an intellectual motivation. For one thing, an intellectual component is built into the notion of *theoria,* which also has the sense "philosophical contemplation," and it can be argued that there was a conceptual link between the two. First, being a spectator at the panhellenic games was sometimes used as a symbol for the *theoretikos bios* (the life of contemplation lived by philosophers), which is opposed to the *praktikos bios* (or practical life, lived by politicians and by most citizens).[38] Second, philosophers seem to exploit the idea of pilgrimage as a journey culminating in *theoria* as a symbol for the path of reasoning, consisting of dialectic and culminating in rational enlightenment; a particular factor in the background here may have been the Eleusinian Mysteries, where the enlightenment that comes at the end is particularly dramatic.[39] The "philosophy" sense of the word may even color the "pilgrimage" sense. Solon's famous *theoria,* in Herodotus 1.29, seems to have had a philosophical dimension. An Athenian inscription has been reconstructed to say that a young man from Pergamon who came as a *theoros* to Athens decided to stay there so that he could study philosophy: *theoria* in the ritual sense is a pretext for *theoria* in the philosophical sense.[40]

But pilgrimage is often about religious learning. The best examples come from Egypt, largely because the data there are better preserved. At Abydos, there is a *proskunema* by a certain Bagas who does not ask anything of the god but speculates on his identity: "some say you are Asclepius, but I that you are Dionysus; others that you are Phoibos and Hermes and Harpokrates . . ."[41] A more developed example of the same pattern comes from Kalabsha (Talmis), on the Nile in Nubia, the site of a temple of Mandaules/Merwul, perhaps a Blemmyan deity. A number of inscriptions survive from the walls, all from the Imperial period. An anonymous inscription records a vision received in the temple (the subject of a famous article by Arthur Darby Nock); the writer describes the motivation for his pilgrimage as desiring to know if Mandoulis was really Helios:

> Beaming Shooting Master, Mandoulis Titan, Makareus, watching the bright signs of you I considered and was busy, wanting to know for sure whether you are the sun. I made myself free of all vice and impiety, and having been holy for a long time, I sacrificed what was necessary for the sake of divine piety. And I had a vision and rested. For you granted my prayer and showed yourself to me . . . heavenly . . . washing yourself meanwhile in the holy water of immortality, you appear again. You came at the right time, making a rising toward your enclosure, bringing breath to your statue and the temple and great power. There I recognized you, Mandoulis, as the son, the all-seeing master, king of all, all-ruling Aion. O most fortunate people who dwell in sacred Talmis, which Mandoulis the sun loves, which is beneath the scepter of beautiful-haired Isis of the thousand names.[42]

In order to ask this question, he says he has purified himself. Subsequently, he relates that Mandoulis revealed himself, perhaps in a dream, as Helios. The pilgrim is motivated by a desire for mystical knowledge, and it is duly revealed to him: the god is not an obscure local deity but has a universal status.

It is also around this time that the oracle of Claros started delivering explicitly mystical, theosophical messages. It has long been believed that some of the so-called theological oracles, such as those transmitted in the so-called Tübingen Theosophy, go back to genuine oracles delivered at Claros and Didyma. In the most famous one, a certain Theophilos asked Apollo: Are you god or is it another? And the reply was:

> There is a flame situated above the superheavenly container, immense, moving, an insatiable Eternity [Aion], and it is beyond the grasp of the immortals, unless the great father contrives that he be seen where neither aither bears bright stars, or the clear moon hovers, nor does a god meet on the path. Nor do I grasp him and scatter on him my rays as I whirl through the heaven. But god is a

very long channel of fire, creeping, whirling in a circle. If one touched the heavenly fire, one would not divide its heart[?]. For it does not admit division, and in continuous practice Eternity is united with eternities, self-generated from god himself. Untaught, motherless, unstruck, not yielding even its name in word[?], dwelling in fire, this is god. We messengers are a small part of god.[43]

A version of the last three lines also survives in a recently discovered inscription from the temple of Theos Hypsistos at Oenoanda, perhaps a record of a real Clarian oracle. The theology is striking: Apollo himself is but a messenger; god is the universal Aion. Another oracle, cited by Macrobius (*Saturnalia* 1.18–19) makes generalizing syncretistic statements about divinity, identifying Apollo with other Greek deities and even with the Jewish Yahweh (Iao). Nock relates this to the theology of Middle Platonism.[44]

Pausanias's confession at 8.2.3 can be compared to that of the *proskunema* at Kalabsha. What brings the writer to make the pilgrimage is a general sense that divine *numen* is more readily accessed at sacred sites, though he remains skeptical of details of local theological doctrine (the myth of Cronos, the equation of Mandoulis with the Sun). The pilgrimage in some way brings about a religious revelation, so the pilgrim returns with greater faith than he set out with. The pattern is common in pilgrimage; according to the Epidaurian Iamata, some pilgrims on arrival disbelieved the accounts of Asclepius's power described to them but become convinced before they left; and yet they must have had some faith in the deity to make the pilgrimage in the first place. The point of such stories of religious revelation in the Epidaurian Iamata is didactic: pilgrims should trust the god's power. Does Pausanias's confession at 8.2.3 make a similar point?[45]

Pausanias and the Pilgrimage Environment of the Second Sophistic

General

Although Pausanias's pilgrimage fits into a long tradition in ancient Greece, it can also be read as typical of its times. In the Second Sophistic, pilgrimage assumed a high profile, manifesting itself in many different traditions and undertaken by different types of participants and with varying motivations. New geographical areas became important. Particularly well documented is pilgrimage to sanctuaries in Roman Egypt, including that of Imhotep-Asclepius at Deir el-Bahari, that of Isis at Philae, and that of Mandoulis Aion at Kalabsha (as we saw in the last section).[46] Greek-speaking pilgrims to Egyptian sanctuaries very often left inscriptional evidence, most commonly *proskunemata,* which served as permanent records of their visit and of their friends and relatives.

There is great variety in the participants of pilgrimage. Philosophers are one class of pilgrims in this period; some of the journeys of Apollonius of Tyana described by Philostratus resemble pilgrimages.[47] Roman emperors make up another class. Hadrian was initiated at Eleusis, as Augustus had been, and he

visited Ajax's tomb at Troy in A.D. 132. Following in the footsteps of Trajan
(A.D. 113), in A.D. 129 Hadrian visited Mount Kasion (Jebel al-Akra), which is
on the Syrian coast to the north of ancient Ugarit (Ras Shamra) and south of
the mouth of the Orontes and was famous for its view of the sunrise. He also
traveled to Egypt and made a pilgrimage to hear Memnon greet the dawn.[48]

More traditional forms of pilgrimage, going back to the civic culture of
Archaic and Classical Greece, also continued to flourish. Athletic competitions,
for which we find evidence all over the Greek world, must have attracted pilgrims; besides the great panhellenic competitions, which remained important,
numerous regional festivals came into being as well, for example, the Gorgas
festival in Phocian Ambrussos, attested during the Severan period.[49] Pilgrimages
undertaken for healing increased in importance, and state pilgrimages both continued and were revived. Athens, for instance, sent official delegations to Delphi
and Delos, accompanying offerings of twelve oxen (*dodekaides*).[50] Asia Minor
seethed with religious activity: one of the most important sanctuaries in this
period was the sanctuary of Apollo at Claros, a center for visitation from all
over Asia Minor, and here we find a self-conscious emulation of Greek cities
in the classical period, as evidenced by the use of terms like *theopropoi* and
theoroi in inscriptions.[51] This conservative tendency is shown also in the self-
presentation of the temple staff: many of the officials at Claros, and also some
prophets, traced their descent to "the Heraclids from Ardus" (Ardus was one of
the early kings of Lydia), and by referring to him, the *thespiodes* seem to claim
an ancient pedigree, and indeed a Greek one.[52]

Pausanias is aware of these varieties of pilgrimage tradition. For example,
in his account of Arcadia, he describes how Argives carry away fire from the
temple of Artemis Pyronia on Mount Krathis, just as Athenians do in the Pythais
(8.15.9).[53] In his account of Thebes, he describes how the men of Titheorea in
Phocis raid the tomb of Amphion and Zethus in Thebes, a sort of covert pilgrimage (9.17.4). Interestingly, he ignores one of the great religious innovations
in pilgrimage in this period: in A.D. 131 or 132, Hadrian set up the Panhellenion
in Athens, a religious center for the whole Greek world, including Asia Minor;[54]
it must have been visited regularly by delegations. Pausanias does not mention
this institution, though he does mention Mount Panhellenion on Aegina, a traditional national center (1.44.9, 2.29.8).

Besides the evidence of Pausanias himself, a considerable amount of pilgrimage literature from this period exists. The *Life of Apollonius* by Philostratus
can be read as a pilgrimage text, as can Lucian's *De dea Syria*. Philostratus's
Heroicus describes a pilgrimage from Thessaly to Troy. Plutarch (*Quaestiones
Graecae* 26) describes a pilgrimage made by the Aenianes in Thessaly to Cas-
siopaea in Epirus. Pilgrimage was also a theme in the Greek novel: for example,
state pilgrimage from Byzantium to Tyre plays an important role in the plot of
Cleitophon and Leucippe, by Achilles Tatius.[55]

The Antonine Age thus emerges as a golden age for pilgrimage. It is in this
context that the *Periegesis* of Pausanias should be read. The pervasiveness of
pilgrimage and quasi pilgrimage in the period creates a presumption that Pausanias is writing for pilgrims, and even that he may have been a pilgrim himself.

Identity Is Territory: Pausanias and Aelius Aristides

One of the most important pilgrimage texts of this period is the account given by Aelius Aristides in his *Sacred Tales* of the minor pilgrimages to healing spas in northwest Asia Minor. This is the earliest detailed first-person account of pilgrimage that survives from antiquity, and it reveals many interesting themes, such as the notion of ritual purification (*katharsis*) as the culminating activity of a pilgrimage, and the link between pilgrimage and physical suffering.

Aristides's illness began on a pilgrimage. In A.D. 143, he went to bathe in the river Aisepos, probably at Gönen in north Mysia, where there were baths of Artemis Thermaia. Unexpectedly, he got ill, and this illness proved to be a major problem when he set off to Rome shortly afterward. He left Rome to embark upon a period of *kathedra,* a kind of retreat, at Pergamum (A.D. 145–47), during which he was frequently ordered by Asclepius to take baths in the sea or at local spas.[56] At the end of the *kathedra,* Asclepius sent him on many pilgrimages round Asia Minor. Three are particularly important. In January of A.D. 149, Asclepius dispatched him from Pergamum to the island of Chios "for a purgation," but this turned into a much more complicated journey (48.11–17).[57] He set sail at Clazomenae, but the wind blew in the opposite direction, and Aristides decided that it was fated for him to cross back to Phokaia, where he received the purgation. Subsequently, Aristides came to believe that Asclepius had remitted the pilgrimage to Chios (48.17).

A second major pilgrimage took place in December A.D. 152, the tenth year of the illness, when Aristides set off for the river Aisepos, having been instructed in a dream to return to where his illness had started.[58] He broke the journey at the way station of the Asclepieion at Poimanenos (now Eski Manyas). More than on any other journey, Aristides emphasizes his deep emotional involvement (50.1–7, *Sacred Tale* 4). Having stayed several days, he returned home when a voice in a dream instructed him to do so (50.6).

Some years later, in A.D. 165, Asclepius instructed Aristides, who was in Smyrna, to go "to the land of Zeus," which he initially interpreted as Pergamum, the sanctuary of Zeus-Asclepius.[59] He had three sleepless nights en route, unable to find suitable hotels, and finally, after visiting the sanctuary of Apollo Gruneion, he reached Pergamum, where he had another dream, in which Asclepius told him to press on "since they are in pursuit." At that point, he became convinced that the "land of Zeus" that Asclepius mentioned was not Pergamum at all but the temple of Olympian Zeus close to his estate in central Mysia. There he went, arriving on the "second or third day."

On the face of it, the differences between the pilgrimages of Aristides and Pausanias are striking. Pausanias makes a continuous tour around mainland Greece; Aristides makes individual trips starting from and returning to a fixed location. Aristides travels for the sake of his health; Pausanias to visit and pay homage to religious sites. Aristides is always motivated by divine instruction; Pausanias never mentions it. Aristides stresses the difficulty of the journey— indeed, he is the first pilgrim in Western history to dwell on the physical and mental suffering that the journey imposes; Pausanias tell us little about the journey and nothing about his body.

But there are also similarities. Some of Aristides's pilgrimages take him on routes as circuitous and meandering as those of Pausanias. And, cumulatively, Aristides's crisscrossing journeys cover the whole region of northwest Asia Minor; he must have come to know the territory as well as Pausanias knew the mainland. As for the distinctive suffering body of Aristides, in another respect their physicality might be judged to be another factor that Aristides and Pausanias share, insofar as they both use their relationship to territory to define their experience of themselves: Pausanias uses it to define his identity as a Hellene; Aristides to chart the stations of his illness, defining his relationship with Asclepius. In both cases, travel, space, and the personal view of the narrator/traveler/ritual-actor intersect in a relentlessly religion-focused set of contexts.

This chapter offers support for Elsner's argument that the *Periegesis* is pilgrimage literature, but it differs from him in one crucial respect. Elsner chooses to treat pilgrimage as a very broad, transcultural category, but this tactic lays him open to the criticism that this was not what pilgrimage was for the Greeks and Romans. I have tried to illuminate the status of Pausanias's text through the traditions of Greek pilgrimage, showing that the elements of sacred vision and intellectual contemplation are rooted in Greek religious practice. If it is true that these parallels do not provide conclusive proof that Pausanias is a pilgrim, it is equally true that they effectively undermine the argument that he is not. But what is really at stake here is that the distinction between pilgrimage and tourism is an artificial one in Greek tradition. Finally, it may be that Pausanias's relationship to his tradition is more complex than I have presented it: although in some respects the *Periegesis* continues traditional Greek *theoria,* in other respects it may go beyond Greek religious tradition, for example, in taking in a broader geographical scope than any normal pilgrimage would have done.

Reflections on Context

One of the main issues to occupy critics of Pausanias's text in the last two or three decades is undoubtedly the placing of his *Periegesis* in its correct historical setting. It is not by chance, therefore, that that question is the main subject of this collection of essays. We are familiar with the fact that Pausanias has been (and to some extent is bound to remain) one of the favorite *livres de chevet* of archaeologists, of historians of Greek religion, and, in a broader sense, of all scholars of *Altertumswissenschaft,* who have invariably attempted to reconstruct *Realien.* This is a scholarly perspective which, insofar as it relates to the *Periegesis,* is—if not devoid of history—at least metahistoric.

As a matter of fact, both historians of Greek religion and scholars of Greek institutions have rarely made serious efforts to understand the reasons for the selection made by Pausanias out of the totality of monuments and pious practices he had the chance to see or to hear of while visiting the various towns and sites of the *Periegesis.* As Elsner duly notes in chapter 1, classicists have been more anxious to retrieve the fragmentary testimonies of individual, timeless antiquarian evidence than to make all possible efforts to reconstruct the formation of the man Pausanias. Even when attempted, this reconstruction has normally taken place without any endeavor to understand what significance any given piece of information had for Pausanias, a circumstance that may even affect the reliability of our text. It should instead be self-evident that the meaning of a building, of a local mythical tradition, or of a particular *aition* in the eyes of the writer is crucial for that information's correct historical assessment. With the exception of the well-known preferences of our author for mystery or soteriological cults, such as those related to Demeter or Asclepius, and for religious matters whose antiquity can be documented by especially old *xoana,* or cult statues, and by ancient myth-historical traditions, we have to admit that the reasons for Pausanias's selections are hardly explicit—indeed, even obscure, apparently due to what seems to be a rather casual approach. In fact, it is not rare to find commentators blaming unspecified local *exegetai* for the fantasies or patently unfounded *aitia* of the text, and often we see modern scholars ready to credit

53

Pausanias with superficial attitudes or distractions to explain inclusions and ex-
clusions in his treatment of monuments, cities, religious practices, or political
events. We have to conclude, sadly, that the traditional, scholastic way of reading Pausanias—in little fragments as parts of antiquarian treatises—is extremely
persistent.

Quite similarly, archaeologists too have often tried to find mechanical and
direct correspondences between the text and the topographical and monumental
situations revealed by a survey or an excavation. Of course, this does not mean
that archaeologists usually fail to take into account the chronology of the monuments they excavate. In excavations we do normally encounter clear cases of
the addition of monuments later than Pausanias's visit and that therefore escaped
the record of the *Periegesis*. One of the best examples of this is attested in
Corinth, where during the reign of Commodus (i.e., a few years after Pausanias's
visit to the town), two temples partially superseded the monuments built in the
agora in the age of Augustus by Cn. Babbius Philinus,[1] which were (incom-
pletely!) described by Pausanias. Contemporary archaeologists are normally
aware of such situations, since the enormous progress in excavation techniques
has made us more attentive to architectural chronology and therefore prevents
us from making serious mistakes along these lines.

It is instead more unusual to find archaeologists who are ready to attempt
to integrate fully the topographical data and the culture of Pausanias, and to
understand the profound reasons motivating Pausanias's choices while he is
describing buildings, statues, and paintings in full accord with the taste and the
cultural needs of an average Greek of the second century A.D.[2] It may sometimes
happen that Pausanias, while describing particular topographical situations,
avoids the mention of a building that to his eyes is not interesting or, even
worse, ideologically "unappealing." It is, for instance, interesting to see to what
extent Pausanias understands and accepts the magniloquent imperial propaganda
created by means of specific monuments, a weighty concern in the building
policy of local ruling classes throughout the Roman empire and a popular theme
of contemporary archaeological research. If, for instance, we move to the description of the monuments in the forum of the Roman colony of Corinth,[3] we
reach the unmistakable conclusion that Pausanias does not at all share the formal
enthusiasm of Roman colonial elites for all forms of imperial propaganda and
therefore deliberately ignores the monumental strategies that characterize such
ideological expressions of loyalty to the central imperial power. As a matter of
fact, writing (with D. Musti) the commentary on three books of Pausanias, with
a fourth currently in preparation,[4] has taught me that Pausanias's selection within
monumental contexts, far from being the result of distractions or of superficial
decision making, is more frequently the product of cultural and political choices,
which can be both conscious and unconscious but always derive from a profound
adherence to the values that monuments, be they mentioned or discarded, embody within the Hellenistic taste of this particular Greek of the second century
A.D.

Most of the chapters of the present volume deal with this problem, which—
inevitably—is crucial for the archaeologist, who, like myself and hundreds be-

fore and after me, is bound to use Pausanias to reconstruct the topography and the history of ancient Greek cities. In the first of the three parts of this volume, entitled "Pausanias and His *Periegesis,* the Traveler and the Text" we find good treatments of the important issues of the literary antecedents of the *Periegesis* and of the use and the literary genre of our text. Moving from the justly famous work of Habicht,[5] Jones (chap. 3) effectively traces the profile of Pausanias's oral sources and classifies our author as one of the numerous members of "the kind of society that Plutarch portrays in his Pythian dialogues and his *Table Talks,* with its mixture of sophists, professors of literature, philosophers, lawyers, doctors, and wealthy amateurs," belonging "at that middle level of Greek intelligentsia which is perhaps represented better by inscriptions than by literature." Not by chance was this kind of society particularly appealing to the positivistic minds of the Victorian bourgeoisie, with all its interests and its (apparent) analogies with the cosmopolitan Greek cultivated milieux of Hellenistic and Roman times: thence the interest for Pausanias in scholars like Farnell, as described by Henderson in Chapter 11.

Intellectuals belonging to Pausanias's social context had a sort of sacred view of the common past. Pausanias appears to have been very piously attentive to the political uses of this attitude: describing the vain attempts made in the past to cut the isthmus of Corinth, he concludes, οὕτω χαλεπὸν ἀνθρώπῳ τὰ θεῖα βιάσασθαι "So hard is it for man to do violence to the works of God" [2.1.5]), but avoids mentioning the most recent (and aborted) project by Herodes Atticus.[6] A few lines later (2.1.7–8), though not mentioning Atticus explicitly as dedicant, Pausanias gives a careful description of the wealthy *anathema,* an impressive chryselephantine group of cult statues, that he had consecrated in the temple of Poseidon at Isthmia. It is therefore tempting to interpret the silent contrast between a pious act (the dedication of a precious *agalma*) and an impious project (the cutting of the isthmus) as a rhetorical (and cautious) strategy to signal the existence of a polemic with the most powerful personality of the circles to which our author belonged: notice that both the main point and the arguments of this polemic are of religious significance.

Pausanias's text is crowded with similar contemporary debates founded on religious arguments. An example found immediately after the case just mentioned occurs in Pausanias's account of the Isthmian sanctuary, where it is not difficult to discover traces of the "reforms" of local rituals, obscurely alluded to in the description of the sanctuary and introduced by the *archiereus* P. Licinius Priscus Iuventianus. Religion, in the age of Pausanias more than in the past, included the traveling of cultivated men disguised as devout pilgrims. The practice had started in the form of *theoriai* centuries before him, as a simple means to strengthen the links between the Greeks of the diaspora and their cultural roots. As happened centuries later, with the "Grand Tour" of those eighteenth-century aristocracies of Europe close to the end of their world, the looser such roots grew, the longer and more universal these pilgrimages became. Both Elsner (chap. 1) and Rutherford (chap. 4) rightly emphasize this aspect, stressing the effect of such travels as a powerful stimulus for the recollection of past glory. For the Greeks of the Hellenistic and Roman age, and therefore for

Pausanias, this memory was to be activated by the vision of monuments, *agal-mata,* and places, from which *logoi,* myths, and very old traditions were revived. The yeast, however, was invariably piety: but in the view of a Greek of the Second Sophistic, piety could become "true" only by means of rhetoric, as shown by Snodgrass in his elegant essay (chap. 7) on Pausanias and the Chest of Kypselos. According to Snodgrass, the ekphrastic genre, applied to a most unusual monument such as this chest, could provide "an ideal opportunity to inculcate certain academic and pedagogic principles for the description of works of art."

Religion and literary glories of Classical Greece go together much as do religion and traveling through old, glorious landscapes. Pausanias gives a special place to the great books that shaped Greek culture from Classical times on—Homer, Pindar, Herodotus—as Musti has effectively emphasized in his intro-duction to Book I of the Lorenzo Valla edition, in my view the most sensible contemporary profile of Pausanias's cultural background.[7] In such a culture you easily sense not only the flavor of the educational modes of the gymnasia, typical of the Greek Hellenistic middle class and giving great emphasis to the common heritage of Hellenic culture, but also the tradition of the search for *aitia,* specific to antiquarians and local historians, one of the most significant cultural trends of the Hellenistic period. Alcock, in her essay on Book IV (chap. 8), stressing the selective character of Pausanias's description of Messenia, is particularly surprised by the gap between historical narration and archaeological evidence. This happens, however, because, as she says, "an underlying theme of the entire *Periegesis* is the celebration of *eleutheria*"—that is, of that value which together with *autonomia* was the pillar of Greek civic consciousness and of the same cultural history of the Greek world.[8] Together with their sequels and supple-ments composed in Roman times, local histories of the Hellenistic period (of which Pausanias's long Messenian digression is one of the most monumental examples) can be considered an excellent way to secure an identity for the cultivated citizen of a Greek city in Roman times. They could also be the sole possible response to the despotic pressure of the imperial power, similar to that exerted in the Hellenistic period over the ruling classes of "free" Greek *poleis* by the kings and their courts.

Religion, rhetoric, literary education, and nostalgia are thus the ingredients of Pausanias's book, to which we shall always look for a better understanding of its author's world, something too often overlooked by modern scholarship: a good lesson taught by this volume.

Commentary

DAVID KONSTAN

The Joys of Pausanias

Pausanias's personality is baffling. On first acquaintance, he has the bland anonymity of a writer of guidebooks. As Sutton and Wagstaff show in this volume (chaps. 9–10), the resemblance is not coincidental: guidebooks to Greece have taken their inspiration from Pausanias, right down to the present moment. Pausanias thus seems similar to us on the most prosaic and yet private of levels—that of our leisure pursuits. He is fellow tourist or connoisseur, and it is easy to think of him as a well-traveled, somewhat garrulous neighbor.

Nor is there anything odd about Pausanias's fixation on the Classical past. Guidebooks invariably emphasize bygone eras: ancient art and architecture have an aura that overshadows modern monuments, quite apart from their aesthetic or historical significance. The map that emerges from a modern guide to Rome, for instance, is just as skewed, temporally, as that of Pausanias. When we travel to distant places, we incline to make a parallel excursion into other times. Sometimes, for no apparent reason, a particular item, like the Chest of Kypselos, catches Pausanias's fancy and he dwells lovingly on it, passing rapidly over other monuments that to us, at least, seem to have a comparable importance (see Snodgrass, chap. 7, this volume). These quirks of taste may tell us something about Pausanias's personal interests but do not seem to reflect a systematic bias on his part.

But can Pausanias's voyages, nearly two millennia ago, have had no other motive than recreation and antiquarianism? It is tempting to suppose that his painstaking researches and travels on the Greek mainland reflect nostalgia for the great age of Greece, before it was reduced to a province of Rome called Achaia. This would explain Pausanias's concentration on monuments that date to the time when Greece, or rather some Greek cities, were free and independent. Elsner, Rutherford, and Porter, for example, all regard Pausanias's explorations as a form of pilgrimage, by which he paid homage to a past that was, for him, the privileged locus of a specifically Greek identity, before the coming of Rome (see chaps. 1, 4–5, this volume).

Undoubtedly, Pausanias loved old Greece. Ascribing a political or religious motive to his travels, however, is more problematic. Consider, for example, the geographical entity that Pausanias calls "Greece." It includes the Peloponnesos and some of the peninsula to the north; it thus falls within the boundaries of the modern Greek state. Pausanias himself hailed from a city in Lydia, located in what is now the western part of Turkey. He was a native speaker of Greek and acquired an excellent education, very likely in his home province. It is clear from incidental remarks in his travelogue that he had considerable local pride (see Bowie, chap. 2, this volume). There is no reason to suppose that he imagined himself as part of a diaspora, or that he harbored sentiments for mainland Greece as his ancestral homeland and aspired in his journeys to reconnect with an authentic past. We may recall that Greeks had occupied Asia Minor for a millennium or more in Pausanias's day and had, after the conquests of Alexander the Great, constituted the dominant caste in cities from Egypt to Syria, a position they retained even after the region was absorbed into the Roman empire. To the extent that Pausanias had a notion of a unified Greek territory, it was constituted precisely by the borders of the Roman province of Achaia.

Imagine a New Zealander of Scottish descent, on tour in Scotland. He or she is fascinated by ruined castles, faded inscriptions that testify to ancient majesty, monuments older than the Scottish things back home. We can appreciate such a visitor's eager interest in records and legends of the time of the great clans, before Scotland was part of Great Britain, and would not be surprised to find that his or her notebooks contained a mélange of old myths and historical details alongside scrupulous, if amateur, commentaries on objets d'art. Some years later, let us suppose, a travel book is published: it is comprehensive, idiosyncratic, and reveals frustratingly little about the author. What was the motive for it? Did the writer harbor a vision of Scottish independence? Was it inspired by a kind of religious quest? Does it betray the author's search for identity, for roots? Or might the enchantment of old places that is evident in its pages be in no way different from that which an Italian or American without a drop of Scottish blood in their veins might have experienced? Of course, the very idea of such a comparison between ancient and modern sensibilities is fanciful; I offer it merely as a complement to other, more charged scenarios.

Book VI of Pausanias's description of Greece finds him in Elis and begins with an account of the statues he saw there. Pausanias notes that he will not list all the Olympic victors, since some had no statues, and even among those who did, he has selected only those that represent well-known individuals or are distinguished by the excellence of their crafsmanship. Pausanias continues:

> On the right of the temple of Hera is the statue of a wrestler, Symmachus the son of Aeschylus. He was an Elean by birth. Beside him is Neolaïdas, son of Proxenus, from Pheneüs in Arcadia, who won a victory in the boys' boxing-match. Next comes Archedamus, son of Xenius, another Elean by birth, who like Symmachus overthrew wrestlers in the contest for boys. The statues of the athletes mentioned above were made by Alypus of Sicyon, pupil of Naucydes of Argos. The inscription on Cleogenes the son of Silenus declares that he was a native, and that he won a prize with a riding-horse from his own private stable. Hard by Cleogenes are set up Deinolochus, son of Pyrrhus, and Troïlus, son of Alcinoüs. These were both Eleans by birth, though their victories were

not the same. Troïlus, at the time that he was umpire, succeeded in winning victories in the chariot-races, one for a chariot drawn by a full-grown pair and another for a chariot drawn by foals. The date of his victories was the hundred and second Festival. After this the Eleans passed a law that in future no umpire was to compete in the chariot-races. That statue of Troïlus was made by Lysippus. The mother of Deinolochus had a dream, in which she thought that the son she clasped in her bosom had a crown on his head. For this reason Deinolochus was trained to compete in the games and outran the boys. The artist was Cleon of Sicyon. (6.1.3–5; trans. W. H. S. Jones, Loeb Classical Library).

The description of the statues goes on for sixty or seventy pages more, occasionally enlivened, as here, by anecdotes or historical comment.

Let us compare with this narrative an excerpt from a work published about fifty years after Pausanias's book, also written in Greek; the author was a native of the old Greek city of Naucratis in Egypt but later moved to Rome. He is Athenaeus, who is known to us, like Pausanias, by a single text, in this case the *Deipnosophistae,* or "Table-Talkers." The passage, which comes from Book I, is part of a discussion of dance steps:

> National dances are the following: Laconian, Troezenian, Epizephyrian, Cretan, Ionian, and Mantinean; these last were preferred by Aristoxenus because of the motion of the arms. Dancing was held in such esteem and involved such art that Pindar calls Apollo "dancer": "Dancer, Lord of beauty, Thou of the broad quiver, Apollo!" And Homer, or one of the Homeridae, in the *Hymn to Apollo* says, "Apollo, with lyre in hand, harped sweetly the while he stepped forth high and gracefully." And Eumelus of Corinth (or was it Arctinus?) introduces Zeus as a dancer with the words: "And in their midst danced the father of gods and men." But Theophrastus says that Andron, the flute-player of Catana [in Sicily], was the first to add rhythmical motions of the body to the playing of the flute; hence, "to do the Sicel" meant "to dance" among the ancients. After him there was Cleolas of Thebes. Famous dancers also were Bolbus, mentioned by Cratinus and Callias, and Zeno of Crete, a great favourite of Artaxerxes, mentioned by Ctesias. Alexander, too, in his letter to Philoxenus, mentions Theodorus and Chrysippus. (22b–d; trans. C. B. Gulick, Loeb Classical Library)

Athenaeus (or his excerptor) passes from the catalogue of dances to other convivial topics at this point.

I have quoted these two passages at some length to convey the dogged quality of Pausanias's and Athenaeus's narratives, and I have juxtaposed them because I think that Athenaeus's love for old authors and the evidence they provide for symposiastic practices of yore is analogous to Pausanias's passion for ancient monuments and the stories associated with them. I do not wish to push the similarity between Pausanias's oeuvre and that of Athenaeus any further, save to note that both authors are something of a mystery to modern readers because their grab-bag surveys seem so monotonous as literature. Is it possible, we wonder, that anyone ever enjoyed such stuff?

Of course, people did enjoy it—not just ancient Greeks living under Roman rule but modern Europeans and others from the Renaissance down to the eighteenth century, at least. Both books are mines of information. I do not know whether travelers in antiquity regularly carried the ten papyrus rolls of Pausanias's *Periegesis* with them when they visited Greece; I imagine that the volumes were just as entertaining to read at home. We should recall that educated people at that time cultivated their memories to a far greater extent than we do now and could learn by heart long catalogues and lists. What is more, they had a vivid sense of spatial orientation, as witnessed, for instance, by the extraordinary achievements of the ancient geometers, who saw with the mind's eye complex three-dimensional figures undergoing complicated rotations. The favored mnemonic technique, as described, for example, by Cicero, involved attaching facts or names to imagined locations—buildings in the forum, or objects in a mansion of many rooms—and recalling each item through its association with a visualized feature. Ancient readers were thus ideally trained to envisage and recollect the combination of topographical and historical particulars recounted by Pausanias.

To be sure, Classical Greece had great cultural prestige, and this gave added interest to its treasures, whether literary and linguistic or artistic and architectural. But this legacy was not necessarily the unique heritage of Greeks. Greek-speaking Romans participated in the pedantic dinner conversation recorded by Athenaeus, and I see no reason why they might not have responded with equal enthusiasm to Pausanias's review of the chief physical sites of Achaia. They too would acquire in this way a fund of useful or decorous knowledge, just as they might do in the Latin pages of Pliny's encyclopedic *Natural History* or Aulus Gellius's *Attic Nights*.

Pausanias lived in an age when it was highly esteemed to have a well-stocked memory and fund of knowledge. He made his contribution to this learned pastime in the form of a survey of Greek monuments in Achaia. That he chose this strenuous project rather than a more philological pursuit, like Aulus Gellius and Athenaeus, tells us something about Pausanias's temperament and conceivably too about his values. Among these latter, there was, perhaps, a tenuous form of patriotism or ethnic identification, although I am not convinced that this is so. But whatever the causes of his particular affection for old Greece, Pausanias's researches belong to the genre of collections of information that his contemporaries prized and perused for the noteworthy bits of knowledge they could find in them. I expect that many got, or could get, substantial parts of such treatises by heart. In thinking about Pausanias's purposes in compiling his encyclopedic guide to Greece, it may be best to put aside the topographical maps and photographs that accompany modern editions, and ignore the erudite reconstructions of ancient sites provided by archaeologists, valuable as these are for understanding the Classical world. Instead, just read a stretch of the *Periegesis* aloud, slowly, as the ancients would have done. At a certain point, the long sequences of anecdotes and artifacts begin to numb reflection and leave only the irreducible pleasure—it is, I think, a genuine pleasure—of scanning an intelligently itemized inventory of precious things and places. For us armchair sightseers, that is the joy of reading Pausanias.

PART II

STUDIES AND COMPARISONS

Ideals and Ruins

*Pausanias, Longinus, and
the Second Sophistic*

The Greeks entered into Death backward:
what they had before them was their past.
                         Roland Barthes

Time Travel through Culture(s)

This chapter sets out to explore affinities of mind and attitude between two Greek authors from the Roman Imperial period: Pausanias (fl. A.D. 170) and pseudo-Longinus (henceforth "Longinus"), author of *On
the Sublime* (Περὶ ὕψους). The juxtaposition of these two writers may at first
glance seem unlikely. The riddle of the latter's precise dates and name aside,[1]
what might an antiquarian and a literary critic have in common? And yet their
very location as Greeks in a Roman world, each gazing longingly upon a distant
past, that of Classical Greece, makes the comparison irresistible. Both authors
practice a form of travel (in the first instance) through time, and they seek out
monuments as their landmarks. Longinus tours the literary remains of his heritage in much the same way as Pausanias collects a material record of the past—
its monumental, historical, mythological, and religious remains—in an attempt
to hold that record together in his imagination. Each in his own way writes a
guidebook to the great monuments of Greece. In doing so, they share and exhibit
a cultural imaginary that is typical of Greek writers in the Imperial period who
are conventionally grouped together under the rubric of the "Second Sophistic,"
a point that will be confirmed through a side-glance at Dio of Prusa (fl. late first
century) toward the end of this chapter. Their strategies of narrative and authorial position, used for identifying their surroundings and themselves, and their
ways of shaping readerly desire, ought prima facie to be comparable as well.

Attempting the comparison, it is hoped, will help us deepen our appreciation of this later period of Greek literary culture and its sense of itself.

What all these writers share is a reverence for the Greek past and a capacity to travel large distances through time and space. These two characteristics are closely connected. There are, to be sure, important differences as well, but the similarities are striking, and it is these I want to focus upon. We may start with the notion of traveling. Travelers who describe what they see are interesting cases of mediation. They have no fixed location, whether in time or in space. They live in a present that is fluid, not fixed, in part because traveling takes time and is displacing. Their gaze is divided into a here and a there, and consequently so is that of their readers. Pausanias's project took several decades to record (ca. A.D. 150–80), and its production is intimately bound up with and practically "indexed" by the sites he visited (or so he would have his readers believe).[2] Longinus's project, a fraction of the size of Pausanias's work in ten books, may have taken anywhere from a few days to several years to set down, but it contains a lifetime of cultural attainments, for, as he says, "literary judgment comes only as the final product of long experience" (6.1). Furthermore, the effects of sublime literature are as strongly indexical, as burned into a reader's experience, as any form of travel can produce. This brings us to a further meaning in the idea of displacement. Longinus's position as a writer is determined by his objects in as self-effacing and self-constructing a way as that of Pausanias: each creates his persona by interacting with the distantly located and remembered, and in any event imaginatively experienced, objects of his treatise. As agents of their descriptions, they vanish into their objects, only to emerge at the other end as the framers of what they describe. Dio is in some ways more complex, because his output is more varied and his face is more overtly turned toward the present. But as a traveler into the past, a stance he gladly affects when it suits him to do so, he too falls within the general paradigm just outlined.

I want to suggest that this displacement from the present and this shoring up of the past go hand in hand with a sublime sensibility. This sensibility is a clue to the aesthetics of a certain cultural experience that our authors share. They display what T. S. Eliot would call a monumental, "historical sense" that "involves a perception, not only of the pastness of the past, but of its present."[3] Bringing the past into the present is one way in which writers of the Second Sophistic interpret their own contemporary reality: it imparts a depth to their own self-understanding and self-location, in the absence of which they would simply have no identity at all.[4] What interests me here is the ambivalent nature of this act of reflection, the fact that there is a certain artifice and even trompe l'oeil involved in putting oneself in relation to the past in this way. The sublime, which is intimately connected up with historical feeling and not just with historical knowledge, authorizes and naturalizes the perspectival effects of history, particularly those that conform to the ideology of classicism which runs through the Second Sophistic. Consequently, the sublime too must be considered a marker and an effect of cultural ideology. Putting the sublime into closer contact with classicism so understood will be one of my goals in this paper. Character-

izing the experience of Greek authors under Roman rule in terms of the sublime
will also help give more depth to this aesthetic category, which is too often
reserved for a narrowly defined literary experience. And so the present chapter
aims to contribute not only to our understanding of Greek cultural experience
as it was shaped in the first few centuries of our era but also, indirectly, to our
understanding of the sublime. A brief explanation of the way in which these
two faces of cultural and literary analysis can come together perhaps needs to
be made.

That cultural experience is mediated by aesthetic experience and vice versa
is well enough established today. Starting from Longinus, who develops a language for naming *hypsos* (or the "sublime"), we can, I believe, move forward
without anachronism to a more recent analysis of culture and ideology. According to this later view, the sublime is any confrontation with "a positive, material
object elevated to the status of [an] impossible Thing" that, simultaneously fascinating and fearful, both invites and resists integration into symbolic frameworks of understanding.[5] The experience of the sublime is the gamut of responses one has in the face of such an object, although ultimately the experience
one has before a sublime object is, on this view, of the contingency of one's
own frameworks of meaning and understanding.[6] Is that not the effect of a
sentence from Demosthenes that, thanks to the "hazards of his long hyperbata,"
Longinus says, threatens to collapse into nonsense and to draw us into itself
(22.3–4); or of the glimpse given by Homer into "how the earth is torn from
its foundations" (9.6)? I believe that the writings of Pausanias and Longinus are
organized around encounters with sublime objects construed in this way, which
explains the powerful grip that these objects exercise upon their respective imaginations. Each author is brought face-to-face with a void. But before turning to
the specifics that will justify this claim, let us first consider some of the more
general reasons for setting up Pausanias and Longinus for comparison.

Both Longinus and Pausanias seek out large reminders of their purpose,
objects that can be seen at a distance and that cannot be missed, as well as
objects that can only be viewed from afar, from a reverential distance. Such
items radiate a compelling aura. The tantalizing mention in *On the Sublime*
(36.3) of a colossus, possibly the Colossus of Rhodes or the image of Zeus at
Olympia by Phidias (and described by Pausanias at 5.11.9), is one such instance.[7] The naming of natural wonders like the Nile, the Danube, the Rhine,
the Ocean, and spewing Etna (35.4) is another. These are among the seemingly
few purely "periegetic" moments of Longinus's treatise, which otherwise is
given over to literary description. But they also illustrate a maxim that applies
to the whole of his work and that appears earlier in the same context: "our
thoughts often travel beyond (ἐκβαίνουσιν) the boundaries of our surroundings"
(35.3). In the light of this maxim, we can recognize how Longinus's work is at
once periegetic and hyperbatic—that is to say, never purely periegetic but always aimed in excess of itself. Pausanias's mentions of colossi at Rhodes, Athens, Rome, and elsewhere, and his extended account of the sanctuary of Apollo
at Delphi in Book X, in which he describes the divine vapors of the place, are
characteristic of his treatise and parallel to the interests of Longinus, who treats

the Pythian shrine as a symbol for poetic inspiration, in language reminiscent of Pausanias (13.2).[8] The connection between grandeur and the inspirational (or the divine) is for both authors an intimate one, and this co-implication will be crucial in what follows—for the sublime dwells in this connection.

Another way to approach the comparison is to ask about the two writers' attitudes toward evidence and its persuasive appeal. If Longinus can take Orestes's madness as a token of what the poet Euripides "saw" and of how he has nearly "made his audience see what he imagined" (15.2), Pausanias can go a step further and claim to have seen the tomb where Orestes bit off his finger while he was haunted by the Eumenides to the verge of madness (8.34.2). Given the prominence of the visual record in Pausanias and of the general criterion of visibility in Longinus, we can say that visualization (φαντασία) is their common coin. They are both operating within the conventions of a visual culture. And these conventions are most energetically at work at that place where the dimensions of the imaginary begin to overtake those of vision and where vision simultaneously leaves a trace and becomes a material deposit in the mind.[9] That place is where memory becomes visible.

A further—as it were, outward—mark of comparison between these two writers is the way in which their historical memories are sharply bounded, based as they are on a selective amnesia. In Longinus, achievements in Greek culture down to the firm cutoff date of the fourth century are monumentalized and sacralized, and so made coherent as a whole.[10] Pausanias's boundary for the authentic Greek past is only a little more generous. As Bowie observes, the author of the *Description of Greece* "almost completely neglects monuments and dedications later than c. 150 B.C.," although as a rule his cutoff point falls closer to Longinus's.[11] The literary writers cited by Pausanias suffer a similar fate. Further, both authors heroize and even divinize the great historical agents of the circumscribed past. For Pausanias, "men were raised to the rank of gods in those days [in the mythical—for Pausanias, the historical—past], and are worshipped down to the present time" (8.2.4), while for Longinus sublime writers are "heroes" (4.4, 36.2) and "divine" (4.6, 35.2).[12] To be sure, in this both authors are following traditions rather than inventing them. Thus, the Phigalians sacrifice every year to the self-sacrificing Oresthasians, treating them "as heroes" (8.41.1), while Longinus's claim that Demosthenes, in his famous Marathon oath, "deifies his audience's ancestors . . . as though they were gods" (16.2) is a conventional one (cf. Plut. *Moralia* 350C) that is borne out by the emotions of the original passage (μὰ τοὺς Μαραθῶνι προκινδυνεύσαντας, etc. [Demosthenes 18.208]). Underlying these attitudes is the recognition that heroic risk-taking (παρακινδυνεύειν [Pausanias 3.6.5; Longinus 33.2]) in the name of Classical ideals leaves the most memorable impressions (ἄξιον μνήμης [Pausanias 3.6.5; Longinus 8.4; cf. 33.3]). And underlying these convictions is the view that memory and vision are underpinned by the twin criteria of what Greenblatt has termed "resonance and wonder."[13] Things are "worth seeing" (θέας ἀξία) for just these reasons, and all of Greece concurs.[14] Thus, Pausanias seems willing to endorse a predecessor or possibly a contemporary, Cleon of Magnesia, who "used to aver that people who have not happened in the course of their own lives to see extraordinary sights [τὰ παράδοξα] are incredulous about marvels [θεάμωσιν]. Whereas he himself, he said, believed that Tityus and others had been just as tradition describes them" (Pausanias 10.4.6).[15] So, too, Longinus: "the unusual always excites our wonder [θαυμαστὸν ἀεὶ τὸ παράδοξον]" (35.5).

This selectivity, the preference for artifacts of Archaic to fourth-century Greek culture and a depreciation of the Hellenistic period (not to mention the contemporary, Romanized present), seems to have been in vogue at the time. The same attitude is found in Apollodorus, in Arrian, and in countless other authors from the period.[16] Yet what is striking in both cases is the way in which the imaginary wholeness of a Greece that was is made to contrast sharply with the ruined condition of the monuments presented. Pausanias dwells upon monuments that are in fragments. Longinus serves up an antique past that is itself fragmented, and deliberately so, in the form of quotations torn from their original seats and contexts.[17] The invitation to readers is that they restore the ruins in their minds. But there is a violence to this imaginary viewing on both sides, both in the fragmentation and in the desperate acts of reintegration, while the desire for an integral past is elicited precisely through the obstruction of the view of it. *Enargeia* (or "vividness of description") here serves two distinct functions: it simultaneously conceals and reveals. Roland Barthes's familiar insight, occasioned by his reading of the nineteenth-century novel, is none the less apt for being addressed to the question of a "modern" sensibility:

> What pleasure wants is the site of a loss, the seam, the cut, the deflation, the *dissolve* which seizes the subject in the midst of bliss . . . Is not the most erotic portion of a body *where the garment gapes?* . . . It is this flash itself which seduces, or rather: *the staging of an appearance-as-disappearance.*[18]

What is the peculiar modernity of the ancient texts to be considered below? What is the textual pleasure or bliss, the pleasurable discomfort, that they encourage and possibly stage? And consequently, how natural or calculated is their classicizing ideology? These will be the questions that guide the present inquiry into time travel in later Greek literature.

Guardian of Memory: Pausanias's *Description of Greece*

Despite his frequent statements to the contrary, and despite their reiteration by scholars, Pausanias's objective is not to record "all things Greek."[19] "All things" clearly would be impossible to capture, for what would such a description amount to? The object of the *Description of Greece* is saner and more selective, as Pausanias is well aware:

> To prevent misconceptions, I stated in my *Attica* [1.39.3] that I had not described everything, but only a selection of the most memorable objects [⟨τὰ δὲ⟩ μάλιστια ἄξια μνήμης]. This principle I will now repeat before I proceed to describe Sparta. From the outset I aimed at the most valuable traditions [τὰ ἀξιολογώτατα] from out of the mass of insignificant stories which are current

among every people. My plan was adopted after mature deliberation, and I will not depart from it. (3.11.1)

His reasoning, which is adamant, borders on the defensive. One wonders what the objection he is warding off might be.[20] But it is plain that his work is meant to cull what is of value and significance; it is to be a discriminating account. Yet within these bounds the *Description* is also intended to be truthful, which means exhaustive (within Pausanias's human limits) and, in its own way, indiscriminate. Duty-bound by a kind of ἀνάγκη (6.3.8), like an ethnographic camera, he will record whatever he encounters in the form in which this information is given to him. Yet he will not believe all that he hears and sees (6.3.8). There is a conflict in this program. What makes an incredible story worth recording, which is to say valuable and significant? Without any discriminating distance at all, Pausanias would be an unreliable narrator of his encounters. And without a certain indiscriminateness he would be equally unreliable as an observer. For the value of his account principally resides, not in its being critical, but only in its being accurate.

Much of Pausanias's account is taken up by local traditions, which he does not necessarily expect his readers to believe, or about which he is happy at least to affect a stance of tempered skepticism.[21] But what lends these a credibility of another kind, lends them the very memorability and value they might be thought intrinsically to lack, is their proximity to the real stuff of his *Description*: the exiguous or monumental traces of the Greek past. What Pausanias gives his readers is a fantasy of Greece, of the prodigious phenomenon that Greece once was, made credible by its physical and contemporary attestations.[22] Empiricism here subserves a romanticizing imagination. Thus, there is no real (and no felt) contradiction between Pausanias's claims to be describing "all things Greek" (πάντα τὰ Ἑλληνικά [1.26.4; cf. 9.15.6]) and his claims *not* to be doing this, if he is setting out to describe a Greece that no longer exists: the object of his descriptions is a fantasy image, a false and indeed impossible totality, that can only exist by dint of a formal gesture that magically converts the contingent, scattered, and empirical details of fact into the hallowed remnants of a once-cohesive whole.

This gesture, which is at once memorializing and canonical, is one of sublimation. Yet there is nothing ahistoricizing about the move. Pausanias's fantasy is, on the contrary, grounded in precise historical coordinates, which fall between the defeat of the Persians in the fifth century and the defeat of Philopoemen, the "last of the Greeks" (Plutarch, *Philopoemen* 1.7), at the beginning of the second century, when Greece lost its bid to unite against Rome: "Miltiades, son of Cimon . . . was the first benefactor of the whole Greek people (κοινῇ τῆς Ἑλλάδος), and Philopoemen, son of Craugis, was the last" (8.52.1), thirty-seven years before Rome crushed the Achaean League in 146 B.C. These are the defining historical points of Pausanias's "whole."[23] Perhaps the simplest solution to the problem is to take the phrase πάντα τὰ Ἑλληνικά in the way that Pausanias's model Herodotus would have done: τὸ Ἑλληνικόν (Herodotus 8.144.2) designates "Greekness," pure and simple; Pausanias will be describing Greek identity in an exhaustive way.[24] But this still leaves us with the problem, for Pausanias's notion of Greekness covers much more ground than this historical span of three centuries: his account runs from the dark reaches of the Greek past well before Homer, right down to Greece in the Roman present. A primary tension, accordingly, runs through Pausanias's account: the totality of Greece he describes is *larger* than the historical totality that grounds it (itself a fantasy of unity). There is "Greece" the numinous whole, and there is "Greece" at its most powerful and purest—to wit, in its brief moment of political hegemony.[25] The relative lack of fit between these two modes of perception, the gap between them, is the actual object of Pausanias's attention. And yet, as we shall see, no material object, however small or large, can fail to evoke this antagonism of proportions. Rather than overromanticize Pausanias's position, we might say that he suffers, not from an excess of loss, but from an excess of *presence*: the past bulks all too large in his field of vision, it is far too *immediate,* to be balanced by the actual present. And that is the source of the sublimity of his account. But in order to understand how this is so, we must unpack further the logic of his work.

Pausanias scans the landscape and reads it for the traces of memory it contains: sites encountered become texts to be read, while encountered texts (inscriptions, oral histories, miracles, marvels, poetic accounts) are transformed into sites of memory.[26] But Pausanias's account is not merely in the third person, transmitting the memories of others. It is an autobiographical, participatory account that produces first-personal memories. Pausanias relates his own travels and experiences, and this direct contact with the soil of Greece lends more than mere vividness to his account: his wanderings are a participation in the numinousness of the Greece he is re-creating. Partaking of mysteries and sacrifices when he can, and often guiding his travels by these landmarks of cult activity (e.g., "chiefly, for the sake of this Demeter I went to Phigalia"; 8.42.11), Pausanias makes of his travels a performative ritual. But the record of his travels has an exemplary function as well. Through Pausanias's experience, readers can enjoy the benefits of an imaginary re-creation of Greece's rituals and its numinous dimensions.[27] There is a ritual feel to Pausanias's account in the mere rhythms of its narrative as it proceeds, periegetically, through its descriptions, and it is this attitude of tender reverence that ought to be part of any description of his work.

Because Pausanias's eye is drawn to traces of the canonical past surviving into the present, no object that he enters into his account will fail to evoke that past. Such is the lavish generosity of memorialization and the actual meaning of Pausanias's trademark formula, "the things worth seeing are these" (e.g., at 3.18.7). It is also the source of his fixation upon fragments. The most compelling details are those which point to the absence of the totality they evoke and confirm, the way pedestals point to statues that no longer exist. The pedestals literally support the memory of the statues. Thus, the memory of Philopoemen is sustained by one such vital sign:

> Not far from the market-place is a theater, and beside it are pedestals of bronze statues, but the statues are no longer there. On one of the pedestals is an elegiac

inscription stating that the statue is that of Philopoemen. The memory of Philopoemen is fondly cherished by the Greeks. (8.49.1)

The identity of Greece exists in this system of tokens; Pausanias's description, in turn, re-creates the memory-system of Greece. Ruins, foundations, half-memories, echoes, unheard voices, and missing objects are the floor plans, as it were, of "Greece": they are its archaeology. Much of Pausanias's *Description* compulsively circles around such trace-objects, which are intrinsically worth mentioning and remembering (ἀξιόχρεα), literally "handed over to memory" (παρείχετο ἐς μνήμην [8.32.2]), as though their sole purpose were to document the "now gone" character of Greece.[28] Mere columns, bare of walls and roofs (such as the temple of Carnean Apollo in Sicyon), lonely altars (the temple of Athena in the same place), empty sepulchers (as in the grave of Hyrnetho in Argos), villages that formerly were cities (such as Gortys), emptied sanctuaries (as in the temple of Nemean Zeus), tales of nymphs who once gave oracles (as in a cave at Cithaeron) or of places haunted by mere echoes (as in Thebes, "where they say the Muses sang at the wedding of Harmonia")—these are the sorts of traces that attract Pausanias's eye.[29]

There is, of course, a certain sleight of hand here. Objects do not evoke the past of themselves. They may commemorate histories, but histories in turn provide the context by which objects become visible as partial objects, metonyms of missing wholes. Thus, the historical sources very occasionally cited by Pausanias are one element of the invisible framework of his *Description,* while Greek patriotism, generally understated in his narrative and existing more as a mood than a clear political message, provides another.[30] Pausanias freely crosses back and forth between these two frameworks, which never go unlinked. And they come together again in his reliance on oral local histories.[31] Much of the time Pausanias is actively searching for a historical framework to make sense of what he finds. For the only real way in which his objects can speak to him at all is through this insistence upon their historicity, the value of which is never put into doubt. Still, we should acknowledge that this "speaking" is never in the form of an immediate communication. Just as the eye is conditioned by its perspective, so too do the sublime objects of the past always reach Pausanias, always address him, in the form of a quotation.

At the limit, and I believe at the core of his project, Pausanias's Classical past is backlit by a still more recessed, if dim, memory of an even further past, that of the Archaic age (τὸ ἀρχαῖον [9.3.9]). One element of this prehistory is the mythological and legendary past of "what the Greeks call the heroic age" and its proximate sequel ("not long afterwards"), the age of the "Epigoni" (9.9.1, 9.9.4). This background is not so carefully marked out in Pausanias as it is for us today, to be sure; but it is nonetheless part of the historical and value-laden picture of Greece that he inherits and then refashions for himself. What is arguably of interest to Pausanias here is simply the blurry impression of a past dimension, the mere fact of its indisputable presence. This encapsulation of a memory within a memory is a valid constituent of Pausanias's image of "Greece": it gives "Greece" a greater depth and enhances its memorableness "today." The obscure but ever-present antiquity of Homer, Hesiod, ancient and "hard to make out" epigraphical scripts, and other found objects all lend a hoary penumbra to the brighter, clearer image of "Greece." These objects fulfill three functions. Time-worn (6.15.9), they provide an index of "antiquity" itself and for that reason are an intrinsic source of attraction and worth; they tend to "poeticize" Greece, thereby recalling the archaisms of literature which do just this ("for it is a Greek custom to introduce the older [ἀρχαιότερα] instead of the later names into poetry"; 7.17.7); and at the limit they pass over into the dimension of the numinous, like the names of the gods that populate the landscape of Pausanias's Greece. Archaic Greece is useful to examine, for it is the place where some of the stress lines of Pausanias's project appear on the surface.[32]

The deep past of Greece is its most illegible feature, a reminder of the near-illegibility of present-day Greece (which, as it were, lacks all depth; it has no history and no commemorative value) and of the difficulty of reading the past, which suffers, as it were, from an *excess* of depth ("I cannot tell who made these images, but they seem to me to be also extremely ancient [ἐς τὰ μάλιστα ἀρχαῖα]" [5.17.3]).[33] The double helix of archaic lettering on inscriptions (*boustrophedon*) is only the most literal form of this disconcerting illegibility (5.17.6).[34] At times, it is reassuring to draw a line between the past that can be known and the past that is beyond one's ken, and that is how Pausanias sets off darker antiquity. Older images are cruder and stranger, frequently geometric, aniconic, or colossal. "The images [of Gracious Zeus and Artemis Paternal at the altar to Isthmian Poseidon] are rude [σὺν τέχνῃ πεποιημένα οὐδεμιᾷ]: that of Zeus resembles a pyramid and that of Artemis a column" (2.9.6; here, we have only Pausanias's account to go by). The offering at Amyclae, a thronelike image of the god of the place (Apollo) from around 530 B.C., is "an ancient and rude image [ἀρχαῖον καὶ οὐ σὺν τέχνῃ πεποιημένον]; for except that it has a face and feet and hands, it otherwise resembles a bronze pillar" (3.19.2). Such primitive artifacts recall the disturbing strangeness of Greece itself. But they are as venerable—and, by the second century A.D., as mythical—as the myths and divine presences they tell: they point to history in its larger-than-life dimensions.

Pausanias is careful to let us know which of the remains "are the most ancient Greek images in stone that I have seen" (1.43.8). These signs of antiquity are crucial to his project of description. Impressive despite their aesthetic deficiency when viewed from the classicizing perspective he cherishes, they evoke a dimension beyond superficial beauty. Thus, "the works of Daedalus [one being a "naked wooden image" of Heracles in Corinth] are somewhat uncouth [ἀτοπώτερα] to the eye, but there is a touch of the divine in them [ἔνθεόν τι] for all that" (2.4.5). Habicht suggests that Pausanias here "has the discernment, despite the sculpture's lack of elegance and refinement, to recognize a kind of sublime inspiration and to value that."[35] Whatever the truth about the sculpture's circumstances of production may be, it is the attribution of divinity by Pausanias that is significant. And this is to be connected with the sublime aesthetics of his traveling eye.[36]

Sublimity in its most startling form is to be found in the wondrous and the miraculous, the outsized and the venerable, and above all in what lies beyond

reach in the present: Mycenae and Tiryns (with their cyclopean walls) and colossal images of all kinds, whether Greek or Egyptian, such as the famous
resonating statue of Memnon (1.42.3), which would later be a staple of the
Romantic sublime tradition,[37] or the "huge bone" of a sea monster on display
in Sicyon, "big in its bigness" (μεγέθει μέγας [2.10.2]).[38] These are all artifacts
that, like the rustic antiquities mentioned above, are notable primarily for the
sheer bulk of their dimensions and their loftiness, for their being ὑψηλά (a term
that is reserved for this meaning when it is not topographically descriptive), but
not for their beauty.[39] The statue of Zeus at Olympia is a case in point. Framed
by an impressive Doric temple, whose dimensions Pausanias sees fit to cite
(5.10.3), the image of Zeus is by contrast huge beyond measure. Those who
took the measure of its literal dimensions (ἐς ὕψος τε καὶ εὖρος) are to be
faulted, he claims, "for even the measurements they mention fall far short of
the impression [δόξα] made by the image on the spectator" (5.11.9). The people
of the place know the true measure of the statue, however. "For when the image
was completed Phidias prayed that the god would give a sign if the work was
to his mind, and straightway, they say, the god hurled a thunderbolt into the
ground at the spot where the bronze urn stood down to my time" (5.11.9).

The logic here, which is one of overwhelming (if deceptive) appearances,
is unmistakably that of the sublime, an aesthetic category that is as old as Greek
literature itself and that will later find canonical expression in identical terms:
from Longinus to Kant, sublimity consists in magnitude beyond measure. "Nature," Longinus writes, "implanted in our minds from the start an irresistible
desire for anything which is great [τοῦ μεγάλου] and, in relation to ourselves,
supernatural [δαιμονιωτέρου]" (35.2). Thus, "the gods' thundering horses" of
Iliad 5.770–72 evoke a measure that can only be called "cosmic" due to the
impressiveness of the image, which exceeds all ordinary comparisons (διὰ τὴν
ὑπερβολὴν τοῦ μεγέθους [9.5–6]). Similarly, objects are "colossal" for Kant if
they defeat all relative measure, be they Egyptian pyramids, the Basilica in Saint
Peter's Cathedral in Rome, or (optimally) a piece of nature: their only true
measure is in the imagination. These objects embody what Kant calls "absolute"
magnitude. Literally big in their bigness, they comprise "a magnitude that is
equal only to itself." They are compelling *qua* magnitude (as opposed to any
other criterion)—that is, in virtue of their just being big (*schlechtin groß*), and
not of this or that size (*eine Größe*).[40] Small wonder that Pausanias would later
appeal to the European Romantic imagination (as several other contributors to
this volume bring out). In their sublimity, objects such as these embody a paradox for the mind (Kant talks about "the bewilderment or kind of perplexity
that is said to seize the spectator" in the face of sublime objects).[41] They provide
a benchmark for ordinary dimensionalities, as well as (in Pausanias's book) a
confirming map of decline. More so than for Kant, the perception of "loftiness"
and "antiquity" go hand in hand for both Pausanias and Longinus: these qualities
in objects make for memorable impressions, and so too they are the true constituents of antiquarian memory. Pausanias has a deep view of the past which,
however, exceeds that of either Longinus or Kant. Peering into the darkest
reaches of the past, one occasionally glimpses its gigantic inhabitants, literal

Giants, originally sprung from India (for no land can have "produced men earlier or bigger"; 8.29.1–4). Pausanias knows: he has laid eyes on the bones of Greek superhumans himself (8.32.5).[42]

There is a sublimity to this glimpse into the vanished, as well as an overriding sense of paradox. Megalopolis, located in the heartland of the Greek rustic world (Arcadia), elicits some of Pausanias's most eloquent remarks about this aspect of his commemorative archaeology of Greece. Perhaps it is the place-name (the "Great City") that prompts the thought. Or else it is simply the place that does:

> Megalopolis, the foundation of which was carried out by the Arcadians with the utmost enthusiasm, and viewed with the highest hopes by the Greeks, now lies mostly in ruins, shorn of all its beauty and ancient prosperity. I do not marvel at this, knowing that ceaseless change is the will of God, and that all things alike, strength as well as weakness, growth as well as decay, are subject to the mutations of fortune, whose resistless force sweeps them along at her will. Mycenae, which led the Greeks in the Trojan war; Nineveh, where was the palace of the Assyrian kings; Boeotian Thebes, once deemed worthy to be the head of Greece: what is left of them? Mycenae and Nineveh lie utterly desolate, and the name of Thebes is shrunk to the limits of the acropolis and a handful of inhabitants. The places that of old surpassed the world in wealth, Egyptian Thebes and Minyan Orchomenus, are now less opulent than a private man of moderate means; while Delos, once the common mart of Greece, has now not a single inhabitant except the guards sent from Athens to watch over the sanctuary. At Babylon the sanctuary of Bel remains, but of that Babylon which was once the greatest city that the sun beheld, nothing is left but the walls. And it is the same with Tiryns in Argolis. All these have been brought to nought by the hand of God. But the city of Alexander in Egypt and the city of Seleucus by the Orontes, founded but yesterday, have attained their present vast size and opulence because fortune smiles on them. Yet does she [i.e., Fortune] display her power on a still grander and more marvelous scale [μείζονα καὶ θαύματος πλείονος] than in the disasters and glories of cities. A short way across the sea from Lemnos lay the island of Chryse, where they say that Philoctetes met with his mishap from the water-snake. The billows rolled over all that island, and it went down and vanished [ἠφάνισται] in the depths . . . So transient and frail are the affairs of man. (8.33.1–4)

Pausanias's professed philosophical indifference to Megalopolis ("I do not marvel at this"), while confirmed by his unusual refusal to describe the site, is contradicted by the philosophical passion that the place elicits, by the glow of its past political glory (7.6.8–9), and perhaps by the quasi-conversional moment that the larger region of Arcadia, traditionally and mythologically the paradigm of archaism, famously occasions in him (8.8.3).[43]

"Marveling" is for the most part equivalent to "describing" in Pausanias, but there is another kind of marveling that passes all words. In revisiting his own *Description* in this retrospective mood here in Book VIII, now naming the highlights of his work and adding to them as well, Pausanias makes it clear that the whole of his work is governed by this spectacle of changing fortunes, the very view of which is breathtakingly grand.[44] The workings of fortune are in some sense the true subject of his ten books, as the sheer frequency and prominence of his descriptions of sanctuaries to Tyche throughout Greece might suggest alone. Prompted by "an ancient image" at the temple of Fortune in Pharae and by the widespread practice of representing Fortune with a celestial crown (inaugurated by the sculptor Bupalus at Smyrna in the sixth century), Pausanias credits Homer with being the first to mention the goddess but then faults him for failing to acknowledge her as "the mightiest of divinities and wielding the greatest influence over human affairs" (4.30.4–6). Fortune's workings are perceptible only, so to speak, from the bottom up, at the nadir of history.[45]

Similarly, the view of lofty heights is attainable only when that view is obstructed and so can only be imagined. This too is part of the paradoxes that typify the sublime. Thus, in Phigalia:

> The image made by Onatas was no longer in existence in my time, and most of the Phigalians were not aware that it had ever existed; but the oldest man we met said that three generations before his time some stones from the roof had fallen on the image, smashing and annihilating it; and sure enough in the roof we could still clearly see the places from which the stones had broken off. (8.42.12–13)

Greece falls into place only when it no longer exists as such, when it has the status of Delos in the passage from book VIII quoted above, lovingly and religiously watched over by guardians of memory like Pausanias. But nowhere are the sites of memory more compelling than where they are least visibly supported, as in the example of empty sepulchers, which are literal monuments to memory (2.23.3), or else in those unmistakable signs of absence, mere gaping holes. At the furthest remove are the ultimate kinds of remains, those that are denoted not by missing objects but by their absence—that is, by pure loss— and that thus designate *the very loss of loss*. Remains like these, overwhelmingly oppressive in their felt material presence, are the most resistant to the project of description and therefore the sublimest sites of all: "*No ruins of Parapotamii remained in my time, and the very spot on which the city stood is forgotten*" (10.33.8).[46]

What this last train of images brings us closer to is the secular—or, rather, purely memorializing—counterpart to what Elsner rightly points out as moments of breakdown in Pausanias's narrative:

> The description . . . broke down precisely at some of the sights that Pausanias deemed most worth seeing. At the sacred centres to which the pilgrimage of his text moves there is an absence . . . What all the instances in which Pausanias signalled his inability to describe an object have in common is ritual and the difference of an initiated viewer from the ordinary person.[47]

In what sense does Parapotamii fit this account? It is of course possible to say that this aspect of Pausanias's writing, its lapse into embarrassed or ritual silence, constitutes "a catalogue of instances where the ideology constructed by the rest of his text failed to apply,"[48] notably those touching sacred mysteries, purely numinous and ineffable (or ritually protected) accounts and experiences. But if we turn the logic around, we can see how such moments, far from being instances of failure, are in fact the fulfillment of Pausanias's ideology and of his text, which circles around a loss that is made palpable in two ways. From one perspective, the loss that is gestured toward antedates and exceeds the inscriptions of religion or patriotism. For at the heart of the account is the fundamental shock of contingency—the "transience and frailty" of fortune—that is itself elevated to a sublime status and projected "on a still grander and more marvelous scale" onto the cosmos. From another perspective, the loss exists and can be perceived only within the framework of these inscriptions, at their place of intersection: for the contingency of the historical real, operating with all the force of a necessity, is a palpable and material one. This coincidence of opposites within a sublime object is what today in some quarters is called the "Real," whether the Real of history or of symbolic structures of meaning. In Pausanias's terms, it is whatever occupies the place of a traumatic loss, materialized and palpable in the sublime remains (signs) of a particular past. The place-holder for this loss exists in the paradoxical form of a memory that, strictly speaking, ought to be forbidden, traceless, unreconstructable, like the non-ruins of Parapotamii.[49] The moments of blank wordlessness of Pausanias's text, where words fail, are moments when this loss comes to be invested with a numinous presence. Far from debarring readers from an experience, these moments initiate readers into the desire to know and to see, and thus into the collective ritual of cultural memory.[50]

Pausanias's project combats the loss of memory. It is a memorial project, but also a monitory one. In reconstituting the memory of a lost Greece and in documenting its fall into decline, Pausanias is doing more than commemorating the freedom that "the whole of Greece" once enjoyed. He is preserving the possibility of freedom itself, by performing the imaginative act that in his eyes is constitutive of freedom to begin with. Not for nothing does he report the remark made by the emperor Vespasian in A.D. 69 when he rescinded the freedom that Greece had so recently regained from Nero in exchange, no less, for the mere possession of Sardinia: because "Greece *had forgotten* what it was to be free," Vespasian felt justified in claiming it as his possession again (7.17.4; cf. Suetonius, *Divus Vespasianus* 8.4). The whole of Pausanias's *Description of Greece* exists to counteract the reality of this statement; it reclaims as a possession the memory lost by the Greeks themselves. That is the ultimate source of the selectivity of his work and of its sheer imaginative power. If Pausanias's readers have found Pausanias to be unimaginative, it is because they have failed to appreciate the act of mind that makes his project cohere at all.[51] For the same reason, nothing could be more wrong than to distinguish between the "historical" and the "descriptive" aspect of Pausanias's writing (as Frazer does)[52] or between the "aetiological" and the "historiographical" aspects (Veyne).[53] Such compartmentalizations miss the point of the totalizing power of Pausanias's selectivity, the ability of his project to flood all of its objects with meaning. Pausanias's selective history is descriptive and his descriptions are historically inflected in the precise senses given above; that is, they are commemorative and laden with historical meaning—they are signs of lost value. In this way, Pausanias makes memory into an antidote against decline. But what is even more important, he makes memory into an antidote against insignificance, in the face of the inexorable "mutations of fortune," of which (he would have us believe) Greece is but the nearest, and so too the most compelling, example. Pausanias makes memory sublime.

The Rhetoric of Classicism: Longinus's *On the Sublime*

Although often credited with being the most eloquent spokesperson for the sublime in antiquity, Longinus in no way holds a unique patent on the concept. There are good reasons, however, to want to connect the particular form that sublimity takes in Pausanias with the form in which we find it in Longinus, starting with the broader cultural attitudes that the two authors seem to have held in common.

Of these, the most immediately obvious is their shared moral and political pessimism, or at least the appearance of it that they both give. Pausanias's attitude is nowhere more clearly put than in Book VIII. Whereas in the distant past,

> men were raised to the rank of gods . . . and are worshipped down to the present time . . . , in the present age, when wickedness is growing to such a height, and spreading over every land and every city, men are changed into gods no more, save in the hollow rhetoric which flattery addresses to power; and the wrath of the gods at the wicked is reserved for a distant future when they shall have gone hence. (8.2.4–5)[54]

The closing chapter of *On the Sublime* is likewise an elegy on the theme of decline:

> "Are we to believe . . . the common explanation that democracy nurtures greatness, and great writers flourished with democracy and died with it? Freedom, the argument goes, nourishes and encourages the thoughts of the great, as well as exciting their enthusiasm for rivalry with one another and their ambition for the prize . . . We of the present day, on the other hand, . . . seem to have learned in infancy to live under justified slavery, swathed round from our first tender thoughts in the same habits and customs, never allowed to taste that fair and fecund spring of literature, freedom. We end up as flatterers in the grand manner." (44.2–3)

A question that has exercised commentators is how closely Longinus is to be identified with the speaker of this passage, who is introduced as "one of the philosophers" in recent dialogue with Longinus ("the other day"). Perhaps a better question to start with is how closely the speaker is to be identified with the notions he retails ("the argument goes"). The philosopher's complaint is routinely taken as evidence of the date of the treatise itself, alluding as it does to "the political change from republican to monarchical government" and excluding, inter alia, a date during the Second Sophistic, when "Greek literary men were no longer as modest as is Longinus about the achievements of their own age."[55] But in Longinus you will look in vain for a reference so precise as any of this.[56] Longinus goes on to dismiss as a factor in the current moral state of affairs "the peace of the world [ἡ τῆς οἰκουμένης εἰρήνη]" (44.6), a political condition that could refer to any time under the imperial pax Romana. Pausanias's perspectives on political and cultural decline are not substantially different from the views represented in Longinus's treatise, which are general and philosophical and shaped by a diffuse romanticizing of the Greek past.[57] Dio of Prusa's attitudes are of a similar cast, as will be seen below.[58]

At first sight, Longinus's own views might appear to be distinct from those put forward by his philosopher friend. Longinus bemoans "a universal dearth of literature" and of "sublime or really great minds" (44.1). That his sights are trained on targets larger than mundane corruptions is suggested by the word "universal" (κοσμική; cf. 35.3: οὐδ' ὁ σύμπας κόσμος ἀρκεῖ).[59] His vision points beyond this world: it looks to transcendent values unconditioned by material circumstances, by contemporary materialist ideologies, or by politics or the social, for these are not eternal, timeless, or a source of sublimity. And it points inwardly, to the soul and its capacity to circumvent the narrow impingements of the present, for the soul "is spontaneous, uninhibited, and therefore least affected by external social and political factors."[60] This is indeed the surface ideology of the Longinian sublime. And in fact, on such a view, one would not only be hard-pressed to compare Longinus's treatise with Pausanias's. It would be impossible to date Longinus's treatise at all: the work is simply there, transcending (in its aspirations) time and space, the product of no external circumstances but merely of a direct communication with the divine logic of the cosmos.

But Longinus knows better. He knows, for instance, that the soul is vulnerable to external factors ("I cannot see how we can honor, or rather deify, unlimited wealth as we do without admitting into our souls the evils which attach to it . . . These evils then become chronic in people's lives . . . It is an inevitable process"; 44.7–8).[61] This knowledge is what informs his complaint about his age, about its "universal dearth of literature" and its turning away from the sublimity of the past; and it is this same knowledge that informs the dire pessimism of his reflections ("Perhaps people like us are better as subjects than given our freedom. Greed would flood the world in woe, if it were really released and let out of the cage, to prey on its neighbors"; 44.10). Longinus also knows that despite its universal pretensions, sublimity cannot be free of external determinations, whether this means transcending cultural barriers or even time itself. That it can is part of the official ideology of the sublime, which suggests that we may "reckon those things which please everybody all the time as genuinely and finely sublime," where by "all the time" is meant "people of different trainings, ways of life, tastes, ages, and manners" (7.4). However appealing it may be, this last point is marred by the polemical nature of Longinus's treatise and thus by the very contestability of its own assumptions. (Longinus from first to last is disputing the views of an opponent, Caecilius, probably of Calacte from the late first century B.C., who had himself written a treatise entitled *On the Sublime*.) What is more, the range of Longinus's tastes is narrowly circum-scribed by his classicism, which is transparent on every page of his work. Not a single Greek author from after the fourth century is viewed by him as sublime, while those who do come in for praise are part of the Classical canon, which his treatise exists to reaffirm, to renew, and in ways to deform, at times by offering novel arguments that would justify this selection and its perpetuation. One of these arguments is about the paradox at the heart of his treatise and announced on the first page: "How can we develop our nature to some degree of greatness" in a world that is now definitively in decline?

The solution that Longinus's treatise is most frequently seen to commend is the imitation and emulation of sublime literature. But for all of its pretenses to rhetorical instruction, *On the Sublime* is not a how-to book on sublime writing. We need not write like Herodotus in order to appreciate his "inimitable" sentences (28.4). On the contrary, the aim of the treatise is to cultivate a reader's receptivity to sublimity. It is a pragmatic manual in identifying sublime litera-ture, in reading the signs of sublimity, and in reproducing the effects of sublimity in one's responses to the great canonical works of the past. In a move typical of post-Classical literature, *On the Sublime* is addressed to the reader as critic: the reader must cultivate himself and so become a "free, uncorrupt judge [κριτής] of great things of permanent value" (44.9); the aim is to "achieve a genuine understanding and appreciation [ἐπιστήμην καὶ ἐπίκρισιν] of true sub-limity" (6.1). Hence the shift from the addressee *qua* potential writer to the same *qua* potential "nature": if what counts is developing "our nature to some degree of greatness," the nature developed is one that will help us cultivate a unanimous judgment of what counts as sublime. Sublimity thus has a canonical function: it is what defines the very best literature, while cultivating an appreciation for the sublime is how the canon comes to be pleasurably enforced.

Plainly, nothing is more determined culturally, politically, or socially than this use of sublimity. Sublimity, meanwhile, is the momentary illusion that the opposite is the case.[62] Like any gripping ideology, sublimity rests on the argu-ment of sheer self-evidence ("Caecilius tries at immense length to explain to us what sort of thing 'the sublime' is, as though we did not know"; 1.1). In the-oretical and ideological terms, sublimity spells out the criteria and conditions for sublime identifications whose nature is beyond all doubt. In literary terms, which give the narrower, pragmatic object of the treatise, sublimity is a property of great literature, "a kind of eminence or excellence of discourse" (1.3). To recognize this property wherever it occurs is to commemorate a past literary achievement, that of the classics. So, unless Longinus is to run into the seem-ingly fatal contradiction of pointing out the obvious, his treatise has to be seen as having another purpose. Perhaps that purpose is to help readers discover the true goal of literature and to give them reasons for accepting what they already intuitively know. If so, then his treatise is a defense of an illusion.

Through their sublimity, the classics are made so vivid that the past seems to be awakened and lived out in the present once again. In this way, the classical canon justifies itself incontrovertibly. Accordingly, for Longinus the museal past is not permanently frozen; it is mobilized in the reproductive imagination of its readers.[63] The line between reproduction and production is thus blurred to the point of indistinction: "It is our nature to be elevated and exalted by true sublimity. Filled with joy and pride, we come to believe we have created what we have only heard" (7.2). In this reverential yet proudly appropriative identification, this highly constrained "freedom" (which is that of the collector and the *bricoleur*), Longinus is at one with Pausanias. Both validate the achievements of a past—the selfsame past—through its vivid experience in the present. Both *arrange* the past in order to be able to recall it.[64] The pleasure taken is partly surreptitious. It is like the pleasure that arises when we find something we pretend we had lost.

Hence arises the extraordinary emphasis in Longinus's treatise on the memorial function of reading great literature. So, for instance, Longinus will write that while minor literature "comes to seem valueless on repeated inspection" and "endures only for the moment of hearing," "real sublimity contains much food for reflection, is difficult or rather impossible to resist, and makes a strong and ineffaceable impression on the memory" (7.3).[65] Sublime literature is of an "eternal" duration (1.3): it lasts for an αἰών, and αἰών (eternity) here is synonymous with posterity (14.3, 36.2). Sublimity, produced, looks forward to posterity ("How will posterity take what I am writing?" 14.3); read by us, it looks back to the eternal posterity of the past (τῶν ἔμπροσθεν [13.2]). Analogously, writers who lapse from sublimity "forget themselves" and their higher purpose (4.4), which is to project their memory into the future and to recall, in turn, the great models of the past ("it is good to imagine how Homer would have said the same thing" or reacted to it; 14.1–2). The sublime is thus an exponentially heightened form of remembrance: it is the vivid preservation of the past in the latter's most memorable aspects. *Phantasia,* if not fantasy, is only one of the critical components of the sublime (15.1–12). So viewed, the Longinian sublime captures the intensity of *the experience of canonicity itself*, and as such it is a purely ideological effect. On one reading of Longinus's treatise, which may not be the most complete or necessarily even the best reading of the treatise, *On the Sublime* is itself an attempt to (re)produce such canonical effects. At the very least, his treatise is an account of how the ideological subject of Greek literature is itself (re)produced.[66]

Let us explore a little further the workings of this cultural ideology as it is put on display in Longinus. Sublimity for Longinus never truly belongs to the present save in one sense: it exists in a present experience of the past—or in its projection into the past (as an experience that any fourth-century Athenian, e.g., would have had).[67] But this barely begins to capture the great power of sublimity. Sublimity nearly obliterates the present with a kind of violence, with an "invincible power and force": "produced at the right moment, [it] tears everything up like a whirlwind"; it leaves a subject in a state of "wonder and astonishment," and even of "ecstasy" (1.4). Its effects are like those that Demosthenes's speeches have. "Demosthenes burns and ravages; he has violence, rapidity, strength, and force . . . ; he can be compared to a thunderbolt or a flash of lightning" (12.4), or better yet, to an eclipsing light that dazzles and blinds, as if by overexposure: "its very brilliance conceals . . . ," the way "fainter lights disappear when the sunshine surrounds them" (15.11, 17.2). Sublimity is thus linked to the near-death—the "beautiful death"—of posthumousness.[68] And yet death assumes different guises in Longinus's treatise. For the past, when it comes to life, obliterates the present. Here, Longinus comes into contact with Pausanias again. Their works do not merely celebrate the past. They linger over it, at the cost of eclipsing the present.

Capturing thematic moments of near-death and resurrection, and then reenacting these experiences upon the reader (who is blinded and subjected to a kind of literary violence through ἔκπληξις [15.2]),[69] the sublime passes over into the realm of the numinous, the supernatural, and the divine; it takes the form of possession and inspiration. "Many are possessed by a spirit not their own" (13.2). The Pythia at Delphi is adduced as a (reported) example ("so they say") but also as a metaphorical parallel: "Similarly, the genius of the ancients (τῶν ἀρχαίων) acts as a kind of oracular cavern, and effluences flow from it into the minds of their imitators"—or their readers (13.2). Part of the meaning of the parallel lies in its reported nature: the sublime exists only in a chain of citations.[70] The resumption of the Pythian oracle under Hadrian is a specimen case of classicism intervening powerfully in culture.[71] But it also points to the felt need for a shadowy recess behind the bright façades of Classical appearances. Longinus's sublime expresses some of this need.

There is an "archaicism" to the classicism of the sublime.[72] In the light of the discussion of Pausanias above, this taste for the old and the archaic should no longer appear a strange overlay on top of classicism. On the contrary, this taste is an essential component of the classicizing ideology: it signifies the very distance of revered classical values, by now half a millennium old. Indeed, classicist criticism of the Imperial period standardly incorporates archaicism into the heart of its aesthetic. As the Augustan Roman literary critic Dionysius of Halicarnassus would say of the austere (impacted) style, "its beauty consists in its patina of antiquity (τὸν ἀρχαϊσμὸν καὶ τὸν πίνον ἔχουσα κάλλος)" (*De compositione verborum* 22). The implication that Antimachus, Empedocles, Pindar, Aeschylus, Thucydides, and Antiphon might themselves be archaizing, not archaic, is left teasingly open by Dionysius. The austere style is at the very least a component of the sublime tradition followed by Caecilius and Longinus and is one of its ideal forms, if not its ideal form, that to which all sublimity aspires: sublimity wants to appear old and venerable. In a similar vein and idiom, Longinus writes about "the choice of correct and magnificent words," a feature that needs to be "cultivated intensely": "it makes grandeur, beauty [κάλλος], old-world charm [εὐπίνειαν], weight, force, strength, and a kind of lustre bloom upon our words as upon beautiful statues; it gives things life and makes them speak" (30.1).[73]

The architectural metaphors are not by chance. The eye in search of "old-world charm" naturally falls upon statuary relics and columns, as in Pausanias (cf. 7.5.5). Thus, for Dionysius,

> the special character of the austere style of composition is this: it requires that the words shall stand firmly on their own feet [ἐρείδεσθαι ἀσφαλῶς] and occupy

strong positions [στάσεις ἰσχυράς] [Rhys: "like columns"] and be seen on all sides [ἐκ περιφανείας ὁρᾶσθαι]; and that the parts of the sentence shall be at considerable distances from one another [ἀπέχειν τε ἀπ' ἀλλήλων], separated by perceptible intervals [αἰσθητοῖς χρόνοις διειργόμενα]. It does not mind admitting harsh and dissonant collocations, like blocks of natural stone laid together in building, with their sides not cut square or polished smooth, but remaining unworked and rough-hewn. It has a general liking for expansion by means of long words which extend over a wide space [εἰς πλάτος]. (*De compositione verborum* 22).[74]

If the distances and proportions of austere language evoke cyclopean structures, they also suggest colossal ruins laid bare by time.[75] The affected "periegetic" feeling of sublime literary criticism, and not only here, is striking, and it is strongly reminiscent of Pausanias. Compare the latter's description of the wondrous throne of Apollo at Amyclae:

The part of the throne where the god would sit is not continuous [συνεχοῦς], but contains several seats. Beside each seat a wide space is left [ὑπολειπομένης καὶ εὐρυχωρίας]: the middle space is widest of all, and here the image stands. I know of no one who has measured the size of the image, but one would guess it to be quite thirty cubits. It is not the work of Bathycles, but is an ancient and rude image [ἀρχαῖον καὶ οὐ σὺν τέχνῃ πεποιημένον]; for except that it has a face and feet and hands, it otherwise resembles a bronze pillar . . . The pedestal of the image is in the form of an altar. (3.19.1–3)

Pausanias's artifact seems to be a virtual template for descriptions of sublime works. Longinus knows the charms of gaping structures too:

The conception [of certain verses from Euripides's *Antiope*] is fine in itself, but it has been improved by the fact that the word-harmony [i.e., the composition] is not hurried and does not run smoothly; the words are propped up by one another [στηριγμοὺς ἔχειν πρὸς ἄλληλα τὰ ὀνόματα] and rest on the intervals between them [καὶ ἐξερείσματα τῶν χρόνων (sc. ἔχειν)]; set wide apart like that, they give the impression of solid strength [πρὸς ἑδραῖον διαβεβηκότα μέγεθος]. (40.4)

So stylized, sublimity cannot help but evoke the noble freedoms of a past glory. In fact, Dionysius makes this very connection in the same passage that was quoted just above, and Longinus follows him implicitly: austere rhythms are "dignified and impressive," and the austere style generally "aims to make its clauses not parallel in structure or sound, nor slaves to a rigid sequence, but noble, conspicuous, and free (εὐγενῆ καὶ λαμπρὰ καὶ ἐλεύθερα)" (*De compositione verborum* 22). Pausanias's tastes are at the very least shaped by the same set of cultural preferences.

I want to suggest that the sublime and its freedoms exist only in the context of threatened or real loss. The gaping nature of the structures above exemplifies this potential and imparts to them the peculiar pathos of the sublime: they suggest their own fragmentation. The sublime is based on an aesthetics not of perfect wholes but of ruptured wholes. That is why modernity is never sublime. Pausanias's eye is not drawn to the polished monuments of his day; these exert no attraction upon his mind. And the same holds for Longinus, who goes a step further and turns the fascination with violent loss into an explicit aesthetic principle. What Longinus admires in Thucydides is his "characteristic" trait: he "shows ingenuity in separating (ἀπ' ἀλλήλων) by transpositions even things which are by nature completely unified and indivisible," and he does this with a violent "willfulness" (22.3). Homer "crushes" his language so as to simulate and heighten the fearful dangers of the stormy sea (10.6). Sappho, "near to dying," is literally dismembered, her body parts enumerated, each overstimulated to incapacity (10.3). Demosthenes's periods display a syntax that is disorderly, disturbed, squall-like, nearly fatally interrupted, and consequently they "throw the hearer into a panic lest the sentence collapse altogether" (20.1–3, 22.3–4). Immeasurable intervals and abysses of various kinds yawn open, threatening every sense of intactness and measure: "the interval between earth and heaven," "a cosmic distance," suggesting how "there [is] not enough room in the world," "Tarturus laid bare," "the sea part[ing] in joy," "the universe" when it is viewed as "not [being] wide enough for the range of human speculation and intellect" and thus rent by the energy of the mind (9.5–8, 35.3), and so on. The logic of the sublime is a relational logic of gaps and crevices, of the interstitial, the fragmentary. It thrives on interruption; it points to something that is lost or nearly so.[76]

By the same token, the sublime may be associated with ideals of heroism and freedom, but these are sublime only when they are imperiled, when they are imagined as potential, or simply when they are no more.[77] The sublime appeal of freedom is freedom on a razor's edge, as in Herodotus (22.1); or freedom mourned, as in Hyperides's and Demosthenes's responses to the battle of Chaeronea (15.10, 16.2–4); or the prospect of release from enslavement and imprisonment (9.7, 15.9–10, 21.2, 32.5, 44.4–5 and 10, etc.). Proud heroism is forever pitched on the brink of extinction, whether literal (Ajax, 9.10) or metaphorical (the pulverization of the reader, 1.4, etc.). Freedom that is secure is never sublime: for sublimity resides less in the moral dimension of heroism and freedom than in the emotional experience of freedom at critical junctures (cf. 16.3).[78] If ideologies have emotions bound up with them, then sublimity would be the emotion of this particular ideological feeling—of the greatness of what it is to be Greek on the verge of the attainment or loss of this greatness. For all its (alleged) ineffability, sublimity uniquely, and adequately, names and captures this quality.

There is a rhetorical character to the sublime that needs to be acknowledged. Description, after all, is an art. Here, in the case of Pausanias and Longinus, it is the art of elevating fragments to a desirable height, of taking, if need be, the apparently small and incidental (a local shrine, a prepositional phrase, or a vowel)[79] and investing it with sublime purpose, literally through a kind of sublimation: "When we are working on something which needs loftiness of expression and greatness of thought, it is good to imagine how . . . Plato or Demosthenes or (in history) Thucydides would have invested it with sublimity (ὕψωσαν ἄν)," literally "would have exalted it" (14.1). "How does Homer make the divine *big*? (ὁ δὲ πῶς μεγεθύνει τὰ δαιμόνια;)" (9.5). Sublimity is something that has to be manufactured, constructed, built up. Hence, again, the multiple building metaphors in Longinus. But there is also his frank recognition of the simulacral and imaginary nature of the sublime, which is in the end but a "mental image"—an appearance—fashioned by writers (and by himself), in part through the technique of visualization (φαντασία or εἰδολοποιία [14.1; 15.1]).[80] Sublimity dwells in fragments. A sublime effect is generated by the juxtaposition of fragments in tension, against the background of loss, violence, speechlessness, or blinding. For "juxtaposition," Longinus will say "combination" of elements that have survived a "selection" (10.1), as in the case of Sappho, whose "skill" as a poetic fashioner of lifelike illusion lies "in [her] selecting the outstanding details and making a unity of them": "Do you not admire the way in which she brings everything together—mind and body, hearing and tongue, eyes and skin? She seems to have lost them all, and to be looking for them as though they were external to her [Grube: "as if they were scattered elements strange to her," πάνθ᾽ ὡς ἀλλότρια διοιχόμενα] . . . . Sappho's excellence, as I have said, lies in her adoption and combination of the most striking details" (10.1–3).

The shrewd artfulness of the example (δεινότης) puts the emotional sincerity of Sappho's poem in a somewhat skeptical light. What is more, her example establishes a parallel with Longinus's own practice of writing the sublime into literary history. His technique is likewise one of selection (violent fragmentation) and combination (imagining), of estrangement and rearrangement. In this way, Longinus produces an image of Greek literature as a body that has been dismembered into scintillating literary fragments, snippets of quotations, and, at the limit, into particles of individual words, themselves a brutal locus of clashing forces (as in the Homeric preposition ὑπέκ [10.6]).[81] Literally dwelling in fragments, sublimity by definition breaks literature up into pieces, or rather into fetish-like objects. By producing fragments, sublime criticism renders literary history a survey of remains. That is the source of its canonical energy. In turn, the fragments of the Greek literary past conjure forth, in their sublimity, the fantasy of their totality and simultaneously that of Greece itself. In this way, the past is revived as an authoritative whole.[82] The cult of the ruin here in Longinus, for all its later associations, must have been typical of pedagogical practices from the end of the Hellenistic period onward.[83] And as a rule, Greek literary-critical culture tends to be lemmatic and microscopic, focused on the sentence or the scene, rather than holistic and totalizing. Longinian *hypsos* makes this narrowness of focus into a literary virtue, and a fetish.[84] Needless to say, all of these practices serve a purpose identical to Pausanias's survey of the material remains of the Greek past.

The worry governing Longinus's treatise—how sublimity can be possible in a declining world—is solved by the very nature of the sublime itself. Sublimity is effective *only* as a deracinated moment, one that is cut off from past greatness, in a violent, numbing decontextualization that leaves a reader breathless and disoriented.[85] After all, the sublime exists, as it were (and in fact), only within quotation marks, and its emotional impact on the reader is the violent registration of this alienation.[86] That said, one should be wary of overestimating the nostalgic force of the sublime. The sublime, as Longinus repeatedly reminds us, is a contrived and cultivated effect. Later readings of both Pausanias and Longinus will draw these two writers into the frameworks of Romanticism. Looked upon as themselves fragments of a recuperable Greek past, their works will be seen by the Romantic generations to offer a confirming echo of the modern cult of classical ruins. And yet, paradoxically, Greek re-creators of the past can be assimilated in this way only on pain of a certain loss. They must be brought into literary history as, so to speak, its victims—as secondary, diminished, and never quite canonical—and in this way "pay" for the modern fantasy of antiquity; consequently their own authorial strategies must be misrecognized (disavowed).[87]

Isocrates in his *Panegyricus* (8) had written roughly to the effect that "the power of speech is such that it can make great things lowly, give grandeur (μέγεθος) to the trivial, say what is old in a new fashion, and lend an appearance of antiquity (ἀρχαίως διελθεῖν) to recent events." Longinus objects to this "puerile" remark, not because of its overstatement, but because "it goes too far": it is too flatly *revealing* of the truth of sublime rhetoric (38.1–3).[88] Sublimity requires disavowal if it is to be effective; it must simply *appear,* without appearing to do so. Whether the texts as cited and then exposed by Longinus are self-evidently sublime is a question we may leave aside for now. Suffice it to say that to read this kind of treatise is to change forever one's attitude toward the category of the sublime. To what degree does Pausanias construct the effects of his historical sublime through his own selective procedures and through his active promotion of the fetish-like quality of the fragments he describes? The scholarly practice of referring to the "monuments" in Pausanias obscures this very point—namely, that his description of Greece is a history of fragments, and an unparalleled one at that. The usage also attests to the seductions of Pausanias's approach.[89] Fragments are not intrinsically appealing; the taste for them, on the contrary, has to be cultivated. Consider for a moment Pausanias's lingering over remains in his description of Greece in decline in Book III (3.7.11): "shaken to its foundations" by the Peloponnesian War, "the rickety and decaying structure" that was once "stable and strong" was "brought with a crash to the ground" by Philip. How is it that the images of decay and ruin so repellently presented here come to be endowed with sublime significance in the rest of the work?

One reason has to be that the fascinated extremes of horror and awe are functionally paired: the fetishizing of fragments (the idealizing of ruins) works to obliterate the traumatic memory of the shattering of Greece. That "Greece," so conceived, is itself an ideal only points to the difficulty of returning to the site of a—here, historical and cultural—trauma in its original condition. But *which* trauma? Ideal Greece suffered, we might say, an ideal trauma. Take away the idealization, and all that is left is the broken landscape of Greece, stripped bare of fantasy. The less-than-sublime *or* less-than-hideous nature of the relics from the past must be concealed at all costs. Knowledge of this truth and the attempt to suppress it again are what constitutes the real traumatic core of the memory of Greece. Nostalgia, in other words, is not a simple or straightforward emotion, and it is assuredly not blind to itself. It is a *cultural strategy,* one way of coming to grips with a loss that can only ever be imagined but never experienced as such. Both Pausanias and Longinus owe their places in our histories of antiquity to their successful practice of this strategy. That they were hardly the first to practice nostalgia will be discussed at the conclusion of this essay. I want first to show briefly how they were not alone in this practice in their lifetimes by looking at a final instance of time travel in latter-day Greece, that of Dio Chrysostom, the "Golden-Mouthed," of Prusa.

Dio Chrysostom and the Second Sophistic

> All the former [Hellenes] are past and gone, have perished in an utterly shameful and pitiable way; and as to the rest, it is no longer possible to form a conception of the pre-eminence and splendor of their deeds and, as well, their sufferings, by looking at the men of the present time. Nay, it is rather the stones which reveal the grandeur and the greatness of Hellas, and the ruins of her buildings; her inhabitants themselves and those who conduct her governments would not be called descendants of even the Mysians. So to me, at least, it seems that the cities which have been utterly destroyed have come off better than those which are inhabited as they are now. For the memory of those men remains unimpaired . . . ; just as it is true, I believe, with the bodies of the dead—it is in every way better that they should have been utterly destroyed and that no man should see them any more, than that they should rot in the sight of all! (Dio Chrysostom, *Orations* 31.159–60)

Dio's lament from his *Rhodian Oration* neatly figures the sorrows of the Greeks under the Romans. It is no accident that these words should have found their way into Frazer's preface to his translation of Pausanias. Dio faced a Greek world in which Archaic splendors were in ruins. Yet not a trace of this sorrowfulness is to be found in his Thirty-sixth Oration, the so-called *Borysthenian Discourse,* whose ironies of self-definition read like a patent for Second Sophistic literary culture. The setting of this discourse needs to be unwrapped and then put into relation with the themes discussed above.

The occasion of Dio's writing is a speech addressed to his native audience of Prusans in the Roman province of Bithynia ("The Borysthenian Discourse Which I Read in My Native Land"—so the subtitle transmitted in the manuscripts). Dio relates his visit, while in exile, to Borysthenes, a rustic Greek community in the heart of Scythia, known to Herodotus (4.18) as Olbia. While surveying the site and fulfilling one purpose of his visit, which is ethnographic (1), Dio chances upon a band of natives, led by one Callistratus, a strapping youth, Ionian in his features, and whose—to Dio's way of thinking—questionable homoerotic practices and equally questionable single-minded love of Homer mark him as unquestionably Greek (8–9). Dio appears to this eager outpost of Greek civilization as a beacon of light and wisdom, and he is only more than willing to oblige his hosts. Choosing to pass over the sexual practices of the Borysthenians, he lectures them instead on the virtues of small-scale poetry. A moralizing gnome from the Archaic poet Phocylides provides the desired contrast: Homer is a bit outsized for this tumbledown village on the Black Sea (recalling an image from Longinus illustrating how magniloquence in the wrong place can make for absurdity: "it is like putting a huge tragic mask on a little child"; 30.2); their passion for things Homeric is misguided; and the pithy two verses attributed to Phocylides make the same point again (we will come back to this below). From there, Dio swerves over to some favorite Stoic themes (anthropology, ethics, and civic government) and finally culminates his speech in a fabulous cosmological myth that he claims to have acquired from Persian magi but that resembles nothing so much as a personal blend of Platonic and Stoic philosophy. The sublime vision of divine cosmogony closes upon itself, abruptly, in a confession of ineffability, a failing for which the importunings of the Borysthenians that day are said to be to blame ("if the form of that myth has turned out to be utterly lofty and indistinct, . . . it is not I whom you should blame, . . . because it was they [the Borysthenians] who bade me speak on the subject"). And so ends the discourse to the Prusans.

Dio's Thirty-sixth Oration is a puzzling piece of rhetoric. Rather than be baffled, we can take the speech as a virtuoso display of incongruous, layered frames of reference and thus see in it a self-conscious manipulation of ethical and national identities. The speech has all the earmarks of a piece of novelistic fiction.[90] It is at the very least artfully contrived. Before going into the details, we may consider some of Dio's moves in their sequence. Formally in exile from Rome at the time of the visit, Dio is in fact a Greek in exile from Greece. His flight (φυγή [1]) returns him to a more primitive and original Greece: what he discovers is "Borysthenes," not "Olbia." The choice of names is significant. The resonance of the unused name, "wealth," may be poignant, but the conscious and determined archaism of "Borysthenes" proves double-edged. Traveling back in time is not necessarily a good thing, as we shall see. But first, just where does Dio land? The city is itself doubled. The city that is and that was (ἥ τε νῦν καὶ ἡ πρότερον [1]) overlaps with itself geographically but not physically or symbolically: the present-day Borysthenes is diminished; its size no longer matches its "ancient fame" (4). Borysthenes is dilapidated, the consequence of lost wars and then capture. Its circumference is shrunken; its heights (towers) have been decapitated. A makeshift totality, the enclosure of inner walls points to a whole that once was. Its statues and funeral monuments are fallen (6). All this violent decay and lowliness (ταπεινὸν καὶ ἀσθενές [6]) points to a prior grandeur (μέγεθος [1]). The insistence on the archaic place-name is at first odd but then on reflection entirely apposite. And yet: is Borysthenes Olbia? Dio's *Discourse* circles around this paradoxical starting point. His speech evokes a crisis of proper names, which in turn signals a crisis in other, related (and larger) identifications.[91] The city's ruins are a physical emblem of loss and indeed reflect in miniature the condition of Greece in its contemporary fallen and diasporic state (5). We are reminded of Pausanias's remark from Book VIII that "the name of Thebes has shrunk to the limits of the acropolis and a handful of inhabitants." At the heart of Dio's dilemma is the question, what is "Greek"? Traveling back in time (and not), Dio discovers native descendants of a past culture, a people cut off from the present, strangely archaic, rude, even uncannily Homeric (17), and yet displaced and incongruous. They are Ionian (Milesian) and not Scythian (despite their Scythian dress), warlike and yet literary, Greek-speaking "in the midst of barbarians," and too fondly attached (Dio finds) to Homer's memory (φιλόμηροι), which they preserve in their hearts and on their lips by sheer rote, despite their no longer being in clear command of the Greek language (7–9).[92] A faintly Platonic criticism is probably to be felt here: the rhapsode Ion (hence some of the pun on "Ionian"?) likewise "will hear about no other poet than Homer" (Plato, *Ion* 532b–c).[93] The counterexemplum of Phocylides (11–13), with its formal, self-conscious modesty, its sharp contrasts, and its thematic disdain for greatness, reinforces this criticism:

> This too the saying of Phocylides:
> The law-abiding town, though small and set
> On a lofty rock (ἐν σκοπέλῳ), outranks mad Nineveh. (13; frag. 2 Diehl)

"Aren't these verses as good as the whole of the *Iliad* and *Odyssey* for those who pay heed as they listen?" Dio asks provocatively. Yet the counterexample amounts to more than an exchange of views about literature. It also confirms, and seemingly affirms, the contemporary condition of Borysthenes, and by extension that of diasporic Greece. Pausanias, who also knows about Nineveh, might well agree with Dio's sentiments. But can Dio really be affirming the condition of the ethnic hodgepodge before his own eyes?

The disparities mapped out in these earlier parts of the speech come to a head in the myth of the Magi, with its dressing up of Stoic wisdom in a non-Greek ("barbarian"; 43) tale that in its central vehicle is, as has often been remarked, neither Stoic nor Persian but transparently Platonic. As Russell notes, the confusions involved are witty and meant to surprise and delight Dio's immediate audience, the Prusans, and not the Borysthenians for whose benefit the myth is ostensibly told. "The Borysthenites . . . expected Hellenic culture from Dio, and look at what they got! No wonder he had to apologize. Back home in Prusa, it was different: Dio was a returning traveler, expected to have exotic tales to tell." But as Russell goes on to observe, "there remains, however, a great difficulty."[94] The myth consists of two parts, each of which tells a different tale. The first is about the world's violent, if partial, destruction by fire and flood; the second, loosely appended to the first (πάλιν δὲ ἑτέραν [sc. ἡνιόχησιν λέγουσι]), describes the complete destruction of the universe, not by violence, but by transformation (51–60). The relationship between these two competing stories is anything but clear. Nor do they connect up in any obvious way with the preceding discussion of the perfect form of government (29–38), which itself is a pendant to a discussion of mortal government that never gets told (27). Instead, the connection between the myths and what precedes them is casually bridged over (ἕτερος δὲ μῦθος [39]) and then lost in near-parallels. Dio's discourse threatens to fall apart into a series of non sequiturs. He does little to lift the cloud of confusion and everything, it seems, to foster it. Perhaps his discourse is not about harmoniousness in the cosmos, though it wants to be this (55–57), but about its very own oscillation.

A clue to the problem resides in the second part of the final myth told by Dio. In the first part, four cosmic horses yoked together in a race periodically go awry, dragging the human world along with them, due to the impetuousness of either a fiery or a panicky and copiously sweating horse that, depending on circumstances, fatefully takes the lead. In the second part, the four steeds merge "into one being, having been overcome by that one which is superior in power," the soul of the charioteer. Here, the universe perishes as a whole and is reborn anew. That the myth contains a political allegory seems evident enough, but how does the allegory translate into reality? One possibility is that the nonviolent blending of natures figured in the myth prefigures a hoped-for resolution to racial and political strife besetting the world periodically until Dio's own day, in the new world order of Nerva and Trajan.[95] But the myth is more than a vehicle for toleration and harmony. It speaks of a process of transformation; one might like to call this a process of hybridization and to compare it with the hybrid identities that Dio has been highlighting throughout his speech. The process involves "the movement and change of all four horses, one in which they shift among themselves and interchange their forms"—immanently, not from without—"until all come together into one being" that "appropriates to itself all the substance of them all." "Standing tall and proud, rejoicing in its victory, it not only seized the largest possible region but also needed larger space at that time, so great was its strength and its spirit" (51–53). The metaphors recall nothing so much as imperial expansion, rather than a logical and psychic harmony and subordination.[96] But strangely, once the process of transformation reaches an end, the resulting creature, "having obtained the purest nature of unadulterated light, immediately longed for the existence that it had at first" (55). Which existence is that?

Russell in his note on the passage is right to call this conclusion "paradoxical." The desire expressed here is not for the abstract purity of Stoic logic but for the physical and moral purity of the world in its freshly born state. New things are better than old ones. But old things were once new.[97] Is the wish of Dio's creature nostalgic? If so, the wish reflects the peculiar kind of viewing in which the image of what lies behind in the past is only available from an impossible future vantage point. The cyclical nature of the process described ensures the impermanence of its results (the difference between the two parts of the myth is in the end not all that significant) and sustains the erotic-like potency of the desire that the myth embodies and, relatedly, the fictional and poetic quality of its imagery. The "harmony" celebrated in the end is neither philosophical nor political, but poetic and musical (it can be captured "only [by] the Muses and Apollo with the divine rhythm of their pure and consummate harmony"). It is ineffable (καλοῦ ὄντος ἀμηχάνως). It is indistinct, like the traces of ruins (ἐξίτηλόν). And it is sublime (ὑψηλόν) (60–61).[98]

Dio's own sympathies, and the identity he broadcasts and performs, are as elusive as those he describes. His position is itself the product of a kind of hybridity that fares no better than that which he appears to disdain and to wish to overcome: it combines Greek culture with Roman politics, while Dio seems exiled from both.[99] One might expect Dio to be harking back to an earlier Greek harmony. But it is doubtful that the trick of Dio's barbarian speech lies in its subtle return, as if through a back curtain, to a triumph of "Greekness," any more than it lies in a transcendence, through hybridization, of local identities, of Greeks and barbarians, under Roman rule. We might note, moreover, that Roman identity is simply not an option in the speech: it is more like a formal condition under which genuine identities obtain. Are Romans, then, supposed to become (or continue to become) Greek? Supposing they are, what is it to be Greek? Is being Greek a matter of desiring to hear about Greece, or a matter of a (distant) heritage, or merely a matter of a name?[100] The play of identities in the speech is rampant, and in fact no identities seem finally certain. Simple solutions to the question of identity, and specifically to the question of what it is to be Greek, are ruled out by two further considerations in Dio's speech.

First, ostensive definition, the most intuitive imaginable, is excluded as being "barbaric":

> For most men, said I, know and employ merely the names of things, but are ignorant of the things themselves. On the other hand, men who are educated make it their business to know also the meaning of everything of which they speak. For example, *anthropos* is a term used by all who speak Greek, but if you should ask any one of them what *anthropos* really is—I mean what its attributes are and wherein it differs from any other thing—he could not say, but could only point to himself or to someone else in true barbarian fashion. (18–19)

The universalizing pressure of Dio's position, which abstracts from national particularity, is intense, as are its Cratylean ironies.[101] Just to point to a Greek is to commit a barbarian gesture. But if Greeks are the conventional opposite of barbarians, what is the identity of somebody who can correctly identify what it is to be an *anthropos?* Second, Dio has the barbarian Magi criticize the Greeks for their simplifying memory, which is "weak": it produces the myth of a primordial flood "as a single occurrence," in contrast to the cyclical and plural processes related by the Magi (49). If you want to reach back to your past selfhood, do not try it through the artifices of memory, Dio is suggesting. Here he is at odds with the privileging of memory in the works of Pausanias and Longinus: memory simplifies what was.

But those works are by no means simple in themselves. We are reminded of Pausanias's curious and alienating tactic of presenting Greek history for Greeks, but from the Roman perspective of what "the Greeks" are and do,[102] or of his claim—which flies in the face of any view that would saddle him with having reduced his objects to a naive totality defined by "all things Greek"— that "*most things in Greece* (τῶν ἐν τῇ Ἑλλάδι ⟨τὰ⟩ πλείω) *are subjects of dispute*" (4.2.3; cf. 9.16.7). Longinus's own self-location is emphatically that of a Greek addressing Romans (1.1, 12.5). Yet like Dio he takes refuge in a cosmopolitan, hence placeless and timeless, ideology.[103] But this too is a ruse. Longinus's political sympathies throughout give away the particularism of his cause, which is patently philhellenic and, whatever else he may say in chapter 44 against the alleged spiritual effects of lost political freedoms, prodemocratic. What is more, by identifying himself with the high ground of the sublime, Longinus is simultaneously identified with what he half-evades: the sophistic guile and artfulness that sublimity is calculated to conceal and yet are themselves productive of sublime appearances and impressions (cf. 15.11, 17.1–2, 23.4, and passim). Aesthetics, politics, and rhetoric plainly make for an unstable mix in the treatise *On the Sublime*.[104] Intellectual positionalities become a screen behind which its author can easily hide, luring us into his maze of identifications. Longinus—if not the author, then the authorial instance he projects—might be any or all of these identifications, or none of them. But then is not sublimity, as we saw in the case of Sappho and everywhere else we have been looking, the blissfulness of an alienated identity? Dio's cosmopolitanism, in turn, seems to be fraught with complication and is possibly no more than a cover for his own politics of position(ality). His evasiveness seems characteristically Greek after all.

In what ways are Dio, Pausanias, and Longinus symptomatic of the so-called Second Sophistic? The dates and definition of this rubric are themselves anything but firm, but this very uncertainty is relevant to the point I have begun to underscore.[105] The Second Sophistic is arguably best taken as a loose chronological category rather than as a description by literary genre or profession. Requirements for membership are not sophistication, let alone sophistry, but shared problems of self-definition, and these apply to Greek intellectuals operating under the Roman empire more or less from the time of Augustus on.[106] Indeed, the very uncertainty of the range of "Second Sophistic" in Philostratus (*Vitae sophistarum* 481), who coined the term and improbably dated the *incipit* of the movement to Aeschines in the fourth century B.C., is symptomatic of the phenomenon itself. Greeks under the Roman empire may well have recognized that, insofar as they had so little choice in the matter, they might as well embrace and exploit the uncertainties of their identity. Whenever they succeeded, they passed their uncertainties on to their readership: power, here, could be reclaimed on the level, not of self-fashioned identities, but of *manipulated* identities.[107] This may have been especially typical of the age of the far-flung Empire, where identities were constantly, if imperfectly, blended, and where the uncertainties of what it meant to be Greek played a major part in unsettling all the equations. Indeed, it is likely that the writers of the Second Sophistic would have found no audience at all, or met with only limited success, if they had not played upon anxieties about self-location that were widespread. After all, Hadrian was himself "a Romanized Spaniard masquerading as a Greek."[108] The examples are easily multiplied.[109] Lucian of Samosata seems a particularly vivid instance of anxieties both embodied and voiced. To take one instance that has caused no end of raised eyebrows among scholars, his essay *On the Syrian Goddess* is in ways a mirror image of Dio's Thirty-sixth Oration with its troubling uncertainties of positionality (is its author Greek or barbarian, philhellene or anti-Roman?), and it reads like a virtual parody of Pausanias's travel narrative as well.[110] Whatever else we may wonder about this work, the identity troubles it reflects are self-consciously exhibited and then passed on to his readers. That all three writers examined in this essay were as manipulated by their identities as they sought to manipulate them makes no difference to the problem. Archaism and Hellenism were in fashion, and our writers were in part merely catering to their audiences' needs and desires and in part trumping their audiences. Their trump card lay in their occupying the producing end of fashion and in helping to shape it, but above all in *thrilling* to fashion's dictates and embracing what later would be called (in a Stoicizing idiom) a kind of *amor fati*.[111]

By way of concluding, we might note that the work of negotiating with the past is nothing new in the Greek world. Indeed, it is a constant feature of Greek culture from its first traces. One only needs to think of the Homeric idealization of the past or the Hesiodic myth of the ages. Archaism is as old as the Archaic period itself, as the material record demonstrates.[112] The Alexandrian canonizers, who helped institute this practice for the post-Classical period, in turn became its victims.[113] The mythemes of decline, nostalgia, and irretrievable loss, and the fetishization of the traces of the past at the expense of the present, are not only a persistent feature of Greek writing but arguably one of its least recognized *conventions*.[114] As Longinus says to the philosopher of chapter 44, who could simply be himself,[115] " 'My good friend,' I replied, 'it is easy to find fault with the present situation; indeed it is a human characteristic to do so' " (44.6). Pausanias's historical sublime and Longinus's *periegesis* (tour) of the literary monuments need to be placed within this tradition of pessimism too, and specifically as it develops during the Second Sophistic with a self-consciousness that, not unique in Greek literature, is nonetheless peculiar to the period. All of which is to say that pessimism for these authors is not to be taken at face value: it is converted into a strategy, not only of cultural identification but of hopeful possibilities. Lest there be any doubt about this, one need only consider the closing lines to Pausanias's extant work, with its anecdote about the miraculous healing of Phalysius, the original patron and builder of the Asclepian sanctuary in Naupactus, which at the time of his writing was, Pausanias notes, "in ruins":

> For when his eyes ailed him and he was nearly blind, the god at Epidaurus sent the poetess Anyte to him with a sealed tablet. The woman thought the message only a dream (ὄψις ὀνείρατος), but soon it turned out a waking reality (ὕπαρ); for she found in her hands a sealed tablet, and sailed to Naupactus, and bade Phalysius remove the seal and read the contents. To him it appeared impossible that with his eyes as they were he could see the writing. But hoping for some benefit from Aesculapius he removed the seal, and when he had looked at the wax he was made whole (ὑγιής τε ἦν), and gave to Anyte what was written in the tablet, and that was two thousand golden staters. (10.38.13)

These lines at first blush make for a puzzling conclusion; yet, on reflection, there is nothing odd about them at all.[116] Consciously adopting a Homericism, Pausanias—almost unnoticed—makes the dream of Greece whole again and virtually real himself. As his younger contemporary Aelius Aristides had demonstrated through his own experience (as related in his *Sacred Tales*), there is a performative, therapeutic truth to the worship of the god Asclepius.[117] Pausanias's work closes with an allegory of reading—an allegory about the kind of work that reading his *periegesis* performs, and its therapeutic value. Is he possibly courting his readers for something more than a purely imaginative restoration of his Greek patrimony—such as material patronage (whether for Greece or for himself)?[118] Self-advertisement would certainly not be unique to Pausanias: Dio is a master of these arts, as is Longinus (in less explicit ways). Could self-promotion be the, as it were, bottom-line criterion of Second Sophistic identity? Whatever the case, it is only through the pathways of the imagination that a restoration of physical Greece could ever become real. Pausanias knows this and seems to be winking at his readers as well.

The still-reigning view of the secondariness of the Second Sophistic is no doubt a reflex of our own contemporary nostalgia for a lost Greece, transferred all too one-sidedly onto this vital moment of literary activity, whose very "sophistication" (and individuality) threatens, in fact, to disappear from view under its own shadow. In their skillful manipulation of the past and of the conventions of nostalgia; in their production of an identity for themselves, and not just for the past, out of the ruins and fragments they collect and even manufacture; and in their successful construction of an identity for themselves that is conspicuously hard to pin down (and disquietingly so), Pausanias, Longinus, and Dio tell a different story.

Art, Myth, and Travel in the Hellenistic World

Modern scholarship no longer views Pausanias as a unified subject. Antiquarian and mythographer, travel writer and pilgrim, geographer, cartographer, and ethnographer, historian and art historian, Pausanias has come to exemplify a complex series of overlapping allegiances as regards genre. Although not all scholars agree on the appropriateness of each of the above characterizations, Pausanias's blending of conventions from different genres seems to be smooth and effortless.[1] By contrast, another conjunction of allegiances—cultural and ethnic—speaks to an uneasy and fragmented coexistence. A provincial Greek writing about Greece, Pausanias has been construed as both insider and outsider in the Roman world of the second century A.D. On the one hand, as a member of a well-to-do, educated Greek aristocracy and most likely a Roman citizen, he was privileged enough to take leave from the chores of ordinary life and travel for extended periods of time, not only in Greece but in Italy and the Near East as well. Imperial journeys such as Hadrian's provided a model for him and others of his class to emulate. And because of the dissolution of borders that the Roman empire had brought about, he experienced a world without apparent boundaries.

If his class (and gender) brought security, his ethnicity, on the other hand, seems to have detracted from a fully harmonious sense of belonging. Dominated by the Second Sophistic, the intellectual climate in which Pausanias wrote highlighted the achievements of pre-Roman, independent Greece and held on to the notion of a distinct Greek identity.[2] Through his own single-minded engagement with Greek gods and heroes and his relative neglect of the Roman imprint on Greece's landscape, Pausanias implicitly affirmed a Greek cultural consciousness. Similarly, it was a kind of patriotism that made him cast his eyes on the monuments of Greece's Archaic and Classical past rather than the Roman present. His knowledge of the past was deep and multifarious, and scholars have variously benefited from his diachronic interests.

Pausanias and the Shapes of Time

That Pausanias's work was caught among various configurations of historical time would not have surprised art historian George Kubler, author of *The Shapes of Time*. According to Kubler, it is common for cultural products to exist not only at one absolute calendrical time but at various "systematic" ages as well. Works consist of intricate "bundles" of formal properties from different periods, and—because of the complexity of cultural circumstances—time can exhibit variable lengths. A corollary emerges that two individuals working contemporaneously in the same or contiguous cultural fields may approach similar tasks in competing ways, some adhering to the past, others pushing to change the contingent present.[3]

In this study, I seek to examine Pausanias's work in light of such a competition between his two temporal/cultural dimensions, the Greek accounting for his retrospective orientation, the Roman for his participation in his second-century moment. I will do so in light of Pausanias's exemplary status as representative of the genre of travel literature, as well as in light of this genre's Hellenistic background. It is true that, among the various pasts Pausanias conjures up, he was least interested in the Hellenistic age. Nevertheless, whether he acknowledges this or not, he was the inheritor of the Hellenistic world's intense engagement with travel and geography. Furthermore, the Hellenistic period was the first to display the retrospective mood encountered in Pausanias and some of his contemporaries.

Because the Hellenistic interest in travel and geography manifested itself in both literature and the visual arts and because Pausanias was so intensely concerned with vision and description, I will explore intersections between art and literature. This maneuver will allow us to deal with the practical problems that beset the study of travel in both realms, due to the checkered preservation of relevant textual material, as well as the uneven engagement of the visual arts with this theme. Pausanias is our sole complete source for the ancient genre of travel literature; the discontinuities in the employment of the theme in art will be discussed below. A joining of forces can be illuminating, as long as we do not approach it with the expectation of finding absolute correspondence between the account of travel given in literature, on the one hand, and art, on the other.

Kubler's understanding of the flow of cultural time as having "different kinds of duration" enables a flexible understanding of cultural fields, while maintaining a historical approach. On the present occasion such flexible juxtaposition of different temporal horizons and different states of development within one genre or work seems compelling for another practical reason: the difficulty of negotiating issues of cultural identity in the visual arts of Pausanias's time. Indeed, the impact of Greek identity in a Roman context is much harder to detect in the visual arts, whose "language" speaks its ethnicity much more elusively than texts of the Second Sophistic do. According to literary and inscriptional testimony, as early as the Republic, most artists working for Roman patrons were Greek. Even Roman triumphal paintings, which celebrated the defeat of Greek, among other, territories, seem to have been executed by Greeks.[4] A rare attempt to unravel a distinct stratum of Greek identity in Roman art is R. R. R. Smith's attribution of the harsh, unattractive realism ("verism") of Republican portraiture to the artists' ethnic background. Trapped between their Greek identity and the necessities of working for Romans, these artists captured, according to Smith, not only their patrons' physiognomies without a trace of sympathy or flattery but also their own antipathy and ambivalence.[5] The problems raised by this provocative inquiry are not my present concern. It is sufficient to acknowledge the severe difficulties in identifying the visual elements that might enunciate ethnic consciousness and in disentangling the interpenetrating strands that constituted a Greek artist's social persona in a "Greco-Roman" world. The Hellenistic is the last period to allow confidence in speaking about Greek art as Greek, even though that too was in its own ways a hybrid, rather than a "pure," identity.

Pausanias and the Shapes of Space

One of the most interesting aspects of Pausanias's work is the intersection of geographical (spatial) concerns with mythological (narrative) ones. Consistently, Pausanias describes the natural and cultural landmarks of Greece in light of their mythological and ritual significance. In so doing, he displays a sensibility very different from that of Strabo, his Augustan period fellow Greek, who was so much more comfortably integrated within the Roman worldview. For Strabo, the land is a source of well-being for its inhabitants, as well as a theater for political action.[6] In laying out his theoretical positions at the beginning of his *Geography,* Strabo (1.1.18–20) espouses a strictly utilitarian approach, and posits politics and science (geometry and astronomy) as more important and useful than mythology:

> For instance, if a man should tell the story of the wanderings of Odysseus or Menelaus or Jason, it would not be thought that he was making any contribution to the practical wisdom of his hearers—and that is what the man of affairs demands—unless he should insert the useful lessons to be drawn from the hardships those heroes underwent; still, he would be providing no mean entertainment for the hearer who takes an interest in the regions which furnished the scenes of the myths. (1.1.19; trans. H. L. Jones)

Pausanias's conjuring up of the passage of gods and heroes through the physical landscape was no mere entertainment but a means of presenting Greece's cultural past as a living, still viable present. It has often been noted that—unlike Strabo, who saw his geography as a proper instrument of Roman imperialism—Pausanias ignored those spaces touched by imperial power and populated the land with imaginary superhuman beings. Of course, there was a utilitarian aspect to Pausanias's task as well: his text—with all its interest in spatial orientation and its organization according to geography and topography—echoes cartographic principles and reads like a verbal map; its sequence of chapters, moreover, enacts the process of travel itself.[7]

Maps construct mental worldviews through their selection and encoding of aspects of reality. Inhabited by gods and heroes, Pausanias's own spatial grid is highly selective.[8] He links places by location and distance but constantly interrupts the spatial flow with temporal shifts into mythological (and less often historical) time. As he encounters the land of Greece, memories of bygone stories seem to flood his mind and his writing and to overwhelm the spatial skeleton of his text. Paradoxically, what receives short shrift in the process is the natural landscape itself. There is no description of rolling hills, vineyards, flower beds, or mountain streams, little room for the picturesque. Pausanias does not stop to contemplate fields and forests. Although he is not completely inattentive to these features,[9] such spurts of attention seem driven by a mythological or religious subtext, whereby natural landmarks become noteworthy because of resident deities.

His interest in the mountains of Attica, for example, turns out to be not about them but about statues and altars of gods (1.32.1–2). The "large and beautiful" plane tree he admires at Caphyae in Arcadia is mentioned in the same breath as Menelaus, who allegedly planted it by a spring prior to his departure for Troy (8.23.4). Mention of a cave in the vicinity of the Theater of Dionysus on the south slope of the Athenian acropolis is occasioned by a work of art:

> At the top of the theater is a cave in the rocks under the Acropolis. This also has a tripod over it, wherein are Apollo and Artemis slaying the children of Niobe. This Niobe I myself saw when I had gone up to Mount Sipylus. When you are near it is a beetling crag, with not the slightest resemblance to a woman, mourning or otherwise; but if you go further away you will think you see a woman in tears, with head bowed down. (1.21.3; trans. W. H. S. Jones)

In Pausanias's world it does not rain or shine, and natural phenomena are usually the result of divine activity (e.g., 7.24.6–13).

If his Roman present conditioned the expansiveness of Pausanias's field of vision, Greek tradition may account for his interest in the city more than the countryside, in the signs of culture more than nature, and in the types of human intervention he records. His urban travel shuttles back and forth between a macroscopic mode of apprehension (references to entire regions or cities) and a microscopic mode (descriptions of single architectural monuments and works of art). It is, of course, the latter mode that has sustained Pausanias's usefulness to art historians and archaeologists, but it is the former that interests me here, the all-encompassing view, which allows the world to be experienced as a picture. Anne Jacquemin has drawn attention to Pausanias's appreciation of the form of things, his presentation of the distant view of cities, their high location and steep walls.[10] In this connection, one might remember Strabo's likening of a geographer to an architect or sculptor, who should not be distracted from the mass of detail the observable world presents but should maintain a sense of the whole (1.1.23). This vision accounts for Strabo's description of the Peloponnese as "a leaf of a plane-tree in shape" (8.2.1), Sicily to a triangle, Iberia to an oxhide (2.1.30).

Pausanias often maintains such a sense of the whole and mentions the circular shape and circumference of cities, with the holistic view usually presented first. This is the case with Thebes, which is defined by its ancient enclosure wall with its seven gates (9.8.4). At 4.31.5 he begins his description of Messene thus: "Messene is surrounded by a wall, the whole circuit of which is built of stone, and there are towers and battlements on it" (trans. J. G. Frazer). Only then does he fill the circuit with key monuments. Strabo offers an equally distant view: "The city of the Messenians is similar to Corinth; for above either city lies a high and precipitous mountain that is enclosed by a common wall" (8.4.8; trans. H. L. Jones). Returning to Pausanias, even at Panopeus in Phocaea, a "city" which no longer deserved to be called thus, given its state of decay, the partial remains of an old wall prompted their imaginary completion by the traveler, who conjured up a circuit of "roughly seven stadia" (10.4.2).

As we shall see later on, such macroscopic configurations may be put in the service of a variety of interests. Within traditional Greek thought they were at home, because of a propensity for abstract modes of comprehension. Accordingly, in the fifth century B.C., Herodotus described Athens as a "wheel-shaped city" (7.140). In the fourth/third century B.C., the historian Hecataeus from Abdera described Jerusalem as a fortified city, about fifty stades in circumference (Josephus, *Against Apion* 1.197–98). In the third century B.C., travel writer Heraclides Criticus spoke more than once of the outer perimeter of a city in terms of size and shape, before moving on to the details of layout, landscape, and inhabitants.[11] Thus Thebes "has a circuit of 70 stades [ca. 11.5 km]. It is all flat and circular in shape, with black soil" (1.12; trans. T. S. Brown), and Chalkis has a circuit of seventy stades as well (1.27).

Space and Travel in the Hellenistic World

From the Classical world, and especially from the Hellenistic period, Pausanias inherited not only some of his approaches to space but the very genre of periegetic literature he has come single-handedly to exemplify. It is generally agreed that travel writing as a genre crystallized in the cosmopolitan Hellenistic period, in the third and second centuries B.C., when an intense preoccupation with place, *topos,* also emerged. Formulated by such figures as Diodorus (end of the fourth or the third century B.C.), Heliodorus (late third century B.C.), Polemo of Ilium (early second century B.C.), and Heraclides Criticus (third century B.C.), this literature is largely lost, glimpsed only in fragments and through Pausanias's later, much more ambitious, and in many ways exceptional work.[12]

An intensification of "tourism" as a distinct cultural activity among the elite also belongs to the Hellenistic period, to the aftermath of Alexander's expeditions, which showed the world to be traversable in ways it had never been before and initiated *"l'âge de la curiosité."*[13] An attendant mentality emerged, mixing a demand for curiosities with an aesthetic outlook and calling for specialized services such as guidebooks.[14] Of course, already in the early sixth century B.C., according to Greek tradition, it was possible for Solon, the Athenian lawgiver, to travel overseas for no less than ten years to "see the world" (Herodotus 1.30; Plutarch, *Solon* 25.5). And in the fifth century B.C., Herodotus traveled enormous distances under no practical compulsion to do so. Other forms of travel, such as for trade, had been a reality in all periods of Greek history. Occasional travel by individuals to religious sites for worship and/or medical purposes may go back to the eighth century B.C., and certainly goes back at least as far as the sixth.[15] Yet even "le tourisme religieux de l'époque classique restait encore très largement un tourisme occasionnel."[16] If tourism was not born in the Hellenistic period, its scope and appeal certainly expanded, an expansion coinciding with the development in literary genre mentioned above.

Geography—not only the literary/narrative subgenre but also the scientific one, with its interest in measurements and distances—also crystallized in the Hellenistic period. It produced theoretically inclined works such as Eratosthenes's late-third-century B.C. *Geographica,* predecessor to geographer/cartographer Ptolemy's second-century A.D. *Geography* and its codification of the different concepts surrounding the notion "location."[17] Furthermore, Hellenistic poetry—Apollonius Rhodius's *Argonautica* with its panoramic landscapes, Callimachus's works, and Theocritus's *Idylls*—registered similar concerns.[18] Indeed, these poems have contributed greatly to the belief that corresponding Hellenistic landscape painting must once have existed.

The Telephus Frieze

An important Hellenistic relief, the Telephus Frieze, which once decorated the walls of the interior court of the Altar of Zeus at Pergamum, has helped fill some of the artistic vacuum.[19] Scholars have regarded it as the epitome of the new and forward-looking aspects of Hellenistic art: enlarged spatial scope, continuous narrative, movement through time and space. Dated to the middle of the second century B.C., this unfortunately incomplete sweep of marble slabs narrates the story of Telephus (the mythical founder of Pergamum), from his conception to his death, in a visual counterpart to what Thomas van Nortwick has called in his investigation of the heroic journey in literature "a metaphor for the process of growing up."[20] Because of its incorporation of landscape elements and its travel theme, this monument calls for a brief discussion.

Telephus, son of Heracles and Auge, was conceived despite the design of Aleus, king of Arcadia and father of Auge, to keep his daughter a virgin. Several accounts exist regarding the meeting and sexual union between Auge and Heracles and the subsequent fate of mother and child. None coincides with all the details of the tale as told on the frieze, which must have followed a local variation.[21] Pausanias tells the story of Auge—whose tomb he saw at Pergamum—when discussing her hometown of Tegea. According to his story, Auge had sex with Heracles repeatedly. When she gave birth to Telephus, her father set her and her child adrift on the sea. She reached Pergamum and married the local king, Teuthras (8.4.9; cf. 10.28.8). At 8.47.4, Pausanias alludes to a typical

Greek ambivalence regarding a woman's consent or lack thereof in sexual encounters outside marriage.[22] He notes a fountain where Auge was allegedly raped by Heracles, according to "a local tradition" contradictory to the Milesian Hecataeus's report that the union was mutually desired. At 8.48.7, Pausanias reports on two variant traditions: according to one, Auge gave birth in public on her way to her averted execution; according to the other, she gave birth secretly and abandoned the child, which was nurtured by a deer (cf. 8.54.6).

According to the frieze, the baby was exposed in the wilderness, and Auge was placed on a boat and cast into the sea. Both were luckier than expected. Auge reached Mysia, where she was welcomed by Teuthras. The baby was suckled by a lioness and was eventually found by his father and taken to safety. As an adult, Telephus traveled to Mysia (fragmentary images of ships survive), where he was also welcomed by Teuthras and barely escaped marrying his mother. He eventually settled in the area and fought against the Greeks who arrived at Mysia by mistake en route to Troy (a detail told in Pausanias 1.4.6 and Strabo 1.1.17). Although the Greeks were repulsed, Telephus was wounded by Achilles and traveled by ship to Argos in search of rust from the weapon that had caused his wound. This mission accomplished, he went back to his Mysian home, eventually to be heroized at death.

The frieze communicates these aspects of the story and many others now lost, in a premier example of Hellenistic "continuous" narrative. "Continuous" is the narrative mode that depicts the unfolding of a single story through a series of uninterrupted consecutive compositions in which the main characters appear repeatedly as they enact the story. In this case, Telephus, his parents, Teuthras, and other characters are depicted several times against a continuous ground of landscape elements, shifting from exterior to interior locations, the former sometimes indicated through personification.[23] Scenes are punctuated by trees of various species, rocks, pillars, or columns, whose presence has served as a bone of contention among scholars debating the Hellenistic Greek versus Roman origin of continuous narration. Some emphasize that the protagonists appear several times as their mythical lives unfold and contend that the frieze represents a "true" case of pre-Roman continuous narrative. For those scholars, landscape elements on the frieze facilitate the temporal and spatial flow. Others retort that, instead of enhancing the narrative flow, the landscape and architectural props serve as barriers between scenes. Such props isolate one scene from another and thus prohibit the unfolding of single events because of the abrupt changes of scenery and substantial temporal leaps. According to this view, the frieze is an example of cyclic ("proto"- or "pseudo"-continuous) narrative. Unlike the continuous mode, cyclic narrative comprises a series of independent (although thematically related) "monoscenic" pictures, each one observing the unities of time and space.[24] Accordingly, temporal and spatial transitions materialize only in the viewer's mind as it jumps from frame to frame. In cyclic narrative, artificial physical barriers—such as the triglyphs separating the self-contained metopes on a Doric frieze—usually appear as framing devices.

The scholarly battle over the Hellenistic Greek versus Roman origins of continuous narrative has been fierce. It was initiated at least a century ago, when

Franz Wickhoff argued that continuous narrative was a distinctly Roman imperial mode, which became fully operative in the second century A.D. The Telephus Frieze, however, together with a class of small-scale bowls to be discussed below, leaves no doubt that this type of narrative was quite at home in the Hellenistic world, although not as widespread as in the Roman empire. In fact, Heide Froning has traced continuous narrative back to Greek art of the second half of the eighth century B.C. and found examples in the sixth, fifth, and fourth centuries B.C. as well.[25] She has thus showed that this type of narrative was a flickering phenomenon in Greek art, but one that gathered momentum in the Hellenistic period.

Travel in Hellenistic Arts and Its Predecessors

Because of its experiential nature and inherent incommunicability, travel has had an equally checkered history as a theme in the visual arts,[26] but it too seems to have gathered force in the Hellenistic period. In fact, the two phenomena—continuous narrative and the theme of travel—seem inextricably linked. Continuous narrative is the clearest mode of conveying movement through space and time, and hence a key ingredient when it comes to the suggestion visually of the trope "travel." It is with the Hellenistic period that we can begin unequivocally to speak about "discursive" images, which not only imply the notion of journey but concretely demonstrate the covering of distance and the passage of time as if on a filmstrip.

In order better to assess the Hellenistic treatment of space and time, brief mention of earlier practices is called for. Typically those included images of travelers (individuals bearing accouterments such as special costume, sun hat, or bundle with provisions) but not travel per se. A famous eighth-century B.C. Attic Geometric bowl in the British Museum hints at the potentiality of travel indirectly by means of a large ship, its rowers ready.[27] A man leads a woman (Paris and Helen according to some, Theseus and Ariadne according to others) toward the ship in preparation to board, but departure is suggested rather than depicted. Movement through space was rendered more clearly in Archaic and Classical art, especially in the ritual sphere, where process and short-distance travel were important. One might mention wedding processions, which involved both movement and change of location to signify a woman's change of residence through marriage. Good examples in vase painting are an Attic black-figure lekythos by the Amasis Painter in the Metropolitan Museum, dated ca. 540 B.C., and a red-figure pyxis by the Marlay Painter in the British Museum, dated ca. 430 B.C. Both feature an abbreviated house, which on their rounded bodies acts (in an elastic reading) as both origin (the bride's home) and destination (the groom's home). Thus, in both cases process is still symbolically conveyed.[28]

This propensity for symbolism is evident not only in the suggestion of movement between locations but also in the depiction of spatial context in general, of topography and landscape. Inextricably bound with Greek art's fundamentally anthropocentric outlook, this lack of interest allowed only short-hand markers of location occasionally to appear. Beginning with the Archaic period, doorways, columns, altars, abbreviated architraves, *naiskoi,* fountain houses, caves, stylized trees, and other vegetation entered the visual repertoire to offer the minimum information required for clarifying a story.[29] Our evidence is of course partial and fragmentary, missing the most fragile media such as large-scale painting in general and scenographic painting in particular.[30] Recent extraordinary discoveries of well-preserved wall paintings from Macedonia dating to the second half of the fourth century B.C. (including a hunt scene set within a natural landscape context)[31] have highlighted just how partial our evidence is but have not overturned the main picture of Greek art's anthropocentric outlook.

In this repertoire, whole cities were extremely rarely rendered, although occasionally partial views appeared in a context of warfare. In the early Classical period, Pausanias tells us (10.26.2), Polygnotus's famous *Iliupersis,* painted for the Lesche of the Cnidians at Delphi, showed the walls of Troy. Non-Trojan battles also occasioned the depiction of city walls, as on an Attic red-figure kylix in the J. Paul Getty Museum, dated after ca. 500 B.C. and showing a section of a city wall with two soldiers leaning over its crenellations, trying to spear two hoplite enemies below.[32] In a more speculative case, Evelyn Harrison has envisioned the Amazonomachy on the lost shield of Phidias's Athena Parthenos as a "kind of *topographia,* early and simple, but already serving the purpose of relating events to space as well as to time" by depiction of partial city walls and rocky terrain.[33]

The Mapping of Mythology in Hellenistic Art:
A Case Study

Let us now turn to a Hellenistic relief bowl in the National Archaeological Museum of Athens, whose creation of an urban landscape comes as a surprise when measured against the background mentioned above. Dated to the late third century B.C. or (more likely) the first half of the second, this object also lends support to the proposition that the Hellenistic period holds the key to a cluster of artistic practices conducive to the depiction of travel and its attendant movement through time and space (figs. 4–5).[34] The bowl's subject is mythological, the abduction of Helen by Theseus with the help of Pirithous, the myth being told with an unexpected geographical emphasis and a focus on the journey. Although scholars have noticed and epigrammatically hailed the importance of this work to several aspects of Hellenistic art,[35] its resources have not been fully tapped. It can be made to perform a little more work in the present context, once we recognize that geography is its organizing principle, and travel a dominant trope. Although it belongs to a category of modest and cheap drinking cups, conceptually it opens an ambitious chapter in intellectual history, no less important than that of the vastly more complex Telephus Frieze.

The bowl's pictorial ambition in the depiction of both figures and context makes it stand out from the rest of its surviving corpus of "Megarian" bowls.

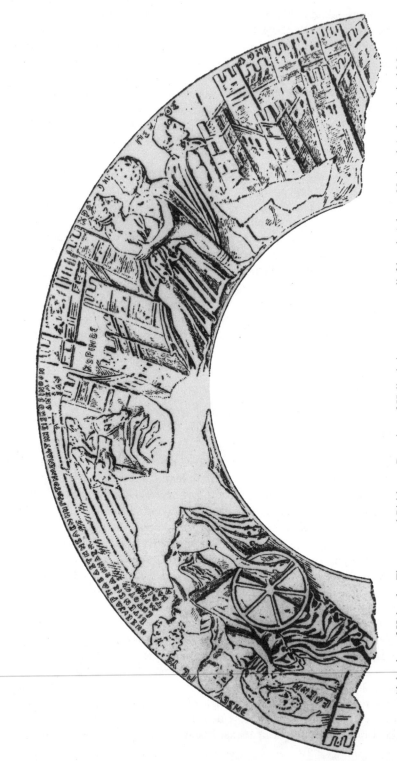

FIGURE 4. Abduction of Helen by Theseus and Pirithous. Drawing of Hellenistic terra-cotta relief bowl; Athens, National Archaeological Museum, inv. 2104. Probably first half of second century B.C. (After C. Robert, *Homerische Becher*, Programm zum Winckelmannsfeste der Archaeologischen Gesellschaft zu Berlin, no. 50 [Berlin, 1890], p. 46.)

FIGURE 5. Abduction of Helen by Theseus and Pirithous. Detail of Hellenistic terra-cotta relief bowl; Athens, National Archaeological Museum, inv. 2104. Probably first half of second century B.C. (Photograph courtesy of the National Archaeological Museum, Athens.)

The term "Megarian" is a conventional and inaccurate one, applied to a category of hemispherical, terra-cotta, mold-made bowls with relief decoration on the outside. They seem to have been invented in Athens ca. 240–220 B.C.,[36] but their manufacture and trade spread quickly in Greece, in the greater eastern Mediterranean, and Italy, becoming a kind of Hellenistic *koiné,* with small variations in shape and decoration. The typical Megarian bowl bears only floral and vegetal decorative motifs or figural decoration consisting of single figures or small groups of two or three: satyrs, tritons, victories, erotes, centaurs, griffins, dolphins, etc., often repeated multiple times but not in narrative unfolding. Scenes with mythological/literary connections—centauromachies, Trojan themes, scenes from the *Odyssey* or from tragedy—also exist, but they are rare by comparison.[37] Because of the prominence of Trojan themes among them, Megarian bowls with narrative subjects have, since the late nineteenth century, been called "Homeric" bowls, even though their repertoire is wider.[38]

Although Homeric bowls have been assigned an important position in the development of continuous narrative,[39] few display the fluent narrativity of our bowl, whose figural zone occupies most of the available space and displays an odd monumentality. In addition, the bowl offers a correlation of textual and visual information that proffers links with the periegetic tradition and the tradition of manuscript illumination. Made of brownish-buff clay with a black glaze, it measures 13 centimeters in diameter at the rim and 7.5 centimeters in height and seems to have been very much used and handled in antiquity, given the wear of the glaze both on the lip and on several spots on the body. Despite some losses, the image is clear.

The Bowl's Narrative Dimension

The bowl depicts a myth whose essential elements crystallized early in Greek literature and remained more or less stable in subsequent antiquity, although there were variations in detail.[40] Together with his Thessalian friend Pirithous, Theseus traveled to Sparta and abducted by force the young and beautiful Helen, whom he took to Attica and entrusted to the care of his mother, Aethra. The heroes then immediately departed for a similar task, to abduct Persephone for Pirithous. This task, however, took them to the Underworld, where they were imprisoned. Pirithous never returned, whereas Theseus was eventually rescued by Heracles. In the meantime, incensed at Helen's abduction, her brothers, the Dioscuri, raised an army, invaded Attica, freed their sister, and carried off Aethra in retaliation. Theseus's political enemies grasped this opportunity to question his leadership, and he fled to Skyros, where he was murdered.

Pausanias's brief references to the seventh-century Spartan poet Alcman (1.41.4) and to the late-seventh-/early-sixth-century Sicilian poet Stesichorus (2.22.6) as sources for aspects of the story are instrumental in establishing the myth's antiquity. That the myth was known already in Homeric times is implied by an oblique reference in *Iliad* 3.144, and it may also have been featured in the largely lost sixth-century epics *Cypria* and *Sack of Troy*.[41] One point of mythological contention was the age of the principal characters. According to most versions, Theseus's escapade occurred in maturity, when he was fifty years old. Helen's age ranges from seven to twelve, but some versions, as well as most images (including the bowl), close the age gap and see a relation between two young adults. The other point of contention was geographical: although the destination of the abductors was Athens, some versions posit Aphidna as the place of Helen's captivity and eventual rescue, as well as the place the Dioscuri destroyed.

Depictions of segments of the story in vase painting exist as early as the seventh century B.C.,[42] while about twenty late-sixth- to late-fifth-century vases show it.[43] Pausanias offers precious information about more fragile media. In discussing the renowned paintings of the Athenian Theseum, he mentions that, while Theseus was held captive in the Underworld, the Dioscuri attacked Aphidna and made Menestheus king of Athens (1.17.5). As is often the case with Pausanias, it is difficult to separate description of the painting from the telling of the story. To Pausanias, furthermore, we owe our knowledge of two famous Archaic representations of the myth. He indicates that an aspect—Helen's rescue and the capture of Aethra—was depicted on the Chest of Kypselos at Olympia in the first half of the sixth century (5.19.2–4) and Helen's abduction on the throne of Apollo at Amyclae in the second half of that century (3.18.15).[44]

Because it showed the abduction itself—Pirithous, Theseus, and the abducted Helen—the throne is especially interesting in the present context, but, unfortunately, Pausanias offers no precise description. He is more forthcoming in regard to the Chest of Kypselos, on the fourth zone of which the Dioscuri were shown with Helen between them after her rescue, while Aethra, dressed in black, was shown on the ground by Helen's feet. There was an explanatory epigram: "Tyndareus's two sons take Helen. They pull Aethra out of Athens" (5.19.3).[45] This "out of Athens" raises the question of how to render a city visually. Taking into account the artistic vocabulary of the Archaic period, the reconstructions of the chest do not mark Athens at all, displaying the four figures against an empty background, assuming that the epigram would have filled the blank in viewers' minds. It is important to reflect on this issue as background to understanding the extraordinary lengths that the Hellenistic bowl has taken to give visual form to the idea of urban landscape.

The fullest textual version of the story is preserved in Plutarch, Pausanias's older contemporary. Plutarch's biographical approach in *Theseus* 31 offers a running account, subordinating geography to storytelling. Unlike the biographer's more discursive approach, Pausanias structures his information according to geographical principles rather than the abduction's plot. It is sites that prompt him to conjure up his characters, and his systematic (relatively speaking) approach to geography results in an unsystematic and discontinuous manner in which biographical stories are told. Near the sanctuary of Sarapis in the vicinity of the Athenian agora, for instance, Pausanias recalls this was the spot where Theseus and Pirithous agreed on their Laconian and then Thesprotian expedition—presupposing the reader knows that the former expedition's purpose was to abduct Helen and the latter's to seize Persephone (1.18.4). Because of a temple to Eileithyia, goddess of childbirth, "nearby," this tale is instantly interrupted by another, Leto's pregnancy. The story of Helen's abduction has already been obliquely referred to at 1.17.5, where Pausanias mentions the attack of Attica by the Dioscuri. Here the reader is expected to know that the purpose of the attack was to liberate the abducted Helen. For a fuller discussion one has to await 1.41.3–5, where a description of Megarian monuments occasions a reference to King Megareus and his son Timalcus, who had fought on the side of the Dioscuri at Aphidna; this occasions reference to the abduction:

> Pindar in his poems agrees with this account, saying that Theseus, wishing to be related to the Dioscuri, carried off Helen and kept her until he departed to carry out with Peirithous the marriage that they tell of [the abduction of Persephone]. (1.41.5; trans. W. H. S. Jones)

In the approach to Athens from Phaliron, Pausanias notes a monument to the Amazon Antiope, whom Theseus and Pirithous also abducted (1.2.1). Another monument catches his attention, and he does not return to that story until 1.41.7 on account of the tomb of Hippolyte, Antiope's sister, at Megara. At Argos he remembers Helen because of a temple of Eileithyia and expects the reader effortlessly to pick up the thread interrupted since 1.17.5 and 1.41.5. This temple was

> dedicated by Helen when, Theseus having gone away with Peirithous, Aphidna had been captured by the Dioscuri and Helen was being brought to Lacedaemon. For it is said that she was with child, was delivered in Argos, and founded there the sanctuary of Eilethyia, giving the daughter she bore [Iphigenia] to

Clytaemnestra, who was already wedded to Agamemnon, while she herself
subsequently married Menelaus. (2.22.6–7, trans. W. H. S. Jones)

At Troezen, Pausanias (2.32.7) locates a temple of Aphrodite, protectress of
marriage, dedicated by Theseus on account of his "marriage" to Helen. Despite
all the discontinuities, it is as if Pausanias's travels pursue in "real" time the
routes earlier taken by countless heroes.

Such linking of locale and mythology goes back to Hellenistic travel literature. A fragment that survives in an ancient scholion to *Iliad* 3.242 indicates
that Polemo told the story of Helen's abduction while describing Attica.[46] He
told of Helen's suspicion that her brothers did not go to Troy because of shame
that their sister was a repeat "offender," abducted not only once (by Theseus)
but for a second time (by Paris); that, because of the first abduction, Aphidna
had been laid siege; that her brother Castor had been wounded in his right thigh
by Aphidnus, king of Aphidna; that the Dioscuri then pillaged Athens in Theseus's absence.

Although, of course, its medium communicates information very differently
from texts, the Hellenistic bowl displays a similar dual concern with myth and its localization. In the bowl's compact wraparound image, the protagonists are repeated
twice, first on a chariot as they begin their journey headed for Corinth, then on foot
as they approach Athens. Athens was Theseus's city from as early as the late sixth
century B.C. to as late as the second century A.D., as articulated on the Arch of Hadrian at Athens.[47] The two cities on the bowl take the form of massive polygonal
rings of wall and are clearly labeled, Corinth inside its enclosure wall, Athens just
above it. Both enclosures are shown in perspective, skillfully employed through
careful use of graded relief: the parts of the wall closest to the viewer are rendered
in significantly higher relief than the rest, thus distinguishing between distant and
foreground areas. Given the small size and humble nature of this bowl, the degree
of descriptive detail and narrative power is impressive. The field is dense, with no
empty ground between scenes, and the notion of "to" and "from," destination and
point of origin, is easily grasped. The conceptual and visual leap from one set of
walls to the other condenses something like a two-day trip: a real second-century
B.C. individual, Aemilius Paulus, who traveled from Athens to Corinth in his 167
B.C. tour of Greece following his Macedonian victory, reached his destination "on
the second day" (Livy 45.27–28).

In the first scene, the chariot—its horses at a speedy gallop, its box rendered
with perspectival gradations of relief—is guided by Pirithous, who looks in the
direction of motion. Theseus is behind him, dressed in a chlamys, and looks in
the other direction, trying with his arms to restrain Helen from jumping off the
chariot. (Some scholars interpret his hair as a helmet.) Helen, supple as a ragdoll,
emphatically arches her torso away from Theseus. Her arms are extended in
distress, framing her face. Her name is legible between her arms; Theseus's
name, next to his head. Pirithous's name appears incomplete in the space between his head and Theseus's, but its restoration poses no difficulty. Of the
three faces, Pirithous's, with a serious and focused expression, is presently the
most legible.

Sandwiched between the walls of Corinth and the walls of Athens, the protagonists reappear on foot, in the second (better-preserved) scene. The disappearance of the chariot from view suggests that the final destination has been reached. Pirithous leads the way, again without interacting with the couple. Theseus, wearing chlamys and boots, is behind him, his attention again focused on Helen, embracing her firmly in a proprietary grasp. If her body language was opposing motion in the previous scene, it now reinforces motion, her legs charging forward underneath the voluminous folds of her dress, her oblique posture adopting the ethos of travel. The small size and overall modesty of this artifact as well as the relative faintness of facial expressions preclude us from settling the question whether Helen is now moving willingly[48] or whether the passage of time brought about a helpless resignation or even a relation of dependency on her captors now that she is away from home. It is similarly unclear whether Theseus's embrace here is required by the possibility that Helen might escape, or whether it is meant visually to instantiate his desire for her. Helen's body is now stiff; she does not try to escape but does not reciprocate the embrace either.[49]

Can we be sure that this second group of figures is identical to the previous? Although the syllables preserved near the heads of the males secure their identities as Theseus and Pirithous, the letters KPA originally read next to the woman's head[50] have raised some questions regarding her identity, thus implicitly casting doubt on the bowl's "continuous" narrative. Recent inspection by the writer, however, showed that the K may be an E and revealed no other legible letters except for a possible partial Λ, which would enable a second reading of Helen's name. In any case, a lengthy but badly damaged inscription above the damaged bodies of the horses in the first scene should dispel all doubt that we are talking about Helen on both occasions. Its opening remarks are preserved sufficiently well to communicate in words the very same information as the image: "Theseus, having abducted Helen, (took her) first to Corinth, then to Athens." We are undoubtedly, then, looking at two phases of the same story and at an unambiguous case of continuous narrative, which sets the image in motion.[51] The story does not merely take place; it unfolds as the drinker turns the bowl in his hands. That the bowl is intent upon depicting transition is made especially clear by the unprecedented inclusion of the second scene—arrival—which is so central to the notion of journey.

The continuous narrative mode of the Theseus-Helen bowl not only thematizes the trope "travel" but also genders this trope. Travel can of course encompass a whole range of experiences, positive and negative, and vantage points of both power or powerlessness. In this geography of gender difference, Helen is assigned a compressed personal space in both scenes, with the attendant existential implications: dislocation, disorientation. She moves unwillingly at least in the first scene, and under constraint in both scenes. The two men's spatial sense of self, in contrast, seems open, full of agency and possibility. The profile view (profile being the traditional view of action), the forward-looking gaze, and upright pose of Pirithous, who guides the couple, speak to that.[52]

With the exception of marriage, when a woman became temporarily mobile in her transition from one home to another, only to substitute one enclosure for another, female travel seems to have been envisioned as displacement.[53] Of course, real women who traveled some distance (usually with relatives) did exist, but the evidence shows them to have been predominantly pilgrims searching for a cure or for pregnancy rather than traveling to see the world.[54] Even the assumption of a more visible public persona by elite women in the Hellenistic period (especially in religious affairs) did not amount to adventurous self-fulfillment or significantly greater mobility.[55]

Greek images imply that women traveled short distances in the company of other women or longer distances in the company of men under strenuous circumstances. To men, images assign a sense of freewheeling privilege, expansion, and opportunity. Mythology furnished such paradigmatic hero-travelers as the Argonauts, Heracles, Theseus, and Odysseus.[56] Even the latter experienced self-growth in his unwilled wanderings. As Strabo put it, "the poets declare that the wisest heroes were those who visited many places and roamed over the world; for the poets regard it as a great achievement to 'have seen the cities and known the minds of many men' " (1.1.16, trans. H. L. Jones). In contrast, those women who traveled alone did so under duress, wandering in Greece and abroad in a state of madness, like Io, or involuntarily cast away, like Danae and Auge. Disguised as a mortal woman and facing mortal dangers, Demeter in the *Homeric Hymn to Demeter* (123–32), when on the move, was abused by Cretan pirates. And the story of Helen and Paris immortalized by Homer, according to which she traveled to Troy willingly, occasioned reinterpretations not only of her agency but also of the extent of her mobility.[57] These reformulations either restrict Helen's travel or argue that she did not travel at all (only her image did).

Returning to the Hellenistic bowl, it is possible to subject it to an alternative interpretation by noticing that Athens looks rather unwelcoming and sterile, from the perspective not only of the uprooted woman but also of the males. No Athenians are greeting their hero, and there is no gate for him to enter. He is left at the threshold of town, and we are left in a state of suspense as to what will happen next. Because Helen's abduction was morally questionable and because it led to the invasion of Attica and Theseus's exile and death, Plutarch had unequivocally negative things to say about this, "one of the greatest crimes laid to his charge" (*Theseus* 29).[58] Already in the early fourth century B.C., Isocrates, although generally complimentary to Theseus, was embarrassed by the decision to abduct Helen: "If the achiever of these exploits had been an ordinary person and not one of the very distinguished, it would not yet be clear whether this discourse is an encomium of Helen or an accusation of Theseus" (*Helen* 21, trans. L. van Hook). Nonetheless, this criticism was not sufficient to dethrone Theseus from his esteemed position.[59] Similarly, were one to detect an implicit criticism of Theseus on the bowl, this would not cancel the overall impression that the simple freedom to travel at will empowers the two male heroes.

Unusual when first published because of its interest in travel, the Theseus-Helen bowl remains unusual today, when the corpus of Hellenistic art in general and of relief bowls in particular has been considerably enlarged. A century after the bowl's discovery, however, an extremely similar, though not identical, scene on a fragmentary relief mold was found at modern Velestino (ancient Pherae) in Thessaly (fig. 6). Three fragments survive, the largest showing bits of Theseus and Helen. Sections of city walls exist as well (fig. 6B). Theseus appears again in another fragment in the company of Pirithous, with another section of walls (fig. 6Δ), while some of Athens's walls survive in a third fragment (fig. 6Γ).[60] A bowl fragment produced from this very mold was also found, showing the upper part of the *symplegma* of Theseus and Helen (figs. 6A and 7). Apparently mold and bowl were locally produced: continued excavation in the area where this and other molds were found produced the remains of two Hellenistic work-shops with kilns.[61] The mass production of bowls such as this ensured their wide dissemination, and it is natural to assume that this motif traveled in the Helle-nistic period more widely than we can know today. Furthermore, the existence of *Odyssey* scenes on fragmentary bowls, including the cave of the Cyclopes and images of ships,[62] suggests that travel imagery encompassed the depiction of other stories.

The Bowl's Mapping Impulse

Let us now take a closer look at the bowl's two remarkable freestanding cities. Athens and Corinth are rendered as independent units, distinct from, but similar to, one another. They are devoid of interior buildings[63] and inhabitants, thus being conceptualized as place rather than body politic. Rendered as if from a distance, they present just as holistic a vision as noted above in relation to periegetic literature. Their steep walls are shown partly in profile, partly obliquely from above. They are externally punctuated by rectangular, crenellated towers, which are further articulated by small apertures and occasional horizontal lines signifying storeys or courses of masonry. Except for the crenellated ram-parts, which seem to have been uncommon from the second half of the fourth century on,[64] the picture does not contradict what we know about the appearance of the circuit walls of Hellenistic Athens and Corinth. It conforms to the roughly circular, imperfectly polygonal outline of both cities.[65] The absence of gateways is, of course, unrealistic, but it reinforces the sense of total vision. This vision materializes Aristotle's prescription that a city be "well able to be taken in at one view" (*Politics* 7.5.2; trans. H. Rackham).

Although rendered at a time when once-strong cities were losing indepen-dence, the commanding views of the walls on the bowl create a sense of com-pactness and power. Even though the formidable strength thus implied was fic-titious, this imagery must have been an effective symbol of resilience, not least because of its activation by archetypal mythological characters.[66] It is regrettable that the dating of Hellenistic relief bowls, even those with clear archaeological contexts, is still so problematical. The rather loose dating of this bowl to the end of the third or first half of the second century B.C. allows for a date very close to 146 B.C., the date of Corinth's sack by Mummius and the destruction of its walls. On the bowl Corinth is rendered only slightly less formidable and imposing than Athens. A not impossible dating of this object just after 146 B.C.[67] would make a fascinating, albeit imaginary, statement on Greek defiance of the

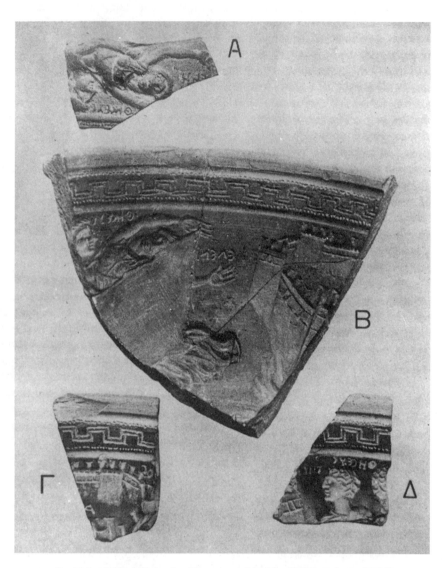

FIGURE 6. Abduction of Helen by Theseus and Pirithous. Fragments of Hellenistic terra-cotta mold (B-Δ) and fragment of relief bowl (A) produced from the mold; Volos, Archaeological Museum, inv. 2291 (mold) and 2290 (bowl fragment). Probably first half of second century B.C. (Photographs courtesy of the Archaeological Receipts Fund [T.A.P.], Greek Ministry of Culture.)

FIGURE 7. Helen and Theseus. Fragment of Hellenistic terra-cotta relief bowl; Volos, Archaeological Museum, inv. 2290. Probably first half of second century B.C. (Photograph courtesy of the Archaeological Receipts Fund [T.A.P.], Greek Ministry of Culture.)

realities of Roman occupation. Centuries later Pausanias still regretted Corinth's sack, most likely exaggerating the extent of its devastation:

> Not one of the Corinthians of antiquity still lives in Corinth; instead they are colonists sent from Rome. . . . When the Romans won the war they took away the armour and weapons of all Greece and the walls of every walled city, and Mummius, the Roman general in the field, systematically devastated Corinth. (2.1.2; trans. P. Levi; cf. 2.3.6, 7.16.7–9).[68]

Despite the possibility that veiled military implications may reside in the bowl, I would argue that its two cities primarily thematize the geographical parameters of the abduction. Corinth's depiction is revealing in this regard, for no ancient writer assigns this city a role in Helen's abduction. Why, then, is Corinth given prominence as the first destination of the abductors, according to both image and text on the bowl? There is no reason to postulate a lost version of the myth or a stray attempt to revise the myth "in favor" of Corinth; nor, given the care lavished on this image, is there reason to assume a mistake on the part of the potter/iconographer. Corinth, of course, lies between Sparta and Athens, and anyone traveling between the two would have to go through the

Isthmus. Thus, the artist lays out a mythological itinerary. Plutarch (*Theseus* 31) equated safety for the abductors with the crossing of the Peloponnese, and it could be that Corinth also signifies that on the bowl: passage to safety, escape from persecution (in mythological "fact," Theseus and Pirithous were not pursued beyond Tegea).

In an earlier chapter (*Theseus* 25), Plutarch had drawn attention to a famous boundary stele set up by Theseus at the Isthmus, marking the border between the Peloponnese and "Ionia" (i.e., Attica). An inscription allegedly clarified matters. On one side, facing east, was the legend "Here is not the Peloponnese, but Ionia"; on the opposite side, "Here is the Peloponnese, not Ionia." Less indulgent in mythology, Strabo assigned the existence of this stone, not to the hero, but to the long-standing dispute between Peloponnesians and Ionians regarding boundaries. He explained this very inscription as the result of an agreement between the two groups (9.1.6).

Pausanias (2.1.4) articulated the geographical transition in terms of mythological deed, Theseus's punishment of the robber Sinis in particular and his clearing of the road between Troezen and Athens from criminals in general. The transition also afforded Pausanias an opportunity for indirect criticism of Nero's failed attempt (in A.D. 67) to dig a canal across the Isthmus.[69] According to Pausanias (and in sharp contrast to the imperial Romans' general admiration for public works that restructured the landscape),[70] such attempts to defy nature rightfully failed: "It is so difficult for human beings to go against the will of the gods" (2.1.5). For him the Isthmus was both a geographical marker and a site of mythological triumph.

The key role of Corinth as a geographical marker was suggested in some unexpected places. In the later first century B.C., for instance, when Propertius (*Elegies* 3.21) made his love-struck hero/self travel to Athens in order to immerse himself in Athenian culture and forget the unresponsive Cynthia, he mentioned the Isthmus as a stepping-stone. Similarly on the bowl, Corinth's presence is required by the maker's effort to think through and visualize the myth's geographical pragmatics.

Predecessors and Successors

In order to understand the boldness of this Hellenistic interest in situating the myth, it is instructive to compare the bowl with a typical example of Classical art with the same subject matter, an Attic red-figure stamnos by Polygnotus in the National Archaeological Museum at Athens (fig. 8).[71] Dated to the 420s B.C., it features Theseus on the left, holding two spears, reaching toward a rather passive Helen. Pirithous mounts a chariot with missing horses. Phoebe, perhaps Helen's sister by that name, waves. All figures display Classical restraint in pose and expression, and all are labeled, the labels almost indiscernible today. What is of interest to us is the complete absence of context in which the scene takes place. The beautiful elaboration of the figures' attire and the attention to detail, together with the large size of this vessel, suggest that its blankness of context is a matter of artistic vision rather than a circumstantial constraint.

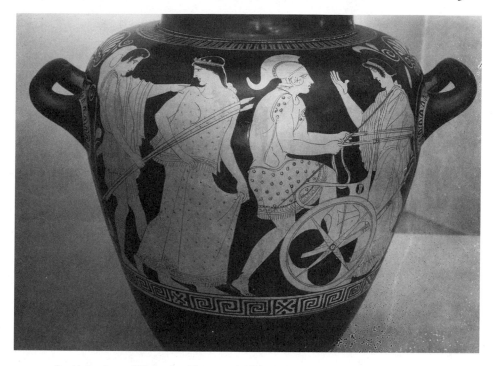

FIGURE 8. Abduction of Helen by Theseus. Attic red-figure stamnos by Polygnotus; Athens, National Archaeological Museum, inv. 18063. Late fifth century B.C. (Photograph courtesy of the National Archaeological Museum, Athens.)

Despite a degree of naturalism in the depiction of the cities on the Hellenistic bowl, stylization and abstraction prevail. This stylization posits a connection with the even more regularized mural crowns frequently worn by female personifications of cities or of their Tyche. Personification was, together with the walled-city motif, the other trope of conceptualizing territory in the Hellenistic period. A Hellenistic relief bowl in the British Museum showing the battle between Eteocles and Polynices fixes its scene geographically by way of a seated female personification of Thebes with mural crown.[72] Known in copy only, Eutychides's famous Tyche of Antioch of ca. 300 B.C. (Pausanias 6.2.7) featured the earliest certain use of the mural crown—a motif with Near Eastern pedigree—in the medium of Greek sculpture.[73] A carved ringstone of the late third or early second century B.C. in the Indiana University Art Museum shows a female head in profile crowned by an enclosure very similar, though geometrically more perfect, to the walls on the Theseus-Helen bowl, down to its uneven crenellations (fig. 9). This representation of Tyche has been convincingly associated both with a Ptolemaic city and a Ptolemaic queen.[74] Just like the motif of the walled city, the image of a turreted woman/personification passed without interruption to the Roman world. Complete with mural crown with gates, turrets,

FIGURE 9. Bust of Tyche. Carved ringstone, garnet; Bloomington, Indiana University Art Museum, Burton Y. Berry Collection, IUAM, no. 76.85.15. Ptolemaic, late third or early second century B.C. (Photograph by Michael Canavagh and Kevin Montague, courtesy of Indiana University Art Museum.)

and windows on the upper level, a marble head from Sparta dated to the second century A.D. makes this clear (fig. 10).[75] The exterior of the mural circuit is populated with figures participating in an Amazonomachy. Fortuna or Tyche or a bit of both, this head exemplifies the difficulties mentioned earlier in identifying and disentangling possible latent statements on Greek identity in the art of Pausanias's era.

If one can argue from later evidence, the crowned personifications of cities and the walled-city motif participated equally in the tradition of mapmaking and became common map symbols. Both types are utilized in the Peutinger Map, a fourth-century A.D. Roman geographical document, preserved in a medieval copy of the twelfth or thirteenth century in the Nationalbibliothek of Vienna. On some occasions (in the rendering of large and important cities, such as Rome, Constantinople, and Antioch), the Peutinger Map combines the city vignette with a personification.[76] We are unfortunately at a loss as to precisely how to reconstruct what this map's predecessors looked like. None survives from Greek antiquity, not even from the Hellenistic period, which witnessed great accomplishments in geographical knowledge and cartography.[77] However, the Peutinger Map offers some clues.

One can further surmise early cartography's pictorial conventions and conceptual principles from a related genre with both medieval and ancient pedigrees. The *Corpus Agrimensorum Romanorum,* a collection of treatises by Roman land surveyors demonstrating land division and demarcation of territory for settlers

FIGURE 10. Tyche. Marble head from Sparta; Sparta Museum, inv. 7945. Second century A.D. (Photograph courtesy of Sparta Museum.)

in Roman colonies, survives in several manuscripts, some illustrated. Although the collection may date to the fourth century A.D. and although the individual treatises were considerably earlier, the surviving illustrated codices, such as an excellent sixth-century A.D. example in the Library of Wolfenbüttel, are medieval.[78] Their cityscape vignettes bear connections with cartography and Roman landscape paintings, as well as the city motif on the Hellenistic bowl.

Purely medieval maps, combining geography with Christian content, also speak to a Hellenistic pedigree. The prominent rendering of Jerusalem on a sixth-century A.D. mosaic from a church at Madaba (Jordan) follows the Greco-Roman tradition. The "Madaba Map" depicts the Holy Land and is only partially preserved (ca. 15.7 m × 5.6 m).[79] It includes a multitude of named towns from the Old and New Testament in accurate relationships, together with villages and geographical features (fig. 11). Jerusalem, the largest city shown, is rendered as an elliptical towered enclosure seen from a bird's-eye view, containing some key buildings, roads, and topographical landmarks (fig. 12). Although humans do not inhabit this world, their presence is implicit, for this map was meant to help pilgrims follow a Christian path to salvation.

Monuments as complexly conceived as the Madaba Map might make the claim that the Hellenistic bowl is governed by a mapping impulse seem overblown. But in the context of the ancient Greek world, the bowl's cognitive boldness seems quite extraordinary and offers a rare glimpse into a changing worldview, in which the representational arts began to render visually ideas whose mental image and literary expression had been formulated even earlier. The striking similarity of the two cities on the bowl suggests that we are dealing with a visual formula no less than an attempt to render reality, the kind of formula later to become a staple in the iconography of maps. Of course, un-

FIGURE 11. Mosaic portraying a map of the Holy Land from a church in Madaba, Jordan. Sixth century A.D. (Photograph courtesy of Archive Studium Biblicum Franciscanum, Jerusalem.)

FIGURE 12. Jerusalem. Detail from the Madaba Map. Sixth century A.D. (Photograph courtesy of Archive Studium Biblicum Franciscanum, Jerusalem.)

like "true" maps such as the Madaba Map, this picture is a metaphorical map, whose graphic rendering of cities is explicitly subordinated to a story line.

That maps existed at least by the Classical period is made clear by literary documents.[80] In Aristophanes's late-fifth-century B.C. *Clouds* (200–217), for instance, a student explains to a farmer named Strepsiades the use of a map:

> STUDENT: Now then, over here we have a map of the entire world. You see there? That's Athens.
>
> STREPSIADES: *That,* Athens? Don't be ridiculous. Why, I can't see even a single lawcourt in session.

STUDENT: Nonetheless it's quite true. It really is Athens.

STREPSIADES: Then where are my neighbors of Kikynna?

STUDENT: Here they are. And you see this island squeezed along the coast? That's Euboia.

STREPSIADES: I know that place well enough. Perikles squeezed it dry. But where's Sparta?

STUDENT: Sparta? Right over here.

(Trans. W. Arrowsmith)

One could not hope for a clearer articulation of the conventional, arbitrary, and, in a sense, naive semiology of maps. It is such an arbitrary topography, one could argue, that we observe on the Hellenistic bowl, and it is language—the inscription—that determines the meaning. That both cities are clearly labeled on the bowl is extremely important. Given the labels, the viewers' imagination would be expected to conjure up the specificity that the image lacks, just as Strepsiades seems to have done once he broke the code of the map. According to Polybius, who paid attention to the geography of travel,[81] "as regards known countries the mention of names is of no small assistance in recalling them to our memory" (3.36.3; trans. W. R. Patton).

There is actually one ancient monument that has been interpreted in light of ancient mapmaking: the famous apsidal mosaic from the sanctuary of Fortuna Primigenia at Praeneste (Palestrina). It measures roughly 6.5 m × 5.3 m and has been heavily restored.[82] Maplike, although not a map per se, it provides a picture of the Nile Valley, sectioned in units, with an aggregate of architectural and landscape elements and with distant sectors raised above those closer to the viewer (fig. 13). The upper region is wild and rocky, inhabited mostly by hunters and exotic animals (reminiscent of the marvelous species Pausanias relishes to mention);[83] the lower region is dominated by the signs of urban culture, with temples, shrines, and boats (in addition to natural features and animals). There is no compositional focus, no holistic view of the river, no explicit overriding narrative, and one can easily imagine the picture expanding in any direction.

Often considered a copy of a Hellenistic painting, this work has recently been examined from the combined perspectives of geography, chorography, topography, cartography, and landscape painting.[84] Nuanced distinctions among geography, chorography, and topography were formulated by the third century B.C. in Hellenistic Greece.[85] The second-century B.C. Alexandrian painter Demetrius, "the topographer" (Diodorus 31.18.2), apparently both painter and cartographer, seems to have put some such distinctions into visual practice. But it was a Roman Greek of the mid–second century A.D., Ptolemy, who transmitted them to us in any clarity (*Geography* 1.1). It is no wonder that, in the absence of unequivocal archeological evidence, the dating of this mosaic has ranged from the late second century B.C. to the third century A.D.

To whatever hybrid genre it belongs, the Palestrina mosaic lacks concern with mythological narrative, thus providing the pictorial counterpart to geographical works such as Strabo's. Despite the connections that have been con-

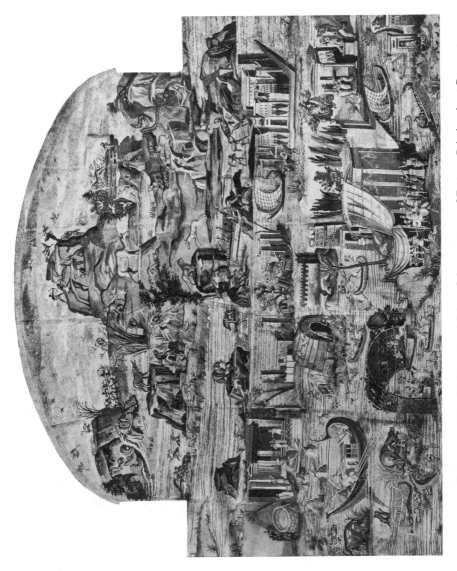

FIGURE 13. Nilotic scene. Mosaic from the vicinity of the sanctuary of Fortuna Primigenia at Praeneste (Palestrina); Palestrina, Museo Archeologico Nazionale, Palazzo Barberini. Probably end of second or beginning of first century B.C. (Photograph: Alinari/Art Resource, New York.)

jured up with a journey along the course of the river, the processional reading solely rests on the viewers' visual scanning of its surface rather than with any procession enacted within the mosaic itself. Mapping, rather than narrating, is this mosaic's focus, and the figures in it are incidental, acting not so differently from the inanimate markers of locale.

By contrast, despite the constraints of their small surface, the Theseus-Helen bowls display an active concern with the notion of journey. Theirs is not only a conceptual attempt at demonstrating the geographical parameters of a story (obviously simplified and condensed) but also an attempt to render transition from one location to another—issues that Pausanias and his Hellenistic predecessors raised through textual narratives and descriptions. (Indeed, the attention to the visual apprehension of travel on the bowls is much more unusual than the attention paid to the city motif, which, as indicated above, did occasionally enter the artistic vocabulary of pre-Hellenistic Greece.) One might consider these unusual objects as symptomatic of a convergence of cultural and epistemological directives in the Hellenistic period, in which we have located an intense preoccupation with geographical science, the intensification of human mobility, and the foundation of travel writing. The minipanoramas on the Theseus-Helen bowls point in this direction, merging biographical narratives in the Plutarchan vein with the descriptive/mythological genre of Pausanias, and a focus on urban landscape. Although acting as a "mediate point in a line of intellectual genesis,"[86] from Classical Greek to Roman concerns, the bowls cannot quite build a case that the focus on travel was a dominant ingredient in the Hellenistic pictorial universe. They do, however, demonstrate that, given a confluence of supporting and reinforcing conditions, this theme became operative in unprecedented ways. In that complex and unstable era, the treatment of space and of human passage within it manifested an interesting dualism: the enlarged spatial scope pointed to future change; the segmentation of space into discreet, plastic entities adhered to traditional Greek modes of looking.

Boundaries and Boundlessness in a Roman World

A Third-Style wall painting of the mid–first century A.D. showing the Fall of Icarus demonstrates how Hellenistic subject matter and motifs were reconceptualized within a Roman context, the Casa del Sacerdos Amandus at Pompeii (fig. 14).[87] The story is told in continuous narrative, with Icarus shown twice— now in flight and falling, now fallen and dead. Located near water, a striking walled city with towers and gates (perhaps Cnossus, where Icarus's failed trip originated) follows the conventions of "Corinth" and "Athens" on the Hellenistic bowl, although, given the wider space available, some interior buildings are also included. The abstract Hellenistic formula is now subordinated to a concrete set of spatial relations and an expansive, continuous flow of space. Granted the seriously incomplete preservation of Hellenistic paintings, it nevertheless seems remarkable how much wider the Roman lens of viewing landscape seems to be, how insignificant the human actors.

FIGURE 14. The Fall of Icarus. Wall painting from the Casa del Sacerdos Amandus, Pompeii. Mid–first century A.D. (Photograph courtesy of Deutsches Archäologisches Institut, Rome [Inst. Neg. 66.1791].)

Recent scholarship has noted a confluence of literal and metaphorical interests manifested in the Roman elite house, its location, interior architectural morphology, and painted decoration working together to construct and to command advantageous and encompassing views of its contingent domain. The voyeuristic preoccupation with the "view"—at times limitless, at times framed and controlled, at times both (as in fig. 14)—manifests a seemingly distinctly Roman delight in possession. No less than the material remains, literary sources suggest that the expression of power was a prime factor in manipulating space.[88] One might be suspicious of the paradox that both visual expansiveness and the drawing of contours (the former opening up horizons, the latter regulating them) would be found to express "power." But ultimately it is extrinsic evidence (historical processes, cultural and personal perspectives brought to the viewing) that assign these values, rather than any absolute meaning inhering in forms and motifs.

Although some might object to such "politicizing" of the real and painted landscape views of the Roman house, no one would deny Trajan's instantiation of empire on his famous column in Rome, dedicated in A.D. 113 Historical in outlook, the column makes the mastery of territory an overt, rather than implicit, message and adapts the city motif to the requirements of this point. Although the notorious difficulty in reading detail compromises the transparency of this signification,[89] the imperial message was undeniably expressed: only an impossible ideal spectator could read the unfolding of the column's multiple substatements, but the real spectators would grasp the monument's statement of power overall—from some distance, in an atemporal way.

Separated by a Victory and a *tropaeum,* Trajan's two campaigns against the Dacians unfold from bottom to top with astonishing topographical and narrative detail along 200 meters of helical frieze. The emperor is the privileged actor, shown repeatedly in continuous narrative (59 times), relentlessly advancing toward victory. His Dacian opponent Decebalus is also shown repeatedly, en route to his eventual demise. Although scenes are usually separated by trees, the impression of continuity is much more dominant than that of fragmentation. Throughout the frieze, the Romans display their technical and tactical expertise in conducting military operations, against a landscape punctuated by mountains, rivers, harbors, and forests (fig. 15). In comparison to paintings such as figure 14, this landscape seems crowded, compressed, and antinaturalistic; in comparison to Hellenistic practices, in contrast, it seems highly particularized and expansive. Prominent within it are a series of mural enclosures: large or small; with angled, curvilinear, or undulating walls; complete, in the process of being built, or in the process of being demolished. We are dealing with the familiar Hellenistic formula, which is here, depending on the narrative circumstances, particularized to stand for Roman forts and camps, Dacian fortresses, or Dacian cities, usually with gates and with figures and structures inside. Precise identification of places is impossible through visual means alone. Utilizing general conventions and codes, the stock motifs subsume reality rather than contradict it.

FIGURE 15. Roman campaign against the Dacians. Lower section of Trajan's Column, in the Forum of Trajan, Rome. Dedicated A.D. 113. (Photograph courtesy of Deutsches Archäologisches Institut, Rome [Inst. Neg. 68.3648].)

The designer of the column seems to have understood that the holistic apprehension of cities could neatly and efficiently symbolize, among other things, control of one's own territory as well as agendas of expansion and appropriation. Dinocrates, architect of Alexander the Great, had allegedly set a precedent, in sentiment although not in execution. This is indicated by Vitruvius, who—with

Augustus in mind—reported that Dinocrates had proposed to shape Mount Athos into the statue of a man, holding in his left hand the walls of a large city (*De architectura* 2, praefatio 1–4). The man, we find out from Plutarch and Strabo, was Alexander himself. Although this plan was never implemented, it was apparently a catalyst for the foundation of Alexandria.[90]

The mythical foundation of Rome was conceptualized in somewhat similar terms: Romulus allegedly described a circle in the place where Rome was to be, then he "fitted to a plough a brazen ploughshare, and yoking together a bull and a cow, drove himself a deep line or furrow round the bounds" (Plutarch, *Romulus* 11; trans. E. Fuller; cf. Livy 1.6). A wall was then built on the furrow. Cato the Elder (*Origines* 1.18a) indicated that this ritual process was typically followed in later times by the founders of Roman colonies. That a city could stand for world empire was understood also by Cassius Dio, a late-second- to early-third-century A.D. Bithynian Greek and often a spokesman for the emperors. Dio "saw the Roman empire as a world-wide *polis.*"[91] If a wall circuit could stand collectively for a city—whether Roman or conquered by Rome—the city could stand for an empire.

Roman triumphal paintings nurtured such ideas by including representations of conquered cities in panoramic or personified form. These paintings go back to the third century B.C. and were influenced by the Hellenistic tradition of battle imagery and visual modes of localization.[92] Models of conquered cities seem also to have been displayed in Roman military triumphs. Interestingly, other ancient cultures (imperialist or aspiring to territorial expansion) utilized the cityscape motif in similar ways: for example, prehistoric Egyptian stone palettes feature an abbreviated enclosure motif to describe conquered territories,[93] while Assyrian reliefs dating from the ninth to the seventh centuries B.C. show panoramic cityscapes of enemy terrain under attack.[94]

To return to Trajan's Column, its utilization of the city formula to signify location also speaks to the cartographic qualities of its relief. In fact, the narrative "skeleton" of the column has been compared to a "colossal geographic map," and some sections have been discussed in light of the Peutinger Map and its schematic suggestion of itineraries.[95] Furthermore, the events depicted on the column have been compared to a biographical journey analogous to that on the Telephus Frieze. More literal depictions of travel also appear, over land and water, with both departure and arrival scenes shown.[96]

Bridge-crossing scenes, cities, villages, and camps also appear on the column of Marcus Aurelius in Rome, dated A.D. 180–92. This monument depicts in continuous narrative Marcus's campaigns against German and Sarmatian tribes. Writing contemporaneously to these campaigns, Pausanias offered at 8.43.6 a unique insight into the Roman side of his identity by conceptualizing the emperor as exacting just punishment for the Germans' and Sarmatians' initiation of an unjust war: "Antoninus the Second [Marcus] brought retribution both on the Germans, the most numerous and warlike barbarians in Europe, and also on the Sarmatian nation, both of whom had been guilty of beginning a war of aggression" (trans. W. H. S. Jones). Marcus Aurelius's Column presented a visual counterpart to this idea. Although introducing several new stylistic ap-

FIGURE 16. The palace of Circe. Panel 6 of the Odyssey Landscapes from the Esquiline Hill, Rome; Vatican Museum. Second half of the first century B.C. (Photograph: Alinari/Art Resource, New York)

proaches, this monument followed (and reinterpreted) the general narrative principles of Trajan's Column.[97]

Taken together, the two columns show that, by the time Pausanias began work on his descriptions of Greece's land and cityscape, the artists of the Roman empire had drastically expanded their visual repertoire to include boundless vistas, as well as to capture travel in its literal and its metaphorical sense and to subject it to political use. They had also reinterpreted Hellenistic mythological depictions, placing them within a similarly boundless spatial framework. As early as the Augustan period, Vitruvius mentioned (7.5.2) that in the previous generation scenes such as the wanderings of Odysseus through landscapes had been prominent on Roman walls. The so-called Odyssey Landscapes (or Odyssey Frieze) from a house on the Esquiline Hill in Rome exemplify this interest. Traditionally dated to the middle of the first century B.C. but recently redated to the end of that century,[98] they display an interest in both space and time and thematize mythical travel. Eight scenes survive, but originally there were at least eleven. Separated by red trompe l'oeil pillars, the scenes derive from Books

X–XII of the *Odyssey* and unfold within a vast panoramic landscape, which overshadows the human protagonists.[99] Although Odysseus does not appear in all extant scenes, he is present in more than one, and on one occasion—his encounter with Circe (fig. 16)—he (together with the sorceress) appears twice within the same frame in continuous narrative.[100]

No picture, however panoramic, can ever re-create the continuous flow of nature. Nevertheless, the Odyssey Frieze and the two columns—in their respective fields of myth and history—strive precisely for that effect, masking as closely as possible the topographical shifts that segment their space. Difficult though it is to negotiate passage from historical circumstance to art and vice versa, one can hypothesize that these new visual notions were conditioned by the experience of a continuous and unified world without boundaries.[101] Not everyone participating in this world experienced it so coherently. Pausanias, for whom "the rural landscape is largely a kind of void that intervenes between each city or sanctuary and its nearest neighbor,"[102] apprehended his world more abstractly. Partly living in a Kublerian "fast time" (the historical time of the Roman empire), partly in the "slow time" of mythical Greece, Pausanias artic- ulated a more fragmented worldview, a world structured more like the Helle- nistic maps to which the Theseus-Helen relief bowl alludes and less like Roman landscape.

Pausanias and the Chest of Kypselos

Plodding the galleries, we ask how can
   That century of the Uncommon Man
Sovereign here in paint, bronze, marble, suit
The new narcissism of the Also-Ran.
      C. Day Lewis, *An Italian Visit,* Part 5,
         "Florence: Works of Art" (1953)

Sightseeing is a notoriously tiring activity. Every user of a guidebook will hope and expect that, from time to time, there will be occasions when the author will call a halt and describe what can be seen from a more or less stationary position. The user of Pausanias's guide will know that he provided a few such occasions for his ancient readers, by offering long and detailed descriptions of objects or groups of objects. This, I suggest, is his counterpart for the *ekphrasis,* in which his more demanding literary forerunners and successors so reveled.[1] Pausanias's passages have not hitherto been taken in this way, because of the extreme restraint and self-effacement with which he presents his material, here and elsewhere; certainly his descriptions, by comparison with the gushing set pieces of some writers of the Second Sophistic, are dry indeed. They are entirely without that overt empathy with the work of art which we encounter in, say, Philostratus or Lucian; and I would not exclude the possibility that this represents an early and deliberate move in the long-running debate between "empathy" and "objectivity" in art criticism, an open espousal of a contrasting approach. Yet their purpose, if I am right, is rather similar: to vary the pace of the itinerary, just as Philostratus varies the pace of his narrative, by calling up a heightened pause and holding the reader's gaze in a single direction.

   This considerate provision on Pausanias's part has earned him scant gratitude from the modern commentators, who for the most part are using his work from the already stationary position of their armchairs and grow impatient at the prolixity of his accounts of long-lost objects. I doubt that W. Gurlitt was the first to call him "dry, sober and pedantic" on the evidence of such detailed excursuses.[2] Even Pausanias's stalwart recent champion, Christian Habicht, has concurred, citing as examples of the author's pedantry the unnecessary enumeration of the sixty-nine altars at Olympia (5.13.4–15.12), the long description of Phidias's statue of Zeus (5.11.1–11), the list of the forty founder-cities of Megalopolis (8.27.3–4), and the accounts of the Chest of Kypselos (5.17.5–19.10) and, longest of all, of the two big murals of Polygnotos in the Lesche of the Knidians at Delphi (10.25.1–31.12).[3]

The simple practical motive that I have ascribed to Pausanias does not apply to all these cases: the founder-cities of Megalopolis are not works of art, and no immediate visual impetus provokes their listing. The artistic set pieces, even if a somewhat deeper programmatic aim lurks behind them as I have tentatively suggested, are perhaps not fully accounted for either. The question, seldom asked, why Pausanias devotes *quite* so much space to these objects may have different answers in different instances. The first, general aim of this chapter is to explore his motivation in the specific case of the Chest of Kypselos; but there are others, which relate to his broader role in the interpretation of early Greek art.

Pausanias's account of the Chest of Kypselos is his second-longest descriptive excursus: even though truncated at its beginning, it takes up some 170 lines in the best-known text,[4] as against 255 for Polygnotos's painting of the Underworld, 164 for his companion piece of "Troy taken," a mere 80 for the statue of Zeus—all of them much better-known works of the fifth century B.C.—and 70 for the Archaic throne of Apollo at Amyklai (3.18.9–19.2). The account of the chest stands out from his work as a whole, even from the last-named monument, because of the very early date of its subject. For the last hundred years, the learned consensus has been that Pausanias had been misled by his guides when he relayed the story that the chest was the actual one in which the infant Kypselos, later tyrant of Corinth, had been concealed; this would have happened at some date in the early seventh century B.C. by our reckoning. Yet the remarkable correspondences between Pausanias's account of the iconography and epigraphy of the chest and the iconography and inscriptions on surviving Corinthian vase scenes are enough to prove beyond reasonable question that he was describing a genuine product of Archaic Corinth, dating perhaps from somewhat after 600 B.C. In principle, I see no reason why the plain cedarwood chest itself cannot have been much older, and the ornate decoration applied to it later in the lifetime of the dynasty that Kypselos founded, precisely because of the dramatic role that it was believed to have once played in the family's fortunes. But that is an unimportant speculation. The interesting issue is Pausanias's choice of a real antique, already some seven and a half centuries old in his time and now long since disappeared, for such full treatment. Apart from the basic circumstance that presumably, because of its location in what was probably then the joint temple of Hera and Zeus, it had once been dedicated to one or both deities, it made an unlikely focus for those religious convictions that Pausanias's subject aroused in him. It was decorated and inscribed in a style that even a Greek-speaker must by then have found obscure, hard to interpret, and aesthetically relatively unrewarding.

The "century of the Uncommon Man," which dominated the impressions of Cecil Day Lewis throughout the long poem which provides my epigraph, was the Renaissance; for Pausanias, the period from the Persian Wars to the time of Epaminondas filled a parallel role, but not to so exclusive an extent. He does show intermittent appreciation of older, Archaic works of art,[5] and doubtless mere age on its own would be the source of a certain interest for the users of his *Guide*. But his whole approach to the chest suggests something far beyond that. In the first place, his own personal interest is clearly aroused: he feels that the chest represents a challenge to his interpretive skills. Thus, after a few perfunctory words on the manner of execution of the decoration and a further few lines on the history of the chest (all in 5.17.5), he proceeds first to the inscriptions, then to his much fuller account of the iconography of the scenes.

The latter has attracted by far the greater attention from modern scholars; yet it is the inscriptions that Pausanias puts first, stressing their unfamiliarity and difficulty of reading, and to which he repeatedly returns later in his text. He reads off the caption inscriptions to identify some of the figures, cites many of the poetic epigraphs in their entirety, gives the exact location of the writing (5.18.2, 5.19.4), comments on the nomenclature used (5.18.5), and, in the case of the metrical inscriptions, specifies the scansion (5.18.2 again, 5.19.3). But for his ability to read the Archaic Corinthian script, he would clearly have been unable to offer a convincing interpretation for many of the scenes, as is shown by his palpably less successful efforts in the case of the third zone from the bottom (5.18.6–8), which evidently lacked inscriptions, and of the fifth and last zone (5.19.7–9), which he specifically states was uninscribed.

Once again, what might have been thought a creditable achievement by a writer of the late second century A.D. has for the most part brought him scorn. Pausanias is the only source for the poetic fragments inscribed on the chest, and it is surely to his credit that he saved them for posterity. But this section of his work, understandably in view of its literary interest, has been claimed by the classical philologists as their property. The tone was set early on by Wilamowitz, whose contempt for Pausanias was based at least partly on the discreditable personal grounds that Habicht has now brought to light.[6] The scribal errors that Pausanias inevitably made in reading and scanning the lines were seized on, at times with something approaching glee, at times with greater patience. Emendations were proposed on the assumption that Pausanias got the meter right but the readings wrong;[7] alternatively, results have been achieved by assuming the opposite, that the readings are more or less correct but the meter not always correctly identified.[8] Some of the lines carry conviction in the form in which Pausanias gives them, while it has proved possible to emend and restore others in a convincing way.

But there was a second line of attack on Pausanias's account of the inscriptions: to deny him the credit for the readings. For a time, the prevailing theory was that the entire description of the chest, along with other extended passages in Pausanias, had been taken over from an earlier writer (Polemo of Ilion being the favorite choice). This view implied an outright rejection of a number of explicit claims to autopsy on Pausanias's part and, in the case of the chest, of his implicit but clear suggestion that he had looked at the object in the same sequence which he prescribes for his readers, since he twice (5.18.7–8, 5.19.7) offers his own interpretation of a scene. I trust that Christian Habicht's reassessment of the work as a whole, in which comparative evidence from every part of it is brought into play, will have done enough to discredit this line of argument permanently.[9] But the persistent skepticism about Pausanias's ability to read Archaic Corinthian script has also taken a more specific form: it is suggested that, for the *inscriptions* (on the chest and elsewhere at Olympia) but not for the rest of his account, he made use of a local repertory of inscriptions and copied its readings.[10] Such an argument overlooks the fact that this is not the only place where Pausanias apparently achieved a reading of a fairly early Corinthian script: he seems to have deciphered, at least in part, the inscriptions on the Corcyrean bull, which was dedicated at Delphi around 480 B.C. and cannot have appeared in any putative handlist of inscriptions at Olympia.[11]

It is surely the most economical hypothesis that he himself managed, no doubt with difficulty and with some help from his guides, to master the letter-forms used in Archaic Corinth and the principle of *boustrophedon* writing, which he evidently (5.17.6) found an interesting curiosity. For the average modern classicist, familiar with the language but epigraphically challenged, Pausanias's efforts with an epichoric Archaic script will excite fellow-feeling and mild admiration rather than contempt. Paul Veyne's assessment of our author—"not a mind to be underestimated . . . the equal of any of the great nineteenth-century German philologists or philosophers. . . . The precision of his descriptions and the breadth of his knowledge are astounding"[12]—may have struck some readers as overenthusiastic, even after the partial rehabilitation of Pausanias that has now taken place; it would certainly have given Wilamowitz apoplexy. But his engagement with the Corinthian script typifies that serious scholarly motivation which Veyne detected in Pausanias.

From the inscriptions, Pausanias moves abruptly to the main subject matter, both of his account and of this chapter: the decorative scenes and their iconography. There were at least thirty separate subjects, almost all of them legendary in nature, treated in different parts of the chest. As with the inscriptions, so here the faithful recording of what Pausanias observed has enabled modern scholars to treat the chest almost as if it still survived. Its decoration has been completely reconstructed on paper more than once[13] (see fig. 17), and the iconographers, like the epigraphists, have been able to offer their own emendations of Pausanias—in this case, of his identifications of certain scenes. In his statistical study of the incidence of legendary subjects in earlier Archaic art, Robert Cook lists the chest in exactly the same way as the surviving vases and sculptures.[14]

It is in fact an observation of Cook's that provides the starting point for this section of my argument. He points out that only a minority of the subjects on the chest (perhaps eight in all) are taken from either the Trojan or the Theban cycle of legends; and that, of these, precisely two figure in the Homeric poems:

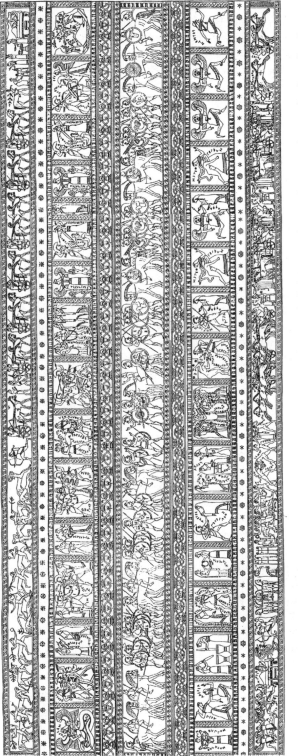

FIGURE 17. Reconstruction of the Chest of Kypselos. (After W. von Massow, "Die Kypseloslade," *Mitteilungen des Deutschen Archäologischen Instituts, Athenische Abteilung,* 41 (1916): 1–117.

the duel between Ajax and Hektor that is portrayed in *Iliad* 7.225–312 and the much more obscure fight between Agamemnon and Koön over the body of Iphidamas, Koön's younger brother, from *Iliad* 11.218–63.[15] Now Cook's calculations reflect the results of modern scholarship, rather than Pausanias's own reckoning, which would have added at least one and probably two scenes from the *Odyssey* and one from the *Iliad,* all in the fifth and uppermost zone of the chest. At 5.19.7, he offers his own identification of a scene showing a man and a woman reclining on a bed in a cave: "I thought [or possibly, since he uses the first-person plural, "The guides and I thought"] that they were Odysseus and Kirke," an interpretation which he backs by a learned comparison of the number and actions of the serving women described in *Odyssey* 10.348–74 with those here shown next to the couple. At 5.19.9, he reports, "As for the two young women riding in a cart drawn by mules . . . they [i.e., his local informants] consider that one is Nausikäa and the other her servant"—thus relating the picture to the episode in *Odyssey* 6.71–84. He does not this time endorse the identification himself, but he offers no alternative view. Both suggestions, however, are weakened by Georg Loeschcke's clever alternative interpretation of well over a century ago that what was really portrayed, in an extensive scene of which the first of the "Odyssean" groups formed the climax, was the wedding of Peleus and Thetis, set in a cave on Mount Pelion according to one tradition at least as old as Euripides (*Iphigeneia at Aulis* 704–707), with the bridal pair reclining and the guests arriving in couples in a row of chariots.[16]

Loeschcke's theory has won almost unanimous support ever since. Much later, K. Friis Johansen added an important gloss to it: that the setting and personae were as Loeschcke had proposed, but that the moment represented was a later one, when Achilles had reached manhood and was about to leave for Troy.[17] Thus the reclining couple would be long since safely married, and decency would be preserved. The only other serious criticism of Loeschcke had come almost immediately, when W. Klein objected that he had not gone far enough: why not also include "Nausikäa and her servant" in the interpretation and make them one of the pairs of divine guests arriving in their chariot?[18] Loeschcke himself refused to go along with this extension of his explanation,[19] and indeed it is not free of difficulty, since it posits a failure on the part of Pausanias's informants (and, by implication, of Pausanias himself) to detect the difference between a cart and a chariot, and perhaps also between mules and winged thoroughbreds; but these would be venial errors. On the whole, it seems easier to reject an incongruous and isolated portrayal of "Nausikäa" amid the two extensive scenes which otherwise take up the whole of the fifth zone—the reception at Peleus and Thetis's cave, and Herakles fighting the Centaurs—and thus to eliminate the second "Odyssean" subject along with the first. If this is right, then there is a nice modern parallel for the same misrecognition of Nausikäa in a scene actually involving Peleus and Thetis.[20]

Assuming that Loeschcke's main interpretation of the setting is sound, there is a third case in this passage where Pausanias entertains the idea of a strictly Homeric setting for a scene that does not truly belong to either Homeric poem. This is where he discusses the arms that Hephaistos was shown bringing to

Thetis. On Loeschcke's account, these must of course be the arms to be presented to Peleus, passed on to his son Achilles as his *first* set of armor, and then in turn loaned, with fatal consequences, to Patroklos.[21] As such, they play a minor part in the narrative of the *Iliad* at several points: they are described in some detail at 16.130–44 and their history is related by Achilles at 18.82–87. But their original *presentation* is not an Iliadic episode. What Pausanias says, once again deferring to his guides, is: "They maintain that this relates to Patroklos's death, with the Nereids in chariots, and Thetis taking the arms from Hephaistos." By these words, he clearly implies that the arms were taken to be the *second* set acquired by Achilles, which were indeed occasioned by Patroklos's death, whose making forms the subject of the famous set piece dominating Book 18 of the *Iliad,* and which are handed over by Thetis (though without the assistance of the Nereids) at the beginning of Book 19.

What is fascinating about the iconographic confusion here (if such it is) is that, once again, precisely the same difficulty has arisen for twentieth-century art historians in establishing the iconographic distinction between the two occasions on which Thetis received armor from Hephaistos and subsequently passed it on to Achilles. The recent consensus has been, following the arguments first propounded by K. Friis Johansen,[22] that the majority of the earlier representations on vases show the *first* presentation, set in Phthia before Achilles's departure for Troy, and with the Nereids often shown in attendance—just as in the scene on the chest, if Loeschcke's view is accepted, the first stage in the history of this armor was portrayed. So, on this view, most of the "Arms for Achilles" scenes cannot after all be taken to illustrate one of the climactic episodes of the *Iliad;* though I must add that, in a recent paper, Steven Lowenstam has dissented.[23] Whatever the true solution to our own problems of interpretation, the strong probability remains that Pausanias's informants were mistaken in *their* identifications, both here and immediately before. Hephaistos, Thetis, and the Nereids from *Iliad* 18–19, cheek by jowl with Odysseus and Kirke from *Odyssey* 10, make an infinitely less convincing reading of an extended scene than one that, like Loeschcke's, binds the figures together. These mistakes are not without bearing on our own deliberations over surviving works.

There is, first, an important general lesson for the art historian, to be learned both from the paucity of truly Homeric scenes on the chest and from Pausanias's palpable errors in trying to add to their number. From the former, the implication is most clearly drawn by Cook when he concludes, from his study of legendary scenes in Archaic art down to about 530 B.C.: "So it seems that there is little or no evidence that artists in this period knew the *Iliad* or the *Odyssey* themselves or, if one or two knew them, that all the others did."[24] This is a theme upon which I have enlarged at much greater length elsewhere.[25] In brief, Cook's view is the one to which any cool and unprejudiced survey of the evidence must point; yet it is difficult to reconcile with the approach of some standard and quite recent works in the field of Homer and early Greek art.[26] There seems to be a predisposition to find a Homeric inspiration for any scene where any case for it at all can be made. Literary scholars too have shown a natural tendency to accept the gift that this approach offers them, of a series of "illustrations" of scenes from the Homeric epic. As Cook points out, this tendency has not gone unchallenged in recent years;[27] but, at least outside the narrower confines of Classical art history, it seems still to hold the field.

The Chest of Kypselos, as we have seen, offers cold comfort for the up-holders of this view. Its makers were familiar with their *Iliad,* as is shown not so much by the often-illustrated duel of Ajax and Hektor, which is prominent in the poem but may well have enjoyed some currency outside it, as by the relatively obscure choice of the fight between Agamemnon and Koön, which passes almost unnoticed in the *Iliad* and is totally unknown from any other source. Yet despite this, neither the Corinthian craftsmen nor the tyrants who employed them show any sign of a wish to privilege Homeric subjects. Long ago, Sir James Frazer, with his eye on the choice of the Muses and the person-ifications of abstract and natural forces shown on the chest, offered the more perceptive comment that the scenes appear to owe more to Hesiod than to Ho-mer.[28]

The inscribed verses, which were evidently composed for the occasion and to which we briefly return, also do little to direct our attention back to Homer. On the contrary, when presented with a rare opportunity, in the scene of Aga-memnon, Koön, and Iphidamas, to cite the Homeric source for a rather obscure episode, the Corinthian poet preferred to improvise two somewhat banal hex-ameters of his own, one describing the whole scene, the other inscribed on the shield of Agamemnon and making perhaps a veiled and incomplete allusion to the description of its device at *Iliad* 12.37–38. Pausanias (5.19.10) offers the conjecture that this poet was Eumelos, author of a processional hymn to Delian Apollo which he elsewhere attributes (4.4.1) and quotes from (4.33.2). Once again, the proposal has met with rejection, mainly on the chronological ground that Eumelos would be far too early for the apparent iconographical dating of the chest. Yet it has the merit of being roughly compatible with *Pausanias's* date for the chest, which could have fallen within the lifetime of Eumelos. Pausanias may well have made his conjecture in awareness of this: if so, it would suggest yet another way in which he has been underrated.

A more specific lesson has emerged from this reexamination of the iconog-raphy of the chest: namely, that the "Homerist hypothesis" in the interpretation of early Greek art, which was alluded to just now and whose impact can be seen in the nineteenth and even more strongly in the twentieth century of our era, may itself go back to Pausanias's time. It is clear that the guides at Olympia, when they fashioned their interpretations of the uninscribed scenes on the chest, were positively looking out for scenes of Homeric inspiration and so settled happily on "Nausikää and her servant" and "after the death of Patroklos." Pau-sanias himself, who had a special interest in things Homeric, followed them with his "Odysseus and Kirke," which is at least as likely to be mistaken. In this predisposition, they may well reflect the prevailing artistic climate of Roman Imperial times, when the long-standing prestige of Homer in literary, political, and philosophical circles had been largely appropriated into the artistic com-munity as well: a series of major and minor works, extending from Sperlonga to the Vatican *Odyssey* landscapes, suggest that this was so. But looking beyond the visual arts, one can see that they also reflect an attitude that finds fuller expression in the movement of the Second Sophistic. Elsner has drawn attention to some passages where the "Homerizing" of Pausanias goes even further than that of other writers.[29] When Homer is treated as the ultimate authority on every subject, it becomes axiomatic that artists too should draw their inspiration from him.

By their readings of the scenes on the chest, Pausanias and his contemporaries betray the assumption that this had *always* been the situation, since the first diffusion of the Homeric epics. Here, as I have said, they pointed a way that modern art historians have eagerly followed. This has not come about by chance: the still largely unacknowledged influence of Pausanias on J. J. Winckelmann, the founding father of Classical art history, is at the very root of the process. There is neither the space nor the appropriate occasion to deploy here the counterarguments to show how improbable a view of Greek art this assumption embodies; but there is some satisfaction in detecting how long it has been around.

This criticism, however, must not be permitted to cloud the broader appreciation of Pausanias as a fellow toiler in the effort to comprehend Greek art. Again and again in his description of the chest, he makes comments that can be heard, in much the same words, in any classroom of the 1990s where Archaic Greek art is being studied for the first time: "The inscriptions are written in twisting lines which are difficult to make out" (5.17.6). "It is perfectly obvious that this is Herakles" (5.18.4). "Artemis (I have no idea why) has wings on her shoulders" (5.19.5). "The Centaur does not have all four horse's hooves, but his front feet are human" (5.19.7). Here is an observant and intelligent mind, confronted with an early or mid-Archaic work for perhaps the first time, and struggling with its many unfamiliarities. Pausanias and his Olympia guides had many advantages over us: the better preservation of what they saw, the sharing of a language with the producers of the art, the possession of a much fuller literary record to help understand it, and, above all, the survival of a rich oral tradition which is almost completely lost to us. True, they lacked the wealth of archaeological comparanda that we have in the shape of excavated vases and bronzes. But there is some comfort in the fact that they still went wrong, and that eighteen centuries later we can still show that they did so.

There remains the question posed at the outset: why did Pausanias devote so much space and trouble to an antique curiosity like the Chest of Kypselos? The same explanation can hardly apply as in the case of his other long excursuses: certainly not that of the throne of Apollo at Amyklai, the nearest parallel in terms of date, where he significantly curtails his account with the words "anyway, most of its workmanship is already familiar" (3.18.10). This judgment stands in stark contrast to that implied by his account of the chest. In a different way, the statue of Zeus was a wonder of the ancient world, the murals of Polygnotos had a literary interest in addition to being masterpieces from the great age of Greek painting, while the foundation of Megalopolis marked perhaps the greatest *bouleversement* in all Greek history: by comparison with these, the chest calls for a special motivation. The decision to include it at all may have been influenced by the fact that, just a century before, Dio Chrysostom (*Orations* 11.45—an early speech, probably of the '70s A.D.), alone of other ancient writers, had made brief mention of the chest; but not the decision to treat it at such length.

Dio remarks that the chest was to be found in the *opisthodomos* of the temple of Hera, an out-of-the-way location which could only be reached after walking all round the temple to its back (western) end. Pausanias may have said the same in the missing opening lines of his account. But Arafat has now drawn a different inference: that the chest had been moved, since Dio's time, into the main *cella* of the temple, where it would have been much more conspicuous.[30] His grounds for this view are that Pausanias has already "visited" the *opisthodomos* (5.16.1) and has now moved on into the *cella*. But the mention in 5.16.1 is part of Pausanias's brief summary of the *architecture* of the temple, where he remarks in passing that one of the columns in the *opisthodomos* was of timber. He next retails a few Olympic legends and then, from 5.17.1 to 5.20.5, he enumerates the *works of art* within the temple. The long description of the chest comes in the middle of this account, it is true; but no seasoned reader of Pausanias can exclude the possibility that he would move from one part of the temple to another (and, for that matter, back again) without explicitly telling us so. It is surely most economical to assume that the chest was still standing where it had been a century earlier, in a spot where it could not impose itself on the casual visitor. Its historical associations with the Corinthian tyranny, though not negligible, represented an episode with which few later Greeks could whole-heartedly empathize. Its materials, which included gold and ivory, were fairly costly, but by no means uniquely so. Most of the scenes carved on it were very small: even if the chest were 2.5 m long, which seems very unlikely, the size of the mostly two- and three-figure compositions in the second and fourth zones would work out at less than 15 cm square—a scale which, like their style, would not have differed markedly from that of a large Corinthian vase. The hexameter inscriptions within these scenes must have been written in tiny letters. The iconography was severely Archaic and, as the description testifies, full of unexpected obscurities. Yet Pausanias persevered until he had given some account of every figure, apart from the groups described collectively in the third and fifth zones, and until he had deciphered every inscription (unlike Dio, who, for the only scene on the chest that he described, was content to report that there was "an inscription in ancient letters" attached to it).

It is possible that the chest had, by Pausanias's time, acquired a certain religious aura as a goal for pilgrimage: if so, this would certainly have been enough to commend it to Pausanias. But two arguments incline me to doubt the force of this explanation. First, many a Greek sanctuary housed relics that purported, however fraudulently, to be of far greater antiquity than the age of tyranny: Pausanias himself saw and described a number of these, but never at anything approaching this length. Second, there is the contrast already noted with his comment on the throne at Amyklai: for me, this carries a strong hint that the chest, far from being spotlighted because of its renown and prestige as a religious attraction, was in fact being picked out for special treatment on roughly the opposite grounds, that its workmanship was *not* "already familiar." I think that we shall move closer to the truth by appealing to the unusual elaboration of the chest's iconographic program: for this is a feature shared by the statue (and especially the throne) of Zeus, the large-scale murals at Delphi, and the throne at Amyklai, on all of which Pausanias also dilates at length.

Besides serving the practical purpose suggested at the very beginning of this chapter, the exposition of this, or any other, lengthy iconographic program provided an ideal opportunity to inculcate certain academic and pedagogic principles for the description of works of art (as I have also, more tentatively, suggested). But what made the chest stand apart was the *difficulty* of its exposition, seven and one-half centuries after it was designed. This, I believe, Pausanias found to be its most attractive aspect. The challenge of its difficult subject matter aroused in him an enthusiasm that he wanted to communicate to his readers. Proud of his newfound expertise as an expositor of very early Greek figural scenes, he felt able to venture on to original interpretations of his own, just as he had done with the less forbidding works of later centuries. Few writers are entirely averse to occasional showing off, and here was an opportunity that ·not even the modest Pausanias could resist.

In his espousal of exact, dry, and objective description of works of art, as in his bent for the *interpretatio Homerica* as a clue to its understanding, Pausanias emerges as the true father of Classical art history. But in his bafflement at the Corinthian letter forms, in his fascination at the surprises of Archaic iconography, and, not least, in his satisfaction at his own success in unraveling it, he is something much closer: he is one of us.

Appendix: J. G. Frazer's (1898) Translation of Pausanias
5.17.5–5.19.10

(5.17.5) . . . There is a chest made of cedar-wood, and on it are wrought figures, some of ivory, some of gold, and some of the cedar-wood itself. In this chest Cypselus, who became tyrant of Corinth, was hidden by his mother when at his birth the Bacchids made diligent search for him. As a thank offering for his escape his descendants, the Cypselids, dedicated the chest in Olympia. Chests were called *kupselai* by the Corinthians of that time, and it was from this circumstance, they say, that the child got the name of Cypselus. (6) Most of the figures on the chest have inscriptions attached to them in the ancient letters: some of the inscriptions run straight on, but others are in the form which the Greeks call *boustrophedon*. It is this: the second line turns round from the end of the first as in the double race-course. Moreover, the inscriptions on the chest are written in winding lines which it is hard to make out.

If we begin our survey from below, the first field on the chest exhibits the following scenes. (7) Oenomaus is pursuing Pelops, who has Hippodamia: each of them has two horses, but the horses of Pelops are winged. Next is represented the house of Amphiaraus, and some old woman or other carrying the babe

Amphilochus: before the house stands Eriphyle with the necklace; and beside her are her daughters Eurydice and Demonassa, and a naked boy, Alcmaeon. (8) But Asius in his epic represents Alcmena also as a daughter of Amphiaraus and Eriphyle. Baton, who is driving the chariot of Amphiaraus, holds the reins in one hand and a spear in the other. Amphiaraus has one foot already on the chariot and his sword drawn, and is turning round to Eriphyle in a transport of rage ⟨as if he could hardly⟩ keep his hands off her. (9) After the house of Amphiaraus there are the funeral games of Pelias, and the spectators watching the competitors. Hercules is represented seated on a chair, and behind him is a woman: an inscription is wanting to tell who this woman is, but she is playing on a Phrygian, not a Greek flute. Chariots drawn by pairs of horses are being driven by Pisus, son of Perieres, by Asterion, son of Cometes (Asterion is said to have been one of those who sailed in the *Argo*), by Pollux, by Admetus, and also by Euphemus. Euphemus is said by the poets to have been a son of Poseidon, and he sailed with Jason to Colchis. He it is who is winning in the two-horse chariot-race. (10) The bold boxers are Admetus and Mopsus, son of Ampyx: between them a man stands fluting, just as it is now the custom to play the flute when the competitors in the pentathlum are leaping. Jason and Peleus are wrestling on even terms. Eurybotas, too, is represented throwing the quoit: no doubt he was some famous quoit-thrower. A foot-race is being run between Melanion, Neotheus, Phalareus, Argeus, and Iphiclus. The last is victorious, and Acastus is handing him the crown. He may be the father of the Protesilaus who went with the army to Ilium. (11) There are also tripods, no doubt prizes for the victors; and there are the daughters of Pelias, though Alcestis alone has her name written beside her. Iolaus, who voluntarily shared in the labours of Hercules, is represented victorious in the four-horse chariot-race. Here the funeral games of Pelias stop. Next we see Hercules shooting the hydra (the beast in the river Amymone), and Athena is standing beside him as he shoots. As Hercules is easily recognised both by the subject and his figure, his name is not written beside him. Phineus, the Thracian, is represented, and the sons of Boreas are chasing the harpies from him.

(5.18.1) In the second field on the chest we will begin to go round from the left. A woman is represented carrying a white boy asleep on her right arm: on her other arm she has a black boy who is like one that sleeps: the feet of both boys are turned different ways. The inscriptions show, what is easy to see without them, that the boys are Death and Sleep, and that Night is nurse to both. (2) A comely woman is punishing an ill-favoured one, throttling her with one hand and with the other smiting her with a rod. It is Justice who thus treats Injustice. Two other women are pounding with pestles in mortars: they are thought to be skilled in drugs, but there is no inscription at them. The man followed by the woman is explained by the hexameters, which run thus:—

> Idas is leading back the daughter of Evenus, fair-ankled Marpessa,
> Whom Apollo snatched from him, and she follows nothing loath.

(3) There is a man clad in a tunic: in his right hand he holds a cup, and in the left a necklace, and Alcmena is taking hold of them. This is to illustrate the

Greek tale that Zeus in the likeness of Amphitryo lay with Alcmena. Menelaus, clad in a breastplate, and with a sword in his hand, is advancing to slay Helen: the scene is clearly laid at the taking of Ilium. Medea is seated on a chair: Jason stands on her right and Aphrodite on her left; and beside them is an inscription:—

Jason weds Medea, for Aphrodite bids him do so.

(4) The Muses, too, are represented singing, and Apollo is leading the song; and there is an inscription at them:—

This is the son of Latona, the prince, far-shooting Apollo;
And round him the Muses, a lovely choir, and them he is leading.

Atlas is upholding on his shoulders, as the story has it, heaven and earth; and he bears also the apples of the Hesperides. Who the man with the sword is that is coming towards Atlas there is no writing beside him to show, but everyone will recognise Hercules. There is an inscription at this group also:—

This is Atlas bearing the heaven, but the apples he will let go.

(5) There is also Ares clad in armour, leading Aphrodite: the inscription at him is Enyalius. Thetis, too, is represented as a maid: Peleus is taking hold of her, and from the hand of Thetis a snake is darting at him. The sisters of Medusa are represented with wings pursuing Perseus, who is flying through the air. The name of Perseus alone is inscribed.

(6) Armies fill the third field of the chest: most of the men are on foot, but some are riding in two-horse chariots. By the attitudes of the soldiers you can guess that though they are advancing to battle, they will recognise and greet each other as friends. Two explanations are given by the guides. Some of them say that they are the Aetolians under Oxylus, and the ancient Eleans, and that they are meeting in recollection of their old kinship, and with mutual signs of good-will. Others say the armies are advancing to the encounter, and that they are the Pylians and Arcadians about to fight beside the city of Phea and river Jardanus. (7) But it is incredible that Cypselus' ancestor, who was a Corinthian, and had the chest made for himself, should have voluntarily passed over all Corinthian history, and should have caused to be wrought on the chest only foreign scenes, and scenes, too, which were not famous. The following conjecture suggested itself to me. Cypselus and his forefathers came originally from Gonussa, the town above Sicyon, and Melas, son of Antasus, was an ancestor of theirs. (8) But, as I have said in my account of Corinth, Aletes refused to allow Melas and his host to enter and dwell in the land, for he was alarmed by an oracle which he had received from Delphi, till at last by coaxing and wheedling, and returning with prayers and entreaties as often as he was driven away, Melas extracted a permission from the reluctant Aletes. We may surmise that it is this army which is represented by the figures wrought on the chest.

(5.19.1) On the fourth field of the chest as you go round from the left there is Boreas with Orithyia, whom he has snatched away: instead of feet he has the tails of snakes. There is also the combat of Hercules with Geryon: Geryon is three men joined together. There is Theseus with a lyre, and beside him Ariadne grasping a crown. Achilles and Memnon are fighting, and their mothers are standing beside them. There is Melanion, too, and beside him Atalanta with a fawn. Hector is fighting Ajax according to challenge, and between them stands Strife, a most hideous hag. In his picture of the battle at the Greek ships, which may be seen in the sanctuary of Ephesian Artemis, Calliphon of Samos represented Strife in a similar way. On the chest are the Dioscuri, one of them beardless still, and between them is Helen. (3) Aethra, the daughter of Pittheus, clad in black raiment, is cast on the ground under the feet of Helen. Attached to the group is an inscription consisting of a single hexameter verse with the addition of one word:—

> The two sons of Tyndareus are carrying Helen away, and are dragging Aethra From Athens.

(4) Iphidamas, son of Antenor, is lying on the ground, and Coon is defending him against Agamemnon. Terror, a male figure with a lion's head, is depicted on Agamemnon's shield. Above the corpse of Iphidamas is an inscription:—

> This is Iphidamas, Coon is fighting for him;

and on the shield of Agamemnon:—

> (5) This is the Terror of mortals: he who holds him is Agamemnon.

Hermes is leading to Alexander, son of Priam, the goddesses to be judged by him touching their beauty. This group also has an inscription:—

> This is Hermes: he is showing Hera, Athena, and Aphrodite
> To Alexander, to judge of their beauty.

I do not know for what reason Artemis is represented with wings on her shoulders: in her right hand she grasps a leopard, and in the other hand a lion. Ajax is represented dragging Cassandra from the image of Athena; and there is an inscription at him:—

> Ajax the Locrian is dragging Cassandra from Athena.

(6) There are also the sons of Oedipus: Polynices has fallen on his knee, and Eteocles is rushing at him. Behind Polynices stands a female figure with teeth as cruel as a wild beast's, and the nails of her fingers are hooked: an inscription beside her declares that she is Doom, implying that Polynices is carried off by fate, and that Eteocles has justly met his end. Dionysus is reclining in a cave: he has a beard and a golden cup, and is clad in a tunic that reaches to his feet: round about him are vines and apple-trees and pomegranate-trees.

(7) The uppermost field, for the fields are five in number, presents no inscription, and we are left to conjecture the meaning of the reliefs. There is a woman in a grotto sleeping with a man upon a bed: we supposed them to be Ulysses and Circe, judging both from the number of the handmaids in front of the grotto, and from the work they were doing; for the women are four in number, and are doing the works which Homer has described. There is a Centaur

not with all his legs those of a horse, but with his forelegs those of a man. (8) Next are the chariots drawn by pairs of horses, with women standing in them: the horses have golden wings, and a man is giving arms to one of the women. This scene is conjecturally referred to the death of Patroclus, it being supposed that the women in the chariots are Nereids, and that Thetis is receiving the arms from Hephaestus. Besides, the man who is giving the arms is not strong on his feet, and behind follows a servant with a pair of fire-tongs. (9) As to the Centaur, it is said that he is Chiron who, having quitted this mortal world, and having been found worthy to dwell with gods, has yet to come to soothe the grief of Achilles. As to the maidens in the mule-car, one holding the reins, the other with a veil on her head, they believe them to be Nausicaa, daughter of Alcinous, and the handmaid driving to the washing-troughs. The man shooting at Centaurs, some of whom he has already slain, is clearly Hercules, and the scene is one of his exploits.

(10) Who the craftsman was that made the chest we were quite unable to conjecture. As to the inscriptions on it, though they may perhaps be by a different poet, yet on the whole I am inclined to guess that they are by Eumelus, the Corinthian, chiefly on the ground of the processional hymn which he composed for Delos.

The Peculiar Book IV and the Problem of the Messenian Past

The most remarkable, and most remarked, feature of Book IV is its imbalance. Pausanias's account of the "many sufferings of the Messenians" is followed by a description of "the country and cities" he sees as he travels from Lakonia to Elis. Pausanias's exploration here of both *logoi* and *theoremata* is obviously not unusual, but the relative emphasis is: some 80 percent of the book recounts the history of the Messenians, in particular their struggles with Sparta in the First and Second Messenian Wars, compared to 20 percent spent on actual sites and monuments.[1] Even when he buckles down to this final section, discussions of unusual water creatures and water bodies also engage his attention.

Explaining this imbalance has, on the whole, been a relatively straightforward matter for later interpreters, with few expressing surprise at this state of affairs. First and most obviously, Pausanias spent little time describing "the things that deserve to be recorded" (1.39.3) because—according to his lights—little in Messenia fell in that category.[2] For much of what today are termed the Archaic and Classical periods, an era in which Pausanias was deeply interested, those Messenians still in Messenia had lain under Spartan domination, subjugated and oppressed, transformed into helots, building nothing for themselves or for their masters.[3] The city of Messene, founded in 369 B.C. after the Messenian liberation by Epaminondas, shattered this pattern, and Pausanias celebrates both its foundation and cityscape at length (4.27.5–7, 4.31.4–33.3; see also 8.52.4–5, 9.14.5). In general, however, the archaeology of Messenia had been left barren ground for Pausanias, and his hasty progress was not to be wondered at. The second straightforward explanation reverts to a familiar approach to Pausanias: consideration of the number and nature of his sources and the assumption that they governed the shape and content of his narrative. The *Quellenforschung* for Book IV, focusing largely on the Hellenistic figures of

Myron of Priene and Rhianos of Bene, has an impressive range and history. The observed deep imbalance between *logoi* and *theoremata,* and indeed any other patterns to be discerned in Book IV, could be thrust back upon these individuals, leaving Pausanias's account a mere reflection of available sources, his relative emphases or gaps in coverage no matter for wonderment.[4]

This chapter takes exception to both these lines of reasoning and reconsiders the peculiarities of Book IV—not least by recognizing that it *is* peculiar and requires more sustained explanation. The fundamental premise here is that, while obviously drawing on and synthesizing literary testimonia (e.g., 4.6.1–4, where he explicitly compares the testimony of Myron and Rhianos), Pausanias nonetheless actively devised his own version of the *Messeniaka,* creating "un 'mosaico,' con l'apporto di sue molteplici esperienze di lettura e di viaggio".[5] If we take Pausanias in his own right, armed with his own authorial agenda, then Book IV becomes a subject for reexamination, not least on the basic question of how Pausanias chose to structure and present the Messenian past. Equally compelling, however, is the "afterlife" of Pausanias's decisions. Rather than looking back in time to locate his sources, we can look forward to his myriad later readers, assessing the impact Book IV has had upon the practice of regional archaeology and regional history in Messenia. This chapter explores these issues, emphasizing in particular some archaeological aspects to these questions and framing the discussion around three archaeological terms: stratigraphy, reconnaissance, and curation.

Stratigraphy

To begin, we can think about the "stratigraphy" of Pausanias's Book IV, the organization of its progression through time (see table 2, which follows the section headings assigned in Frazer's 1898 translation). Already noted is its asymmetrical profile, with an extensive section on the region's past (up to ca. 182 B.C., the death of Philopoemen and Messene's entry into the Achaean League, 4.1–4.29) and a shallow section on its present as viewed by Pausanias (4.30–4.36).[6] The juncture between the two is a very clear turning point in the book:

> Hitherto my account has dealt with the many sufferings of the Messenians, how fate scattered them to the ends of the earth, far from the Peloponnese, and afterwards brought them safely home to their own country. Let us now turn to a description of the country and cities. (4.29.13)

But beyond this division into two distinct horizons, other patterns can be discerned. For example, the history of the Messenians recounted in the first section goes back to its earliest kings and queens and runs through the bitter conflicts with Sparta. With final conquest, however, the focus of attention shifts decidedly away from the inhabitants and topography of Messenia, following instead the fate of the exiles who travel and fight and never forget their native heritage. Little is said in Book IV of the period of Spartan control (usually now recon-

TABLE 2. The "Stratigraphy" of Pausanias's Book IV

Section	Headings in Frazer's 1898 Translation
4.36	Pylus—Sphacteria—Cyparissiae
4.35	Mothone
4.34	The Pamisus—Corone—Asine
4.33	Messene—Oechalia—Andania—Dorium
4.32	Messene
4.31	Thuria—Limnae—Messene
4.30	Abia—Pharae
4.29	Macedonians Seize Messene—Repulse of Macedonians
4.28	Messenians Seize Elis
4.27	Messene Founded (102nd Olympiad, 370 B.C.*)
4.26	Return of Messenians
4.25	Messenians at Naupactus—Siege of Oeniadae
4.24	Revolt of Messenians (79th Olympiad, 464 B.C.*)
4.23	Messenians Take Zancle (29th Olympiad, 664 B.C.; 28th Olympiad, 668 B.C.*)
4.22	The Traitor Aristocrates Is Stoned
4.21	Ira Betrayed—Ira Taken
4.20	The He-Goat—The Cowherd's Leman
4.19	Escape of Aristomenes
4.18	Settlement on Ira
4.17	Battle of Great Trench
4.16	Battle of Boar's Grave
4.15	Battle of Derae—Tyrtaeus (23rd Olympiad, 685 B.C.*)
4.14	Messenian Revolt
4.13	Evil Omens—Ithome Taken (14th Olympiad, 724 B.C.*)
4.12	Oracle of the Tripods
4.11	Battle at Ithome—Messenian Victory
4.10	Death of Euphaes
4.9	Settlement on Ithome—Aristodemus' Sacrifice
4.8	Indecisive Battle
4.7	War with Lacedaemon
4.6	Date of Aristomenes
4.5	Capture of Amphea (9th Olympiad, 743 B.C.*)
4.4	History of Messenia—Affair of Polychares (4th Olympiad, 764 B.C.*)
4.3	History of Messenia
4.2	History of Messenia
4.1	History of Messenia

*Olympiads noted by Pausanias.

Source: After J. G. Frazer, *Pausanias's Description of Greece*, 6 vols. (London, 1898; repr., New York, 1965).

structed as lasting from the late eighth/seventh century to the early fourth century B.C.), and almost nothing of those left behind in the region, those "captured in the country, reduced by force to the position of helots" (4.24.5).[7] Only one episode is reported: after an earthquake punishing the Spartans for their violation of sanctuary, "all the helots who were of Messenian origin seceded to Mount Ithome" in revolt (465/4 B.C.; 4.24.5–7, 3.11.8). Even here, however, much more is made of the actions of these rebels after they left the Peloponnese and were resettled by the Athenians in Naupaktos, notably their subsequent battles with the Acarnanians (4.25.1–10). Events become telescoped at this point in the book—leaping fifty Olympiads without blinking an eye and moving swiftly from the end of the Second Messenian War, to the fifth-century revolt, to the Peloponnesian War, and to the year before Leuktra when omens begin to foretell the return of the Messenians (4.23.4–26.3; see table 2). This acceleration might be taken as a reflection of Pausanias's available sources, but the narrow lens devoted to this time period also suggests a preferred reticence, paralleling his avoidance of the land of Messenia itself.[8]

The narrative both returns to Messenia and slows to provide more detail at the time of liberation, culminating in the foundation of Messene and the return of its exiles, both human and heroic:

> As Epaminondas considered the spot where the city of the Messenians now stands most convenient for the foundation, he ordered inquiry to be made by the seers if the favor of the gods would follow him here. When they announced that the offerings were auspicious, he began preparations for the foundation, ordering stone to be brought, and summoning men skilled in laying out streets and in building houses, temples and ring-walls. When all was in readiness, victims being provided by the Arcadians, Epaminondas himself and the Thebans then sacrificed to Dionysos and Apollo Ismenius in the accustomed manner, the Argives to Argive Hera and Nemean Zeus, the Messenians to Zeus of Ithome and the Dioscuri, and their priests to the Great Goddesses and Caucon. And together they summoned heroes to return and dwell with them, first Messene the daughter of Triopas, after her Eurytus, Aphareus and his children, and of the sons of Heracles Cresphontes and Aeptyus. But the loudest summons from all alike was to Aristomenes. For that day they were engaged in sacrifice and prayer, but on the following days they raised the circuit of the walls, and within built houses and sanctuaries. They worked to the sound of music. (4.27.5–7)

Music, ritual, monuments, repopulation: all come with repatriation and freedom.[9] By contrast, for the exactly calculated 287 years of the Messenian diaspora (4.27.9), "back home" was—in Pausanias's version—an inconsequential and almost invisible landscape. This in turn accords with the lack of monuments and of worthy sights, and the thinness of the section on *theoremata*.

Studying the stratigraphy of Pausanias's discussion in detail, however, forces reconsideration of the relationship between lack of monuments and lack of attention. Was his tour of Messenia so abbreviated because the region's inhabitants had missed out on a "good" period, with noteworthy civic monuments, artworks, and so on? Or because they had experienced a "bad" period, one not worth chronicling with care owing to the region's enslavement? Pausanias throughout demonstrates a sensitivity to issues of conquest and domination; a "refrain of resistance and pride in opposition" seems difficult to deny, as he remembers and celebrates Greek unity, mutual resistance, and defense of Hellenic borders.[10] Praise of those who fought for freedom is recorded, as in a dedication to Epaminondas at Thebes:

> By my counsels was Sparta shorn of her glory,
> And holy Messene received at last her children.

> By the arms of Thebe was Megalopolis encircled with walls,
> And all Greece won independence and freedom. (9.15.6)[11]

Conversely, periods characterized by a lack of autonomy, including Pausanias's own epoch, are met with relative silence. Book IV—with its honoring of Aristomenes, the great local hero of the Second Messenian War, its muteness on the aftermath of defeat, its pursuit of the rebellious as they flee their homeland, its jubilation on their return—fits well within this overriding pattern, a pattern that of necessity demanded that gaps and holes be left in the story.

Commenting on Book IV's imbalance, Habicht is entirely correct: "Nothing illustrates better the lasting effect of Spartan domination over Messenia than this ratio: seventeen pages of description to seventy of history."[12] But the lack of "noteworthy sights" or "memorable things" should be taken as only the surface manifestation of a much deeper-rooted concern and avoidance. The impact of conquest and exploitation, chillingly, still defined what was visible to Pausanias's eyes some half-a-dozen centuries later.

Reconnaissance

This lack of "noteworthy sights" is more often assumed, after a reading of Book IV, than proved on the ground through actual archaeological reconnaissance. Pausanias, as everyone knows, has long been used by Classical archaeologists as a kind of "guidebook" or template in their exploration of regions or specific sites.[13] For Messenia, such reliance on Pausanias has been, if anything, even greater, since he offers our principal source for the area's history and topography. From as far back as the early modern travelers, or early collaborative endeavors such as the Expédition Scientifique de Morée (1832–36), tourists, topographers, and archaeologists have worked to correlate places reported in the text of Book IV with natural features or material remains. For example, the sanctuary of Artemis Limnatis, where Spartan-Messenian hostilities first came to a head in the eighth century B.C. (4.4.2–3, 4.31.3, 3.2.6–7), and the site of Andania, said to be an early royal residence of Messenia and the locus of its mysteries of the Great Goddesses (4.1.3, 4.33.6), have both been continually sought and "found," with their locations still disputed.[14] This exercise of mapping the text of Pausanias against archaeological findings can, for certain inquiries, be exceedingly productive. Habicht has demonstrated that Book IV's tour through Messene is a genuinely helpful account: "In his section on Messene Pausanias has done a careful and thorough job, but that is not surprising—he nearly always did . . . When Pausanias speaks as an eyewitness, he can be trusted."[15] But to what extent is this true elsewhere in the region? Or, to put it another way, how have archaeological approaches to Messenia been shaped by a reading of Pausanias? What questions did he prompt, and which did he fail to prompt?

Two specific influences on the archaeology of Messenia—one temporal, the other spatial—can be traced, at least in part, back to the *Periegesis*. The temporal bias, again, revolves around the disjuncture accompanying Spartan conquest. Pausanias's relative silence about this episode predicted a gap in the archaeological record, a gap so much taken for granted that few attempts have been made to fill it, or even to explore its limits. Little intentional and sustained archaeological attention has been paid to sites of Archaic (ca. 700–480 B.C.) or Classical (ca. 480–323 B.C.) date in Messenia.[16] One of the very few excavated domestic structures of this period—at Kopanaki in the Soulima Valley in northern Messenia—was found during the course of building work in the modern village and dug in a salvage operation in the early 1980s. Its impressive size and the thickness of its walls (suggesting a second storey) initially led to its identification as a huge villa of the late Roman period: certainly an unusually high number (for Greece) of such Roman villas have been noted in the region.[17] These observations, taken in conjunction with the extraordinary discovery of the Mycenaean Palace of Nestor and its Linear B archive in 1939, have worked to incline archaeological attention in the directions indicated by Pausanias: either toward a more distant past or, if less compellingly, toward his Roman present.

As for spatial bias, although Pausanias says relatively little about the region in general, even less is specifically reported about its western coastal zone. Pausanias discusses this coastline—running from Methoni, to Pylos/Koryphasion, to Kyparissia, to Aulon—in fewer than sixty lines; at that point Book IV ends (4.36.1–7; see also 8.1.1; fig. 18). This perfunctory treatment (he may well have sailed this route) led later explorers to adopt similarly low expectations. Frazer, for example, remarked: "The Messenian coast from Cape Coryphasium north to Cyparissiae, a distance of about 20 miles, is of extremely uniform and monotonous character . . . On all this line of coast Pausanias mentions not a single place."[18] The Swedish archaeologist M. N. Valmin began coverage of the west coast in his *Études topographiques sur la Messénie ancienne* as follows:

> La côte ouest de la Messénie, entre l'embouchure de la Néda et Mothon, a été toujours traitée d'une façon superficielle. On a prétendu que pendant la domination spartiate elle était restée déserte, qu'elle avait même été utilisée comme pâturage et qu'elle devait offrir peu d'intérêt au point de vue archéologique et topographique.[19]

Valmin did discover numerous traces of settlement and other human activity in this zone, but few were assigned to the period of Spartan domination.[20] The general temporal bias discussed earlier is clearly to be seen here also; at Classical Pylos/Koryphasion, for example, Pausanias concentrates most attention on monuments of Nestor's time—his house (with a painting of him), his cave for his cattle, his *mnema,* the tomb of his son Thrasymedes (4.36.1–5).[21]

These working assumptions—of the insignificance of Archaic and Classical activity in the region as a whole, of a particularly empty landscape in the west—were of necessity challenged by a disciplinary development in classical archaeology: the introduction of regional survey practices. Messenia was the home of the University of Minnesota Messenia Expedition, often hailed as the first modern, regionally based, scientifically grounded project in Greece.[22] Among its more novel practices, in Mediterranean terms, was surface reconnaissance, seek-

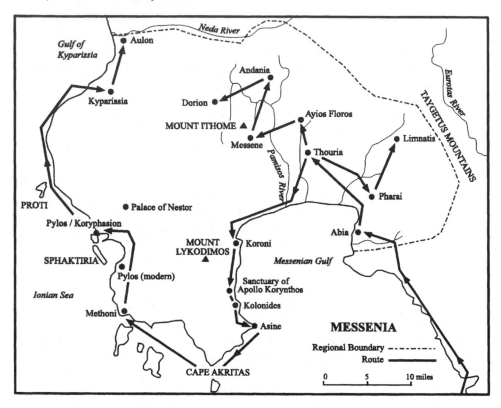

FIGURE 18. Map showing Pausanias's route through Messenia. (After D. Musti and M. Torelli, *Pausania, "Guida della Grecia," Libro IV: "La Messenia"* [Milan, 1991].)

ing out loci of human activity and mapping their distribution by time across the region; a later aspect of the project was the careful excavation of the site of Nichoria, occupied principally in the Bronze and Dark Ages and in Byzantine times. The Minnesota team began work in the 1950s, and its first synthetic volume (*The Minnesota Messenia Expedition: Reconstructing a Bronze Age Regional Environment*) was published in 1972, and with subsequent monographs on Nichoria and its hinterland appearing later.[23] The selection of Messenia for this endeavor followed the original investigators' principally prehistoric (especially Late Helladic, or Mycenaean) preoccupations, as reflected in the first volume's subtitle. Another attraction, however, may have been the marginality of the region to more mainstream classical archaeology (lacking, as it did for the most part, major urban centers or sanctuaries), a marginality that made it less appealing to "normal" archaeological practices and more accessible to innovative research strategies.

Despite their self-admitted Bronze Age chronological focus, the project directors made a considered effort to treat later historical periods as well. They were, however, admirably honest about their relative inability to identify post-prehistoric ceramics, the basic building blocks of survey analysis, and were thus extremely cautious about utilizing these data in any kind of detailed analysis. As a result, their 1972 publication somewhat resembles the "stratigraphy" reviewed above for Pausanias: a heavy concentration on the Bronze Age past, time spent on the ethnographic present, and only limited attention paid to realms in between.[24] Despite the new emphases of this project—its regional approach, its gesture to diachronic coverage, its interest in "man-in-the-environment"—the template of Messenian history presented by Pausanias still seemed pervasive.

Compared to its predecessor, another, more recent venture, the Pylos Regional Archaeological Project (1991–96), was both more genuinely diachronic in scope and more intensive in its methods of reconnaissance. Equally important, the project attempted explicitly to escape the prevailing interpretive framework, recognizing Pausanias, together with other external accounts of the region, as texts requiring more cautious and more questioning engagement. In discussing the goals and background of the project, Jack Davis observed how the region's long-term subordination, from the era of the Spartans to the present-day dominance of Athens, had led to the lack of native historical voices: "For this reason, we believe that any attempt to write a history of Messenia can only succeed if it integrates a vast array of information, gleaned from the careful analysis of artifacts as well as texts."[25] The project's intention here was not to map itself directly against Pausanias's account but rather to offer an alternative frame of reference for the region's past. Results already serve to demonstrate a fuller utilization of the Messenian landscape, including the west coast, than Pausanias had allowed. Several Roman period settlements, for example, have been observed in the project's study region in coastal or near-coastal locations.[26]

The point here is neither to castigate Pausanias for his failure to report such places nor to "test" his account against some archaeologically derived reality. That he largely ignores the day-to-day aspects of life in Roman Greece, for example, is a well-established fact. Comparing these two very different representations of the same landscape does, however, reinforce awareness of the sheer partiality of *panta ta hellenika* (all things Greek). If Pausanias's version of the archaeology of Messenia, and the concentrated power of his determination to record only "the things that deserve to be recorded," have left their mark on regional explorations, other types of reconnaissance are now beginning to challenge that dominance.[27]

Curation

Although it might appear somewhat whimsical to organize this discussion around archaeological terms and metaphors, a central moment of Book IV does involve a specifically archaeological act: the deposition, excavation, and curation (defined here as the safekeeping and preservation) of an artifact. An oracle foretold the failure of Messenian resistance to Sparta, upon which Aristomenes made provision as circumstances demanded. For the Messenians possessed a secret thing. If it were destroyed, Messene would be overwhelmed and lost for ever, but if it were kept, the oracles of Lycus the son of Pandion said that after lapse of time the Messenians would recover their country. Aristomenes, knowing the oracles, took it towards nightfall, and coming to the most deserted part of Ithome, buried it on the mountain, calling on Zeus who keeps Ithome and the gods who had hitherto protected the Messenians to remain guardians of the pledge, and not to put their only hope of return into the power of the Lakedaimonians. (4.20.3–4).

After the battle at Leuktra, Epaminondas summoned back the Messenians to their land and they

with longing for their country and through the hatred which had ever remained with them for the Lakedaimonians, assembled quicker than could have been expected. To Epaminondas it seemed in no way easy to found a city that could resist the Lakedaimonians, nor could he discover where in the land to build it.

At this pass, an "ancient man" (later said to be Caucon, "who came from Athens to Messene the daughter of Triopas at Andania") appeared in dreams to Epaminondas and to Epiteles, general of the Argives, with encouraging messages and an oracle. Epiteles

was bidden by the dream, wherever he found yew and myrtle growing on Ithome, to dig between them and recover the old woman, for, shut in her brazen chamber, she was overcome and well-nigh fainting. When day dawned, Epiteles went to the appointed place, and as he dug, came upon a brazen urn. He took it at once to Epaminondas, told him the dream and bade him remove the lid and see what was within. Epaminondas, after sacrifice and prayer to the vision that had appeared, opened the urn and having opened it found some tin foil, very thin, rolled like a book. On it were inscribed the mysteries of the Great Goddesses, and this was the pledge deposited by Aristomenes. (4.26.5–8)

Epaminondas was thus emboldened to found Messene, which was placed on the slopes of Mount Ithome. This is not the final appearance of the "secret thing." Pausanias cannot speak directly of the mysteries of the Great Goddesses, celebrated at the Karnesian Grove near Andania: "but my dream did not prevent me from making known to all that the brazen urn, discovered by the Argive general, and the bones of Eurytus the son of Melaneus were kept here" (4.33.5).

Hidden on Mount Ithome, by Aristomenes, excavated after an oracle from Caucon, brought for opening to Epaminondas, kept safely at a grove sacred to the Great Goddesses near Andania, where it was seen by Pausanias himself: the burial and recovery of this "secret thing" essentially encompasses within itself the major narrative of the book—the loss and return of the Messenians to their land—while also invoking major places (Ithome, Andania) and major players (Aristomenes, Epaminondas) and linking the entire saga to Pausanias's own personal experience.[28]

By curation, however, more is meant here than the safeguarding of the secret and the later display of the brazen urn. The Messenians themselves are likewise "preserved." If Pausanias's account admits to little left in Messenia after conquest and exile, he does make one exception—this crucial secret thing. The Messenian landscape and its people seem essentialized in this object, suspended in space and time for the duration of Spartan rule. Like "the old woman . . . shut in her brazen chamber," they require liberation in every sense. There is a negative edge to this representation. Pausanias implies that the well-connected, the energetic, and the able go into exile rather than accept servitude (e.g., 4.14.1, 4.23.3, as well as the account of the fifth-century revolt), a pattern prefigured by Thucydides's account of the fifth-century Spartan "purge" of helots in which two thousand potential troublemakers were secretly eliminated, presumably leaving behind the weaker and more submissive (Thucydides 4.80.3–4).[29]

The ensuing vision of passivity, of stagnancy—fostered by the sheer length of their subjugation—became a most insidious way of seeing the inhabitants of Messenia during the years of Spartan domination.[30] Implications of this attitude for archaeological work have already been touched on, not least the unwillingness to choose such periods, and their presumably exiguous traces, for detailed investigation. But such a representation also has a legacy in historical studies of the Messenians, a legacy obviously exacerbated by the scarcity of other sources and the lack of independent local testimonies. As one result, the helots usually tend to be nested within books about Sparta and chiefly tend to be analyzed either in terms of the pressures they placed on Spartan society or of their harsh treatment by Spartiate masters.[31] As in Pausanias, the "high points" of Messenian revolt are certainly acknowledged, and their number and nature much discussed, but little has been done to understand how such revolts were contrived or to investigate other forms of resistant behavior. In other words, until fairly recently, little curiosity was expressed about Messenian internal adaptation—agricultural, social, or ritual—to their altered and exploited lot. Such questions failed to catch fire, in large part thanks to a lack of interest and of relevant textual evidence, which leads back to the influence of Pausanias.

Such problems with sources and resulting scholarly biases are, of course, familiar territory to students of colonial situations elsewhere, and as classicists become more engaged with cross-cultural and comparative analyses, new approaches to Archaic and Classical Messenia have emerged. Placing the helots in relation to chattel slaves in Greece, and employing studies of slave resistance in the New World, allowed Paul Cartledge to explore the difference between "rebels" and "sambos."[32] Research by Stephen Hodkinson on Spartiate-helot economic relations, articulated through a system of sharecropping, unlocks issues of Messenian community structure and internal social stratification.[33] Not surprisingly, archaeological findings can contribute to these reassessments. For example, inhabitants of the Pylos Regional Archaeological Project's study area, arguably part of Messenia's helot population, appear to have dwelt in village-like groupings, not in dispersed and isolated dwellings. This observation, based on the distribution of surface artifacts mapped by the project, has major implications for the processes by which these people communicated and fostered shared memories and identities. Discoveries in ritual settings—for example, later dedications at Bronze Age tholos tombs and in certain sanctuaries—likewise play a part in revealing how Messenian communities operated under Spartan domination, including forms of resistance to that control.[34] Pausanias's version of the history of Messenia has long been perpetuated, but his image of the Messenians under Spartan rule—as a people in limbo, farming and waiting—is slowly beginning to disintegrate.

A provocative parallel to this "curation" of the Messenians, as a people held motionless in time, has been discerned in the presentation of the Minnesota Messenia Expedition:

> In "reconstructing a Bronze Age regional environment" McDonald and his collaborators turned to the ethnographic present as a potential source of knowledge relevant to their reconstruction. They gave to the present a prominent role, on a par with archaeological evidence, Linear B documents, and palynological, sedimentological, and other data, and in the 1972 book they devoted detailed descriptions to modern Messenia in several chapters. . . . Present and past in Greece now were increasingly compared, and, in the process, they became *comparable*.[35]

Fotiadis has suggested that to correlate the present with the past, particularly on the subject of "man-in-the-environment," the Messenians of the present day (for the Minnesota team, chiefly the 1960s) had to be seen and represented in a particular fashion, with the present to be purified "from elements supposedly irrelevant to archaeology." An insistence on the Messenians as fixed to their land, bound to the farmer's cyclical calendar, led to elisions and to silences on topics such as money and banks or technological change. Aschenbrenner's 1970 study of the modern village of Karpofora, for example, mentioned at one point "plowing by tractor." Yet when actual available plowing units were estimated, while each horse and ox was enumerated, the tractors disappeared from sight.[36] The missing tractors of Aschenbrenner's report are more than a little reminiscent of missing elements in Pausanias's account. Such strategic silences served to maintain the Messenians in the place and condition required by these very different authors.

The Messenians, thanks to their peculiar history, were particularly vulnerable to other people's telling of their story:

> . . . the catastrophe that the Messenians have suffered and their long exile from the Peloponnese . . . have obscured much of their ancient history, and, since the Messenians themselves don't know the facts, whoever wants to do so can dispute their claims. (3.13.2)

Pausanias had his own claims to make. If an underlying theme of the entire *Periegesis* is the celebration of *eleutheria,* coupled with relative silence and aversion to its opposite state, then his treatment of the enslaved, then liberated, Messenians takes on special significance. His decision largely to bypass the region and its inhabitants under Spartan rule, or to exhibit them as "frozen" in time and space, both exemplifies and strengthens his association of a people's identity with their freedom: only when the Messenians are liberated and restored to their land can they triumph at Olympia. In the Messenian case, of course, this association was played out and resolved in the past, but for Pausanias it remained an ever-present, and unresolved, concern for the Greeks under Roman rule. In this sense, Book IV may, after all, be less peculiar than paradigmatic for the designs of the *Periegesis* as a whole.

Book IV also served as a paradigm for later students of Messenia, who emulated both Pausanias's reticence about particular periods and his minimalist treatment of particular parts of the region. The impact of reading Pausanias's version of the *Messeniaka* is everywhere manifest, not only in these restrictions and discouragements but also in more positive contributions (such as his "careful and thorough job" on the cityscape of Messene). While it would be foolish to hold Pausanias solely accountable for the attitudes so often brought to the archaeology and history of Messenia, the *Periegesis* must be recognized as an especially potent force in an area not otherwise well documented, where even "the Messenians themselves don't know the facts." As he filled in the history of these people, Pausanias left some holes—not least the "space" he framed so carefully (but ignored so effectively) in his narration of exile and return. Recognizing and challenging the authoritative weight of Pausanias's *Messeniaka* will foster the changes now emerging in analyses of this peculiar region. The use of alternative sources, not least archaeological approaches, is required to liberate still further the study of the Messenian past.

Commentary

BETTINA BERGMANN

Meanwhile, Back in Italy . . .

Creating Landscapes of Allusion

Sometime in the second century B.C., four centuries before Pausanias wrote his *Periegesis,* a *topographos* named Demetrios left Alexandria for Rome. His westward journey paralleled that of many other Greek artists and scientists, who may have traveled on ships bearing loads of sculpture, paintings, mosaics, flora, and fauna from conquered sites of Hellenistic kingdoms into the growing orbit of Rome. About this time, new landscapes began to appear in Italy: publicly, as representations of conquered territories that were paraded in triumphs, displayed in prominent places, and mapped on official plaques; and privately, planted as gardens or depicted in paintings or mosaics. Among the most famous of these early landscapes to survive, the Palestrina Nile Mosaic (ca. 120 B.C.) and the Odyssey Frieze (ca. 40 B.C.) exemplify the Roman interest in foreign environments and the novel ways artisans attempted to capture the dynamics of space and time within a place. The mosaic at Palestrina (see fig. 13, chap. 6) lay on a nymphaeum floor covered with water, so that a viewer standing at the foot of it looked through the water as his eye traveled from Alexandria up the flooded Nile, stopping at famous spots before wandering into the inner reaches of Nubia and the realm of the fantastic. The illusionistic Odyssey Frieze, painted in fresco on the upper part of a peristyle wall, appeared to open onto an expansive panorama of familiar, if unspecific, Mediterranean terrain that gradually assumed identity as the viewer recognized figures of Homeric giants, sorceresses, and residents of the Underworld (see fig. 16, chap. 6). The two late Republican works share a brilliant, innovative pictorial device, the bird's-eye view, with its unified prospect from above of vast stretches of land and sea. Whether or not Demetrios introduced the art of landscape to the Romans, by the time Pausanias wrote his guide, Italy was filled with artificial places evoking famous sites and stories of Greece. And in most cases, these required the participatory engagement of the visitor.[1]

Two themes emerge from several essays in this volume that suggest intriguing links to the art of geographical "lore" that developed in imperial Italy during the empire. One theme is *theoria,* the charged and transformative act of *seeing* a place or monument that was a goal of pilgrimage and visiting sacred sites in antiquity.[2] Another is the experience of "time travel" within a landscape along different routes and discrete tempos, which Pausanias uses as an effective narrative strategy to locate himself and his reader of the "here and now" in relation to the "there and then."[3] The two experiences are interrelated, for seeing a place or thing induces time-traveling, and both result from the guide's artful selection of sights from the world-out-there. The process, first of fragmenting the seen world into selected aspects, and then reintegrating them, characterizes the making of landscapes in Roman art and literature and, as I shall attempt to show here, in actual environments as well.

If we shift the locus of cultural interaction from Pausanias's romanized Greece to Imperial Italy, we find a complementary activity at work in the hellenization of cities, villas, and houses. Indeed, a second-century A.D. visitor to Rome would have encountered Greece at every turn, not just in classicizing buildings and works of art, but in natural areas that were planted and embellished to evoke famous Greek sites. Such evocations were even more apparent in private estates, where since the Republic owners dressed and spoke in Greek while wandering through "Plato's Academy" or the Vale of Tempe or while lingering at the cave where Zeus had been suckled by the goat/nymph, Amalthea.[4]

Scholars have termed this kind of contrived site a *Bildungslandschaft* (translated loosely as a "cultural" or "educative" landscape) because it involved intellectual, as well as physical, engagement with the place. Just as the *theoria* of pilgrimage combined vision with mental inquiry to reach a path of reasoning and eventually revelation, Romans at home cultivated their minds by creating, and then inhabiting, elevated zones of learning. This phenomenon of topographical emulation, which began in Italy in the second century B.C. when Italian magnates saw and were inspired by the estates of Ptolemaic and Pergamene kings, operated during the empire as a familiar and adaptive language of place in nearly all media: poetry, painting, sculpture, architecture, gardens, and full-scale environmental re-creations.[5] Here landscape functioned as far more than backdrop; directive paths, imported plants, and "vestiges" of the past in parks integrated the visitor into a simulated, ideal Greece; poets worked with myths and similes, and painters with pictorial illusions, to achieve the same effect. The only prerequisite was some memory of that past which, once triggered, could stimulate inner contemplation or enlightened conversation.

A look at a few examples of "virtual Greece" made in Italy during the Empire offers a provocative counterpoint to the Greece of Pausanias's *Periegesis,* for the Italian "landscapes of allusion" show similar ways of making, seeing, and experiencing space and time. In particular, they embody a "split vision," a dialectic that characterizes Pausanias's narrative distance from the Greek lands he describes. By excluding features of territories dating after the fourth century B.C. as being less relevant or authentic, he offers to the reader a fictional "deep past" of Greece. It is, as Porter (chap. 5, this volume) puts it, "an ambivalent act of reflection." Cohen, noting a seeming lack of awareness of the physical landscape itself and a gap "between modes of perception" in Pausanias's omission of his present and concentration on early Greece, argues (in chap. 6, this volume) that in fact his worldview is Hellenistic in its scope and nature, an argument that seems supported by the scientific and artistic innovations that occurred at the time Demetrios and his colleagues arrived in Italy. To other authors in the volume, Pausanias represents "the pilgrimage environment of the Second Sophistic" (Elsner, chap. 1, this volume), wherein his focus on the most ancient remains expresses resistance to Roman rule. Pausanias thus emerges as a spokesman of his time, consciously offering an attractively narrow frame of reference to a cosmopolitan audience.

True, a split vision is generally typical of the traveler's desire to be transported to a distant time and place.[6] Yet in their clean sweep of the landscape and with it, the erasure of parts of that landscape's history, Pausanias and the Romans remaking Greek sites in Italy were driven by a desire to remember, preserve, and revive only particular aspects of that world. They employed similar processes in this reconstruction of early Greece, but their goals were very different. There is a fundamental distinction between a nostalgia for one's own lost heritage and the appropriation of another people's past for self-definition. The irony is that these very differently motivated constructions—Pausanias's selective itinerary of sites and the Italian complexes with their rich yield of Greek imitations—have shaped our own inherited picture of the Greco-Roman past and thereby ensured an inherently dichotomous tradition of classicism.

The Verbal and the Visual of Roman Landscape

The Roman language of landscape was bilingual, in that art and architecture visualized literary formulas while verbal formulas articulated place-images. Word and image often were combined physically (an inscription set beside a statue or a bush) or put into dialogue with each other (an epigram addressing a tree). At least in the early empire, the same few recurring images of landscape appear in Latin literature and art. Although one may not find a direct "match" between Pausanias's topographical descriptions and surviving visual evidence, the ancient concept of the environment that these share was clearly unlike our modern, inclusive notion of "landscape." Despite obvious attempts to unify land and sea with devices like the bird's-eye view, ancient authors and artists regarded a place in the plural, as a sum of natural and man-made objects whose association forms one segment of the visual world. Each part has its *topos,* or physical envelope, and it is the relation of one *topos* to another that creates a *choros,* or area. Thus descriptions refer to place in the plural as *topia,* the diminutive form of *topos.*[7]

Such an additive view of the world automatically invites the use of parts as signs or metonyms. From early days in Roman religion, the high priest, or *augur,* would scan the land from a high spot, take sight of certain landmarks, and speak out their names. Thus in augural texts a landscape feature is called a *signum,* a sign that has been selected to represent the place in a new, more meaningful context.[8] The signal value of topography informs landscapes of allusion, as it does Pausanias's tour when he surveys the territory of Greece for "traces of memory it contains." As Porter (chap. 5, this volume) puts it, "sites encountered become texts to be read, while encountered texts (inscriptions, oral histories, miracles, marvels, poetic accounts) are transformed into sites of memory." Four centuries before Pausanias, another Greek, the historian Polybius, almost gave a recipe for landscapes of allusion when he recommended the use of recognizable signs, or archetypes, in order to bring places with which his readers were "unacquainted into connection and relation with those familiar to them from personal knowledge or reading," and adopting "as landmarks harbours, seas and islands, or again temples, mountains . . . as these latter are most universally recognised by mankind."[9]

A comparable visual construction of landscape was said to have been "invented" by the Augustan painter Studius, who was able to capture the variety of all kinds of places with a few key features such as promontories, coasts, rivers, springs, groves, mountains, flocks, and shepherds.[10] From archeological remains, it seems that city and villa designers also responded to the vogue for geographical re-creations by combining generic natural and man-made elements according to an empirical, additive vision. While in texts such geographical lore depended upon associative word-images, in the gardens and representations it was the artful placement of inscriptions, statues, paintings, plantings, and water that stimulated mental links with a specific place or with the general aura of a god or legend. Such experiences of place should recall Pausanias's method, as he moves from site to site and is prompted by artifacts or unusual natural forms to tell a tale.

The desire for a "piece of Greece" in Italy was fueled by travel. Since the establishment of the Pax Romana in the late first century B.C., radiating networks of paved roads and safe open seas allowed wealthy Romans to visit Sicily, Athens, Delphi, and Olympia, even the pyramids of Egypt. For those who could not travel, exotic sites were brought home in the form of recitations of poems, performances of plays, sculptural tableaux in parks, private garden installations, and images on painted walls. By Pausanias's day, some monuments and natural landmarks had assumed meaning independent from their original history and location. Just as today the Elgin Marbles may prompt a European narrative of struggles over cultural property rather than memory of a fifth-century B.C. city celebration, famous markers were dynamic indices of changing values. Pausanias uses the *realia* of sites to stimulate his readers' memories of old stories, and these inspired their re-creation in new environments.[11] Strabo, who came to Rome from Asia in 44 B.C., began his multivolume *Geography,* written in Greek, by claiming that places reflect mythic history as much as mythic history defines the landscapes.[12]

The re-created sites, as is typical for the Roman "culture of the copy," aim, not to reproduce the settings faithfully, but rather to revive them in the viewer's mind. Composed of generic forms with legible cues, they transform an actual locale in Greece into an archetype of another, metaphorical Greece far removed from the vicissitudes of an ever-changing, daily reality.[13]

Virtual Landscapes

Thus, as in Pausanias's *Periegesis,* the remade Greek sites in Italy at times suppressed and at times played upon the most powerful tension within any landscape: that between immutability and inevitable change. The manipulation of time within place was a notable "invention" of Hellenistic art (described by Cohen in chap. 6, this volume): "continuous narrative," the unfolding of events within a seemingly unified and coherent space, accompanied, and was facilitated by, the introduction of the bird's-eye view. The Odyssey Frieze is one of many integrative landscapes in which a story could evolve in stages or a figure enact his life in a kind of cinematic flow. That movement through a constructed realm was physically experienced by visitors to a well-outfitted park or villa garden, who could "travel" the world, from present to past and back again, by passing through provocative zones filled with the appropriate regional vegetation and figures from a myth or historical event.

It is not incidental that Odysseus, the exemplary traveler, was a pervasive figure in the contrived landscapes of Roman Italy. The famous sculptural ensemble in the natural grotto at Sperlonga, we now know, is just one example of a recurring *topos* of villa design, the so-called *antrum Cyclopis,* which became almost standard decor for a wealthy estate.[14] At Sperlonga, four unrelated deeds of Odysseus were integrated physically by the natural frame of the grotto, and thematically by a nearby inscription lauding the hero's stoicism. The experience was interactive, for a visitor could actually reenact Odysseus's deeds by confronting Scylla on a boat or by approaching the sleeping giant Polyphemus on foot. The allegory of travel as a path to salvation coexisted with the familiar story diners enjoyed in spectacular outdoor banquets at the grotto.[15]

In this way, the Italian landscapes of allusion provided a kind of dilatory space for participatory engagement with the metaphor of Greece.[16] Sperlonga is just one example of this engagement on a grand scale, where famous mythological episodes were re-created in the natural environment by placing key figures or signs at a fitting physical spot. Not surprisingly, many of these re-creations were inspired by the most popular tourist sites visited by wealthy Romans. For instance, one distant and exotic goal was the Black Sea, which travelers reached by passing by the ruins of Troy and following the mythical route of the *Argo* through the Hellespont. For Italians who could not make the trip, a boat ride on Lake Avernus simulated the legendary voyage of the Argonauts.[17] They could also continue on a boat up the coast from Naples to the rocky cliffs at Sperlonga, where a marble statue of Andromeda was chained to a rock, recalling another exciting goal for contemporary sightseers, the rocks at Joppa in Palestine, where Andromeda's chains still hung and the teeth of the sea monster were stored in a temple. Pausanias mentions seeing a bloody stretch of water where Perseus slew the sea monster. (Scaurus apparently had brought the monster's bones back to Rome in the first century B.C.)[18] The sight of the Egyptian princess in distress on Italian rocks must have been quite a startling sight for those in passing boats. Despite the poet Propertius's claim that Italian waters do *not* swarm with strange monsters ("not here do Andromeda's chains rattle for her mother's crime"),[19] some patrons clearly wished to create that very illusion by transposing myths to their own coast. For the same reason, perhaps, owners of Campanian villas and townhouses chose the moment of Andromeda's rescue by Perseus as one of the most popular subjects to be painted on their walls (fig. 19).[20]

Among the Greek sites that found their way into Roman poetry, gardens, and interiors was the model sanctuary of a sacred waterway, the river Peneus in the Arcadian valley of Tempe, where the oldest known tree cults, dedicated to Pan and Apollo, were still active. Running between the high mountain cliffs of the valley, its waters diverged around a small island in its center, a configuration similar to many "sacral-idyllic" scenes painted on walls whose atmospheric, unified spaces include those timeless inhabitants of the place, shepherds and fishermen (fig. 20).[21] Copies of such sanctuaries multiplied in Italy as sacred groves assumed a special status, linking Rome's origins back to Arcadian shepherds and evoking the pastoral existence of the early kings of Rome. Augustus restored many of the most ancient shrines in Rome and the countryside as part of his religious revival. Of special prominence were the groves of Diana on the Aventine Hill in Rome and at nearby Lake Nemi, where rites continued to be performed.[22]

Actual views of landscapes through windows and doors were as carefully composed as paintings, with just the addition of a telltale landmark or figure to render that landscape sacred, mythological, and Greek, and many gardens and estates abounded with statues of gods, nymphs, and heroes.[23] Copies of cult images in an archaizing style generated the aura of a *temenos,* for example, in the view from a window of a dining room in the small House of the Moralist in Pompeii that opened onto a grove of Diana identifiable by its tree, shrine, and statue of the goddess.[24] Another window, in a lavish room in the House of Marcus Lucretius painted with themes of Bacchus, offered a view into a planted, watered, and peopled Bacchic realm. The romantic nostalgia for such bucolic *loca sola* of the country was well described by Lucretius, who said that the rustics still claimed that they were animated: "According to local legend, these places are haunted by goat-footed Satyrs and Nymphs . . . Many such fantasies and fairy tales are related by the rustics. Perhaps, in boasting of these marvels, they hope to dispel the notion that they live in the backwoods abandoned even by the gods. Perhaps they have some other motive, since mankind everywhere has greedy ears for such romancing." [25] For Romans returning to Arcadia, such inherited attitudes of reverence combined with nostalgia must have enhanced the experience of authenticity in the ancient groves.

So too would a visit to the fallen city of Thebes, so famous from plays and stories as an example of the ways the maladies of civilization wreak havoc upon humans caught between family and gods by curses passed down through gen-

53.500

FIGURE 19. Perseus rescuing Andromeda, detail of wall painting, Pompeii IX.7.16.
Early first century B.C. (Drawing courtesy of Deutsches Archäologisches Institut,
Rome [Inst. Neg. 53.493].)

FIGURE 20. Sacral-idyllic landscape from north wall, room 16, villa at Boscotrecase; Naples, Mus. Arch. 147501. Late first century B.C. (Photograph by author.)

erations. Sightseers could view remains of the lower city's gates, the grand tomb of the brothers Amphion and Zethus, the funeral pyres and tombs of Niobe's slaughtered children, and even witness ongoing nocturnal rituals to Dirce.[26] Famous Theban episodes pervaded public and private spaces in Italy. On view in Roman parks and villas were three-dimensional sculptural groups of the deaths of the Niobids, which probably were experienced as figures loosely scattered among greenery, linked primarily by glance and gesture, with individual poses suggesting discrete moments of suffering and consciousness, so that the spectator walking among them would have become aware of the charged environment and unknown source of divine arrows piercing the air. Similarly, a version of the famous "Farnese Bull," depicting Amphion and Zethus tying their struggling stepmother Dirce to the bull's belly, had apparently been brought to Rome and set up in the gardens of Asinius Pollio in 43 B.C.; copies of the group followed.[27] Approaching this dynamic, multifigural group in a landscape setting, viewers must have felt temporarily transported back to the cursed Theban countryside, and the beast's imminent charge out into space surely would have arrested their attention.

These and other gripping moments from the Theban cycle also were combined in Roman rooms, most famously in the paired triclinia opening onto the peristyle in the House of the Vettii in Pompeii, which featured a complex interplay of fraught family relations.[28] In order to induce a participatory experience that was so automatic in gardens, painters synchronized the painted light in the scenes with the actual light entering the room through a window or door. Inhabitants of the rooms could spend hours recounting the tales, drawing connections, and discussing the relevance of the ancient outcomes for their own day.[29] Rather than being incidental to the stories, the settings made them more real and enhanced their relevance as reference points for the modern world. And proximity led to conclusions in the mind of the viewer, who became involved in a net of overlapping ideas and themes. For example, in the once-majestic black room of the House of the Marinaio in Pompeii (fig. 21), the viewer encountered four mythological panels, two from Thebes (the slaughter of the Niobids around a rustic sanctuary of Diana and Dirce being tied to the bull) and two seaside scenes (Andromeda being rescued by Perseus at Joppa and Polyphemus wooing Galataea in Sicily; the latter not shown in the reconstruction in fig. 21). The scenes convey starkly alternating moods that correspond to different genres.[30]

In Italy, then, both in public and in private, environmental illusions invited viewers to wander into Arcadian hills, pass the landmarks of heroic feats, and witness the dramatic pursuits, collisions, and transformations of the mythical past—in the very places that now constituted one political and cultural domain. Active viewers in gardens and painted rooms, cutting back and forth between distant sites, remembering the stories that occurred there and bringing them together, found themselves in a kind of ecological paradox of being in several places at once. As the viewers' frame of reference expanded geographically, the division between the imaginary zones and the *peritopos*, the actual lived space of the viewers, dissolved. The sense of "transportation" produced by these com-

FIGURE 21. House of the Marinaio, Pompeii VII.15.1, room z. Left wall: Perseus rescuing Andromeda; back wall: slaughter of the Niobids at the shrine of Diana outside Thebes; right wall: punishment of Dirce. Mid–first century A.D. (Watercolor reconstruction by Victoria I.)

bined illusions reinforced a mental map of the mythical world that had special resonance for Romans in Italy and solidified their status as mobile members of an expansive and absorbent empire.

Two Villas in Italy: Parallel *Periegesis?*

I conclude this brief survey of Italian landscapes of allusion with two second-century A.D. villas that were created in Pausanias's time, one a literary example and the other an actual excavated site. Both employ familiar *topoi* of hellenizing elements that function as metonyms for Greek sites. How might they relate to the Greece Pausanias offered to his readers?

Pliny the Younger (A.D. 61–112), like most wealthy Romans before him, owned estates in various parts of Italy (his beloved villas on Lake Como he nicknamed "Tragedy" and "Comedy"), but his letters dwell on two: the Laurentinum on the beach to the south of Ostia (2.17) and another nestled in the Apennine foothills of Tuscany (5.16).[31] Pliny's narrative follows earlier *Bildungslandschaften* in that he likens his letters to a stroll, with digressions providing rest at designated spots like benches or exedrae and impressionistic phrases conjuring up the pleasurable atmosphere as received through all the senses: sight, hearing, touch, smell. Along the way, he shifts in and out of times and spaces, creating switches in focalization, like "a moving spotlight throwing its rays" on different worlds.[32]

Recently, Drummer has shown how the letters follow the typical steps of an *argumentatio,* in which Pliny uses Greek terms and concepts to demonstrate his erudition. While the villa letters appear to be based upon observation, they follow the same rhetorical principles of compression, antithesis, and recurring rhythmical schemes. Drummer questions them as true descriptions at all and criticizes the search for a "monument" lying behind the letters.[33] His approach marks a shift of interest from an archaeological focus on the villas' realism to their properties in an ideological and symbolic code. Indeed, Pliny was quite self-conscious about his art of describing. At the end of his letter to Apollinaris he even names famous *ekphraseis* by Homer and Virgil as precedents. Yet Pliny's letters, like Statius's villa poems written a few decades earlier, offer rich literary parallels for the heady experience of wandering through a spacious estate with fantastical views populated by Greek mythical figures.[34] Pliny and Statius guide the reader through spatial realms and down imaginary memory paths. The worlds they contrive with words might well be read along with those of Pausanias, whose ostensible goal may appear more documentary and utilitarian, but who achieves many of the same effects of *enargeia* (vivid description) in his reader.

The other example of a second-century villa is the emperor Hadrian's grand complex in Tivoli, built just a few decades after Pliny wrote his letters. Here the *Bildungslandschaften* of earlier descriptions, paintings, and gardens appear to have found epic realization.[35] There are four ancient references to this villa, but three occur in the problematic *Historia Augusta,* which was "compiled" in the fourth century A.D. The most quoted passage states that Hadrian "fashioned the Tiburtine Villa marvelously, in such a way that he might inscribe there the names of provinces and places most famous and could call [certain parts], for instance, the Lyceum, the Academy, the Prytaneum, Canopus, the Poecile, the [Vale] of Tempe. And, in order to omit nothing, he even made an Underworld."[36]

Certain parts of the complex have long been identified with the six sites named in this passage, areas that Hadrian himself visited between A.D. 121–25 and 128–32. In their book on the villa, MacDonald and Pinto are cautious in labeling the remains and actually rename them according to their architectural forms, rather than the sites with which they have been popularly identified.[37] However, they do acknowledge two evocations in the villa: the Vale of Tempe and, curiously, the most fantastic of the six sites, the Underworld. The circular Doric temple in the East Valley, which follows in the tradition of shrines to Aphrodite/Venus, sits on top of a nymphaeum that reaches to the valley below and may refer to the spring of the goddess in Tempe. The topography of the East Valley evidently was altered to resemble the real Vale of Tempe, a natural canyon eight kilometers long through which the Peneus flowed to the sea and which, as we have seen, had long belonged to the vocabulary of popular landscapes in Italy.[38] In the eclectic spirit of the villa, this shrine also may have recalled the most famous of Aphrodite's shrines on the island of Knidos, an identification that seems supported by the discovery nearby of a Roman copy of Praxiteles's Knidian Venus, as well as by Lucian's description of a round, open tholos on the island.

The elusiveness of other parts of the villa is due to the missing semiotic "keys" of buildings and sculpture that, when combined with a particular view, would have incited association with a renowned site. It is clear from the sheer number of imported works of art and stones throughout the villa that the references were overwhelmingly Greek. New versions of Classical statues were made in the Hadrianic style of "enlightened classicism"—for example, those modeled on the caryatids from the Erechtheum on the Athenian acropolis and lining the so-called Canopus (scenic canal) at the villa. MacDonald explains the purpose of Classical statues, whether old or new versions, as secondary to the larger landscape: "surely few cared, as they passed from one statue to another, that some were only copies, for each piece merged equably with the larger whole. Knowledgeable viewers would recognize that whole as an eclectic visual précis of Mediterranean history and memory reaching back a thousand years, a display implying that Roman culture . . . was both its culmination and steward."[39] The desire for an inclusive "set" of Classical sculpture would be echoed centuries later in European collections, where the missing piece of a series, say of emperors, would be replaced with a copy in order to complete the whole. Similarly, while the statuary and landmarks hark back to Greek masters and sites, Hadrian's villa typifies the middle empire's recollective, eclectic nature. It was a "place of remembrance" reinforcing Rome's link to Greece.[40]

What, then, is the connection between the contrived landscapes of Roman Italy and those described in Pausanias's guide? One obvious common denominator is the nature of travel in the second century and the consequent sharing of landscape values. Indeed, "touring" of Greece sometimes involved deeper participation in the rituals of that country's past than the seeming follies of domestic decor in Italy might suggest. Hadrian, like Augustus before him, was actually initiated at Eleusis, and by the Antonine Age, when Pausanias was writing, private individuals increasingly undertook pilgrimages to sacred sites (as Rutherford notes in chap. 4, this volume). The more serious side of topographical emulation can be seen in the example of a villa built right outside Rome on the via Appia in the Antonine period. There the Greek magnate Herodes Atticus re-created a precinct of Demeter and called it the "Triopion" after Eleusis. Along with Demeter and Kore, the empress Faustina the Elder was worshiped as the "New Demeter," joined by Herodes's deceased wife Regilla.[41]

It is entirely possible, then, that MacDonald and Pinto are correct in identifying the High Ground at Hadrian's villa, with its subterranean passages, grotto, and theater, as the Underworld, where the emperor, and perhaps special guests, could reenact that most sacred noctural journey. Around A.D. 112 Hadrian himself had undergone initiation at Eleusis, site of the oldest mystery cult in the ancient world, and was present there again several times between 124 and 131.[42] Pausanias also was an initiate but, like other authors, is generally mute about it: "My dream forbade the description of the things within the wall of the sanctuary, and the uninitiated are of course not permitted to learn that which they are prevented from seeing" (1.38.7). Nevertheless, Pausanias's own participation in various mysteries and rites gives his readers a vicarious sense of Greece's numinous dimensions. There were at least twenty other entrances to Hades in the empire, and many sought the ultimate experience of *katharsis* that had been glorified in the tales of heroes such as Odysseus, Herakles, and, of course, Aeneas. It is no wonder that Hades should become a desirable element of a Roman's private estate.

Pausanias acknowledges Hadrian as one Roman whose mark on Greece should be given due attention, and there even has been some thought that the emperor's travels influenced those of Pausanias.[43] In Book I, for example, Pausanias heralds Hadrian for his many buildings and dedications, also noting where in Greece the emperor's own image could be seen. Of the Olympieion in Athens he says: "Before the entrance to the sanctuary of Olympian Zeus—Hadrian the Roman emperor dedicated the temple and the statue, one worth seeing . . . before the entrance, I say, stand statues of Hadrian, two of Thasian stone, two of Egyptian . . . For every city has dedicated a likeness of the emperor Hadrian, and the Athenians have surpassed them in dedicating, behind the temple, the remarkable colossus" (1.18.6).

The geographical lore created in Italy during the empire invited immersion into an illusory world, an experience not unlike that of *theoria* in pilgrimage. Through the recognition of signs, the memory led to "time travel" within a landscape and a suspension of present time. The imaginary transportation to another place, most often into mythical and legendary Greece, was incited by visual stimuli that, like the guide's vivid anecdote, led the traveler from a landmark to the events that had happened around it.

The examples I have shown pose questions about the perceptions and values of landscape among diverse authors and patrons in the middle empire. The archaeological evidence of this period, and the degree to which it follows earlier trends, need special attention. From a cursory look, it seems that Pausanias and his circle may have been demonstrating resistance to the very "imperative of integration" that was so artfully mastered in Roman contexts in Italy and, of course, elsewhere in the empire. He omits historical episodes leading to the often violent absorption of his ideal Greece into Hellenistic kingdoms and later within Rome's imperial grasp. Yet that omission also served the Italian desire to move easily between a mythical, foreign past and the imperial present. Pausanias sought to separate and preserve past from present; Italian environments, in contrast, seamlessly, seemingly naturally, blended the two.

Commentary

PAUL CARTLEDGE

Sparta's Pausanias

Another Laconian Past

I

"The desire to know may be fabricating its own substantiation": thus Chester Starr in his superbly acerbic deconstruction of the "towering edifice of gossamer" that too often passed for credible early Spartan history a generation ago.[1] A principal building block in that Hans-Andersenian tower was constituted, as Starr immediately went on to observe, by "the historical surveys in Pausanias, Books III and IV," one of the very few "extensive, continuous accounts . . . touching on early Sparta which have survived."[2] Starr's particular concern in that essay was with the (writing of the) history of early— that is, Archaic (seventh to sixth centuries B.C.)—Sparta; but his anathema could be extended without strain to cover Classical Sparta too, as did the relevant books of Pausanias's *Periegesis*.

Today, of course, we read Pausanias differently, as the present collection so splendidly illustrates, firmly placing him in his contemporary intellectual contexts and political milieux; so much so, indeed, that the treatment of him thirty years ago by even as accomplished an intellectual historian as Elizabeth Rawson stands out now in sharply contrasting relief. She, curiously, did not see Pausanias as an important link in the great chain of the "Spartan tradition in European thought" and contented herself with a brief footnoted mention of "the probably recent historical source he uses for this account of Laconia in his huge guide to Greece."[3] Yet the one passage of his that she does specifically cite (3.15.2) actually speaks worlds for his Second Sophistic sensibility: here Pausanias expresses high praise for the melic poems of Alcman (mentioned also at 1.41.4), and this despite the fact that they were written in Lakonian Doric, "the least musical of languages"![4]

Some little disagreement, it is true, would seem to subsist among the experts on the Second Sophistic over whether Pausanias was actually (much) read in his own time. The combined weight of Habicht and Swain inclines firmly to the negative, but Bowie redresses the balance somewhat by throwing into the other pan of the scales Aelian, Philostratus, and Longus, a not inconsiderable literary trio.[5]

There is no questioning, on the other hand, whether Pausanias is much read now, at least within the scholarly community that cares about such things. Among others, Habicht's rehabilitating bio-historiographical study (1985), Elsner's representation of Pausanias as pilgrim (1992, 1995) and Arafat's as art historian (1996), Alcock's exploration of Roman Greece with him as one important guide (1993), a Fondation Hardt Entretiens (Bingen 1996), and now this present volume speak unambiguously to that.[6] Paul Veyne's almost gushing assessment entirely reflects this recent upward reevaluation of our author and, especially for its somewhat odious comparison, bears quotation again: "not a mind to be underestimated . . . the equal of any of the great nineteenth-century German philologists or philosophers."[7] In fact, the danger would now seem to be that we might all turn into "Pausaniacs" (the handy term of D. S. McColl, cited by Henderson, chap. 11, this volume). So it is perhaps worth repeating at the outset Habicht's sober(ing) judgment: "it has to be admitted that he did not have a brilliant mind. He lacked originality and the creative spark."[8]

One upshot of this contemporary reappraisal and revaluation might be to want to disregard Pausanias as a "source" for the (to us, not necessarily in the same way to him) already dim and distant Laconian and Spartan past. However, before pouring the baby out with the bathwater, we might just pause a little to consider what would be lost to the historian of pre-Hellenistic Sparta (Pausanias was, as we shall see, noticeably reticent about almost all things Hellenistic) if— *horribile dictu*—Pausanias's text had not survived. Not, of course, that I mean us to read him as any sort of historian.[9] I simply wish to see what contribution to historical reconstruction his text may legitimately be compelled or persuaded to yield.

I have been encouraged by my generous editors' willingness to countenance a selective focus in this brief essay, even at the cost of rupturing the integrity of the original text, which, in the words of one of our editors, "turned the landscape of Greece into a rhetorical discourse." Since another editor has concentrated on Book IV, I shall look again at Book III, conventionally labeled *Lakonika,* which was originally written perhaps (we have it on the authority of Bowie) within the decade A.D. 165–74.[10]

II

First, we must consider Pausanias on his own terms: what were his declared aims? The *Lakonika* is one of those sections of especial moment to the author in which he steps boldly out from behind the mask to make a ringing declaration of intent:

> Before I speak about the Spartans I must make the same clarification that I made in my essay on Attica [1.39.3]: I am not going through everything in

order, but selecting and discussing the really memorable things (⟨*ta*⟩ *malista axia mnēmēs*). It has been the intention of this book from the beginning to discriminate what truly merited discussion (*ta axiologōtata*) from the mass of worthless stories which every people will tell you about themselves. (3.11.1, trans. P. Levi)

In itself there is nothing particularly startling, or original, in this (variously and energetically fulfilled) statement of intent.[11] For the overall aim of preserving famous achievements from memory loss, and for certain aspects of its implementation, his model was Herodotus.[12] Another Classical mentor along the same general lines, if with a rather wider scope and more moralistic intent than Herodotus, was Xenophon, who differed from his immediate predecessor—and another mentor of Pausanias—Thucydides in seeing merit in preserving the record of rather less grand doings.[13] But was there perhaps some special quality, or aim, to Pausanias's self-consciously selective remembrance of things past?

Lafond has rightly insisted upon the importance of the Peloponnese in general to Pausanias, an Asia Minor Greek from the eastern half of the Roman empire, as the foundation of his inevitably somewhat nostalgic cultural and political identity.[14] That may indeed account for the note of deep Panhellenic despair sounded by his characterization in the *Lakonika* of the effects of the Peloponnesian War: "Until then Greece had walked with her feet well planted on the ground, but that war shook her from her foundations like an earthquake (*dieseisen*)" (3.7.11; trans. P. Levi [slightly modified]). This simile, as Pausanias would have been aware, was one especially well suited to the topography of Laconia and the Spartans' all too familiar experience of seismicity.[15]

So far as his account of Laconia specifically is concerned, we may note that it conforms on the whole to his preference for describing Archaic and fifth-century monuments, and to his corresponding depreciation and scanting of Hellenistic artifacts.[16] With Arafat, we might well wonder whether he would have mentioned Sparta's elaborate stone theater (3.14.1) had he known that it was Augustan—and not even early Hellenistic, as modern scholars used rather optimistically to believe.[17] Porter has observed that Pausanias "chose to narrate fragments and remains."[18] But against the idea that Pausanias always preferred the incomplete and the old, we may note his description of the Panathenaic stadium at Athens of Hadrian as a "wonder to behold" (1.19.6)—the shock of the new could be safely absorbed by resort to a Herodotean and ultimately Homeric trope.[19] Nevertheless, a strong chronological preference for the more antique, allied to a perhaps Thucydidean reserve about personalities, does mean that if we want to learn about, for example, the colorful third-century Spartan kings Agis IV and Cleomenes III, we read Plutarch, not Pausanias.[20]

On the other hand, the example of Thucydides could spur Pausanias to emulation and refutation, as well as imitation. The senior historian had noted the lack of monumental building in Sparta town, predicting brilliantly that it would (mis)lead future observers into underestimating Sparta's one-time power (Thucydides 1.10). Musti has argued the "extreme probability" of the inference that Pausanias's detailed description of the structures of Sparta town (e.g., the Persian Stoa: 3.11.3) constituted a rejoinder to and refutation of his Attic master.[21]

What then was, in Pausanias's prospective view, especially worthy of retrospective commemoration? One passage, rightly singled out by Porter,[22] is especially illuminating, not least for being post-Classical in reference. It occurs in the narrative portion of the *Lakonika,* where the Spartans are said to have been, during the Chremonidean War of the 260s, "ready to put themselves in danger both out of good will towards Athens *and out of their longing to do something future generations would remember*" (3.6.5, my emphasis). This shows clearly enough that in Pausanias's eyes heroic risk-taking was in principle something *axion mnēmēs.* In the event, the Spartans under King Areus actually did nothing, thus confirming Pausanias in his presupposition that post-Classical Sparta was no longer up to accomplishing any such memorable deed.[23]

Another Pausanian category of (com)memorabilia was formed by what Herodotus had called *erga*—that is, especially noteworthy or memorable artifacts or monumental constructions. One such major Laconian monument, of the late Archaic period, that Pausanias (3.18.9–19.5) deemed worthy of minute description was the throne of Apollo at Amyclae designed by his fellow Asia Minor Greek Bathycles of Magnesia on the Meander (not to be confused with Pausanias's own—probable—Magnesia ad Sipylum).[24] But even this description is not furnished for its own sake, out of some appropriate recognition of the monument's historical significance in its original context. Rather, as ever, "textual design controls the release of Pausanias's art historical nuggets."[25] The artistry of Bathycles, in other words, is not the only artistry being put on display in and by Pausanias's description.

III

So much for Pausanias's artful text in ancient context. In this section I proceed in a positive, though not I trust a positivistic, vein, by looking at his *Lakonika* in modern context, asking what sorts of Spartan or Laconian history we could not write but for its availability. Like Pausanias's, my account is selective, as I choose just four topics as most worthy of (my) *logos.*

First is the intricate subject of Spartan religion. For L. R. Farnell, compiling his monumental *Cults of the Greek States,* Pausanias was "the biggest single resource for excerpting attested 'facts' about Greek religion." Likewise, Farnell's contemporary J. G. Frazer had used him as a storehouse to plunder in support of his own, Frazerian, reading of ancient Greek religion.[26] A better approach is to read him against the grain as an ethnographer of ancient Greek religion, as a non-Frazerian proto-Frazer, so to speak.[27] On ancient Spartan religion—Archaic and Classical, as well as that of his own day—the evidence of Pausanias is simply indispensable: heroization, the initiatory system, the militarization of divine representations, the distribution and details of festival practice—to all these and more Pausanias at the very least imparts color and flavor irrecoverable from archeological or epigraphical data alone.[28]

Second is Laconian topography. "Modern reconstructions of ancient cultic landscapes tend to be heavily dependent upon the testimony of Pausanias."[29]

That is no less true of noncultic landscapes as well. Indeed, since Pausanias's political site classifications are generally unreliable, "the main value of Pausanias' work is purely topographical"—indispensable, that is, for putting ancient names to modern places.[30] Hooker rightly singled out Pausanias's account of the Amyclaion, which Colonel Leake first identified in modern times using Pausanias as his guide.[31] Pausanias's topographical value is realized, secondarily, in modern reconstructions of ancient land routes, not least those involving bridges.[32]

My third topic incorporates both religious and nonreligious topography: the Perioikoi. Without Pausanias, we could hardly begin to rescue the Perioikoi from the condescension to which the Spartans and their acolytes generally succeeded in consigning them.[33] One review of my 1979 book *Sparta and Lakonia* was entitled "Promoting the Perioikoi": such an exercise could not have been attempted without Pausanias's Books III and IV, which put flesh on the archaeological and epigraphical skeleton and on such later sources as the bare-bones entries in the Byzantine lexicon of Stephanus.

Fourth, and finally, is Spartan politics. Counterintuitive as it may seem, it is to Pausanias's *Lakonika* that we owe a unique insight into the workings of Classical Spartan politics.[34] It relates to the major political trial of King Pausanias in 403 B.C., for which Pausanias not only specifies the identity of the Spartan "Supreme Court" but actually details the breakdown of the thirty-four votes cast on this momentous occasion. Pausanias's source is unknown, but perhaps ultimately he was drawing here on a near-contemporary, fourth-century B.C. writer.[35]

In case this concentration on the utility of Pausanias to us historians of Archaic and Classical Sparta and Laconia should tend to mislead, it may be worth concluding this section by repeating that Pausanias had his own agenda, one that was not ours, and of which he remained in control throughout. As Henderson has brilliantly put it: "to the Glory of *his* Greece, Pausanias circuits us from Athens to Sparta, Olympia, and on home to Delphi; he models and massages how we are to see Greece, in all its historicality."[36]

IV

To illustrate the lure and frustrations of following closely in the footsteps of the indefatigable periegete, perhaps I may be allowed to end with a personal anecdote. Somewhere in the Tainaron peninsula (the middle prong of the southern Peloponnese) lay ancient Hippola, one of the thirty-nine alleged *poleis* whose ruins (*ereipia*) Pausanias saw for himself (3.25.9).[37] That they were, avowedly, the ruins of a *polis* makes one want to suppose that Hippola had once been a dependent Perioikic *polis,* though, as Rubinstein remarks, no source for possible *polis*-ness is stated, and no foundation myth is given. So far as the site goes, a possible modern identification, at modern Kipoula or Ano Poula, where antiquities including Geometric and black-figure pottery of some description were unearthed at the beginning of this century, would place ancient (Perioikic?)

Hippola, almost unbelievably, right up on top of the inaccessible and inhospitable ridge of the Thyrides cliffs.[38] I have myself tried once to reach that site in order to carry out my own autopsy, but without success.[39] Thanks—or no thanks—to Pausanias, I shall and must try again, with the present volume in hand perhaps, or at any rate in mind.

PART III

NACHLEBEN

A Temple Worth Seeing

*Pausanias, Travelers, and the
Narrative Landscape at Nemea*

In Nemea there is a temple of Nemean Zeus, which is worth seeing,
though the roof had fallen in, and there was no image left. The temple
stands in a grove of cypresses; and it was here, they say, that the
serpent killed Opheltes . . .

Pausanias 2.15.2

A song in the valley of Nemea:
Sing quiet, quite quiet here.

Lawrence Durrell, "Nemea," 1940

In the spring of 1928, W. Macneile Dixon, Professor of English Literature at the University of Glasgow, packed for a much anticipated,
but no longer particularly unusual, journey to Delos and several parts of the
Greek mainland. In these preparations, the reading material Dixon was most
careful to put in his suitcase was what he called "the book of books for travellers
in Greece"[1]—Sir James Frazer's translation of the *Description of Greece* by
Pausanias. Dixon's traveling party of four men and two women was thus to be
guided by an account of the Greek countryside composed roughly 1,600 years
before their excursion. In this, Dixon saw no contradiction, for he was conform-
ing to a pattern followed by most visitors to Greece since the late eighteenth
century, a pattern that, in fact, remains embedded in the core of many tourist
itineraries even today. The journey that Pausanias took and the landscape he
constructed have made themselves felt throughout the period of modern travel
and tourism to Greece. Why this should be so, what it reveals about the narrative
strategies of Pausanias, and how Pausanias's work shapes conceptions of ancient
sites even now are the central themes of this chapter.

In exploring the connection between Pausanias and more recent travel writing, I am also attempting to bring together some strikingly parallel analyses that have occurred in the fields of ancient and modern Greek studies. Recent deconstruction of the notions of landscape and identity embedded in the only-seemingly-straightforward travel narratives inscribed by modern visitors to the Greek countryside[2] has been matched by increasing recognition, well demonstrated in this volume, that Pausanias's account is not the neutral and pedestrian chronicle once assumed.[3] Linking these two discourses makes clear why modern travelers made such constant use of the *Description*. The value of Pausanias's account to these visitors was not simply in locating ancient sites, but also in fashioning a certain image of them. The narrative devices Pausanias employed in creating a landscape of ancient places which often seemed to be entirely removed from present time and circumstance served the needs of more recent travelers as well.

This understanding of the significance of Pausanias's account for modern travel writers is here developed by close examination of the ways in which both he and they represented one particular ancient place. This is the classical sanctuary of Nemea located in an upland valley in the northeastern Peloponnese, a site containing three standing columns of a temple to Zeus as well as the foundations of various other buildings. In noting what it was about Pausanias's discussion of Nemea that resonated with modern travelers, we can explore both how his discursive strategies operated and why they continued to affect the way ancient sites were understood in the modern era. That the travelers made such great use of Pausanias's *Description* says much about the practices of landscape construction common to both.

As an ethnographer of contemporary Greece, my interest in such issues began with a perusal of the travelers for what they might have said about the nineteenth-century condition of the area around the ancient site at Nemea. I was brought to this examination by participation in the Nemea Valley Archaeological Project, for which I was investigating the dynamics of settlement and migration in the region since the time of the modern Greek Revolution.[4] The travel narratives proved something of a disappointment in this regard, for I quickly found that, although they made claims of visual legitimacy, of describing what was tangibly there to be seen, they were nevertheless remarkably myopic. When placed against documentary and archaeological evidence for the modern period, it became clear that the seeming vacuum in which most visitors placed the sanctuary at Nemea was actually a growing agricultural region, with three eighteenth-century hillside villages eventually surpassed by two newly founded ones on the valley floor.[5] That this other history of the contemporary valley was missing from so many travelers' accounts provoked further analysis of their conception of ancient places and archaeological sites,[6] something that, in turn, led me to the ways in which this conception was shaped by their use of Pausanias not only as authoritative testimony but also as rhetorical ally.

The Discursive History of Nemea

This section establishes the chronology of written narratives, both ancient and modern, concerning the Nemea area and thereby sets the stage for examining selected passages from this discursive history in some depth. Pausanias was not, of course, the only ancient author to write about the place. Nemea appears as a matter of course in mythological portrayals of Herakles's first labor, as well as in several versions of the tale of the seven heroes whose stop in the valley, while leading an army against Thebes, resulted in the death of the infant Opheltes.[7] The panhellenic athletic games held at Nemea in three phases from 573 B.C. to roughly 235 B.C.[8] were widely commemorated in lyric poetry, and most particularly in the eleven Nemean odes of Pindar.[9] Ancient historians also wrote of the battles that occurred in the area during the Peloponnesian and Corinthian Wars,[10] while Strabo noted not only the games and the Herakles myth but also the presence of a village known as Bembina.[11] Pausanias's account (2.15.2–4), reflecting his own visit to Nemea in the second century A.D., came late in this literary sequence and was, as it turned out, the last major description of the place for some time to come.

Nemea lay a bit too far inland to make its way into those few travelogues which appeared between Pausanias's *Description* and the later florescence of foreign travel to Greek lands which began in the late eighteenth century.[12] That there had been such a place in antiquity was known to those who studied the classics, but cadastral surveys conducted by the Venetians at the end of the seventeenth century made no use of this toponym, listing instead the small settlements in the valley directly by the names of Koutsoumadhi, Lekosi, and Bekiri Bei.[13] It was not until publication of Richard Chandler's 1766 visit to the valley, traveling on behalf of the Society of Dilettanti, that the ancient name was reattached to the area and the first substantial description of the Classical site since that of Pausanias appeared.[14] Explicitly citing the *Description,* Chandler's passage on the valley at Nemea as a place named for and defined by its ancient qualities became a prototype for the many accounts of the area that were soon to follow.

For the next century, Nemea was a standard stop for those northern European and American travelers undertaking a tour of the Argolid-Corinthia (fig. 22). The valley appeared quite regularly in travel narratives, resulting in the publication of no fewer than seventy-eight accounts of Nemea, in several European languages, between 1760 and 1930.[15] While the first of these visitors generally stayed longer and wrote more elaborate and idiosyncratic accounts than those who came later,[16] these narratives quickly settled into a standardized pattern, heavily influenced by Pausanias's description of the area and only occasionally punctuated with new or unusual information. By the late nineteenth century, the vagaries of railroad placement and package-tour development awarded Nemea a secondary position on most itineraries. The travel memoirs that included it dwindled, soon to be replaced, however, by brief entries appearing in the dozens of tourist guidebooks that emerged as the major form of travel writing on Greece in the twentieth century. These newer passages bear a

FIGURE 22. Map of the Argolid-Corinthia area. (From W. Gell, *Itinerary of the Morea* (London 1817).

remarkable resemblance to the older ones, and indeed consistently read as rather depersonalized and condensed versions of the form modeled by the earlier travelers.[17]

The discussions of the Nemea region by modern Greek geographers and statisticians[18] and the steadily expanding corpus of archaeological studies on the area[19] have had relatively little impact on this travel and tourist literature. Even when cited, these other discourses have hardly altered the manner in which such travel accounts present the area. Pausanias's discussion, by contrast, remains a central element of travel narratives and guidebooks alike. My first thoughts on this pervasive use of Pausanias focused on what I perceived as misuse of ancient authority: that modern writers, in bending an ancient site to their own uses, left out the sacred context of Nemea so clearly important to Pausanias. As I looked more closely, however, I came to see a common framework in the way both constructed the landscape at Nemea: a central theme and shared narrative structure that could be transported from Pausanias to those who came long after him because it created a particular image of ancient places that both sought.[20] It is to this underlying framework that I now turn.

The Recurrent Form of a Nemean Visit

Pausanias's central discussion of Nemea appears in Book II of the *Description*.[21] Frazer's rendering of the full passage follows:

> From Cleonae there are two roads to Argos. One, a short cut, is a mere footpath: the other is over the pass of the Tretus, as it is called. The latter, like the former, is a narrow defile shut in by mountains on all sides, but it is better adapted for driving.
>
> In these mountains is still shown the lion's cave, and about fifteen furlongs from it is Nemea. In Nemea there is a temple of Nemean Zeus, which is worth seeing, though the roof had fallen in, and there was no image left. The temple stands in a grove of cypresses; and it was here, they say, that the serpent killed Opheltes, who had been set down by his nurse on the grass. The Argives sacrifice to Zeus in Nemea as well as in Argos, and they choose a priest of Nemean Zeus. Moreover they announce a race to be run by armed men at the winter celebration of the Nemean festival. Here is the grave of Opheltes enclosed by a stone wall, and within the enclosure there are altars. Here, too, is a barrow, the tomb of Lycurgus, the father of Opheltes. The spring is named Adrastea, perhaps because Adrastus discovered it, or perhaps for some other reason. They say that the district got its name from Nemea, another daughter of Asopus. Above Nemea is Mount Apesas, where they say that Perseus first sacrificed to Apesantian Zeus.
>
> Having ascended to the Tretus and resumed the road to Argos, we have on the left the ruins of Mycenae.[22]

Pausanias's presentation of Nemea thus takes the form of a personal narrative of discovery. It begins by recounting the narrow, mountainous defile from which he approached the valley, noting that the cave of the lion slain by Herakles can still be pointed out there. Nothing is described for the fifteen furlongs or stades that separate this pass from Nemea. Once there, however, Pausanias immediately inscribes the thing he feels is "worth seeing":the temple of Zeus, even with its collapsed roof and missing statue. He connects this monument to the sacred athletic games for which it was built by mentioning a remnant of the older Nemean Games still run in Argos at the temple of Nemean Zeus built when the Games were transferred there in the third century B.C.[23] In addition to this discussion of the temple and Games, Pausanias also notes that this was where a serpent killed Opheltes, where his tomb and that of his father are now located, and that the area takes its name from a daughter of Asopus. The only other sights Pausanias chooses to record are a cypress grove near the temple, a spring possibly named after Adrastus, and an overlooking mountain where Perseus once conducted a sacrifice. He then speaks of resuming the road to Argos, with no place or image mentioned until the ruins of Mycenae.

When Chandler came to the valley, many centuries after, the fact that he carried a copy of the *Description* is both acknowledged and evident.[24] Although he came from the south rather than the north, the form of Chandler's narrative bears a remarkable resemblance to that of Pausanias:

The pass of Tretus is narrow, the mountains rising on each side. The track is by a deep worn water-course, which was filled with thickets of oleander, myrtle, and ever-greens; the stream clear and shallow. . . . Soon after we turned out of the road to the left, and by a path, impeded with shrubs, ascended a brow of the mountain, in which are caves, ranging in the rock, the abode of shepherds in winter. One was perhaps the den of the Nemean lion, which continued to be shewn in the second century. . . . We descended on the opposite side into a long valley, and had in view before us *The Columns,* or the ruin of the temple, by which the village, called Nemea, anciently stood.

The temple of Jupiter Nemeus is mentioned by Pausanias as worth seeing. The roof was then fallen, and the image had been removed. Round it was a grove of cypress-trees. The priest was chosen by the Argives, who sacrificed in the temple, and at the winter congress proposed a race for men in armour; joining this deity in their solemn invocations with Juno. . . .

The Nemean games were triennial, and celebrated in the grove, in memory of Opheltes or Archemorus, a child whom his nurse, while she conducted the Achaean captains, going against Thebes, to a fountain, placed on the grass and on her return, found with a serpent folded about his neck. His tomb was inclosed by a stone-fence, within which were altars, and a heap of earth marked the burial-place of his father Lycurgus. The horse-race for boys, which had been dropped, was restored to this and to the Isthmian festival by the emperor Hadrian. . . .

The temple of Jupiter was of the Doric order, and had six columns in front. The remains are two [*sic*] columns supporting their architrave, with some fragments. The ruin is naked, and the soil round about it had been recently ploughed. We pitched our tent within the cell, on the clean and level area. The roof, it is likely, was removed soon after its fall. A wild pear tree grows among the stones on one side. . . . We were supplied with milk and lambs from a mandra or fold in the valley, and with water from a fountain, once named the Adrastean, at a little distance on the slope of the hill.

Beyond the temple is a remarkable summit, the top flat, and visible in the gulf of Corinth. This was probably the mountain above Nemea called Apesas, on which Perseus was said to have sacrificed to Jupiter. On one side is a ruinous church, with some rubbish, perhaps where Opheltes and his father were said to have been interred. . . .

Between the temple and the church is a road which, branching from that on Tretus, crosses the valley, and passing through the opposite ridge, turns to the right to a village called Hagio Georgio, or St. George, from whence we procured tools to dig, and wine, with other necessaries. Near are vestiges, perhaps of Bembina; a village, from which, as well as Nemea, the region was sometimes named. On the left hand, at a distance from the road, is a small romantic monastery. . . .

We passed by the fountain at Nemea to regain the direct road from Argos to Corinth, re-ascending Tretus. We then travelled over a mountainous tract among low shrubs. . . . We came to a small plain, in which are some vestiges of Cleonae.[25]

Like Pausanias, Chandler thus begins his account of Nemea with an image of the narrow, mountainous Tretus pass, where he too notes caves which might once have been home to the legendary lion. Moving across seemingly uninhabited space to his initial glimpse into the valley itself, Chandler, in continuing parallel with Pausanias, records first and foremost the ruins of the temple. The context with which Chandler then frames the temple also borrows heavily from Pausanias. He discusses the foundation myth and Games connected to the temple, its relationship to Argos, and even Hadrian's restitution of certain races mentioned by Pausanias in a later passage in the *Description*. In terms of physical remains, Chandler again echoes Pausanias, noting the temple's collapsed roof, nearby shrubbery (in this case, a pear tree rather than cypress grove), and the more distant fountain and flat-topped mountain, for both of which he uses the names given by Pausanias. The primary new elements in Chandler's tale are passing mention of shepherds who supplied the group with milk and lambs for supper, and the noting of a detour the next morning to the next town westward to obtain supplies.[26] Following this, Chandler reengaged the Pausanian itinerary, moving across what is described as a barren landscape until reaching the ruins of ancient Cleonae.

The literary travelers who came to the valley in growing numbers over the next few decades were apt to cite Chandler as well as Pausanias,[27] while following their common narrative structure in increasingly formulaic, although generally abbreviated, fashion. The extensive nature of Chandler's account was rarely repeated, a circumstance allowing the bare skeleton of what was borrowed from Pausanias to emerge even more clearly. These visitors universally referred to the area by the site name of Nemea, even though local residents continued to call it by the name of the largest village, Koutsoumadhi, for some time. Furthermore, even in the face of the demographic and agricultural growth discussed earlier,[28] almost all accounts replicated the Pausanian list of what there was to be seen, as if these modern activities and settlements were inconsequential. Only eight of the forty passages published about Nemea before 1880 noted any contemporary settlements in the valley at all, and more cited Pausanias than mentioned conversations with local residents. The temple remained the central theme of their descriptions, juxtaposed with one or two lesser features selected from Chandler's pear tree, the fountain, the stadium (sometimes confused with a theater), the lion's cave, the nearby mountains, and a ruined church near the temple. These accounts were remarkably similar, irrespective of nationality, and even the early Greek geographers Filippidis and Konstantas[29] and the rare nineteenth-century Greek travel writer Paganelis[30] foregrounded Pausanias's discussion in their passages on Nemea.[31] What Pausanias declared to be worth seeing continued to be the measure of an authentic visit to the place. Pausanias found something to muse on in the ruins of a temple that he presented as standing quite isolated from the trappings of contemporary life. So did more recent travelers, for, in ways discussed below, tranquil connection with a glorious Greek past carried as much power in the nineteenth century as it did for Pausanias in the second.

Thus it was that a century and a half after Chandler's visit, even in the midst of a boom in local viticulture production, Durrell characterized the valley at Nemea with the lines which introduce this chapter, and Dixon, from the University of Glasgow, recorded his visit to the place by replicating the distilled model of Pausanias's account which had by then become standard:

> We drove first to Nemea through the pass of the Tretus, which connects Corinth with Argos, a narrow defile by a stream in a deep bed, bordered with thick vegetation, myrtle and oleander. Here in a cave on the mountain side the lion slain by Heracles had his lair, the Nemean lion . . .
>
> The little valley of Nemea, threaded by a brook of the same name, is a sleepy solitude with few habitations. Around the three standing columns of the old Doric temple [fig. 23] are vineyards and wheat-fields, but no human figures enlivened the scene on the day of our visit. A deep silence prevailed . . .
>
> The remains of the stadium, where the contests took place at the great Nemean games, are still visible, but we contented ourselves with an examination of the temple and precincts, for the peace of the surroundings invited to idle dreams.[32]

Although Dixon was able to undertake his visit by motorcar, his account of Nemea is nevertheless remarkably similar to the form that had been established many years before. After noting the narrowness of the Tretus pass, he mentions the lion's cave and nothing else until reaching the valley. While noting a few other sights, Dixon makes it clear that the thing of greatest interest to him is the temple, which invites him to dreams and meditations. Apparently the ability of the temple to invoke such thoughts is at least partially contingent on Dixon's ability to conceive his party as being alone with it during their visit. The narrative is thus accompanied by an engraving in which a single figure,

FIGURE 23. Temple of Zeus. (From R. R. Farrer, *A Tour in Greece, 1880* [London 1882].)

NEMEA

FIGURE 24. Nemea. (From W. M. Dixon, *Hellas Revisited* [London 1929].)

presumably Dixon, leans against one of the columns (fig. 24). Moreover, Dixon explicitly states that there were no other human figures on the scene that day. This hardly seems credible, given the village of nearly five hundred people which then abutted the temple.[33] Even if one gives Dixon the benefit of the doubt by supposing that by "scene," he might have meant the temple foundations only, and that no farmers approached these during his visit, one still has to recognize that by stating it thus Dixon reveals that the only scene he feels worth noticing in the valley is the temple. In final parallel with those who had gone before, Dixon and his party went next to the ruins of Mycenae, in this case describing literally nothing in between.

Dixon's account stands as exemplar of the abbreviated version of Pausanias's description of Nemea which had become standard in modern travel writing. While borrowing the general narrative structure of Pausanias in describing the area, such accounts tended to peel away the social and religious context into which Pausanias placed his characterization. During the entire nineteenth century, fewer than ten passages referred to the athletic games there, and even fewer to the foundation myth behind them or that they were eventually administered by the Argives. Furthermore, the myth of Herakles was given much greater recognition than that of Opheltes. In short, the sacred framework by which Pausanias understood his landscapes was omitted from these narratives.[34] Modern travelers accepted Pausanias's identification of what to notice about an ancient site but inserted this into conceptual settings more meaningful to their own searches for antiquity.

For the first century of such personal travel narratives, this meant that the Pausanian religious context was uniformly replaced with explicit discussions of the sense of isolation, stillness, and melancholy which visitors felt at Nemea,[35] sentiments which contributed to various ruminations on the contrast of past greatness and present circumstance.[36] The area was repeatedly described as having "the dreary vacancy of a death-like solitude" or as "a scene of cheerless desolation," *"un vallon solitaire," "jetzt ode und schweigend,"* and a place of "melancholy loneliness."[37] Although some accounts continued in this mode well into the twentieth century,[38] roughly half the travelogues after 1880 created an alternative context for the temple: a sunny, albeit largely mute, landscape of fields and happy farmers.[39] The valley became a "lovely sight," "a fertile tract," *"ganz von Weinpflanzungen eingenommen,"* and "exquisite in its smiling beauty, full of light and refreshment."[40] This shift represented, not an abrupt change in a valley that had been full of farmers long before 1880, but a general desire in industrial Europe and the United States to experience what were perceived as the timeless and earthy folk. In any case, although local residents and their vineyards came to grace these narratives more often, they were rarely developed in detail and remained picturesque background to the temple. Frazer, whose commentary was written just as this shift was occurring, seems to have tried to reconcile these two positions, although he ultimately sided with the older one:[41]

> But if the valley itself, especially after rain, is green and smiling, the surrounding hills, scarred and seamed with the beds of torrents, are of a dark and melancholy hue, and, combined with the absolute solitude—not a human habitation being visible through the length and breadth of the dale—affect the mind with a sense of gloom and desolation. The solitude is only broken by the wandering herds of cattle, and from time to time by a group of peasants who come over from *St. George* to till their fields in this secluded valley.[42]

The standardized guidebooks that eventually surpassed such reflective travel narratives in volume and usage began with those of Murray, Joanne, and Baedeker in the mid–nineteenth century[43] and slowly grew into the myriad handbooks now marketed for mass tourism.[44] Throughout this process, the descriptions accorded Nemea have remained remarkably stable. It is usually accorded a single paragraph, which reads as a capsule version of the form regularized by the literary travelers. All present the temple as the thing worth seeing in the area, and most still cite Pausanias in this regard.[45] With great regularity, these guidebook passages surround the temple with the familiar list of fountain, stadium, mountains, ruined church, and/or lion's cave. This is now sometimes supplemented by brief mention of recent archaeological work as well as of wineshops along the main road, but only half, even now, mention contemporary settlements in the valley. The current edition of the *Blue Guide* gives a detailed discussion of the architecture of the site but still begins by labeling Nemea a "lonely little plateau,"[46] something mirrored by the *Eyewitness Travel Guide*'s much briefer entry, which sees the site as "evocatively occupying an isolated rural valley."[47] The first sentence of the passage on Nemea in the 1998 edition of the most widely read English-language handbook, *Let's Go: Greece and Turkey,* is both telling and familiar:

> Pausanias wrote in the 2nd-century A.D. edition of *Let's Go: Nemea,* "Here is a temple of Nemean Zeus worth seeing although the roof has fallen in and the cult statue is missing."[48]

Past Sites in Present Times

What is happening that an account written nearly two millennia ago should still structure how so many people see a place? Fundamentally, I have come to understand that the travelers adopted Pausanias not just because he lent ancient authority in helping them locate sites but also because he created the very same type of selective landscape they too were seeking. Were the *Description* only useful in finding one's way to places, eighteenth- and nineteenth-century travelers might well have supplemented their discussion of Nemea with the testimony of other ancient authors, as well as other kinds of material. That they made rare use of other sources suggests that they found Pausanias's account useful in ways that went beyond site identification. In this final section, I examine how the narrative structure shared by Pausanias and modern travelers functioned to make a particular understanding of ancient sites seem self-evident. Pausanias and more recent visitors alike wished to see the site at Nemea as an isolated place of peace and meditation, where the past spoke directly to the viewer, and their descriptions mirror this desire.

As has been fruitfully explored by various scholars over the last two decades, both Pausanias and more recent travelers were interested in the ruins of Classical Greece for points that they wished to make about the present day of their respective periods.[49] Both felt they could make experiential contact with this ancient past by visiting special places. The narrative structure that they had in common operated and gained its effectiveness in this context. In this light, as attested by other authors in this volume, Pausanias's account may be seen as a construction of Greek identity under the conditions of Roman imperialism. It drew power from its invocation of a time when Romans were not in charge, its assertion of the Hellenic nature of the lands through which Pausanias traveled, and ruminations on what Porter (chap. 5, this volume) identifies as themes of decline, nostalgia, and irretrievable loss. Modern travel writing is also illuminated by recognition of what Greek antiquity has signified to these more recent wayfarers, whose senses of truth, beauty, justice, and status have been strongly intertwined with their idealization of the Greek past. The meditative qualities of ancient places could be fitted to the ponderings of a variety of travelers, ranging from those who employed ancient Greece in a social critique of their own societies, to those who copied and admired its aesthetic qualities, and even to those who simply checked off such visits as appropriate markers of class and culture.

Knowing that both Pausanias and modern travelers were interested in direct contact with an earlier Greece illuminates their shared rhetorical devices, which mirrored the conventions of literary travelers in many places[50] but were, in this case, bent to the specific purpose of experiencing Greek antiquity. The casting of many accounts as personal stories rather than encyclopedic geographies, for example, evoked the sense of individual contact and drama of discovery that rendered such sites as ancient Nemea appropriable for personal use. As Augustinos has pointed out, these places seemed to belong, at least for the moment, to those who encountered them while wandering the countryside.[51]

In continuing rhetorical parallel, Pausanias and the modern travelers chose to comment only on certain places within what was, of course, a continuous topographical surface. This unacknowledged selectivity gave the appearance of describing an entire region while highlighting certain spots and omitting others. Snodgrass has recognized that, for Pausanias, "the rural landscape is largely a kind of void that intervenes between each city or sanctuary and its nearest neighbor."[52] As many have now argued, in selecting which spots to record, Pausanias showed marked preference for the remains of an earlier period of Greek history than his own.[53] Pausanias did sometimes write about Roman Greece, as Arafat has pointed out,[54] but such passages seem to have been restricted to certain places, while other sites clearly functioned to remove him from that world and connect him to a past one. Thus it was that Pausanias omitted the nymphaeum of Herodes Atticus at Olympia, as well as the temple of Roma and Augustus on the Athenian acropolis. For Pausanias, such places belonged to the past, and it was clearly onto such a prior landscape that he also set Nemea. Because modern travelers were similarly predisposed, the itinerary of Pausanias became theirs as well, with the added twist that the distinction between Roman and Classical Greece embedded in Pausanias's narrative no longer mattered because, from their point of view, all places he described were suitably ancient.

In many ways, those who established the canon of modern literary travel in Greece moved across two landscapes: that of Pausanias (which was the driving force of their journeys) and that of the modern settlements (where they sometimes spent the night or obtained supplies, before reengaging the Pausanian world). Given the degree to which they incorporated images of ancient Greece into their understanding of the world, both landscapes may have seemed equally real. Sometimes, as at Athens, these two landscapes were in sight of each other, but at other times, as in the area around Nemea, they were not. Indeed, the entire region between Corinth and Argos was, for Pausanias and modern travelers alike, anchored only by ancient sites which seemed to stand amid, and gain power from, their contrast with an otherwise uninhabited and mute environment. Even those writers who, in other places, discussed contemporary Greek commerce and politics fell silent on such matters at Nemea.[55] This was an area that belonged to the past, and to this day the package tours for foreign visitors through this stretch of the Argolid-Corinthia stop only at the sites of Pausanias, though Greek excursion buses traveling the same stretch never fail to point out the Revolutionary War sites in the area, even when they bypass Nemea completely.[56]

The unspoken site selectivity found in the writings of both Pausanias and more recent travelers worked to disconnect the site at Nemea from broader networks, rendering it a place out of present time and context. Indeed, Nemea became precisely the kind of countersite to ordinary experience that Leontis, in her discussion of the Acropolis, has labeled a "heterotopia."[57] The closest neighbors consistently recorded were two other ancient sites, at Mycenae and Cleonae. Even within this context, Nemea has seemed to stand by itself, off the major road, with little described along the way. This image has been reinforced by accompanying references to the mountains which cut the valley off from the outside world, the time and distance necessary to reach the valley, and the empty plateau crossed in the approach from the east. In this regard, it is worth noting that copying Pausanias's itinerary also blinded the travelers to a world of market towns and mountain commerce well established in the areas west of the valley in the eighteenth century.[58]

Selectivity in what sites to place on the itinerary was mirrored by selectivity in discussing the features of the site itself, once at Nemea. Following the general conventions of travel writing, this second kind of selectivity was, however, masked by the implication that both Pausanias and later writers were simply recording what there was to be seen.[59] Pausanias's pattern of brief, unexamined entries projected a misleadingly simple matter-of-fact positivism. At Nemea, as in so many other places, Pausanias identified what he believed to be important about the area—the temple—in a manner suggesting that this emerged quite naturally from what was in front of him.[60] His passage on the temple and selected features around it thus gave every impression that not only was this a thing worth seeing in the valley, but indeed it was the only thing to be seen in the first place.

This was, of course, not the case. One might argue that Pausanias's account is generally as notable for what it omits as for what it actually discusses.[61] At Nemea, this is immediately instantiated by his somewhat puzzling oversight of the ancient stadium, whose outline in the hillside remained readily apparent up to the modern period. Less obvious, but equally telling, was his recounting of sacred myths connected to the place but not the intra-Hellenic battles reported by ancient historians. Nor did Pausanias discuss the farming settlements that archaeological work has revealed near the sanctuary at the time of his visit.[62] And while he used his preceding section on Corinth as the opportunity to vilify the Roman general Mummius, all Roman presence seemed to have vanished by the time he reached the temple of Zeus.[63] In short, Pausanias constructed Nemea as a place where a harmonious period of mythic Greek history could still be felt.

A very similar selective description of the visible was repeated time and again by modern visitors to Nemea. The site of Pausanias suited their interests well, and the canonical presentation continued to single out the temple in what was otherwise left as an undifferentiated landscape encircled by a wall of mountains. Knowledge of recent conditions makes clear what they left out of this only seemingly intact scene: villages in clear view of the sanctuary and a dense network of fields, field houses, and chapels reflecting a vigorous, export-oriented agricultural economy. At Nemea, visitors came to contact the past, and even when local settlements and vineyards sometimes found their way into its description after 1880, these remained passive elements. The neglect and miscomprehension of modern Greek life, which Angelomatis-Tsougarakis has noted for Greek travel literature in general, are fully evident at Nemea.[64] Visitors to this site pursued personal, experiential contact with an imagined Greek past, and their accounts emphasized the elements making this possible.

The Nemea of both Pausanias and the modern travelers was thus a place that temporarily freed them from their own time while also allowing them to comment upon it. Like other ancient sites, it provided them with moments of innocence, transport from current political and economic entanglements, and the opportunity, as Elsner has stated, to fashion a self from history.[65] Such understandings illuminate why modern travelers selected Pausanias over all others who might have guided them through the Greek countryside, why they rarely confronted the partial nature of his landscapes, why the work of eighteenth- and nineteenth-century geographers and administrators was generally overlooked in their narratives,[66] and why recent archaeological research developing a more complex view of the past has made little headway in recent guidebooks.[67] As Habicht has noted, Pausanias was the one who told these wayfarers about that which they had come to see.[68]

This tacit understanding, shared by Pausanias and the travelers, that ancient sites are places alone and apart from their surroundings, continues to make itself felt in multiple ways outside the realm of literature. It reverberates in the physical and conceptual separation of many archaeological sites from their surrounding areas, particularly when such sites are fenced and locked, standing as separate worlds visited and controlled largely by outsiders. It feeds into the alienation that many who live near these sites feel, especially in areas where a tourist-based economy has not developed and houses or fields have been expropriated. It accounts for the bafflement of tourists who now dutifully report to these sites but are generally given few guideposts for interpretation and no longer share the knowledge base or compelling interest in antiquity held by earlier travelers. And it provides slippery territory for archaeological work, especially when the concept of site is unproblematized.[69] In such situations, the bounded site can too quickly become the sole means of accessing antiquity, and the roots of local disinterest or antagonism toward the place can easily be misunderstood. Over the last two decades, Stephen Miller, who has supervised recent excavations at the sanctuary of Nemea, has made remarkable efforts to involve local residents in activities at the site and to provide expanded interpretive context for visitors.[70] In a parallel vein, the Nemea Valley Archaeological Survey has gathered much information on other periods and places in the area.[71] Both efforts, however, have had to work against a long history of other, narrower visions of this place.

In these other visions, the site at Nemea has operated as an emblem that could be severed from its moorings and made to sail under a variety of flags of convenience, an emblem dependent on partial description and flattening of context. The Nemea of Pausanias, shorn of its religious quality, became that of modern travelers as well. Both wanted to find and isolate past places within present landscapes. The parallel ways they pursued this goal illuminate the rhetorical strategies of both. The major ancient guide for modern travelers was not just a locator of sites, but a fellow traveler on a very similar journey of historical displacement.

Pausanias and the Topographers

The Case of Colonel Leake

The aim of this contribution is to examine the ways in which Pausanias's *Description of Greece* was used by Colonel Leake, one of the most highly regarded commentators on the geography of ancient Greece. First, I will explain who he was and what he did. Then, I will attempt to reconstruct his view of Pausanias. Next, I will show how Leake used the text of Pausanias, choosing as examples his study of the topography of ancient Athens and his travels in the Peloponnese. Finally, Leake's use of Pausanias will be discussed in relation to that of earlier and contemporary western visitors to Greece.

Background and Career

Leake (1777–1860) came from a line of distinguished English public servants, the Martin Leake family. For example, his grandfather Stephen Martin Leake (1702–73) spent some years in the Navy Office and then the Treasury, before becoming a herald and rising to the position of Garter King of Arms (1754–73).[1] Leake's father, John Martin Leake (1739–1836), was also a herald (1743–91) but held a commission in the Essex Militia (1759–62) and then entered the Treasury. He rose steadily through the ranks (1763–83), became one of the Commissioners for Auditing the Public Accounts (1783–94) and ended his career as a Comptroller of Army Accounts (1794–1811).[2]

Our subject, William Martin Leake, became a gentleman cadet at the Royal Military Academy, Woolwich (21 February 1792–1 January 1794), and entered the Royal Artillery. His first posting was to the West Indies (1795–98). Service with the British Military Mission to Turkey followed (1799–1802). This gave Leake the opportunity to cross Anatolia, visit Cyprus, travel in Palestine, Egypt, and Syria, and make his first excursions in Greece (July–September 1802), as well as take part in the battle of El Khanka (16 May 1801). He returned to Greece in 1804 when the British and Ottoman governments expected a French attack, either on the Morea (Peloponnese) or Epirus, and British ministers were anxious to give some support to their Turkish allies. Leake's task was to liaise with the local Ottoman authorities about defense, to assess whether local people would support the French in the event of a landing, and to collect geographical information which would be useful in dealing with a French advance into the interior. Leake traveled widely in the Peloponnese and central Greece before being put under house arrest in Salonika (February 1807) when the Ottoman government decided to throw in its lot with France in the hope of stemming Russian military advances in the Danubian Principalities and the Balkans. Immediately upon release (October 1807), Leake was sent to Epirus by the British ambassador to the Porte in an attempt to establish whether Ali Paşa, the most powerful of the virtually autonomous governors in the south Balkans, would support the French or the British. After a short stay in Britain, Leake returned to the court of Ali Paşa in 1809 with a cargo of munitions and the object of securing support for British action against the Ionian Islands, then occupied by France. It was during this residency that Byron encountered Leake and found him "taciturn," ill-dressed, and quite unlike "an (English)man of this world."[3] Fearing for his life from the threats of Ali Paşa, Leake left Epirus in April (?) 1810. He never returned to Greece, except in his imagination.

Back in Britain, Leake was elected as a fellow of the Royal Society (1815), became a member of the Association for the Exploration of the Interior Parts of Africa (1813), and joined the Society of Dilettanti (1814), whose members supported archaeological and architectural studies in Classical lands, especially Greece. He remained in the army, but much of his time over some four years seems to have been available for scholarly activity. His projects included collecting and collating information for a map of Greece and putting together a study of the languages found there in the early nineteenth century.[4] All this came to an end in March 1815 with the return of Napoleon Bonaparte from exile in Elba. As the allied armies reformed to face the French, not knowing where the main attack would come, Leake was sent to act as a military advisor to the army of the Swiss Cantons. He saw some action against the French in the Jura and on the upper Rhine and returned home in 1816.

Leake attained the rank of lieutenant colonel in the Royal Artillery in 1820 (he had enjoyed the brevet rank in the army since 1813) and remained a soldier for another three years. In 1823 his own ill-health, the apparent lack of prospects for promotion, and the "downsizing" of the Artillery encouraged him to leave, a decision which he later regretted. He married Mrs. Elizabeth Marsden in 1838. She was the widow of William Marsden (1754–1836). He was a former Secretary to the Board of Admiralty, and a historian of Sumatra and fellow numismatist; she was the eldest daughter of another Orientalist, Sir Charles Wilkins (1749?–1836).

Even in the army, Leake was able to resume his scholarly work. By the time he died in January 1860, he had published thirty-three articles in learned journals—eight of them in the *Classical Journal* (1814–22) and twenty in the *Transactions of the Royal Society of Literature* (1829–51)—as well as eight books, including his *Topography of Athens* (1821; 2d ed., 1841), *Travels in the Morea* (in three volumes, 1830; a supplement entitled *Peloponnesiaca* appeared in 1846), *Travels in Northern Greece* (in four volumes, 1835), and the catalogue of his extensive coin collection, *Numismata Hellenica* (1856; 2d ed., 1859). Leake also found time to edit and publish some of the papers left by the Swiss traveler Jean-Louis Burckhardt[5] and to produce the first background study in English to the Greek War of Independence.[6] Through letters to such newspapers as the *Morning Chronicle* and the *Daily News* and some ten pamphlets (1847–58), he showed himself a steady supporter of Greek independence and a severe critic of British policy toward Greece and Russia, especially during the Crimean War.

Despite a "singular modesty,"[7] Leake was an active member of early-nineteenth-century London's intellectual elite. He was a founding member of two gentlemen's clubs which still survive (Travellers, 1819; Athenaeum, 1824), a dining club (the Raleigh, 1826–54), and two learned or scientific societies (the Royal Society of Literature, 1821; the Royal Geographical Society, 1830). He served as a vice-president of both societies and became a member of the inner circle of the Dilettanti, its Publications Committee (1823). Not surprisingly, the major newspapers and the *Illustrated London News,* as well as several learned journals, carried fulsome obituaries in 1860. The president of the Royal Geographical Society described him as a *"model geographer"* (original emphasis) on account of the "well-weighted arguments and accurate observations" that constituted his "valuable and standard" topographical works on Greece.[8]

Leake's View of Pausanias

Colonel Leake compiled a catalogue of his library in 1858. It shows that he then possessed nine editions of Pausanias's *Descriptio Graecae* (table 3). This is perhaps a measure of the importance that he attached to the source, as well as an indication of the scholarly need to compare different texts. When he went to Greece in 1804, though, he may have owned only the poor-quality English translation by Thomas Taylor (1758–1835)[9] that has "W M Leake, 1804" written on the title page of his copy and contains many annotations, including corrections to the translation. He could have carried one of the Aldine Press Greek texts with him (but surely not both), whereas the 1613 Hanover edition was probably too large, as a folio volume, to fit easily into a saddlebag or a traveling box.

Leake's own comments on Pausanias appear for the most part in the introduction to his *Topography of Athens*.[10] They are comparatively brief. For Leake, Pausanias was at once the chief source for the ancient topography of Greece, whose text contained "the only consecutive description which we possess of the topography of Athens"[11] and at the same time preserved

TABLE 3. Editions of *Descriptio Graecae* in Leake's Library, 1858

Date of Edition	Editor	Place of Publication
1516	M. Musurus	Venice (Aldus Manutius, quarto)
1516	M. Musurus	Venice (Aldus Manutius, duodecimo)
1613	G. Xylander and F. Sylburg	Hanover
1794	T. Taylor (trans.)	London
1814	F. Clavier (after Corais)	Paris
1822	C. G. Siebelis	Leipzig (quarto)
1826	I. Bekker	Berlin
1832	C. G. Siebelis	Leipzig (octavo)
1838	J. H. C. Schubart and C. Watz	Leipzig

Sources: Catalogue dated 29 March 1838 (Museum of Classical Archaeology, University of Cambridge); texts identified from Rocha-Pereira 1989, vol. 1: xxi.

much important information . . . upon the history of those arts in which the Greeks have so peculiarly excelled all other nations. From him alone [Pausanias] do we derive an adequate idea of the brilliant genius, profound study, and unrivaled skill, which they applied to the arts of design; of the private economy, and public magnificence, which must have conspired to adorn every small city with so many elegant buildings and works of art.[12]

As a result and somewhat optimistically, though thoroughly in accord with the attitudes of his circle,[13] Leake was

much inclined to believe, that the descriptions which the ancient traveler has given of the cities of Greece—of their distribution, mode of decoration, monuments, and productions of art, would, if better known, be useful to the cultivators of the fine arts in general; that they might have a tendency to assist the public discrimination on these subjects; and that they are particularly worthy of the attention of those upon whom depends the erection of monuments and public works of every kind, in regard to which few persons will be so hardy as to assert that the good taste of this nation has kept pace with its wealth and expenditure.[14]

Otherwise, Leake concluded that "the minuteness of his [Pausanias's] remarks" indicated that Pausanias had spent several years traveling in Greece and that the internal evidence showed that this was at the time of the Roman emperor Antoninus Pius (A.D. 138–61) or Marcus Aurelius (A.D. 161–80),[15] views that subsequent commentators have shared.[16] He also thought that Pausanias used a deficient method in organizing his material, while expressing the view (again shared by later scholars)[17] that his very conciseness suggested that Pausanias "faithfully described Greece as he found it." Leake was not aware of (or made no reference to) the marked avoidance of most things Roman;[18] the very idea that Pausanias himself could have "constructed" a Hellenic identity[19] would probably not have occurred to anyone in the early nineteenth century. However,

Leake was certainly acutely aware of the ambiguity that a concise style created when it came to using Pausanias to reconstruct the cultural geography of an ancient city, and he alluded to a degree of selectivity—for example, in Pausanias's all too brief description of monument-rich Athens.[20] Other sources had to be used to fill the gaps and particularly to clarify Pausanias's own descriptions. Leake met the challenge by developing a method involving the collection of all the available literary references, cross-checking between them, and comparing the ancient texts with the ground. Coins and inscriptions were pressed into service where appropriate, together with maps and the accounts of recent travelers to Greece.

Leake's Use of Pausanias

Leake admitted that most of his work with Pausanias's *Descriptio Graecae* was done at "leisure," although he took the opportunity of his journeys in Greece to confront "the texts of the ancient authors with the actual locality to which they relate."[21] The long gestation period before Leake's major publications appeared suggests that much of this scholarly work was probably done in Britain, but there were long periods of "leisure" in Greece when he was not traveling but, for example, writing his reports for the Foreign Office on landing places and invasion routes and drafting his maps. These breaks would have provided time for Leake to read the ancient authors. It is not possible to say whether he was proficient in ancient Greek at this stage. He certainly had some texts with him, including one or more of Pausanias. However, his methods for collating ancient literary material on specific sites have yet to be discovered: did he employ an early form of card-index system, for example?

The fieldwork for his studies was carried out as Leake traveled. The broad strategy of his major journeys (1804–1807) was dictated by the terms of his mission to collect information on contemporary geography and to meet local officials. The detailed routes, however, were determined in two ways. One was Leake's wish to visit the major sites then known or tentatively identified already. The other was a keenness to investigate reports from local people about the existence of ancient remains at particular places. Leake's journeys in 1809–1810 were more of his own making. On the one hand, he needed to occupy himself during the long intervals between his discussions with Ali Paşa. On the other hand, he wished to complete his earlier investigations, and the opportunity to make a long excursion into Thessaly arose on at least one occasion.

Leake's working of the literary and the topographical data into a synthesis is best demonstrated by consideration of two contrasted examples. I have chosen his *Topography of Athens* and *Travels in the Morea*. The first is Leake's major attempt to reconstruct the cultural geography of an important settlement, though apparently without seeking to locate his reconstruction on a specific time horizon. *Travels in the Morea* is structured around a conventional travel narrative and is representative of his other works in this genre.

The Topography of Athens

My discussion of the *Topography of Athens* is based upon the first edition of 1821, which shows Leake's initial approach to the problems posed by a complex historical site. The second edition, published twenty years later, is seven or eight thousand words longer. Careful comparison shows that Leake undertook considerable revisions to the text in the light of recent research while retaining the basic structure of the original work.[22] He also increased his seventeen "Additional Notes" to twenty-one appendices, running to 176 pages, and finished with 12 pages of addenda.

The first edition contains ten sections, including the introduction. In the introduction Leake claims only to outline "those parts of the history of Athens, whether real or fabulous, which are most necessary to the elucidation of its topography and antiquities."[23] This runs down to the Venetian attack of 1687 and the resulting damage to the Parthenon. In fact, Leake actually does much more than present an outline history. He also provides the assessment of Pausanias mentioned above,[24] reviews the work of previous travelers and their writings on Athens,[25] sketches the "considerable alterations" ("dilapidations" in the second edition)[26] undergone by the town and its monuments since the visit of Richard Chandler in 1764,[27] evaluates the prospects for making further interesting discoveries through excavation,[28] explains the superiority of ancient Greek art,[29] and concludes by arguing that a knowledge of Greek sculpture (including small objects like coins and gems) and Greek architecture would lead to considerable (and desirable) improvements to the arts and architecture of contemporary Britain.[30] The first edition contains eight plates; in the second edition, six rather different plates are used.

Section I consists of an edited translation of Pausanias's account of Athens, which deliberately omits the greater part of the history and mythology and is rounded off by some observations on the incompleteness of the text.[31] Leake points out here that Pausanias named some buildings and monuments without locating them, omitted some famous objects mentioned by other authors, and ignored some structures, the remains of which survived into the early nineteenth century (e.g., the Horologium of Andronicus Cyrrhestes and the Arch of Hadrian). Section II deals with the locations and identification of structures about which, on the basis of the ancient authors and local evidence, there "can be little or no doubt."[32] There were twelve of these (table 4). Subsequent research has shown that Leake's identifications were correct in every case except two: the Theseum and the Fountain of Enneacrunus. The problem posed by the latter site is discussed below. "The identity of the temple of Theseus," Leake wrote, "may be presumed from the importance of the existing building and from its vicinity to the ruins of the Gymnasium of Ptolemy, but the best proof is to be found in some of the remaining sculptures of the temple" which show the labors of Heracles and Theseus.[33] Leake was not alone in his identification, but scholarly opinion now supports the view that the Doric temple which overlooks the site of the ancient Agora was probably dedicated to Athena and Hephaestus.[34]

TABLE 4. Locations in Ancient Athens That Leake Believed Were Firmly Identified*

Position	Mentioned by Pausanias
River Ilissus	1.19.5
Acropolis	1.22.4–1.28.3
Areiopagus	1.24.2; 1.28.5
Theseum	1.17.2, 6
Museum	1.25.8
Pnyx	Not mentioned (Frazer 1898, vol. 2: 375)
Temple of Jupiter Olympius	1.18.6
Fountain of Enneacrunus	1.14.1
Stadium	1.19.6
Dionysiac Theater	1.21.1
Odeium of Herodes	7.20.6
Agora of the time of the Romans	1.18.9

*In Leake's words: "The positions which ancient history and local evidence concur in determining with the greatest certainty."

Sources: Positions: W. M. Leake, The Topography of Athens (London, 1821), 50. Presence in Pausanias: J. G. Frazer, Pausanias's "Description of Greece" (London, 1898), vols. 2 and 6, indexes.

Section III of the *Topography of Athens* attempts to locate "some of the other principal places of ancient Athens" about which there was "a considerable degree of probability." Leake mentions forty-one such places. In the light of later scholarship, he correctly located fourteen (34 percent) of these, was partly right with perhaps six (15 percent), and offered viable possibilities for ten others (24 percent). He was plainly wrong in eleven cases (27 percent).

Sections IV–VIII trace five routes which Pausanias appears to have adopted to structure his account of ancient Athens and to describe the monuments that would be encountered. The final section (IX) deals with the ports of Athens, the Long Walls, and the other fortifications of the city. "Additional Notes" conclude the volume.[35] It is clear, then, that Leake's *Topography of Athens* does not attempt simply to elucidate Pausanias's presentation of the topography of Athens. Leake, in fact, uses the *Descriptio Graecae* as the basis for his own reconstruction of the ancient city. His method emerges in Sections I and II. It is essentially scientific, fixing known points and then trying to locate those about which there was some doubt, moving from near certainty to degrees of probability. His sources are the other ancient authors, as well as Pausanias, the researches of recent travelers, and the results of his own "local observations."[36] Leake's observations must have been made principally in 1802, when he spent about five weeks in the town (30 June–9 July, August). He was on his way back from serving with the Military Mission to Turkey and awaiting passage on Lord Elgin's brig, the *Mentor,* with a consignment of marbles being loaded at the Piraeus by his traveling companion and lifelong friend, Elgin's secretary, W. R. Hamilton (1777–1859). These initial observations were probably supplemented when Leake spent three weeks in Athens during January 1806.[37] Some instrumented survey is indicated by the plans that Leake published in his first edition of the *Topography of Athens*—Plan of Athens and its Harbours with the Surrounding Country from an actual Survey and Plan of the Antiquities of Athens (fig. 25)—both of which have at the bottom "W.M.L met." The surveys were probably carried out in 1802 with the assistance of Lt. John Squire, who was also traveling home with Leake and Hamilton.

Pausanias provided Leake with the basis for reconstructing the topography of ancient Athens. According to Leake when he came to revise his views and had a paper read to the Royal Society of Literature in 1835 ("On some disputed positions in the topography of Athens"), the key to understanding Pausanias was to determine two locations: (1) the Peiraic Gate (as Leake, following Plutarch, called the gate by which Pausanias envisages his traveler arriving at Athens from Piraeus) and (2) the Fountain of Enneacrunus.[38] Of these, the first was absolutely critical, since Pausanias began his description there. Accordingly, Leake spends twelve pages in the first edition of his *Topography of Athens* fixing the location of the Peiraic Gate, one of his certain positions. He does this by drawing upon four lines of evidence. I will outline these to demonstrate how Leake constructed his argument. It is typical of his way of proceeding and of how he uses Pausanias.

Leake begins by identifying the monument of an armed man standing by a horse (described by Pausanias as located at the relevant, but unnamed, gate) with the heroic Monument of Chalcodon which Plutarch specifically stated stood at the Peiraic Gate. Leake then examines the location of this gate with respect to the Dipylum, which he had previously located and equated with the entrance to the town from the Peloponnese, and to the Cerameicus; ancient authorities suggested that both were near the Peiraic Gate. Next he draws into the argument the line of the eighteenth-century wall of Athens and the position of the Aslan Kapesi (Turkish, "the Lion Gate"), that is, the gate leading out toward Aslan Limani (Turkish, "the Lion Harbor"; Porto Leioni, as Piraeus was then called) and compares them with the traces of the ancient defensive wall. Finally, Leake draws upon topographic elements in the descriptions of military operations by Xenophon and Appian, as well as in Plutarch's biography of Theseus, to clinch the argument.[39] He later modified his views as a result of more recent research,[40] but his suggested location was substantially correct.

Leake locates the second critical point, the Fountain of Enneacrunus, in much the same way, pointing out that it was "the most important point in Athens for the elucidation of the topography of Pausanias, inasmuch as the simple text of his narrative, uncompared with other authorities, generally leaves an impression on the reader's mind that this fountain was towards the central or western part of the city."[41]

Partly on the basis of topographical references in other ancient authors and partly because a spring existed there (and was still a fountain when Spon and Wheler were in Athens in 1675), Leake fixes this point at the southeastern extremity of the town, on the bank of the river Ilissus.[42] Subsequent research has suggested that this may be incorrect and has equated the actual site with the

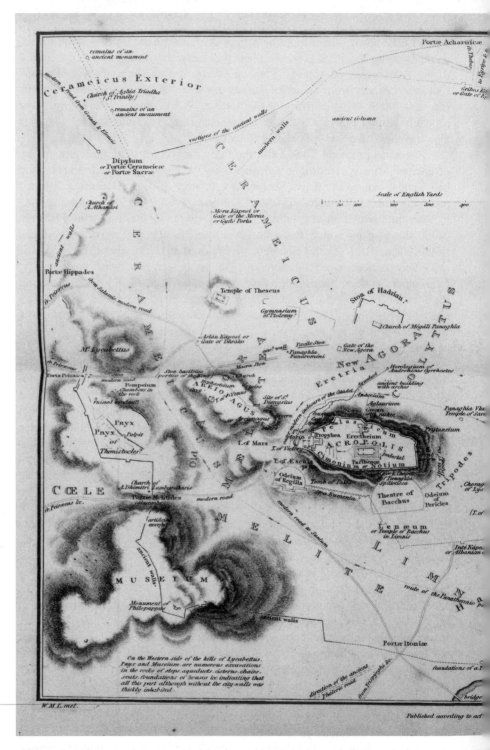

FIGURE 25. W. M. Leake's Plan of the Antiquities of Athens, 1821. (Reproduced by permission the British Library.)

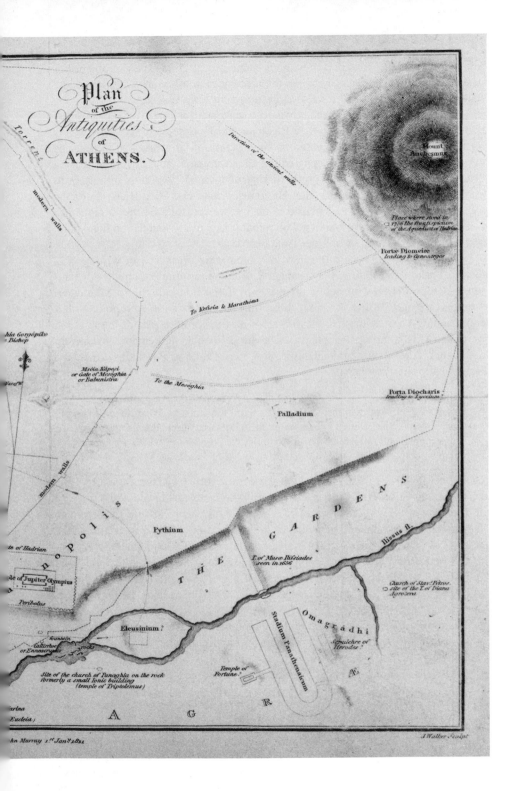

Plan
of the
Antiquities
of
ATHENS.

Torrent

modern walls

Direction of the ancient walls

Mount
Anchesmus

Place where stood in 1756 the front opinion of the Aquaduct of Hadrian

Porte Diomeire
leading to Cynosarges

hia Gorgópiko
Bishop

To Kefisia & Marathona

ara W.

Meóia Kũpeçi
or Gate of Mesághia
or Bubunistra

To the Mesághia

Porta Diocharis
leading to Lyceium

Palladium

modern walls

nopolis

Pythium

T. of Masæ Ilisiades
seen in 1656

THE GARDENS

Ilisus fl.

te of Hadrian

Church of Stav. Petros.
Site of the T. of Diana
Agro. Xent.

le of Jupiter Olympius

Peribolus

Eleusinium ?

fountain
Kallirhoe
or Enneacrunos *rock*

Site of the church of Panaghia on the rock
formerly a small Ionic building
(temple of Triptolemus)

Temple of
Fortune ?

Stadium Panathenaicum

Omagrádhi

Sepulchre of
Herodes ?

Æ.

arina
Eucleia)

A   G   R

John Murray 1st Jan.y 1821

J.Walker Sculpt.

Southeast Fountain House on the Agora excavated in 1952.[43] The problem lies in the confusing differences between the references in other ancient authors and Pausanias's description.[44] Leake's suggestion is at least plausible.[45]

The Fountain of Enneacrunus was the terminus for one of the two routes that Pausanias traced from the Stoa Basileius. Leake argues in *The Topography of Athens* that Pausanias's objective in this section of his work was to describe the southern side of the Areiopagus and the Acropolis, and to follow it by a description of an area on the northern side of these. It was thus important to Leake's research to locate the Stoa Basileius. Leake classified it as one of the more uncertain positions but placed it on the western end of the Areiopagus. Leake was wrong: excavation has shown that it is actually located on the Agora, between the Stoa of Zeus and the Panathenaic Way.[46]

The Prytaneium, where the laws of Solon were preserved in writing (following Leake's translation of Pausanias)[47], was the terminus of another of Pausanias's routes. Leake places it on the site of the house built by M. Lusieri "some years ago,"[48] that is, under the northeast angle of the Acropolis with a commanding view of the sea, as well as of all the northern part of the city and its plain. This is at least a plausible location, though agreement is far from complete.[49] After making this identification, Leake follows Pausanias around the Acropolis to the Propylaea.

> It cannot be doubted that Pausanias, in his description of the Acropolis, adopted some particular order in mentioning the several monuments. What the order is appears from the relative situations of the Parthenon, Erechtheium and four other monuments, which no longer exist, but the positions of which are known from a comparison of other authorities with that of Pausanias.[50]

Leake then proceeds to suggest where the various structures mentioned by Pausanias were located. His method is essentially the same as that adopted elsewhere in *The Topography of Athens,* but it is worth considering a little further since he also introduces numismatic evidence into his argument, notably to locate "the brazen colossus of Minerva by Phidias . . . commonly called Minervas Promachus." Leake uses the image stamped on an ancient Athenian coin (which he publishes opposite his title page) to suggest a location between the Parthenon and the Propylaea, but on the north side of the Acropolis. Testimony from Herodotus, as well as from Pausanias, is used to confirm the position. Again the suggestion has been accepted by later scholars.[51] Leake's descriptions of the buildings on the Acropolis draw less on Pausanias than on his own firsthand observations, and he waxes quite lyrical about their sublime architectural qualities, as well as about the superb sculptures that adorned them.

Travels in the Morea

Travels in the Morea[52] is based on journeys made by Leake between 22 February and 11 June 1805, and between 22 February and 29 May 1806. Leake does not explain very clearly why he decided to publish, but his purpose seems to have been threefold.[53] First, he aimed to provide an account of the Peloponnese on

the eve of its emancipation from Ottoman rule. This was of topical interest at
the time, following the establishment of an independent state of Greece that
consisted principally of the Morea (Peloponnese). Second, Leake wanted to provide information about the interior of the region which had been "little explored"
before his own time. Third, he wished to provide the means whereby a
nineteenth-century reader could compare "every part of the Peloponnesus as
Pausanias found it, with the view which it presented to the follower of his steps,
after an interval of sixteen centuries."[54] The *Descriptio Graecae* is thus basic to
Leake's purpose, and to aid the reader he provides abridged versions of Pausanias's descriptions of ancient cities at appropriate points in his text. As mentioned above, he hoped that these would also help to improve the taste of the
nation. But Leake did not rely entirely on Pausanias for his information: he
summarizes Strabo and other ancient sources where appropriate.

Leake made no attempt to lead the reader along Pausanias's routes through
the Peloponnese. Rather, his narrative follows his own itineraries, and as already
explained, these were determined by the military and political needs of his mission. He turns to Pausanias only when he encounters a major ancient site of
known identity that needs elucidation, or when he attempts to give a name to a
set of ruins pointed out to him by his hosts and guides. To illustrate his approach,
I have chosen to examine his account of Sparta (to balance that of its rival,
Athens) and his suggested location for ancient Amyclae, which, according to
Pausanias, was nearby.

The site of ancient Sparta was already well known to Western travelers
when Leake visited it with William Gell on 21 March 1805.[55] Leake's account
begins with their approach from Mistra, where they were staying, and the few
ancient remains that they could see as they rode along. He then describes the
relief of the site in some detail, before isolating "the only considerable relics of
Hellenic workmanship" that they could see. These were the theater, two facing
doors (partially buried), four more doors (also partially buried), and an ancient
bridge over the Trypiotiko. But Leake also observed that "every part of the site
of Sparta is covered with fragments of wrought stone, among which . . . are
found pieces of Doric columns of white marble, together with other fragments
of architecture of different orders and dimensions," and that similar materials
were built into the almost entirely ruined Roman defense walls surrounding the
principal height on the site. At this point, Leake introduces Pausanias. He writes:

> Before I attempt to render intelligible any observations on the ancient topog-
> raphy of the city, I shall give an abstract of the description of Sparta by Pau-
> sanias; in which, by attempting a division of it under several heads, we shall
> be enabled perhaps to discover a greater degree of method in his description,
> than is at first apparent.[56]

There are nine divisions:[57]

1. The Agora, with its buildings and statues
2. The street Aphetae or Aphetais leading from the Agora
3. The street of Scias

4. The area west of the Agora, including a magnificent theater of white marble
5. A place called Theomelida and the surrounding area
6. "That which appears to form a sixth division in the description of Pausanias begins abruptly as follows: 'In Sparta there is a Lesche called Poecile, where are heroa of . . . ' "
7. The area of the temple of Lycurgus
8. The place called Limnaeum, with temples of Diana Orthis and Latona
9. The Acropolis, with its temples, other structures and statues

The only one of these points that Leake could identify with complete certainty was the theater: the remains were clearly visible and their purpose obvious.[58]

> But it is a point [i.e., the theater] which throws great light on the whole description of Pausanias. Between the western side of the Agora and the theater, he mentions only one monument, the tomb of Brasidas. We have the situation, therefore, of the Agora in the hollow of the great height behind the theater. Thus placed, the eastern extremity of the Agora would be not far removed from an opening, partly natural and partly artificial, which is still observable towards the middle of that bank of hills which overlooks the valley of the Eurotas, and forms the front of Sparta to the north-east. This opening, it is further remarkable, is immediately opposite to the remains of a bridge over the Eurotas.[59]

Leake goes on to deduce the location of the streets Aphetae and Scias. He does this mostly by topographical argument from the terrain and Pausanias's account of the city, but he also draws into the argument some evidence from Livy's account of the attempt by the Roman commander Titus Quinctius Flamininus (d. 174 B.C.) to take Sparta.

"For the rest of the topography of Sparta the most important point to determine is the Acropolis."[60] From the remark of Pausanias that the Acropolis was the highest hill in Sparta, Leake tried to work out where it would be. He confesses that Pausanias is ambiguous "as there is little or no apparent difference" in height across the site. He opts for the northern hill, on the grounds that it is somewhat separate from the others and at an angle to the rest of the site.

Having identified the key positions—the theater and the acropolis—Leake goes on to suggest locations for the other points mentioned by Pausanias, basing his suggestions on the coherence of the ancient literary sources with the ground as surveyed (fig. 26).[61]

Leake and Gell had tried to find ancient Amyclae on the previous day (20 March 1805) because some ruins at the nearby village of Sklavokhori had been identified by "the learned of Mistra" as its site.[62] Pausanias himself had described a number of objects worth seeing at Amyclae, which he called a village.[63] At the site the two Englishmen found eight or nine ruined churches containing ancient materials and about thirty "much dispersed" houses. Despite the existence of a fragmentary inscription containing the Greek letters AMYKΛ, Leake rejected the equation of Amyclae with Sklavokhori. He did so because the situation of Sklavokhori did not agree with the indications of its position given by Polybius and Pausanias, both of whom (in Leake's view) put Amyclae much

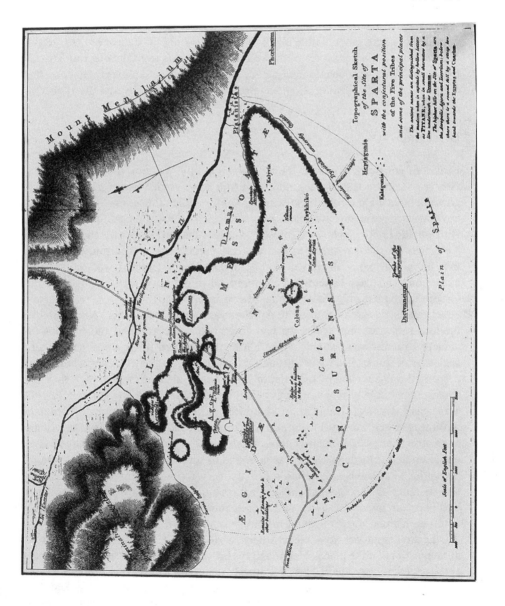

FIGURE 26. W. M. Leake's Topographical Sketch of the Site of Sparta, 1830.

nearer to both the river Eurotas and Sparta. He then summarized Polybius's description of the expedition of Philip son of Demetrius against Sparta in 218 B.C.[64] Leake maintained that this account put Amyclae about two and a half miles from Sparta, near the right bank of the Eurotas, and argued that the location agreed with what Xenophon said about the position of Amyclae in his description of the invasion of Laconia by Epaminondas after the battle of Leuctra.[65] He concluded that Amyclae was actually "not far from Aia Kyriaki," even though the distance from the center of ancient Sparta was more than two and a half miles. This site has "such a commanding position as the early Greeks usually chose for their towns." Moreover, it is one of only two eminences of any considerable height in the little chain of hills following the course of the Eurotas and separating the low levels of the vale of the Eurotas from the plain of Mistra. Pausanias's sparse topographical detail, which Leake summarizes, clinched the argument. Leake's identification was proved correct by excavation in 1890.[66]

Discussion

Leake, of course, was neither the first nor the only Western visitor to Ottoman Greece to carry a text of Pausanias with him and to make use of the *Descriptio Graecae*. Once a published text was available (Aldine Press, 1516), most Western travelers seem to have taken one with them.[67] Even the military engineer Rinaldo de la Rue, who was present at the bombardment of Athens by the Venetians in 1687, referred to Pausanias,[68] though it is not absolutely certain that he had a text with him in the field. Dr. Henry Holland was one of the exceptions and later lamented what more he might have done on his visit to Greece in 1812 if only Pausanias had been in his hands.[69]

Leake's research on ancient Athens was not unique either. Many of his predecessors traveling in Greece had sought to make sense of the remains of ancient structures embedded in the fabric of a modern town, often using Pausanias as a guide. This was difficult not only because the modern buildings prevented a clear view of the relationships of the ancient remains but also because comparatively few structures could be identified with enough certainty to act as marker points. The work of Stuart and Revett in 1751–53 was exceptional, but it was largely confined to careful measurement and depiction of the surviving ancient structures.[70] William Wilkins's *Atheniensia,* published in 1816 but based on observations made in 1802, was intended to supplement their work. Although he outlines Pausanias's description of Athens, Wilkins—a professional architect and designer of the National Gallery in London—was primarily concerned with buildings, architectural styles and architectural sculpture, and what principles could be learned for application in improving modern architecture.[71]

Leake's approach to ancient Athens is different. He sets out to fix the relative positions of the places mentioned by the ancient authors, chiefly Pausanias, and thereby to provide at least a framework for unraveling the topography of the whole city. The publication of *The Topography of Athens* thus marked "an epoch" for "every one who . . . paid any attention to Greek topography," for it replaced fanciful and ignorant conjecture with knowledge and conscientious, learned inquiry.[72] Contemporaries were convinced that such a formidable piece of scholarship would form the basis of all subsequent research on the subject.[73] This has proved to be the case. Leake's views are so well founded that even today they must be taken seriously, while his test of "coherence" applied to all the available evidence is widely accepted.[74]

Pausanias may have suggested interesting places for Western travelers to visit, but most of them used him in an often perfunctory way to describe or to locate an ancient site.[75] There was little else they could do, of course. Information available locally was suspect; modern guidebooks did not exist; the accounts left by recent travelers were rarely satisfactory. In any case, travelers were expected to display a little erudition, and reference to Pausanias could provide it. The account published by one of Leake's exact contemporaries in Greece will illustrate the general use of Pausanias. Edward Dodwell drew upon Pausanias for the early history of Patras, where he began his travels in 1801. When he gets to Sparta (1805 or 1806), he remarks:

> A traveller must not expect to derive any information whatever from the generality of Greeks upon the antiquities of their country, but must extricate himself as well he can, from the dark mazes of conjecture and uncertainty, by the topographical light of Pausanias, and by the few scattered materials of some other authors.[76]

But he then makes very few references to Pausanias. Typical are:

> According to Pausanias there were several hills in Sparta.
> According to Pausanias, the monuments of the Spartan kings Pausanias and Leonides were opposite the theatre.

Dodwell's use of Pausanias in describing the ruins of Athens is little better.[77]

Richard Chandler, who visited Greece forty years earlier, is much closer to Leake in spirit. His expedition was sponsored by the Society of Dilettanti and conceived by them as a serious contribution to scholarship. Accordingly, the text that Chandler produced uses plain, matter-of-fact language. It consolidates previous research on ancient Greece and synthesizes material from relevant ancient and recent descriptions.[78] Typically, these digests begin with a translation of a few pages from Pausanias.[79] The order is inverted, however, in his much-quoted account of the "rediscovery" of the temple of Apollo at Bassae, but in characteristic fashion Chandler simply reports what he learned in Zante from the French engineer Joachim Bocher and adds Pausanias's account without comment.[80]

As we have seen, Leake also summarizes passages from Pausanias, usually omitting the historical and mythical sections, but his use of the *Descriptio Graecae* goes much further than that of either his predecessors or his contemporaries. Although acknowledging the difficulties in the text, he uses it as the basis for systematic investigation of ancient topography. It was much the most comprehensive and coherent ancient source available. Other ancient evidence is drawn in to clarify and extend Pausanias's account. Coherence is sought and, where found, used as the basis for suggesting a location or an identification. Modern maps, as well as the accounts of recent Western travelers, are consulted (rarely) as appropriate. Careful checking against the ground is essential to Leake's approach, whether this was done by simply viewing the land while traveling on public service (usually the case) or (more rarely) through more careful, instrumented survey. Leake could then "rectify" the ancient evidence and fix a location or establish an identity.

Leake was a thorough master of his methodology, but he did not invent it. Similar methods had been developed by generations of cartographers in compiling maps of Greece.[81] They were also followed by most geographers in the early nineteenth century. A notorious example is Leake's contemporary W. D. Cooley, also a fellow of the Royal Geographical Society. Cooley applied essentially the same methods as Leake to the elucidation of the geography of Africa, often preferring conclusions derived from applying his "principle of rectification" and "rule of reason" over firsthand modern field evidence, with some absurd results.[82] There was little alternative to adopting such methods of compilation and rectification when so much of the world remained inaccessible and unexplored, but the results of scientific survey were already becoming available in the transition phase of the early nineteenth century. At this time the topography of modern, let alone ancient, Greece was still as unknown as much of interior Africa. Little systematic exploration had taken place before Leake went there, and archaeological investigation had been limited. Pausanias's *Descriptio Graecae* filled many of the informational gaps in ancient Greek topography, thereby establishing its fundamental importance, not only to curious Western travelers but also to serious geographers, among whom Colonel Leake was so eminent.

Farnell's *Cults*

The Making and Breaking of
Pausanias in Victorian Archaeology
and Anthropology

Whate'er of heaven a seer hath told,
  In vision or fancy overbold,
Is naught to the Afric marigold . . .
    L. R. Farnell, "The Marigold
        of Morocco" (1927)

The twentieth century ended like its predecessor with a crescendo of
attention paid to Pausanias. The nineteenth-century surge was intimately bound up with thoroughgoing revision of classical studies. The challenge then was to accommodate the astonishing profusion of archaeological finds
and to evolve methodologies that would think Hellenism into a viable bond
between established philological scholarship and a new cultural history securely
founded on material remains. Specifically, three scholarly projects—Jane Harrison and M. de G. Verrall's guide to Attica, *Mythology and Monuments of
Ancient Athens* (1890, nicknamed the "Blue Jane"), J. G. Frazer's vast commentary on the *Description of Greece* (1898), and L. R. Farnell's eventually no
less vast synthesis of *Cults of the Greek States* (1896–1909)—represent scholarly initiatives that grew from broadly similar exposure to the same mid-
Victorian of waves of intellectual energy and institutional reform.[1] In the wake
of Empire, comparativist theorizing was responding to seemingly boundless and
seething vistas of human behavior planet-wide by casting Science ("scientific
naturalism") as heroic conqueror of the unruly riot of chaotic phenomena. The
giant monument of intellection was prized and desiderated—as "a vast symbol
of encyclopaedic knowledge."[2] Pages by the thousand would explain civilization's contents, wherein rival "Old Rat[ionalist]s" contrived to subdue all oth-

ernesses as so many evolutionary preludes, shortfalls, or mutant eccentricities.[3] Origins were all the rage: aetiology could redescribe any data, read right through all narratives, tell every informant and item just where they belonged in the order of things. But if our trio of "Loxbridge" classicists (i.e., from the London-Oxford-Cambridge triangle)[4] got into Pausanias in the same intellectual carriage, their futures took them on such different routes that it is hard to recover the outset from retrospect, whether ours or theirs. All three invested heavily in the buzz area of incipient anthropology, as they animated their training in Classics with cross-culturally oriented technologies of knowledge; but if each set out to relaunch Hellenism, as once more the fountainhead of authoritative knowledge about human culture, they went about it in dramatically different ways.

Frazer was bound for *The Golden Bough* (1st ed., 1890; 2d ed., 1900; 3d ed., 1906–1915), his ever-expanding universal mythic map of mankind; for just as universal an impact, collecting veneration and a knighthood; and for the felicitous *longue durée* of uninterrupted research in the bosom of the academy, free from obligation and luxuriant in facilitation. Not much less distracted, but in Newnham College, Cambridge, not Trinity, Harrison would spread her net ever wider until her *chef d'oeuvre, Themis* (1912), looked clean through Greece, to find the nature of the human animal in the murky pre-Olympian world of primitive violence barely masked by our patriarchal repression. Spat out by the (Olympian males of her) profession and aghast at (their) World War, she would eventually quit Greece for Russia in her head, burn her boats (and papers), and swap an equivocal position in the academy for Parisian bohemia—a heroine for certain modernist literati but, most of all, the complex myth of a modern heroine.[5] Farnell, by contrast, was dug in, for life. As we shall see, his tiny College was the world, and he had it taped and under control. But there were aliens across the Broad (in Balliol); someone had to do the dirty work if Greece was to be saved for the higher morality ("Greats," i.e., Literae Humaniores, the final part of the Oxford B.A. in Classics); and conservative Antiquity had made such heroes gods . . . In this chapter, I shall calibrate Farnell's launch into the politics of scholarship (I) against that of the others (II), then block out his take on their later divergence, using his intellectual and institutional entrenchment (III) to check out our own appropriation of Pausanias within contemporary theorizing/propagandizing of Classics and Hellenism (IV). Farnell is, mind, *anti*-hero.

I

when / Archaeology began to be scientific. Round about the year 1880 . . .
>   A. B. Cook, *The Rise and Progress of Classical Archaeology*
>   (1931:41–42)

The Mods don at Exeter College (teaching Honour Moderations, the first part of the Oxford B. A. program), Rev. H. F. Tozer, took the occasion of the first volume of the neophyte nation-wide journal *Classical Review* (*CR*) as an opportunity to let the combined audience of schoolteachers and university staff know that:

A complete edition of Pausanias is one of the greatest desiderata of modern classical scholarship. The importance which is attached at the present day to epigraphy, as one of the most trustworthy sources of our knowledge of the life of the ancients, and the rapidly increasing study of archaeology and classic art, together with the kindred subjects of mythology and legendary history, tend more and more to increase the estimation in which his *Description of Greece* is held. But the time for such an edition has not yet come. . . . When that period comes, the editor must be a many-sided man.[6]

A year later, Tozer's former pupil Lewis R. Farnell supplied the second volume of *CR* with a pithy note, "A misinterpreted passage in Pausanias," to save the city of Boura in Achaea, and the world, from the scandal of a (spurious) "undraped Eileithyia";[7] and a couple of years later, Farnell managed a brief speculation on ambrosial significance for the lilies attributed to Phidias's Zeus Olympios in Pausanias's description.[8] Between them, as we shall see, these thoughts capture in miniature the scholarly profile maintained through the bulk of his long career. To suggest what he was about, I must look back over the decade leading up to Tozer's fanfare, starting from 1878–79, when Walter Pater delivered the first lecture-course on Greek art ever given in the University of Oxford—featuring the Archaic art from Aegina and Pausanias's purplest passage, on the "Chest of Kypselos."[9]

Pater inspired the newly departed Trinity College, Dublin (TCD) and Oxford student Oscar Wilde to descend on Greece, in the company of Professor Mahaffy from Dublin and the leading Hellenophile and publisher George Macmillan. It was a tense time of reform and resistance. True, the Royal Commission (1877) charged with restructuring British higher education was not making much of a dent in the college bastions of Oxford and (their pride and joy) the unique coupling of text-based Classics in Mods with the (moral) philosophy and (ancient) history of Greats. Yet the astonishing discoveries of Schliemann at Troy and Mycenae (made, the saga had it, with trusty Pausanias in hand—and with everything crossed), matched by the prolific and publicity-sensitized parade of scientific practice put on by the German excavations at Olympia, had already made Archaeology a coming thing.[10] In Loxbridge, the cause already had a small but strategically placed band of determined proponents and something of a bridgehead in the Universities. But what was it to be, whose dream?

Charles Newton at the British Museum (BM) and Sidney Colvin at the Fitzwilliam in Cambridge were the masterminds. In 1877, Newton had taken his BM protégé Percy Gardner along to visit the sites just mentioned. When Macmillan came back from Greece with the idea of forming a "Hellenic Society," Gardner came up with the title for their magazine, *Journal of Hellenic Studies* (*JHS*), and he got down to work as editor, at the BM base, while Macmillan served in the twin roles of publisher and Hon. Sec. (for just the first fifty-five years).[11] The first volume was ready for 1880. Frazer and Harrison were founding members, both just graduated, with Frazer winning a Fellowship at his

College (with his thesis "Plato's Ideal Theory"), and doubtless enthused and recruited by Richard Jebb's high-profile promotion of the new Society in Cambridge;[12] and Harrison homing on Newton at the BM, ready and willing to train for museum and lecture work (and see what opportunities came her way). Farnell had just graduated too and, after the usual wobbles (including a cameo from rival examinee Oscar Wilde), won a Fellowship at *his* College, in 1880; somehow or other, he only became a member of the Hellenic Society in their second year, 1881. But, by 1886, he was up there on the Council and had contributed mightily to the cause, with his tripartite study "The Pergamene Frieze: its relation to literature and tradition."[13] Further orthodox art historical research into the stylistics of Greek sculpture would ensue: "On some works of the school of Scopas," "The Works of Pergamon and their influence," and (when *JHS* enlarged to its full-size format) "Some museums of northern Europe" and "Various works in the Pergamene style."[14]

To look at the first number of the *Hellenic Journal* (as it was soon dubbed) is to meet the powerhouse that meant to propel classical archaeology into a new British Classical Studies which could catch up with the market-leader of German *Altertumswissenschaft*. There on the first Council sit Mahaffy and Wilde (with J. A. Symonds for company). But Farnell's tutor in History, Henry Pelham (of *Pelham's Outlines of Roman History* fame),[15] is there as well, and this will cue us to a particular "tendency" in the cohort. Among the contingent of thirteen contributors to *JHS* 1 are the stars of Cambridge: Jebb, Colvin, and (besides the maverick A. W. Verrall) the newly arrived Charles Waldstein—in his mid-twenties and let loose on Cambridge via Newton through Colvin, soon to elicit a new Readership in Greek Archaeology for himself (1883).[16]

But Oxford—a particular slice of Oxford—is in on the act too. Newton's "An introductory address" (1880) had been the inaugural meeting's curtain-raiser and duly opens the journal. Keeper of Greek and Roman Antiquities at the BM since 1861 (after turning down the Chair of Greek in 1855),[17] Newton doubles as the newly installed first Yates Professor of Archaeology at University College London (UCL) (1880–88), bringing out the manifesto *Essays on Art and Archaeology* (1880), which cements his claim to father the cause: "the object which Archaeology would achieve if possible is not less than Exhibition of the Industry of all nations for all time," as he had put it in his Oxford lecture from 1850, "On the study of Archaeology"—the essay that leads out the 1880 collection.[18] Newton would be immortalized as impresario of the Mausoleum sculptures; but he had started out as a product of *Exeter College, Oxford*. The great(s) scholar Ingram Bywater, "bosom-friend" of Pater,[19] and the worst of teachers[20] Henry Tozer are two more Exon(ian)s on the team; and William Ramsay would cross from St. John's to join the Fellows of Exeter from 1882 (before moving along the Turl to Lincoln College as first Professor of Classical Archaeology in 1885–86). The little college founded to give Devon and Cornwall a share of the action had a total Fellowship *in single figures* (Rector plus nine in 1891).[21] Farnell tells how in 1879 Exeter compounded its investment in material culture by importing anthropology to its Fellowship, in the shape of Henry Moseley, "who had just returned from a scientific world-travel in *Challenger*

[and] brought us into touch with the dawning science of anthropology. . . . He seems to have given our society a predilection for anthropology."[22] R. R. Marett, Farnell's long-term colleague, eventual successor as Head of House, and principal obituarist, came to "incarnate" the subject (and to give the long line of Frazer's works fierce reviews!).[23] Archaeology *and* Anthropology: *not* a commonplace Oxford Common Room.

Back at the start of the 1880s, however, the novice Fellow Farnell showed no alarming potential in that direction. Rather, he assumed forever the College's hostility to the rigged system of language- and composition-based Classics bossed from Jowett's Balliol and was prompted to make a beeline for Germany, for a crash course in *Kunstgeschichte* (Art History) from the horse's mouth and for (eminently publishable) raids on museum holdings across Europe, pencil in hand. Already in 1880 and 1881, he was off to soak up Weimar culture, then get a grounding in Pergamene sculpture in Berlin (whence the *JHS* articles— "over-Teutonic in style").[24] By 1882, he was tagging along with Professor Percy Gardner and his brother Ernest, for a spell in Munich, memorable for one of the traumas of Farnell's bioscript: allowed a private key to the *Glyptothek,* he crashed out after a long day's solitary note-taking, and waking in the dark "imagined I had passed away into some mystic phantom-world where pale spectral forms were pointing at me and beckoning me with long outstretched arms."[25]

Through the 1880s, Farnell kept up his travels in search of Greek Archaeology-as-Art, visiting Pompeii and Rome with his predecessor as Rector of Exon, W. W. Jackson, and then Athens (whence the research on Skopas)[26] and central Greece with Pelham. When he struck off alone to salutiferous Epidauros, Farnell was drawn there by "the theatre constructed by Polukleitos the sculptor, the work that roused the sober Pausanias to an enthusiastic outburst: 'What architect could rival Polukleitos for harmony and beauty?' "[27]

These same years wrapped Farnell's life around the pair of Gardners: Percy, who had been at the same school as fellow "Citizen" Farnell (i.e., products of the City of London School), had (after a hiccup) followed his teacher J. R. Seeley to Christ's College, Cambridge, and hated Classics there: "they liked to see a man, as they put it, translate through a brick wall."[28] Exchanging sisters with schoolchum J. S. Reid (later Cambridge's first Professor of Ancient History), Gardner had jumped (out of still celibate Oxbridge) into the Department of Antiquities at the BM purely for the salary, with *no* previous interest in "memorials of the past" whatever, and would spend the 1870s cataloguing the Greek coins for R. S. Poole, the Keeper of Coins. In the fallout from the Royal Commission shake-up at Cambridge that hatched the new Classical Tripos with the specialism of Archaeology integrated into the structure of Part II (= "Section D"), Gardner was fetched in as first Disney Professor of Archaeology (1880).[29] Launching the *Hellenic Journal,* to which he allowed himself to contribute (with F. Imhoof-Blumer) a massive—and tripartite—"Numismatic Commentary on Pausanias,"[30] he hid his real obsession, theological reconciliation of *Faith and Conduct,*[31] but was soon lured over by Mark Pattison, Rector of Lincoln, to take *up* that fledgling Chair of Classical Archaeology there (1887) and to take *on* the establishment of Oxon Classics. With Arthur Evans and Farnell, Gardner straightaway rejigged the Oxford Philological Society to cut out "comparative and English philology" and stick to "classical subjects";[32] but thereafter he endeavored to introduce "specialist" archaeology into the Oxford syllabus, not as handmaiden to history but for the monuments' "style [and] intrinsic interest"— and (of course) lost.[33]

In praeposital retrospect,[34] Farnell thoroughly mythologized (and falsified) his side of Gardner's arrival next door at Lincoln College. Entitling chapter 15 of his memoirs "CANDIDATURE FOR OXFORD CHAIR OF ARCHAE-OLOGY," he makes Percy Gardner's election in 1887 "one of my happy failures in life." His ex-colleague at Exeter Ramsay (who back in 1879 had got the new Craven Fellowship for travel in Classical lands ahead of the graduand Farnell, who was busily cramming for the competition on a reading list extracted from Newton) had resigned the infant Chair after just a year or so, trooping off to head Humanity (Latin) in Aberdeen (escaping the lot of them?).[35] Farnell could not think of any plausible BM or Cantab (Cambridge) candidate, so he put in for the post and rustled up references:

> Soon after, I learned that Percy Gardner, at that time an official of the Coin Department of the British Museum . . . , had resolved to be a candidate . . . [T]he electors inevitably did the right thing in electing him. . . . Our relations became very cordial and intimate, growing into a life-long friendship. . . . Looking back . . . I can now discern my good fortune in missing that professorship. Had I been elected, I should not have been able to devote my whole life to the service of the College that I loved best, nor able to help the University at a time of need.[36]

Farnell will not mention it, but we happen to know that the (massive) reference exercise did not go to waste, for in the very next year, when old Newton vacated the Yates Chair in London, among the outside-bet applicants who were pipped by the successful candidate, Poole, was a certain L. R. Farnell.[37] Much further on too, Farnell kept among his Papers the record of another application for a Chair (Edinburgh 1903), where success would have returned him to the bosom of his ancestors[38] but torn him from that of his beloved College; no mention of this in the retrospect either (its terms are that *An* Oxonian *looks back!*). Instead, "in the summer of 1887, the wonderful summer of the Jubilee, I felt a certain chill of disappointment, and determined to throw it off by distant and arduous travel"—to Russia, Sweden, and northern Italy[39]—and "I covered more ground and did more work in these seven weeks than ever before or since. I had picked up a touch of ophthalmia. . . . I also inhaled some miasma. . . . I had a slight break-down. . . . I have no doubt the cause of it was mainly physical, the cumulative overstrain of a very restless travel. . . . I tried to shake off the effect by a twenty-five miles' walk. . . . Then . . . I collapsed. . . . A slight case of what is now called 'neurasthenia.' "[40] Farnell dug in, churning out the papers, serving as Lecturer and Tutor in Exeter (from 1883 and 1884 on), and making the role of College policeman (Subrector = disciplinary Dean) his very own (1883–93). And the epic rowing and canoeing exploits down German and adjacent riverways which he and his chums had dreamed up intensified from 1884 to reach their peak in 1888 (a teacher-contact wheedled [*this*] *Englishman's Adventures on German Rivers* out of him, as an English-language text for German school-girls to hate making sense of).[41] When Farnell recovered from the multiple shocks of 1887–88, we can understand how he "finally conceived the ambition ... to achieve an authoritative work that might fill the gap [on Greek religion in English scholarship, 'the main and the highest theme of the Greek art that I was minutely studying'—'as archaeology and philology were "equi-pollent" sources of evidence, I should be able to gratify my equal love of the literature and the art']. But aware of the vastness of the field, I decided to limit myself to a treatise on the public cults of Greece."[42]

He soon dropped his agreeably varied schedule of shuttling between student discipline, shooting rapids, and stylistic sorting of marbles. First he would "do" the rest of the Greek world: Sicily in 1890, then Asia Minor, and a final *peri-egesis* of the Peloponnese, in Pausanias's footsteps, from the Acropolis to Sparta, round wildest Arcadia, and on to his terminus at "the world's wonder, the Her-mes of Praxiteles, the statue that has no equal on the earth for beauty of form and surface" (found [?] in 1877 on the spot at Olympia just where Pausanias describes it). "Thus ended my ten years of archaeological exploration." It was all (going to have been, all along) a well-laid plan: "After my return from Greece in 1891, thinking that I had then acquired by original observation sufficient archaeological material, I at once began to get forward with the *Cults of the Greek States*."[43] And Farnell got a move on with getting his life together too: of a sudden, we find him honeymooning by canoe in 1893 and starting his twenty-year stint as Exeter's Senior Tutor (1893–1913). He would stay put, earn the salary to raise and keep a family,[44] and work up the *opus maius,* to see if it would land him a post, near the dreaming spires—or far far away. All the notes, and the precious photos, were safe in his study. He had the Art; now he would plug his skills into the unfolding and rumbustious world of Classical studies *with Archaeology.*

II

> I picture Athens crowded with eminent Oxford dons turned Pausan-
> iacs, each with a copy of Harrison and Verrall under one arm, and
> Schuchardt (is it?) under the other.
>   D. S. MacColl to E. Sellers in Athens, 18 January 1891[45]

Meantime, Frazer had caught the tide and begun work towards a new translation of Pausanias for the use of George Macmillan and other tourists (negotiations with the press opened in 1884).[46] He was soon diverted from the task, switching on to Robertson Smith's "anthropological" theorizing, getting married, and plunging into Comparative Religion's "dark wood of savage superstition": the proofs of his *Golden Bough* were with Macmillan when he headed off to visit Greece for the first time in 1890.[47] The *Pausanias* would eventually come out in six volumes, 3,000 pages plus and a decade over deadline, in 1898, distended by lavish commentary to accompany the translation. The work still posed as a travelers' *vade mecum* round Pausanias's circuit, including items foreign to Pausanias's *Guide* but also recording Frazer's own trip in diary form and parading portentous passages of scenic description for the armchair (soon gathered for a spin-off [money-spinning? -recouping?] compilation-volume of 1900).[48] Most of Frazer's information stands as echt Classical scholarship of the day, doubtless pedestrian on art history and generally short of archaeological grip,[49] but alive to Pausanias's vast stores of information about ancient cult and with the nerve to write up Hellenism into the aether. With (e.g.) four assorted notes in the second *CR* and no textual-critical ability or pretensions, Frazer had got in on the ?archaeology? scene in the early days—in the large sense of the jumbled realm(s) of art history–monuments–numismatics–epigraphy–topography–myth–religion–folklore–cultural history.[50] His *Pausanias* got a fine reception from the management:

> [C]ompared with [Harrison and Verrall 1890] Mr. Frazer's shows far greater solidity of judgement, power of weighing evidence, breadth of view . . . There is something very impressive and manly in the way in which Mr. Frazer deals with the hundred bitter controversies as to topography, art and antiquities in Greece . . . , a cold and severe air to his work.[51]

Frazer of Trinity was an asset, still, for all that "Mr. Frazer's *tendo Achillis* [exposed him] at his weakest when dealing with works of art."[52] By the time the commentary was done, however, its author's signature had come to signify fame in the hyperinflating stakes of *Anthropology,* and Pausanias was, first and foremost, à quarry for juicy data demanding assignment to their rightful place in the grand(iose) picture of the evolutionary course of human history from savagery to civilization. The new century's Classics, however, would opt out; it became less mad for totemism, taboo, Aborigines, and aboriginal savagery by the academic year, as the Classical Association (established 1903) rallied round to stave off the forces of darkness and save civilization—their subject.[53]

By the time that Frazer got round to taking ship to explore Greece for his *Pausanias,* Macmillan had found a winning team prepared to deliver on a contract, like true professionals, like anyone short of clout. Frazer took to Athens the brand-new Macmillan travel guide just produced under the direction of Jane Harrison (1890). Verrall's wife, Margaret, turned out a translation of the tour of Attica in Pausanias's Book I, cutting all the "digressions" (mostly historical narratives); Harrison wrote both the long introductory essay and the very substantial "Archaeological commentary" on each of the sections presented.[54] The *Blue Jane* was a working-book, the commercial success that Frazer would not (could not) turn out: clear structure and dotty illustration somehow managed to outweigh all the untranslated quotes and impenetrable erudition. The archaeological establishment welcomed the guide—just the ticket for all the Hellenophile and classical visitors they were drumming up with the Society for the Promotion of Hellenic Studies and the British School at Athens (BSA): "It is no exaggeration," promised the *JHS* reviewer, "to say that this book is the most important archaeological publication that has appeared in England for some time."[55]

On the one hand, the London-based Harrison had become a high-profile expert on Greek mythography, out in Greece most summers and well known both to the Hellenic Society stable and to real excavators on site, a striking lecturer and contributor of scholarly articles, with a particularly handy investment in the sideline specialism of the images on lowly Greek ceramics.[56] On the other hand, she had, of course, no university post and would need to break new ground to land one. Runner-up for the Yates Chair at UCL (to the BM's numismatist Poole) in 1888, she was off that same year researching for *Mythology and Monuments* with Dörpfeld, Schliemann's lieutenant and exemplary excavator of Olympia;[57] and Poole's successor (in 1896) would be, not Harrison, but Ernest Gardner, rather handily placed, you could say, as Percy's brother, and whose institutional authority as Director of the BSA (1887–95) she *could not* match.[58] By this time, Gardner minor was working toward his *Ancient Athens*:[59] an in-house challenge for the *Blue Jane*. At one level or another, the brew of "anthropological" rant and radicalism Harrison lent, put, and lost her name to was making her the perfect candidate for round rejection by hordes of classical men, and she was back with her society of women at Newnham (1898), teaching girls Archaeology for the Cambridge Tripos, dreaming up an outrage, big-time: *Prolegomena to the Study of Greek Religion* (1903).

Back at the end of the 1880s, as Beard conclusively demonstrates,[60] Harrison's strain of weirdness made her no more of an outlaw than Frazer's made of him; and Percy Gardner and associates, determined to knit art, archaeology, and the whole range of cultural-material disciplines into the portfolio of Hellenism, as the legit business of an integrated Classics, had no call to distance or disown the Cambridge pair, yet embrace the emergent Farnell—even now that he was sloughing his "Teutonic" novitiate and stepping out as the well-prepared and uniquely trained would-be practitioner of the trendy science of Comparative Religion.

It would be easy to pick out both moments in Frazer's *Pausanias* that shout "totemism" and moments that proclaim "Winckelmann" and show the work as bridge between the thought-worlds of his past and his future. So too we can pick out the emphasized slogan *"ritual practice misunderstood"* or, say, the menacing position statement "The *nomina numina* method I have utterly discarded" from Harrison's preface[61] if we want to accentuate her nascent dogmatism and pugnacity. Or, contrariwise, we can work through her treatment of variant stories, such as those around Theseus, and applaud her scholarly recognition of the difficulties presented by "the 'tangled jungle' of classic polytheism":[62] listing the literary sources, as between Apollodorus's supposed second century B.C. and Pausanias's second century A.D., she insists that "were these our only authorities, it would be impossible to state that their exploits were matters of popular faith in the fifth century B.C. Fortunately, art comes to our aid"; that any *Dictionary of Myth* summary always "wholly neglects the consideration of the local form of the myth and accepts without question the version based on Attic tragedy"; that "it is clear that Pausanias heard from the local priesthood an account very different from that which, through the drama of Euripides, had become canonical."[63] Sense and, surely, sanity; and just what reading Pausanias was *about,* for the Classics of Newton and Gardner (and Farnell).

The Farnell of *Cults* stepped before his public meticulously rehearsed.[64] A "compendious account" was lacking, to extricate Greek Religion from confusion with Myth. In *Cambridge* (he name-dropped), a "new interest in Greek ritual and myth" was in inspirational evidence: Farnell could for his part decoct from the latest *scientific* anthropology a higher application to the comparative study of religion. His aim was to "giv[e] a complete account of the names and ideas that were attached, and of the ceremonies that were consecrated, by the Greek states to their chief divinities." The three volumes announced (vols. 1–2 ready; vol. 3 had to wait until 1909) work down from "the Zeus-cult," through "the worships of Hera, Athena, Artemis, and Aphrodite [& c.]": "it is natural to study the cults of Zeus and Hera side by side, and . . . convenient to group the other goddesses with Hera in order to appreciate their traits of affinity and points of contrast."[65] Each deity is given both "literary" and "archaeological" chapters, aiming "to enumerate all the cult-monuments, so far as anything definite is known about them; this is not so difficult a task, as these are comparatively few." By contrast, in "the chapters on the ideal types of each divinity my task has been mainly one of selection; I have tried to confine myself to those of which my studies in the various museums and collections of Europe have given me personal knowledge" (plus a stock of photos). A table of *"Schriftquellen"* follows each "cult," listing in full the quotations from Classical texts and inscriptions that were cut and pasted to make the narrative account (the design-feature that really sold *Cults* to me: see my n.1).

The Introduction proceeds with a review of relevant theory for window dressing; "origins" are "put aside":

> In dealing with so complicated a phenomenon as the religion of a people, it is surely advisable to consider separately and first the actual facts, the actual beliefs in the age of which we have history, rather than the prehistoric germ from which they arose.[66]

German mythologists had had this all wrong. But Farnell has a much more exalted goal before him: "the twofold question, what was the average meaning of the religion for the nation, and what ideal expression did it occasionally receive . . . [T]he art and literature were not mere records of the religion; they were forces that directly or indirectly assisted its growth." He will show us how Homer's legacy was "a higher and clearer religious view . . . but when Greek art developed it became a truer record of the national and popular belief than the literature." The major arts exerted "their refining influence," for "the gross and barbarous elements in the myths and lower folklore intrude themselves but rarely even into vase-painting, the lowest of all the Greek arts of design, and scarcely at all into monumental sculpture and painting. These dealt with the highest forms of Olympian religion."

The image is an assured fusion of tried expertise and trusty uplift with new-wave proto-"science." Force a Life-Work's imposing scale onto the solemn acclamation of Hellenic glory as he might (the final span of five volumes was completed in 1909, but only by a feat of "literary superfetation," when he reserved *Greek Hero Cults* for a later occasion [1921]);[67] and ham up the leap into anthropology as he pleased: still it takes just the merest glance through one short review he wrote in late 1887 to find that Farnell had the whole enterprise staked out in advance, fully formed even before he got it started. For the second year of *CR,* he contributed a report on (the first installment of) W. Roscher's *Ausfürliches Lexikon der griechischen und römischen Mythologie.*[68] His appraisal of this vast collectively produced work of reference—"an equal statement of the literary and monumental evidence and a complete account of the facts of the myths and cults"—bemoans the obvious lack of a single coordinating control and criticizes both excess in "reducing to a logical unity or order the manifold characteristics" of the Greek gods and shortfall in treatment of "the imaginative aspect." He extracts and analyzes the formulaic pattern normally followed by each entry:

- the original and essential conception of the divinity
- local beliefs and centers of worship
- myths in which the divinity figures
- account of the monuments

For content, Farnell chooses to air early versions of his views on a series of gods—Aphrodite, Apollo, Artemis, Asclepios, Athene, Dionysos, Giants, Hades, and Hekate. He makes a point too of both trotting out references to his *Hellenic Journal* papers on "high art" (a domain left in the cold by Roscher's *Lexikon*) and pressing home references to Pausanias, as the prime source for information about Greek cults.

Of course *Cults* was to be a Titanic labor, and Farnell was no slouch, but he never wavered from complete faith in (t)his project.[69] What offended him in *Roscher,* and the fact that it offended him, catalyzed the whole thrust of his scholarship: helped make him *Farnell*. No one could say he did not pitch in dry-eyed or claim that they were not warned:

> It has been my object to restrict myself as far as possible to the statement of the facts, and not to wander too far into the region of hypothesis and controversy. One's work thus incurs the risk of a dryness and coldness of tone; and the risk is all the greater because, while Greek mythology was passionate and picturesque, Greek religion was, on the whole, sober and sane. An exposition of it may be of great value for the purposes of literature; but for the purposes of science it is best to exhibit the facts, as far as possible, in a dry light.[70]

Just put this beside Frazer's (standard, if jazzed-up) pen-portrait of Pausanias:

> In the writings of Pausanias we certainly miss . . . warmth and colour. . . . His book is too much a mere catalogue of antiquities, the dry bones of knowledge unquickened by the breath of imagination. Yet his very defects have their compensating advantages. If he lacked imagination he was the less likely to

yield to that temptation of distorting and discolouring the facts to which men of bright fancy are peculiarly exposed, of whom it has been well said that they are like the angels who veil their faces with their wings.[71]

Today we acknowledge no "compensatory" trade-off between "dry style" and "unmediating reportage," whether in Pausanias or in the rhetoric of any other Plain Man.[72] We need not play blind to the drive (commitment, aggression, passion) masked by Farnell's level, and level*ing,* deployment of writerly power/knowledge. In a nutshell, he disciplined and drilled his work, first, to show that "Greek religion was, on the whole, sober and sane" and, second, *because* that was the case. Only take a look at those indexes to *Cults,* screamingly severe with their stark lists of the chief gods; those unalleviated pages with their long columns of sub-head "cult epithets": the whole point is to rivet Greek religion to *these* "merely barren, mere names"; to demonstrate their indispensability to serious scholarship, to scholarly seriousness;[73] and to finesse the "hypothesis and controversy" of all-comers, by restricting the text to the (exhaustive) cataloguing of local cult nomenclature and accompanying ceremony, in closest paraphrase of the ancient sources. Naturally, Pausanias is the compiler's biggest single resource for excerpting attested "facts" about Greek religion. Pausanias's style of brief and unproblematized observations models for a "scientistic" detail-*cult,* a matter-of-factness that projects taut objectivism. Deliberately cultivated scholiastic aridity powers a strenuous regime of intellectual hygiene and wards off, keeps at bay, all threats to the assured hierarchies of the universe: high above low, Hellenic over barbarian. This way, idealizing Greek Art and Literature are the trump cards. They import moral transcendence in the panhellenic register and sublate the egregious heroism of "paragons of academic virtue who, with intellects purged of all subjective failings, claim communion with *a higher order of reality.*"[74] They are to be segregated from the quaint "popular" customs that bond societies to localities. They belong in separate chapters. Everything we can know of Greece must be foil to the pure core of culture—between Pindar and Euripides. Because earlier is inferential and later is lower, both are at a discount: "There is no inner reform traceable in Hellenic religion after the fifth century [B.C.]."[75] Just as Homer troubles the interdiction on "prehistorical" speculation on Origins, so Pausanias and the rest of the testimonia provided by "post-Classical" materials must somehow elude the taint of postlapsarian deviance. Indeed a heroic challenge, then and now: "a severe ordering of our methods is most imperative."[76]

III

Archaeology has always seemed to me a vast sea, at present almost without a shore, and archaeological studies to be in a position which does not make them easy or profitable to teach.
                    J. P. Postgate to E. Sellers, 2 March 1889[77]

L. R. Farnell, Exon: matriculated 1874, B.A. 1878, Fellow 1880–1913, M.A 1881, Subrector ("those long ten years of hard service")[78] and Lecturer 1883–

93, Tutor 1884–93, Senior Tutor 1893–1913, D.Litt. 1901, twenty-fourth Rector 1913–28, Honorary Fellow 1928–34. Fifty-four years at the College = "private greatness," combining "a surprising austerity and a surprising warmth"; "travelled, well-informed, genial, the somewhat arid lecturer would completely unbend in his home."[79] College parties—whether boaties or Sylvia and her cello—brought intramural success, after a dodgy start as "something of a martinet" of a Subrector, this "very manly man . . . tough as whipcord, though of light build,"[80] needed to get tough in Exeter at just one critical juncture: as the demanding 600th anniversary loomed, he had seventy-five-year-old Jackson step down as "Ruggins" (emphasizing his right to run College by organizing a *Bibliography of the Fellows* [1914]).[81] Getting the birthday-do done was a doddle—but fate at once dreamed up the ordeal of the Great War ("The memories of last term are as a golden vista seen across a dark and perilous flood").[82] The Rector came through with flying colors, penning for the Subrector hero's Victoria Cross some rousing war poetry and an obit to match.[83] Only the charge that he had conspired to bring down "the college system" ever queered his home pitch. "For him the College was the centre of the Universe. It is easy to scoff at the notion."[84]

The parallel lines of Farnell's University academic and administrative careers tie in with the Exeter front with fearful symmetry: the Senior Tutor won the D.Litt. (1901),[85] a University Lectureship in Classical Archaeology (1903–1914), and publication of *The Evolution of Religion* (in 1905), as well as *Cults*. Abortive efforts to introduce (Natural and) Comparative Religion into Oxford as a discipline climaxed in his appointment as first Wilde Lecturer in the subject (1908). But *The Higher Aspects of Greek Religion* (published 1912) twinned with elevation to Head of House (and Fellow of the British Academy [FBA] 1916); so did *Attributes of God* (published 1924), written by "the Iron Vice-Chancellor" in the third and last year of his term of office as "a refreshing nepenthe" (1920–22).[86] Between retirement and death (1928, 1934), there was exactly enough time for his labor of love, *Pindar* (1930–32), and his *Oxonian* retrospect (1934)—for this neat-lived man "finished this book on the evening of March 21st . . . , told [his wife] of his happiness in having been able to complete his work," and died on 28 March.[87]

So far as Farnell impinged on Oxford beyond Exeter, it was as the memorable "banning" V-C (Vice-Chancellor, the chief administrator of the University).[88] Getting the University into shape after the War (back- or forward) was a specially tricky challenge calling for tact and liaison skills. "Farnell was a stubborn man. Some thought him pig-headed. He had certainly a talent for doing the right thing the wrong way."[89] He tried to ban the O.U. Labour Club, then had to ban the Conservatives too, for parity (commuted to one meeting *per annum*); stopped lectures by Bertrand Russell and a public meeting to be addressed by Marie Stopes on "the sex-problem" (birth control); leaned on a French Club production of Molière (Bloodbath!); scotched a toffs' Oxford versus Cambridge aeroplane race; tried to put cafés (teashops) out of bounds, and dances in Town;[90] and (the scandal!) had one Arthur E. C. Reade, 1920 Worcester, sent down for publishing a "Red Terror" magazine (this victim of the "old brute" surmised in his last number that it could not be "feeble Farnell's" doing, but the Chancellor's, and in a trice the *"Free Oxford* affair" was all over the *Times*); a nasty plot to stop the V-C getting the last year of the usual term of office then stained our wounded Cicero's big moment.[91]

But Farnell had also made other bad moves: drilling an Afrikaaner Rhodes Scholar–elect on the politically correct position to adopt on Empire, and coming across, at least, as racially prejudiced against the presence of Indian students in Oxford.[92] *The* Farnell anecdote is linked to this: "Toothpowder plot: Professor Hoaxed" (1922). A box of chocolates is anonymously sent the wicked V-C as a student jape but its contents then analyzed (by Professor Soddy, Exon) as "poison" (ground glass). The student confesses: it wasn't arsenic powder (as in a murder case hot in the headlines), but "Old Dutch Cleanser" (apparently made of volcanic glass, and for *false* teeth). Rumor knew it was an anarchist; "an Indian criminal"; or a Central African witch doctor—perhaps a "ploughed" or "progged" Rhodes Scholar? Should the V-C watch out for "an assegai at the next Encaenia"?[93] "Possibly he was a bit of a disciplinarian," confided the new Rector to the College, on Farnell's retirement. "He was not afraid to say no. But he fought without bitterness and was a good loser."[94] R. M. Dawkins (Fellow of Exeter) liked to sum up *this* Olympian Farnell—"an erudite scholar of excellent manners, but wanting in humour"—as delightfully short on self-awareness, "notably when he referred to his book *The Attributes of God,* as 'my attributes.' "[95] Which must forcefully remind us that our chief source for Farnell is the retrospect of a bruised administrator and figurehead. This former Head of House and Vice-Chancellor had scores to settle with the world, and his nineteenth-century past must, to an extent, be re-told to lead up to his vindication at the point where it mattered.

His longevity also helped obituarists to burnish the old boy's memory: "We shall no longer 'see what Farnell thinks about it' when dealing with any of a wide range of difficulties."[96] But still rancor invades even this familiar Oxonian haze: "There was something of antiseptic cleanness in his thought, fatal to the swarming bacteria of absurdity and crudeness, and making it not rash to foretell that what he wrote will live when much that was for a time more popular has been forgotten."[97] If a target is wanted, who else could this be but *J. E. Harrison?* Through citation of Nestorian Gilbert Murray paraded on the first page of Stewart's preface, Harrison's "biographer" makes sure we see Farnell as Harrison's dark other, gratuitously contrasting with her achievements "the five learned volumes of L. R. Farnell [which] now seem to belong to the Dark Ages," on the first page.[98]

Retired Farnell knew he had been right to help block the (premature) admission of women to Oxford back when *Cults* first entered the world (1896); he could "discern how the writings of the gifted Jane Harrison, the leading woman scholar of the time, were marred by the spirit of feminist propaganda."[99] Women earned Oxford in the War (whereat Harrison quit), and this V-C's tenure (and problems) began with the tasks of matriculating Oxford's first women students, a thousand in the morning, and the same afternoon of awarding the first ever Oxon. degrees to women.[100] As well as coping with all the demobs, Farnell had the invention of a regimen for undergradu*ettes* on his plate. In his academic persona (in fact at the British Academy), he had just been preaching methodology in myth studies, deploring how "the efforts of trained thinkers to establish critical and sane methods" had been ruined by tosh put out recently (i.e., when the men had a war on): "The whole field . . . appears to be especially alluring to the feminine mind."[101] By then, perhaps, the two major spats Farnell had had with Harrison were a world (war) away (and she was lost to Russia-n). In their time, however, their swapped reviews had seethed with energetic spleen: *Themis* versus *Higher Aspects* in 1912, when both scholars had severed their roots in Classical Archaeology; and *Prolegomena* versus *Evolution of Religion* in 1903–1905, when J. E. H. still launched her anthropological flights from her specialist base in Classical mythography, but L. R. F. was already flirting with *his* full-blown general "Anthropology" (a.k.a. Natural and Comparative Religion).[102] In both rounds Farnell went after the matriliny and gynaecocracy postulated by Harrison for the Ur-culture of the "Eniautos-Daimon, who lies behind each and every particular god," before the macho Hellenes of history suppressed the pre-conscious "*durée,* life," and installed their Olympian cults.[103] He damned all "sociological hypotheses concerning the position of women" (i.e., primeval matriarchy).[104] He scolds her "dogmatism," scolds her "two dominant prejudices—the prejudice against the personal individual God and the matriarchal prejudice," scolds her scolding:

> She scold[s] . . . the "Olympian" and the poets and artists who glorified him: she scolds Homer . . . ; she scolds Pindar . . . ; and she scolds Praxiteles . . . We do not find in *Themis* the great tradition of Cambridge scholarship.[105]

Years before, Harrison had written off feeble Farnell for good (to Murray, in correspondence):

> Those two volumes [*Cults,* vols. 1–2] are just *nil* & now I shall have to try & be kind & Xian just because woe is me—I have the fear of you before my eyes. . . . If you say Farnell is "important" I should send for my neo-lithic club—he is essentially insignificant.

> I didn't think it was possible for him to grow duller but with academic officials all things are possible.[106]

For the pair of them, more was at stake than intellectual rift or personal-political style war: their standing and good name, their prospects and life course.[107] For Classics, their Titanomachy (melo)dramatizes the ongoing struggle to locate the thrust of the discipline by finding its borders. The revalorization of Hellenism after the Romans under way as the twentieth century ended was another round in the perpetual negotiation between our institutional practices and our investment in them. As Beard has theorized,[108] Classical Archaeology (in the large sense) names the no-man's-land between the discipline and the interdisciplinary, where the point of our work is on the line. ⁊Pausanias⁊ stands for this question of cultural identity, for Hellenism and for Hellenists. In "traversing all that is Hellenic alike" (πάντα ὁμοίως ἐπεξιόντα τὰ Ἑλληνικά [1.26.4]), Pausanias invites us to join him in the quest to situate, in relation to the history of precedents and predecessors, our own determination of what we mean to see *as* "Greek—*all this, this* totalization."[109]

IV

> The record we have to read is the record of what we have lost.
>
> J. E. Harrison and M. de G. Verrall, *Mythology and Monuments of Ancient Athens* (1890: xi)

> What we think about Greek religion affects what we think about everything else.
>
> J. E. Harrison, *Themis* (1928: xxii)

Pausanias has appeared in no literature course in Classics. His contribution to Hellenism is as tour guide, for travelers *en grand seigneur* and in packages, for lecture-room and armchair imaginations. To the Glory of *his* Greece, Pausanias circuits us from Athens to Sparta, Olympia, and on home to Delphi; he models and massages how we are to see Greece, in all its historicality. But his audience is, all too clearly, coming late to the panorama and, like all Hellenists, blotting out the centuries between *classicizing* Now and the *classical* Then. So rich are the pickings, if we disregard his *narration* and cream off his *compilation!* So many of our data for *Altertumswissenschaft* are in Pausanias's gift, most of all for *Kunstgeschichte*—and yet *not one* item can but be framed by the *textual* economy of the *Description*. Each classic lemma, from a late twentieth-century perspective, signifies through relations with neighbors, nestles within larger thematic plotting. These are neither entries in a catalogue nor notes toward preparing one; rather, they are vectors of narrative, and Pausanias's Greece is, "more than an enumeration, . . . an *experience,* a journey into identity."[110] How, then, did it matter neither to Pater's inaugural party-piece of *epideixis* on the "Chest of Kupselos" nor to Farnell's acclamatory halt to his travels before the "Hermes of Praxiteles" that the pre-Classical box and the masterpiece of Greek sculpture share the same textual scenario of Pausanias's Olympia: the essay of 1,789 words on the heirloom covered with antique writing dominates the book and presents a self-reflexive image of Pausanian interpretivity (5.17.5–19); whereas "the statue that has no equal on the earth" is appended in a throwaway "afterwash of later features in the Heraeum"—in just *ten* subordinated *words* (5.17.3)?[111]

An answer might find, in traditional processing of Pausanias's text into "lexicographical" formats such as Farnell's *Cults,* a good part of the secret menace for Hellenizing Classics represented by the current revision of *Roman Pausanias. What we think about Pausanias affects what we think about every*thing else to do with Ancient Greece. With the *Description*, the hostility to the quest for Origins which *our* cultural history of Classical Greece shares with Farnell's—"neither survival nor prefiguration"—runs into the intransigent fact that Pausanias is "describing the cults and sanctuaries *still in existence in Greece* *in his day,* together with their historical background and the myths attached to them." Swapping a functionalist for an evolutionary paradigm for understanding the *Cults of the Greek States* makes no difference to this basic condition of Hellenism as retrospect and reconstruction from the perspective of Roman Greece.[112]

Moreover, our current "Ways of Approaching the Pantheon"[113] are just as vulnerable to the same Pausanian crisis of historicality as the nineteenth-century paradigms we have demolished. To catalogue the Greek gods as Farnell did, from Zeus and his wife (women) on down through the deities, providing each god with a "history" and "geography" dictionary-fashion, is indeed to miss and destroy (and lack) "the inherent requirements of an organized system," and so to obscure the functioning in each city of a "symbolic system with its own peculiar logic and coherence." But there is no possibility of decocting from the accounts of the cultic heritage that Pausanias wrote up for his Roman provincial cities anything like "a rigorously logical ensemble" for each town (or, rather, territory).[114] Rather, Pausanias's own Hellenism informs a narrative predicated on a classicism constructed out of "survival" and "prefiguration."

Imagin*ative* travel on a post-Classical tour of (extant) Graeco-Roman antiquities affords only the possibility of imagin*ary* travel through the (lost) post-savage cityscapes of Classical Greece. Though the analytical mode of sociological idealization of Functional System has scotched that of lexical idealization of hierarchic procession, there is no denying the underlying continuity in classicizing Classics of nostalgia for heroized loss. When Farnell cultivated the differences within Greek cults to show how much there was about Greek culture that even the exhaustive devotions of the ultraspecialist scholar (L.R.F.) could know so little about, the name of the game was to exploit "archaeology" for the devotions of an integrated Classics at the shrine of the "Olympian" civilization imagined for the fifth century, between Pindar and Euripides; comparativism was harnessed to elevate, not to relativize, Hellenism.[115] When Harrison cultivated the untidy and untidiable differences within ?Greek? cults, her wild speculations in the visual periphery and along the byways of Pausanias's synthesis tilted at the *rigging* of the game: why should some "Greeks," however congratulated since, be so absolutely a cut above the rest?[116]

> Pausanias lets out quite unconsciously a good part of the secret.
> J. E. Harrison and M. de G. Verrall, *Mythology and Monuments of*
> *Ancient Athens* (1890: clii)

> *Floreat Exon! Floreat Oxon!*
> L. R. Farnell, *An Oxonian Looks Back* (1934: 344, finale)

"Pausanias in Petticoats,"
or *The Blue Jane*

Microcosmographia Academica

The academic wrangles of earlier generations are always liable to provoke our scorn. It is hard to take seriously the bitter controversies that preoccupied our predecessors, the scholarly battles long ago won and lost: the Peace of Kallias, the Terminal Date of Caesar's Command, the "Greekness" of Linear B. . . . It is hard not to mock the overinvestment of energy and emotion on all sides of these debates, by winners as much as losers. Unfairly perhaps, the mavericks who strenuously backed the wrong side often seem more appealing than those whom time has proved right (Richard Jebb and his glorious conviction that the ruins of Mycenae were medieval is easily more engaging than the repulsive Schliemann with his Tomb of Agamemnon). More often than not, of course, it turns out not to have been a question of winning or losing at all: the controversies are not settled, they just fade away. No one has ever conclusively demonstrated whether or not Kallias did make a "peace" with the Persians; nor has anyone successfully unscrambled the relationship between Athenian ceramics and precious metals. But these problems have outlived their usefulness, and we have left them behind.

Throughout the nineteenth century, the text of Pausanias (in particular, the chapters on Athens in Book I) was a breeding ground for just such (long-lost) disputes. The identity of the gate (Dipylon or Piraeic?) through which he entered the city and so—for this is what hung on it—how the buildings around the Agora were arranged, sparked a major controversy that did not survive the twentieth-century American excavations of the site; for these literally unearthed the answer (and, incidentally, proved almost every competing theory wrong).[1] The so-called Enneacrunus episode, on the other hand, was never entirely resolved—but had faded to oblivion by the end of the twentieth century.

This problem was as stark as it now seems trivial. Pausanias mentions the famous Pisistratid Fountain (with its nine spouts, hence the name) in the course of his trip around the Agora, "near" (πλησίον) the Odeum (1.14.1). Thucydides, by contrast, seems to locate it nowhere near the Agora at all, but south of the Acropolis in what he judged to be the oldest settlement area of Athens, making it identical with the spring Kallirhoe in the bed of the river Ilissus (Thucydides 2.15). For generation after generation, this conflict of evidence engaged some of the best brains of the Western world; it claimed appendices to itself; it guided excavation programs; it was quite simply "the most important point in Athens for the elucidation of the topography of Pausanias."[2] If you assumed (as most did) that Thucydides could not be wrong, then was Pausanias simply digressing in his account of the Agora? Had he misidentified some other fountain there as the Pisistratid monument? Or was there a confusion in the manuscript tradition? Alternatively, was it possible to reconcile the two versions—locating the Ennea-crunus so that it would (almost) match up with both Thucydides's and Pausa-nias's accounts? Some participants were confident that they had got the answer ("now at last the 'Enneakrounos Episode' may be laid to sleep in peace," crowed Jane Harrison, prematurely, in 1906);[3] others would lovingly rehearse all the arguments but ultimately opt for a judicious "don't know" ("Each of the three theories has found advocates whose opinions are entitled to the highest respect, and it is certainly open to any one to hold any of the three without the possibility of a dogmatic assertion that he is wrong" was Ernest Gardner's magisterial way of having his cake and eating it).[4] Today it is largely the sheer unanswerability of the question—to that extent we are on Gardner's side—that has taken it right off *our* intellectual map.[5]

Yet, for all our derision, there are wider issues at stake in such apparently narrow disputes. Scratch their surface, and—more often than not—you will quickly find much more significant controversies of theory, method, and ap-proach lurking just underneath.[6] Hence, of course, the enormous amount of emotional and scholarly energy poured into questions that seem, at first sight, so trivial. In the case of Pausanias, the "Enneacrunus episode" was not only a linchpin for a whole series of other topographical inferences[7] but a crucial testing ground for any theory of how the "Periegete" was to be read, under whose authority, and within what disciplinary framework.

Obviously it reflected the burning issue (fueled by Wilamowitz and his successors) of the authenticity of Pausanias's journey:[8] how far could you re-construct the details of his trip from his text? Do digressions (and "misplace-ments" of famous monuments) support the idea that Pausanias's *Periegesis* was very much a desk job? Or do they merely hint at an author with an idio-syncratic itinerary? ("Pausanias was staying with friends near the Ilissus, and went home to lunch," as Jane Harrison satirized one explanation for the intru-sion of the fountain into his tour round the Agora).[9] But the Enneacrunus ep-isode also plugged into topical questions about disciplinary boundaries within Classics and the role of Archaeology. Was Pausanias to be read entirely within the confines of traditional philology, his oddities ascribed to a jumbling of the manuscript leaves and the old standby of inaccurate excerption from his sources? Or could he be properly understood only against the background of the material culture and topography of Greece? Was Pausanias Book I inseparable from the physical remains of Athens, an archaeologist's (rather than a philologist's) text?

Pausanias *der Perieget*

Pausanias was high up on the academic agenda for much of the nineteenth century, and particularly for its last two decades or so. The *Periegesis* lay at the center of a whole stream of books and articles, on a scale unparalleled even in the "rediscovery" of Pausanias in the late twentieth century. Between W. M. Leake's *Topography of Athens* of 1821 (which was in essence a translation of "relevant" passages of Pausanias Book I, with an extended commentary)[10] and J. G. Frazer's six-volume blockbuster at the end of the century (1898), you find not only a kaleidoscope of editions, translations, commentaries, and studies coming out of Germany, France, and Britain[11] but also some of the most imaginatively cranky contributions to scholarship that there have ever been. Pride of place here must go to Imhoof-Blumer and (Percy) Gardner's *Numismatic Commentary on Pausanias,* separately issued in the late 1880s as a monograph after a three-part serialization in the fledgling *Journal of Hellenic Studies.*[12] It was exactly (as mad) as its title suggests: a complete collection of coin types which appeared to show statues that happened to be mentioned by Pausanias. "The importance of the work cannot be doubted" was the authors' bland and reassuring opening. Those of us who *have* doubted suspect a desperate attempt to get numismatics in on the Pausanian boom (if not a cynical ploy for filling up the new journal with some lengthy copy).[13]

The main factors that lay behind this enthusiasm for Pausanias are clear enough. First was tourism—or, more precisely, the gradual opening up of Greece to the (more or less) academic visitor, keen to explore the material culture of Classical lands firsthand and at the same time experience the exotic charm of a country that was in the ideal state of being still romantic but was no longer particularly dangerous.[14] From the 1870s on, Athens and the Peloponnese was almost uncomfortably full of Euro-dons and their friends (stalwart supporters of the new archaeological schools in Athens, eager visitors to the ever increasing numbers of excavations[15]—but at the same time enjoying the donkey rides, the nights under canvas, the peasant hospitality, and the gratifying *frisson* of encounters with the Other). In the spring of 1886, for example, John Edwin Sandys (and Mrs.) set out for *"An Easter Vacation in Greece,"* "undeterred" (as he is careful to boast in his account of the trip) "by rumours of impending war between Greece and Turkey": across the channel, train to Marseilles, steamer to Athens, followed by just under a month doing the northern Peloponnese, Delphi, Olympia (where he decides that the statues are much better seen in the Cast Gallery at Cambridge), and Zante, before heading for Corfu and home (via Trieste and Harwich) by the end of April.[16] A couple of years later, a rather more racy party led by Jane Harrison and D. S. MacColl (and including Mr. and Mrs. Arthur Sidgwick from Oxford) made what was basically the same journey—though lasting three months and with some rather more dar-ing excursions for the particularly keen participants.[17] In the middle of the trip, Harrison and MacColl made a quick dash east to take in Constantinople (Harrison forgot her passport on this excursion and had—naughtily—to be passed off as MacColl's wife; wives did not need passports). But the highlight of the whole trip came on their return to the Peloponnese when they spent a night camping out in the temple at Bassae, in the pouring rain. In fact, romantic and remote as Bassae was, they only just missed bumping into their friend Wilhelm Dörpfeld (whose four-hour on-site lecture on the Theater of Dionysus had thrilled Harrison, and bored MacColl silly, during their Athenian stay).[18] Dörpfeld was at that point passing through on the first of his famous archaeological tours, or *Peloponnesos-Reisen*; with him were eighteen students and assorted grandees (including Professors Overbeck and Lipsius from Leipzig, Professor Maaß from Grießwald, and Professors Waldstein and Tarbell from the American School at Athens). After Bassae, this group went on to Olympia, where "an der Hand des Pausanias wurden die verschiedenen Wanderungen dieses Periegeten durch die Altis wiederholt."[19]

Pausanias was a mainstay of travel of this kind[20]—and not merely as a guidebook to the ruins, to supplement the modern Baedekers and Murrays (which were useful on hotels but unreliable on archaeology, as on much else). For sure, on some sites, it was possible (and enormous fun) to tour the remains with Pausanias in hand, to move from building to building under his guidance, to re-create from his text the lost statues and paintings, as well as the rituals and stories. This was one of the special thrills of Olympia, as Dörpfeld well knew when he took his party to do just that in 1888. But more often Pausanias was the crucial entry point to the site as a whole—not the useful ancillary to a stroll round the ruins, but the indispensable link between the small fragments that survived and the whole ancient landscape, its religion, culture, and politics. In Athens, in particular, the expectations of many classicists must have been frankly disappointed by the extent of what remained to be seen. Outside the Acropolis, the survivals could only seem perverse to late Victorian academics bred on the texts of the fifth and fourth centuries B.C.: nothing in the Agora (apart from the disputed "Theseion," which until 1874 doubled as the main Athenian archaeological museum); the Theater of Dionysus was only just being uncovered (in bursts between the 1860s and 1880s); and far too much of what *was* left standing was Roman. Pausanias, especially with his emphasis on earlier monuments, was the key to the city they wanted to find; as Leake saw, in the 1820s, the "Topography of Athens" could only be a version of Pausanias Book I (certainly until more was excavated).[21] When we mock the naiveté of those early scholars who tried to reconstruct the layout of Athens from what seems a crudely literal reading of Pausanias, we would do well to remember that it was their only option for re-creating the ancient cityscape.

This exploration of Greece on the ground went hand-in-hand with the invention of Archaeology as one of the subdisciplines of Classics in British universities (and more widely).[22] Not surprisingly, many of our Greek tourists were also driving forces behind the introduction of Archaeology into the university classical curriculum. Here too Pausanias turns out to have been a linchpin.

Late Victorian England put most educational certainties on the line. In Classics the main dispute lay between, on the one hand, those who wished at all costs to preserve the classical curriculum as "pure" philology (i.e., composition, "unseens," a bit of linguistics, and not much else) and, on the other, a very mixed group, with very mixed motives, who advocated extending the range of what was to count as "Classics" into philosophy, history, material culture, and literary criticism.[23] It was, of course, the latter group who "won" and who now stand (awkwardly in some cases) as the heroic founders of Classics as we know it.[24] But victory did not come without a whole series of improvisations and compromises at all levels. In Cambridge (and similar, though differently nuanced, solutions were adopted elsewhere),[25] the Classics course was divided into two parts, as it still remains (Part I and Part II): the first part was more or less the "Palace of Philology"[26] that the conservatives had wanted; only in the second (and, to begin with, optional) part was much room made for nonlinguistic specialisms, and even then, the price of inclusion within the Classics degree was that each subdiscipline was to be substantially based around ancient *texts*. This was easy enough for history and philosophy, where Plato and Thucydides, Aristotle and Tacitus, flowered, but it created a paradox for Classical Archaeology, which some of its proponents had explicitly defined as those areas of Classical studies that were not based on literary sources.[27]

There were few texts that would fit the bill; those that would had to be squeezed for all they could offer. At the heart of the new Archaeology papers, and central to the preparation of any student who opted for them, was a startling series of authors (emphatically not—in the jargon of the time—"the best"): Pliny the Elder, Vitruvius, and, of course, Pausanias.[28] The early examinations in Classical Archaeology, taken by students in Cambridge for the first time in 1883, were littered with quotations from all three; students were to translate, analyze, and comment. For the most part, the quotations were the pegs on which more general questions were hung: "Translate the following passage [a hefty ten lines of Pausanias 1.26, on the Erechtheum], and describe the existing remains of the Erechtheum, giving the probable date of its completion" (Paper on "Inscriptions, Arts and Handicrafts," 3 June 1889); "τοῦ ναοῦ δέ ἐστι πέραν ᾿Απόλλων χαλκοῦς (Pausanias 1.24.8). Describe the statue here mentioned; and also the building omitted at this point by Pausanias" (i.e., the temple of Rome and Augustus outside the Parthenon's front door; Paper on "Architecture and Special Subject," 27 May 1901); and so on. But pegs or not, it is clear that anything less than a good working knowledge of most of Pausanias risked a very bad mark, if not failure.[29]

It was not just the students, of course, who needed to have Pausanias at their fingertips; so did their teachers. The shifting reciprocities between research and teaching were no less complex in the nineteenth century than they are today. But inserting Pausanias for the first time into the pedagogical agenda could not fail to have had an impact on academic projects at every level, on common-room talk, and on publishing ambitions. Even the formal examination questions that I have quoted hint at shared areas of interests between students and their teachers and at the content of the lectures and supervisions that prepared the way for the final exam. To ask explicitly about Pausanias's omission of the Roman temple on the Acropolis strongly suggests that, just under the surface of these technical questions, lies a (disarmingly up-to-the-minute) concern with the author's aims, his selective vision, and his construction of the past.

But nineteenth-century Archaeology was more than material culture and in all kinds of ways quite different from its modern homonym. To be sure, it included art and architecture, inscriptions, coins, and pots. But it equally embraced the study of religion, ritual, and mythology (not to mention "daily life" and a smattering of what we would call "social history");[30] and it was closely bound up with the development of comparative anthropology, discussed in detail by John Henderson elsewhere in this book (chap. 11). You could want no sharper symbol of that integration than the list of examiners for the first-ever papers in Classical Archaeology in Cambridge in 1883: for the name of J. G. Frazer—soon to be hard at work on *The Golden Bough*—leaps out among them.[31]

The drive to investigate the world's religions, myths, customs, and folklores under a vast comparativist umbrella—in many ways the defining fashion of late Victorian academe—is the final factor I shall point to behind the nineteenth-century Pausanian boom. And it neatly squares the circle. For not only was Pausanias himself a mine of religious information, quaint customs, and myths, all *begging* to be set down next to similar stories from the heart of Africa or the margins of the Pacific; but also those academic tourists who tramped round Greece, Pausanias in hand, inevitably found themselves face-to-face with yet another range of rural folktales and colorful ceremonies—present-day equivalents (indeed, on many an attractive evolutionary scheme, *descendants*) of what Pausanias had seen and described. The figure of Frazer again points up the connections here. No sooner had he finished with the proofs of *The Golden Bough* in 1890 than he set out for Greece to work on *Pausanias*. He was not at that point changing academic direction or "returning" to Classics but was pursuing the same intellectual project—and one to which Pausanias was central.[32]

Pausanias *als Schriftsteller*

This complex investment in Pausanias and his text helps to explain the richness and variety of nineteenth-century studies on the *Periegesis,* as scholars across Europe and America staked out their different positions on the author. There was plenty of intense discussion of detail (such as the Enneacrunus episode), but also debates that broached big questions head-on. What was Pausanias's book *for?* What was *his* investment in the account? How did the *Periegesis* fit into the cultural politics of the second century A.D.? At the same time, Pausanias's position outside the canon of "best authors" also encouraged a wide range and diversity of approach. Quite simply, you could do things with (and say things about) Pausanias that would not have gone down well had he been one of the "best."[33] And you were not required to have top-notch philological credentials to be allowed to join in the game. Most top-notch philologists looked elsewhere for their material.

But not all. Wilamowitz, the doyen of philology with a finger in every pie, made a notorious contribution to the Pausanian debate, staking the claim—lovingly amplified by his students—that the *Periegesis* was (literally) no such thing, but fantasy-cum-pastiche, written by a charlatan who need never have set foot outside his own hometown.[34] This prompted all the predictable defenses of Pausanias's trustworthiness as a reporter, traveler, and guide (to his supporters, it must have seemed too good to be true that the Hermes of Praxiteles was discovered at Olympia in exactly the spot Pausanias said he saw it—in the very year that Wilamowitz's paper appeared).[35] But it also had the effect of focusing attention back on the text of Pausanias—*as a text*. If the *Periegesis* was not the practical guidebook/eyewitness account that it seemed, then it was (in some sense) "literature." Wilamowitz and most of his clones resisted this idea. For them it was always a scissors-and-paste job by (at best) an incompetent or (at worst) a crook. But in 1909 C. Robert turned the tables with a study of Pausanias's *rhetoric,* arguing for the highly *literary construction* of what most of his supporters took as artless description.[36]

Most of those who championed Pausanias as reliable guide to the topography of ancient Greece were happy to grant that he was not a major intellectual figure ("intelligent sometimes with that depressing form of intellect to which all things are interesting" is Harrison's characteristic put-down).[37] In fact, it was precisely his lack of discrimination that made him so useful for the modern scholar. According to Harrison again, "the intellectual shortcomings constitute in a sense his peculiar merit. A more able man might often have been a less trustworthy guide."[38] Twenty years earlier Thomas Dyer had made a similar point, if more clumsily:

> It is perhaps a fortunate thing for us, that Pausanias possessed no false and affected enthusiasm for art. He does not, like some of our aesthetical critics, treat us to long disquisitions intended rather to display the beauties of the writer's style than that of the objects on which it is employed. Hence he has not only more space for the enumeration of works of art, but we may also have a more confident reliance that those mentioned, were really masterpieces.[39]

Not that Pausanias was deemed to have had no ideas of his own at all. There was plenty of speculation about what this plodder ("a man made of common stuff," as Frazer had it)[40] thought he was doing, and why. How far was the whole project essentially a religious one by a "devout pagan"?[41] Or was it a museum work, compiled by a man with a strongly nostalgic or antiquarian turn—and a soft spot for the ancient glories of Greece? (Frazer again: "if Pausanias chose to chronicle the masterpieces of the great age of art rather than the feeble productions of the decadence, we can only applaud his taste. Yet we may surmise that his taste was here reinforced by his patriotism. . . . He was a patriot who warmly sympathised with the ancient glories of his country and deeply mourned its decline.")[42] None of this, of course, was very far from politics. Did Pausanias's selective vision of the sites he visited imply a political agenda? Did he acquiesce "in the Roman dominion as inevitable" but a regrettable lapse from Greek freedom?[43] Or was he (as Jane Harrison saw it) "distinctly *imperial* in tone," with a fatal weakness for tales (wearisomely repeated) of "the mutations of empires and the illustrious transactions of kings."[44]

It is hard to gauge through all the late Victorian jargon quite how "modern" these debates are. In exploring scholarship's history, we are always caught between, on the one hand, writing off our predecessors as almost an alien species (engaged in arguments which we may observe with curiosity but which are emphatically *not ours*) and, on the other, conscripting them all too easily into our own world, translating the idiom and reading our debates into theirs. All the same, many late nineteenth-century pages on Pausanias do have a disconcertingly familiar ring; for they repeatedly go out of their way to place the *Periegesis* at the center of issues of cultural identity, imperialism, pilgrimage, and the politics of representation. Or at least, that is how *we* would put it.

The Blue Jane

For the rest of this chapter, I shall be exploring the history of one of the most famous books on Pausanias to be written in Victorian England, a radical contribution to Archaeology (myth and religion included) and for years an indispensable guidebook for the up-market tourist to Athens.[45] Affectionately called by its admirers *The Blue Jane*, it is Harrison and Verrall's *Mythology and Monuments of Ancient Athens, being a translation of a portion of the "Attica" of Pausanias by M. de G. Verrall, with introductory essay and archaeological commentary by J. E. Harrison;*[46] over 600 pages issued by Macmillan in 1890 for the commensurately hefty price of sixteen shillings.

Today *Mythology and Monuments* is almost entirely forgotten. Even leading Pausanians have let it quietly slip from their footnotes and bibliographies.[47] It retains a foothold only in the narrower subdiscipline of the historiography of ancient religion. For Harrison's renown has turned on her role as a leading figure in the early years of the twentieth century among the so-called Cambridge Ritualists—an informal group (including Francis Cornford and Gilbert Murray), whose modern nickname derives from one of their main arguments: that *ritual is central to the understanding of Greek religion*.[48] It was in the preface to *Mythology and Monuments,* long before she had ever met either Cornford or Murray, that Harrison first put such a ritualist manifesto into print: "My belief is that in many, even in the large majority of cases *ritual practice misunderstood* explains the elaboration of myth."[49] This has given the book a historical status as *fons et origo* of "ritualism,"[50] even though—so far as Pausanias is concerned—it is emphatically off the map.

The origin, production, impact, and *Nachleben* (up to 1953) of *Mythology and Monuments* is well documented. In following its story, my aim is not to resurrect a lost classic; some of it *is* brilliant and (as often with Harrison) disconcertingly witty, but too many pages now seem unreadably convoluted, as well as archaeologically obsolete.[51] My aim is rather to shed light on part of the history of nineteenth- and twentieth-century Pausanias studies, through the history of a forgotten commentary.

Pausanias in Petticoats

Jane Ellen Harrison and Margaret de Gaudrion Verrall (née Merrifield) were both "distinguished quasi-graduates of Newnham College" in Cambridge, as Percy Gardner put it, with chilling accuracy.[52] Harrison had come up to (the newly-founded) Newnham in 1874 to read Classics, already trumpeted as the "cleverest woman in England."[53] A glamorous, self-glamorizing, charismatic, and ambitious student, in 1879 she sat the Tripos examination (in the unofficial way then open to women—hence Gardner's "quasi-graduates") and was dismayed to be awarded only a (quasi-)second class result.[54] Although she had hoped to be taken on by the College as a resident Classical Lecturer, the authorities may well have been relieved to have a ready-made excuse to offer the job in due course to a far less dangerous candidate: Margaret Merrifield, Harrison's slightly younger contemporary and college friend.[55] Harrison left Cambridge for London, where she became the protegée of Charles Newton, keeper of Greek and Roman antiquities in the British Museum. Throwing herself into archaeology (particularly the interface between material culture and mythology), she soon acquired a huge reputation as an independent lecturer and teacher (archly describing herself as "fatally fluent")[56] and began publishing the series of books and articles that would eventually lead her back to a post in Cambridge.[57] Merrifield meanwhile did not last long in her Newnham job. In June 1882 she married A. W. Verrall (classicist and later Professor of English Literature in Cambridge); and on her marriage, as was required, she resigned her lectureship.

We do not know exactly when Harrison and Verrall decided to collaborate on Pausanias Book I. But Verrall had approached a publisher (Macmillan) by August 1888,[58] and Harrison was certainly working on the project during her stay in Athens in the spring of that year. (Her preface refers to Dörpfeld's marathon theater lecture, as well as to help with inscriptions from one of her traveling companions on that trip; D. S. MacColl is credited with some of the translations of Greek verse that were included in the commentary.) According to Harrison, the final version was pulled together with extreme speed, thanks to Verrall, who presumably had no wish for the whole process to drag on:

> I shall never forget the three weeks I spent with her pulling together the MS draft. With characteristic alacrity and precision she said at the outset "I can give you three weeks and we must finish it up." In the little inn at Robin Hood's Bay which to me now has its special sanctity I laid before her a frightful tangled mass of material and what is worse, conflicting opinion. She sifted it and sorted it and saw through it with a swiftness that was then and still is to me little short of miraculous.[59]

The book that resulted is a much stranger product than the straightforward title *Mythology and Monuments of Ancient Athens* would immediately suggest.

For a start, the text of Pausanias has been violently chopped: anything that was not directly related to Athens and the Athenians has been omitted ("when he digresses to tell the fortunes of foreigners and barbarians, because his story is no longer serviceable to my pupose, I omit or curtail it"—so exit the Gauls, Attalus, Ptolemy, Lysimachus, Pyrrhus, and Seleucus; altogether more than half the book);[60] and what is left is carved up into short sections and translated under headings that refer to the monuments described, followed by a long commentary. There is no Greek text, nor even a continuous translation, but a series of topographical chapters, each introduced by the relevant passage of Pausanias.

The book opens with a typically swashbuckling preface by Harrison (well worth reading on its own, even if you get no further). These are deliciously provocative pages which range from the anthropology of the Greeks ("in regarding the myth-making Greek as a practical savage rather than a poet or philosopher,—I follow, *quam longo intervallo,* in the steps of Eusebius, Lobeck, Mannhardt, and Mr Andrew Lang")[61] to some clever reflections on Pausanias and the impetus driving his work ("When we become *interested* in the gods, when we study the minutiae of their worship and recount their various legends, the days of love and fear are long since over and gone").[62] But the main point she has to emphasize is that the focus of her interest is indigenous Athenian myth and the topography of the city *as it bears on mythology.* The reader has been warned. Now follows an introduction of more than a hundred pages: a "Mythological Essay" written explicitly with the specialist in mind,[63] which relentlessly pursues primitive Athenian religion, particularly the hero-kings and their associated rituals and myths. By comparison, her lengthy commentaries on the sections of Verrall's translation are easy going ("addressed, not to the professional archaeologist, but to the student, whose needs I have constantly borne in mind").[64] True, they include a good deal of high-level mythography (unbelievably bravura chains of argument that scour Greek art and literature to explicate a brief phrase of Pausanias), as well as far-too-intricate discussions of the latest archaeological theories of the ever-present Dr. Dörpfeld. But they are constantly enlivened by Harrison's directness ("The new theory adopted is revolutionary. It simply changes the whole lie of the agora"),[65] by her sense of *presence* ("The inscription is not easy to find; it is inside the garden of the observatory on the top of the hill, to the right-hand side of the path as one enters"),[66] and by her engaging—to some readers, no doubt, irritating—jokes ("it was expressly forbidden that any one who had eaten garlic should enter the Metröon—an enactment that might advisably be made in modern sanctuaries").[67]

There were also to be lavish illustrations and photographs. But here trouble lay ahead. Between summer 1888 and spring 1890, when the book finally appeared, almost two years were taken up with hitches, disputes, cost-cutting, complaints, and near-disasters over the pictures. By the end of August 1888, Macmillan had already insisted that Harrison's original list of illustrations be reduced to 200 or 250;[68] not only was it a question of the total number, but it was also the size, the method of reproduction, its expense, and the clarity (or otherwise) of the result. Basically, Macmillan was trying to avoid the high-quality (but extremely costly) process of engraving, making do with a cheaper alternative on offer from "Messrs Boutall and Walker." Harrison was prepared to compromise but predictably worried about the final appearance of the book ("I do not *like* their process—it has a *veiled* unpleasant appearance").[69] The dispute rumbled on for the next year or so. Harrison tried to dig her heels in ("I saw Mr Walker at the Museum. I am distressed to find from him that the clearness of the pictures suffers far more by reduction than I had any idea of. In fact he says most of the inscriptions disappear altogether. . . . I fear the *illustrations* will be rather *disastrous*");[70] and other firms (and methods) were canvassed. But, in the end, Macmillan got his way with the economies, as publishers usually do.

Harrison was right to be worried. When the book eventually came out, reviewers lamented the atrocious quality of the pictures: "those of sites and buildings often too indistinct to be of much value."[71] "Many of the reductions of photographs are unfortunately blurred and useless";[72] and so on.[73] Indeed, where Harrison in her preface thanked "Mr J. S. Furley" for the photograph that became "the beautiful view of the Epidaurus theatre (p. 294)," in his own copy A. B. Cook underlined "beautiful" and penciled next to it "?practical joke."[74] But it was not only the pictures that provoked some carping phrases in the reviews. Mrs. Verrall's translation was good enough if you did not scrutinize it too carefully. On the other hand, there *were* some embarrassing errors,[75] not to mention the fact that, throughout, Greek accents appeared to have been scattered with a degree of abandon that would horrify any decent philologist; and that Harrison's mind had clearly not been on the job when she read the proofs. ("Greek words are printed with great disregard of the rules of accent, and the proof reading generally is very careless," summed up Tarbell in the *Classical Review*.) As for MacColl's lusty "translations" of various snatches of Greek verse throughout the Commentaries, the less said about *them* the better. He might at least "have spared us the rhyme of 'brighten' and 'Aristogeiton' " chipped in the *Oxford Magazine*.[76]

The reviewers could not overlook the fact that here was a substantial book on a Classical topic written by a pair of women. That, after all, was what lay behind all the nasty insinuations about Greek accents. And it infected their comments on the style and content of *Mythology and Monuments* more generally. Few of them went quite so far as (the appropriately pseudonymous) "Nemo" in the *Revue des études grecques,* who rounded off his review by slavering over the thought of visiting ancient Athens with this "Pausanias in Petticoats" ("il n'est pas un ami de l'antiquité qui ne trouve plaisir à visiter les monuments d'Athènes sous la conduite de ce Pausanias en jupons").[77] But even the more restrained British commentators resorted to a predictable range of girly adjectives when applauding Harrison's writing: "Her style is so extremely fresh and vivacious that her pages are pleasant reading";[78] "Miss Harrison's style is lively and vivacious to the last degree";[79] "Miss Harrison's style, which is delightfully fresh and lively, at times becomes almost too vivacious."[80] When it came to the *arguments,* on the other hand, there was a distinct tendency to *chercher l'homme.* One reviewer even claimed the *real* author of some of the most important sections was not Harrison or Verrall at all: "It is no discourtesy to these ladies . . . to say that the element in this book which makes it indispensable to all students, even the most advanced, of Athenian topography is not contributed by either of them." It was, of course, Dörpfeld, "who has enriched Miss Harrison's pages at every turn."[81] Others took a similar line, suggesting that Harrison had merely "appropriated" her mentor's work;[82] or that *Mythology and Monuments* simply "embodied" Dörpfeld.[83]

But the reaction to the book was not all carping or patronizing. Even those who oozed about the "vivacious style" saw that this was a substantial contribution to Greek archaeology and that radical claims were at stake. Harrison knew Athens "on the ground" and was as up-to-date as you could be on all the excavations and topographical theories (with or without Pausanias): "It is incomparably the best Guide to the Acropolis, and ancient Athens generally, which has yet appeared."[84] "It is no exaggeration to say that this book is the most important archaeological publication that has appeared in England for some time past."[85] Besides, it clearly heralded a whole series of new approaches to the mythography of Athens. There may have been some who felt that it was two books rolled awkwardly into one: "Indeed I venture to think that both mythology and monuments would have gained by being completely separated in treatment."[86] But no one missed (even if they did not approve) Harrison's claims about early Athenian religion and about how it might best be uncovered. Some reviews picked on the key phrase about myth (*"ritual practice misunderstood"*).[87] Others astutely summarized the book's implications, emphasizing the way Harrison exploited the shrines of Athens combined with Pausanias's information and (for this was her stock-in-trade) the evidence from Greek vase-painting to open up a religious world far more lost than any of which Pausanias could have dreamt. The anonymous reviewer in the *Spectator* put it as briskly as any: "She is bent on going behind the orthodox Hellenic pantheon, and even the Homeric theology, and recovering for us the old local cults that lingered in the several Attic demes, and the primitive forms of ritual which gave rise to curious explanatory legends, or were but clumsily adapted to the more developed and centralised worships of later Athens."[88] Vintage Harrison.

And yet, from a distance of more than a hundred years since it first appeared, we may now feel it odd that Harrison's contemporaries were not *more* puzzled by the book, and, in particular, that they did not stop to ask what kind of reading of Pausanias she was offering. I have, for example, found no objections raised to her radical dissection of the text (or even comments on it) and the sometimes brutal excision of any part not strictly "relevant" to the project. But there are still more fundamental issues about the *function* of Harrison's commentary and its relationship to Pausanias himself that are almost bound to strike a modern reader.

It is a truism that (on the "dogs and their owners" principle) commentators come to resemble their authors; or rather that, in the very process of writing a commentary, they are always liable to construct their author in their own intellectual image. So, for example, it is commonly said that, when he picked on Pausanias for his vast commentary, J. G. Frazer was homing in on his intellectual twin: a hugely industrious compiler, whose overriding interests lay in the study of religion. Or, to put that the other way round, Frazer's commentary was partly an exercise in constructing Pausanias in Frazerian terms—terms that are now so dominant that we cannot entirely "unthink" them.[89]

In Harrison's case similar points could be made. In fact, it is hard not to notice how much of the criticism sharply directed against Pausanias in her preface could so easily be turned against her own essay and commentary. What are we to make of a commentator who derides her author for dwelling at such length on the "illustrious transactions of kings" and then opens with more than a hundred pages on the mythography of the Athenian *kings?* Is it *our* category mistake? *Her* authorial blindness? Or is she actively conscripting us into a much more complicated game of reading and doublethink between academics and their subject?

But there is a sharper irony, and one with implications for our own understanding of Pausanias, in the subsequent *use* of Harrison's *Mythology and Monuments*. The nickname *Blue Jane* says it all. The book soon became the traveler's *vade mecum*. Pausanias was (as I have already argued) the key to the ancient Athenian cityscape; Harrison's Pausanias showed you *how* that key unlocked the monuments "on the ground" (as well as taking you on a quite different, imaginary, journey into primitive cultic history). Almost every reviewer hinted that the book would be invaluable in this way; and as early as 1891 we find it entering the symbolic economy of late Victorian academe, as an icon of the "travellers guide." In January 1891 MacColl wrote to his friend Eugénie Sellers in Athens as follows: "I picture Athens crowded with eminent Oxford dons turned Pausaniacs, each with a copy of Harrison and Verrall under one arm, and Schuchardt (is it?) under the other."[90] More than just a flattering—and evenhanded—reference to female literary production (for Sellers herself had recently translated Schuchhardt's *Schliemann's Excavations*), this neatly conjures up the world of academic tourism, with Harrison and Verrall as its pocket-book.

At this point, we must remember that Harrison herself never suggests this function for *Mythology and Monuments*. Admittedly, her detailed site descriptions in the commentary repeatedly emphasize her own *autopsy*. Referring back to her own visit and to the obstacles—in various different forms—that confront the modern visitor to Pausanian monuments, she offers in passing all kinds of useful information for those attempting to repeat the experience for themselves. Yet, when she laid out the purpose of her book and its intended readership in her preface, she made no mention at all of the traveler to Athens. She foresaw two readership groups: specialists in ancient myth and religion and Archaeology students (for whom, as we have seen, Pausanias was a central set text).[91] The Pausanian parallels are unmissable. During the very years when the controversy over *Pausanias der Perieget* was at it most intense (ancient Baedeker or desk-bound fantasy?), Harrison writes a book explicitly for desk-bound readers, which instantly turns into a *Blue Jane*. How far she anticipated that, or even planned it, we do not know. But for us, it is a telling reminder of the necessary fluidity of all travel writing (ancient or modern), always precariously lodged *between* home and abroad. In every *Periegesis* there is pleasure for the reader by the fireside, but there is *also* a trip to be repeated; in that sense, every *Periegesis* can always be a Baedeker.

Pausanias's Description of Greece, 6 volumes (1898)

The *Blue Jane* was a huge success. Two thousand copies were printed and sold.[92] Its principal author went on to be a notable archaeologist and the most famous female classicist in history. So why has it been so comprehensively forgotten?

The developments in archaeology are partly the answer. Harrison herself had been contemplating a second edition, according to the notes she wrote into her own copy;[93] but at least by 1906 she realized that archaeology had moved on too quickly for any simple "revisions" to be appropriate.[94] *Mythology and Monuments* captured an exciting moment in the uncovering of Athens, but it was locked into the theories and debates of the late 1880s. By the 1930s, with the American excavations of the Agora, Harrison's archaeology would seem even more irrelevant; and by that stage (probably more crucially) even Pausanias had been dethroned as the key to the understanding of Athenian topography. If you wanted to explore the cityscape of ancient Athens, you no longer started with Pausanias Book I; you looked at what had been excavated.

Even the "mythology" of *Mythology and Monuments* did not keep the book in people's hands. Although historians of scholarship regularly note it as the "origin" of "Ritualism," no one who wanted to explore Harrison's contribution to Greek religion would ever sensibly start here. By 1903 you could turn to her famous *Prolegomena to the Study of Greek Religion,* where she did it more fully and (probably) better, and where you got translations by Gilbert Murray, not the dreadful versifying of D. S. MacColl.[95] *Mythology and Monuments* came to be of interest only in the archaeology of Harrison's thought.

But *The Blue Jane* has not only been forgotten; it has also been *obscured*— by the vast six volumes of Frazer's Pausanias, whose appearance in 1898 obliterated its rivals and has held center stage as the Pausanian commentary for the English-speaking world until this day.[96] *Blue Jane* with her select passages of Book I did not survive the advent of Mr. Frazer.

His victory was largely by bulk. Like the complete version of *The Golden Bough,* the sheer size of the book defeats most readers, at the same time securing its status as a monument. Frazer may have had a lot that he wanted to say, but he certainly understood the reputational advantages of writing *at length* and of cleaning up on the competition.[97] We know that he had little time for Harrison's work on Pausanias. He bought a copy of *Mythology and Monuments* in Athens in 1890 and fulminated copiously in its margins: "This is quite wrong. The *altar* was dedicated by *Callistratus,* but nothing whatever is said of his archonship." "This is either wrong or implies a different reading." "This is as if one were to speak of a faithful *kuon* or a spirited cob *hippos.* Greek is a noble language, and so is English, but a jumble of the two is detestable. And when this jumble is, as it sometimes is, interlarded with tags of German, the result is quite unbearable." "It may be observed that the emphasis of a statement is usually in inverse proportion to the evidence on which it is based." And so on and on.[98] Nevertheless, throughout his commentary on Book I, Harrison's views are repeated and referenced. If you wanted to know what she (or any other earlier commentator) thought, it was simplest just to go to Frazer.

When his multivolume Pausanias appeared in 1898 (one thousand copies printed, for the vast sum of six guineas a set), it was well received.[99] True, there were worries about Frazer's status as a philologist (he had not after all reedited the Greek text or printed one); and despite his pilgrimages around the sites of Greece and enormous bibliographic expertise, he still seemed "at his weakest when dealing with works of art."[100] Nevertheless, overall the book was a pillar of judicious scholarship, applauded for its cool assessment of many of the intricate controversies that dogged the history and topography of Athens and Greece as a whole. Harrison and Verrall's fate was sealed—and quite explicitly. Percy Gardner, Professor of Classical Archaeology in Oxford, had been one of their most glowing reviewers in 1890, with a high-profile (if anonymous) piece in the *Quarterly Review,* hailing it as an archaeological milestone, while lamenting the "bondage" of Oxford "Greats" ("prone to regard any study of antiquity which does not confine itself to philosophy and the workings of political forces as certainly frivolous and probably useless").[101] When he came to review Frazer in the *Classical Review* of 1898, he opened with a direct comparison with *Mythology and Monuments:*

> Miss Harrison's book has great merits; it is fresh and interesting and full of appreciation. But compared with it Mr. Frazer's shows far greater solidity of judgement, power of weighing evidence, breadth of view . . . There is something very impressive and manly in the way Mr. Frazer deals with the hundred bitter controversies as to topography, art and antiquities in Greece . . . For example, in dealing with the Theseum, he sums up thus (ii. 155): "The view which identifies the so-called Theseum with the temple of Hephaestus, though it is not free from difficulties, seems less open to serious objection than any of the others. It may therefore be provisionally accepted." Miss Harrison had accepted it with fervour: but Mr. Frazer's well-weighed words express the exact truth.[102]

The "quasi-graduates" of Newnham had done their (vivacious) work; they could now get out of the limelight.

Postscript: *The Ancient City of Athens* (1953)

But Jane Harrison's partisans were not prepared to let the book pass away quite so easily. Her enormous reputation throughout much of the twentieth century has been largely due to the willful refusal of her pupils and her college to let her memory die.[103] While other pioneers were gracefully forgotten, Harrison's supporters competed in their efforts to keep her name, personality, and writing on the academic agenda. Part of this campaign involved *Mythology and Monuments.*

A few years after Harrison's death (in 1928), the Jane Harrison Committee at Newnham came up with the plan of producing an updated edition of the book. Leading light in the project was Jessie Stewart, Harrison's pupil and first biographer, a woman scarcely rivaled in the energies that she poured into ensuring her teacher's posthumous fame.[104] In 1934 she drafted a formal proposal, justifying the project to potential supporters and publishers: "though an early work of Miss Harrison, it has all the fascination of her later style." And shortly (it is not clear on exactly what financial terms) she had enlisted Ida Thallon Hill (an American archaeologist, and wife of Bert Hodge Hill, who had been Director of the American School in Athens until 1927) to undertake the revisions.

It was to be a publishing saga that dwarfs Harrison's own relatively good-humored scraps with Macmillan. The truth was, of course, that no publisher really wanted to take on this white elephant, even though, when confronted with Stewart's passionate commitment to the whole idea (and promises of subventions from the college), they did not always have the heart to say *no* right away. The archaeological fraternity too had its doubts, among other things about the timing of the project. "The whole of the section on the Agora is at the moment in the melting pot, and the solutions of the chief problems will be available in a couple of years," explained Humfry Payne in a letter to Stewart.[105] Behind her back, he was franker to D. S. Robertson: "she seemed to me not altogether to appreciate what the task of bringing up to date so learned a work would involve . . . ⟨it is⟩ not the ideal moment to write anything about Athenian topography. I say all this because I have reason to believe that even after what I said she may have thought I accepted her plan rather more completely than was the case."[106]

Nonetheless, after rejections from Cambridge University Press, Oxford, Macmillan, and Methuen, Leonard Woolf seemed to blow warm enough for Stewart and Hill to be happy to press ahead. By 1939, however, when they had a very long manuscript to show, Woolf blew considerably cooler and would only offer quite impossible financial terms.[107] Negotiations of a kind dragged on through the war, ineffectually. By the late 1940s, the Jane Harrison Committee decided to pull the plug on the project; and Hill to cut her losses and use the material she had gathered to write a new book on the same subject: *The Ancient City of Athens: Its Topography and Monuments.*[108] This is dedicated "To the imperishable memory of Jane Ellen Harrison, Guide, Philosopher and Friend" and, in its preface, offers a rather sanitized account of its origins in *Mythology and Monuments*;[109] but it is essentially a quite different enterprise, a topography of Athens no longer guided by the thread of the Pausanian account.

The sting in the tail comes (again) with the reviews. Two very different responses came out of Cambridge: some judiciously light irony from R. M. Cook ("Here is a book that most Hellenists not only need but can afford");[110] some characteristically intelligent thundering from Hugh Plommer ("H. seldom stands on her own feet, partly because she knows too little architecture." "Should a second edition be deemed necessary, the following passages should be reconsidered . . .").[111] But on one thing both were agreed: the book would have been greatly helped if it had brought Pausanias back into the picture; Plommer even advocated printing a translation of Pausanias's chapters on Attica in their entirety. How far either of these were aware of the complicated history of the book, whether or not they realized that Hill had in practice been forced to cleanse it of its Pausanian origins, I simply do not know.[112] But the fact that *Mythology and Monument*'s direct (though arguably illegitimate) descendant should find itself criticized for *not* paying due attention to Pausanias, all too neatly squares the circle of my story.

"The Other in the Note"

Chateaubriand's Rediscovery of
Ancient Sparta

Close to the beginning of his *Itinéraire de Paris à Jérusalem,* Chateaubriand breaks off his expansive description of the view from the citadel of Sparta to make a brief comment on the temple of Athena, "Lady of the Bronze House":

> Chalcioecos, house of bronze. One must not take the text of Pausanias and Plutarch literally, and imagine that this temple was all of bronze: it simply means that the temple was covered with bronze on the inside, and perhaps on the outside. I hope that no one will confuse the two Pausaniases that I mention here, the one in the text, the other in the note.[1]

Chateaubriand's annotation suggests a momentary solicitude for his future readers. First published under the Empire in 1811, and running into three editions in two years, the *Itinéraire* fulfilled its mission of paying all the author's debts with its initial print run of 3,200 and rapidly developed a celebrity which spawned a series of parodies. He could not assume in advance that these readers would pick up the passing reference in the text to "the foundations of the temple of Minerva Chalciúcos, where Pausanias vainly sought refuge and lost his life." "Pausanias" was, after all, primarily a textual reference for him, one that he could invoke to demonstrate his awareness of the Classical sources and throw into relief his present perceptions of the scene. So we read a few pages later: "We know from Herodotus that there was a lion of stone on the tomb of Leonidas; circumstance which is not recorded by Pausanias."[2] The Chateaubriand who is author of the text assures us that he sought vainly to discover any trace of this imposing monument, but the Chateaubriand in the note, who is allowed second thoughts, is ready to confess his error (and vindicate Pausanias's accuracy): "My memory let me down here; the lion that Herodotus mentions was at Thermopylae."

What appears important for Chateaubriand, if we go by these examples, is a textual system that allows him to gloss, and occasionally correct, the recorded experience of his travels in Greece. The Classical (and more recent) sources provide him with information that can be tested in the field, and by the same token they supply a check on his spontaneous enthusiasms, forcing him to recognize that he has sometimes committed himself to a wild goose chase. However, the fact that Chateaubriand does not actually eliminate the references to his misguided quests is significant. "I redoubled my ardor," he insists in the text when recounting his fruitless search for the lion of Leonidas. Yet "all my efforts were useless." The note explains to the reader that he had no edition of Herodotus to hand while he walked among the ruins of Sparta. But this unsurprising detail is upstaged by the rather more extraordinary information that his luggage did contain the works of Racine, Tasso, Virgil, and Homer, "the latter with white sheets to write notes." As he is a writer, Chateaubriand judges it essential to travel in the company of the works of other writers, chosen not for their pertinence to the sites visited on the journey but to form a paradigmatic set of "classic" texts. Homer, Virgil, Tasso, and Racine (to list them chronologically, and not as they subtend from Chateaubriand's point of view) traverse the gap between Classical antiquity and modern France, and he is poised to inscribe his continuing text as a supplement to the most ancient of them all.

This means that Pausanias (the one in the note) is the grit in the oyster incubated by the writer and actor Chateaubriand. His agency diminishes to a minimal trace in the saga of discovery. Visiting Mycenae, Chateaubriand refers to Pausanias's tale that the name of the town itself is etymologically linked to the Greek word for "mushroom," deriving from the fountain that Perseus discovered under a convenient fungus. But, having mentioned Pausanias's name, Chateaubriand is launched on his personal mythmaking:

> Wishing to find the way back to Corinth, I heard the ground resonate under the steps of my horse. I dismounted, and I discovered the vault of another tomb.
>
> Pausanias counts five tombs at Mycenae: the tomb of Atreus, that of Agamemnon, that of Eurymedon, that of Teledamus and Pelops, and that of Electra. He adds that Clytemnestra and Aegisthus were buried outside the walls: so would this be the tomb of Clytemnestra and Aegisthus that I had found? I mentioned it to M. Fauvel, who will seek it out on his first journey to Argos: a singular destiny which has me leave Paris expressly to discover the ashes of Clytemnestra![3]

Here Chateaubriand not only dramatizes the point that he has located the tomb that Pausanias merely cites in passing but links his discovery to the mysterious intervention of "destiny." This is despite the fact that "the ashes of Clytemnestra" remain no more than a promissory note, dependent on the future exertions of the archaeologist. It is easy to appreciate why Chateaubriand's host at Argos, an Italian doctor named Avramiotti, later took the trouble to write a detailed refutation of several of Chateaubriand's claims, including this particular one: "These underground chambers, I saw them in 1803, as I have already mentioned, and there is no herdsman or shepherd who does not know them, because they are accustomed to looking for animals that get lost. So why exclaim with an emphatic voice: 'Singular destiny' . . . ?"[4]

The answer to Avramiotti's exasperated question is not as easy as it may seem, since it touches the heart of Chateaubriand's conception of his role as a writer and the particularly complex notions of agency and experience that he built into it. If travel writing is a particularly unstable genre, linked to the making and remaking of the traveling subject, then Chateaubriand is one of the first writers to exploit that instability to the full, celebrating in turn the alternating moments of doubt and certainty as the journey unfolds. Chateaubriand is invariably anxious that we should observe him casting himself for the role that he has been destined to play. We are called in on the sudden moments of illumination, when the self-dramatizing subjectivity fuses memory and experience. So, like the uneven paving stones of the courtyard of the Hôtel de Guermantes for Proust's Marcel, the resonant vaults of Clytemnestra's tomb cause Chateaubriand to revisit a tissue of memories whose enchainment seems for that moment to be necessary rather than contingent. The difference, of course, is that *A la recherche du temps perdu* derives that necessary enchainment from the fictional construction of the written text, while the *Itinéraire,* like the subsequent *Mémoires d'outre-tombe,* in which Chateaubriand reflects upon the whole of his autobiography, explicitly courts the risk of contingency that any adventure, or any life, needs to encounter.

This implies, once again, that the difference between agency and authority in the "text" and in the "note" is bound to be a crucial one. There must be a functional division corresponding to the roles of actor and commentator, even when (or perhaps because) they are one and the same person. It is perhaps an overinterpretation to see in Pausanias's text hints of a certain emotional investment in passages where the Spartan heroes who bore his own name are featured. There is "Pausanias the son of Cleombrotus," who never became king but won the important battle of Plataea. Of the general's clemency to those caught up in the battle, the writer Pausanias states: "I cannot praise too highly the way in which Pausanias treated the Coan lady . . . [he] sent the lady back to Cos, and she took with her the apparel that the Persian had prepared for her as well as the rest of her belongings" (3.4.9–10). But there must also be a mention of the later Pausanias, son of Pleistoanax, who also never became king and was brought to trial in his native Sparta after refusing to press home his victory over the Athenians. Pausanias records that exactly half of the Spartan elders, together with the king of the other house, Agis, judged him guilty (3.5.2). He goes on to record, as Chateaubriand does, that Pausanias took refuge in the temple of Athena Alea in Tegea.

Whether or not Pausanias is being elliptical about his unfortunate namesake here, it is worth taking further, despite the risk of anachronism, the comparisons between the ancient travel writer and the modern. The subjective investment of each, so far as it can be gauged, is necessarily relative to the Mediterranean world as they saw it. But we find tantalizing similarities as well as points of difference. Pausanias, as is noted several times in this collection of essays, holds to an ideal, even a "sublime," view of Greek monuments, Greek art, and Greek religion. A member of the "well-to-do, educated Greek aristocracy," as Cohen puts it (chap. 6, this volume), he is distinctly neglectful of the Roman contribution to the sites that he describes and gives no explicit attention to the political situation of Greece within the Roman empire of the second century A.D. Again, in Cohen's terms, it would appear that "the intellectual climate in which Pausanias wrote highlighted the achievements of pre-Roman, independent Greece and held on to the notion of a distinct Greek identity."

The Breton aristocrat Chateaubriand had, by comparison, two scarcely reconcilable models of identity in mind when he made his decision to set out from Paris to Jerusalem in 1806. One was born of the prediction of the Benedictine prior of Plancoët, that he would visit the Virgin of Nazareth. He would travel in the footsteps of the medieval Comte de Chateaubriand who had fought in the Holy Land with Saint Louis and served a period of captivity with the Saracens.[5] The writer who had recently published his *Génie du christianisme* to confute the Voltairean ideals of the eighteenth century was all too ready to envisage his journey to Jerusalem as a modern pilgrimage. The other model of identity came, however, from a more present reality. It was Napoleon who by signing a concordat with the papacy paved the way for Chateaubriand's success as a neo-Christian author, and it was Napoleon who, after his Egyptian expedition, had led a second French army into the Holy Land. As Chateaubriand expressed it in the Egyptian section of his *Itinéraire,* the sad day of Mansourah (when Saint Louis was defeated by the Saracens) was avenged by the Battle of the Pyramids.[6] Though he excised specific references to the emperor from editions of the *Itinéraire* coming out after 1815, he was still very much in awe, in his journey of 1806, of the force that had tamed the revolution: the "necessary man." He was also, in practical terms, reliant as a traveler on the network of French governmental representatives overseas.

It would be fair to say, nevertheless, that the descendant of pilgrims and crusaders predominates in the *Itinéraire,* at the expense of the imperial servant. Chateaubriand finds on entering Sparta that he can convince a Turkish interlocutor of the purpose of his journey only by explaining it as a pilgrimage to Jerusalem. "This Turk could not understand that I would leave my country for a simple motive of curiosity; but he found it quite natural that I would undertake a long journey to go and pray at a tomb."[7] Equally, when he has finally located the site of the ancient city, his most emotive tribute to its reputation is: "When Nero visited Greece, he did not dare to enter Lacedaemon."[8] When Chateaubriand finally broke with the emperor in 1807, it was through a carefully coded newspaper article that invoked Nero in connection with the imperial court.[9]

Is there any helpful comparison to be drawn in this connection between the travel writing of the Greek gentleman who reverently explores the Greek past and that of the Breton embarked on a voyage of discovery in which his own identity is put so egregiously into play? The very fact that they both choose to list sites and objects, rather than describe events, is a minimal indication. Thucydides begins his *Peloponnesian War* (I.I.I.) with the statement that this was to be a war "more worth writing about" than any other. Pausanias uses exactly the same word (*axiologotata*) to explain that he has "not mentioned everything in order" (3.9.1) but selected according to this criterion of worth. In so doing, he picks up the use of same term by Herodotus (2.148), who assesses the temples of Ephesus and Samos as "worth writing about." Perhaps the very judgment that sites and objects remaining from the past (as opposed to great contemporary events) are "worth writing about" is a cultural phenomenon of unusual specificity. It depends radically on the possibility of constituting a "writing subject" who is free to make such discriminations.

Having said this, however, it must be obvious that Chateaubriand pursues a strategy entirely different from that of "the other in the note." It is precisely because Pausanias, and indeed the other authorities he has consulted, cannot indicate the site of ancient Sparta to a modern traveler that Chateaubriand must stage an amusing *peripeteia* for the reader's benefit. On arrival at "Misitra" (i.e., Mistra), the Byzantine town overlooking the valley of the Eurotas, he believes himself to be already on the venerable site and arranges a day's excursion to Amyclae in anticipation of his intensive sightseeing on the day that follows. Unfortunately, he has not resolved the problem, and the reported dialogue with his *cicerone* renders in comic terms the impossibility of communicating to a modern Greek the question of "whether Mistra is Sparta."[10] Chateaubriand has to present the preexisting literary authorities as inconclusive, and the nineteenth-century population as uncomprehending, in order for his own rediscovery to make its mark.

But how will that rediscovery be signaled? Here there is a significant innovation to note, and one that allies Chateaubriand with the visual sensibility of the new century in its most advanced form. It would be absurd to try and sum up briefly the visual character of Pausanias's descriptions, and other contributors to this volume have in any case clarified many of their aspects. As a generalization, however, it could be said that his listing of monuments and works of art proceeds by contiguities, for which the syntactical protocols are prepositions like "above," "beside," and "near," as well as indexical markers referring to the position of the spectator, such as "to the right" and "to the left." Nowhere is the scene exhaustively described from a single viewpoint. Chateaubriand, on the other hand, explicitly adopts the panoramic point of view, in which the whole aspect of the site is displayed to the observer. He does so, in fact, on two occasions: first of all, in relation to the delusory spectacle of the plain as seen from the heights of Mistra:

> So here I am mounted on the ramparts of the castle of Mistra, discovering, contemplating, and admiring all of Laconia. But when will you speak of Sparta, the reader will say to me? Where are the remains of this town? Are they contained within Mistra? Are there no traces remaining?[11]

The answer comes soon enough. The next day Chateaubriand is standing on the highest point overlooking the site of ancient Sparta, in the plain many miles from Mistra: "If you place yourself with me on the hill of the citadel, this is what you will see around you."[12] There follows a lengthy description of the geographical and natural setting and the monuments to be seen all around, which Chateaubriand confesses to be in part the emanations of his own scholarly fantasy: "I counted in this vast space seven ruins standing above ground, but completely shapeless and degraded. As I could choose, I gave one of these remains the name of the temple of Helen; the other, that of the tomb of Alcmeon . . . So I took the side of fable and recognized for history only the temple of Lycurgus."

In saying that Chateaubriand cultivates the panoramic point of view, one is doing no more than repeating his own, quite justified claim to have influenced the development of this distinctive new form of spectacle, which was available in Paris from the beginning of the century but acquired new popular appeal and technical perfection with the Restoration. Pierre Prévost inaugurated his *Panorama of Jerusalem* in 1819 and his particularly acclaimed *Panorama of Athens* in 1821.[13] Chateaubriand confirms that his previously published descriptions were not superseded: "my exactitude was found to be such, that fragments of the *Itinéraire* were used in the popular programme and explanation of the pictures of the *Panorama*."[14]

No visual panorama of Sparta was ever put before the French public. Yet in staging his rediscovery of the ruined city at the beginning of the *Itinéraire,* and in framing a comprehensive view which demonstrably owed much of its detail to his own literary and historical imagination, Chateaubriand marks a new stage in the vivid apprehension of the Classical past. Because he is a poet, he has the liberty of *preferring* to think, not about the Spartans' black gruel, but rather about the memory of "the only poet that Lacedaemon produced, and the crown of flowers that the daughters of Sparta collected for Helen"—the latter reference being explained by a quote from one of the books that he no doubt carried in his baggage: Virgil's *Georgics.*

Chateaubriand's travel writing thus embodies the revelation that the past can be reinvoked rhetorically on the basis of the modern subject's desire for it. This is an intuition that will form the grounding of Michelet's *History of France.*[15] But it can never have been more transparently conveyed than in the description of Chateaubriand's meeting, on his journey out of Laconia, with a young peasant who had "the air of Meleager, in his build and in his clothing."[16] Pausanias would recall of his visit to Sicyon: "It is also said that in this temple Meleager dedicated the spear with which he slew the boar" (2.7.9). But his formulation makes it undecidable whether Meleager has, for him, a real or a fictive status.[17] Chateaubriand stages the incident in such a way that the distinction can simply be transcended by the intensity of the encounter, and by its rhetorical resolution. He sees Meleager first of all in the dress of the young man, in his tunic, sandals, and distinctive coiffure. But the important point is that Chateaubriand's folkloric gaze is then reciprocated: the young man seems no less fascinated by Chateaubriand. "My new companion, seated, as I have said, in front of me, surveyed my movements with an extreme ingenuousness. He said not a word, and devoured me with his eyes."[18] When Chateaubriand starts on his journey again, the young man follows in his tracks running for more than half an hour, without speaking or indicating what it is that he might wish to convey. So there comes to be a mysterious contract between the Breton traveler and the person he conceives to be a "descendant of the true Spartans," which can be expressed in the form of a perfect chiasmus. "I was touched, I know not why, perhaps in seeing myself, me a civilized barbarian, the object of the curiosity of a Greek become barbarian." The message could be that such an encounter epitomizes the magnetic lure of the classical past.

Commentary

JOHN F. CHERRY

Travel, Nostalgia, and Pausanias's Giant

> Nostalgia, they say, is an exercise in grammar wherein you find the
> present tense and the past perfect.
> P. O. Whitmer, *When the Going Gets Weird* (New York 1993): 267

Now I think about it, my own first foray into the Peloponnese had
a Pausanian flavor. As we traveled together down from the Isthmus
to the Argive Plain, my then-professor, at that time working on a study of the
topography of the ancient Corinthia,[1] began to wax lyrical about the Tretos Pass,
through which we were driving. His words, though, were not so much a personal, traveler's-eye response to the inspiring landscape as a mélange of loosely
remembered phrases from the colorful passage in volume 3 of Sir James Frazer's
1898 commentary on Pausanias:

> The more convenient way from the valley of Cleonae to the plain of Argos . . .
> was the pass of the Tretus. . . . In antiquity it was, as Pausanias tells us, a
> driving road, and the ruts worn by the chariot-wheels can still be seen in many
> places. . . . The road runs by a deeply worn watercourse, at the bottom of which
> a clear and shallow stream finds its way amid luxuriant thickets of oleander,
> myrtle, and arbutus. The lower slopes of the mountains are also green with
> shrubs, but their upper slopes are grey and rocky. . . . At the southern outlet of
> the pass the whole plain of Argos, with the mountains on either hand and the
> sea in the distance, bursts suddenly on the view.[2]

As Sutton (chap. 9, this volume) reminds us, Pausanias himself in fact says
almost nothing about the Tretos or its surrounds: for him, here as elsewhere,
the rural landscape amounted merely to "a void crossed by the lifeline of the
road system."[3] Frazer's lengthy commentary on the Tretos (and the nearby cave
of the Nemean lion) is thus a hyperelaborated gloss on just a few phrases of
Pausanias (2.15.2, 4).

247

But if we travelers of the 1970s were unable to "see" the Tretos without the literary mediation of Frazer (and Pausanias), the same, *mutatis mutandis,* is certainly true of Frazer also. The passage in question manages in four pages to look over its shoulder at, and is quite clearly colored by, the *récits de voyages* of a veritable procession of some twenty earlier Tretos-travelers whom he cites—from Chandler, Dodwell, and Gell to the *Baedeker* and *Guide-Joanne* of Frazer's own day (not to mention a number of ancient testimonia). An edifice of textuality intervenes between Frazer and Pausanias, between Frazer and the place "Tretos." Millennia of writing/reading have transformed a physical location into, as it were, a "textual zone"—or what Michel Butor, in his justly famous 1974 essay "Travel and Writing," terms an *espace de lecture.*[4] Neither we nor Frazer and his many precursors nor Pausanias himself entered the Tretos as textual innocents. This example may seem jejune; but behind it lie some points I think we would do well to keep in mind as we approach Pausanias.

Elsner (chap. 1, this volume) rightly castigates classicists for their reticence, at least compared to a number of other disciplines, in taking the literature of travel seriously as a genre.[5] His own contributions to Pausanian studies, specifically, have greatly enhanced appreciation of Pausanias's travel writing as a subtle literary artifact, a self-consciously elaborated textual performance, a vehicle of cultural self-perception—in the sense of an actor-centered, experiential account of "a journey into identity." More controversially, he has made a case for taking Pausanias's account, not as that of an antiquarian intellectual, but as a "pagan pilgrimage," in many respects anticipating that of later Christian pilgrims such as Egeria.[6] This reading too has opened up valuable insights. We understand much better, for example, the ideology driving Pausanias's seeming obsession with religious monuments; his work becomes intelligible as a highly wrought narrative of a transformative encounter with the sacred Other; seemingly pedantic descriptions, "digressions," and myth-historical interpretations, which many have supposed were introduced "to relieve the tedium of the topographic part of his work,"[7] come into proper focus as a carefully selected set of elements intended to structure a *Grèce imaginaire,* meaningful to provincial Greeks under Roman rule as they wrestled with problems of cultural and political identity.[8]

There is a great deal to commend this line of analysis, especially if we take "pilgrimage" in its widest sense as "a journey to those places which speak, which tell us of our history and ourselves" (the resonant phrases, again, of Michel Butor).[9] On the other hand, so strong a focus on the religious experience in Pausanias carries with it the commensurate danger of generating too unidimensional a reading, one that elides too many of his other interests and agenda. Cohen is quite correct in noting that Pausanias is no longer a unified subject for modern scholarship, and I warm to her opening remark (in chap. 6, this volume) that he "has come to exemplify a complex series of overlapping allegiances as regards genre." That comes as no surprise: travel writing, something quite hard to define, is an unstable and hybrid genre that straddles categories.[10] As Jonathan Raban puts it: "As a literary form, travel writing is a notoriously raffish open house where very different genres are likely to end up in the same bed."[11]

Pausanias, to be sure, was in part pilgrim, mythographer, ethnographer, cartographer, geographer, historian, art historian, antiquarian; but overriding, or binding together, all these interests is the characteristic discourse of *travel* writing—that is, a literary work constructed, however artificially or imaginatively, from the raw material of journeys Pausanias had himself undertaken. Styling him too restrictively as (merely) a religious tourist visiting sacred sites (i.e., as the author of a pilgrimage narrative, one very specific form of travel writing) somewhat occludes the possibility of treating Pausanias comparatively and critically alongside the many other forms of literary production, both ancient and much more recent, that we might classify as the literature of travel.[12]

Reading the chapters of this volume, I am struck by how some aspects of "Pausanias's project" (as Elsner, Porter, and others like to refer to it) in fact mirror features that one could argue to be virtually endemic to most forms of travel writing, irrespective of cultural context.[13] Putting this another way, my response to a number of rather specific claims about the ways in which structure or selection or emphasis or omission in the *Periegesis* serves this particular author's aims in his "project" would be: "But *così fan tutti!*"[14] This observation could lead in several rather different directions, but I will expand here on just two (closely related) points by way of example: the preconditioning of travel by text; and the rhetoric of nostalgia and belatedness.

Travel and Textual Mediation

As Heil recently remarked, "de auctore nihil constat nisi quod ex eius opere colligitur."[15] This statement applies just as much to Pausanias's compositional methods as it does to the man himself and his intentions in writing. That he was well educated and widely read is everywhere apparent. Since his travels and writing were spread over many years, and his text is crisscrossed with a network of over a hundred backward-looking or anticipatory self-references, one may imagine a protracted dialectical process involving the mutual confrontation of (i) what Pausanias already knew or had read, (ii) preparatory library researches (Pergamum, we may note, was handily close to Pausanias's own probable home area in Magnesia ad Sipylum), (iii) personal autopsy on the road, (iv) evaluation of the testimony of the *exegetai,* and (v) subsequent checking and follow-up reading. This does not seem very controversial.

Exactly *what* he had read, or at least what he mentions explicitly, is a matter that the publication of comprehensive indexes to Pausanias has now made it easier to explore.[16] It is the wide range and sheer quantity of it that are impressive. He names 125 different authors, some (such as Homer, Hesiod, and Pindar) repeatedly, and he quotes directly from a good many of them; in the *Periegesis* as a whole, in fact, there are nearly 700 such references, either to authors' names or works or to their actual words. The true figure is higher yet, since one must also take account of "hidden" allusions (e.g., to Herodotus), demonstrable evidence of his familiarity with known works never mentioned explicitly by name (e.g., several of Plutarch's *Lives;* and his reliance on Polybius for the history of

Achaea in Book VII), and the hugely problematic identification—usually inconclusive—of sources, whether historical or periegetic, that are no longer fully extant.[17]

Virtually every Pausanian scholar of this century has gone over this ground. My own amateur reading does not see much of a hidden subtext in Pausanias's choice of sources. Avoiding mention of any contemporary or Roman writer might indeed have been conscious strategy: but he *was* writing in Greek, as a Greek himself, about mainland Greece, primarily for Greeks wherever they lived within the empire, and it is not obvious what these "omitted" Roman sources would have added to his already comprehensive coverage. He emphasizes the epic and lyric poets, references all of the canonical tragic and comic dramatists, shows interest in any author with things to say about myth and cult, and is thoroughly familiar with all the historians, even the unfashionable Hellenistic ones. His choices appear to be determined by a mixture of personal preference, the taste of his age, and, above all, relevance to the themes and authorial agenda of his work (hence, perhaps, his disinterest in the philosophers). Pausanias's "project" may indeed have centered on the construction of the mythical ideal of a glorified Greek past set in a much earlier age than his own; but that emerges far more strongly from his lopsided predilections concerning art and architecture, and from what he chose to "see" and record at the sites he visited, than it does from his selection of written sources.

In fact, I would direct the emphasis in the rather different direction hinted at in my opening paragraphs. It is less the selectivity than the *range* and *richness* of literary reference, with an example on almost every one of his 900 pages, that I find conspicuous—something that surely distinguishes him from other ancient travel writers (insofar as we can know them). For Pausanias, others' writings traveled with him in imagination, and shaped his choices and perceptions: he was visiting—rereading, so to speak—an *already written landscape.* Another way of expressing Pausanias's "project," one might say, is that what he had seen in his imagination, through the literature he had read (as well as via the words of others he heard on-site), was really more vivid to him than what he had seen with his own eyes. Significantly, however, "this curious interplay between literary experience and lived experience forms one of the defining characteristics of the genre of travel literature."[18]

The perceptive article "The Travel Writer and the Text" by Heather Henderson, from which the quotation just cited is drawn, borrows for its subtitle a phrase of Ralph Waldo Emerson, "My giant goes with me wherever I go." As she explains:

> The giant that accompanies every travel writer is constructed in part by the books he or she has read. . . . The literate traveler cannot escape the literature that preconditions his experience of travel. Where he goes, as Emerson observed in "Self-Reliance" [1841], the traveler carries his "giant" with him.[19]

Henderson is hardly alone among modern critics in emphasizing the importance of such "textual mediation," the interposition of texts between the traveler and sights/sites. It is, of course, a particularly prevalent feature of self-conscious forms of modern travel writing in the postcolonial age of globalization, which offers vanishingly few uninscribed landscapes about which to write; but it is likewise a strand in most travel writing about the Classical lands and the Orient ever since people began to travel with Homer in their heads. Monuments, places, landscapes, assume their interest, not so much for any intrinsic qualities, as from the fact that they already have a place in literary representation, and that others have seen and mentioned them before.[20]

A consequence of such an attitude is the preference for traces of the past over observable present-day conditions; travel writing is full of authors working themselves up into a suitably historical frame of mind to imagine scenes from the past in the very places they occurred, meanwhile ignoring all to be seen around them (the central point, of course, of Sutton's chapter in this volume). In *Eothen* (1844), arguably the first truly modern travel book, Alexander King-lake wrote that

> there are people who can visit an interesting locality, and follow up continu-ously the exact train of thought which ought to be suggested by the historical associations of the place. A person of this sort can go to Athens, and think of nothing later than the age of Pericles; can live with the Scipios as long as he stays in Rome.[21]

And we encounter precisely the same sentiment in a narrative of travel over much the same route as Kinglake's, one and a half centuries later: "For there to be any point in travelling, you have always to be looking at things as they were, and dodging things as they are."[22]

This, obviously, comes close to Pausanias's viewpoint. One of the *Peri-egesis*'s defining features is its very *lack* of the expectable stuff of a journey's narrative: nothing about the passing landscape and its inhabitants, chance en-counters along the way, food and accommodation, or indeed the privations and pleasures of travel in general—merely the relentless ". . . resuming the road to Argos, we have on the left the ruins of Mycenae. The Greeks are aware that the founder of Mycenae was Perseus," etc. (2.15.4). Plenty of this could have been written without leaving the armchair. Pausanias travels as much through his literary imagination as through "real" experience. Certainly, it is hard to point to passages in Pausanias that do not relate to *loca sancta,* to landscapes with myth-historical associations, or to storied places in the history of a *Grèce imaginaire.* Pausanias's trip to Greece began in reading and in images derived from reading. It shares with most travel narratives a fundamental and unresolved tension between the nature of a lived experience and reading and writing about that experience.

Here we return to Butor, who has explored with great subtlety the complex dialectic of this nexus of traveling, reading, and writing. Other francophone writers have taken this further still. Philippe Dubois, for instance, speaks in terms of what he calls "le triangle butorien." Christian Jacob refers to Pausa-nias's myth-historical space, specifically, as a place "où le parcours est aussi une lecture, où l'espace est un récit."[23] And Sophie Basch, in her *Le voyage imaginaire,* has exposed the essentially "bookish" character of most twentieth-century French travel writing about Greece:

> Les voyageurs du XXe siècle se rendent en Grèce malgré la Grèce moderne, dans une Grèce entre guillemets. Leur vrai Grèce est une Grèce de cabinet, la Grèce livresque . . . Au fond, ils n'ont pas tellement envie de partir.[24]

Belatedness and Nostalgia in Pausanias

Pausanias's account is imbued with a strongly elegiac strain of disappointment. It is full of descriptions of ruin and sorry delapidation, of temples whose roofs have collapsed, of places whose Time has Passed; there is a stubborn unwillingness to give much, if any, credit for the brushed-up conditions of at least some parts of Greece under Roman rule (for which we now have independent archaeological evidence). Sorting out the extent to which Pausanias can be read as a blueprint of a "real" experience, rather than a literary trope, is understandably crucial for those who would like to suppose he can provide useful historical material on Roman Greece. Pausanias's negativity is mirrored, of course, in writers both Greek (Polybius, Strabo, Plutarch, Dio Chrysostom) and Roman (Cicero, Horace, Ovid, Seneca), but Alcock has shown how easy it is to identify in them rhetorical stances underlying such "obsession with past glory compared with present obscurity."[25]

From what I have already said, however, it should be no surprise that the themes involved here pervade much travel writing and are hardly unique to Pausanias, even if he does put them to work for his "project." These themes I take to be an awareness of *belatedness* and a rhetoric of *nostalgia.*

The *locus classicus* for the former is Lévi-Strauss's tirade against travel writing in the early pages of his *Tristes Tropiques*—ironic precisely because it introduces a massive ethnographic travel narrative:

> Journeys, those magic caskets full of dream-like promises, will never again yield up their treasures untarnished. . . . The perfumes of the tropics and the pristine freshness of human beings have been corrupted. . . . I wished I had lived in the days of *real* journeys, when it was still possible to see the full splendor of a spectacle that had not yet been blighted, polluted and spoilt; I wished I had not trodden that ground as myself, but as Bernier, Tavernier or Manucci did. . . . Would it have been better to arrive in Rio in the eighteenth century with Bougainville, or in the sixteenth with Léry and Thevet? . . . In short, I have only two possibilities: either I can be like some traveller of the olden days . . . or I can be a modern traveller, chasing after the vestiges of a vanished reality.[26]

Such conceits, understandably, have taken center stage in much nineteenth- and twentieth-century travel writing, whose authors struggle to accommodate the loss of the object of their desires: in the former case, for instance, the dissolution of the Orient under European colonialism, in the latter, the loss of empire itself.[27]

But belatedness is a perennial preoccupation, and these same ideas run like a ground bass through the travel literature of many eras. In a sense, they go with the turf: for those who travel through already-inscribed landscapes, it proves almost impossible to avoid dreaming of a past that has already passed into myth, yearning to have been a "real" traveler *then—When the Going Was Good,* as the title of Evelyn Waugh's book about his pre-war travels famously put it.[28] This sense of studied anachronism, an unwillingness or inability to see his world as having changed irrevocably, lies at the very heart of Pausanias too. The "Greece" through which he traveled, both in reality and in imagination, was several hundred years too late. He is scarcely alone among travel writers in working through his anxieties about cultural displacement by "seeking solace for a troubled present in nostalgic cultural myths."[29]

Nostalgia for other times and places, in fact, is a fundamental quality of travel writing. Although Arafat's 1996 book *Pausanias' Greece* has demonstrated that Pausanias's attitude to things Roman was less straightforward than some have maintained, by his silences and deliberate omissions Pausanias everywhere makes apparent his muted enthusiasm for *Romanitas;* he was a less than fully signed-up participant in empire (even though, paradoxically, it was the settled conditions of empire that made his travels and writing possible in the first place). The reverse of this coin, then, is his intense nostalgia for a lost authenticity that exists only in the past. He seeks a free and independent Greek past of his own invention, knowing in advance that this is both spurious and impossible. Here is the traveler "chasing after the vestiges of a vanished reality" (Lévi-Strauss, again), torn between describing the world he sees and his desire to make it conform to preconceptions of it derived from religious experience, myth-history, and literature—an instance, that is, of the tension between "travel writing's desire to come to terms with a complex world in transformation and its nostalgic need to restore the imaginary site of a 'simpler' past."[30]

The playful definition of nostalgia embodied in the quotation at the head of this commentary—"the present tense and the past perfect"[31]—is one with which Pausanias would have agreed absolutely. Nostalgic reimagining of the past is central to his entire work, just as it is one of the basic preoccupations of all travel literature.[32] Literary journeys usually turn out to be much more about time than place, just as the landscapes they traverse are intrinsically temporal.[33]

Pausanias's Readers?

These remarks arise, not as a critique of the excellent contributions to this volume, but from the wish to build on them, by reconnecting Pausanias to some pervasive themes in later travel writing. If this makes the *Periegesis* both a more powerful and (conceivably) a more influential work, it also raises the matter of his *reception*—or, more bluntly, the question of whether anyone ever read him.

Knowing what we do of the literary culture of the Second Sophistic, guesses about the audience he might have aimed for (well-educated literary connoisseurs like himself?) are certainly possible;[34] but Pausanias says barely a word about his overall intentions—his "project"—and the missing nonintegral preface, which Bowie (in chap. 2, this volume) plausibly proposes might have offered a statement of purpose, remains missing. I am amused by the arguments swirling around the notion that Pausanias's systematic coverage of different regions, starting from their central places, made his work usable by at least some of his readers on-site, in *Blue Guide* fashion. Habicht envisages the impracticability of open-air wrestling with armfuls of book rolls, in search of the passage appropriate to the moment; Bowie counters by pointing out that only one roll at a time would be needed, and roll-handling duties would likely be in the hands of a slave of the leisured, well-to-do πεπαιδευμένος; Elsner cuts the Gordian knot by raising the (slim) possibility of availability in codex form.[35] Whatever the case, not a shred of evidence exists to indicate that anyone actually did (or, for that matter, did not) make use of the *Periegesis* in this way; and yet so discursive a work seems more fit for armchair-bound literary delectation, at least compared to the many more practical guidebooks, enumerative lists, itineraries, regionaries, *periploi,* etc., that existed in the Roman world. And then there is the question, exhaustively considered here by Bowie, of ancient readers and writers who signal some knowledge of Pausanias's text. We have only three nominations: one (Aelian) possibly suspect; one (Philostratus) perhaps only using a source that Pausanias also used; and one (Longus) providing, at best, the faintest of verbal echoes. On the whole, I prefer Diller's more forthright view: that Pausanias's work "made no impression or very little on contemporary literature," and if published at all, "it was in a limited issue for private circulation among the author's acquaintances"; quite possibly, a single copy was simply "deposited in some great library in Rome or the East," ensuring its preservation and availability to Stephanus Byzantius, after whom we find no trace of knowledge of the work until Arethas, archbishop of Caesarea, in the tenth century.[36]

I confess no expertise in any of these matters, but I detect a "wish it were so" attitude underlying much discussion of Pausanias's seeming failure to attain literary fame, and I certainly side with Habicht in his opinion that Pausanias's chief miscalculation may have lain in writing for an audience that did not really exist.[37] Habicht's excellent 1985 book marks a turning point, in its demonstration that the *Periegesis* is both more trustworthy and a great deal more sophisticated than the late-nineteenth-century "Pausaniacs" allowed. But has the pendulum now swung too far? If nobody much read him (in his own day or in later antiquity), if he never became a model for emulation, if the ways in which he made sense of his "Greece" seemingly made no sense to or had little influence on his contemporaries, then what price the vaunted "Pausanian project" of recent scholarship? If it is really so powerful an exploration of identity through memory and myth-history, and if its primary discourse concerns cultural anxiety about, and resistance to, Roman imperialism ("how to be a Roman Greek"),[38] then why did it not resonate more widely?

I wonder, in fact, if we shouldn't face the fact that the work is simply less successful than some modern readers (and presumably Pausanias himself) would like it to have been. Notwithstanding the web of textuality that I have suggested as fundamental to his account, perhaps not *every* phrase counts, not *every* example is replete with significance, and perhaps *some* aspects of the work's structure simply reflect how Pausanias encountered or remembered things. Notwithstanding Konstan's apt remarks (this volume) about the pleasures the ancients derived from exercising a well-stocked memory, did anyone—then, at least—either need or want to encounter, in a literary work, such things as the excruciatingly detailed enumeration of the 203 most notable victor statues standing in the sanctuary of Zeus at Olympia (6.1–18)? Was Pausanias just badly in need of a good editor? No matter how useful he may be to modern scholars or how intriguing the interpretive challenges of his *Periegesis,* as a habitual reader of travel writing I am glad that there is many a more lively work out there to be read.[39]

A Pictorial Postscript

Joseph Michael Gandy (1771–1843)
The Persian Porch and Place of Consultation of the Lacedemonians. Watercolor
and gouache over pen and pencil; 43.4 × 64.3 cm; ca. 1816. (See fig. 27.)

The watercolor reproduced in figure 27 was shown at the Royal
Academy in the Exhibition of 1816 ("the Forty-eighth") under the
title *The Persian Porch and place of consultation of the Lacedemonians* [*sic*].[1]
The artist, Joseph Michael Gandy, an architect who spent much of his career as
the "perspectivist" employed by Sir John Soane,[2] inscribed this title along with
the notation "Vide Pausanias B.III C 11" in ink on a sheet accompanying the
picture.[3] The explicit reference to Pausanias marks this image as a special instance of the *Nachleben* of the *Description of Greece*. It stands out as one of a
remarkable series of visual interrogations of Pausanias's text, realized as architectural fantasy, that Gandy exhibited at the Royal Academy throughout his
lengthy career. These have never been studied as a group—indeed, most are
known only from the Academy exhibition catalogues, though some (such as the
one illustrated here) have come to light in recent years. Table 5 provides a list
of those pictures by Gandy (mainly watercolors) whose titles specifically cite
Pausanias and usually also a given portion of his text.[4] As a group, they indicate
a remarkable and persistent interest in Pausanias over the course of more than
twenty years, in which the Periegete's text served as inspiration for a highly
exceptional antiquarian vision.[5]

Gandy's watercolor *The Persian Porch* was deliberately conceived and ad-
vertised, like the others in the series, as a visual engagement with, and interpretation of, a passage in Pausanias's text. As such, it is—in its own way—no
less compelling or far-fetched than the nineteenth-century travelers' and archaeologists' use of Pausanias as guide, or the scholars' urge to follow him through
the byways of ancient ritual. Gandy's vision has a neoclassical grandeur in
which the old agora of Sparta (itself probably romanticized in Pausanias's account) becomes an imperial fantasy hardly matched by the best actual architecture of any modern European capital (let alone London, whose Greek Revival

FIGURE 27. Joseph Michael Gandy, *The Persian Porch and Place of Consultation of the Lacedemonians*, ca 1816. (Courtesy of the Getty Research Institute, Research Library, 910072*.)

TABLE 5. Citations of Pausanias in the Titles of Pictures by Joseph Michael Gandy

1. *Subterranean Temple: The hint of this design is taken from the caverns and temples of the oracles of the Cybell* [sic] *on the lake of Avernus, near Naples, and from the Adytum of the Greeks. Vide Pausanias* . . . (no. 373, 1802, p. 18).

2. *The Odeum, or Music-school. — Vide Pau. Att.* (no. 906, 1806, p. 34).

3. *The Open Temple and Temple Tower of the Greeks, designed from various remarks in Pausanius's* [sic] *Description* (no. 355, 1808, p. 19).

4. *The interior part of a sea-port. — Vide Pausanias b ii, c xii* (no. 359, 1809, p. 18).

5. *A composition in Greek architecture, designed from Pausanius's* [sic] *description of Greece. — Vide Achaias* [sic] *chap xxi* (no. 844, 1812, p. 37).

6. *Architectural composition: The vapour rising from the miraculous fountain of Agno to supply the earth with rain, in the mountains of Lycaeus, agreeably to the wishes of the Arcadians. — Vide Pausanias b viii c 38* (no. 835, 1813, p. 35).

7. *The great temple of Ceres at Eleusis: A composition of Greek embellishments from Pausanias and other authors, and from discoveries made on the spot by the last mission of the Dilettanti Society* (no. 770, 1815, p. 34).

8. *The Oracle of Mercury: A Hermes in the market-place of Patrae. Vide Taylor's Pausanias, Achaiacs* [sic] *book vii, c 22. — The Hermes were not only used as markers for boundaries to land, amongst the ancients, but adorned the door-posts of the Athenian homes and temples, as the god protector against thieves* (no. 858, 1815, p. 38).

9. *The Persian Porch and place of consultation of the Lacedemonians* [sic]. *— Vide Pausanias B.III C 11* (no. 806, 1816, p. 36).

10. *Idea of a bridge and path amongst the Platxenses* [sic] *to commemorate the victories by sea and land against the Persians. — Vide Pausanias* (no. 903, 1817, p. 40).

11. *Jupiter Pluvius, Lebedea — Vide Pausanias' Greece, B ix c xxxix to xli* (no. 1086, 1819, p. 45).

12. *An architectural composition, from an idea of the hollow way between Argos and Mysenae* [sic], *on reading Pausanias book ii. chap. 23 and 24* (no. 969, 1823, p. 40).

Note: The references are to the picture number in the relevant exhibition, the year shown, and the page in that year's Royal Academy catalogue.

was reaching its peak around 1820).[6] Yet the impulse to fantasy—hardly checked by the details of Pausanias's text—is (in the title) apparently subordinated to the scholarship of the learned reference.

All the painting's many details—statues, temples, urns, flowerpots—seem to come from Gandy's fertile imagination, suggested perhaps by the vividness of Pausanias's account but not actually commensurate with it. Here is the relevant portion of the text in Frazer's version:

> The Lacedaemonians of Sparta have a market-place that is worth seeing, and in the market-place are the Council House of the Senate and the offices of the Ephors, of the Guardians of the Laws and of the so-called Bidiaeans . . . The most striking monument of the market-place is a colonnade which they name the Persian Colonnade. Built originally from the spoils of the Persian war, it grew in course of time into the spacious and splendid edifice which it now is. On the pillars are figures of Persians in white marble: one of them is Mardonius, son of Gobryas. Artemisia, daughter of Lygdamis, Queen of Halicarnassus, is also represented. . . . In the market-place there is a temple of Caesar, the first Roman who aspired to the throne, and the founder of the present system of

government. There is also in the market-place a temple to Caesar's son Augustus, who placed the monarchy on a firmer basis, and attained a height of dignity and power which his father never reached. His name Augustus is equivalent in Greek to *sebastos* ("august," "reverend"). Beside the altar of Augustus they show a bronze statue of Agias. . . . In the market-place at Sparta there are images of Pythaean Apollo, Artemis, and Latona. This whole place is called Chorus, because of the festival of Gymnopaediae, to which the Lacedaemonians attach the greatest importance, the lads dance choral dances in honour of Apollo. Not far from these is a sanctuary of Earth and of Market Zeus; another of Market Athena and Poseidon, whom they surname "Asphalius" ("securer"); and a third of Apollo and Hera. There is also a colossal statue of the Spartan people. . . . The Lacedaemonians also have a sanctuary of the Fates, and beside it is the grave of Orestes, son of Agamemnon. For in obedience to an oracle they brought the bones of Orestes from Tegea and buried them here. Beside the grave of Orestes is a statue of Polydorus, son of Alcamenes. . . . There is also a Market Hermes carrying the infant Dionysus; also what is called the old Ephorea (office of the Ephors), containing the tombs of Epimenides the Cretan, and of Aphareus, son of Perieres. (3.11.2–11)

Gandy's watercolor is not an archaeologically or textually accurate rendition of Pausanias's chapter.[7] It does not even attempt to render all the text's monuments in a plausible order or arrangement. Rather, Gandy allows the themes implicit in Pausanias's enumeration of buildings and statues to inspire him: his concern is not with the list of items—or indeed the items in the list—but with the visual evocation of what he took to be the main themes underlying Pausanias's account. These focus on conquest (in the Greek victory over the Persians, in Gandy's own period perhaps redolent of recent British victories over the French), on imperialism and monarchical power (in all the official buildings of government with which Pausanias prefaces his description, as well as in the references to Caesar and Augustus, which allow Gandy to turn Sparta into a modern imperial capital), on religion (not only in all the temples, but also in the smoking altar at the picture's center right), as well as on death (suggested by Pausanias's closing notes on tombs and evoked by the commemorative resonance of Gandy's monuments and the urn to the picture's right). What he takes from the text's careful listing is the "feel" of a richly adorned public ceremonial center, whose columns, statues, and buildings emerge from Gandy's imaginative vision.[8] In the specific instance of temples to Roman emperors in juxtaposition to the Persian colonnade, Gandy misreads Pausanias. For Gandy these things go together as a general picture of antique imperial glory, but for Pausanias—one suspects—the pairing is highly ironic, creating an implicit contrast between the monument to Greek liberty erected by the city most responsible for freeing Greece from the Persian threat and the temples to Roman rulers, which signal nothing less than contemporary enslavement. Yet even in this misunderstanding, Gandy is right to see the text as far more than just an architectural record; for what he paints is its "imaginary"—that is, his version of what the agora of Sparta is made to mean in Pausanias's description. The golden coloring and the dramatic sky add luster to the vision.

Yet this is a visual interpretation that radically transgresses aspects of the tenor of Pausanias's writing. Famously, Pausanias hardly peoples his text with any of his contemporaries and with little local color (except when he recounts ritual activity).[9] Gandy, however, brings his *Persian Porch* to life with a few characters wandering through the colonnade, which he casts in a beam of brilliant sunshine,[10] and with the rather odd couple in the front, of whom the man appears to be wielding a spear (is this one of the dances mentioned in the text?).[11] While Pausanias needs to exclude the present in order to render his monuments more directly redolent of the glorious fifth and fourth centuries B.C., Gandy's Sparta is indeterminately placed at any time in antiquity: both in the fifth century B.C. and in the second century A.D., when his source described the site. Here Gandy does more than simply break with Pausanias in envisioning a pristine yet peopled world, free of the ruins which dominate much of the text. He also moves beyond the unwritten rules governing the British tradition of illustrating antique sites in Greece and the eastern Mediterranean, established in the classic volumes of Wood, of Stuart and Revett and of Adam, all published in the 1750s and 1760s. These supplemented printed descriptions with two kinds of engravings: contemporary glimpses of ruins peopled by a genre world of colorful locals, on the one hand, and restored ideal views, on the other, bereft of settings and humans, presented as carefully measured model studies of canonical buildings.[12] Instead of this division prompted by the author-traveler's autopsy, Gandy's vision, inspired by his reading of Pausanias and his reworking of the text, renders Sparta as a restored and ideal view of a city in its context, populated with antique figures and set in a fantasy of a real antique world. Effectively, the shift from actual travel and archaeology (in the form of measuring monuments in situ) to reading a text and imagining the objects of its description leads to a transformation in the artist's interpretation of his subject matter. While the engravings of Wood, Stuart and Revett, and Adam still belong to the order of Classicism and remain grounded in an objective reality (which other travelers could always verify), the drawings of Gandy take the Classical toward a Romanticism of the sublime in which the grandeur of vision takes precedence over any kind of potentially "objective" evaluation. Only in the entablature on the right-hand side of the drawing—a kind of framing device—is the foliage of ruination allowed to impinge into Gandy's fantasy of classical perfection, allowing the smallest entrée of Pausanian desolation about the present (which is the condition for his nostalgia for the past) into the golden serenity of Spartan glory.

Notes

Abbreviations

Abbreviations generally follow the conventions of the *American Journal of Archaeology* 104 (2000): 3–24, and *The Oxford Classical Dictionary,* ed. S. Hornblower and A. Spawforth, 3rd ed. (Oxford, 1996).

AJA	*American Journal of Archaeology.*
AM	*Mitteilungen des Deutschen Archäologischen Instituts, Athenische Abteilung.*
ANRW	H. Temporini, ed. *Aufstieg und Niedergang der römischen Welt.* Berlin, 1972—.
BABesch	*Bulletin antieke beschaving. Annual Papers on Classical Archaeology.*
BCH	*Bulletin de correspondance hellénique.*
BICS	*Bulletin of the Institute of Classical Studies of the University of London.*
BSA	*Annual of the British School at Athens.*
CQ	*Classical Quarterly.*
CR	*Classical Review.*
EchCl	*Echos du monde classique/Classical Views.*
FGrHist	F. Jacoby, *Fragmente der griechischen Historiker.* (Berlin and Leiden 1923–58).
GRBS	*Greek, Roman, and Byzantine Studies.*
IG	*Inscriptiones Graecae.* (Berlin 1873–).
JdI	*Jahrbuch des Deutschen Archäologischen Instituts.*
JHS	*Journal of Hellenic Studies.*
JRS	*Journal of Roman Studies.*
JWalt	*Journal of the Walters Art Gallery.*
LSJ	H. G. Liddell and R. Scott, *Greek–English Lexicon* (9th ed., rev. H. Stuart Jones). (Oxford, 1925–40).
PCPS	*Proceedings of the Cambridge Philological Society.*
RA	*Revue archéologique.*
RE	G. Wissowa, E. Kroll et al., eds. *Paulys Real–Encyclopädie der klassischen Altertumswissenschaft.* (Stuttgart, 1893–).
REA	*Revue des études anciennes.*
REG	*Revue des études grecques.*
RM	*Mitteilungen des Deutschen Archäologischen Instituts, Römische Abteilung.*

TAPA   *Transactions of the American Philological Association*
YaleBull   *Yale University Art Gallery Bulletin.*
YCS   *Yale Classical Studies.*
ZPE   *Zeitschrift für Papyrologie und Epigraphik.*

Preface

1. Elsner 1992; Alcock 1993.
2. Arafat 1996; Pritchett 1998, 1999.
3. Bingen 1996; Aupert and Knoepfler, forthcoming.
4. Pirenne-Delforge and Purnelle 1997.
5. These are the Fondazione Lorenzo Valla series (e.g., Musti and Torelli 1986), of which five volumes have appeared at the time of writing this preface, and the Budé series (e.g., Casevitz, Pouilloux, and Chamoux 1992), of which three volumes have appeared.
6. Frazer 1898, vol. 1: viii.
7. Frazer's Pausanias, published in six volumes in 1898, occupied the bulk of his scholarly agenda before the first edition of *The Golden Bough* (1890) in two volumes and between this and the second, three-volume edition of 1900. Frazer had been contracted to produce a translation of Pausanias by Macmillan in 1884 and worked solidly on it until the end of 1886. For discussion of Frazer's Pausanias in the context of his life and works, see Ackerman 1987: 54–58, 127–42, 302. In Ackerman's judgment, not only was *Pausanias' "Description of Greece"* "the prototypical Frazerian opus" (1987: 57), but it was also key to the genesis of *The Golden Bough.*
8. Habicht 1985: 5.

Chapter 1

My thanks, as ever, are due to my fellow editors for their careful and critical perusal of an earlier draft. In general, I use the Loeb translation of Pausanias, often somewhat emended, throughout this chapter.

1. Honorable exceptions—both French—include Jacob 1991 and Hartog 1996.
2. The literature one might cite is vast. For accounts with a literary emphasis, see Pratt 1992; Islam 1996; Cardinal 1997. Up-to-date bibliographies, along with collections of new essays, may be found in Elsner and Rubiés 1999; Duncan and Gregory 1999.
3. On the notion of *"Grèce imaginaire"* in Pausanias, see Jacob 1980b: 37. On the text of Pausanias as discourse, and as an attempt to observe and enunciate an anthropology of Greek cult, see Calame 1995 and further in this area the series of essays in Pirenne-Delforge 1998b.
4. On this passage, see Alcock 1996: 267 and, at length, Nörenberg 1973.
5. See Habicht 1985: 6–7, with bibliography at nn. 33–34; Habicht here dismisses the theory of a lost Book XI (or even XII–XIV).
6. Generally, on the periegetic background to the genre Pausanias chooses, see Bowie 1974 (esp. 184–89); Habicht 1985: 2–4; Arafat 1996: 22–24 (both of the latter with further bibliography).
7. See Habicht 1985: 7–8, 11. Passages such as 8.8.3 certainly imply that the writing of the later books belongs relatively late in the Pausanian project—i.e., where they stand in the order of reading the text.
8. See the incomplete list in Settis 1968: 61–63, with Habicht 1985: 7; Elsner 1995: 137–40.

9. Note, however, that the existing manuscripts are descended from a single lost exemplar known to have been in Florence in 1418. On the manuscript tradition, see Casevitz 1992; Rocha-Pereira 1989, vol. 1: v–xxi; Diller 1956, 1957.

10. The manuscript of Planudes is Laur. LIX 30: see Diller 1937: 298–99, 1956: 90–91. This, of course, only proves that the book titles go back beyond the thirteenth century into the depths of the now-lost medieval manuscript tradition—perhaps to an early editor. Nonetheless, the internal evidence of the text (e.g., in the discussion of herms on the borders of Argolis and Sparta, which defines the division of Books II and III; see further, below) implies that the book divisions themselves (if not their transmitted titles) go back to the author.

11. On this aspect, see Habicht 1985: 19–21; Snodgrass 1987: 75–89; Elsner 1995: 134–37; Alcock 1996: 244–45; Hartog 1996: 151–58.

12. On this formulation and its meanings, see Frazer 1898, vol. 1: lxxv; Habicht 1985: 6; Arafat 1996: 8–9. Note the critique of traditional interpretations of this phrase by James Porter (chap. 5, this volume).

13. See de Certeau 1986: 67–79, esp. 67–69. On Pausanian phenomenology, see Elsner 1995: 134–37.

14. On Herodotus Book IV, see esp. Hartog 1988. On Pausanias's debt to Herodotus, see Arafat 1996: 23–24, with bibliography at n.55; Musti 1996: 11–12, 35–39; Moggi 1996: 83–87; Ameling 1996: 146–51; Kreilinger 1997: 471–72.

15. For Pausanias as "ethnographer . . . an individual who travelled among and wrote of a people from the outside looking in," see Alcock 1996: 242–43; see also Jacob 1980b: 44–45, 54–56.

16. See de Certeau 1986: 68. Needless to say, this is a relatively unusual (a pre-anthropological) tradition in travel writing, in that the emic is given its own space to speak, by contrast with much more clearly Romanocentric texts (e.g., Tacitus's *Germania*).

17. This idea is currently controversial. In favor, see Elsner 1992: esp. 20–27, followed by Hornblower 1994: 51, n.130; Woolf 1994: 125; Alcock 1996: 247; Auffarth 1997: 222–23. Against, see Swain 1996: 342, n.50 (who thinks that belief "in full" is a precondition for pilgrimage, which is certainly a Christianizing assumption since this notion of "belief" is a Christian innovation in Greco-Roman thinking), and Arafat 1996: 10–11 and n.22 (who believes that being interested in anything other than religion disqualifies a pilgrim from being a pilgrim, though the problem of how to align "curiosity" with the business of religious devotion is in fact central to pilgrimage discourse, not only in the Christian Middle Ages but also elsewhere). In my view, both these objections arise from drastic simplifications of the problematic phenomenon of pilgrimage. Further on the issue of pilgrimage, see Rutherford, chap. 4, this volume; on Pausanias and religion, at length, see Heer 1979; Pritchett 1998: 61–363.

18. On the act of recounting one's travels as a *rite de passage,* see Harbsmeier 1987: 337.

19. On Apollonius of Tyana as pilgrim, see Elsner 1997 (esp. 25–28).

20. Generally on the landscapes of Roman Greece, see Alcock 1993. For Pausanias in the sacred landscape, see Alcock 1993: 173–79, 200–208.

21. For Attica, see the commentaries by Frazer 1898, vol. 2; Beschi and Musti 1982; Chamoux 1992. For Delphi, see Kalkmann 1886: 109–119; Frazer 1898, vol. 5; Daux 1936; Jacquemin 1991b: 221–29; Lacroix 1992.

22. On Pausanias in Olympia, see esp. Kalkmann 1886: 72–109; Gurlitt 1890: 341–430; Trendelenburg 1914; Meyer 1971. On the site, see Herrmann 1972: 183–99.

23. See Strabo 8.3.30–31 ("the greatest games in the world") and also the representation of Apollonius at Olympia in Philostratus, *Vita Apollonii* 8.15–18 (see Elsner 1997: 27–28).

24. On this, see, e.g., Pirenne-Delforge 1998a: 129–33.

25. For Book II, I take the introduction to be 2.1 and for Book IX to be 9.1. "Teubner pages" refers to the edition of Pausanias by Rocha-Pereira (1989).

26. For Book V, I take the introduction to be 5.1.1–5.5.2; for Book VIII, 8.1.1–8.6.3; for Book X, 10.1.1–10.3.4. In Book VIII, however, note the long excursus on Philopoemen, 8.49.2–8.52.6.

27. For Book III, I take the introduction to be 3.1.1–3.10.5; for Book IV, 4.1.1–4.29.13; for Book VII, 7.1.1–7.17.4.

28. The description of the Messenian monuments (4.30.1–4.36.7) takes up eighteen Teubner pages, as opposed to the sixty-nine given to their history.

29. Hence the frequent critical distinction in reading Pausanias between "digressions" and "his main theme": e.g., Frazer 1898, vol. 1: xl; Habicht 1985: 96; Arafat 1996: 9, n.15 (whence come the two quotations given in this note).

30. On the popularity of Herodotus in the Second Sophistic, consider (apart from frequent references to him in all kinds of texts) the attack written by Plutarch in *De malignitate Herodoti* and also *De dea Syria,* an interesting imitation, in Ionic Greek, almost certainly written by Lucian—on which, with further bibliography, see Elsner, forthcoming.

31. On the Roman discourse of empire, see esp. Nicolet 1991 (in particular, Agrippa's Map and Augustus's *Res gestae,* which was exported in Greek translation, as well as Latin original, and inscribed into the temples and cities of Asia Minor; Nicolet 1991: 15–56, 95–122). The geographic parts of Pliny's *Natural History* represent the (surviving) apogee of this tradition as it was developed in Rome; see Carey 1998: 41–78. A later example of the practical-imperial discourse of travel writing—with its concern to label, acquire, and mark out possession—is Arrian's *Periplus Ponti Euxini,* probably written during its author's tenure as imperial legate in Cappadocia (A.D. 131–37); see Swain 1996: 243–44.

32. Other Second Sophistic writers who composed periegetic works in addition to volumes in other genres include Plutarch (although his *On the Festival of Statues in Plataea* hardly survives except for two fragments) and Telephus of Pergamon, whose *Periegesis of Pergamon* and *On the Temple of Augustus at Pergamon* are attested alongside philological, literary, and historical treatises. On all this, see Bowie 1974: 185.

33. On some of the issues at stake in the debate about Lucian's authorship of *De dea Syria,* see Elsner, forthcoming. Though most Lucian scholars have now come round to including the book in the Lucianic corpus (see Swain 1996: 304–308, with bibliography), there are regular dissenters—most recently Dirven 1997.

34. I quote Frazer 1898, vol. 1: xlix. Others have broadly concurred, e.g., Casson 1974: 299; Habicht 1985: 161–62 ("dry, sober and pedantic. He can also be dull . . . It has to be admitted that he did not have a brilliant mind. He lacked originality and the creative spark"!).

35. Frazer 1898, vol. 1: xl.

36. Cf. Trendelenburg 1914: 13–17.

37. My division differs from those of Robert 1909: 82 and Trendelenburg 1914: 22–24, in that they attempt to divide the description according to the topography of the site, whereas I prefer to follow the structure of Pausanias's written discourse. See also Schneider 1997: 497–502, who emphasizes the centrality of the Mendean monument (5.27.12) within the text of Pausanias as a whole, as well as within the two books on Elis.

38. Wycherley (1935: 57) believes that "the author's classification is artificial—the statues of victors would be offerings no less than the others." Trendelenburg (1914: 22,

49–53) treats the statues of Zeus and the votive offerings together, ignoring Pausanias's deliberate and repeatedly signaled attempt to separate them. These approaches, broadly typical of early- and mid-twentieth-century readings of Pausanias, represent a patronizing attitude to the text that overrides even the text's own careful signals of how it should be read.

39. For discussion, see Frazer 1898, vol. 5: 489–90.

40. On the topography of the Altis, see Gardiner 1925: 173–92.

41. On Pausanias and the altars, see Robert 1888: 429–36; Frazer 1898, vol. 3: 559–74; Trendelenburg 1914: 39–45; Etienne 1992: 292–97 (with an attempt to map the siting of the altars and Pausanias's route, which is to say the monthly ritual, in fig. 2); Elsner 2000: 53–57. For an archeological account of the altars, see Gardiner 1925: 193–205.

42. The passage describing the third altar is corrupt in the manuscripts, so I have excluded it. See the discussion of Maddoli and Saladino 1995: 262.

43. See further on this Elsner 1996: 518–28.

44. "Pedantic," Habicht 1985: 161, n.82; "erratic," Wycherley 1935: 56.

45. Note, however, that in 5.15.4 the mss. read ἐντός and have been corrected.

46. See Chamoux 1974: 85–86; Habicht 1985: 19–20; Snodgrass 1987: 81–84 (on Thebes).

47. Cf. the comments of Maddoli and Saladino 1995: 346–47, effectively following Trendelenburg 1914: 51.

48. On this *"kryptisches Denkmal"* placed at the very center of Pausanias's text, see Schneider 1997.

49. See Maddoli and Saladino 1995: 356, following Settis 1968: 48.

50. The most comprehensive discussion is Herrmann 1988.

51. Hyde 1921: 339–61, esp. 339; Herrmann 1988: 132–37.

52. Hyde 1921: 361; Habicht 1985: 65, n.4, 149, n.35 (with bibliography). Generally on Pausanias and inscriptions, see Habicht 1985: 64–94; Whittaker 1991.

53. Habicht 1985: 149–51.

54. Codices (papyrus and parchment) certainly existed in Pausanias's time, although for the turn of the second and third centuries the statistics of papyrus finds (of non-Christian literary material) give only 4.5% codices, compared to 95.5% rolls, indicating the relative popularity of the forms in Pausanias's time; see Roberts and Skeat 1983: 36–37. However, for utilitarian use on a religious site (and especially for travelers, as already implied by Martial's famous passage at 1.2.1–6), codices would certainly have been more serviceable, as was recognized by the Christians, who showed an almost exclusive preference for the codex from the second century A.D. (the earliest date of surviving Christian writings). See Roberts and Skeat 1983: 38–44; Gamble 1995: 42–81.

55. On the temple and image, see Ashmole and Yalouris 1967; Mallwitz 1972: 211–34. For Pausanias's account, see Trendelenburg 1914: 71–102.

56. See Arafat 1995 (esp. 466, on crowding; 470–73, on museum function).

57. See, e.g., Becker 1995: 4 (quoting G. Graff) for *ekphrasis* as "a miniature replica of a text embedded within that text; a textual part reduplicating, reflecting or mirroring (one or more than one aspect of) the textual whole." For some acute remarks on *ekphrasis* in Euripidean drama, see Goff 1988; Zeitlin 1994. For *ekphrasis* as "a significant paradigm for the framing narrative," see Goldhill 1991: 240–46, 308–11 (quotation from 308). On *ekphrasis* in the novel, see Bartsch 1989.

58. On Pausanian absence, see Foccardi 1983; Elsner 1995: 144–52; Dalfen 1996; Porter, chap. 5, this volume.

59. See Jacquemin 1991a; Jacob 1993; Birge 1994 (esp. 238–45).

60. Cf. Philostratus, *Imagines* 2.6.1 (purportedly describing a painting of the site): "The land furnishes a stadium in a simple glen of sufficient extent, from which issues the stream of the Alpheius, a light stream . . . and about it grow wild olive trees of green-gray color, beautiful and curly like parsley leaves."

61. On Pausanian decline, see Elsner 1994: 244–52; on ruins, see Jacob 1980b: 44–48.

62. Frazer 1898 (in six vols.), followed by Frazer and Van Buren 1930, as a supplement. The selections appeared as Frazer 1900, subsequently reissued as Frazer 1919.

63. On Frazer's selectivity, Mary Beard notes that he hardly mentions "sacred groves" anywhere in his commentary, although Pausanias is full of them and they were hardly incidental to Frazer's non-Pausanian anthropological interests (Beard 1993b: 175).

64. Yates 1966: 1–26; Carruthers 1990: 16–32; Coleman 1992: 39–59; Small 1997: 95–137; Webb 1997. For some art historical explorations of this material, see Bergmann 1994; Elsner 1995: 76–79.

65. See the interesting discussion by Goldmann 1991: 148–52.

66. As has been argued particularly by Goldmann 1991 and (from a different angle) by Alcock 1996.

67. See Theon 11 (ed. Spengel 1853–56, vol. 2: 118); Hermogenes 10 (ed. Rabe 1913: 22); Aphthonius 12 (ed. Rabe 1926: 36). There is a brief but acute discussion of this issue by Dubel (1997: 254–59).

68. Cf. Bowie 1996b: 208.

Chapter 2

All translations from the Greek are those of the author.

1. For a fuller discussion of the evidence, see Habicht 1985: 9–12.

2. Cf. *Anthologia Palatina* 7.157; Bowie 1990: 67–69.

3. For evidence on the senator's career, see Halfmann 1979: no. 89; note esp. *Supplementum Epigraphicum Graecum* 4.407.

4. ἀπὸ δὲ τοῦ Περγαμηνῶν Σμυρναίοις γέγονεν ἐφ' ἡμῶν Ἀσκληπιεῖον τὸ ἐπὶ θαλάσσῃ (And it was from the Asclepieion in Pergamon that in my time the Asclepieion by the sea was established in Smyrna).

5. Aelius Aristides 50.102, for whose date I follow Behr 1981, vol. 2: 338. Habicht (1985: 10, n.54) dates this part of Aristides's adventures to A.D. 151 and takes the Asclepieion of 47.17 to be the same, and hence supposes that the Asclepieion referred to in 50.102 was finished by the time narrated by Aristides in 47.17 (i.e., A.D. 166).

6. Habicht 1985: 9.

7. Pausanias 10.34.5.

8. Cassius Dio 72.23.5; see Millar 1964: 28–32.

9. The bulkier works were the *History of the Period after Alexander,* in ten books according to Photius, *Bibliotheca Codex* 92, 69a3 (Τὰ μετὰ Ἀλέξανδρον frag. 1 Roos); and the *Parthian History,* in seventeen books, Photius, *Bibliotheca Codex* 58, 17a23 (*Parthica* frag. 1 Roos). For Arrian's claim of lifelong commitment to the *Bithynian History,* see Photius, *Bibliotheca Codex* 93, 73b14–18 (*Bithynica* frag.1 Roos).

10. Scrutinized by Habicht 1985: 176–80.

11. ἐγὼ δὲ μετ᾽ ἀνθρώπων μὲν ἔτι αὐτὸν ὄντα οὐκ εἶδον, ἐν δὲ ἀγάλμασιν εἶδον καὶ ἐν γραφαῖς (8.9.7).

12. See Ihnken 1978: no. 27, where Straton son of Tyrannos is called Ἰουδαῖος.

13. Scriptores Historiae Augustae, *Antoninus Pius* 7.8.

14. E.g., Athenaeus (probably writing between A.D. 192 and 195) 8.361F: "the emperor in all respects best and most given to the Muses" (τοῦ πάντ᾽ ἀρίστου καὶ μουσικωτάτου βασιλέως); Athenaeus 13.574F: "the emperor who was best in all respects" (τοῦ πάντ᾽ ἀρίστου Ἀδριανοῦ βασιλέως); Philostratus, *Vitae sophistarum* 1.24, 530 (probably composed ca. A.D. 230): "the most suited of all the emperors of past times to foster excellence" (ἐπιτηδειότατος τῶν πάλαι βασιλέων γενόμενος ἀρετὰς αὐξῆσαι).

15. Habicht 1985: 13–15. Chronology does not exclude his identification with the sophist in Philostratus *Vitae sophistarum* 2.13, Pausanias from Caesarea in Cappadocia, who was indeed a pupil of Herodes Atticus, but the range of interests of these two seems hardly to overlap, and I do not share the view of Heil (1998: 64) that they could be the same.

16. Cf. Jacob 1980a: 73–75.

17. This status requires us to qualify the presentation of Pausanias as a "pilgrim in his own land" by Elsner 1992.

18. For accounts and explanations, see most recently Swain 1996; Schmitz 1997.

19. Robert 1977: 120–29. For honors to poets, see Bowie 1989: 201–203. Note especially the honors offered by Halicarnassus to C. Iulius Longianus of Aphrodisias: it was decided that his statue should be erected near that of "old" (παλαιός) Herodotus (*Monumenta Asiae Minoris Antiquae* 8.418a and b).

20. See Deichgräber 1952.

21. Among mannerisms common to Herodotus and Thucydides, note, e.g., Pausanias's claim "I have found" (εὕρισκον) at 1.14.6, 1.28.7, 2.24.7, 2.26.10, etc.; and cf. Herodotus 1.60.3, 1.105.3, 4.15.1, etc., and Thucydides 1.21.1, 1.135.2, etc. For echoes, cf. "For the disaster at Chaeroneia initiated evil for all the Greeks and enslaved not least those who ignored it and who aligned themselves with the Macedonians" (τὸ γὰρ ἀτύχημα τὸ ἐν Χαιρωνείᾳ ἅπασι τοῖς Ἕλλησιν ἦρξε κακοῦ, καὶ οὐχ ἥκιστα δούλους ἐποίησε τοὺς ὑπεριδόντας καὶ ὅσοι μετὰ Μακεδόνων ἐτάχθησαν), 1.25.3, echoing Homer, *Iliad* 11.603, and Herodotus 5.97.3.

22. Strid 1976: 99 ("The language and style of Pausanias are marked by a fundamental classicism which bears a chiefly Herodotean stamp. Alongside Herodotus, Thucydides above all served as a model").

23. The *Indike* was written after the *Anabasis,* in which (5.4.3–5.1, 6.28.6) its composition is heralded by Arrian, but the *Indike* cross-refers so often to it (19.8, 21.8, 23.6, 32.1, 40.1, 43.14) that it is unlikely to have been composed very much later. Bosworth argues (1972, 1980: 9–11) that the *Anabasis* is an early work, i.e., of the 120s, but even if it was written after Arrian's retirement from his Roman career in Athens in the 140s (where he was *archon* in A.D. 146/7), the *Indike* could well have been published by the mid-150s.

24. See Bosworth 1993: 274, with n.241.

25. Lucian, *De historia conscribenda* 16, 18.

26. I.e., the Σμυρναειταί of Ihnken 1978: no. 18.2 (and in the Hellenistic period a *sympoliteia;* Ihnken 1978: no. 1).

27. Strid 1976: 47–66 *(Wortstellung),* 99–103 *(Zusammenfassung).*

28. Szelest 1953; cf. Strid 1976: 65.

29. Cf. 1.20.5 with Habicht 1985: 15.

30. *FGrHist* 1F1: Ἑκαταῖος Μιλήσιος ὧδε μυθεῖται.

31. For Amyntianus, see Photius, *Bibliotheca cod.* 131, 97a9–15 (= *FGrHist* 150F1); for the *Bithynica* cf. *eund. cod.* 93, 73b14–18 (frag. 1 Roos).

32. Habicht (1985: 18) thinks that it would have been out of character for Pausanias to open his work with a dedication to a prominent contemporary. Although my argument is in favor of the probability simply of a preface, I doubt if our understanding of Pausanias's character is sufficient to exclude a dedication.

33. For details, see the edition of Winterbottom 1971: xix–xx. I am grateful to Professor Winterbottom for drawing my attention to this parallel.

34. I am grateful to Professor Roland Mayer for calling my attention to this parallel.

35. For an example of self-confident assertions, see 3.11.1 (on his selectivity).

36. Habicht 1985: 164 (drawing, in n.88, upon Reardon 1971: 221), 163 (citing Ebeling 1913: 139).

37. οἱ πλεῖστοι τῶν περὶ συγκομιδὴν ἱστορίας ἀσχοληθέντων ἔργων τε πάλαι γεγονότων μνήμην ἀνανεώσασθαι σπουδασάντων, παιδείας κλέος ἀίδιον μνώμενοι, ὡς ἂν μὴ σιωπήσαντες λάθοιεν ἐς τὸν πολὺν ὅμιλον ἀριθμούμενοι . . . (The majority of those who have worked on the gathering together of history and have expended effort in renewing the memory of events which took place long ago, wooing deathless fame for their learning, so that they should not, by reason of their silence, slip into aggregation with the majority of mankind . . .), Herodian 1.1.1.

38. Strid 1976: 103 ("What he wanted to achieve in literary terms—the outcome may please us moderns or not—was actually attained by him").

39. So Habicht 1985: 140, on Pausanias 9.30.3.

40. His three uses of the term seem to give it the sense "philosopher" or "intellectual" rather than "virtuoso practitioner and teacher of rhetoric": 6.18.5 of Anaximenes of Lampsacus; 6.24.5 of Pyrrho; 8.49.3 of the serious literature read by Philopoemen.

41. Cf. Bowie 1994, 1996a.

42. Cf. 6.23.7 with Habicht 1985: 8, n.43; and for Olympia, cf., e.g., Dio of Prusa, *Oration* 12, for which see the introduction and commentary of Russell 1992; for Delphi, the performances of Aufria, cf. Colin et al. 1930: no. 79.

43. Kalinka and Heberdey 1901–, vol. 2: 910 (= Cagnat et al. 1906: 733).

44. *Anthologia Palatina* 7.158; cf. Bowie 1990: 67.

45. "[H]is failing to find the audience he had hoped for" (Habicht 1985: 22); "if through the centuries he was never read" (24); "he seems to have failed with all of them" (26).

46. Dickie 1997: 15–20, noting the links between Philostratus, *Apollonius* 6.10–11, and Pausanias on the temples of Apollo at Delphi, 10.5.9–13, and justly emphasizing the verbal similarity of Pausanias 10.5.9 (καλύβης δ'ἂν σχῆμα οὗτός γε ἂν εἴη παρεσχηματισμένος ὁ ναός) and *Apollonius* 6.10 p. 214 K. (καλύβη αὐτῷ ξυνεπλάσθη μικρά . . .) and 6.11 p. 221 (οἴκου σχῆμα).

47. τὰ δὲ ἐν τῇ Μεσοποταμίᾳ καί φοβερώτερα, καὶ ἀληθέστερον δέος σύμπασιν (Cassius Dio 80.3.1–2).

48. Habicht 1985: 22.

49. Habicht 1985: 26, quoting Regenbogen 1956: 1093.

Chapter 3

I am very grateful to the editors and to Glen Bowersock for their help. All translations from the Greek are my own.

1. The standard treatment is now Habicht 1985 (revised ed., 1998). Kreilinger 1997 is an excellent treatment of Pausanias's artistic interests.

2. For Pausanias as a "pilgrim," see Elsner 1992 (revised in Elsner 1995: 125–55). For the recent volume in the series Fondation Hardt, Entretiens sur l'antiquité classique, see Bingen 1996.

3. This is a major theme of Habicht 1985.

4. Habicht 1985: 139–40.

5. On the acquaintances, a full list and discussion can be found in Habicht 1985: 144–45. On the expounders, a useful list, more complete than in the editions of Pausanias, and good discussion are in Pandiri 1985: 134 n.7 (I owe this reference to Jaś Elsner; I have not yet seen Pirenne-Delforge and Purnelle 1997.) "Those who recall the antiquities": Habicht 1985: 145 n. 19. "The expounder of local matters": 1.13.8, 1.41.2, 7.6.5, 9.3.3. Cf. "expounders of portents and dreams" (*teratōn kai enupniōn exēgē tas*), 5.23.6; "expounders" as interpreters of oracles, 10.10.7. Lydia: 1.35.8. Cities: Megara, 1.42.4; Sicyon, 2.9.7; Argos, 2.23.6; Elis, 5.6.6, 5.21.8–9; Patrae (in the dative), 7.6.5; Delphi, 10.28.7. Inferred from the context: Athens, 1.31.5; Oropos, 1.34.4 (but see below); Troezen, 2.31.4; Andania, 4.33.6; Plataea, 9.3.3. "The expounder at Olympia" 5.10.7, *en Olympiai;* 5.20.4, *Olympiasin.* "The expounder" as participating in sacrifices: 5.15.10.

6. Thus in the fifty or so sentences or clauses with *Homēros* as the subject, the verb is in the present, aorist, or perfect tense, never in the imperfect; 1.28.7, "Homer prevented me (*ouk eia*) from taking on trust the account of Sophocles" is not a true exception. Nor have I found examples of the imperfect with the names *Aischylos, Hērodotos,* or *Pindaros.* For all these searches I am indebted to the *Thesaurus Linguae Graecae* (Irvine).

7. For *elegen,* etc., see 1.35.8, 5.6.6, 5.20.4, 7.6.5; 9.3.3; *pareitai,* 1.42.4; *lelēthen,* 2.23.6, 5.21.8; *homologeitai,* 4.33.6. Cf. Goodwin 1889: 12: "In narration [the imperfect] dwells on the course of an event instead of merely stating its occurrence."

8. In general, Chantraine 1968–80, vol. 2: 405–406; for *perēgeomai,* LSJ cites Herodotus 7.214.1, *hoi periēgēsamenoi to oros toisi Persēsi* (those who showed the Persians the way round the mountain). For *perēgeomai/periēgēsis* in inscriptions from the fourth century on, see Habicht 1985: 2, n.5, to which add *Supplementum Epigraphicum Graecum* 40.991, lines 6–7.

9. 1.41.2.

10. 1.13.8, etc. Cf. Kroll 1927; *FGrHist* 312 (suggesting an Imperial date); Lloyd-Jones and Parsons 1983: 527–30 (agnostic).

11. See the examples cited by Stephanus 1831–63, vol. 6: 827, and by *LSJ.* Athenaeus (*Deipnosophistae* 5.210A = Müller 1883: 3: 133, frag. 58) is the first author to call Polemo of Ilion a *periēgētēs.*

12. For Greek words meaning "to read," see Chantraine 1950: esp. 121 on *epilegesthai.*

13. 1.34.4. By a curious coincidence, an Iophon son of Iophon from Magnesia on the Maeander is honored at Knossos ca. 200 B.C.; see Kern 1900: no. 67 = Guarducci 1935–50, vol. 1: 65, no. 10. On the Amphiaraion, see Bethe 1894; Petrakos 1968.

14. 5.20.4–5; cf. 5.27.11; Habicht 1985: 146.

15. 1.35.7–8. On Temenouthyrae, see Drew-Bear 1979. Pausanias's information about Gadeira (Cadiz) might have come from his fellow citizen Cleon (10.4.6); his use of the verb *ephasken* goes against the view of Jacoby (1921) that this was a written source.

16. 2.23.6.

17. For his comments on Theseus, see 1.3.3 (for a parody of such complaints, see

Dio Chrysostom 11.2). See also Plutarch, *Moralia* 14D–37B. For his use of the term *philēkooi*; see 9.25.5; and cf. Dio Chrysostom 36.16, on the orator's audience at Borysthenes, *philēkooi kai tō tropō Hellēnes.*

18. Preller 1838: 162–69; there is also a very good collection of references in Reinach 1892: 885–86.

19. Preller 1838: 167.

20. Frazer 1898, vol. 1: lxxvi–lxxvii, cited by Habicht 1985: 145. A rather similar view is expressed by Casson (1974: 264–67) in his standard book on ancient travel. The fragment of Varro (frag. 34 Bücheler = 35 Cèbe) cited by Casson and others is obscure but appears to have nothing to do with guides or tourism: see Cèbe 1972–94, vol. 1: 134–38.

21. Strabo 17.1.29, C. 806. Note that Strabo here uses the same "imperfect of recollection" as Pausanias: *edeiknunto, parēkolouthei.*

22. Longus, *Daphnis and Chloe* pref., 4.39.2; cf. Schissel von Fleschenberg 1913 (esp. 93–97); Pandiri 1985: 117. It is relevant to remember the Greek practice, which continued into late antiquity, of worshiping in caves and decorating them: see Robert 1977: 79 (= Robert 1987: 37), discussing Pausanias 10.32.2–4. On Plutarch and the inscription of Lesbos, see below.

23. I am of course omitting *exēgētai* who are clearly not guides but expounders of other kinds, such as those concerned with the Eleusinian rites (on whom see Oliver 1950).

24. For inscriptions at Olympia, see Dittenberger and Purgold 1896: nos. 59–141, with Dittenberger's discussion, cols. 137–42; the only additions (some of them joining stones already known) are noted or published by Kunze 1956: 173–75. Inscriptions referring to *periēgētai* are nos. 77, line 9; 83, line 2; 110, line 17; 120, line 10. On monthly sacrifices, see Pausanias 5.15.10. On Pausanias at Olympia, see Elsner, chap. 1, this volume.

25. All my examples are from the excellent article by Bischoff (1937: 725–26).

26. *IG* IV.723. On local grants of the title *archiatros,* see Nutton 1971 (esp. 54–55).

27. *IG* XII.2.484, lines 23–29. On the immunities available to local and other doctors, see Nutton 1971. For *prothytai* in the imperial cult, see Robert 1960: 323–24 (= Robert 1969b: 839–40). For *theiotatos* (most divine), indicating a date not earlier than Hadrian, see Rougé 1969; Robert and Robert 1970: no. 136.

28. Plutarch, *Moralia* 394D–409D. On these persons, see Puech 1992: 4846 (Diogenianus II), 4869 (Philinus).

29. *De Pythiae oraculis* 395A–397E, 400D–E.

30. *Quaestiones convivales* 675E; cf. Pausanias 2.1.3 (pine), 723A–724F (palm).

31. On Charon and Hermes, see *Contemplantes* 2. On Aeacus and Menippus, see *Dialogi mortuorum* 6 (20) 1. On guides, see *Verae historiae* 2.31. On Tychiades, see *Philopseudes* 4. On Lycinus, see *Amores* 8 (on the date and authenticity of this work, see Jones 1984).

32. [Justin], *Cohortatio ad Graecos* chap. 37; Migne 1857: 305–310; Marcovich 1990: 75–76. On this testimony in relation to the actual cave, see Parke 1988: 84. On Pausanias in Cumae, see 8.24.5, 10.12.8.

Chapter 4

1. See Dillon 1997; Coleman and Elsner 1995; Chelini and Branthomme 1987.

2. Cf. Morinis 1992: 4.

3. Elsner 1992: 8 ("A religious tourist visiting sacred sites is *not* simply a tourist: he or she is also a pilgrim"), 13–14 (identity), 22–23 (religious sensibility).

4. Arafat 1996: 10.

5. Sourvinou-Inwood 1990: 297 ("The *polis* anchored, legitimated and mediated all religious activity"). She shows this is true of contact between different *poleis*—e.g., Delphi, where the "non-Delphians were treated on the model of *xenoi* worshipping at the sanctuary of the *polis*."

6. On pantheons in Pausanias, see now Pirenne-Delforge 1998b.

7. Arafat 1996; for sacrifice on Aegina, see Pausanias 2.30.4.

8. *Theoria* is somewhat neglected in Dillon's (1997) account.

9. Eck 1985; Morinis 1984: 73.

10. There is a good account of pilgrimage and vision in a later era in Lane Fox 1986. See also Rutherford 2000.

11. On this passage, see Rutherford 1998b.

12. Elsner 1992: 8.

13. See Cohen 1992. On tourism in Roman Egypt, Frankfurter (1998: 218–19) comments that "early tourism almost always had a religious component, the acquisition of a series of encounters with holy places; but in the Roman period, tourism to Egypt tended increasingly to function as pilgrimage."

14. Perdrizet and Lefebvre 1919: no. 424; Masson 1961: no. 379; Bernand 1988. On Aramaic-speakers, see Fitzmyer and Kaufman 1992—: B.3.f.23.

15. *P. Tebtunis* I, 33 (112 B.C.). On pilgrim and tourist, see Festugière 1970: 191; Bernand 1969: I, 22–28; Malaise 1987: 63.

16. Such a distinction might be sought in the ancient tradition that the word *theoros* means a divine envoy sent to oracles, whereas a *theates* is a spectator of shows (Ammonius, *Peri diaphoron lexeon* = Lysimachides, *FGrHist* 366F9). But notice that Lysimachides was arguing against Caecilius's view that *to theorikon* (the theoric fund) is derived from *thea,* a move that would collapse the distinction between *theoros* and *theates.*

17. Robert and Robert 1989: 3–6.

18. Morinis (1992: 26), in a survey of pilgrimage, suggests that we think of it as a movement between two poles: familiar (known, human, social, imperfect, mundane) and other (mysterious, divine, ideal, perfect, miraculous). This leaves out one very important dimension: that of the national.

19. This point is made by Ross Holloway (1967) in an analysis of the frieze on the temple of Zeus at Olympia: "Whether the visitor came from Asia Minor or Thrace, Thessaly or Boiotia (the birthplace of Heracles), Attica or the Peloponnese, there was something that he could call his own."

20. Snodgrass (1986: 54) comments: "But, given that its initial successes were the foundation of its subsequent prestige, how was Delphi able to embark on this career in the first place? Like the Pope, it had no divisions, yet the most powerful cities felt the need of its sanction. If its role had been exclusively a religious one, and if the motive for soliciting its approval had been only piety, it seems unlikely that it could have played so complex a role. The explanation must surely be that a culture so fragmented as early Greece was very much in need of a common arena, in which innovations, advances and attainments of each individual *polis* could be rapidly communicated to others, when desired, or could, more simply, be displayed for admiration. The alternation of direct interaction, when there were more than two hundred separate polities, often many days' travel apart, would have required an extremely elaborate network of communication."

21. Similarly, according to Thucydides (8.10.1), at the Isthmian Games of 412 B.C., to which the Athenians sent an embassy (*etheoroun*), since they had been invited, they learned more about the imminent revolt of Chios and as a result took steps to stop it.

22. Morgan 1990: 18. Particularly instructive in this regard are dedications purporting to be the spoils of victory by one state over another, of the sort criticized by Plutarch (*Moralia* 401d: *De Pythiae oraculis* 15).

23. On periegetic historiography in Hellenistic times, see Bischoff 1937; Pasquali 1913. On Ion of Chios, see Pfister 1951: 48–64, who (p. 62) finds an intimation of the genre as early as Solon's *theoria* described in Herodotus 1.29.

24. Dittenberger, 1915–24, vol. 2: 585.114 (dating to 177/6 B.C).

25. Preller 1838: 44 (Athens), 48 (Sparta), 67 (Samothrace), 53–54 (Thebes), 55 (Delphi).

26. Preller 1838: 50–51, frag. 22 (see also 56, frag. 28); on ascription, see Athenaeus 11.479f.

27. Preller 1838: 63–65, frag. 31–33.

28. Philostratus, *Heroicus* (De Lannoy 1977: 53–55). The pilgrimage tradition at Troy could be very old indeed, to judge from the archaeology.

29. Preller 1838: 140–44, frag. 87–88, quoted in Athenaeus, *Deipnosophistae* 11.478c-d (trans. C. B. Gulick, Loeb Classical Library).

30. Preller 1838: 95–96, frag. 53.

31. Pfister 1951. Notice that "Herakleides" (at 3.5) shares the concern with Greek identity that Elsner finds in Pausanias: *he de kaloumene nun Hellas legetai men, ou mentoi esti* ("Greece," as it is called, is a word but not a reality).

32. On Agaklytos, see Müller 1851: 288; on Anaxandrides, see *FGrHist* 404.

33. The route of the Delphic festival announcers is: Delphi–Aegina–Argolid–Achaea–Messenia–Laconia–Arcadia–Elis–Ithaca–Aetolia. Pausanias's route is different; once he has entered the Peloponnese, he circles it the other way, going west via Sparta to Messenia and Elis, before returning to Achaea and Arcadia, and then on to Boeotia.

34. Giovannini 1969; Nachtergael 1975.

35. *IG* II² 3563 (the Sarapion Monument).

36. Bischoff 1937: 726; Dittenberger and Purgold 1896: 141, no. 59; see also Jones, chap. 3, this volume.

37. Swain 1996: 342, n.50. Swain also criticizes Elsner's point about Greek identity, on the grounds that Pausanias was not from Greece but from Magnesia ad Sipylum; but surely we would expect feelings of identity to be at their strongest among Greeks who grew up away from mainland Greece.

38. Heraclides of Pontus, frag. 88 Wehrli; cf. Burkert 1960.

39. Plato, *Republic* 517b, *Symposium* 210d–e; Riedweg 1987.

40. *IG* II² 886; see Robert and Robert 1989: 27; Tod 1957: 137, n.91.

41. Perdrizet and Lefebvre 1919: no. 498.

42. Nock 1934; Totti 1985: no. 40. The translation given here is by the author.

43. TT13-Theosophistae Tubingensis 13; see Erbse 1995: 7–8.

44. Parke 1985; Erbse 1995; Nock 1928.

45. The man called Apistos at *IG* IV² 121–33; Ambrosia of Athens at *IG* IV² 133–48. On the Iamata, see Dillon 1994.

46. On Deir el-Bahari, see Bataille 1951; on Philae, see Rutherford 1998a; on Kalabsha, see Nock 1934.

47. Elsner 1997.

48. On Eleusis, see Clinton 1989; Halfmann 1986: 116. On Ajax's tomb, see Halfmann 1986: 199; Philostratus, *Heroicus* (De Lannoy 1977: 8, line 19). On Mount Kasion, see *Anthologia Graeca* 6, 332; Spartianus, *Vita Hadriani* 14.3. On Memnon, see Bowersock 1984; Théodoridès 1989; Bowie 1990. For the significance of Hadrian's pilgrimages, see Holum 1990.

49. Dittenberger 1915–24, vol. 3: 1063; Spawforth 1989: 194–95.

50. *Dodekaides* (sacrifices of twelve oxen) were sent from Athens to Delphi in the time of Augustus and in the early empire. There was a later sequence of *dodekaides* from Athens to Delos in the early to mid–second century A.D.; a *dodekais* was also sent from Keos to Delos in the Imperial period. This seems to represent a revival of earlier traditions. For Delphi, see Bruneau 1970, 139–43; Colin 1909–13: 59–66; for Delos, see Dürrbach 1923–37: 2535–38.

51. Inscriptions recording a delegation: from Tabai (Robert and Robert 1954: n. 24); from Laodiceia on the Lycos (Robert 1969a: 299); from Parion (Robert 1955: 275); from Sagalassus (MacCridy 1905: 167, III.3). The last of these uses the word *molpoi,* one with a rich background in Ionian cult.

52. Picard 1922: 211, 238, 410–11.

53. Boethius 1918: 74.

54. See Jones 1996.

55. On Philostratus's *Life of Apollonius,* see Elsner 1997; on Lucian's *De dea Syria,* see Elsner, forthcoming.

56. Behr 1968: 43.

57. Behr 1968: 69–70.

58. Behr 1968: 80–81.

59. Aristides 51.1–10 (*Sacred Tale* 5); Behr 1968: 97; Rutherford, forthcoming.

Commentary (Torelli)

1. Cf. Scranton 1951: 36–51.
2. On these issues, see now Arafat 1996.
3. Torelli, forthcoming.
4. Musti and Torelli 1986, 1991a, 1991b.
5. Habicht 1998.
6. Philostratus, *Vitae sophistarum* 2.1.6.
7. Musti, in Beschi and Musti 1982: xxiv–xxxv.
8. Musti 1989: 9.

Chapter 5

Thanks go to Sally Humphreys and Deborah Lyons for marginal queries, circlings, underlinings, and other expressive signs that accompanied me throughout my revisions. Sally Humphreys's article from 1995 probably inspired me more here than I inspired her there. Tom Rosenmeyer's comments on a later draft saved me from a number of infelicities. I am especially grateful to the editors, whose work led me to appreciate Pausanias for the first time while I was teaching a survey of later Greek literature in the spring of 1997—and to put him on the syllabus in the future. Their generous editorial comments, suggestions, and encouragement were invaluable to me. Finally, I would like to acknowledge the support of the Alexander von Humboldt–Stiftung during 1997–98 while I conducted the preliminary research that went into this essay.

1. Guesses range from as early as the first century B.C. (Goold 1961; but see Porter 2001: n.100) to the mid–third century A.D. (see Russell 1964: xxii–xxx). One broad consensus opinion puts the treatise in the first century A.D. (Roberts 1899; Kroll 1940: 1124.60; Segal 1959; Russell 1964; and others). If Pausanias's name is uncertain, his dates are less so; see Habicht 1985: 8–9. Translations of Longinus below are by Russell, in Russell and Winterbottom 1989; those of Pausanias are from Frazer 1898, vol. 1; those of Dionysius of Halicarnassus and Dio of Prusa are from the Loeb Classical Library.

2. On the dates, see Frazer 1898, vol. 1: i, xvi–xviii; Habicht 1985: 8–12; Arafat 1996: 8.

3. Eliot 1950: 4; cf. 5: "The existing monuments form an ideal order among themselves."

4. In psychoanalytic terms, one might say that the monumental gaze is not a perspective that is first-personal but is rather a gaze *of* (i.e., *possessed by*) *the Other*: one sees the past through the eyes of another agency, from an utterly "imaginary point of the infinite axis of perspective . . . which confers on the field of vision its depth" (Žižek 1991: 61). This would be a promising way of turning round the problem of self-identification in the Second Sophistic, and I merely mention it here as a further possibility. See, however, n.67, below.

5. See Žižek 1989: 71.

6. This is also how Kant took the sublime (1987).

7. This obscure passage is usually taken as a defense of literature over sculpture (see Russell 1964 *ad loc.*). But Longinus could as easily be defending an aesthetics that is tolerant of mistakes in the name of grandeur as opposed to Classical perfection. Through its sheer size and bulk, and even due to its inevitably strained technique (Strabo 1.1.23), a colossus—a work that resembles a force of nature more than a work of art (cf. ἐπὶ δὲ τῶν φυσικῶν ἔργων [Longinus] 36.3—could suggest the superhuman dimension (τὸ ὑπεραῖρον τὰ ἀνθρώπινα [Longinus] 36.3) that sublime literature strives to put before our eyes. The sculptural metaphors to be noted below eliminate any prima facie doubts about the potential force of this analogy.

8. In the case of the colossi, both Pausanias (1.18.6) and Longinus (36.4) find reasons to excuse flaws in the monuments described. In the case of the Pythian shrine, their language is quite similar (although this may only reflect a common source), as is their stance of circumspection: πολλοὶ γὰρ ἀλλοτρίῳ θεοφοροῦνται πνεύματι τὸν αὐτὸν τρόπον ὃν καὶ τὴν Πυθίαν λόγος ἔχει τρίποδι πλησιάζουσαν, ἔνθα ῥῆγμά ἐστι γῆς ἀναπνέον, ὥς φασιν, ἀτμὸν ἔνθεον, αὐτόθεν ἐγκύμονα τῆς δαιμονίου καθισταμένην δυνάμεως παραυτίκα χρησμῳδεῖν κατ' ἐπίπνοιαν ([Longinus] 13.2); ἤκουσα δὲ καὶ ὡς ἄνδρες ποιμαίνοντες ἐπιτύχοιεν τῷ μαντείῳ, καὶ ἔνθεοί τε ἐγένοντο ὑπὸ τοῦ ἀτμοῦ καὶ ἐμαντεύσαντο ἐξ Ἀπόλλωνος (Pausanias 10.5.7). See further Russell 1964: ad loc.

9. On the inscriptional nature of vision in Second Sophistic narratives, see Morales, forthcoming; Goldhill, forthcoming.

10. See Roberts 1899: 216 for a conspectus of authors mentioned. Hellenistic authors (Apollonius, Theocritus, Eratosthenes, Aratus) are damned with faint praise ("flawless," "felicitous," "blameless" [33.4–5], "smooth" [10.6]) or else simply damned (Hegesias, Matris, Amphicrates, and Alexander's historian Timaeus [3.2, 4.1]).

11. Bowie 1974: 188; cf. Habicht 1985: 23, 134–35. A prominent exception is the colossal statue of Zeus dedicated by Hadrian in Athens (1.18.6), although Pausanias's praise of this work is somewhat qualified (cf. Frazer 1898, vol. 1: lxiii). Another exception is the statue of Hadrian in the Parthenon, which, however, receives a bare mention (1.24.7). As Elsner (1998: 120) notes, Pausanias "pointedly ignores" the remaining Ro-

man additions to the Parthenon, quietly subtracting them in his account of what is to be seen, or at any rate is worth seeing, at the monument the way it looked at around A.D. 160. For further exceptions, see Arafat 1996.

12. This theme in Longinus is analyzed in Segal 1987.

13. Greenblatt 1990: 161–83. Greenblatt's essay is valuable above all for reminding us that the smallest and apparently most insignificant of things are capable of radiating "a tiny quantum of cultural energy" (162) and thus of being transmuted into sublime objects. See also Stewart 1984 [1993]; Žižek 1989.

14. Cf. 3.5.6, on the sanctuary in the temple of Athena Alea in Tegea, where the Spartan general Pausanias took refuge in ca. 470/471 B.C.: "From of old (ἐκ παλαιοῦ) this sanctuary had been looked upon with awe and veneration (αἰδέσιμον ἦν) by the whole of the Peloponnese," as were many other objects elsewhere in Greece. No reason is given for the veneration in the present case, because none is needed: veneration accrues upon itself; by 471 the shrine was venerable just because it once was. Elsner (1994: 245) reminds us that the notion of recounting *thaumata* (wonders) is a trope that goes back at least to Herodotus. The phrase θαῦμα ἰδέσθαι, "a wonder to behold," of course goes all the way back to Homer.

15. Jacoby (1921) takes Cleon to be an indubitable contemporary, and ἔφασκε to refer to private conversations with Pausanias.

16. See Bowie 1974: 189–91 and passim. This position is modified in Bowie 1996b (esp. 208), where Pausanias is considered both typical and atypical of his age.

17. In the depiction of the earth torn open from 9.5, the effect is heightened by Longinus's having violently conflated (and reversed) verses drawn from three passages lying books apart: the theme and the critical operation work in tandem.

18. Barthes 1975: 7, 9–10; final emphasis added by Porter.

19. E.g., Elsner 1994: 245, 247, 252; 1992: 11. Habicht (1985: 6) and Arafat (1996: 8–9) take the phrase in a literal, not a rhetorical, sense, as though it indicated Pausanias's actual objective. Frazer (1898, vol. 1: xxv) is quick to note the self-contradiction.

20. See Frazer 1898, vol. 1: xviii for one suggestion.

21. See generally Veyne 1988b.

22. Bowie 1974: 197; Elsner 1994: 248.

23. Cf. in the same context the phrases ἅπαν τὸ Ἑλληνικόν (8.52.2) and ἁπάντων Ἑλλήνων (8.52.5).

24. "Many very powerful considerations prevent us [from going over to the Persians and helping them enslave our fellow-Greeks]: first and foremost, the burning and destruction of our temples and the images of our gods . . . ; then, *to Hellenikon* [literally, 'the Greek thing,' so 'Greekness']—our common language, the altars and sacrifices we all share, our common mores and customs" (trans. and glossed as in Cartledge 1995: 82). See n.23, above.

25. Cartledge's argument (1995: 79) that the consolidation of a panhellenic identity resulted only after the Persian Wars would seem to confirm and to clarify Pausanias's double approach to Greece: the ahistorical fantasy of "Greece" has a historically precise emergence.

26. Alcock's term "landscapes of memory" is apt (Alcock 1996; cf. Goldmann 1991). As Young (1993: 7) writes, in a remote but relevant context, "the reciprocal exchange between a monument and its space is still too little studied. For a monument necessarily transforms an otherwise benign site into part of its content, even as it is absorbed into the site and made part of a larger locale." As Pausanias shows, however, "this tension between site and memorial" can work in both directions: sites that exist in the Greek historical imaginary can turn anything in their midst into a memorial. They

transform place into memorial content, just because they are conceived as *"lieux de mémoire"* (Nora 1984)—viz., as leftovers of history. That is, Greek sites are for Pausanias memorials in and of themselves.

27. See Lane Fox 1986: 90–95, 110–11; Elsner 1992.

28. This is true even if, on occasion, Pausanias will say of sites that they are not "worth seeing," as with the sanctuary of Lycian Apollo in Sicyon, which despite being "in ruins" seems to be worth mentioning, describing, and annotating (2.9.7); or if he will claim, as of the once magnificent temple of Athena in Sicyon, that the "memory [of a monument] was doomed in time to pass away": for God destroyed this temple "by thunderbolts" (2.11.1). But the very mention of the temple gainsays Pausanias's own claim.

29. 2.11.2, 2.11.1, 2.23.3, 8.28.1, 2.15.2, 9.3.9, 9.12.3.

30. "Pausanias nowhere makes explicit his vision of the past" (Arafat 1996: 75).

31. Habicht 1985; Meadows 1995 (on historical sources).

32. On Pausanias's (admittedly vague) sense of historical layers within and behind the Classical past, see Pollitt 1974: 157; Habicht 1985: 102–103; Veyne 1988b: 210–16 (see n.53, below); Arafat 1996: 43–75. I differ slightly from Bowie in viewing the Classical past as something Pausanias takes to be ideologically proximate rather than historically "recent" (Bowie 1996b: 214; either way, an apparent discrepancy—that of Pausanias's approval of Roman restorative building policies, wherein new monuments and restorations are juxtaposed fittingly with the old ["the old must be left, the new must seem in some way to complement it" 225]—disappears), and as consistent nonetheless with his strong obsession with prior antiquity (Bowie 1996b: 210). I differ from Arafat (1996: 76) in viewing the "wonder" and "awe" that Pausanias shows toward the Archaic past as a core element of his vision of the (idealized) past. To what degree Pausanias's interest in and his uses of the pre-Classical past reflect views, in Greek antiquity generally, of the "Archaic" as a bounded period (and the various forms of attachment it generates) is a subject that would be worth developing. I am aware of no study that undertakes this in a synthetic way.

33. See Bowie 1974: 182, citing Strasburger 1966.

34. Similarly, Arrian, *Periplus Maris Euxini* 2, on presumably Archaic Greek inscriptions that are badly and indistinctly chiseled, as if by barbarian hands; but for Arrian these traces are not worthy of "memory eternal," though others are—such as the Palaeolithic, very stonelike remains of the *Argo*'s anchor (at *Periplus Maris Euxini* 11). These parallels were brought to my attention by Timothy Spalding.

35. Habicht 1985: 131.

36. Deborah Lyons reminds me that the attribution is conventional; see Donohue 1988. The passage cited needs to be viewed in the context of other references to Daedalus in Pausanias and elsewhere; see Morris 1992: 247–54 (esp. 248 on the fact that for Pausanias the divinity of this work and others like it derives from their presumed antiquity); Arafat 1996: 67–74.

37. As in Hegel's lectures on aesthetics. It is worth noting that where the modern tradition draws a line between the sublime (Memnon, Saint Peter's) and the beautiful (Polyclitus, Classical beauty [Kant 1987: 83]), the ancient tradition puts the Archaic in tension with the Classical, both being, from a later perspective, suffused with sublimity.

38. μεγέθει μέγας is a recurrent formula: 2.17.4, 2.34.11, 5.20.9, 8.16.4, etc.

39. Words in ὑψ- (ὕψος, ὑψηλός, etc.) abound in Pausanias (see Pirenne-Delforge and Purnelle 1997, vol. 2: 1012–1013, for a concordance). But one should also pay attention to the (actual and conceptual) coupling of such terms with μεγ- words (e.g., ἐπὶ μέγα [6.21.9]), as in the sublime tradition that culminates in Longinus, wherein the words

are virtually synonyms. Monuments and monumental objects tend to be either located on high or to be physically lofty and imposing (cf. διὰ τὸ ἄγαν ὑψηλόν [5.11.10]), and so Pausanias's gaze—real and imaginary—is inevitably directed upward throughout much of his travels, even when all he has before him are ground plans and pedestals.

40. Kant 1987: 103–105 (§25), 108–109 (§26). For the tradition of the sublime prior to Longinus, see Quadlbauer 1958; Russell 1964: xxx–xxxiii; Ford 1992; Porter 1992, 2001. Whereas Plato (*Sophista* 235e–36c) scoffs at architectural and other visual illusions of grandeur, Longinus (17.2 and passim) condones them, in the name of (the rhetoric of) classicism (see the section on Longinus, below). While we are on the subject of the exotic East, a perennial fascination for Greeks (see, e.g., Elsner 1992), it is worth mentioning that the "archaicist" core of classicism is nearly on a par with the latter's Orientalist fantasies. See, e.g., Pausanias 1.33.6 on Atlas, a mountain near the Nile that is so ὑψηλός as to be "said to touch the sky with its peaks." On Longinus, see West 1995, tracing Longinus's Near Eastern inspirations—a thesis that may, however, reflect West's own Orientalist fascinations more than Longinus's. Thus, the claim that the Homeric passages cited by Longinus, which are "out of the ordinary," "certainly do not reflect normal Greek conceptions of the gods and their workings" (West 1995: 338) begs its own premise of what counts as "normal": the passages, and the conception, do after all occur in Homer! Hugo von Hoffmannstahl (1928, 101) would later tellingly describe the real spirit of Classical antiquity—its "numen"—as "our true inner Orient, our open, incorruptible secret."

41. Kant 1987: 108.

42. Lest we be disturbed by the reference to India, we should note how India serves as a backdrop to the Classical fantasy here: it designates an impenetrable strangeness within the most familiar and intimate essence of "Greece." Cf. Virgil, *Georgics* 1.493–97 (where the helmets of the heroes' bones are, precisely, *inanis*); Pausanias 5.20.8 (both suggesting a kind of protoarchaeology); Homer, *Iliad* 21.403–405. See also Pausanias 6.5.1 on the superior height of men in the age of heroes and in that of their predecessors. See also 10.4.4–6. Considerations like those adduced by Innes 1979, which touch on the sublime aspects of the ancient mythological and geographical imagination, need to be thrown into this mix.

43. Megalopolis was, moreover, the place where Arcadia was once politically consolidated, after 279 B.C. (7.6.8–9).

44. As is, occasionally, the image of Tyche, for example at Elis, where a colossus (μεγέθει μέγα) of gilt wood and white marble commands attention (6.25.4).

45. The view is not always so grand, however. Cf. 2.33.3: "Never, I think, did fortune (τό δαιμόνιον) show her spiteful nature so plainly as in her treatment, first of Homer, and afterwards of Demosthenes." Daimon and Tyche are paired at 9.39.5.

46. Cf. Wolf 1985 [1795]: 209 (chap. 49, ad fin.): "For here too in some fashion even the ruins have perished," said of Homer; the allusion is to Lucan 9.969 (*etiam periere ruinae*).

47. Elsner 1992: 26.

48. Elsner 1992: 26.

49. Thus, the claims that Pausanias "had no need to evoke a Greek past by reference to what is no longer there, since his purpose was fulfilled simply by description of what was there," or that he was "presenting not a 'memory,' but a very tangible reality of the past" (Arafat 1996: 33, 214) make Pausanias at once too positivist and too literal-minded, and they omit any reference to, as it were, the purpose of his purpose, viz., the motives for his description and the form it assumed. On the concept of the historical Real, see Jameson 1981 (esp. 34–35, 82, 100–102). The term, borrowed from Lacan, designates

an experience that resists symbolization (it is a traumatic, empty gap) and yet is simultaneously the imaginary product of an existing symbolic field (it is a leftover). See further Žižek 1989.

50. When Pausanias writes that "surely it is clear that the uninitiated may not lawfully hear of that from the sight of which they are debarred" (1.38.7), he is spelling out the conditions of his narrative as a whole. In the place of seeing, from which readers by definition are debarred, Pausanias substitutes—literally *supplies*—the experiences of imagining and of (collective) memory. His text is performative in this precise sense. Cf. the elaborate, substitutive logic of ritual as described in 1.27.3; cultural memory works in an analogous fashion. The failure of words, likewise troped as a moment of ruination ("when the ecphrasis 'fails,' when words revert to being words, tapestries revert to thread, and architecture to rubble"; Bryson 1994: 270), occurs in Philostratus's *Imagines* (2.28). See Bryson 1994: 270 for the argument that "this effect of negativity [is] a figure for Philostratus' own ecphrastic enterprise." The same principle holds true for Pausanias, whose enterprise (which is ecphrastic in its own way) is, to be sure, not identical with Philostratus's.

51. E.g., Frazer (1898, vol. 1: xlix), states that "he lacked imagination"; Habicht (1985: 162) concurs: "Much can be said in Pausanias' favor . . . but it has to be admitted that he did not have a brilliant mind. He lacked originality and the creative spark." To put my point in classical rhetorical terms, Pausanias has not merely selected his materials but combined them into a meaningful whole. See the next section, below.

52. "The matter of his work is of two sorts, historical and descriptive: the one deals with events in the past, the other with things existing in the present" (Frazer 1898, vol. 1: lxxi).

53. See Veyne 1988b: 25, where these are made radically distinct: "Once born, a city has only to live its historic life, which is no longer a concern of etiology," viz., of what one might call commemorative archaeology. Cf. Veyne 1988b: 101: "in religion . . . in history. . . ." Veyne's conceit is premised on an idea foreign to Pausanias (though he claims the opposite): "The implicit idea . . . is that our world is finished, formed and complete." This likewise affects Veyne's severely disjunctive ("balkanizing") approach to the concept of the "archaic" (see Veyne 1988b: 18, 48–49, 56), which overlooks the fact that the archaic exists *only in the present,* in the form of charged memory traces and is thus only the most potent species of memory. Signs of the archaic point exponentially to the *loss*—the gap—that is constitutive of memory. Cf. further Habicht 1985: 163.

54. See Habicht 1985: 162, for further examples; and Dio 36.17 on flattery as cultural and political betrayal.

55. "The sole argument for this [the proposed date of the first century A.D.]—and it is a convincing one—is derived from the last chapter (44), in which the author discusses the relation betwen the decline of literature and the political change from republican to monarchical government. This topic occurs frequently in writers of the first century or so of the Roman principate—e.g. in the two Senecas and in Tacitus. It does not occur much after A.D. 100, and is inconceivable in the disturbances of the third century" and "after the rise of the Second Sophistic." So Russell and Winterbottom 1989: 461, reiterating Russell 1964: xxv, the source of the final quotation about the Second Sophistic; see also Russell 1995: 146–47.

56. See Russell 1964: ad loc., on δημοκρατία: "here particularly the Republic as opposed to the Principate." See also, e.g., Segal 1959: 121: "the change from democracy to empire," cited as one of "the common *topoi* for rhetorical writers of the first century A.D."

57. Although Pausanias is conscious of writing in the more settled and benign reign of Hadrian (during which time Athens could "flourish again"; 1.20.7), he is no more prepared to attribute to Roman hegemony and stability any positive effects than is Longinus; see Habicht 1985: 124.

58. See Bowie 1974: 189 and passim on Pausanias's perspectives and on those of his contemporaries. Dio's attacks on the corruptions of the present are legion; he abhors the moral and political slavery of non-Roman subjects (see Moles 1995: 178, n.5); and he uses the shining image of Classical Greece, the Greece of Phidias and of Homer, to scourge the present (see Dio Chrysostom, *Orations* 12, *Olympicus,* passim). The mixture of cosmic homilies and specific political messages in Dio is, moreover, conventional (as Longinus and Pausanias independently testify); see also Moles 1995: 184.

59. See also Segal 1959: 139.

60. Segal 1959: 131.

61. "Longinus seems to imply that the corruptive influences of his time have in fact penetrated far enough to pervert the whole *psyche,* even the faculty of spontaneous emotional reaction to the sublime" (Segal 1959: 133). This conclusion might not sit well with Longinus ("he would not agree, for example, that the entire personality of man is a product of the material forces about him"; Segal 1959: 133); but, if not, then what this shows is not what Longinus believes but how he can be deeply at odds with himself, which is the more promising way to begin proceeding here.

62. See Segal 1959: 125: "Thus through his ideal of eternity he returns to canons of literary criticism which go far beyond the limitations of a particular political and social situation." This is indeed the self-erasing and circular logic of the Longinian sublime.

63. Differently, Segal 1959: 125: "The classicism of Longinus, however, is not . . . fixed and does not at all imply the unattainability of the sublime of the great writers," who occasionally " 'forget themselves' (4.4)"—as do, by definition, all sublime readers.

64. Cf. Greenblatt 1990: 166: "The order of things is never simply a given: it takes labor to produce, sustain, reproduce, and transmit the way things are." See further n.85, below.

65. Recalling Thucydides 1.22.4; cf. Dionysius of Halicarnassus, *De compositione verborum* 22 (108.11–12 U–R).

66. The ideology of literary culture, exemplified by modern notions of the canon (always in relation to the "classics"), is usefully discussed by Guillory (1993); see also Beard and Henderson 1995.

67. Far from being direct and immediate, the sublime, we might say, is experienced through the agency of an imaginary, ideal audience, one that is contemporary with the Classical past. This is the correlative of Longinus's rule that in order to write sublime Greek you have to imagine, through an act of intense visualization, Homer or Demosthenes as your audience (14.1–3). See n.4, above.

68. See Vernant 1991: 50–74 on this Homeric concept; Hertz 1983 and Segal 1987 each develop this differently. I am interested here in yet another set of possibilities for understanding the metaphors of death in Longinus. One wonders whether Longinus's mention (and inversion) of the *cognomen* of his addressee, Postumius Maurus Terentianus (1.1; Roberts 1899: 18–21), has any point, but this is not worth pressing too far.

69. "It would be easier to open your eyes to an approaching thunderbolt than to face up to [Demosthenes's] unremitting emotional blows (πάθεσιν)" (34.4).

70. For an acute reading of the poetics of quotation in Longinus and for a useful parallel to Walter Benjamin, an inveterate collector of quotational fragments, see Hertz 1983.

71. See Swain 1991. Cf. Pausanias. 1.42.5 on another Hadrianic restoration and, more generally, Lane Fox 1986: 215–37 (esp. 228, on Plutarch's wistfulness toward "the old days" of oracular activity).

72. I am using "archaicism" to refer to the critical valorization of Archaic qualities and to avoid confusion with "archaism," the stylistic affectation of Archaic qualities.

73. The parallel is noted by Russell 1964: ad loc.

74. Translation modified from Russell 1964. Cf. Dionysius of Halicarnassus, *De Demosthene* 38, for a less graphic and less extended version of the same metaphor.

75. A little further on, at *De compositione verborum* 22 (109.16–17 U–R), Dionysius speaks of a "rupturing" of the continuity of a structure (a *harmonia*) and the intrusion of a "gap" of time (a *chronos*) required by a hiatus between vowels. In the sequel he talks about the "disjoining" of the parts of a structural whole. Time literally intrudes into the spatial visualization of the scene—in the form of a gap.

76. The passage at 10.7 might appear to be an exception: "one might say that these writers have taken only the very best pieces, polished them up and fitted them together. They have inserted nothing inflated, undignified, or pedantic. Such things ruin the whole effect, because they produced, as it were, gaps or crevices, and so spoil . . . a structure whose cohesion depends upon their mutual relations," etc. This is not an exception, however, for here the objectionable gaps and crevices in question are whatever ruin the construction of sublimity, which itself is built (συντετειχισμένα) upon relations that, at their most dramatic, include fissures, gaps, etc. The sublime is a body in disintegration: its law of cohesion (τῇ πρὸς ἄλληλα σχέσει) resides in this fact alone. Cf. Dionysius of Halicarnassus, *De compositione verborum* 20 (91.14–17 UR), which names the kind of gaps of which Longinus would only approve (τὸ δὲ μεταξὺ τῶν ὀνομάτων ψύγμα, where "chink" means "breathing space," i.e., "pause"). As Russell 1964: at 22.3–4 observes, the passage, 10.7–11, just quoted is closely echoed in the later passage from 22 on syntactical ruptures (*hyperbata*). They have more in common than at first meets the eye.

77. See Segal 1987 (esp. 217).

78. Cf. Dionysius of Halicarnassus, *De compositione verborum* 22 (97.7–8 U-R) sublimity seeks "to portray emotion (πάθος) rather than moral character (ἦθος)."

79. See Dionysius of Halicarnassus, *De compositione verborum* 20 (91U–R) for an analysis of vowels conceived as sublime magnitudes.

80. The connection between sublimity and greatness of thought (8.1) is a function of this imagining (see 15.1).

81. See 32.5, a literal reorganization of Plato's somatic metaphors from *Timaeus* 65–85.

82. For a related problem, see Humphreys 1995: 210: "Conceptions of authority and authorial identity are complicit in the construction of our desires and fetishes and, in complex ways, in the processes by which fragments and canons are produced."

83. See Marrou 1956: 160–75; Kaster 1988: 11–13. Cf. Innes 1995: 112: "Longinus . . . uses the formal structure of a textbook."

84. Needless to say, in scholiastic commentary the effects of sublimity are transposed from the text—not all lemmata will be sublime, and ironically *most* are *not*—to the act of cultivating the text itself. For Longinus's dependence on the Greek scholiastic tradition, see Bühler 1964.

85. Deracination clears the way for reorganization in fantasy. See Stewart 1984: 158 on the rituals of collecting: "Not simply a consumer of the objects that fill the décor, the self generates a fantasy in which it becomes producer of those objects, a producer by arrangement and manipulation. . . . The economy of collecting is a fantastic one." See Stewart 1984: 19–20 on the power and vulnerability of the severed quotation.

86. I take this to be the force even of Longinus's statement about Ajax's sublime silence in *Odyssey* Book XI, which is "quoted" at the start of chap. 9 so as to illustrate the maxim (itself—ironically—a self-quotation by Longinus): " 'Sublimity is the echo of a noble mind.' "

87. On the disavowals at the heart of modern German classicism, see Porter 2000.

88. As Hertz 1983 notes to good effect.

89. See Alcock 1996 on Pausanias's choice of models and their significance for his criteria of selection. To this consideration may be added the simple fact that Pausanias chose to narrate fragments and remains, to give a "fragmentary" history of Greece—a choice that has no obvious literary antecedents, although this kind of historical fascination is abundantly paralleled among Pausanias's contemporaries.

90. See Braund 1997: 126 (with further references). The novelistic quality of a similar speech (Dio Chrysostom, *Orations* 7, the *Euboicus*), has been frequently pointed out; see Russell 1992; Sidebottom 1996: 455, with n.69.

91. Braund (1997: 126) sees in the choice of names "an indication of the distance between [Dio's] account and Olbian actuality," but this seems to get things backward: it is Dio's account that is doubled and at odds with itself. It is not the case, for instance, that Dio simply "seems to locate the barbarians outside the city" and thus has "oversimplified" the reality, which points instead to "a substantial 'barbarian' presence within the population of the city" (Braund 1997: 129): Dio's Olbians are, precisely, these "barbarians" (see below). The political treatment of cities in the Black Sea region under Hadrian's Panhellenion as "Greek, but not Greek enough," and Bion of Borysthenes's earlier sensitivity to his own mistrusted origins (Braund 1997: 133–34) confirm Dio's wariness toward the Borysthenians' identity in the Thirty-sixth Oration. Another, this time minor, instance of a crisis in naming is Dio's contradiction of Herodotus (ὡς ἐμοὶ δοκοῦσι) over the identification of the "Blackcoats" as Scythian (7). Where Herodotus suspends judgment (4.20), Dio pretends to decide in favor of Scythian identity. But the overall effect of this dispute is a suspension of certainty. A final example is the unnamed referent of μητρόπολις in 8, which is usually taken to refer to Miletus (see Russell 1992: ad loc., and the gloss in the Loeb text), but which could simply (poetically) refer to Borysthenes itself, prior to its conquest (cf. ἥ τε νῦν καὶ ἡ πρότερον [1]; *LSJ* s.v. II.1: "mother-city," "home"). Either way, the true origins and identity of Olbia/Borysthenes are left uncertain by Dio. See further n. 100, below.

92. Cf. Dio, Orations 53.6. There may be a playful erotic connotation in φιλόμηροι.

93. Is the name "Ion" in Plato already a calque on "Ionia," the home of the rhapsodic tradition? "Nothing is known about Ion apart from what Plato tells us" (Murray 1996: at *Ion* 530a1). Surely Ion the Ephesian looks to be a pure fiction and indeed an emblem for the rhapsodic tradition—both its most recent instantiation ("apparently the finest rhapsode in all Greece," Murray 1996: 96) and therefore, so far as Plato is concerned, "the last and weakest . . . replicant" of Homer (Nagy 1996: 60, 77). A homonymical play, by allusion, on the name "Ion" may likewise occur in Callimachus's *Iambus* 13; see Hunter 1997: 46–47 for this suspicion.

94. Russell 1992: 232.

95. So Russell 1992: 22–23, 223; Moles 1995: 190–92.

96. See Moles 1995: 182 on a different political allegory at Dio's *Olympicus* 37.

97. Hieroson and Callistratus are literally inverted in Dio's speech: the younger man represents the older, Homeric literary culture (14), while the older man (indeed the oldest of the Borysthenians) represents a more recent and advanced literary culture (Hieroson has some familiarity with Plato and begs Dio for more of the same [24–27]).

98. Cf. "the gods' thundering horses" in Longinus, who require a "cosmic measure": were they to take two more strides, "they would find there was not enough room in the world" (9.5). The parallels to Longinus are remarkably close, despite the obvious differences. See further Russell 1992: 2–3, 53; Porter 1992: 97–99.

99. On the concept of hybridity, see Bhabha 1994. See also Moles 1995: 190, who points to the "hybrid nature" of the myth but then argues that this hybridity "seems to suggest the ultimate harmony of Greek and barbarian peoples within the universe."

100. A nice irony is the Olbians' self-distancing from "those who come here who are nominally Greeks but actually more barbarous than ourselves" (25). The multiple embarrassments in the speech caused by the term of disdain used here and implied everywhere else, βαρβαρώτερος, is crystallized, and somewhat defused, by this joke.

101. Cratylus refused to name objects; instead he would merely point to them with his finger (Aristotle, *Metaphysica* Γ.5, 1010a11–13). Dio's irony is an inversion of a Socratic irony; see Plato, *Cratylus* 439b5–7, a concluding thought in the dialogue: "knowledge of things does not derive from names; rather it is to be sought in things themselves." (The etymology of *anthropos* at Plato, *Cratylus* 399c6, is less relevant here.) But see also Lucian, *De domo* 2, where mute gesturing at an object (τὴν χεῖρα ἐπισείεσθαι) in place of verbalization, is deprecated as uncultured. The prejudice may be older than Cratylus.

102. Cf. 2.16.4: "in the epic which the Greeks call the *Great Eoeae*. They say . . ."; more emphatic is a passage like the following (10.17.13): "My reason for introducing this account of Sardinia into my description of Phocis is that the island is but little known to the Greeks."

103. Note how easily talk of philhellenism can slide into talk of broader ideals in Favorinus, [Dio] 37.17: "lovers of Hellas, of justice, of freedom, and haters of villainy and tyranny."

104. Some of this is caught by Hertz 1983—for instance, the contradictions between the sublime's enslavement of the audience (15.9) and the freedoms it seems to promise (9.3, 21.2, and passim).

105. For some different views, see Bowersock 1969, 1974; Bowie 1982; Branham 1989; Anderson 1990; Brunt 1994; Swain 1996.

106. Arguments for the general coherence of the literary culture of this age may be found in Bowie 1974; Dihle 1994.

107. Cf. Gleason 1995.

108. Elsner 1998: 121.

109. The sheer fascination exerted by a figure like Favorinus surely stemmed, not from the oddity of his physical appearance alone, but also from the spectacle of identities at odds and overcome which he staged through his performances of himself, viz., of his self. See [Dio] 37 (the *Corinthian Oration*), discussed by Gleason 1995: chap. 1 (cf. esp. p. 16).

110. For one summary of the debate, see Swain 1996. The narrator seems to be (at times) a philhellenic barbarian (an acculturated Assyrian) or else a barbarophilic Greek (or a barbarophilic Roman in Greek guise), fascinated with the foreign and unfamiliar, yet translating everything back, almost blindly, into the familiar again (through hellenizing analogies and namings). In fact, he is none of these alternatives but is rather the point of antagonism among these competing tugs of identification: the narrator literally represents *the problem* of identity in the Second Sophistic world; and the attempt to pin him down to one identity or another merely indulges the fantasies of this symptomatic formation. The truest emblem for the unintegrated persona that the narrator ultimately is comes in *De dea Syria* 33, a culminating iconic description in the travelogue—not the "polymorphic" and, as it were, hybridistic statue of Hera (32), which "as you look at her

projects a wealth of forms" (she seemingly could be a Hera, an Athena, an Aphrodite, a Silene, a Rhea, an Artemis, etc.), but an adjacent image of gold that is literally *"unlike itself"*: lacking any "proper form" (μορφὴν ἰδίην οὐκ ἔχει), it only *recalls* other gods and is therefore variously identified (as Dionysus, Deucalion, and Semiramis). Not πολυείδεια but unknowable *formlessness,* a question mark of form, is the ultimate paradox at the heart of this "centauric" writing by Lucian (as Dryden also saw, albeit from a more purely formal perspective; see Branham 1989: 214–15). As for the Pausanian echoes, these are arguably everywhere to be found in Lucian's piece (cf. the circumspect weighing of informants' tales at 11), although the whole hagiography of the foreign seems to constitute a further jab at the reverential attitude of a Pausanias. Is Lucian poking fun at the tradition out of which Pausanias emerges (as in *Dialogues of the Dead* 6) or possibly at Pausanias himself (i.e., the first and partial "edition" of his *Description*)?

111. Nietzsche, *Ecce Homo,* "Why I Am So Clever," 10: "My formula for greatness in a human being is *amor fati:* that one wants nothing to be other than it is, not in the future, not in the past, not in all eternity. Not merely to endure that which happens of necessity, still less to dissemble it—all idealism is untruthfulness in the face of necessity—but to *love* it . . ."

112. See Snodgrass 1980; Humphreys 1981; Ford 1992: 141–46; Morris 1992: 248. New evidence generally confirms this picture; see Antonaccio 1998. On the Classical period, see now Higbie 1997.

113. See Quintilian (10.1.54), who explains why Apollonius of Rhodes never appeared in the Alexandrian lists of authors even after his death: the *practice* of the grammarians Aristarchus and Aristophanes of Byzantium, which was never to include a living author in their lists, became a *principle* of exclusion and thus was frozen in time. In this way, through a cruel irony, the Alexandrians managed to exclude themselves for ages to come from their own mausoleum to Greek literary culture, the Museum. But they also knew how to play at the game of nostalgia by manipulating its conventions, as is gradually coming to be realized. See Hutchinson 1988; Goldhill 1991; Hunter 1997; Selden 1998.

114. See Bhabha 1994: 161 for a relevant definition of fetishism: fetishism is an obscuring of differences that are "disavowed by the fixation on an object that masks the difference and restores an original presence," in an "archaic affirmation of wholeness/ similarity," an affirmation that is made in the intimation of its own incompleteness. On the parallel practices in fourth-century Greek historiography, described as "responding to major changes in the distribution of power and the boundaries of political action and/ or [as] engaging in dialogue with an imperial power from a peripheral, subaltern position," see Humphreys 1995: 212 and passim. Exemplary for a wariness toward the face value of Second Sophistic productions is Branham 1989: 214.

115. As Gibbon suspected early on (cited in Roberts 1899: 13–14, n.6).

116. Habicht (1985: 6–7) doubts whether Book X is complete, not whether Book X is the last in Pausanias's work. But the evidence for incompleteness is circumstantial and in any case too weak for drawing firm conclusions of any kind.

117. See King 1999.

118. On Pausanias's attitude to restorations, see Bowie 1996b (esp. 220–30).

Chapter 6

1. Chamoux 1974; Jacob 1980a, 1980b; Habicht 1985; Elsner 1992, 1994, 1995: 125–55; Bowie 1996b; Alcock 1993: passim, 1996; Arafat 1996; essays in Bingen 1996 (with discussion); Jacquemin 1996; Frazer 1898, vol. 1: xi–xcvi.

2. On ethnicity and the Second Sophistic, see Bowie 1991; for a nuanced discussion

of identity conflicts, see Elsner 1995: 125–55 (esp. 125–27, 138–44); see also Woolf 1994 (esp. 125–30).

3. Kubler 1962, 1985.

4. Holliday 1997: 143–44.

5. Smith 1981.

6. Jacob 1991: 147–66; Dilke 1985: 62–65.

7. Elsner 1995: 132–37.

8. For insights, see Snodgrass 1987: 67–92 and fig. 16, which maps out the region of Boeotia in light of Pausanias's spatial grid; see also Chamoux 1974; Jacob 1980b: 39–41.

9. Jacquemin 1996; Jacob 1980b on natural marvels.

10. Jacquemin 1996: 127; Jacob 1980b: 37–41.

11. On contrasts between Pausanias and Heraclides Criticus, see Snodgrass 1987: 89–91.

12. Frazer 1898, vol. 1: lxxxii–lxxxix, with focus on Polemo; Bischoff 1937; Casson 1974: 292–99; Elsner 1995: 131–32; Chamoux 1974: 83–84; Jacob 1980b: 36; Arafat 1996: 23, n.57. On Heraclides Criticus (whose work is sometimes attributed to pseudo-Dicaearchus: Müller 1848: 254–61, 1855: 97–110; Frazer 1898, vol. 1: xliii–xlviii; Elsner 1992: 10), see Brown 1965: 245–54; Austin 1981: 151–54; Pfister 1951; Snodgrass 1987: 89–91; Perrin 1994; see also Ferguson 1911: 261–63; Bischoff 1937: 738–39. On Polemo, see Preller 1838; Müller 1883: 108–48; Deichgräber 1952; Habicht 1985: 2–3.

13. André and Baslez 1993: 62, 75–76.

14. Casson 1974: 85, 94; Habicht 1985: 2; Arafat 1996: 22–24; André and Baslez 1993: 34–36, 43–76 (64–68 on guidebooks).

15. Dillon 1997: xiii–xix; André and Baslez 1993: 18–24, 28–29.

16. "In the classical period tourism for religious purposes still remained for the most part occasional" (André and Baslez 1993: 24).

17. See Dilke 1987b; Jacob 1991: 126–31; Thrower 1996: 18–24.

18. On Hellenistic poetry, see Phinney 1967; Williams 1991; Hunter 1996; Fowler 1989: 110–36 (on connections with the visual arts). Of course, kernels of concern both with location and with travel between locations were embedded within pre-Hellenistic texts, whether historical, philosophical, or poetic in orientation (Lukermann 1961: 196–97). Oldest among these were the *Iliad* (esp. the description of the shield of Achilles; see Hardie 1985) and the *Odyssey*.

19. For recent thorough discussions, bibliography, and photographs, see Dreyfus and Schraudolph 1996–97 (see esp. Stewart 1996a on matters of narrative); see also Pollitt 1986: 198–206; Froning 1988: 174–76; von Hesberg 1988: 342–43, 355–56.

20. Van Nortwick 1992: x.

21. Heres 1997; see also Stewart 1996b, on another visual variation.

22. See Cohen 1996; Stewart 1996b.

23. On this mode, see Wickhoff 1900; for a somewhat different understanding, see von Blanckenhagen 1957: 78–79; Weitzmann 1947: 69–70. A review of narrative theories is in Meyboom 1978, with emphasis on the continuous mode; see also Swift 1951: 58; Dawson 1944: 188–96; Pollitt 1986: 200–205. Occasionally the requirement of an unchanging landscape (going back to Wickhoff 1900; but see Weitzmann 1947: 35; Schefold 1960: 89) is needlessly and problematically added to the definition of continuous narrative. Adherence to this requirement would mean that the Telephus Frieze's narrative is not continuous.

24. Swift 1951: 59–61 on the Telephus Frieze. The cyclic was an old mode of narration going back to the Archaic period; see Froning 1988: 177–80, 1992. The continuous method is sometimes conflated with the cyclic, notably in Weitzmann 1947: 17–

33. Weitzmann utilizes the term "cyclic" in a more encompassing way, with formal subdivisions, to describe a variety of methods, including both the depiction of a single event in stages (which we commonly call continuous) and the series of independent but interconnected scenes. I will not uphold this conflation. See also Hanfmann 1957: 73, with definition of "cycle" in n.14; Meyboom 1978: 60–63.

25. Froning 1988; cf. Meyboom 1978 (esp. 64–69, on pre-Hellenistic occasions of continuous narrative). On a likely case of continuous narrative on an Apulian lekythos by the Underworld Painter, dated ca. 350–340 B.C. and now in the Virginia Museum of Fine Arts, Richmond (80.162), see Boardman 1990: 61–62; it shows the abduction of the Leucippidae by the Dioscuri and its aftermath.

26. Interestingly, one of the clearest representations, rather than simple insinuations, of the idea of travel belongs to Aegean prehistory. Traditionally dated ca. 1500 B.C. and more recently ca. 1620 B.C., the so-called Naval Fresco from the upper storey of the "West House" at Akrotiri, Thera, is the earliest semicartographic document in the Aegean; see Televantou 1994.

27. London, British Museum, 1899.2-19.1; Fittschen 1969: 51–59.

28. New York, Metropolitan Museum of Art 56.11.1 (Oakley and Sinos 1993: 29–30); London, British Museum 1920.12-21.1 (Oakley and Sinos 1993: 31; see 26–34 on wedding processions in general).

29. Dawson 1944: 4–49; Borchhardt 1980; Nelson 1977; Wegener 1985; Carroll-Spillecke 1985; Childs 1978: 86–89; von Hesberg 1988: 348–49.

30. Romano-Campanian painting of the first centuries B.C. and A.D. is sometimes used to shed partial light on this lost medium: see Fowler 1989: 168–86; Leach 1982; Pollitt 1986: 187–88; Tybout 1989: 109–150, 187–98.

31. See Andronikos 1984: 101–119.

32. Malibu, J. Paul Getty Museum, inv. 84AE, 38, attributed to the Kleomelos Painter. The exact subject is unknown. On this object and its parallels in late Archaic and Classical vase painting, see Childs 1991.

33. Harrison 1981: 309, fig. 5; Childs 1991: 37; Hanfmann 1957: 77.

34. Athens, National Archaeological Museum, inv. 2104. See Koumanoudis 1884; Robert 1890: 46–50; Courby 1922: 292–93 (no. 18); Biebel 1938: 343, pl. LXXXVII, c; Ghali-Kahil 1955: 311–12; Weitzmann 1959: 43, fig. 48; Childs 1978: 65–66, fig. 31; Carder 1978: 190–91; Sinn 1979: 101–102, fig. 7,3; Brommer 1982: 95; Hausmann 1986: 198, 201 n.5; von Hesberg 1988: 353–54, fig. 25; Schefold and Jung 1988: 263, fig. 313; Byvanck-Quarles van Ufford 1954: 38, with n. 33. All publications indicate that the bowl was found in a grave at Tanagra. However, the very first document of its existence, a handwritten record of the Athens Archaeological Society, purchaser of the bowl in 1883, mentions the area of Demetsana in Arcadia as provenience.

35. Schefold and Jung 1988: 263; Childs 1978: 65–66.

36. Rotroff 1982: 10–11.

37. It is indicative that in the rich corpus of molds recently discovered in the agora of Pella, 89.5 percent are vegetal and only 10.5 percent are narrative; see Akamatis 1993: 344.

38. On terminology, see Robert 1890: 1–7; and now Rogl 1997: 318–20.

39. See Weitzmann 1947, 1959, who draws attention to narrative sequences with as many as five and as few as two consecutive scenes on Homeric bowls. However, Wickhoff (1900: 16, 21, 110–114, 154–57) argues that the bowls' narrative mode is not yet truly continuous, because they string along isolated moments in the lives of their protagonists. See Weitzmann 1947: 35–36 for critique of Wickhoff's arguments. See also Swift 1951: 58–59; Horsfall 1983; Brilliant 1984: 41–43; Pollitt 1986: 200–202.

40. Herodotus 9.73.2; Isocrates, *Helen* 18–22; Apollodorus, *Epitome* 1.23 and *Li-*

brary 3.10.7; Diodorus 4.63; Plutarch, *Theseus* 31; Pausanias 1.17.4, 1.18.4, 1.41.4, 2.22.6; Hyginus, *Fabula* 79. See Brommer 1982: 93–97; Garland 1992: 87–88; Ghali-Kahil 1955: 305–313; Calame 1977: 281–85, 1990: 262–65; Neils 1987: 7–8. See also Despinis 1966. On the variations on the myth and its depiction, see Shapiro 1992.

41. Davies 1988: 39, frag. 12; see Mills 1997: 6–7; Walker 1995: 18; von Steuben 1968: 98, n.99; Weitzmann 1959: 43.

42. On a famous Protocorinthian aryballos from Thebes (Paris, Louvre CA 617), dated ca. 680–70 B.C., see *Lexicon iconographicum mythologiae classicae* 4.1 (1988) s.v. "Helene" (L. Kahil), p. 507, with bibliography; Ghali-Kahil 1955: 309, pl. 100; von Steuben 1968: 35; Fittschen 1969: 186, 189–90.

43. Shapiro 1992: 233–34.

44. On the chest, see Stuart Jones 1894 (esp. 76–77 on the rescue of Helen); von Massow 1916 (esp. 81–84); Lacroix 1988; Snodgrass, chap. 7, this volume. On the throne, see Martin 1976.

45. There is a possibility that the epigram is corrupt in Pausanias's transmitted text and that "out of Athens" may have been "out of Aphidna."

46. Müller 1883: 118, frag. 10; Preller 1838: 43, frag. 10.

47. Neils 1987: 1–3; Adams 1989.

48. Schefold and Jung 1988: 263.

49. See Cohen 1996; Stewart 1996b (on the complexities of rendering, and reading, a woman's attitude in circumstances of abduction).

50. See Robert 1890: 47–48; Sinn 1979: 102.

51. On earlier vases showing consecutive elements of the story, but without any hint of travel, see Shapiro 1992: 233, n.8.

52. See Schapiro 1973: 43 for the observation that in the visual arts profile and frontal views are "coupled in the same work as carriers of opposed qualities" and along with other features mark "polarized individuals." Juxtaposed with a profile face (in Greek art the fundamental view of action and power), a frontal face, such as Helen's in the first scene, connotes a passive or constrained person (44). Helen is shown in profile in the second scene on the bowl, where her pose is determined by Theseus and their joint movement forward.

53. The polarity between male and female mobility in relation to the home has been explored by Jean-Pierre Vernant, who took the contrasting roles of two deities, Hermes and Hestia, as his point of departure for understanding Greek social customs. The former god, a wanderer, represents "movement and flow, transience, mutation and transition"; the latter is stable, home-bound, immobile, tied to domesticity; see Vernant 1969: 133–34.

54. Dillon 1997: 183–203.

55. Van Bremen 1996: passim (especially 205–225).

56. Lacroix 1974. On Theseus, see Neils 1987.

57. On Stesichorus's *Palinode*, see Plato, *Phaedrus* 243a-b (cf. Pausanias 3.19.13). For Herodotus's account see *Histories* 1.1–4. See also Euripides's *Helen* and Isocrates's *Helen*. Discussion in Austin 1994: 1–13, 102, n.23, 118–36, 137–203.

58. According to Plutarch, the Athenians did not appreciate the provocation Theseus gave to the Dioscuri and did not take his side in this dispute. Plutarch was critical of Theseus also because of his entanglement in various sexual exploits for pleasure rather than honor. Theseus's allegedly advanced age in relation to Helen possibly also mattered, for similar situations occasioned Plutarch's critique in the telling of Roman lives, although not as explicitly in the case of this Greek one: see Stadter 1995 (esp. 225–27, 230). See Garland 1992: 97–98 on the morally ambiguous character of Theseus, hero

and rapist at once. On the confluence of positive and negative characteristics in his persona, see Mills 1997: 97–104, and on this hero's openness to varying interpretations, Calame 1990.

59. In the Hellenistic period, Theseus was a popular figure in Athens, and the festival of the Theseia was celebrated with splendor, as inscriptions from the second century B.C. indicate: see Bugh 1990; Habicht 1997: 237, 240–41; cf. Hollis 1992.

60. Volos, Archaeological Museum, inv. 2291 (mold) and 2290 (bowl fragment); Kakavoyannis 1980: 271–75.

61. Doulgeri-Intzesiloglou 1990: 122.

62. Hausmann 1986.

63. But see Childs 1978: 66, who detects such buildings.

64. Winter 1971: 138–41, 328.

65. Winter 1971: fig. 48 (Corinth), fig. 79 (Athens); see 152–203 on towers.

66. Alcock's comment that the Hellenistic *poleis*'s loss of prestige and power brought about a "conscious archaism in their self-representation" is relevant in this connection. "Myth, legend, and heroic genealogies were increasingly invoked to provide a sense of identity and of purpose, as well as to spin a web of interrelationships among the political units of the Mediterranean world." See Alcock 1994b: 258; cf. Alcock 1994a (esp. 223). On Athens's evolving circumstances in the Hellenistic era, see Habicht 1997.

67. See Byvanck-Quarles van Ufford 1954: 38, with n.33, for an unusual late dating of the bowl in the first century B.C.

68. On Pausanias's and other ancient views on this event, see Arafat 1996: 89–97. Strabo (8.6.23) understood Corinth's predicament as a just punishment.

69. See Suetonius, *Nero* 19 and 37. Roux (1958: 88–89) draws attention to Pausanias's reluctance to name the agent behind this attempt. Such plans predated Nero, but he was the first to attempt implementation; see Alcock 1993: 141.

70. Bergmann 1991: 58–59.

71. Athens, National Archaeological Museum, inv. 18063; Karouzou 1970; Matheson 1995: 64, 224–25, fig. 53.

72. London, British Museum, G. 104; Sinn 1979: 107 (MB 45), pl. 18, 4; von Hesberg 1988: 353–54, fig. 26.

73. On such crowned female figures and their antecedents in the Near East, see Metzler 1994; Childs 1978: 81–82. See Pollitt 1986: 3, fig. 1, for the best-known Roman copy of Eutychides's Tyche, now in the Vatican. See also Gardner 1888. Interestingly, Helen herself is on rare occasions shown wearing a mural crown, as if to underscore her connection to cities and their fall. On a large Apulian lekythos showing her abduction by Paris (private collection, on loan to the Musée d'Art et d'Histoire, Geneva), see Aellen, Cambitoglou, and Chamay 1986: 136–49, with pl. on p. 140. On a volute krater showing her arrival at Troy and presentation to Priam (Geneva, Collection Hellas et Roma, inv. HR 44), see Aellen, Cambitoglou, and Chamay 1986: 97–108, with fig. on p. 99. Both are dated ca. 340–330 B.C. and attributed to the circle of the Darius Painter.

74. Bloomington, Indiana University Art Museum, inv. 76.85.15; Smith 1994: 91–92, with fig. 59; Spier 1989: 24 (no. 28), 32, fig. 20 (cf. figs. 21, 22, 42, for similar ringstones).

75. Sparta Museum, inv. 7945; Palagia 1994: 65–75, with figs. 35, 39–43. Compare Edwards 1990: 529–31 and pl. 83a on a roughly contemporary turreted head of Tyche from Corinth (S 802).

76. Biebel 1938: 345; Ehrensperger-Katz 1969: 2, fig. 3; Levi and Levi 1967: 134–50 (on city walls), 151–59 (on personifications); Bosio 1983: 83–89 (on personifications),

89–92 (on walled cities); Dilke 1987c: 238–42. On cartographic conventions, see Dilke 1987a; Aujac et al. 1987a, 1987b; Johnston 1967; Nicolet 1991: 4.

77. But see Johnston 1967, on a fourth-century B.C. Ionian coin type, whose reverse is interpreted as a relief map of the hinterland of Ephesus.

78. Herzog August Bibliothek, Wolfenbüttel, Codex 36.23. Aug. 2° (see fol. 55ᵛ); Weitzmann 1959: 6–7, fig. 3; Dilke 1967, 1987d: 217–21; Carder 1978; Geyer 1989: 67, pl. 10,2; cf. Nicolet 1991: 150–52, figs. 47–49. See also Dilke 1985 (esp. 145–53, 156–65); Campbell 199 (esp. 99 and pl. 1); Ehrensperger-Katz 1969: 2, fig. 5.

79. Avi-Yonah 1954; Donceel-Voûte 1988; Piccirillo 1993: 26–34, 94–95, 1989: 76–95; Donner 1992.

80. See Johnston 1967: 86, 92–93; André and Baslez 1993: 29–31; Jacob 1980a: 69–70, 1991: 41–47 (on Herodotus 5.49–54 and his connecting of maps with conquest); Prontera 1985.

81. Nicolet 1991: 30–31; Walbank 1948; Dilke 1985: 60–61; Zecchini 1991.

82. See Meyboom 1995, with bibliography; Pollitt 1986: 205–208; Ling 1991: 7–8, fig. 3; Steinmeyer-Schareika 1978; Tybout 1989: 340–41, 344–45. Panayides (1994) dates the mosaic to the second century A.D.

83. Pausanias 1.12.3–4, 1.33.6, 2.28.1, 9.21.1–4; Jacob 1980a: 71–72, 1980b.

84. Moffitt 1997: 227–47. The Roman cityscape newly discovered at the Baths of Trajan in Rome and tentatively dated to the last third of the first century A.D. seems to conjure up these same genres: within a towered city wall lie buildings such as temples, a courtyard surrounded by porticoes, houses, a theater, a bridge over a river; see *Archaeology* 51 (May/June 1998): 23.

85. On these distinctions, see Lukermann 1961: 194–96; Nicolet 1991: 4, 100–101, 119, n.23; Moffitt 1997.

86. Lukermann 1961: 195, discussing Ptolemy.

87. 1.38 m × 0.89 m (Pompeii 1,7,7); Dawson 1944: 99, 121; Schefold 1960: 88, with fig. 2; Peters 1963: 93–95; von Blanckenhagen 1968; Ling 1991: 114–16, fig. 116; Pugliese Caratelli 1990: 594–97; Leach 1988: 346, 349, fig. 32. Another painting from Pompeii, in the British Museum, shows the same subject and a walled city largely seen from above; see Hinks 1933: 15–16 (cat. no. 28), pl. XII; cf. Schefold and Jung 1988: 263.

The city motif had a long life in medieval mythoreligious narrative manuscripts; see Biebel 1938; Ehrensperger-Katz 1969. On the early-fifth-century Vatican Vergil (Rome, Vatican Library, cod. Vat. lat. 3225), see Geyer 1989; on the early-sixth-century Vienna Genesis (Vienna, Österreichische Nationalbibliothek, cod. Vindobonensis. theol. graec. 31), see von Hartel and Wickhoff 1895. On the tenth-century Joshua Roll (Rome, Vatican Library, cod. Vat. gr. 431), see Weitzmann 1948. On the Gospels of Otto III of ca. A.D. 1000 (Munich, Bayerische Staatsbibliothek, Clm. 4453), see Dressler et al. 1978.

88. Bergmann 1991; Wallace-Hadrill 1994; Elsner 1995: 74–85. See Mitchell 1994 for the claim—intended and received as a general proposition—that the interest in pictorial landscape is intimately connected with notions of power.

89. Veyne 1988a, 1991: 311–42. But on narrative principles and ways of enhancing the viewer's comprehension of the frieze, see Settis 1988: 107–114, 202–210; Brilliant 1984: 90–108. Generally on the column, see Settis 1988; Kleiner 1992: 212–20, with bibliography on 263–64.

90. Plutarch, *Alexander* 72.5.7; Strabo 14.1.23, who speaks of two cities rather than one. See Stewart 1993: 402–407, on these and other ancient testimonia with translations; see 28–29 on the variant names assigned to this architect, as well as fig. 1.

91. De Blois 1998: 361.

92. Holliday 1997; Kleiner 1992: 47–48.

93. The Narmer Palette of the Egyptian First Dynasty, ca. 3100 B.C., features a rectangular plan in the lower register of its reverse. The slightly earlier Towns Palette shows on its lower section several rectangular enclosures with protruding bastions, symbolizing cities in plan, each subjugated by a different animal symbol. Both palettes are in the Egyptian Museum, Cairo; see Spencer 1993: figs. 32–33.

94. On the extensive low reliefs of the palace of Ashurnasirpal II (883–859 B.C.) at Nimrud, now in the British Museum, see Frankfort 1970: 158–59, figs. 182–84. The Assyrian army, fully armed, is shown attacking battlements of cities defended energetically by their inhabitants. In the second half of the ninth century B.C., Ashurnasirpal's son Shalmaneser III made geography—natural landscape features and human structures—central to the depictions of his expeditions: see Marcus 1987; Reade 1980. In the second half of the eighth century B.C., the motif of the walled city participated again in the imperialist visual messages of Tiglathpileser III (Frankfort 1970: 168–69, fig. 194) and Sennacherib (Childs 1978: pls. 27.1–4). Lycian funerary relief monuments of the early fourth century B.C., such as the "Nereid Monument" from Xanthos and the "Heröon" from Gjölbaschi-Trysa, inherited this tradition. The Heröon, with its panoramic landscape backgrounds, features natural or architectural elements throughout but no complete enclosure can be made out. The Nereid Monument, in contrast, features on one of its podium friezes not only partially viewed cities but also two fully enclosed. On the Trysa reliefs in Vienna, see Childs 1978: 13–14, 31–36, fig. 20, pls. 14–17; Wegener 1985: 74–79; Oberleitner 1994: 36, figs. 74–76, 81. On the Nereid Monument in the British Museum, see Childs 1978: 12–13, 28–31, figs. 11, 18, 19, pls. 12.1, 12.2; Wegener 1985: 72–74.

95. Torelli 1982: 119–20. See also Settis 1988: 97–99, 112; Koeppel 1980. On stock motifs, see Gauer 1977: 13–18 (14 on cityscapes); Settis 1988: 120–37, 188–202.

96. Winkler, in Baumer, Hölscher, and Winkler 1991: 271–77.

97. Kleiner 1992: 295–301, with bibliography on 314; Brilliant 1984: 114–15; Wegner 1931.

98. Biering 1995: 190. Today the paintings are for the most part in the Vatican Museum.

99. Dawson 1944; Schefold 1960: 94–95; Andreae 1962; von Blanckenhagen 1963; Pollitt 1986: 185–89, 208–209; Froning 1988: 173–74; von Hesberg 1988: 343–48; Ling 1991: 107–111; Biering 1995; Lowenstam 1995. For this monument's position within Odyssean imagery, see Buitron et al. 1992; Andreae and Presicce 1996.

100. Thus, even if one reads the pillars as frames and dividers, which would speak to "cyclic" narrative, "continuous" would still be an applicable term, given the occasional repetition of figures within a single visual unit. But see Biering 1995: 193 (reviewed by Bergmann 1997), who rejects the widely held view that the frieze employs continuous narrative.

101. On the creation of this world in the Augustan period, see Nicolet 1991.

102. Snodgrass 1987: 77.

Chapter 7

1. See esp. Elsner 1992.
2. Gurlitt 1890: 126.
3. Habicht 1985: 161 and n.82.
4. Hitzig and Blümner 1896–1910.
5. See Habicht 1985: 131–33; and now Arafat 1996: 43–79.

6. Habicht 1985: 165–75 (Appendix I: "Pausanias and His Critics").

7. As by Robert 1888: 436–44.

8. As by Gallavotti 1978: 12–14.

9. Habicht 1985.

10. Gallavotti 1978: 3.

11. See Vatin 1981: 440–49, on the now rediscovered inscriptions; Habicht 1985: 75–77.

12. Veyne 1988b: 3.

13. E.g., Stuart Jones 1894; von Massow 1916 (from whom fig. 17 is taken).

14. Cook 1983.

15. Cook 1983: 3–4.

16. Loeschcke 1880: 5ff. [*non vidi*].

17. Johansen 1967: 247–49.

18. Klein 1885: 16.

19. Loeschcke 1894: 512–13, n.2.

20. See the exchange between Brommer 1980 and Boardman 1981.

21. So von Massow 1916: 96.

22. Johansen 1934: 52–72, 1967, 92–127.

23. Lowenstam 1993.

24. Cook 1983: 5.

25. Snodgrass 1998.

26. Most notably, Johansen 1967; Schefold 1964, 1978, 1981, 1989, 1993; Schefold and Jung 1988.

27. Cook 1983: 1, n.1.

28. Frazer 1898, vol. 3: 606.

29. Elsner 1995: 316–17, n.30.

30. Arafat 1995: 465.

Chapter 8

Thanks to Geoff Compton of the Interdepartmental Program in Classical Art and Archaeology, Univeristy of Michigan, for help with illustrations. I would also like to thank the following for comments and advice: my co-editors, Jaś Elsner and John Cherry; Paul Cartledge; Jack L. Davis; Stephen Hodkinson; and Sally Humphreys. Remaining problems are all my own. Translations of Pausanias are from the Loeb Classical Library, with slight emendations.

1. Calculated, as Habicht did, by counting pages in the Teubner edition (Rocha-Pereira 1989); Habicht 1985: 37; Musti 1996: 17–18; Kiechle 1959: 3.

2. This focus on "the most noteworthy," "the really notable," "the most remarkable," "the memorable," is expressed in various ways and repeated throughout the *Periegesis:* for lists, see Elsner 1992: 11, n.37; Alcock 1996: 246, n.8.

3. Habicht explains the imbalance as follows: "Messenia . . . was a region of Greece that for centuries had been subject to Sparta and, consequently, had no history of its own and only a small number of important sites and monuments" (1985: 21); see also Shero 1938: 500; Torelli and Musti 1991b: ix. Musti (1996: 17) regards the imbalance as the result of cultural loss stemming from Spartan domination, and argues that Pausanias compensates for this by his longer mythic and historical section, working to bring the account of Messenia into greater conformity with other areas of Greece.

4. A further wrinkle is the suggestion that Pausanias may only have known Myron and Rhianos through an intermediate source. For bibliography on this complex issue, see Shero 1938; Pearson 1962 (esp. 397, n.2); Habicht 1985: 96–97, n.5; Torelli and Musti 1991b. For a sophisticated study of Pausanias's historiography of neighboring Lakonia, see Meadows 1995.

5. Torelli and Musti 1991b: xxvi. "A 'mosaic,' with the contribution of his multiple experiences of reading and of travel."

6. The death of Philopoemen (the "last of the Greeks," Plutarch, *Philopoemen* 1.4) by poison in Messene was clearly a significant turning point to Pausanias: "After this Greece ceased to bear good men" (8.52.1).

7. More mentions are made, in passing in Book III, to the Messenian Wars and to the subjection or banishment of the Messenians: 3.3.2, 3.4-5, 3.7.6, 3.14.4, 3.18.7, 3.20.6.

8. "Il risultato fu che i *Messeniaka* non divennero mai storie della Messenia, ma storie dei Messeni. Fu una letteratura interessata a un popolo, non a un territorio, alle vicende dei 'fichi buoni' in esilio, non a quelle dei 'fichi cattivi' rimasti in patria" (Asheri 1983: 41). Pausanias commits a major chronological "gaffe" in this section of the book (4.23.6-9), on the date of Anaxilas, tyrant of Rhegium: he assigns his seizure of Zancle to the Twenty-ninth Olympiad (664–661 B.C.), whereas Anaxilas was actually, as Frazer (1898, vol. 2: 418) puts it, "a contemporary of Darius and Xerxes" (494–476 B.C.); Kiechle 1959: 119–23; Pearson 1962: 421–22; Shero 1938: 525–31; Torelli and Musti 1991a: 237–39, 1991b: xviii. Explanations for the confusion vary (see Luraghi 1994 on just how far it *is* a confusion), but the ultimate result is to "lose" almost two centuries between the conquest and the liberation of Messenia (see table 2).

9. "The Messenians were not truly themselves until their return" (Elsner 1992: 16). As another sign of Messenia retaking its place in the Greek world, a Messenian, Damiscus, later a victor at Nemea and the Isthmus, won the Olympic footrace for boys "in the year after the settlement of Messene." No Messenian had won at Olympia, Pausanias was "exceedingly surprised" to learn, during their years of exile; with their return, "their luck in the Olympic games came with them" (6.2.10–11).

10. Alcock 1996: 250–60 (quote at 259). The most pervasive example of this, of course, is Pausanias's frequent invocation of the Persian Wars as a kind of panhellenic charter of identity; his decision to follow Herodotus as a model cannot wholly account for the compelling role of *ta Medika* in his account. On the Persian Wars tradition in Roman times, see Spawforth 1994.

11. See also Elsner 1992: 17–20, 1994: 244–52.

12. Habicht 1985: 37.

13. For examples of such work at Athens, see e.g., Thompson and Wycherley 1972: 204–207; Wycherley 1959; at Delphi, see e.g., Daux 1936. For more regional studies, see Roux 1958; Jost 1973.

14. Only some of the principal reports are listed here. For Artemis Limnatis, see, e.g., Frazer 1898, vol. 3: 427 (with nineteenth-century references); Valmin 1930: 12–13, 187; Hope Simpson 1966: 115–16; McDonald and Rapp 1972: 316, no. 548; Breuillot 1985: 794. For Andania, see, e.g., Frazer 1898, vol. 3: 444 (with nineteenth-century references); Hiller von Gaertringen and Lattermann 1911; Valmin 1930: 92–99, 1938: 13; Roebuck 1941: 7–10; Breuillot 1985: 799–802; McDonald and Rapp 1972: 316, no. 607. On the Expédition scientifique de Morée, see esp. Bory de Saint-Vincent 1834–36.

15. Habicht 1985: 36–66 (quote at 63). For recent reports on excavations at Messene, see, e.g., Orlandos 1976; Themelis 1993, 1994a, 1994b.

16. Exceptions, not surprisingly, are long-lived sanctuaries mentioned by Pausa-

nias. On Apollo Korynthos, 4.34.7, see Versakis 1916; Jeffery 1990: 203–204, 206. On Ayios Floros/Pamisos, 4.3.10, 4.31.4, see Valmin 1938: 419–65; Jeffery 1990: 202, 206.

17. Kopanaki: *BCH* 107 (1983) 764; *Archaeological Reports* 29 (1982–83) 30. Kaltsas (1985) reports that the structure actually dated from the sixth century B.C. to the second quarter of the fifth, when it was violently destroyed. The identification of the structure's residents remains open. The excavator, Kaltsas, suggested it as the residence of a Spartiate absentee landowner and his helot underlings; see also Harrison and Spencer 1998: 161–62. On Roman villas, see Alcock 1993: 64–71, table 6; Lukermann and Moody 1978: 99–100, table 7–1.

18. Frazer 1898, vol. 3: 462.

19. Valmin 1930: 126. "The west coast of Messenia, between the mouth of the Neda and Mothone, has always been dealt with in a superficial fashion. It has been claimed that during the period of Spartan domination the area remained wild, that it had even been used for grazing, and that it could offer little of interest from an archaeological or topographical point of view."

20. Valmin 1930: 126–63.

21. Also mentioned by Pausanias is Sphaktiria, which provokes a comment about how "human fortunes can confer renown on places previously unknown. . . . So Sphaktiria is known to the world for the disaster that there befell the Spartans" (4.36.6). Classical Pylos/Koryphasion and Sphaktiria might at first seem major exceptions to the general neglect of the west coast. Thucydides's account (in Book IV) of events in 425 B.C. has generated great interest among travelers and military historians eager to refight that famous encounter of the Peloponnesian War (Wilson 1979, for bibliography). Yet this fascination does not really alter the basic pattern of indifference to the region's own history. Thucydides and his followers were concerned with the conflict of outside forces as played out in this locale, Pausanias with musing upon the vagaries of human fortune. Nowhere is there a desire to investigate the local trajectories of "places previously unknown" (Torelli and Musti 1991a: 271). The local Messenian population remains invisible in Pausanias's account.

22. On the goals and scholarly reception of this project, see McDonald 1984; Fotiadis 1995. For its place in the history of Classical and Messenian archaeology, see Cherry 1983: 392–93; McDonald 1984; Davis et al. 1997: 394–96; Spencer 1998: 39–41.

23. McDonald and Rapp 1972; Rapp and Aschenbrenner 1978; McDonald, Coulson, and Rosser 1983; McDonald and Wilkie 1992. See Coulson and Wilkie 1983 for the fairly scanty remains of Archaic through Roman date at Nichoria.

24. Of the analysis of the initial regional survey results, about 80 percent is devoted to prehistoric and 20 percent to "post-Mycenaean" times: McDonald and Hope Simpson 1972: 130–46; see also McDonald and Rapp 1972: 310–21 (Register B). For comments explaining this imbalance, see McDonald and Hope Simpson 1972: 123, 143; Lukermann and Moody 1978: 82, 84. The Bronze Age emphasis grew less pronounced in the project's later years, notably with the valuable publication of Nichoria's Dark Age and Byzantine occupation.

25. Davis 1998: xl and (on "Travelers' Views") xxxiv–xxxix; Davis et al. 1997: 454–55.

26. Such as Gargaliani *Ordines* (K1); Marathoupolis *Dialiskari* (G1); Vromoneri *Ayia Sotira* (G2); Vromoneri *Pigadia* (G3); Romanou *Romanou* (I4). See Davis et al. 1997: 454–74, esp. fig. 20 (map showing distribution of Roman finds); Alcock 1998; Alcock et al., in prep.; *The Pylos Regional Archaeological Project Internet Edition* (http: //classics.lsa.umich.edu/PRAP.html), for further information on these specific sites, some

of which had previously been noted by investigators such as Valmin. On the results of the survey for the period of Spartan conquest, see below.

27. On Pausanias's "construction of authority," see Alcock 1996: 260–61.

28. The name of the town Koroni was also validated through the recovery of a buried object: a bronze crow discovered while digging the foundation of the city walls (4.34.5–6). On other "buried talismans" in Pausanias, see Frazer 1898, vol. 3: 433–34. Elsner (1992: 25) emphasizes the secrecy of the object and its burial, noting "that Pausanias' narrative told his readers all and yet missed the crucial precisions of what was buried and where it was concealed." Only after its recovery is the identity of the "secret thing" revealed.

29. Even Aristomenes, the great hero of the struggle, leaves Messenia to die and be buried in Rhodes; only after liberation are his bones recovered, by order of the god of Delphi, and honored in Messene (4.24.3, 4.32.3). The Messenian exiles too are represented by Pausanias as in some ways unchanging, or "frozen," if in a different fashion: "But the wanderings of the Messenians outside the Peloponnese lasted almost three hundred years, during which it is clear that they did not depart in any way from their local customs, and did not lose their Doric dialect, but even to our day they have retained the purest Doric in the Peloponnese" (4.27.11). For other evidence and discussion of this linguistic archaism, see Hall 1997: 180.

30. "By the fifth century generations of subjugation had eventually conditioned most helots in both Laconia and Messenia to accept their inferior condition. . . . The evidence suggests that helots smarted under Spartiate haughtiness and brutality, but endured them passively" (Talbert 1989: 39; for a rebuttal, see Cartledge 1991: 380); "l'oppression dont les Hîlotes étaient traditionnellement les victimes ne provoquait pas chez eux la colère ou la contestation, mais la résignation et la conscience de leur infériorité" (Ducat 1974: 1452). See also Roobaert 1977 on "inertie" among Laconian helots.

31. For recent major discussions of the Spartans (and thus the Messenians), see Cartledge 1979, 1987; Powell 1988, 1989. On helots specifically, see Ducat 1978, 1990. For reviews from the Messenian point of view, see Roebuck 1941 (although this focuses on the years 369–146 B.C., thus beginning only after liberation and ending with Roman intervention); Lazenby and Hope Simpson 1972. Treves (1944) is an early prescient voice on "the problem of a history of Messenia"; Whitby (1994) touches on different national traditions in this scholarship.

32. Cartledge 1985, 1991; see also de Ste. Croix 1983. For comparative discussions of the problems inherent in the study of subordinate peoples, see Comaroff 1985; Miller, Rowlands, and Tilley 1989; McGuire and Paynter 1991; Pratt 1992; van Dommelen 1998.

33. Hodkinson 1992.

34. Davis et al. 1997: 455–57; Alcock et al., in prep. On tomb cult and sanctuaries, see Bauslaugh 1990; Coulson and Wilkie 1983; Alcock 1991 (esp. 456); Antonaccio 1995: 70–102; Alcock, forthcoming. Stephen Hodkinson is currently preparing a systematic study of tomb cult in Archaic and Classical Messenia and its sociopolitical implications.

35. Fotiadis 1995: 61–62.

36. Aschenbrenner 1992: 57–58; Fotiadis 1995: 70, though he notes (p. 72) that Aschenbrenner elsewhere expanded his analyses and drew a radically different picture of Karpofora.

Commentary (Bergmann)

1. The term *topographos* may mean a mapmaker or landscape painter; the distinction did not exist in antiquity. For bibliography on Demetrios, see Rouveret 1989: 331–

36; on the Palestrina Nile Mosaic, Meyboom 1995; on the Odyssey Frieze, Biering 1995; see also Cohen, chap. 6, this volume.

2. Rutherford (chap. 4, this volume) discusses the appropriation and awe of *theoria;* its meaning ranged from being a spectator at panhellenic games to a symbol for the contemplative life of philosophers.

3. Addressed by both Porter and Cohen (chaps. 5 and 6, respectively, in this volume).

4. Many of the villa *topoi* are first named by Cicero: Schmidt 1899. On Amalthea, see Callimachus, *Hymn* 1; Ovid, *Fasti* 5.111–28. Cicero (*Epistulae ad Atticum* 1.31.1) mentions his Amaltheum in a letter of 61 B.C. (Neudecker 1988: 9–11). On imperial villas, see the invaluable, unpublished dissertation by Leppert (1974).

5. Schneider 1967: 498, 630; Mielsch 1987: 94–111. In general on villa culture, see D'Arms 1970; on adopting a Greek lifestyle among Romans, see Griffin 1986.

6. Elsner and Rubiés 1999: 7: "modernity is constituted in opposition to a past, for which there is also desire."

7. *Topion* is a term known only from the Roman period: Daremberg and Saglio 1877–1919: s.v. *topia* (G. Lafaye); Rouveret 1989: 323–31.

8. On the augural process, see Cancik 1985–86.

9. Polybius 5.21, quoted from van Paassen 1957: 300.

10. Vitruvius, *De architectura* 7.5.1–3; Pliny, *Naturalis historia* 35.116; Ling 1977.

11. Travel, enjoyed by the elite since the fourth century B.C., was more in vogue than ever in the second century A.D. On visiting famous sites, see Polybius 1.4.6; for the typical travel itinerary in Greece, see Livy 45.27–28; Friedländer 1908–1913, vol. 1: 323–428; Casson 1974: 174–96; André and Baslez 1993.

12. Strabo 1.2.12.

13. Alcock 1993, 1994a, 1996, chap. 8, this volume.

14. As, e.g., at the villas of Castelgandolfo, Tivoli, and Piazza Armerina (Neudecker 1998: 44–45; Andreae and Presicce 1996: 252–375).

15. On Odysseus as *exemplum* of traveler/pilgrim, see Elsner and Rubiés 1999: 8–9; Ewald 1999.

16. Barthes 1977: 73.

17. On Lake Avernus, see Ammianus Marcellinus 28.4.18; Neudecker 1988: 40. Cicero (*Tusculanae disputationes* 1.20.45) recommended seeing the mouth of the Black Sea first entered by the *Argo*. For Hellenistic and Roman visitors to Troy, see Vermeule 1995.

18. Pausanias 4.35.9; Strabo 16.2.28; Pliny, *Naturalis historia* 5.69. On Scaurus, see Pliny, *Naturalis historia* 9.11; also Suetonius, *Divus Augustus* 72 and Pausanias 8.46 on collections of bones of monsters and heroes. On the exhibition of natural curiosities in Rome, see Friedländer 1908–1913, vol. 4: 6–11.

19. Propertius 3.22.29 (trans. G. P. Goold). On the statue, see Conticello 1969; Ridgway 1971; Neudecker 1988: 222.

20. Phillips 1968; Bergmann 1999: 92, 98–99. It is interesting that Josephus (*Bellum Judaicum* 3.419–21), describing Joppa in the late first century A.D., when these images had been long visible, wrote as if he were seeing a landscape painting.

21. On tree cults in Arcadia, see Pausanias 8.23.4–5. Virgil describes how a shepherd departing from the river Peneus stood at its sacred source crying out to his divine mother underwater (*Georgics* 4.317–32; cf. 2.469). A similar waterway is experienced by Aeneas during his subterranean journey when he stops to behold the sacred fountainhead of *amoenus* Pater Tiburinus, one of the earliest *numina* to whom the Romans offered worship (*Aeneid* 7.30-34). On the paintings, see Bergmann 1992.

22. On Diana of Nemi, see Frazer 1890: 1–9; on the Julio-Claudian elaboration of the site, see Moltesen 1997.

23. Pliny, *Epistulae* 2.17.5; Martial 10.30; Drerup 1959. Statius (*Silvae* 2.2) envisions Galataea and Leander, along with famous Hercules and famous landmarks, in his patrons' Italian villas (Bergmann 1991).

24. Zanker (1998: 135–203) has revised his earlier argument (Zanker 1979) that the fantasies painted on Pompeian walls and re-created three-dimensionally in small gardens emulated the installations in grand estates; rather they are part of a much broader cultural phenomenon in Roman society.

25. Lucretius 4.576–94 (trans. R. E. Latham); Dionysius Halicarnassensis, *Antiquitates Romanae* 2.18.3; Fantham 1997; Segal 1981; Kegel-Brinkgreve 1990: 1–190.

26. Pausanias 9.16.7, 9.17.2. Thebes had been rebuilt by Kassander in 316 B.C., captured by Licinius in 173 B.C., destroyed by Mummius in 146 B.C., and barely rebuilt before again being sacked by Sulla (Symeonoglou 1985: 193–94).

27. On the sculptural groups of the Niobids and Dirce, see Grimal 1984: 339–41; Geominy 1982; Pliny, *Naturalis historia* 36.34; Pozzi 1991.

28. Wirth 1983. Juxtapositions of Theban scenes appeared elsewhere, for example, in the black triclinium of the House of the Fruit Orchard and the House of the Marinaio (Bergmann 1999).

29. Similarly, the visitor walking in a garden might chance upon statues evoking different sites and stories; remains have been found in villas of the Muses, a Ganymede, the sleeping Ariadne, young Hylas, and Actaeon being seized by his dogs (Neudecker 1988: 39–47, 136–37). In a cave at Capri, sea gods emerged from the waters (De Franciscis 1965).

30. I have argued elsewhere (Bergmann 1999) that although the individual stories and pictorial compositions may derive from Greek prototypes, their revised visual vocabulary and coexistence in rooms called for an analogical process of reception that was inherently Roman.

31. See Förtsch 1993; Pliny's letters share villa lore with descriptions by Horace, Cicero, and Statius.

32. Eco 1985: 301.

33. Drummer 1993.

34. Bergmann 1991.

35. MacDonald and Pinto 1995.

36. Scriptores Historiae Augustae, *Hadrian* 26.5–6 (quoted in MacDonald and Pinto 1995: 7).

37. For a summary and critique, see Packer 1998.

38. MacDonald and Pinto 1995: 58–59.

39. MacDonald and Pinto 1995: 146. Habicht (1985: 131) claims that Pausanias's mention of 179 Greek sculptors reflects the taste of his time for Archaic and Classical works.

40. MacDonald and Pinto 1995: 196–97.

41. *IG* XIV.1389; Tobin 1997: 82–83.

42. On Hadrian at Eleusis, see MacDonald and Pinto 1995: 132–38, 351 (bibliography); Porter, chap. 5, this volume.

43. Habicht 1985: 162–63; Garzetti 1973: 393.

Commentary (Cartledge)

1. Starr 1965: 258, 272.

2. Starr 1965: 258.

3. Rawson 1969: 113, n.2. The standard commentary on all Pausanias remains Frazer 1898. On the sources for Book III, see Immerwahr 1889 (an uninspired 150-page

pamphlet, soundly critiqued by Meadows 1995); for the genealogical narrative at the start of Book III, Calame (1987: 186, n.55) envisages tentatively an oral Lacedaemonian tradition. On Pausanias's sources generally, see Musti, in Beschi and Musti 1990: xxiv–xxxv.

4. Trans. Levi (1971). For the development of Lakonian Doric in the last two centuries B.C., see Brixhe 1996. On the still allegedly "purest" Doric of the Messenians (4.27.11), see Hall 1997: 180.

5. Habicht 1985: 22, 24, 26; Swain 1996: 31; Bowie, chap. 2, this volume.

6. Older literature is given in Regenbogen 1956; also in Beschi and Musti 1982; Casevitz, Pouilloux, and Chamoux 1992. For two general assessments, one ancient and one modern, see Frazer 1900: 1–159; Pouilloux, in Casevitz, Pouilloux, and Chamoux 1992: ix–xxix.

7. Veyne 1988b: 3.

8. Habicht 1985: 162 (also cited by Porter, chap. 5, n.51, this volume).

9. Habicht (1985: 95) is of course right that Pausanias "is not, and does not intend to be a historian, and should not be judged by the standards applied to historians."

10. See, in this volume, Elsner, chap. 1; Alcock, chap. 8; Bowie, chap. 2. In addition to the work cited in previous footnotes, see the useful commentary on Book III by Musti and Torelli (1991a).

11. Other relevant Pausanian passages are listed in Elsner 1992: 11, n.27; Alcock 1996: 246, n.8.

12. See Bowie, chap. 2, this volume; as Porter (chap. 5, this volume) nicely puts it: "Pausanias's project combats the loss of memory. It is a memorial project, but also a monitory one"; cf. Hartog and Casevitz 1999: esp. 49–51 = Pausanias 8.33.1–4, a reprise but also a transformation of the Herodotean themes of great cities becoming small and of the instability of human affairs.

13. On the *Hellenica*'s objectives, see Cartledge 1987: esp. 61–66; Gray 1989.

14. Lafond 1996: 170.

15. Cartledge 1976.

16. E.g., Porter, chap. 5, this volume; cf. Bowie 1996b.

17. Arafat 1996: 130–31; Waywell and Wilkes 1995 (probably 20s B.C.); cf. Waywell, Wilkes, and Walker 1999.

18. Porter, chap. 5, n.89, this volume.

19. Kennell 1997: 232; cf. Porter (chap. 5, n.14, this volume).

20. For an account of Agis and Cleomenes, see, e.g., Cartledge and Spawforth 1989: chap. 4.

21. Musti 1996. See also Stibbe 1989; but note the proper caution of Wycherley 1935: text to pl. 52: "Identifiable points . . . are too few to determine the topography of Pausanias' account."

22. Porter, chap. 5, this volume.

23. Cartledge and Spawforth 1989: 37, 40.

24. Refs. in *Lexicon iconographicum mythologiae classiace* 2.1 (1988), s.v. "Apollon," no. 55, and V.1 (1990), s.v. "Hyakinthos," A(a) no. 1; a full study by A. Faustoferri has recently been published (1996). The throne is, interestingly, cited thrice elsewhere in the present volume, by Porter (chap. 5), Cohen (chap. 6), and Snodgrass (chap. 7).

25. Henderson, chap. 11, n.111, this volume; cf. Kreilinger 1997.

26. Farnell 1896–1909; Henderson, chap. 11, this volume.

27. Calame 1995, 1998.

28. Parker 1989, probably the best short account of Classical Spartan religion, is

littered with references to Pausanias; likewise Pettersson 1992. Also relevant to Pausanias's take on religion is Pritchett 1998.

29. Hall 1997: 100.

30. Rubinstein 1995: 217 (responding to Alcock 1995); cf. Hooker 1980: 16 (Pausanias was "the earliest, and by far the most important, of all travellers who have left an account of their journeys" and made "an honest attempt to fit his observations into the framework of history and legend").

31. Hooker 1980: 20; cf. Wagstaff 1992. As Wagstaff points out (chap. 10, this volume), when Leake was traveling during the early nineteenth century, "the topography of modern, let alone ancient, Greece was still as unknown as much of interior Africa"; see also n.24, above, for the throne of Bathycles.

32. Armstrong, Cavanagh, and Shipley 1992; Pritchett 1980, 1982, 1989; Shaw 1997.

33. Alcock, chap. 8, this volume; Shipley 1992, 1997; for Perioikic religion, cf. Parker 1989: 145 and n.15.

34. Generally for Pausanias and Classical Spartan history, from the point of view of his "working method and reliability," see Meadows 1995 (with excellent bibliography).

35. Cartledge 1987: 134–35, cited by Meadows 1995: 104.

36. Henderson, chap. 11, this volume.

37. Cf. Rubinstein 1995: 218.

38. References and discussion in Cartledge 1975: 52–53; Cavanagh et al. 1996: 304; Shipley 1997: 191, 245 (Hippola is attested only after the Classical period).

Chapter 9

1. It is not clear if Dixon packed merely the translation or took along the commentary as well. His debt to this rendition of the *Description,* however, is beyond doubt. As he states in the preface to his travelogue: "To the book of books for travellers in Greece, Sir James Frazer's magnificent *Pausanias,* I cannot, as will be manifest, measure my obligations; I have spent with it many of my happiest hours, and should be glad, and satisfied that I had acquired merit, if to that great work my own served as a signpost" (1929: viii).

2. Angelomatis-Tsougarakis 1990; Augustinos 1994; Constantine 1984; Dimaras 1968; Eisner 1991; Spencer 1954; Stoneman 1987; Tsigakou 1981.

3. Alcock 1995, 1996; Arafat 1996; Elsner 1992, 1994; Habicht 1985; Levi 1971: 1–5.

4. The Nemea Valley Archaeological Project has aimed at illuminating settlement and economy in the area from earliest habitation to the present, through a combination of full surface survey and excavation, accompanied by ethnographic, geological, botanical, and other research. It has been funded primarily by the National Endowment for the Humanities and the National Geographic Society and directed by James C. Wright, John F. Cherry, Jack L. Davis, and Eleni Mantzourani. See Wright et al. 1990.

5. The valley's population grew from 184, as recorded in the Grimani Census undertaken by the Venetians in 1700 (Panayiotopoulos 1985: 21), to 704, as recorded during the Greek National Census of 1991. During this time, the area also became a major producer of currants, wine, olives, and selected other crops. For more detailed discussion of this demographic and economic growth, see Sutton 1988, 1994, 1995a.

6. Sutton 1995b, 1997.

7. Apollodorus 1.104, 2.71, 2.75, 3.64–66; Bacchylides 7.36; Hesiod, *Theogony* 325, 330; Sophocles, *Trachiniae* 1090; Strabo 8.6.19.

8. These Games ran initially from 573 B.C. to the early fourth century, then from the late fourth century to the 270s B.C., and finally for a very brief period around 235 B.C.: see Miller 1990.

9. Bacchylides 7.35, 7.36, 7.37, 7.40; Lysias 19.63; Plato, *Lysis* 205c, *Laws* 950e; Pindar, *Nemean Odes* 1–11; *Isthmian Odes* 5.15, 6.1, 6.45, 6.60; *Olympian Odes* 7.8, 8.15, 8.55, 9.85, 13.32, 13.95.

10. Diodorus 14.83.2; Plutarch, *Pericles* 19.3; Thucydides 3.96, 5.59, 5.60; Xenophon 4.2.14, 4.7.3, 7.2.5–7.

11. Strabo 8.6.19.

12. Good accounts of the history of modern travel to Greece are given by Spencer 1954: 126–53, 196–210; Tsigakou 1981: 15–78; Stoneman 1987; Eisner 1991. Such travel intensified in the late eighteenth century, as commercial, diplomatic, and pilgrimage journeys were surpassed by those directed toward personal reflection informed by a knowledge of Classical texts.

13. Pacifico 1704: 118–19; Panayiotopoulos 1985: 241.

14. Chandler 1776: 243–46.

15. A search of the Gennadeios Library in Athens, as well as the libraries of the University of Cincinnati and Indiana University, has revealed seventy-eight passages on Nemea by literary travelers of this period. That there are still others in works not held by these institutions is very likely.

16. Among those who wrote more extended accounts were Chandler 1776; Clarke 1814, vol. 3: 709–715; Dodwell 1819, vol. 2: 207–211; Gell 1817: 158–60; Leake 1830, vol. 3: 330–35; Pouqueville 1826, vol. 5: 301–304.

17. This analysis is based on my examination of over three dozen guidebooks spanning the period from 1845 to the present.

18. Gritsopoulos 1971; Miliarakis 1886: 160–65; Noukhakis 1901, vol. 2: 488–89; Ragkavis 1853, vol. 1: 382.

19. For good histories of archaeological work at Nemea, see Blegen 1966; Stephen G. Miller 1983, 1990: 13–15; Wright et al. 1990.

20. In comparing Pausanias's treatment of the Boeotian countryside with that of Leake, Snodgrass (1987: 79) has noted similar parallels, particularly in terms of what he calls "purpose and background."

21. In addition to this central passage, there are twenty-four other references to Nemea in the *Description*. Most describe victors at the Games there (1.22.6, 6.1.8, 6.2.11, 6.3.9, 6.4.5–6, 6.4.11, 6.6.3, 6.7.10, 6.8.1, 6.11.5, 6.12.8, 6.13.8, 6.14.2, 6.15.1, 6.15.6, 6.17.2, 6.20.19, 7.27.2). Others repeat mythological references from the central passage (5.22.6, 5.27.7, 6.5.5). Two discuss the continuing practices of the Argives with respect to the Nemean Games (2.19.4, 6.16.4), and yet another identifies the victory wreath as made of celery (8.48.2).

22. Pausanias 2.15.1–4, as translated by Frazer 1898, vol. 1: 92–93.

23. Arafat (1996: 210) has noted that, in 6.16.4, Pausanias gives the emperor Hadrian credit for reintroducing the winter Nemean Games. Archaeological work in the valley (Miller 1990: 141) and Pausanias 2.20.3 strongly indicate that these renewed Games were held in Argos, not Nemea itself.

24. As Spencer (1954: 133) points out, Jacob Spon and George Wheler were the first modern travelers to be guided by Pausanias (in 1675–76); they did not, however, stop at Nemea.

25. Chandler 1776: 243–46.

26. Chandler 1776: 244–46. This passage also mentions buying "tools to dig," but this is difficult to decipher. There is no mention of digging at the temple. It is possible that these tools were for pitching the tent or excavating at sites they expected to encounter later in the trip.

27. E.g., Clarke 1814, vol. 3: 709–716.

28. For detailed accounts of this growth, see Sutton 1994, 1995a.

29. Filippidis and Konstantas 1791: 61.

30. Paganelis 1891: 53–60.

31. That Pausanias's account could be combined with a less-selective description of the contemporary landscape is evidenced by the fact that two of the most thorough Greek geographers mentioned both the *Description* and the modern settlement and economy of the valley (Miliarakis 1886: 160–65; Noukhakis 1901, vol. 2: 488–89).

32. Dixon 1929: 133–38.

33. According to the 1920 national census, the village of Iraklio had 499 de facto residents.

34. Several scholars have recently underscored the sacred nature of Pausanias's landscapes: see Elsner 1994; Arafat 1996: 76; Levi 1971.

35. Stella Miller (1983) has written an excellent and very parallel discussion of this imagery surrounding the temple at Nemea.

36. Such imagery was not restricted to the site at Nemea but is quite typical of what travelers found important about ancient sites in general (Augustinos 1994: 204; Eisner 1991: 98–100; Tsigakou 1981: 27).

37. Respectively, Dodwell 1819, vol. 2: 210–11; Holland 1815: 421; Pouqueville 1826: 301; Ross 1851: 136; Hettner 1854: 156.

38. E.g., Dixon 1929; Hausenstein 1934: 127–28.

39. Hutton (1928: 204–205) explicitly remarked on this changing imagery by discussing the difference between his perception of the valley and that of earlier travelers, concluding that these others must have been influenced by the belief that the ancient Games were funerary in nature, because he could not imagine the place anything but sunny.

40. Respectively, Saunders-Forster 1887: 154; Sandys 1887: 57; Philippson 1892: 117; Hutton 1928: 204.

41. It should be noted that—in small print—Frazer (1898, vol. 3: 90) also stated: "In recent years the foundation of the new village of *Herakleia* has somewhat broken the solitude of the pastoral valley."

42. Frazer 1898, vol. 3: 90.

43. Murray 1845: 147; Joanne and Isambert 1861: 183–84; Baedeker 1883: 224–25.

44. E.g., Barber 1995: 212; Dubin 1997: 167; Ellingham et al. 1992: 141.

45. E.g., Barber 1995: 212; Lyons and Munson 1998: 145. The *Knopf Guide* places Pausanias's statement that the temple is the thing worth seeing in a special box at the top of the page (Roberts 1994: 299).

46. Barber 1995: 212. The *Blue Guide* has recently been revised to include archaeological material from recent work in the valley, but little else yet appears.

47. Dubin 1997: 167.

48. Lyons and Munson 1998: 145.

49. See nn.2 and 3, above.

50. For insightful discussions of recent literary travel in general, see, e.g., Pratt 1992; Mills 1991; Lowe 1991.

51. Augustinos 1994: 227.

52. Snodgrass 1987: 77.

53. Arafat 1996: 4; Elsner 1992; Snodgrass 1987: 80.

54. Arafat 1996.

55. E.g., Anderson 1830: 60; Hughes 1820: 238; Pouqueville 1826, vol. 5: 301; Ross 1851: 136.

56. Many excursions designed for Greeks citizens do make an additional stop in this area—at the monument to the Greek Revolutionary War battle of Dervenakia. In some ways, there are now two sets of tourist itineraries: those of foreigners and those of Greeks.

57. Leontis (1995: 40–66) borrows the term "heterotopia" from Foucault's general discussion of the ways in which places and landscapes are constructed.

58. Most travelers approached Nemea from the Corinth-Argos road, thus entirely missing the town of Ayios Georgos, which was a major market center for the interior Corinthia and the hub of a network which made the Nemea valley anything but isolated.

59. Pratt 1992: 228.

60. Alcock 1996: 246; Habicht 1985: 21.

61. Alcock 1996: 245; chap. 8, this volume.

62. Birge 1992: 53–57; Wright et al. 1990: 610.

63. Arafat (1996: 89) discusses this passage of Pausanias (2.1.2) at some length.

64. Angelomatis-Tsougarakis 1990.

65. Elsner 1992. That modern travelers wished to make parallel use of the power of ancient Greek history for their own lives has been well discussed by Augustinos 1994: 13; Eisner 1991: 81; Stoneman 1987: 143; Tsigakou 1981: 27.

66. See n. 18, above, on the geographers. It should also be noted that Venetian administrators (Pacifico 1704: 118–19) and the French Scientific Expeditions (Bory de Saint-Vincent 1834–36, vol. 2: 67–68) left detailed accounts of the contemporary Peloponnese that included Nemea; but they were not used.

67. See n. 19, above. While some guidebooks include the architectural findings of archaeological work at the sanctuary, they rarely discuss the broader social conclusions reached by archaeologists working in the area.

68. Habicht 1985: 16.

69. Fotiadis 1992.

70. Stephen G. Miller 1990, 1994; Marker 1996.

71. Wright et al. 1990.

Chapter 10

1. Markham 1895; Wagner 1967.

2. J. Martin Leake n.d.

3. Marchand 1973: 102.

4. Leake 1814.

5. Burckhardt 1819, 1822.

6. Leake 1826 (first published anonymously in 1825).

7. Marsden 1864: 42.

8. De Grey and Ripon 1860.

9. Leake 1830, vol. 1: viii; Taylor 1794.

10. Leake 1821: xxix–xxxviii.

11. Leake 1839.

12. Leake 1821: xxxv

13. Turner 1984: 15–61.

14. Leake 1830, vol. 1: viii–ix.
15. Leake 1821: xxix–xxxviii, 63.
16. Frazer 1913, vol. 1: xv–xvi; Habicht 1985: 9.
17. Alcock 1996; Elsner 1992; Habicht 1985: 59–63.
18. Alcock 1995.
19. Elsner 1992.
20. Leake 1821: 46–49.
21. Leake 1830, vol. 1: vii–viii.
22. Stanley 1844.
23. Leake 1821: i.
24. Leake 1821: xxix–xxxviii.
25. Leake 1821: xciv–cv.
26. Leake 1841: 98.
27. Leake 1821: cv–cix.
28. Leake 1821: cx–cxi.
29. Leake 1821: cxii–cxiii.
30. Leake 1821: cxii–cxiv.
31. Leake 1821: 1–35, 46–49.
32. Leake 1821: 50–67.
33. Leake 1821: 31.
34. Frazer 1898, vol. 2: 153–55; Travlos 1971: 578–79.
35. Leake 1821: 300–362, 377–429.
36. Leake 1839.
37. Leake 1835, vol. 2: 416–49.
38. Leake 1839.
39. Leake 1821: 72–97.
40. Leake 1839.
41. Leake 1821: 45.
42. Leake 1821: 45–59.
43. Travlos 1971: 204.
44. Frazer 1898, vol. 2: 112–17; Travlos 1971: 204.
45. Binder 1976.
46. Leake 1821: 99; Travlos 1971: 580.
47. Leake 1821: 19.
48. G. B. Lusieri (1751–1821) was a Neapolitan painter and Elgin's agent in Athens.
49. Leake 1821: 19, 133; Binder 1976: 21; Wycherley 1978: 5, 45–48.
50. Leake 1821: 238–39.
51. Leake 1821: 241–44; Travlos 1971: 54, 55.
52. Leake 1830.
53. Leake 1830, vol. 1: v–ix.
54. Leake 1830, vol. 1: viii.
55. Leake 1830, vol. 1: 150–85.
56. Leake 1830, vol. 1: 160.
57. Leake 1830, vol. 1: 160–70.
58. Leake 1830, vol. 1: 170.
59. Leake 1830, vol. 1: 170–71.
60. Leake 1830, vol. 1: 173.
61. Topographical Sketch of the Site of Sparta in Leake 1830, vol. 1.
62. Leake 1830, vol. 1: 133–47.
63. Pausanias 3.18.6–3.19.5.

64. Polybius 5.18.9–5.19.8.
65. Fought in 371 B.C.
66. Frazer 1898, vol. 3: 348–49.
67. Angelomatis-Tsougarakis 1990: 27; Spencer 1954: 133.
68. Paton 1951: 145, 146, 147, 150, 154.
69. Holland 1872: 50.
70. Stuart and Revett 1762–1816.
71. Wilkins 1816.
72. Stanley 1844.
73. See, e.g., *The Classical Journal* (1822): 237–47; Wordsworth 1836: 53–54; Stanley 1844.
74. Binder 1976; Camp 1986: 15–18; Habicht 1985: 59; Wycherley 1978.
75. Constantine 1984: 149.
76. Dodwell 1819, vol. 2: 403–404.
77. Dodwell 1819, vol. 1: 288–415; vol. 2: 404, 408.
78. Chandler 1776.
79. Constantine 1984: 188–209.
80. Constantine 1984: 204.
81. See Zacharakis 1992, as well as the notes published on their sources by Barbié du Bocage (1814) and d'Anville (1755).
82. E.g., Cooley denied the existence of snow on Mount Kilimanjaro and of the Mazitu, a group of Ngomi people, and argued that there was only one great lake in East Africa; see Bridges 1976.

Chapter 11

I must thank the Librarian and Sub-Librarian of Exeter College Library heartily for allowing me to consult the Farnell Papers (a modest box of documents, carefully selected by Farnell when he cleared his rooms on retirement and duly delivered to the College Library by his trusty widow). Fascination with Farnell's *Cults* goes back to my happening on them as an undergraduate exploring the mighty shelves of the Bodleian Library (next to Exeter): I just *knew* I had hit on the genuine "stuffage" of Hellenism here. But my acquaintance with the pupation of classical archaeology and with the academic politics of Frazer, Harrison, and their world(s) is nearly all due to Mary Beard's brilliant exegeses, which I shall pillage mercilessly (esp. 1992, 1993a, 1999, 2000); she cannot, however, be held *responsible* for anything here.

1. Farnell disappears, or skulks at the margin, in classicist–anthropological–history of scholarship revaluations of "the days of Frazer and Jane Harrison" (Dodds 1977: 181; material on Farnell listed at Naiditch 1991: n.80). Nor has *Cults* (or *COGS*) thus far, *interested* the new Pausaniacs: yet "the beliefs of the average individual," as Farnell would intone, are the touchstone for all *Higher Aspects* (1912a: 69; cf. 134).
2. Beard 1992: 224.
3. Harrison's nickname: "the really uncongenial influence of the Later Victorian rationalists (the Old Rats, as she came to call them)" (F. M. Cornford, cit. Africa 1991: 35). For "Darwinism" as a threat to the Classical, cf. Fitton 1996: 38, with P. Gardner as Canute.
4. As we shall see, not least in the instance of Miss Harrison, the British Museum

in London was a crucial matrix in the formation of classical archaeology; University College London was also part of the alchemy.

5. Beard 2000. The Provost of King's College's all-out attack on her "confused and confusing . . . grossly misleading" work and her suitability to be trusted with "the direction of young students" gives some idea of the odium she quit. The indictment runs: "Loose thinking, exaggeration of resemblances, ignoring of differences, and downright falsification of evidence . . ." (James 1917). Harrison 1917 is her reply; Murray (1917) gives chivalrous but palpably faint support; Jessie Stewart (1959: 88) memorializes the victimization (she had been "one of the earliest of Jane Harrison's pupils . . . in the rather new Part II of the Classical Tripos" [Stewart 1959: 13; cf. 13–18, "Cambridge Archaeology"]). *CR* would give Farnell and Frazer obits (Rose 1934, 1941), but not Harrison.

6. Tozer 1887: 101.

7. Farnell 1888a.

8. Farnell 1890a.

9. "Wholly 'unscientific' ": "all that he really had to say about the Chest of Kupselos was that 'it must have been a very beautiful thing' " (Farnell 1912b: 147–48, 1934: 76–77). But the lectures still did hook the student. On the Chest, see Snodgrass, chap. 7, this volume.

10. On the Irish/British politics of the famous cavalcade to Greece, I have learned much from current work in progress by A. E. Doody, esp. her unpublished Cambridge M.Phil. thesis (1999) "Landscape as Monuments: Pausanias' Guide to Attica and Its Nineteenth-Century Reception." On Schliemann, and esp. on the German campaigns at Olympia (from 1875 on), see Marchand 1996 (esp. 84–91).

11. Gardner 1933: 32, 38–40.

12. Stray 1998: 138–40.

13. Farnell 1882, 1883, 1885.

14. Farnell 1886a, 1886b, 1888c, 1890b.

15. His lectures on Greek religion for Greats get plaudits from Farnell (1934: 42); cf. Clarke 1959: 120 for Pelham on Roman history.

16. Gardner 1933: 51–52: Beard 1993a.

17. Clarke 1959: 120; Farnell (1912b: 145–46) regrets eternally that Jowett—"the grave of free research"—not Newton, took the Chair and went on to dominate Oxford's late 1880s as Vice-Chancellor and high-profile Master of ascendant Balliol (1870–93). (For Jowett's victory in College over the "research institute" lobby see Heyck 1982: 174–75.) Was Jowett's Oxford a "liberal education" (lege: bogus "atmosphere"? Syndicated "exam grind"? Hotbed of freethinking godlessness? Cradle of freebooting protocapitalism? Et alii alia.)? As the tribute of malice had it: "My name is Ben Jowett:/ All there is to know I know it. / I am the Master of Balliol College. / What I know not is not knowledge" (Petrie 1960: 23). Jowett's triumph over Anglican orthodoxy and its congeners united and brokered all manner of antagonisms: "in Balliol Chapel Jowett used to interpolate *sotto voce* the words 'used to' after 'I' and before 'believe,' so that he could still recite the Creed" (Petrie 1960: 22; see Hinchliff 1987). Farnell's pitch on this will become clear(er) as we proceed.

18. Newton 1880: 35 (alluding to and outdoing the Great Exhibition of 1851). Cf. the definition in Cook 1931: 59–60, "Classical Archaeology is nothing less than the attempt mentally to reconstruct, at least in its outward and material aspects, a whole bygone civilisation."

19. Farnell 1934: 42–44.

20. Historical geographer/gentleman-traveler and editor of *Childe Harold*, Tozer

was all "Piccadilly" whiskers and abysmal retsina, says Farnell (1934: 38–40); "he took immense pains and put great effort into his teaching; but the greater his effort, the more complete was his failure."

21. How 1928: xix.

22. Farnell 1934: 109.

23. Obits: Marett 1934a, 1934b; reviews: Ackerman 1987: 201–203. Reviews by Farnell (1905–1906, 1906–1907), held Frazer accountable for the nonsense about "matriarchy" in Cambridge. Marett delivered *both* a Frazer Lecture (in 1927; Farnell advised: "Either summarise your well-known views about *mana,* and they will nod their heads, and say 'Just what we thought'; or else pitch into somebody hard, and they'll be all attention!" so Elliot Smith was for it [Marett 1941: 245]) *and* a Jane Harrison Memorial Lecture (in 1932–33; in his memoirs he professed a—then highly unfashionable—"deep sense of the value of her work. . . . Her books will be found to have a timeless quality, in that they reach farther than they grasp, and by their overmeaning inspire, even when their meaning fails to inform," a canny enough view [Marett 1941: 251–52]).

24. Farnell 1934: 199.

25. Farnell 1934:91–92; Gardner 1933: 38.

26. Farnell 1886a.

27. Farnell 1934: 180–81: "My own impression was no less ecstatic. . . . I wonder if I could recapture such emotions now; at all events it is something to have had them." Beard 2000 captures vividly how imaginative travelers thronged mid-Greece in more- and less-scholarly droves through the 1880s.

28. Farnell 1934: 7, 13: "One turned classical phrases into elegant English, and English prose or verse into readable Greek and Latin, without troubling oneself as to what was the full bearing of the passage."

29. Beard 1999; cf. Henderson 1998 (esp. 3–5).

30. Gardner and Imhoof-Blumer 1885–87.

31. Gardner's *Faith and Conduct* was published anonymously (1887). His *Exploratio Evangelica* (1899) was, he tells us, the pinnacle of this dark horse and melancholic numismatist's other persona, the incorrigible essayist on evolutionary religion (Gardner 1933: 75). *The Hibbert Journal—A Quarterly Review of Religion, Theology and Philosophy* (certain we all agree that "the goal of religious aspiration is One" [editorial, 1902–1903: 3])—was another initiative with Percy G. in on the act from the start (on the Editorial Board and a heavy contributor in the first decade—until he jumped ship and got the Church of England–anchored *Modern Churchman* off the ground, in 1911: Ruston 1984: 34). It was, or was supposed to be, militant Unitarian evangelism, but its "liberal" blend of religious philosophy and Bible criticism caused a great stir across the whole spectrum of punters (Ruston 1984: 29–45); and it was another journal that had Farnell climbing aboard for the *second* issue: 1903–1904a; 1903–1904b.

32. Gardner 1933: 44.

33. Cit. Stray 1998: 51, *q.v.* 149–54: Gardner became a leading figure in "The Museum Vote" (*for* research-science-professoriate, *against* college-library-text) and a member with Pelham, Evans, and Farnell, of a sinister Dining Club (*for* Pattison, *against* Newman and Jowett). See Gardner 1933: 71; Farnell 1934: 267–68. Of course, the sides actually majored in murk and menace—a blur well beyond the purchase of such schematic antitheses as " 'Young Oxford' [= *Against*] Versus the 'Ageing Radicals' [= *For*]," as in Engel 1983: 207–16, 232–34.

Greek sculpture was a Mods option from 1890, but Greats was kept archaeology-free: Clarke 1959: 120. Farnell was squeezed off the Classical Board by the opposition, for good. The credit for the New Ashmolean setup complete with cast collection is Gardner's: Farnell 1934: 266–67.

Gardner's assault on the Oxford experience as inane finishing school (1903) drew instant rebuttal (e.g., Warde Fowler's [1903] parable on "atmosphere"). Twenty years later, Vice-Chancellor Farnell would try leaning on the Faculty of Literae Humaniores to "make some study of the monuments of Greek Art an integral and essential part of our teaching of Hellenism." All Mods candidates would be required to show "outline knowledge of the highest monuments of Greek Art" (and Greek oratory texts plus verse composition would be sacrificed) (Farnell Papers). And in his fifteen minutes of fame as host to the (British-imperial-academic) universe (Farnell 1921b), our V-C would open the first session, on "The Universities and the Balance of Studies," by deploring " 'formal scholarship,' a familiar friend, who is obviously dying and whose funeral I shall be glad to attend . . . , the narrow spirit of a mutually admiring coterie, that wrote Latin and Greek verses to each other and to no one else . . . , ignorant of so many of the things that Greece means for us, ignorant of its art, its monuments, its religion and, strange to say, of much of its literature." Between rallying the Congress to carry on despite the overnight decease of the Chancellor of Cambridge (A. J. Balfour) and accepting the Vote of Thanks for supervising arrangements for the week's grueling jamboree, Farnell told humanity (under "University Finance") that universities must specialize, and (under "universities and Research") that teaching worthy of a University depends on a continuum with intensive academic research (Farnell 1921b: 7, 235, 428, 327–29, 380–82).

34. Retired Oxbridge Heads of House traditionally make a bid in print to reorient their times around their lives, if only for the benefit of "their" College.

35. Boardman (1985: 44–46) tells the official reason, the usual failure to attach salary to a new Chair.

36. Farnell 1934: 199–200.

37. Calder 1991b: 51.

38. Farnell in Forfarshire/Angus was, as the Exon anecdote had it, Viking home of the clan. The local Dominie, asked if "any eponymous descendants now survive [] . . . up here," tells Farnell, "No, there's none here. But there's the great Doctor Farnell of Exeter College in Oxford, ye ken. I doubt he'll be one of the auld stock" (Anon. 1928: 211; N. C. 1934: 385, with the coda, "But the rector said nothing").

39. Whence Farnell 1888c (in Percy Gardner's *JHS* 9).

40. Farnell 1934: 199–200, 209–210: no, "a dire accident" to his "best and nearest friend" did *not* unman our hero, perish the thought! The denial goes into overdrive, as Farnell sets the record straight for us, and for his pal (Sidney Ball): "owing to the incredible carelessness of the doctor [Ball] had picked up a loaded pistol in the dark and inadvertently shot himself. Ball pulled himself out of the valley of the shadow . . . : the bullet had healthily occupied his thoughts with something tangible . . . The pistol . . . saved the undeserving doctor's life a few weeks after, when he was attacked by a murderous gipsy on the roof of the Cathedral of Cordova." No way is any picture of *Farnell* going under going to lodge in his or his readers' image-repertoires.

41. Farnell 1891, 1909: 185. "Rollicking" *adventures* according to Marett 1934b: 295.

42. Farnell 1934: 339–40.

43. Farnell 1934: 239–41, with a double séance before the Hermes and on the vacant site of Phidias's Zeus Olympios in preparation for the immortal accounts that frame Farnell's *Cults,* vols. 1 and 5: "long contemplation" of the Praxitelean ?original?

(lately impugned, by Blümel in 1927; see Ajootian 1996: 103–10), plus "long hours in the museum [and] near the place where the lightning had struck the floor when Zeus showed by a sign to Pheidias that this was the very image of his person in which he was well-pleased," as Pausanias had (almost) told (5.11.9, "at the spot where down to my time stood a *hydria* of bronze"; cf. Cook 1914–40, vol. 3: 958). Farnell had "done" the Athens-Delphi circuit in 1886: ecstatic at Bassai, "I felt that most of my earthly aspirations were satisfied"; nostalgic at Delphi, "No divinity can survive the aesthetic blight of the motor" (Farnell 1934: 237, 190).

44. His wife, Sylvia, only appears in the autobiography as the bride put on the train while brave Farnell shot the worst rapids alone (Farnell 1934: 264–65); of their three sons and a daughter, there is not a word, even a name (in 344 pages).

45. Strong Papers, box 13, cit. Beard 2000: ch. 6. "Schuchhardt" refers to E. Sellers's (Mrs. Arthur Strong, the later doyenne of Roman art and of the British School at Rome) translation of Schuchhardt's *Schliemann's Excavations* (1891).

46. Baedeker's first guide to Greece appeared precisely in 1883.

47. Harrison on *The Golden Bough*: cit. Peacock 1988: 182.

48. Ackerman 1987 (esp. 55–69, 127–42). The well-timed second edition of *The Golden Bough* (1900) would boost sales?

49. Frazer (1898, vol. 1: 7) makes a prefatory (so rhetorically dense) claim that he would have stopped, or never started, a commentary if he had known that Hitzig and Blümner were at work on their edition (Book 1 appeared in 1896).

50. Frazer 1888a–d. See Beard 1999 passim.

51. Gardner 1898: 465–66. " 'Old Percy' whom I adore . . . his dear foolish head is stuffed with cotton wool," so Harrison told Gilbert Murray (Peacock 1988: 215), had no time for women in the academy and had just made an ass of himself in the 1896 campaign to keep them out (won by a vote of 165 votes to 55), claiming that admission would unman Oxbridge and render "both our great Universities . . . sexless" (letter to the *Times,* 31 January 1896, cit. Balsdon 1970: 89). Farnell (1934: 280–81) "advocated a separate women's university," anxious (he says) not to involve suffrage politics in Academe.

52. Gardner 1898: 465–66.

53. Stray 1998: 235–70; see esp. Gardner and Myres 1901 for concrete proposals for archaeology in school.

54. When Stewart (1959: 11) has Harrison polish the project off in three weeks flat, this concerns the "writing up," not the gathering of materials from scratch. (Ackerman 1972: 224, 226, n.33, may mislead on this.)

55. R[ichards] 1890: 218, drawing attention to the book's method for approaching Greek myth as well as applauding it as "scholarly guide-book." I *think* he means "for some *considerable length of* time."

56. Her first Hellenic Society appearance on 7 May 1885; papers in *JHS* 4, 6, 7, 8, 9 (Harrison 1883; 1885; 1886; 1887; 1888b), and in *CR* 3 (1889a–c).

57. Dörpfeld lived to be best buddy of the Kaiser and fan of Nazi *Lebensraum* (Marchand 1996: 242, 345).

58. Calder 1991a: his conclusion betrayed by his evidence; Ackerman 1991: 7. Professor E. A. Gardner, with a First (distinction) in Section D in the new Part II of the Cambridge B.A. (1884), took over the *JHS* "Archaeological Report from Greece," as Director of the BSA (Gardner 1889, after Harrison 1888a). Ernest G.'s blessing on *Cults,* vol. 5, would make pleasant reading when Farnell consulted Percy G.'s favorite quarterly review: Gardner 1909–1910. (Uncomprehending Ernest does, however, find the index meager.)

59. Gardner 1902 (published by Macmillan).

60. Beard 2000.

61. Harrison and Verrall 1890: iii.

62. Harrison and Verrall 1890: xiv.

63. Harrison and Verrall 1890: cx, cli, clii.

64. Farnell 1896–1909, vol. 1: preface and introduction.

65. Farnell really did idolize "the archetype of the monogamous Aryan marriage" and "this virile race of men of clear and sane mental vision" (1912a: 30, 23); *he* really did mean to rescue manly Hellenic Aryans from fanatical Semitic contamination (1911: 8–16, 106; on occasion, his Orientalism could pay off, as when he abjected "sacred prostitution" Hellenism; see Beard and Henderson 1998). His xenophobia against "the Teutonic race" really was virulent too—and not just after the War, though the memoirs cannot, of course, be trusted on this.

66. Farnell 1896–1909, vol. 1: 1, whence also the quotations in my next paragraph.

67. Marett 1934b: 295.

68. Farnell 1888b.

69. This despite Farnell (1921a: v) candidly owning that the "hero-cults" had been prepared "many years ago" as a sixth volume of *Cults,* but explaining a change of design: "I did not wish to write a mere Encyclopaedia, and scholars can always avail themselves of Roscher's *Lexikon.*" He will drop "geographical" arrangement and instead classify "the different hero-personalities," then deal with "the greater personages of saga." The shift makes little impact on the bulk of the book, but this was a course of *lectures,* calling for broad scope and no lists, and "heroes" was a chance to descant on favorite themes of religious belief (Euhemerism, Orphism, etc.) and in particular to work *Homeric* heroes into a prominent place in "Greek cult" (with disastrous consequences for British archaeology; see Snodgrass 1988).

70. Farnell 1896–1909, vol. 1: x.

71. Frazer 1898, vol. 1: xlix.

72. Frazer 1898, vol. 1: lxix: "He was an honest, laborious, plodding man of plain good sense, without either genius or imagination, and his style is a faithful mirror of his character." Pausanias's rhetoric of authorization: Alcock 1996 (esp. 241–43).

73. Larson (1995: 4) cites Farnell (1921a: v) as if he meant to lament the impossibility of expatiating on Greek hero*ine*s (which she disproves): but this was fine by Farnell, just what he willed: skepticism betokens and affirms assured judiciousness, as in Pausanias (e.g. Farnell 1919: 14–15; cf. Alcock 1996: 263).

74. Shanks 1996: 103.

75. Farnell 1896–1909, vol. 1: 87.

76. Farnell 1919: 10.

77. Trying to dissuade Harrison's younger equivalent from taking up archaeology: Strong Papers, box 2, cit. Beard, 2000: ch. 2. But the next year (1890) Sellers became the BSA's first female student: back home, Leaf saw her translation of Schuchhardt through the press, as Schliemann expired—and was canonized (December 1890; cf. Marchand 1996: 149–50).

78. Farnell 1934: 130–48, at 148: in his element.

79. "N. C." 1934: 383, citing as eloquent conversation (at breakfast), "My dear Sir, since women have joined the ranks of journalism, journalism has become more vituperative, more mendacious, more insolent, and more obscene"; Clunes Gabell 1934 (clipping in Farnell Papers).

80. Marett 1934a: 380–81. (In student days, he had lobbed "a bomb-like firework" at Sub-Rector Farnell: Marett 1941: 69.) "Martinet" (drillmaster) was exactly what Far-

nell became as inventor of the squad of "Mounted Infants" that kept the O.U. Volunteer Corps its War Office grants (Farnell 1934: 149–57: harbinger, he claims, of Territorials, Officer Training Corps, and Victory in the Great War).

81. Farnell 1914a. A copy is in the Farnell Papers. Farnell 1931 tells of explaining *to* the Rector that "Ruggins" in Harrovian/Exonian dialect meant Rector. Jackson lived on to reach ninety-three before his death in 1931.

82. Farnell 1914c. (Floodwaters dominated his image-repertoire of anxiety his life through.)

83. "Thronged as we stand with fears, / Beset with traitors' whisperings and chill doubt, / Still to our hearts across the gulf of years / Against the phantom host our fathers' cry rings out." Lt. Cuthbert Francis Balleine of the Royal Army Medical Corps "was not only a man of high intellectual powers, but also of splendid physique, perfect nerve, and an iron constitution" (Farnell 1915).

84. "N. C." 1934: 385–60. Cf. Farnell 1934: 324–37, ch. XXVI, ECHOES AND VISITANTS FROM THE OUTER WORLD. Inevitably, Farnell played College chronicler (1914b).

85. Prime lobbyist and one of the first recipients of the degree (Barber 1931–40: 269).

86. Farnell 1934: 342: his nomination for best of his books; like the *Hero Cults* (1921a), *Attributes* was the proceeds of Gifford lectures at St. Andrews, a Scottish judge's freethinking endowment for the promotion of "Natural Theology": "The Knowledge of God, the Infinite, the All, the First and Only Cause, the One and the Sole Substance, the Sole Being, the Sole Reality, and the Sole Existence, the Knowledge of His Nature and Attributes, the Knowledge of the Relations which men and the whole universe bear to Him, the Knowledge of the Nature and Foundation of Ethics or Morals, and of all Obligations and Duties thence arising . . . The lecturers to treat their subject as a natural science, the greatest of all possible sciences, indeed, in one sense, the only science, that of Infinite Being, without reference to or reliance upon any supposed special exceptional or so-called miraculous revelation" (Jaki 1986: 72–74). "Iron V-C": Marett claims the heroic title for Farnell (1941: 223). "The Chancellor" is titular head of the University administration, above the fray except in crises (in Farnell's case, the worthy collecting this gong was Marquess Curzon of Kedleston).

87. Farnell 1934: preliminary "NOTE" by S. F. (the widow). The book's first chapter elaborately writes the career back into childhood: a "hero-cult" on Hampstead Heath, the "hero" Garibaldi; Greek sculpture in the BM, Kingsley's *Heroes,* Rollins's *Universal History,* permanent antipapal bias ("a vaguely religious temperament with a Christian colouring but with no fixed belief in prevailing theology"), and old folklore names picked up on Oxfordshire walks—in short, a systematic exercise in "Origins" story*telling*. So too, College discipline (e.g.) resurrects the "dromena" of ritual "orgy," "Bacchanalian" rout, "pharmakos" behavior, and "epinician" . . . (Farnell 1934: 130–38; a local conceit: Anon. 1910 ends his review of *Cults,* vol. 5: "Speakers in Oxford . . . may obtain useful practice in the use of the Comparative Method by comparing Greek *orgies* with those that occasionally obtain in College quadrangles"). Valediction to Exon: Farnell 1928.

88. Farnell has suppressed from our view much of his activity as a player in Oxon politics: we catch him brokering the Chair of Greek for Gilbert Murray in 1908 (on the retirement of Bywater), calling on Murray's wife on "a delicate personal matter" but sending out confusing signals and giving her a false lead on (his fellow "Citizen") the Prime Minister's intentions for the appointment: West 1984: 128; Wilson 1987: 129.

89. Grundy 1945: 138.

90. Farnell 1934: 290–97; Hollis 1976: 44; Mabbott 1986: 39–40. In retirement,

Farnell would suppress Germans, cars, golf, the General Strike, the "Usurpations of the Trades Unions," and Poole Harbour bridge (Farnell Papers).

91. Farnell 1934: 314–18. Reade's letter of 1940 (to Professor John Mavrogordalo at Exeter College, from Traveller's Club, Pall Mall, S.W.1; in Farnell Papers) still rakes over the affair (Farnell 1934: 297–99; the book had to be recalled and reissued minus two pages after threats of a libel action; see Balsdon 1970: 123–24). The V-C's address is among the Farnell Papers (10 October, 1923: 10, "The modern city of Oxford [is] no longer a desirable place for a University"), with the 1922 equivalent, where S.F. tells us "space forbade" inclusion in the memoirs.

92. Symonds 1986: 168, 260–61: at a meeting called by him in Exeter Hall, the participants are supposed to have set the place on fire.

93. Farnell 1934: 303–305; Bickerton (the former Head Porter of University College, Oxford) 1953: 39–41: "ploughed" = sunk in exams; "progged" = caught gownless after dusk; cf. Masterman 1975: 141–42; Hollis 1976: 44, Mabbott 1986: 39–40 (a "friend" of the student involved).

94. Marett 1928: 207. Turner (1984: 129) can brand Farnell's "conservatism bordering on priggishness," but it is (was) an elaborately constructed package of ideology and persona that commanded/commands attention, not assent or dismissal.

95. Bowra 1966: 252.

96. R[ose] 1934.

97. R[ose] 1934.

98. Stewart 1959: xi.

99. Farnell 1934: 281: her only (un-indexed) mention, now notorious (e.g., Africa 1991: 23; Hoberman 1997: 20).

100. Balsdon 1970: 90; Brittain 1960: 154; for a photo of the V-C and the first *graduandae,* see Farnell 1934: pl. IV. Dreadful patronizing remarks mar his "Addresses" (Farnell Papers).

101. Farnell 1919: 1. The violent attack by the Monty James gang, remember, had been delivered in 1917 (see n.5, above).

102. My schematic story elides overlap: e.g., keen exchanges were sparked in 1907 by Harrison's *Cambridge Review* of *Cults* (30 May: 440–41) versus P. Gardner's protest (13 June: 408) versus her reply (13 June 483): cf. 27 January 1910: 226. Cf. Anon. 1907, on *Cults*: "The author has no axe to grind, but what he says will retain its value long after most of the brilliant hypotheses which now constantly disturb our notion of Greek religion are disarmed of their most aggressive qualities and retire to a modest seclusion beside the solar myth." The sensational "discovery" of "Dionysiac" mummery alive and theoretically sound in Dionysus's Thrace galvanized the feud (Dawkins [of Exeter] 1906). In the 1928 second edition (ix), Harrison kidded herself that *Themis* had won the argument, if not in Classics, then in the New Archaeology; but cf. Stray 1998: 283–86.

103. Harrison 1928: vii, xiii. "Their Olympians represent that tendency in thought which is towards reflection, differentiation, clearness, while the Eniautos-Daimon represents that other tendency in religion towards emotion, union, and invisibility" (xxi).

104. Farnell 1904; cf. 1903–1904b; 1912a: 25, 1912–13. The 1904 piece (in Usener's journal) names no culprits. But Harrison became his bête noire long before the subtitle of *Themis* perpetrated its double affront: *Social!* ... *Origins!*

105. Farnell 1912–13: 453, 455, 458. Cf. 1903–1904b; Africa 1991: 23. A draft of the *Themis* review preserving Farnell's deletions and insertions is itself preserved, by Farnell, in the Farnell Papers. Even vitriol is paraded as under strict control.

106. Cit. Peacock 1988: 214.

107. See Turner 1984: 133–34. Twentieth-century Frazer became unplaceable and untouchable, a sui generis autotelic institution: the living legend (Beard 1992). (Seamless between the minutiae of Ovid's *Fasti* and oceanic ethnography, between classical studies and the horizon beyond—(as Marett [1941: 302] commented, how *did* he "g[e]t through all that work"?)

108. Beard 1999.

109. The ever-to-be-contested slogan for Pausanias's project: Arafat 1996: 8–9. *Our* modeling by (past) Pausanias(es) is spliced into our every attempt to model (with) him: Alcock 1996: 266.

110. Elsner 1992: 12; cf. Veyne 1983 (esp. 105–12), "Pausanias n'arrivant pas à échapper à son programme."

111. The syntax mimes how even this grudging mention is grudgingly *extracted* from a reluctant author, in triple globs of mimimal annotation: χρόνῳ δὲ ὕστερον καὶ ἄλλα ἀνέθεσαν ἐς τὸ Ἡραῖον· Ἑρμῆν λίθου, Διόνυσον δὲ φέρει νήπιον, τέχνη δέ ἐστι Πραξιτέλους, καὶ. . . . This reveals a lemma at the core of Farnell's Hellenism, as well as of his specialism. Textual design controls the release of Pausanias's art historical nuggets; see Kreilinger 1997.

112. Bruit Zaidman and Schmitt Pantel 1992: 4, 18 (my emphasis); "a good part of our reconstruction of the cult life of the Greek states depends on Pausanias"; paradigm: cf. 5–6. Pausaniacs should carefully scrutinize the example they explore: "The Pantheon in Mantineia," 207–214, with Pausanias 8.9–10 as the "principal source of information."

113. A term I borrow from Bruit Zaidman and Schmitt Pantel 1992: 183–86.

114. Bruit Zaidman and Schmitt Pantel 1992: 183–86, 183 (citing J.-P. Vernant), 185. *Ancient* Greek works did address the festivals and cults of individual cities; but we have only vestigial survivals; see Tresp 1914: 2–29.

115. When Cook was expanding his comparative explorations of Omnipotence, from Zeus through the Celtic-Germanic and Letto-Slavonic realms and beyond, "Dr Farnell in the friendliest fashion put a spoke in my wheel by convincing me that the unity of an ancient god consisted less in his nature than in his name. Thereupon I decided to abandon my search for 'The European Sky-God' " (and . . . homed in on Classical Archaeology, and the Laurence Chair) (Cook 1914–40, vol. 1: xi). Farnell himself (1911: 4) saw his work as integrative, working away from "attributes and titles" toward "relation to nature and to the social sphere of law, politics, morality, and therefore interaction of religion, social organization and ethics." Naturally, Farnell never stooped to *negotiate* his Hellenism: e.g., the newly decorated D.Litt. preached that Greek worship (nearly) matches Christianity for civilizing uplift (1903–1904a), the Tutor devoted his life to "The Moral Service of the Intellect" (1910–11), and the newly elevated Rector proclaimed that civilized thought has existed (since its Origins) to save us "from the *mirage sauvage*" (1913–14). H. D. would play vengeful fury to "the whole tribe of Academic Grecians," underlining *"hieros gamos"* in her copy of *Cults* to mark her mystic vision on Corfu (Gregory 1999: 66–121, 160).

116. Her anthropology leveled the Greeks from their classic(ized) sublimation by the institutionalized official Farnell but also broke ranks, with the idealizing (pan-) Hellenism of her ally the progressivist liberal Gilbert Murray; see Fowler 1991: 90, 94; Turner 1984: 129–33. Travel and imagination in post-Roman Greece proved to Farnell that no political unity was to be expected from such diffracted terrain as the valley systems of Greece (1934: 234).

Chapter 12

This chapter obviously intersects closely with that of John Henderson—to whom it owes a lot. Thanks are also due to the preternaturally patient editors. Note: my spelling of Greek names and places generally, but not entirely consistently, follows the normal nineteenth-century "Roman" style.

1. The "right" answer is Dipylon. The point was that different gates would take Pausanias into the Agora from quite different directions, and so suggest a quite different orientation for many of the buildings in and around it. As usual, Frazer (1898, vol. 2: 42–45) gives a full resumé of the main views; Hitzig and Blümner (1896–1910, vol. 1: figs. 2–6) offer a series of plans of different nineteenth-century reconstructions of the layout of the Agora. Even the "best" ones bring the Agora much too far south, to hug the slopes of the Areopagus—not entirely their fault ("It is startlingly evident that no reconstruction [of the Agora] even approaching completeness and correctness could have been made on the basis of Pausanias' description alone" [Wycherley 1959: 23]).

2. Leake 1821: 45. The state of play in 1898 is reviewed by Frazer 1898, vol. 2: 112–18; Carroll 1907: 242–51 (a clear-speak introduction for American college students, as well as disgraceful plagiarism of E. Gardner 1902: 535–38). Judeich (1931: 193–201) brings it up to the eve of the major program of Athenian excavations in the 1930s.

3. Harrison 1906: 158. Her optimism stemmed (as often) from her faith in the excavations of Wilhelm Dörpfeld, who believed that he had found the actual fountain at the foot of the Pnyx (Dörpfeld 1892, 1894).

4. Gardner 1902: 538.

5. What Pausanias saw is now generally agreed to be the excavated "Southeast Fountain House" in the Agora; whether or not this was (or came in antiquity to be *thought of as*) the Pisistratid Enneacrunus is frankly anyone's guess. See the refreshingly brief pages in Thompson and Wycherley 1972: 198–99; Camp 1986: 42–43. (For the Indian summer of the controversy, see Levi 1961–62, who suggested applying the name "Enneacrunus" to the whole Pisistratid water supply, with nine *fountains*.)

6. No one entered the recent "Greek ceramics vs. metalwork" dispute without (at some level) being aware that more was at stake than a few pieces of lost Greek silverware: where were the boundaries of Greek art history to be set; how was the subject to be defined; who was to control it?

7. As Harrison and Verrall (1890: v) point out.

8. Though others had in fact raised the question before, the origin of discussions of Pausanias's autopsy is usually taken to be Wilamowitz 1877: 344–47 (this and further contributions are amply reviewed by Frazer 1898, vol. 1: lxxvii–xcvi; Habicht 1998: 165–75). For Enneacrunus as part of an argument for Pausanias's desk-top method, see Kalkmann 1886: 70–72.

9. Harrison 1906: 157.

10. As usual, Colonel Leake was leading the academic pack (see Anon: 1864; Wagstaff, chap. 10, this volume). It is instructive to compare his sense of Pausanias as a structuring principle of the study of Greek topography with the views of Bishop Christopher Wordsworth (1839, and much reprinted). Far from appealing to Pausanias, Wordsworth conjures Greece as a real-life version of Hadrian's Villa at Tivoli (Wordsworth 1839 [1882]: ix–x); only with the revision by H. F. Tozer in 1882 does Pausanias play any part in the book.

11. References are collected in Frazer's preface (1898, vol. 1: xiii–xcvi) and—more systematically—in Carroll 1907: 216–27. Even so, some contributions tend to slip

through the bibliographic net: notably the embarrassingly inadequate translation of the complete text by A. R. Shilleto (1886), certainly not to be confused with his father, the famous Cambridge Classical "coach" Richard Shilleto.

12. Imhoof-Blumer and Gardner 1887, reprinted from *JHS* 6 (1885), 7 (1886) and 8 (1887). For reasons that defy comprehension, it was reprinted in 1964.

13. Imhoof-Blumer and Gardner 1887: 1. The fact that the Gardner brothers (Ernest and Percy) between them were responsible for no fewer than six articles in *JHS* 6 (1885)—the "Numismatic Commentary" weighing in satisfyingly at over fifty pages— suggests something of the microeconomy of the new journal.

14. The growth of tourism (and its links with the sometimes inconveniently turbulent politics of the new Greek nation) is sketched by Tsigakou 1981: 63–78; for the cause célèbre murder of a party of up-market British and Italian visitors in 1870, see Jenkins 1961. The transition from a journey to Greece as serious adventure, to be undertaken only by the very rich, very brave, or very determined, to a relatively routinized holiday for the chattering classes is nicely captured by Clark 1858 (Clark was one of the most spirited of the mid-Victorian reformers of the Classical Tripos in Cambridge [Beard 1999: 105–106] and, as he describes himself [1858: ix], a "gleaner after Leake"). The chronology of this significant shift matches A. B. Cook's attempt to chart the history of archaeology as a development from the "Age of Topographers" (1800–1860) to the "Age of Excavators," inaugurated between 1850 and 1880 (Cook 1931: 36–39).

15. And not-so-new Schools: the French had established a base in 1846; the Germans followed in 1874; then the Americans (1882); and finally the British (1886). Apart from ongoing projects in Athens, the major excavations were at Mycenae (in the 1870s and again from 1884), Olympia (from 1875), and Delphi (from 1892).

16. Sandys 1887: 99 (Olympia versus the Cambridge Cast Gallery). You get a sense of the thriving industry of such tourism when Sandys (1887: 78) describes his visit to a peasant(?) cottage in Delphi, whose owner enterprisingly kept a Visitors Book. He spots the names of several friends (though only one woman for several years back) and is surprised to discover that (in early April) he and his wife are the first English of the year (though a party of Americans had already passed through).

17. The main sources for this trip are letters from Harrison to Mrs. E. Malleson (copies in Newnham College, Harrison Papers, box 8) and letters from MacColl to various members of his family (notably Glasgow University Library, Department of Special Collections, MacColl Papers, M252–256, E59). MacColl was a charismatically frank Scot, art critic, and champion of the avant-garde (who was later Keeper of the Tate). For a fuller account of the travels and the personalities, see Beard, 2000: ch. 5.

18. Harrison to Mrs. E. Malleson, 6, June 1888 (Harrison Papers, box 8); MacColl to Mrs. J. S. M. MacColl, 12, April 1888 (MacColl Papers, M253).

19. "Pausanias in hand, the different routes of this guide through the Altis were repaired." The itinerary is noted in *Archäologischer Anzeiger* 4 (1889): 63. Waldstein was another friend or acquaintance of Harrison, who combined his post at the American School with a Readership in Classical Archaeology at Cambridge. See Beard 1999: 117–23.

20. And so a commercial proposition. On 6 July 1884, James Gow wrote to George Macmillan explicitly in those terms: "I think a moderately cheap translation of Paus [*sic*] would pay very well just now" (he was angling, needless to say, for a contract for his friend J. G. Frazer) (British Museum Add. MSS 55257, quoted by Ackerman 1987: 55).

21. This fact is enshrined in most nineteenth-century discussions of ancient Athens. See, e.g., Dyer 1873; though not including a text of Pausanias or a detailed commentary, his description of the city is structured according to Pausanias's six "tours."

22. At this point it becomes almost impossible to take any general *European* perspective, for the genesis of Archaeology and its relations with cognate disciplines have been dramatically different in different educational systems throughout Europe. What follows here is a strictly British (even English; Scotland being another story) account.

23. This characterization inevitably oversimplifies a much more complex set of issues; for which, see Stray 1998; Beard 1999.

24. The main players are noted in Stray 1998: 119–66, 202–232. They include some whom we can easily conscript as our intellectual ancestors. Above all stands Henry Jackson, Professor of Greek in Cambridge, 1906–1921, whose radical rhetoric (ridiculing, e.g., those who could translate Plato but knew nothing of the Theory of Forms) was instrumental in widening the range of specialisms in Cambridge Classics. It is less easy now to feel quite so at home with his partner in crime, B. H. (Primer) Kennedy. See Beard 1999.

25. For late Victorian Classics in Oxford (up to 1872), see Jenkyns 1997; Murray 1997. Part of the story of the early years of Oxonian Archaeology is told by John Henderson (chap. 11, this volume).

26. The words of A. A. Vansittart, Flysheet, 16, May 1866 (Cambridge University Archives, CUR 28.7).

27. This is essentially the position taken in Charles Newton's groundbreaking 1850 lecture "On the Study of Archaeology": the subject's aim was, he suggested, "to collect, to classify, and to interpret all the evidence of man's history not already incorporated in Printed Literature" (Newton 1880: 2).

28. In this sense the victory of the philologists, in ensuring that texts remained at the heart of all classical disciplines, was a hollow one: for it served to thrust into prominence classical authors that conservative voices dismissed as a bad influence on the student's most important skill (i.e., his [*sic*] ability to write "good" Latin and Greek). Something of this lingers on: to my knowledge Pausanias has never been set in a Cambridge Tripos "unseen" examination (though we would now say that it was because he was too "difficult").

29. Desperate question-spotters would probably have risked concentrating on Books I, V, and VIII.

30. Whole papers in the Archaeology section of the Cambridge Classical Tripos were devoted to "Myth, Religion, and Ritual" and variants on the same theme. I discuss the changing definition of "Archaeology" in Beard 1999.

31. Beard 1999: 104.

32. Ackerman 1987: 111–13, 127–29.

33. So, e.g., Frazer can get away without reediting the text; Jane Harrison can subject Pausanias to the kind of idiosyncratic and self-serving dismemberment that would have been unthinkable with Thucydides or Plato (Harrison and Verrall 1890: passim).

34. Following Wilamowitz 1877, the most strident attack on Pausanias is Kalkmann 1886. See Ackerman 1987: 133–36.

35. These arguments are rehearsed at great length in Frazer 1898, vol. 1: lxvii–xcvi; for reactions to the discovery of the Hermes of Praxiteles (if indeed it was "of Praxiteles"), see Frazer 1898, vol. 3: 595–99.

36. Robert 1909.

37. Harrison and Verrall 1890: viii.

38. Harrison and Verrall 1890: ix–x; echoed by Gardner 1902: 533.

39. Dyer 1873: 183.

40. Frazer 1898, vol. 1: xlix.

41. The phrase is Dyer's (1873: 183).

42. Frazer 1898, vol. 1: xxxiv; contra Harrison and Verrall 1890: vii ("essentially an antiquarian, and only by parenthesis either politician and [*sic*] patriot").

43. Frazer 1898, vol. 1: lxix.

44. Harrison and Verrall 1890: ix.

45. Jessie Stewart (pupil, biographer, and devoted champion of Harrison) was still—absurdly, it must be said—claiming it as "a requisite of travellers to Athens" in 1959 (Stewart 1959: 12).

46. Harrison and Verrall 1890: title page. Verrall's role was strictly translation, and there is no reason to assume that she had much informal input into the essay or commentary; hence I normally refer to Harrison alone as the effective "author" of the book (though see below, n. 75)

47. Harrison and Verrall do not rate a reference in Arafat 1996 or Habicht 1998—nor, for that matter, in any of the contributions in Bingen 1996. Happily they are *not* forgotten—albeit slightly misspelled!—by Elsner (1992: 4, n.8).

48. This is fully discussed in Beard 2000: ch. 8 (where cold water is poured on the idea that the so-called "Ritualists" were ever much of a coherent "group").

49. Harrison and Verrall 1890: iii, a widely quoted phrase in studies of history of religion.

50. See Schlesier 1991: 189; Ackerman 1972: 225–26 (somewhat modified in Ackerman 1991: 7).

51. Harrison herself would have been the first to admit its obsolescence; see Harrison 1906: vii, rejecting the idea of a reprint.

52. Gardner 1890: 123–24.

53. Paley (Marshall) 1947: 20–21.

54. The story goes that the examiners gave her the highest marks of any candidate in philosophy and were divided over whether to award her a notional "second" or a notional "first"; see Peacock 1988: 54 (with references).

55. Awarded a notional "second" in 1880; it would, presumably, have been impossible to appoint her if Harrison had secured a "first."

56. Harrison 1925: 63.

57. Harrison's early career (and the considerable problems of disentangling it) is the focus of Beard 2000.

58. Harrison to F.(?) Macmillan, 17 August 1888 (University of Reading, Macmillan Archive, 201/284): "I am very glad to hear from Mrs Verrall that you think it may be possible for you to undertake our book"; later in the letter she explains that she had left Verrall to make the first approach "because it might be easier to you to return a flat negative to one less intimately concerned."

59. Stewart 1959: 11.

60. And the geographic extent of "Athens" is defined very strictly too; so out goes the very beginning of Pausanias's text (on the Piraeus) and everything on Attica and its surroundings (after 1.30).

61. Harrison and Verrall 1890: iii.

62. Harrison and Verrall 1890: x.

63. Note the *faux* modesty of "I venture to hope the specialist may find material worthy of his criticism" (Harrison and Verrall 1890: i).

64. Harrison and Verrall 1890: i.

65. Harrison and Verrall 1890: 40.

66. Harrison and Verrall 1890: 108.

67. Harrison and Verrall 1890: 53. The joke was not lost on A. B. Cook, who (in

his copy now held by Newnham College Library) penciled two exclamation marks in the margin.

68. Harrison to F.(?) Macmillan, 28 August 1888 (University of Reading, Macmillan Archive, 201/284).

69. Harrison to F.(?) Macmillan, 12 October 1888 (University of Reading, Macmillan Archive, 210/284).

70. Harrison to F.(?) Macmillan, 4 February 1889 (University of Reading, Macmillan Archive, 7/5).

71. Tarbell 1890: 432.

72. "R." 1890: 393.

73. E.g., R[ichards] 1890: 219; the only discordant note was P. Gardner ("Small they necessarily are, and quite without pretensions to style, but, for purposes of help to students, admirable" [1890: 125]).

74. Harrison and Verrall 1890: xiii (copy held in Newnham College Library).

75. Various inaccuracies were picked out by reviewers; but the best compilation of Verrall's mistakes (e.g., a dreadful howler on p. 239, making αἰτεῖν mean "to ask a question" rather than "ask *for* something"—and so entirely overturning the sense of the anecdote) is in Frazer's own copy of Harrison and Verrall 1890 (in Trinity College Library, Cambridge, Adv. d. 21.2). Quite how much help A. W. Verrall gave to the translation is unknown (though he did contribute a short appendix on a textual problem).

76. "R." 1890: 393.

77. "There is not a lover of antiquity who does not find pleasure in visiting the monuments of Athens under the guide of this Pausanias in petticoats," "Nemo" 1891: 411

78. "R." 1890: 394.

79. R[ichards] 1890: 220.

80. Anon. 1890a: 698.

81. Anon. 1890b: 841. In some ways, perhaps, Harrison was asking for this reaction, with her fulsome thanks to the Master and her almost wholesale acceptance of his every theory. Unlike many other English classicists, who were extremely suspicious of the "German School," she was an enthusiastic convert. And she championed Dörpfeld at a time when most of the English archaeological establishment were gunning for him (notably over the "Greek Theatre Controversy" [see Beard 2000: 66–70]; in this context her fulsome introduction may have been an intentional provocation). Yet she makes it absolutely clear in the book that (while she may embrace his views en route) her central mythological project is quite different from his.

82. Tarbell 1890: 431; Tarbell certainly knew Dörpfeld's views firsthand, having been a participant in the first *Peloponnesos-Reise*.

83. "R" 1890: 394.

84. Gardner 1890: 125.

85. R[ichards] 1890: 218.

86. Tarbell 1890: 431.

87. Cook 1890: 380; Tarbell 1890: 432.

88. Anon. 1890a: 697.

89. Ackerman 1987: 127 ("Pausanias and Frazer were made for one another"); Fraser 1990: 39–41.

90. MacColl to E. Sellers, 18 January 1891 (Girton College Archive, Strong Papers, box 13).

91. There is no reason to suppose that "students" here is shorthand for "students

visiting Athens." Harrison repeatedly put the book on the reading lists for her students in University Extension Classes in London (a selection can be found in Newnham College Archive, Harrison Papers, boxes 9 and 18), and she wrote to Macmillan about it in those terms (Harrison to F.[?] Macmillan, 4 January 1889 [University of Reading, Macmillan Archive, 204/192]: "I specially ask [about the publication date] because of putting the book on lists of 'books to be read' in various schemes of approaching lectures").

92. Information from the Macmillan Archive, Basingstoke.

93. Kept in Newnham College Archive. The marginalia all seem to date to the 1890s (most of them in the years immediately following the publication of the book).

94. Harrison 1906: vii.

95. Harrison 1903.

96. Frazer 1898.

97. The investment of modern commentators in exposing Frazer's *argument* (here or in *The Golden Bough*) goes against the grain of most readers' experience of his text as endless detail, brightened by some self-consciously fine writing. His introduction to Pausanias is a case in point (Frazer 1898, vol. 1: xiii–xcii). Although it is possible to admire the thoroughness with which he discusses, e.g., the relationship of Polemo and Pausanias, it is more tempting to detect undiscriminating prolixity.

98. Notes from J. G. Frazer's copy of Harrison and Verrall 1890 (Trinity College Library, Cambridge, Adv. d. 21.2); see pp. 130, 515, 521, 456.

99. The history of Frazer's Pausanias is more fully covered by Ackerman 1987: 127–42.

100. Gardner 1898: 466

101. Gardner 1890: 126.

102. Gardner 1898: 465–66.

103. This is a major theme of Beard 2000, where the awful truth about the lengths to which her champions went (and, of course, the rivalry between them) is exposed.

104. Her main competitor as most active disciple was the sub-Bloomsbury poet and novelist Hope Mirrlees. See Beard 2000: 129–60.

105. "Friday"(?) 1934 (Newnham College Archive, Harrison Papers, box 16).

106. H. Payne to D. S. Robertson, 27 May 1934 (Newnham College Archive, Harrison Papers, box 16); Robertson disloyally (or loyally?) sent a copy straight on to Stewart (which is what is preserved in the Newnham Archive).

107. L. Woolf to J. Stewart, 21 July 1939 (Newnham College Archive, Harrison Papers, Box 16): "I am afraid that financially it is impossible for us now to offer to do anything except publish it for you on a commission basis at 10 per cent." Woolf, by this point, was not the leading managerial force in the firm. In an earlier letter (2 December 1938), J. Lehmann (of Hogarth) wrote more frankly to Miss [*sic*] A. J. B. Wace, who had been advising Stewart: "Dear Madam . . . under the present circumstances there would be hardly any chance of our being able to undertake it" (Newnham College Archive, Harrison Papers, box 16).

108. Hill 1953.

109. Hill 1953: vii–viii.

110. Cook 1954.

111. Plommer 1955.

112. And R. M. Cook was not prepared to pretend that he could recall. They may both have had in mind such work as Vanderpool 1949 (reexamining Pausanias's text, but this time as a direct spin-off of the Agora excavations); cf. Wycherley 1959.

Commentary (Bann)

1. Chateaubriand 1969: 823.
2. Chateaubriand 1969: 828.
3. Chateaubriand 1969: 839.
4. Chateaubriand 1969: 1698–99.
5. Chateaubriand 1969: 683.
6. Chateaubriand 1969: 1137, 1735.
7. Chateaubriand 1969: 808.
8. Chateaubriand 1969: 827.
9. See Bann 1988: 245–48.
10. Chateaubriand 1969: 816.
11. Chateaubriand 1969: 814.
12. Chateaubriand 1969: 824.
13. See Comment 1993: 21.
14. Chateaubriand 1969: 696. The quotation is from the author's preface to his *Oeuvres complètes* (1826).
15. See Bann 1984, 1995.
16. Chateaubriand 1969: 833.
17. This is, of course, to oversimplify an issue that is considered exhaustively by Veyne (1983). Veyne finds it helpful to prolong the doubt as to whether Pausanias is speaking as a philologist or as a historian in cases such as this. However, he recognizes the post-Rankean tendency to separate out the two modes of inquiry. My inclination is to signal the rhetorical underpinning of narrative structures especially when (as with Chateaubriand) the relation to the past is worked through in terms of the incorporation of the Other.
18. Chateaubriand 1969: 833.

Commentary (Cherry)

I am grateful to my fellow editors, Paul Cartledge, Jack Davis, and Jim Porter for reactions to this commentary, not all of which I have heeded.

1. Published half a dozen years later than this trip, see Wiseman 1978.
2. Frazer 1898, vol. 3: 85–89 (quotations from 85–86): an instance of Henderson's "portentous passages of scenic description for the armchair" (chap. 11, this volume).
3. Snodgrass 1987: 77.
4. Butor 1974: 5.
5. A general reticence compounded, in the case of Pausanias, by the distaste that most philologists share for the alleged inelegance of his style, and by his position outside the canon of "best authors," thus making him unworthy of being read, taught, or examined; see Beard, chap. 12, this volume.
6. Elsner 1992, 1994, 1995: 125–55, 1998: 203–204. For some reactions to this suggestion, see Elsner, chap. 1, n.17, above. "A journey into identity" (or "a journey into his own cultural roots"): Elsner 1992: 9, 10, 12.
7. Frazer 1898, vol. 1: xl.
8. On *Grèce imaginaire,* see Jacob 1980b; Basch 1991. For wider discussion of pagan (and later) cult, travel, and pilgrimage, see, e.g., Hunt 1984; Lane Fox 1986; Ousterhout 1990; André and Baslez 1993; Dillon 1997; Elsner and Rubiés 1999: 8–29.

Rutherford's chap. 4 (this volume) is explicitly intended to bolster Elsner's arguments on pilgrimage.

9. Butor 1974: 9.

10. It straddles contemporary disciplines too, both borrowing from and appealing to cultural and literary studies, history, human geography, anthropology, social science, religious studies, etc. Travel writing, and its criticism, can also display considerable erudition (as, of course, does Pausanias), without necessarily following the disciplinary codes of conventional scholarship.

11. In his essay "The Journey and the Book" (a review of Fussell 1980), reprinted in Raban 1987: 253–60.

12. Elsner and Rubiés 1999 is the best attempt so far to produce a comparativist, cultural history of travel and its literature, although their focus is on the construction of modernity (going so far as to claim [p. 4] that the literature of travel is "one of the principal cultural mechanisms, even a key cause, for the development of modern identity since the Renaissance").

13. I do not mean in any way to imply that the travel writing of every period is somehow "all the same." Duncan and Gregory (1999: 5–6) outline some of the key ways in which travel and travel writing have been transformed since the eighteenth century by entering into the Euro-American project of modernity; cf., more comprehensively, Elsner and Rubiés 1999.

14. The masculine form of *tutti* is deliberate, in recognition of the overwhelmingly male history of travel writing, although Robinson's 1990 biographical directory of women travelers lists some four hundred since Egeria in the fourth century. For an up-to-date critique of gender issues in travel writing, see Holland and Huggan 1998: 111–55; cf. also Mills 1991.

15. "Nothing is certain about the author [Pausanias], except what is to be inferred from his work" (Heil 1998: 64).

16. Rocha-Pereira 1989, vol. 3: 189–328; Pirenne-Delforge and Purnelle 1997.

17. Habicht 1985: 97 and n.9, with refs. (Herodotus); 98 and n.10 (Plutarch); 133 (Polybius). Habicht's excellent chap. 4, on Pausanias and history, should now be read alongside Meadows 1995; Bingen 1996.

18. Henderson 1992: 230.

19. Henderson 1992: 230, 239.

20. This is, equally, a central element in tourism as a cultural practice, in which sightseers are engaged in reading cities, landscapes, and cultures as symbolic complexes or semiotic systems, already fully formed in their minds as a consequence of prior expectations based on what others have seen and described before. See Mac-Cannell 1976; Culler 1988: 153–67 ("The semiotics of tourism"); Adler 1989a, 1989b; and, in a somewhat different direction, Barthes 1972: 74–77 ("The *Blue Guide*").

21. Kinglake 1844: 94.

22. Cited in Henderson 1992: 232, from Glazebrook 1984 (an admittedly extreme example of a travel writer straining to see only that about which he has already read—in this case, the experience of Victorian era travelers in the Ottoman empire).

23. Butor 1974; Dubois 1981: 153; Jacob 1980b: 43.

24. Basch 1991: 38. "Twentieth-century traveler go to Greece despite modern Greece, to a Greece within quotation marks. Their true Greece is a "cabinet" Greece, the bookish Greece. . . . basically, they don't much want to set out."

25. Alcock 1993: 24–32, 145–49 (with table 7, p. 146, listing communities de-

scribed by Pausanias as abandoned or "in ruins"), 173–79; cf. also Arafat 1996 and, most recently, Pritchett 1999.

26. Lévi-Strauss 1955: 29, 35–36 (emphasis in the original).

27. See esp. Leed 1991; Porter 1991; Pratt 1991; Behdad 1994.

28. Waugh 1946.

29. Holland and Huggan 1998: xi (and, more generally, 1–25). Postcolonial and postmodern interests in exile, diaspora, migration, borders, anxiety about identity, etc., have led scholars in cultural studies, anthropology, and literary theory to take an interest in travel as a metaphor (on which, see Van den Abbeele 1992) for forms of cultural displacement; the literature is vast, but see esp. Said 1983: 226–47 ("traveling theory"); Robertson et al. 1994; Kaplan 1996; Clifford 1997: 17–46 ("traveling cultures"). For the crude clichés that the "true age of travel writing" has ended and that "other travelers are always mere tourists," see, e.g., MacCannell 1976; Fussell 1980; Raban 1987: 256–57; Culler 1988; Henderson 1992.

30. Holland and Huggan 1998: 24.

31. Whitmer 1993: 267.

32. On the relationship between travel writing and nostalgia, see esp. Frow 1991; Holland and Huggan 1998: passim. See also Rosaldo's (1989: 69–70) influential concept of "imperialist nostalgia"; cf. Kaplan 1996: 33–40.

33. On the temporality of landscape, see Ingold 1993.

34. Habicht (1985: 21–27) provides what seems to me a balanced review of varied opinions about readership and audience.

35. Habicht 1985: 22; Bowie, chap. 2, this volume; Elsner, chap. 1, this volume. Casson 1974 goes so far as to entitle his chapter on Pausanias (292–99) "Baedeker of the Ancient World." The notion of Pausanias as a *vade mecum* is surely undercut to some extent by the fact that those modern versions intended explicitly for use as tourist travel guides have felt the need for either drastic excision of "digressions" (e.g., Harrison and Verrall 1890: see Henderson, chap. 11, this volume) or radical restructuring (e.g., Levi's 1971 two-volume translation for Penguin Books; see Elsner 1992: n.2).

36. Diller 1956: 84–86. My Michigan colleague James Porter has pointed out to me that other authors too (e.g., Longinus, Philodemus) failed to receive much, if any, later citation; the key point may be that Pausanias was not a writer whose work was *taught*—which, of course, has to do with institutional politics and authority.

37. Habicht 1985: 22.

38. Elsner 1992; Woolf 1994; Alcock 1993, 1996.

Coda (Elsner)

1. See Anon. 1816: 36 (no. 806); Graves 1905 [1970]: 199; Roth, with Lyons and Merewether, 1997: 74. The picture was hung in the "Architectural Drawings &c" section in the Library of the Academy at Somerset House.

2. Gandy was the only architect added to the list of Associates of the Royal Academy during the long presidency of Benjamin West (1792–1820); see Sandby 1822: 400. On Gandy and Soane, see Lukacher 1987: 51–64; on Gandy's life and work, see Summerson 1963: esp. 114–23.

3. The sheet is now in the possession of the Getty Research Institute in Los Angeles. It reads "Joseph Gandy Association R.A., The Persian Porch and place of consultation of the Lacedemonians [*sic*]. *vid* [*sic*] Pausanias B.III C XI," and finally the artist's ad-

dress, 58 Greek Street, Soho Square (my thanks are due to Claire Lyons for supplying me with this information). Since all this material appears (in different places) in the Royal Academy Exhibition catalogue, one may infer that the Getty sheet was the manuscript from which the catalogue entry was made.

4. Not all have been found in modern times or reproduced, but see Roth, with Lyons and Merewether, 1997: 46–47 (as well as fig. 27 in this volume), for no. 9; Harris 1983: 92, for no. 1; Lukacher 1983a, for no. 11.

5. Although Gandy's picture titles, as recorded in the Royal Academy's annual exhibition catalogues, engage with other ancient authors (notably the tragedians), his most systematic focus is on Pausanias. He may be described as one of Pausanias's most dedicated early commentators.

6. See Jenkins 1992.

7. On the fanciful nature of Gandy's "scholarship," see Summerson 1963: 129.

8. This vision is unique in English architectural drawing, in which Gandy is the supreme architectural fantasist. See Summerson 1963.

9. See Frazer 1898, vol. 1: xxx–xxxiii, xlii–xlix.

10. On Gandy's lighting effects, see Lukacher 1983b.

11. This "transgression" also characterizes the two other examples from the series I have seen (nos. 3 and 11 in table 5). The latter of these, an oil painting rather than a watercolor, which elicited some contemporary debate (see Lukacher 1983a), evokes Pausanias's interest in ritual with a grand sacred procession.

12. See the great sets of engravings published by Wood (1753, 1758), Stuart and Revett (1762–1816), and Adam (1764). The illustrations of all these conform to the division of modern populated ruins and restored ancient buildings divorced of context. The earliest, Wood's *Palmyra* and *Baalbec,* are relatively restrained in their peopling of modern views, but ruined antiquity as a backdrop to a capriccio of Oriental exotica rapidly became a significant part of the publishing enterprise; see Tait 1993: 103–110.

Bibliography

Ackerman, R. 1972. "Jane Ellen Harrison: The early work." *GRBS* 13: 209–231.

———. 1987. *J. G. Frazer: His Life and Work.* Cambridge.

———. 1991. "The Cambridge group: Origins and composition." In Calder 1991a: 1–20.

Adam, R. 1764. *Ruins of the Palace of the Emperor Diocletian at Spalatro in Dalmatia.* London.

Adams, A. 1989. "The Arch of Hadrian at Athens." In *The Greek Renaissance in the Roman Empire (BICS* Supplement 55), ed. S. Walker and A. Cameron, 10–15. London.

Adler, J. 1989a. "Origins of sightseeing." *Annals of Tourism Research* 16: 7–29.

———. 1989b. "Travel as performed art." *American Journal of Sociology* 94: 1366–91.

Aellen, C., A. Cambitoglou, and J. Chamay. 1986. *Le peintre de Darius et son milieu: Vases grecs d'Italie méridionale* (Hellas et Roma 4). Geneva.

Africa, T. W. 1991. "Aunt Glegg among the dons or Taking Jane Harrison at her word." In Calder 1991a: 21–36.

Ajootian, A. 1996. "Praxiteles." In *Personal Styles in Greek Sculpture* (YCS 30), ed. O. Palagia and J. J. Pollitt, 91–129. Cambridge.

Akamatis, I. M. 1993. *Πήλινες Μήτρες Αγγείων από την Πέλλα · Συμβολή στη Μελέτη της Ελληνιστικής Κεραμικής. Δημοσιεύματα του Αρχαιολογικού Δελτίου* 51. Athens.

Alcock, S. E. 1991. "Tomb cult and the post-classical polis." *AJA* 95: 447–67.

———. 1993. *Graecia Capta: The Landscapes of Roman Greece.* Cambridge.

———. 1994a. "The heroic past in a Hellenistic present." *EchCl* 38 (n.s. 13): 221–34.

———. 1994b. "Minding the gap in Hellenistic and Roman Greece." In *Placing the Gods: Sanctuaries and Sacred Space in Ancient Greece*, ed. S. E. Alcock and R. Osborne, 247–61. Oxford.

———. 1995. "Pausanias and the *polis*: Use and abuse." In Hansen, 1995: 326–44.

———. 1996. "Landscapes of memory and the authority of Pausanias." In Bingen, 1996: 241–67.

———. 1998. "Liberation and conquest: Hellenistic and Roman Messenia," In *Sandy Pylos: An Archaeological History from Nestor to Navarino*, ed. J. L. Davis, 179–91. Austin.

———. Forthcoming. *A Matrix for Memory: Landscapes, Monuments and the Greek Past.* Cambridge.

Alcock, S. E., A. Berlin, A. Harrison, S. Heath, N. Spencer, and D. Stone. In prep. "The Pylos Regional Archaeological Project. Part IV: Historic Messenia, Geometric to Late Roman." *Hesperia*.

Ameling, W. 1996. "Pausanias und die Hellenistischen Geschichte." In Bingen 1996: 117–66.

Anderson, G. 1990. "The Second Sophistic: Some problems of perspective." In *Antonine Literature*, ed. D. A. Russell, 91–110. Oxford.

Anderson, R. 1830. *Observations upon the Peloponnesus and Greek Islands Made in 1829*. Boston.

André, J. M., and M.-F. Baslez. 1993. *Voyager dans l'antiquité*. Paris.

Andreae, B. 1962. "Der Zyklus der Odysseefresken im Vatikan." *RM* 69: 106–117.

Andreae, B., and C. P. Presicce, eds. 1996. *Ulisse: Il mito e la memoria* (Catalog of the Exhibition, Feb. 22–Sept. 2 1996, Palazzo delle Esposizioni, Rome). Rome.

Andronikos, M. 1984. *Vergina: The Royal Tombs*. Athens.

Angelomatis-Tsougarakis, H. 1990. *The Eve of the Greek Revival: British Travellers' Perceptions of Early Nineteenth-Century Greece*. London.

Anon. 1816. *The Exhibition of the Royal Academy MDCCCXVI: The Forty-Eighth*. London.

———. 1864. *A Brief Memoir of the Life and Writings of the late William Martin Leake*. London.

———. 1890a. Review of *Mythology and Monuments of Ancient Athens, being a translation of a portion of the "Attica" of Pausanias by M. de G. Verrall, with introductory essay and archaeological commentary by J. E. Harrison* (London and New York, 1890). *The Spectator*, 17 May: 697–98.

———. 1890b. Review of *Mythology and Monuments of Ancient Athens, being a translation of a portion of the "Attica" of Pausanias by M. de G. Verrall, with introductory essay and archaeological commentary by J. E. Harrison* (London and New York, 1890). *Atlantic Monthly* 66: 839–44.

———. 1907. Review of L. R. Farnell, *The Cults of the Greek States* III–IV. *The Guardian cit. Stapeldon Magazine* I. 7: 294.

———. 1910. Review of L. R. Farnell, *The Cults of the Greek States* V. *Stapeldon Magazine* II. 12:220.

———. 1928. College notes. *Stapeldon Magazine* VII. 42: 211–15.

Antonaccio, C. M. 1995. *An Archaeology of Ancestors: Tomb Cult and Hero Cult in Early Greece*. Lanham, Md.

———. 1998. "The archaeology of ancestors." In *Cultural Poetics in Archaic Greece: Cult, Performance, Politics*, ed. C. Dougherty and L. Kurke, 46–70. Oxford.

Arafat, K. W. 1995. "Pausanias and the Temple of Hera at Olympia." *BSA* 90: 461–73.

———. 1996. *Pausanias' Greece: Ancient Artists and Roman Rulers*. Cambridge.

Armstrong, P., W. G. Cavanagh, and G. Shipley. 1992. "Crossing the river: Observations on routes and bridges in Laconia." *BSA* 87: 293–310.

Aschenbrenner, S. 1972, "A contemporary community." In McDonald and Rapp 1972: 47–63.

Asheri, D. 1983. "La diaspora e il ritorno dei Messeni," In *Tria Corda: Scritti in onore di Arnaldo Momigliano*, ed. E. Gabba, 27–42. Como.

Ashmole, B., and N. Yalouris. 1967. *Olympia: The Sculptures of the Temple of Zeus*. London.

Auffarth, C. 1997. " 'Verräter-übersetzer?' Pausanias, das römische Patrai und die Identität der Griechen in der Achaea." In *Römische Reichsreligion und Provinzielreligion*, ed. H. Cancik and J. Rüphe, 219–38. Tübingen.

Augustinos, O. 1994. *French Odysseys: Greece in French Travel Literature from the Renaissance to the Romantic Era*. Baltimore.

Aujac, G., et al. 1987a. "The foundations of theoretical cartography in Archaic and Classical Greece." In *The History of Cartography*, vol. 1, ed. J. B. Harley and D. Woodward, 130–47. Chicago and London.

———. 1987b. "The growth of an empirical cartography in Hellenistic Greece." In *The History of Cartography*, vol. 1, ed. J. B. Harley and D. Woodward, 148–60. Chicago and London.

Aupert, P., and D. Knoepfler, eds. Forthcoming. *Traduire, commenter, éditer Pausanias en l'an 2000*. Lausanne.

Austin, M. M. 1981. *The Hellenistic World from Alexander to the Roman Conquest*. Cambridge and New York.

Austin, N. 1994. *Helen of Troy and Her Shameless Phantom*. Ithaca and London.

Avi-Yonah, A. 1954. *The Madaba Mosaic Map*. Jerusalem.

Baedeker, K. 1883. *Griechenland: Handbuch für Reisende*. Leipzig.

Baladié, R. 1980. *Le Péloponnèse de Strabon: Étude de géographie historique*. Paris.

Balsdon, D. 1970. *Oxford Now and Then*. London.

Bann, S. 1984. *The Clothing of Clio: A Study of the Representation of History in Nineteenth-Century Britain and France*. Cambridge.

———. 1988. "Romanticism in France." In *Romanticism in National Context*, ed. R. Porter and M. Teich, 240–59. Cambridge.

———. 1995. *Romanticism and the Rise of History*. New York.

Barber, E. A. 1931–40. L. R. Farnell. *Dictionary of National Biography*, 269.

Barber, R., ed. 1995. *Blue Guide: Greece*. New York.

Barbié du Bocage, J. D. 1814. *Carte de la Morée dressée et gravée au Dépôt Géneral de la Guerre per Ordre du Gouvernement en 1807*. Paris.

Barthes, R. 1972. *Mythologies*. New York.

———. 1975. *The Pleasure of the Text*. New York.

———. 1977. "Diderot, Brecht, Eisenstein." In *Image, Music, Text*, by R. Barthes (trans. S. Heath), 69–78. New York.

———. 1981. *Camera lucida*. New York.

Bartsch, S. 1989. *Decoding the Ancient Novel*. Princeton.

Basch, S. 1991. *Le voyage imaginaire: Les écrivains français en Grèce au XXᵉ siècle*. Athens.

Bataille, A. 1951. *Les inscriptions grecques du temple de Hatshepsout à Deir el Bahari*. Cairo.

Baumer, L. E., T. Hölscher, and L. Winkler. 1991. "Narrative Systematik und politisches Konzept in den Reliefs der Traianssäule: Drei Fallstudien." *JdI* 106: 261–95.

Bauslaugh, R. A. 1990. "Messenian dialect and dedications of the 'Methanioi.' " *Hesperia* 59: 661–68.

Beard, M. 1992. "Frazer, Leach, and Virgil: The popularity (and unpopularity) of *The Golden Bough*." *Comparative Studies in Society and History* 34: 203–24.

———. 1993a. "Casts and cast-offs: The origins of the Museum of Classical Archaeology." *PCPS* 39:1–29.

———. 1993b. "Frazer et ses bois sacrés." In *Les bois sacrés (Collection du Centre J. Bérard* 10), 171–80. Naples.

———. 1999. "The invention (and re-invention) of 'Group D': An archaeology of the Classical Tripos, 1879–1984." In *Classics in Nineteenth and Twentieth Century Cambridge: Curriculum, Culture and Community (PCPS* Supplement 24), ed. C. Stray. 95–134. Cambridge.

————. 2000. *The Invention of Jane Harrison*. Cambridge, Mass.

Beard, M., and J. Henderson. 1995. *Classics: A Very Short Introduction*. Oxford.

————. 1998. "With this body I thee worship: Sacred prostitution in antiquity." In *Gender and the Body in the Ancient Mediterranean*, ed. M. Wyke, 56–79. Oxford. Originally published in *Gender and History* 9.3 (1997): 480–503.

Becker, A. S. 1995. *The Shield of Achilles and the Poetics of Ekphrasis*. Lanham, Md.

Behdad, A. 1994. *Belated Travelers: Orientalism in the Age of Colonial Dissolution*. Durham, N.C.

Behr, C. A. 1968. *Aelius Aristides and the Sacred Tales*. Amsterdam.

————. 1981. *P. Aelius Aristides: The Complete Works, Translated into English*. Leiden.

Bergmann, B. 1991. "Painted perspectives of a villa visit: Landscape as status and metaphor." In *Roman Art in the Private Sphere: New Perspectives on the Architecture and Decor of the Domus, Villa, and Insula*, ed. E. K. Gazda, 49–70. Ann Arbor.

————. 1992. "Exploring the grove: Pastoral space on Roman walls." In *The Pastoral Landscape* (Studies in the History of Art 36), ed. J. D. Hunt, 21–46. Washington, D.C.

————. 1994. "The Roman house as memory theater: The House of the Tragic Poet in Pompeii." *Art Bulletin* 76: 225–56.

————. 1997. Review of Biering 1995. *AJA* 101: 802–804.

————. 1999. "Rhythms of recognition: Mythical encounters in the Roman landscape." In *Im Spiegel des Mythos: Bilderwelt und Lebenswelt* (Palilia 6), ed. F. de Angelis and S. Muth, 81–107. Wiesbaden.

Bernand, É. 1969. *Les inscriptions grecques et latines de Philae*. Paris.

————. 1988. "Pelerins dans l'Égypte grecque et romain." In *Mélanges Pierre Leveque* I (Annales litteraires de l'Université de Besançon 367, Centre de Recherches d'Histoire Ancienne, 79), ed. M.-M. Mactoux and E. Geny, 49–63. Paris.

Beschi, L., and D. Musti, eds. 1982. *Pausania, "Guida della Grecia," Libro 1: L'Attica*. Milan.

————. 1990. *Pausania, "Guida della Grecia," Libro 3: Laconia*. Milan.

Bethe, E. 1894. "Amphiareion." *RE* 1: 1893–97.

Bhabha, H. 1994. *The Location of Culture*. London.

Bickerton, F. 1953. *Fred on Oxford*. London.

Biebel, F. 1938. "The walled cities of the Gerasa mosaics." In *Gerasa: City of the Decapolis*, ed. C. H. Kraeling, 341–51. New Haven.

Biering, R. 1995. *Die Odysseefresken vom Esquilin*. Munich.

Binder, J. 1976. *Athens Survey 1976: The Monuments, Sites, Place-Names and Cults of Athens Known from the Written Sources and the Remains*. Limited ed. Athens.

Bingen, J., ed. 1996. *Pausanias historien* (Fondation Hardt, Entretiens sur l'antiquité classique 41). Geneva.

Birge, D. E. 1992. "The Sacred Square." In *Excavations at Nemea*, vol. 1: *Topographical and Architectural Studies*, by D. E. Birge, L. H. Kraynak, and S. G. Miller, 1–98. Berkeley.

————. 1994. "Trees in the landscape of Pausanias' *Periegesis*." In *Placing the Gods: Sanctuaries and Sacred Space in Ancient Greece*, ed. S. E. Alcock and R. Osborne, 231–45. Oxford.

Bischoff, H. 1937. "Perieget." *RE* 19.1: 725–42.

Blegen, C. W. 1966. Foreword to *The Temple of Zeus at Nemea*, by B. H. Hill, v–vii. Princeton.

Boardman, J. 1981. "No, no Nausicäa." *JWalt* 39: 38.

————. 1985. "100 years of classical archaeology in Oxford." In *Beazley and Oxford*, ed. D. C. Kurtz, 43–55. Oxford.

————. 1990. "The Greek Art of Narrative," in *EUMOUSIA: Ceramic and Iconographic Studies in Honour of Alexander Cambitoglou*, ed. J.-P. Descoeudres, 57–62. Sydney.

Boethius, A. 1918. "Die Pythaïs: Studien zur Geschichte der Verbindungen zwischen Athen und Delphi." Ph.D. diss. University of Uppsala.

Borchhardt, J. 1980. "Zur Darstellung von Objekten in der Entfernung: Beobachtungen zu den Anfängen der griechischen Landschaftsmalerei." In *Tainia* (Festschrift Roland Hampe), ed. H. A. Cahn and E. Simon, 257–67. Mainz.

Bory de Saint-Vincent, J. B. G. M. 1834–36. *Expédition scientifique de Morée: Section des sciences physiques*. Paris.

Bosio, L. 1983. *La tabula peutingeriana: Una descrizione pittorica del mondo antico*. Rimini.

Bosworth, A. B. 1972. "Arrian's literary development." *CQ* 22: 163–85.

————. 1980. *A Historical Commentary on Arrian's History of Alexander*. Vol. 1, *Commentary on Books i-iii*. Oxford.

————. 1993. "Arrian and Rome: The minor works." *ANRW* II Principat, 34.1: 226–75.

Bowersock, G. W. 1969. *Greek Sophists in the Roman Empire*. Oxford.

————. 1984. "The miracle of Memnon." *Bulletin of the American Society of Papyrologists* 21: 21–31.

————. ed. 1974. *Approaches to the Second Sophistic: Papers Presented at the 105th Annual Meeting of the American Philological Association*. University Park, Pa.

Bowie, E. L. 1974. "Greeks and their past in the Second Sophistic." In *Studies in Ancient Society*, ed. M. I. Finley, 166–209. London. Originally published in *Past and Present* 46 (1970) 3–41.

————. 1982. "The importance of Sophists." *YCS* 27: 29–59.

————. 1989. "Poetry and poets in Asia and Achaea." In *The Greek Renaissance in the Roman Empire* (*BICS* Supplement 55), ed. S. Walker and A. Cameron, 198–205. London.

————. 1990. "Greek poetry in the Antonine Age." In *Antonine Literature*, ed. D. A. Russell, 53–90. Oxford.

————. 1991. "Hellenes and Hellenism in writers of the early Second Sophistic." In Ἑλληνισμός: Quelques jalons pour une histoire de l'identité grecque (Actes du Colloque de Strasbourg, 25–27 octobre 1989), ed. S. Saïd, 183–204. Leiden.

————. 1994. "The readership of Greek novels in the ancient world." In *The Search for the Ancient Novel*, ed. J. Tatum, 435–59. Baltimore and London.

————. 1996a. "The ancient readers of the Greek novels." In *A Companion to the Ancient Novel*, ed. G. Schmeling, 87–106. Leiden.

————. 1996b. "Past and present in Pausanias." In Bingen, 1996: 207–239.

Bowra, C. M. 1966. *Memories, 1898–1939*. London.

Branham, R. B. 1989. *Unruly Eloquence: Lucian and the Comedy of Traditions*. Cambridge, Mass.

Braund, D. 1997. "Greeks and barbarians: The Black Sea region and Hellenism under the Early Empire." In *The Early Roman Empire in the East* (Oxbow Monograph 95), ed. S. E. Alcock, 121–36. Oxford.

Bremmer, J., ed. 1987. *Interpretations of Greek Mythology*. London and New York.

Breuillot, M. 1985. "L'eau et les dieux de Messène." *Dialogues d'histoire ancienne* 11: 789–804.

Bridges, R. C. 1976. "W. D. Cooley, the RGS and African geography in the nineteenth century." *Geographical Journal* 142: 27–47, 274–86.

Brilliant, R. 1984. *Visual Narratives: Storytelling in Etruscan and Roman Art*. Ithaca and London.

Brittain, V. 1960. *The Women at Oxford: A Fragment of History*. London.

Brixhe, C. 1996. "Les IIe et Ier siècles dans l'histoire linguistique de la Laconie et la notion de Koina." In *La Koine grecque antique*, vol. 2, *La concurrence*, ed. C. Brixhe, 93–109. Paris.

Brommer, F. 1980. "Theseus and Nausicäa." *JWalt* 38: 119–20.

———. 1982. *Theseus: Die Taten des griechischen Helden in der antiken Kunst und Literatur*. Darmstadt.

Brown, T. S., ed. 1965. *Ancient Greece: Sources in Western Civilization*. London and New York.

Bruit Zaidman, L., and P. Schmitt Pantel. 1992. *Religion in the Ancient Greek City*. Cambridge.

Bruneau, P. 1970. *Recherches sur les cultes de Délos à l'époque hellénistique et à l'époque impériale* (Bibliothèque des Écoles Françaises d'Athènes et de Rome 217). Paris.

Brunt, P. A. 1994. "The bubble of the Second Sophistic." *BICS* 39: 25–52.

Bryson, N. 1994. "Philostratus and the imaginary museum." In *Art and Text in Ancient Greek Culture*, ed. S. Goldhill and R. Osborne, 255–83. Cambridge.

Bugh, G. R. 1990. "The Theseia in late Hellenistic Athens." *ZPE* 83: 20–37.

Bühler, W. 1964. *Beiträge zur Erklärung der Schrift vom Erhabenen*. Göttingen.

Buitron, D., B. Cohen, N. Austin, G. Dimock, T. Gould, W. Mullen, B. B. Powell, and M. Simpson. 1992. *The Odyssey and Ancient Art: An Epic in Word and Image*. Annandale-on-Hudson, N.Y.

Burckhardt, J.-L. 1819. *Travels in Nubia*. London.

———. 1822. *Travels in Syria and the Holy Land*. London.

Burkert, W. 1960. "Plato oder Pythagoras? Zum Ursprung des Wortes 'Philosophie.' " *Hermes* 88: 159–77.

Butor, M. 1974. "Travel and writing." *Mosaic: A Journal for the Comparative Study of Literature and Ideas* 8.1: 1–16.

Byvanck-Quarles van Ufford, L. 1954. "Les bols homériques." *BABesch* 29: 35–40.

Cagnat, R., et al. 1906. *Inscriptiones Graecae ad res Romanas pertinentes*, vol. 3. Paris.

Calame, C. 1977. *Les choeurs de jeunes filles en Grèce archaïque*. Vol. 1, *Morphologie, fonction religieuse et sociale*. Rome.

———. 1987. "Spartan genealogies: The mythological representation of a spatial organisation." In Bremmer 1987: 153–86.

———. 1990. *Thésée et l'imaginaire athénien: Légende et culte en Grèce antique*. Lausanne.

———. 1995. "Pausanias le Périégète en ethnographe, ou comment décrire un culte grec." In *Le discours anthropologique: Description, narration, savoir*, ed. J.-M. Adam, M.-J. Borel, C. Calame, and M. Kilani, 205–226. Paris.

———. 1998. "Logiques du temps légendaire et de l'espace cultuel selon Pausanias: Une représentation discursive du 'panthéon' de Trézène." In Pirenne-Delforge 1998b: 149–63.

Calder, W. M., III, ed. 1991a. *The Cambridge Ritualists Reconsidered: Proceedings of the First Oldfather Conference, Held on the Campus of the University of Illinois at Urbana–Champaign April 27–30, 1989* (Illinois Classical Studies Supplement 2). Atlanta.

———. 1991b. "Jane Harrison's failed candidacies for the Yates Professorship (1888, 1896): What did her colleagues think of her?" In Calder 1991a: 37–60.

Camp, J. M. 1986. *The Athenian Agora: Excavations in the Heart of Classical Athens*. London.

Campbell, B. 1996. "Shaping the rural environment: Surveyors in ancient Rome." *JRS* 86: 74–99.

Cancik, H. 1985–86. "Rome as a sacred landscape: Varro and the end of Republican religion in Rome." *Visible Religion* 4–5: 250–63.

Carder, J. N. 1978. *Art Historical Problems of a Roman Land Surveying Manuscript: The Codex Arcerianus A, Wolfenbüttel.* New York and London.

Cardinal, R. 1997. "The passionate traveller: Goethe in Italy." *Publications of the English Goethe Society* 67: 17–32.

Carey, S. 1998. "Cataloguing Culture: Pliny the Elder's Presentation of Art in His *Natural History.*" Ph.D. diss., Courtauld Institute, University of London.

Carroll, M. 1907. *The Attica of Pausanias* (College Series of Greek Authors). Boston.

Carroll-Spillecke, M. 1985. *Landscape Depictions in Greek Relief Sculpture: Development and Conventionalization.* Frankfurt and New York.

Carruthers, M. 1990. *The Book of Memory.* Cambridge.

Cartledge, P. A. 1975. "Early Sparta c. 950–650 B.C.: An Archaeological and Historical Study." D.Phil. diss., University of Oxford.

———. 1976. "Seismicity and Spartan society." *Liverpool Classical Monthly* 1: 25–28.

———. 1979. *Sparta and Lakonia: A Regional History, c. 1300–362 B.C.* London.

———. 1985. "Rebels and sambos in Classical Greece: A comparative view." *History of Political Thought* 6: 16–46.

———. 1987. *Agesilaos and the Crisis of Sparta.* Baltimore.

———. 1991. "Richard Talbert's revision of the Spartan-helot struggle: A reply." *Historia* 40: 379–81.

———. 1995. " 'We are all Greeks?' Ancient (especially Herodotean) and modern contestations of Hellenism." *BICS* 40: 75–82.

Cartledge, P. A., and A. Spawforth. 1989. *Hellenistic and Roman Sparta: A Tale of Two Cities.* London.

Casevitz, M. 1992. "La tradition du texte de Pausanias." In M. Casevitz, Pouilloux, and Chamoux 1992: xxxi–xlvi.

Casevitz, M., J. Pouilloux, and F. Chamoux. 1992. *Pausanias, Description de la Grèce.* Vol. 1, *L'Attique* (Budé edition). Paris.

Casson, L. 1974. *Travel in the Ancient World.* London and Toronto.

Cavanagh, W. G., J. H. Crouwel, R. W. V. Catling, and G. Shipley. 1996. *Continuity and Change in a Greek Rural Landscape: The Laconia Survey.* Vol. 2, *Archaeological Data (BSA* Supplementary Vol. 27). London.

———. Forthcoming. *Continuity and Change in a Greek Rural Landscape: The Laconia Survey.* Vol. 1, *Methodology and Interpretation (BSA* Supplementary vol. 26). London.

Cavanagh, W. G., and Walker, S., eds. 1999. *Sparta in Laconia: Proceedings of the 19th British Museum Colloquium.* London.

Cèbe, J.-P. 1972–94. *Varron, Satires Menippées: Édition, traduction et commentaire* (Collection de l'École Française de Rome 9.1–9.10). Rome.

Chamoux, F. 1974. "Pausanias géographe." In *Littérature gréco-romaine et géographie historique (Mélanges offerts à Roger Dion),* ed. R. Chevalier, 83–90. Paris.

———. 1992. "Commentaire." In Casevitz, Pouilloux, and Chamoux 1992: 135–274.

Chandler, R. 1776. *Travels in Greece, or an Account of a Tour Made at the Expense of the Society of Dilettanti.* Dublin.

Chantraine, P. 1950. "Les verbes grecs signifiant lire." In *Mélanges Grégoire,* vol. 2 (Annuaire de l'Institut de Philologie et d'Histoire Orientales et Slaves 10), 115–26. Brussels.

————. 1968–80. *Dictionnaire étymologique de la langue grecque: Histoire des mots.* Paris.

Chateaubriand, F.-R. 1969. *Oeuvres romanesques et voyages*, vol. 2, Ed. M. Regard. Paris.

Chelini, J., and H. Branthomme. 1987. *Histoire des pèlerinages non chrétiens. Entre magique et sacré: Le chemin des dieux.* Paris.

Cherry, J. F. 1983. "Frogs round the pond: Perspectives on current archaeological survey projects in the Mediterranean region." In *Archaeological Survey in the Mediterranean Area* (British Archaeological Reports, International Series, 155), ed. D. R. Keller and D. W. Rupp, 375–416. Oxford.

Childs, W. A. P. 1978. *The City Reliefs of Lycia.* Princeton.

————. 1991. "A new representation of a city on an Attic red-figured kylix." In *Greek Vases in the J. Paul Getty Museum*, vol. 5 (Occasional Papers on Antiquities 7) 27–40. Malibu, Ca.

Clark, W. G. 1858. *Peloponnesus: Notes of study and travel.* London.

Clarke, E. D. 1814. *Travels in Various Countries of Europe, Asia and Africa.* London.

Clarke, M. L. 1959. *Classical Education in Britain, 1500–1900.* Cambridge.

Clifford, J. 1997. *Routes: Travel and Translation in the Late Twentieth Century.* Cambridge, Mass., and London.

Clinton, K. 1989. "The Eleusinian mysteries: Roman initiates and benefactors, second century B.C. to A.D. 267." *ANRW* II Principat, 18.2: 1498–1539.

Clunes Gabell, A. V. 1934. Obit L. R. Farnell. *Morning Post*, 3 April 1934.

Cohen, A. 1996. "Portrayals of abduction in Greek art: rape or metaphor?" In *Sexuality in Ancient Art*, ed. N. B. Kampen, 117–35. Cambridge and New York.

Cohen, E. 1992. "Pilgrimage and tourism: Convergence and divergence." In Morinis 1992: 47–61.

Cole, S. G. 1989. "Mysteries of Samothrace during the Roman period." *ANRW* II Principat, 18.2: 1564–98.

Coleman, J. 1992. *Ancient and Medieval Memories: Studies in the Reconstruction of the Past.* Cambridge.

Coleman, S., and J. Elsner. 1995. *Pilgrimage: Past and Present in World Religions.* London.

Colin, G. 1909–1913. *Fouilles de Delphes*, vol. 3.2: *Inscriptions du trésor des Athéniens.* Paris.

Colin, G. et al. 1930. *Fouilles de Delphes*, vol. 3.4: *Les inscriptions de la Terrasse du Temple et de la région nord du Sanctuaire.* Paris.

Comaroff, J. 1985. *Body of Power, Spirit of Resistance: The Culture and History of a South African People.* Chicago.

Comment, B. 1993. *Le XIXᵉ siècle des panoramas.* Paris.

Constantine, D. 1984. *Early Greek Travellers and the Hellenic Ideal.* Cambridge.

Conticello, B. 1969. "The one-eyed giant of Sperlonga." *Apollo*, March : 188–93.

Cook, A. B. 1890. Review of *Mythology and Monuments of Ancient Athens, being a translation of a portion of the "Attica" of Pausanias by M. de G. Verrall, with introductory essay and archaeological commentary by J. E. Harrison* (London and New York, 1890). *Cambridge Review*, 5 June: 379–80.

————. 1914–40. *Zeus: A Study in Ancient Religion.* 3 vols. Cambridge.

————. 1931. *The Rise and Progress of Classical Archaeology, with Special Reference to the University of Cambridge: An Inaugural Lecture.* Cambridge.

Cook, R. M. 1954. Review of I. T. Hill, *The Ancient City of Athens: Its Topography and Monuments* (London, 1953). *CR* 68: 318.

————. 1983. "Art and epic in Archaic Greece." *BABesch* 58: 1–10.

Cooper, F. A., S. G. Miller, S. G. Miller, and C. Smith. 1983. *The Temple of Zeus at Nemea: Perspectives and Prospects*. Athens.

Coulson, W. D. E., and N. Wilkie. 1983. "Archaic to Roman times: The site and environs." In McDonald, Coulson, and Rosser 1983: 332–50. Minneapolis.

Courby, F. 1922. *Les vases grecs à reliefs*. Paris.

Culler, J. 1988. *Framing the Sign: Criticism and Its Institutions*. Oxford.

Dalfen, J. 1996. "Dinge, die Pausanias nicht sagt." In *Worte, Bilder, Töne: Studien zur Antike und Antikerezeption*, ed. R. Faber and B. Seidensticker, 159–77. Würzburg.

d'Anville, J. B. B. 1755. *Les Côtes de la Grèce et l'Archipelago*. Paris.

Daremberg, C., and E. Saglio, eds. 1877–1919. *Dictionnaire des antiquités grecques et romaines d'après les textes et les monuments*. Paris.

D'Arms, J. 1970. *Romans on the Bay of Naples: A Social and Cultural Study of the Villas and Their Owners from 150 B.C. to A.D. 400*. Cambridge, Mass.

Daux, G. 1936. *Pausanias à Delphes*. Paris.

Davies, M. 1988. *Epicorum Graecorum Fragmenta*. Göttingen.

Davis, J. L. 1998. "Glimpses of Messenia past." In *Sandy Pylos: An Archaeological History from Nestor to Navarino*, ed. J. L. Davis, xxix–xliii. Austin.

Davis, J. L., S. E. Alcock, J. Bennet, Y. G. Lolos, and C. W. Shelmerdine. 1997. "The Pylos Regional Archaeological Project. Part I: Overview and the archaeological survey." *Hesperia* 66: 391–494.

Dawkins, R. M. 1906. "A modern carnival in Thrace and the cult of Dionysus." *JHS* 26: 191–206.

Dawson, C. 1944. *Romano-Campanian Mythological Landscape Painting* (YCS 9). New Haven.

De Blois, L. 1998. "The world a city: Cassius Dio's view of the Roman empire." In *L'ecumenismo politico nella coscienza dell'Occidente: Atti del convegno, Bergamo 1995, 18–21 settembre*, ed. L. Aigner Foresti, 359–70. Rome.

de Certeau, M. 1986. *Heterologies: Discourse on the Other*. Minneapolis.

De Franciscis, A. 1965. *Le statue della Grotta Azzurra nell'isola di Capri*. N.p.

de Grey and Ripon, Earl. 1860. "Address to the Royal Geographical Society of London; Delivered at the Anniversary Meeting on 28 May 1860." *Journal of the Royal Geographic Society* 30: cxiii–cxvi.

Deichgräber, K. 1952. "Polemon (9)." *RE* 21: 1288–1320.

De Lannoy, L. 1977. *Flavius Philostratus, "Heroicus."* Leipzig.

Demakes, D. 1938. "Proti-Dialiskari." *Messiniakon Etos*, 87–93.

Despinis, G. I. 1966. "Ἡ ''Αρπαγὴ τῆς Ἑλένης'." *Archaiologikon Deltion* 21A: 35–44.

de Ste. Croix, G. E. M. 1983. *The Class Struggle in the Ancient World from the Archaic Age to the Arab Conquests*. London.

Dickie, M. W. 1997. "Philostratus and Pindar's eighth paean." *Bulletin of the American Society of Papyrologists* 34: 11–20.

Dihle, A. 1994. *Greek and Latin Literature of the Roman Empire: From Augustus to Justinian*. Trans. M. Malzahn. London.

Dilke, O. A. W. 1967. "Illustrations from Roman surveyors' manuals." *Imago Mundi* 21: 9–29.

————. 1985. *Greek and Roman Maps*. Ithaca, N. Y.

————. 1987a. Cartography in the ancient world: An introduction." In *The History of Cartography*, vol. 1, ed. J. B. Harley and D. Woodward, 105–106. Chicago and London.

————. 1987b. "The culmination of Greek cartography in Ptolemy." In *The History of*

Cartography, vol. 1, ed. J. B. Harley and D. Woodward, 177–200. Chicago and London.

———. 1987c. "Itineraries and geographical maps in the early and late Roman empires." In *The History of Cartography*, vol. 1, ed. J. B. Harley and D. Woodward, 234–57. Chicago and London.

———. 1987d. "Roman large-scale mapping in the early empire," In *The History of Cartography*, vol. 1, ed. J. B. Harley and D. Woodward, 212–33. Chicago and London.

Diller, A. 1937. "Codices Planudei." *Byzantinische Zeitschrift* 37: 295–301.

———. 1956. "Pausanias in the Middle Ages." *TAPA* 87: 84–97.

———. 1957. "The manuscripts of Pausanias." *TAPA* 88: 169–88.

Dillon, M. P. J. 1994. "The didactic nature of the Epidaurian Iamata." *ZPE* 101: 239–60.

———. 1997. *Pilgrims and Pilgrimage in Ancient Greece*. London and New York.

Dimaras, K. F., ed. 1968. *Periiyiseis ston Elliniko Khoro*. Athens.

Dirven, L. 1997. "The author of the *De Dea Syria* and his cultural heritage." *Numen* 44: 153–79.

Dittenberger, W. 1915–24. *Sylloge Inscriptionum Graecarum*. 3d ed. Leipzig.

Dittenberger, W., and K. Purgold. 1896. *Olympia V: Die Inschriften von Olympia*. Berlin.

Dixon, W. M. 1929. *Hellas Revisited*. London.

Dodds, E. R. 1977. *Missing Persons: An Autobiography*. Oxford.

Dodwell, E. 1819. *A Classical and Topographical Tour Through Greece During the Years 1801, 1805, and 1806*. London.

Donceel-Voûte, P. 1988. "La carte de Madaba: Cosmographie, anachronisme et propagande." *Revue biblique* 95: 519–42.

Donner, H. 1992. *The Mosaic Map of Madaba: An Introductory Guide* (Palaestina antiqua 7). Kampen, The Netherlands.

Donohue, A. A. 1988. *Xoana and the Origins of Greek Sculpture*. Atlanta.

Dörpfeld, W. 1892. "Die Ausgrabungen an der Enneakrunos." *AM* 17: 439–45.

———. 1894. "Die Ausgrabungen am Westabhange der Akropolis 1." *AM* 19: 496–509.

Doulgeri-Intzesiloglou, A. 1990. "Φεραϊκά Εργαστήρια 'Μεγαρικών Σκύφων'." In *Β´ Επιστημονική Συνάντηση για την Ελληνιστική Κεραμεική, Ρόδος, 22–25 Μαρτίου 1989*, 121–34. Athens.

Drerup, H. 1959. "Bildraum und Realraum in der römischen Architektur." *RM* 66: 147–74.

Dressler, F., et al. 1978. *Das Evangeliar Ottos III*. Frankfurt.

Drew-Bear, T. 1979. "The city of Temenouthyrai in Phrygia." *Chiron* 9: 275–302.

Dreyfus, R., and E. Schraudolph, eds. 1996–97. *Pergamon: The Telephos Frieze from the Great Altar*. 2 vols. Austin and San Francisco.

Drummer, A. 1993. "Villa: Untersuchungen zum Bedeutungswandel eines Motivs in römischer Bildkunst und Literatur." Ph.D. diss., Ludwig-Maximilians-Universität zu München.

Dubel, S. 1997. "*Ekphrasis* et *enargeia*: La description antique comme parcours." In *Dire l'évidence (philosophie et rhétorique antiques)*, ed. C. Lévy and L. Pernot, 249–64. Paris.

Dubin, M. 1997. *Eyewitness Travel Guides: Greece, Athens, and the Mainland*. New York.

Dubois, P. 1981. "Le voyage et le livre." In *Arts et légendes d'espaces: Figures du voyage et rhétoriques du monde*, ed. C. Jacob and F. Lestringant, 149–201. Paris.

Ducat, J. 1974. "Le mépris des hilotes." *Annales: Économie, sociétés, civilisations* 29: 1451–64.

———. 1978. "Aspects de l'hilotisme." *Ancient Society* 9: 5–46.

———. 1990. *Les hilotes* (*BCH* Supplément 20). Athens.

Duncan, J., and D. Gregory, eds. 1999. *Writes of Passage: Reading Travel Writing*. London.

Dürrbach, F., ed. 1923–37. *Inscriptions de Délos*. Paris.

Durrell, L. 1980. *Collected Poems, 1931–1974*. Ed. J. A. Brigham. New York.

Dyer, T. 1873. *Ancient Athens: Its History, Topography and Remains*. London.

Ebeling, H. L. 1913. "Pausanias as an historian." *Classical Weekly* 7: 138–41, 146–60.

Eck, D. L. 1985. *Darśan: Seeing the Divine in India*. 2d ed. Chambersburg, Pa.

Eco, U. 1985. "A portrait of Pliny the Elder as a Young Pliny: How to build fame." In *On Signs*, ed. M. Blonsky, 289–302. Baltimore.

Edwards, C. M. 1990. "Tyche at Corinth." *Hesperia* 59: 529–42.

Ehrensperger-Katz, I. 1969. "Les représentations de villes fortifiées dans l'art paléochré-tien et leurs dérivées byzantines." *Cahiers archéologiques* 19: 1–27.

Eisner, R. 1991. *Travelers to an Antique Land: The History and Literature of Travel to Greece*. Ann Arbor.

Eliot, T. S. 1950. "Tradition and the individual talent." In *Selected Essays*, by T. S. Eliot. New York.

Ellingham, M., M. Dubin, N. Jansz, and J. Fisher. 1992. *The Real Guide: Greece*. New York.

Elsner, J. R. 1992. "Pausanias: A Greek pilgrim in the Roman world." *Past and Present* 135: 3–29.

———. 1994. "From the Pyramids to Pausanias and Piglet: Monuments, travel and writing." In *Art and Text in Ancient Greek Culture*, ed. S. Goldhill and R. Osborne, 224–54. Cambridge and New York.

———. 1995. *Art and the Roman Viewer: The Transformation of Art from the Pagan World to Christianity*. Cambridge and New York.

———. 1996. "Image and ritual: Reflections on the religious appreciation of Classical art." *CQ* 46: 515–31.

———. 1997. "Hagiographic geography: Travel and allegory in the *Life of Apollonius of Tyana*." *JHS* 117: 22–37.

———. 1998. *Imperial Rome and Christian Triumph: The Art of the Roman Empire, A.D. 100–450*. Oxford.

———. 2000. "Between mimesis and divine power: Visuality in the Graeco-Roman world." In *Visuality before and beyond the Renaissance*, ed. R. Nelson, 45–69. Cambridge.

———. Forthcoming. "Describing self in the language of Other: Pseudo(?)-Lucian at the Temple of Hire." In *Being Greek under Rome: Cultural Identity in the Second Sophistic*, ed. S. Goldhill. Cambridge.

Elsner, J. R., and J.-P. Rubiés, eds. 1999. *Voyages and Visions: Towards a Cultural History of Travel*. London.

Engel, A. J. 1983. *From Clergyman to Don: The Rise of the Academic Profession in Nineteenth-Century Oxford*. Oxford.

Erbse, H. 1995. *Theosophorum Graecorum Fragmenta* (Bibliotheca Scriptorum Grae-carum et Romanorum Teubneriana). 2d ed. Stuttgart.

Etienne, R. 1992. "Autels et sacrifices." *Entretiens Hardt* 37: 291–319.

Ewald, B. C. 1999. "KAKOMOUSIA: La Virtù di Ulisse e il potere della musica." In

Im Spiegel des Mythos: Bilderwelt und Lebenswelt (Palilia 6), ed. F. de Angelis and S. Muth, 143–54. Wiesbaden.

Fantham, E. 1997. "Images of the city." In *The Roman Cultural Revolution*, ed. T. Habinek and A. Schiesaro, 122–35. Cambridge and New York.

Farnell, L. R. 1882, 1883, 1885. "The Pergamene Frieze: Its relation to literature and tradition, Parts I–III." *JHS* 3: 301–338; 4: 122–35; 6: 102–142.

———. 1886a. "On some works of the school of Scopas." *JHS* 7: 114–25.

———. 1886b. "The works of Pergamon and their influence." *JHS* 7: 251–74.

———. 1888a. "A misinterpreted passage in Pausanias." *CR* 2: 325.

———. 1888b. Review of *Ausführliches Lexicon der griechischen und römischen Mythologie*. Herausgegeben von W. H. Roscher. Parts 1–12 (A–Hera), each part 2 mks. *CR* 2: 133–38, 164–67.

———. 1888c. "Some museums of northern Europe." *JHS* 9: 31–46.

———. 1890a. "Pausanias V. 11, 1." *CR* 4: 68–69.

———. 1890b. "Various works in the Pergamene style." *JHS* 11: 181–209.

———. 1891. *An Englishman's Adventures on German Rivers*. Berlin.

———. 1896–1909. *Cults of the Greek States*. 5 vols. Oxford and New York. Reprinted New Rochelle, N.Y., 1977.

———. 1903–1904a. "Press. Sacrificial communion in Greek literature." *Hibbert Journal* 2: 306–22.

———. 1903–1904b. Review of *Prolegomena to the Study of Greek Religion*, by J. E. Harrison (Cambridge 1903). *Hibbert Journal* 2: 821–27.

———. 1904. "Sociological hypotheses concerning the position of women in ancient religion." *Archiv für Religionswissenschaft* 7: 70–94.

———. 1905. *The Evolution of Religion: An Anthropological Study*. London.

———. 1905–1906. Review of *Lectures on the Early History of the Kingship*, by J. G. Frazer (London 1905). *Hibbert Journal* 4: 928–32.

———. 1906–1907. Review of *Adonis, Attis, and Osiris: Studies in the History of Oriental Religions*, by J. G. Frazer (London 1906). *Hibbert Journal* 5: 687–90.

———. 1909. "Reminiscences." *Stapeldon Magazine* II.12: 181–89.

———. 1910–11. "The moral service of the intellect." *Hibbert Journal* 9: 513–28.

———. 1911. *Greece and Babylon: A Comparative Sketch of Mesopotamian, Anatolian and Hellenic Religions* (Wilde Lectures). Edinburgh.

———. 1912a. *The Higher Aspects of Greek Religion* (Hibbert Lectures). London. Reprinted Chicago, 1977.

———. 1912b. "Reminiscences. No. II: *Ecce iterum Crispinus*." *Stapeldon Magazine* III.17: 143–53.

———. 1912–13. Review of *Themis: a Study of the Social Origins of Greek Religion*, by J. E. Harrison (Cambridge 1912). *Hibbert Journal* 11: 453–58.

———. 1913–14. "The presence of savage elements in the religion of cultured races: An application of the methods of anthropology to early Mediterranean civilization." *Hibbert Journal* 12: 804–818.

———. 1914a. *Bibliography of the Fellows and Tutors of Exeter College, Oxford, in Recent Times*. Privately printed, May 1914.

———. 1914b. "Exeter College in the past." *Stapeldon Magazine* IV.21: 51–58.

———. 1914c. "Sexcentenary celebration of the College." *Stapeldon Magazine* IV.22: 108–109.

———. 1915. *A message from Senlac, 1066*. Obit Lt. Cuthbert Francis Balleine of RAMC. *Stapeldon Magazine* IV. 23: 140–42.

————. 1919. "The value and the methods of mythologic study." *Proceedings of the British Academy* 9: 1–15.

————. 1921a. *Greek Hero Cults and Ideas of Immortality* (Gifford Lectures). Oxford.

————. 1921b "The present and the future of Hellenism." In *Second Congress of the Universities of the Empire, 1921, Report of Proceedings*, 7–15, 235, 327–29, 380–82, 428. London.

————. 1924. *Attributes of God* (Gifford Lectures). Oxford.

————. 1927 "The marigold of Morocco (Rabat-Casablanca), Feb. 1927." *Stapeldon Magazine* VII.40: 122.

————. 1928. "A message from the Rector." *Stapeldon Magazine* VII.42: 208–210.

————. 1930–32. *A Critical Commentary on the Works of Pindar.* 3 vols. London.

————. 1931. "Obit William Walrond Jackson." *Stapeldon Magazine* VIII.49: 193.

————. 1934. *An Oxonian Looks Back.* London.

Farrer, R. R. 1882. *A Tour in Greece, 1880.* London.

Faustoferri, A. 1996. *Il trono di Amyklai e Sparta Bathykles al servizio del potere* (Aucnus 2). Naples.

Ferguson, W. S. 1911. *Hellenistic Athens.* London.

Festugière, A. J. 1970. "Les proscynèmes de Philae." *REG* 83: 175–97.

Filippidis, D., and G. Konstantas. 1791. *Geografia neoteriki peri tis Elladhos.* Athens. Reprinted 1970.

Fitton, J. L. 1996. *The Discovery of the Bronze Age.* Cambridge, Mass.

Fittschen, K. 1969. *Untersuchungen zum Beginn der Sagendarstellungen bei den Griechen.* Berlin.

Fitzmyer, J. A., and S. A. Kaufman, eds. 1992–. *An Aramaic Bibliography.* Baltimore.

Foccardi, D. 1983. "Silenzio religioso e reticenze in Pausania." In *Le regioni del silenzio: Studi sui disagi della communicazione*, ed. M. G. Ciani, 79–120. Padua.

Ford, A. 1992. *Homer: The Poetry of the Past.* Ithaca, N.Y.

Förtsch, R. 1993. *Archäologischer Kommentar zu den Villenbriefen des jüngeren Plinius.* Mainz.

Fotiadis, M. 1992. Units of data as deployment of disciplinary codes." In *Representations in Archaeology*, ed. J.-C. Gardin and C. S. Peebles, 132–48. Bloomington.

————. 1995. "Modernity and the past-still-present: Politics of time in the birth of regional archaeological projects in Greece." *AJA* 99: 59–78.

Fowler, B. H. 1989. *The Hellenistic Aesthetic.* Madison.

Fowler, R. L. 1991. "Gilbert Murray: Four (or five) stages of Greek religion." In Calder 1991a: 79–96.

Fowler, W. W. 1903. *An Oxford Correspondence.* Oxford.

Frankfort, H. 1970. *The Art and Architecture of the Ancient Orient.* 4th rev. impression. Harmondsworth.

Frankfurter, D. 1998. *Religion in Roman Egypt: Assimilation and Resistance.* Princeton.

Fraser, R. 1990. *The Making of the Golden Bough: The Origins and Growth of an Argument.* Basingstoke.

Frazer, J. G. 1888a–d. "Ares in the brazen pot. Coins attached to the face. Hide-measured lands. The bedstead of the Flamen Dialis." *CR* 2: 222, 261, 322 *bis*.

————. 1890. *The Golden Bough: A Study in Comparative Religion.* In vols. 2d ed., 1900; 3d ed., 1906–1915. London.

————. 1898. *Pausanias's "Description of Greece."* 6 vols. London. Reprinted New York, 1965.

————. 1900. *Pausanias and Other Greek Sketches.* London.

————. 1913. *Pausanias's "Description of Greece."* 2d ed. London.

————. 1919. *Studies in Greek Scenery, Legend and History.* London.

Frazer, J. G., and A. W. Van Buren. 1930. *Graecia Antiqua: Maps and Plans to Illustrate Pausanias' Description of Greece.* London.

Friedländer, L. 1908–1913. *Roman Life and Manners under the Early Roman Empire.* London and New York.

Froning, H. 1988. "Anfänge der kontinuierenden Bilderzählung in der griechischen Kunst." *JdI* 103: 169–99.

————. 1992. "La forma rappresentativa ciclica nell'arte classica." In *Coloquio sobre Teseo y la copa de Aison* (Anejos de archivo español de Arqueología 12), ed. R. Olmos, 131–54. Madrid.

Frow, J. 1991. "Tourism and the semiotics of nostalgia." *October* 57 (Summer): 123–51.

Fussell, P. 1980. *Abroad: British Literary Traveling between the Wars.* Oxford.

Gallavotti, C. 1978. "Le copie di Pausania e gli originali di alcune iscrizioni di Olimpia." *Bollettino del Comitato per la Preparazione dell'Edizione Nazionale dei Classici Greci e Latini* (*Accademia dei Lincei*) n.s. 26: 3–27.

Gamble, H. Y. 1995. *Books and Readers in the Early Church.* New Haven and London.

Gardiner, E. N. 1925. *Olympia: Its History and Remains.* Oxford.

Gardner, E. A. 1889. "Archaeology in Greece, 1888–89." *JHS* 10: 254–80.

————. 1902. *Ancient Athens.* London.

————. 1909–1910. Review of *The Cults of the Greek States,* vol. 5, by L. R. Farnell (Oxford 1909). *Hibbert Journal* 8: 927–30.

Gardner, P. 1887. *Faith and Conduct.* London.

————. 1888. "Countries and cities in ancient art." *JHS* 9: 47–81.

———— [writing anonymously]. 1890. Review of *Mythology and Monuments of Ancient Athens, being a translation of a portion of the "Attica" of Pausanias by M. de G. Verrall, with introductory essay and archaeological commentary by J. E. Harrison* (London and New York, 1890). *Quarterly Review* 171: 122–49.

————. 1898. "Frazer's *Pausanias's Description of Greece.*" *CR* 12:465–69.

————. 1899. *Exploratio Evangelica: A Brief Examination of the Basis and Origins of Christian Belief.* London.

————. 1903. *Oxford at the Crossroads.* London.

————. 1933. *Autobiographica.* Oxford.

Gardner, P., and F. Imhoof-Blumer. 1885–87. "Numismatic commentary on Pausanias." *JHS* 6: 50–101; 7: 57–113; 8: 6–63.

Gardner, P., and J. L. Myres. 1901. *Classical Archaeology in Schools.* Oxford.

Garland, R. 1992. *Introducing New Gods: The Politics of Athenian Religion.* Ithaca, N.Y.

Gauer, W. 1977. *Untersuchungen zur Trajanssäule.* Berlin.

Gell, W. 1817. *The Itinerary of Greece.* London.

Geominy, W. 1982. "Die Florentiner Niobiden. Dissertation," Rheinische Friedrich-Wilhelms Universität zu Bonn. Rev. ed. published Bonn, 1984.

Geyer, A. 1989. *Die Genese narrativer Buchillustration: Der Miniaturenzyklus zur Aeneis im Vergilius Vaticanus.* Frankfurt.

Ghali-Kahil, L. B. 1955. *Les enlèvements et le retour d'Hélène dans les textes et les documents figurés.* Paris.

Giovannini, A. 1969. *Étude historique sur les origines du catalogue des vaisseaux.* Bern.

Glazebrook, P. 1984. *Journey to Kars: A Modern Traveller in the Ottoman Lands.* New York.

Gleason, M. 1995. *Making Men: Sophists and Self-Presentation in Ancient Rome*. Princeton.

Goff, B. 1988. "Euripides' *Ion* 1132–65: The tent." *PCPS* 34: 42–54.

Goldhill, S. D. 1991. *The Poet's Voice: Essays on Poetics and Greek Literature*. Cambridge.

———. Forthcoming. "The erotic eye: Visual stimulation and cultural conflict." In *Being Greek under Rome: Cultural Identity in the Second Sophistic*, ed. S. D. Goldhill. Cambridge.

Goldmann, S. 1991. "Topoi des Gedenkens: Pausanias' Reise durch die griechische Gedächtnislandschaft." In *Gedächtniskunst: Studien zur Mnemotechnik*, ed. A. Haverkamp and R. Lachmann, 145–63. Frankfurt.

Goodwin, W. W. 1889. *Syntax of the Moods and Tenses of the Greek Verb*. London. Reprinted 1965.

Goold, G. P. 1961. "A Greek professorial circle at Rome." *TAPA* 92: 168–92.

Graves, A. 1905. *The Royal Academy of Arts: A Complete Dictionary of Contributors and Their Work from Its Foundation in 1769 to 1904*. Vol. 2. London. Reprinted 1970.

Gray, V. J. 1989. *The Character of Xenophon's "Hellenica."* London.

Greenblatt, S. J. 1990. *Learning to Curse: Essays in Early Modern Culture*. London.

Gregory, E. 1999. *H. D. and Hellenism: Classic Lines*. Cambridge.

Griffin, J. 1986. *Latin Poets and Roman Life*. Chapel Hill, N.C.

Grimal, P. 1984. *Les jardins romains*. 3d ed. Paris.

Gritsopoulos, T. A. 1971. "Statistikai eidiseis peri Peloponnisou." *Peloponnisiaka* 8: 411–59.

Grundy, G. B. 1945. *Forty-five Years at Oxford: An Unconventional Autobiography*. London.

Guarducci, M., ed. 1935–50. *Inscriptiones Creticae*. 4 vols. Rome.

Guillory, J. 1993. *Cultural Capital: The Problem of Literary Canon Formation*. Chicago.

Gurlitt, W. 1890. *Über Pausanias Untersuchungen*. Graz.

Habicht, C. 1985. *Pausanias' Guide to Ancient Greece* (Sather Classical Lectures 50). Berkeley.

———. 1997. *Athens from Alexander to Antony*. Trans. D. L. Schneider. Cambridge, Mass., and London.

———. 1998. *Pausanias' Guide to Ancient Greece* (Sather Classical Lectures 50). Rev. ed. with new preface. Berkeley.

Halfmann, H. 1979. *Die Senatoren aus dem östlichen Teil des Imperium Romanum bis zum Ende des 2.Jh.n.Chr.* (Hypomnemata 58). Göttingen.

———. 1986. *Itinera Principum: Geschichte und Typologie der Kaiserreisen im Römischen Reich*. Wiesbaden.

Hall, J. M. 1997. *Ethnic Identity in Greek Antiquity*. Cambridge.

Hanfmann, G. M. A. 1957. "Narration in Greek art." *AJA* 61: 71–78.

Hansen, M. H., ed. 1995. *Sources for the Ancient Greek City-State* (Acts of the Copenhagen Polis Centre 2). Copenhagen.

———. 1997. *The Polis as an Urban Centre and as a Political Community* (Acts of the Copenhagen Polis Centre 4). Copenhagen.

Hansen, M. H., and K. A. Raaflaub, eds. 1995. *Studies in the Ancient Greek Polis* (Historia Einzelschrift 95). Stuttgart.

Harbsmeier, M. 1987. "Elementary structures of Otherness." In *Voyager à la Renaissance*, ed. J. Céard and J. C. Margolin, 337–55. Paris.

Hardie, P. R. 1985. "Imago Mundi: Cosmological and ideological aspects of the Shield of Achilles." *JHS* 105: 11–31.

Harris, J. 1983. "Wizard Genius." *AA Files: Annals of the Architectural Association School of Architecture* 4: 91–94.

Harrison, A., and N. Spencer. 1998. "After the palace: the early 'history' of Messenia." In *Sandy Pylos: An Archaeological History from Nestor to Navarino*, ed. J. L. Davis, 147–62. Austin.

Harrison, E. B. 1981. "Motifs of the city-siege on the Shield of Athena Parthenos." *AJA* 85: 281–317.

Harrison, J. E. 1883. "Monuments relating to the Odyssey." *JHS* 4: 248–65.

———. 1885. "Odysseus and the Sirens. Dionysiac boat-races. A cylix by Nikosthenes." *JHS* 6: 19–29.

———. 1886. "The judgement of Paris: Two unpublished vases in the Graeco-Etruscan Museum at Florence." *JHS* 7: 196–219.

———. 1887. "Vases representing the Judgement of Paris. Itys and Aedon: A Panaitios cylix." *JHS* 8: 268, 439–45.

———. 1888a. "Archaeology in Greece, 1887–1888." *JHS* 9: 118–33.

———. 1888b. "Some fragments of a vase, presumably by Euphronios." *JHS* 9: 143–46.

———. 1889a. "The central slab of the E. Parthenon frieze." *CR* 3: 378.

———. 1889b. "The festival of the Aiora." *CR* 3: 378–79.

———. 1889c. "On the meaning of the term Arrephori." *CR* 3: 187.

———. 1903. *Prolegomena to the Study of Greek Religion*. Cambridge.

———. 1906. *Primitive Athens as Described by Thucydides*. Cambridge.

———. 1912. *Themis: A Study of the Social Origins of Greek Religion*. Cambridge.

———. 1917. [Correspondence.] *CR* 31: 63.

———. 1925. *Reminiscences of a Student's Life*. London.

———. 1928. *Themis: A Study of the Social Origins of Greek Religion*. 2d ed. Cambridge.

Harrison, J. E., and M. de G. Verrall. 1890. *Mythology and Monuments of Ancient Athens, being a translation of a portion of the "Attica" of Pausanias by M. de G. Verrall, with introductory essay and archaeological commentary by J. E. Harrison*. London and New York.

Hartog, F. 1988. *The Mirror of Herodotus: The Representation of the Other in the Writing of History*. Berkeley and Los Angeles.

———. 1996. *Mémoire d'Ulysse: Récits sur la frontière en Grèce ancienne*. Paris.

Hartog, F., and M. Casevitz. 1999. *L'histoire d'Homère à Augustin: Préfaces d'historiens et textes sur l'histoire*. Paris.

Hausenstein, W. 1934. *Das Land der Griechen*. Frankfurt.

Hausmann, U. 1986. "Zu neuen Odyssee- und Odysseus-Bildern auf hellenistischen Reliefbechern." In *Studien zur Mythologie und Vasenmalerei* (Festschrift Konrad Schauenburg), ed. E. Böhr and W. Martini, 197–202. Mainz.

Heer, J. 1979. *La personalité de Pausanias*. Paris.

Heil, M. 1998. "Pausanias." In *Prosopographia Imperii Romani* vol. 6, ed. L. Petersen, K. Wachtel, M. Heil, K.-P. Johne, and L. Vidmann, 64–65. Berlin and New York.

Henderson, H. 1992. "The travel writer and the text: 'My giant goes with me wherever I go.' " In *Temperamental Journeys: Essays on the Modern Literature of Travel*, ed. M. Kowalewski, 230–48. Athens, Ga. Reprinted, with modifications, from *New Orleans Review* 18.2 (1991): 30–40.

Henderson, J. 1998. *Juvenal's Mayor: The Professor Who Lived on 2^D. a Day (PCPS Supplement* 20). Cambridge.

Heres, H. 1997. "The myth of Telephos in Pergamon." In Dreyfus and Schraudolph 1997, vol. 2: 83–108.

Herrmann, H.-V. 1972. *Olympia: Heiligtum und Weltkampfstatt.* Munich.

———. 1988. "Die Siegerstatuen von Olympia." *Nikephoros* 1: 119–83.

Hertz, N. 1983. "A reading of Longinus." *Critical Inquiry* 9: 579–610.

Hettner, H. 1854. *Athens and the Peloponnese with Sketches of Northern Greece.* Edinburgh.

Heyck, T. W. 1982. *The Transformation of Intellectual Life in Victorian England.* London.

Higbie, C. 1997. "The bones of a hero, the ashes of a politician: Athens, Salamis, and the usable past." *Classical Antiquity* 16: 278–307.

Hill, I. T. 1953. *The Ancient City of Athens: Its Topography and Monuments.* London.

Hiller von Gaertringen, F. F., and H. Lattermann. 1911. *Hira und Andania* (Einundsiegzigstes Programm zum Winckelmannsfeste der Archaeologischen Gesellschaft zu Berlin). Berlin.

Hinchliff, P. 1987. *Benjamin Jowett and the Christian Religion.* Oxford.

Hinks, R. R. 1933. *Catalogue of the Greek, Etruscan, and Roman Paintings and Mosaics in the British Museum.* London.

Hitzig, H., and H. Blümner. 1896–1910. *Pausaniae Graeciae Descriptio.* 3 vols. Leipzig.

Hoberman, R. 1997. *Gendering Classicism: The Ancient World in Twentieth-Century Women's Historical Fiction.* New York.

Hodkinson, S. 1992. "Sharecropping and Sparta's economic exploitation of the helots." In Sanders 1992: 123–34.

Hoffmannstahl, H. von. 1928. "Vermächtnis der Antike: Rede anlässlich eines Festes von Freunden des humanistischen Gymnasiums gehalten." *Die Antike* 4.2: 99–102.

Holland, H. 1815. *Travels in the Ionian Isles, Albania, Thessaly, Macedonia, etc. during the Years 1812 and 1813.* London.

———. 1872. *Recollections of a Past Life.* London.

Holland, P., and G. Huggan. 1998. *Tourists with Typewriters: Critical Reflections on Contemporary Travel Writing.* Ann Arbor.

Holliday, P. J. 1997. "Roman triumphal painting: its function, development, and reception." *Art Bulletin* 79: 130–47.

Hollis, A. S. 1992. "Attica in Hellenistic Poetry." *ZPE* 93: 1–15.

Hollis, C. 1976. *Oxford in the Twenties: Recollections of Five Friends.* London.

Holum, K. G. 1990. "Hadrian and St. Helena: Imperial travel and the origin of Christian Holy-Land pilgrimage." In Ousterhout 1990: 66–81.

Hönle, A. 1968. *Olympia in der politik der griechischen Staatenwelt.* Tübingen.

Hooker, J. T. 1980. *The Ancient Spartans.* London.

Hope Simpson, R. 1966. "The seven cities offered by Agamemnon to Achilles." *BSA* 61: 113–31.

Hornblower, S. 1987. *Thucydides.* Baltimore.

———, ed. 1994. *Greek Historiography,* Oxford.

Horsfall, N. 1983. "The origins of the illustrated book." *Aegyptus* 63: 199–216.

How, A. B. 1928. *Register of Exeter College Oxford, 1891–1921.* Oxford.

Hughes, T. S. 1820. *Travels in Sicily, Greece and Albania.* London.

Humphreys, S. C. 1981. "Death and time." In *Mortality and Immortality: The Anthropology and Archaeology of Death,* ed. S. C. Humphreys and H. King, 261–83. London.

———. 1995. "Fragments, fetishes, and philosophies: towards a history of Greek historiography after Thucydides." In *Collecting Fragments/Fragmente sammeln*, ed. G. W. Most, 207–24. Göttingen.

Hunt, E. D. 1984. "Travel, tourism and piety in the Roman Empire." *EchCl* 28: 391–417.

Hunter, R. 1996. *Theocritus and the Archaeology of Greek Poetry*. Cambridge and New York.

———. 1997. "(B)ionic Man: Callimachus' iambic program." *PCPS* 43: 41–51.

Hutchinson, G. O. 1988. *Hellenistic Poetry*. Oxford.

Hutton, E. 1928. *A Glimpse of Greece*. London.

Hyde, W. W. 1921. *Olympic Victor Monuments*. Washington, D.C.

Ihnken, T. 1978. *Die Inschriften von Magnesia am Sipylos* (Inschriften der griechischen Städter Kleinasiens 8). Bonn.

Imhoof-Blumer, F., and P. Gardner. 1887. *A Numismatic Commentary on Pausanias*. London. Originally published in *JHS* 6 (1885): 50–101; 7 (1886): 57–113; 8 (1887): 6–63.

Immerwahr, W. 1889. *Die Lakonika des Pausanias auf ihre Quellen untersucht*. Berlin.

Ingold, T. 1993. "The temporality of the landscape." *World Archaeology* 25: 152–74.

Innes, D. C. 1979. "Gigantomachy and natural philosophy." *CQ* 29: 165–71.

———. 1995. "Longinus: structure and unity." In *Greek Literary Theory after Aristotle: A Collection of Papers in Honour of D. M. Schenkeveld*, ed. J. G. J. Abbenes, S. R. Slings, and I. Sluiter, 111–24. Amsterdam.

Innes, D. C., H. Hine, and C. Pelling, eds. 1995. *Ethics and Rhetoric: Classical Essays for Donald Russell on His Seventy-fifth Birthday*. Oxford.

Islam, S. M. 1996. *The Ethics of Travel: From Marco Polo to Kafka*. London.

Jacob, C. 1980a. "The Greek traveler's areas of knowledge: Myths and other discourses in Pausanias' *Description of Greece*." *Yale French Studies* 59: 65–85.

———. 1980b. "Paysages hantés et jardins marveilleux: La Grèce imaginaire de Pausanias." *L'ethnographie* 76: 35–67.

———. 1991. *Géographie et ethnographie en Grèce ancienne*. Paris.

———. 1993. "Paysage et bois sacré: ἄλσος dans la *Périégèse de la Grèce* de Pausanias." In *Les bois sacrés* (Collection du Centre J. Bérard 10), 31–44. Naples.

Jacoby, F. 1921. "Kleon (7)." *RE* 21: 718.

Jacquemin, A. 1991a. "Les curiosités naturelles chez Pausanias." *Ktema* 16: 123–30.

———. 1991b. "Delphes au IIᵉ siècle après J.-C.: Un lieu de la mémoire Grecque." In Ἑλληνισμός: *Quelques jalons pour une histoire de l'identité grecque, Actes du Colloque de Strasburg, 25–27 octobre 1989*, ed. S. Saïd, 217–31. Leiden.

———. 1996. "Les curiosités naturelles chez Pausanias." In *Nature et paysage dans la pensée et l'environnement des civilisations antiques. (Actes du Colloque de Strasbourg, 11–12 juin 1992)*, ed. G. Siebert, 121–28. Paris.

Jaki, S. L. 1986. *Lord Gifford and His Lectures: A Centenary Retrospect*. Macon, Ga.

James, M. R. 1917. "Some remarks on 'The Head of John Baptist.'" *CR* 31: 1–4.

Jameson, F. 1981. *The Political Unconscious: Narrative as a Socially Symbolic Act*. Ithaca, N.Y.

Jeffery, L. H. 1990. *The Local Scripts of Archaic Greece*. Rev. ed. by A. W. Johnston. Oxford.

Jenkins, I. 1992. "'Athens Rising near the Pole': London, Athens and the idea of freedom." In *London: World City, 1800–1840*, ed. C. Fox, 143–54. New Haven.

Jenkins, R. 1961. *The Dilessi Murders*. London.

Jenkyns, R. 1997. "The beginning of Greats, 1800–1872: I. Classical studies." In *The History of the University of Oxford*, vol. 6, *The Nineteenth Century*, pt. I, ed. M. G. Brock and M. C. Curthoys, 513–20. Oxford.

Joanne, A., and E. Isambert. 1861. *Itinéraire descriptif, historique et archéologique de l'Orient*. Paris.

Johansen, K. F. 1934. *Iliaden i tidlig graesk Kunst*. Copenhagen.

———. 1967. *The Iliad in Early Greek Art*. Copenhagen.

Johnston, A. E. M. 1967. "The earliest preserved Greek map: A new Ionian coin type." *JHS* 87: 86–94.

Jones, C. P. 1984. "Tarsos in the *Amores* ascribed to Lucian." *GRBS* 25: 177–81.

———. 1996. "The Panhellenion." *Chiron* 26: 29–56.

Jost, M. 1973. "Pausanias en Mégalopolitide." *REA* 75: 241–67.

Judeich, W. 1931. *Topographie von Athen*. 2d ed. Munich.

Kakavoyannis, E. C. 1980. "Ὁμηρικοὶ Σκύφοι' Φερῶν Θεσσαλίας." *Archaiologika Analekta ex Athinon* 13: 262–84.

Kalinka, E., and R. Herberdey. 1901–. *Tituli Asiae Minoris*. Vienna.

Kalkmann, A. 1886. *Pausanias der Perieget*. Berlin.

Kaltsas, N. 1985. "H archaïke oikia sto Kopanaki tes Messenias." *Archaiologike Ephemeris* 1983: 207–37.

Kant, I. 1987. *Critique of Judgment*. Trans. W. S. Pluhar. Indianapolis.

Kaplan, C. 1996. *Questions of Travel: Postmodern Discourses of Displacement*. Durham, N.C., and London.

Karouzou, S. 1970. "Stamnos de Polygnotos au Musée National d'Athènes." *RA*, 229–52.

Kaster, R. A. 1988. *Guardians of Language: The Grammarian and Society in Late Antiquity*. Berkeley.

Kegel-Brinkgreve, E. 1990. *The Echoing Woods: Bucolic and Pastoral from Theocritus to Wordsworth*. Amsterdam.

Kennell, N. 1997. Review of K. Arafat, *Pausanias' Greece: Ancient Artists and Roman Rulers* (Cambridge, 1996), and J. Bingen, ed., *Pausanias historien* (Fondation Hardt, Entretiens sur l'antiquité classique 41) (Geneva 1996). *Phoenix* 51: 229–33.

Kern, O., ed. 1900. *Die Inschriften von Magnesia am Maeander*. Berlin.

Kiechle, F. 1959. *Messenische Studien: Untersuchungen zur Geschichte der Messenischen Kriege und der Auswanderung der Messenier*. Kallmünz.

King, H. 1999. "Chronic pain and the creation of narrative." In *Constructions of the Classical Body*, ed. J. I. Porter, 269–86. Ann Arbor.

Kinglake, A. W. 1844. *Eothen, or Traces of Travel Brought Home from the East*. Reprinted Marlboro, Vt., 1992.

Klein, W. 1885. *Zur Kypsele der Kypseliden*. Vienna. Originally published in *Sitzungsberichte der phil.-hist. Classe der Kaiserlichen Akademie der Wissenschaften* 108 (1884) 51–83.

Kleiner, D. E. E. 1992. *Roman Sculpture*. New Haven and London.

Koeppel, G. M. 1980. "A military *Itinerarium* on the Column of Trajan: Scene L." *RM* 87: 301–306.

Koumanoudis, S. A. 1884. "Σκύφοι Βοιωτικοὶ Δύο." *Archaiologike Ephemeris* 1884: 60–66.

Kreilinger, U. 1997. "Τὰ ἀξιολογώτατα τοῦ Παυσανίου: Die Kunstauswahlkriterien des Pausanias." *Hermes* 125: 470–91.

Kroll, W. 1927. "Lykeas 2." *RE* 13: 2266.

———. 1940. "Rhetorik." *RE* Suppl. 7:1039–1138.

Kubler, G. 1962. *The Shape of Time: Remarks on the History of Things.* New Haven and London.

———. 1985. "*The Shape of Time* revisited." In *Studies in Ancient American and European Art: The Collected Essays of George Kubler,* ed. T. F. Reese, 413–30. New Haven.

Kunze, E. 1956. "Inschriften." In V. *Olympia-Bericht über die Ausgrabungen in Olympia,* 149–75. Berlin.

Lacroix, L. 1974. "Héraclès, héros voyageur et civilisateur." *Bulletin de l'Académie Royale de Belgique (Classe des Lettres)* 60 (5e série): 34–59.

———. 1988. "Pausanias, le coffre de Kypsélos et le problème de l'exégèse mythologique." *RA* 1988: 243–61.

———. 1992. "A propos des offrandes à Apollon de Delphes et du témoinage de Pausanias: Du réel à l'impression." *BCH* 116: 157–76.

Lafond, Y. 1996. "Pausanias et l'histoire du Péloponnèse depuis la conquête romaine." In Bingen 1996: 167–98.

Lane Fox, R. 1986. *Pagans and Christians.* New York and San Francisco.

Larson, J. 1995. *Greek Heroine Cults.* Madison.

Lawrence, A. W. 1979. *Greek Aims in Fortification.* Oxford.

Lazenby, J. F., and R. Hope Simpson. 1972. "Greco-Roman times: Literary tradition and topographical commentary." In McDonald and Rapp 1972: 81–99.

Leach, E. W. 1982. "Patrons, painters, and patterns: The anonymity of Romano-Campanian painting and the transition from the Second to the Third Style." In *Literary and Artistic Patronage in Ancient Rome,* ed. B. K. Gold, 135–73. Austin.

———. 1988. *The Rhetoric of Space: Literary and Artistic Representations of Landscape in Republican and Augustan Rome.* Princeton.

Leake, J. M. n.d. *Memoir.* Microfilm, Hertfordshire County Record Office, Hertford.

Leake, W. M. 1814. *Researches on Greece.* London.

———. 1821. *The Topography of Athens with some remarks upon its Antiquities.* London.

———. 1826. *Historical Outline of the Greek Revolution.* London. First published anonymously in 1825.

———. 1830. *Travels in the Morea.* 3 vols. London.

———. 1835. *Travels in Northern Greece.* 4 vols. London.

———. 1839. "On some disputed positions in the topography of Athens." *Transactions of the Royal Society of Literature* 3: 183–237.

———. 1841. *The Topography of Athens with some remarks on its Antiquities.* 2d ed. London.

———. 1846. *Peloponnesiaca: A Supplement to "Travels in the Morea."* London.

Leed, E. 1991. *The Mind of the Traveler: From Gilgamesh to Global Tourism.* New York.

Leontis, A. 1995. *Topographies of Hellenism: Mapping the Homeland.* Ithaca, N.Y.

Leppert, M. 1974. "23 Kaiservillen. Vorarbeiten zur Archäologie und Kulturgeschichte der Villegiatur der hohen Kaiserzeit." Diss., Universität Freiburg.

Levi, A., and M. Levi. 1967. *Itineraria picta: Contributo allo studio della Tabula Peutingeriana.* Rome.

Levi, D. 1961–62. "Enneakrounos." *Annuario della Scuola Archeologica di Atene e delle Missioni Italiane in Oriente* n.s. 23–24: 149–71.

Levi, P., trans. 1971. *Pausanias: "Guide to Greece."* 2 vols. Harmondsworth.

Lévi-Strauss, C. 1955. *Tristes Tropiques.* Paris. Trans. J. Weightman and D. Weightman (New York, 1997).

Ling, R. 1977. "Studius and the beginnings of landscape painting." *JRS* 67: 1–16.

————. 1991. *Roman Painting*. Cambridge and New York.

Liritizis, S. 1969. "H arhaia polis tis dytikes Messinias Erana." *Platon* 21: 152–80.

Lloyd-Jones, H., and P. Parsons, eds. 1983. *Supplementum Hellenisticum, Texte und Kommentare*. Vol. 11. Berlin and New York.

Loeschcke, G. 1880. *Archäologische Miscellen*. Dorpat.

————. 1894. "Korinthische Vase mit der Rückführung des Hephaistos." *AM* 19: 510–25.

Lowe, L. 1991. *Critical Terrains: French and British Orientalism*. Ithaca, N.Y.

Lowenstam, S. 1993. "The arming of Achilleus on early Greek vases." *Classical Antiquity* 12: 199–223.

————. 1995. "The sources of the Odyssey landscapes." *EchCl* 39 (n.s. 14): 193–226.

Lukacher, B. 1983a. "Jupiter Pluvius." *AA Files: Annals of the Architectural Association School of Architecture* 4: 95.

————. 1983b. "Phantasmagoria and emanations: Lighting effects in the architectural fantasies of Joseph Michael Gandy." *AA Files: Annals of the Architectural Association School of Architecture* 4: 40–48.

————. 1987. "John Soane and his draughtsman Joseph Michael Gandy." *Daidalos* 25: 51–64.

Lukermann, F. 1961. "The concept of location in Classical geography." *Annals of the Association of American Geographers* 51: 194–210.

Lukermann, F., and J. Moody. 1978. "Nichoria and vicinity: settlements and circulation." In Rapp and Aschenbrenner 1978: 78–112.

Luraghi, N. 1994. "Pausania e la fondazione di Messene sullo stretto: Note di lettura." *Rivista di filologia e d'istruzione classica* 122: 140–51.

Lyons, P. K., and Z. W. Munson, eds. 1998. *Let's Go: Greece and Turkey*. New York.

Mabbott, J. 1986. *Oxford Memories*. Oxford.

MacCannell, D. 1976. *The Tourist: A New Theory of the Leisure Class*. New York.

MacCridy, T. 1905. "Altertümer von Notion." *Jahreshefte des Österreichischen archäologischen Instituts in Wien* 8: 155–73.

————. 1912. "Antiquités de Notion II." *Jahreshefte der Österreichischen Akademie der Wissenschaft* 15: 36–67.

MacDonald, W., and J. Pinto. 1995. *Hadrian's Villa and Its Legacy*. New Haven and London.

Maddoli, G., and V. Saladino, eds. 1995. *Pausania, Guida della Grecia*. Vol. 5, *L'Elide e Olimpia*. Verona.

Malaise, M. 1987. "Pèlerinages et pèlerins dans l'Égypte ancienne." In Chelini and Branthomme, 1987: 55–82.

Mallwitz, A. 1972. *Olympia und seine Bauten*. Munich.

Marchand, L. A., ed. 1973. *Byron's Letters and Journals*. Vol. 2, *1810–1812*. London.

Marchand, S. L. 1996. *Down from Olympus: Archaeology and Philhellenism in Germany, 1750–1970*. Princeton.

Marcovich, M., ed. 1990. *Cohortatio ad Graecos, De monarchia, Oratio ad Graecos*, by Pseudo-Iustinus (Patristische Texte und Untersuchungen 32). Berlin and New York.

Marcus, M. I. 1987. "Geography as an organizing principle in the imperial art of Shalmaneser III." *Iraq* 49: 77–90.

Marett, R. R. 1928. "L. R. Farnell. Rector 1913–28." *Stapeldon Magazine* VII.42: 205–207.

————. 1934a. "Obit L. R. Farnell." *Stapeldon Magazine* VIII.54: 379–82.

————. 1934b. "Obit L. R. Farnell, 1856–1934." *Proceedings of the British Academy* 20: 285–96.

————. 1941. *A Jerseyman at Oxford*. London.

Marker, S. 1996. "Where the Games began." *New York Times*, 28 April.

Markham, C. R. 1895. *Life of Captain Stephen Martin, 1666–1740* (Navy Records Society 5). London.

Marrou, H. I. 1956. *A History of Education in Antiquity*. Madison.

Marsden, J. H. 1864. *A Brief Memoir of the Life and Writings of the Late Lieutenant Colonel William Martin Leake*. London (privately printed).

Martin, R. 1976. "Bathyclès de Magnésie et le 'trône' d'Apollon à Amyklae." *RA* 1976: 205–18.

Masson, O. 1961. *Les inscriptions chypriotes syllabiques: Recueil critique et commente*. Paris.

Masterman, J. C. 1975. *On the Chariot Wheel: An Autobiography*. Oxford.

Matheson, S. B. 1995. *Polygnotos and Vase Painting in Classical Athens*. Madison.

McDonald, W. A. 1984. "The Minnesota Messenia Survey: A look back." In *Studies Presented to Sterling Dow on His Eightieth Birthday*, 185–91. Durham, N.C.

McDonald, W. A., W. D. E. Coulson, and J. Rosser, eds. 1983. *Excavations in Nichoria in Southwest Greece*. Vol. 3, *Dark Age and Byzantine Occupation*. Minneapolis.

McDonald, W. A., and R. Hope Simpson. 1972. "Archaeological exploration." In McDonald and Rapp 1972: 117–47.

McDonald, W. A., and G. R. Rapp, Jr., eds. 1972. *The Minnesota Messenia Expedition: Reconstructing a Bronze Age Regional Environment*. Minneapolis.

McDonald, W. A., and N. Wilkie, eds. 1992. *Excavations at Nichoria in Southwest Greece*. Vol. 2, *The Bronze Age Occupation*. Minneapolis.

McGuire, R. H., and R. Paynter, eds. 1991. *The Archaeology of Inequality*. Oxford.

Meadows, A. R. 1995. "Pausanias and the historiography of Classical Sparta." *CQ* 45.1: 92–113.

Metzler, D. 1994. "Mural crowns in the ancient Near East and Greece." *YaleBull* 1994: 77–85.

Meyboom, P. G. P. 1978. "Some observations on narration in Greek art." *Mededleelingen van het Nederlands Historisch Instituut te Rome* 40: 55–82.

———. 1995. *The Nile Mosaic of Palestrina: Early Evidence of Egyptian Religion in Italy*. Leiden and New York.

Meyer, E. 1971. *Pausanias: Führer durch Olympia*. Zurich.

Mielsch, H. 1987. *Die römische Villa: Architektur und Lebensform*. Munich.

Migne, J.-P. 1857. *Patrologiae Cursus Completus. Patrologiae Graecae Tomus 6: S. Justinus [etc.]*. Paris.

Miliarakis, A. 1886. *Geografia politiki nea kai arkhaia tou Nomou Argolidhos kai Korinthias*. Athens.

Millar, F. 1964. *A Study of Cassius Dio*. Oxford.

Miller, D., M. Rowlands, and C. Tilley, eds. 1989. *Domination and Resistance*. London.

Miller, Stella G. 1983. "The early travellers, 1766–1883." In Cooper et al. 1983: 16–39.

Miller, Stephen G. 1983. "The archaeologists, 1884–1979." In Cooper et al. 1983: 40–49.

———. 1994. *The Ancient Stadium of Nemea: A Self-Guided Tour*. Walnut Creek, Calif.

———. ed. 1990. *Nemea: A Guide to the Site and Museum*. Berkeley.

Mills, Sara. 1991. *Discourses of Difference: An Analysis of Women's Travel Writing*. London.

Mills, Sophie. 1997. *Theseus, Tragedy and the Athenian Empire*. Oxford and New York.

Mitchell, W. J. T. 1994. "Imperial landscape." In *Landscape and Power*, ed. W. J. T. Mitchell, 5–34. Chicago.

Moffitt, J. F. 1997. "The Palestrina mosaic with a 'Nile scene': Philostratus and ekphrasis; Ptolemy and Chorographia." *Zeitschrift für Kunstgeschichte* 60: 227–47.

Moggi, M. 1996. "L'*Excursus* di Pausania sulla Ionia." In Bingen 1996: 79–116.

Moles, J. 1995. "Dio Chrysostom, Greece, and Rome." In Innes, Hine, and Pelling 1995: 177–92.

Morales, H. Forthcoming. *Vision and Narrative in Achilles Tatius.* Cambridge.

Morgan, C. 1990. *Athletes and Oracles: The Transformation of Olympia and Delphi in the Eighth Century B.C.* Cambridge.

Morinis, E. A. 1984. *Pilgrimage in the Hindu Tradition: A Case Study in West Bengal.* Delhi.

————, ed. 1992. *Sacred Journeys: The Anthropology of Pilgrimage.* New York.

Morris, S. P. 1992. *Daidalos and the Origins of Greek Art.* Princeton.

Müller, C. 1848. *Fragmenta Historicorum Graecorum.* Vol. 2. Paris.

————. 1851. *Fragmenta Historicorum Graecorum.* Vol. 4. Paris.

————. 1855. *Geographi Graeci Minores.* Vol. 1. Paris.

————. 1883. *Fragmenta Historicorum Graecorum.* Vol. 3. Paris.

M[urray], G. 1917. [Correspondence]. *CR* 31: 63–64.

Murray, J. 1845. *Handbook for Travellers in Greece.* 2d ed. London.

Murray, O. 1997. "The beginning of Greats, 1800–1872: II. Ancient History." In *The History of the University of Oxford, vol. 6, The Nineteenth Century,* pt. I, ed. M. G. Brock and M. C. Curthoys, 520–42. Oxford.

Murray, P., ed. 1996. *Plato on Poetry: "Ion," "Republic" 376e–398b, "Republic" 595–608b.* Cambridge.

Musti, D. 1989. *Storia greca: Linee di sviluppo dall'età micenea all'età romana.* Bari and Rome.

————. 1996. "La struttura del discorso storico in Pausania." In Bingen 1996: 9–43.

Musti, D., and M. Torelli. 1986. *Pausania, "Guida della Grecia," Libro II: "La Corinzia e l'Argolide."* Milan.

————. 1991a. *Pausania, "Guida della Grecia," Libro III: "La Laconia."* Milan. 2d ed., 1992.

————. 1991b. *Pausania, "Guida della Grecia," Libro IV: "La Messenia."* Milan.

Nachtergael, G. 1975. "Le catalogue des vaisseaux et la liste des Théorodoques de Delphes." In *Hommages à Claire Préaux,* ed. J. Bingen, G. Cambier, and G. Nachtergael, 45–55. Brussels.

Nagy, G. 1996. *Poetry as Performance: Homer and Beyond.* Cambridge.

Naiditch, P. G. 1991. "Classical studies in nineteenth-century Great Britain as background to the 'Cambridge ritualists.'" In Calder 1991a: 123–52.

N. C. 1934. "A great rector." *Stapeldon Magazine* VIII.54: 383–86.

Neils, J. 1987. *The Youthful Deeds of Theseus.* Rome.

Nelson, L. G. 1977. "The Rendering of Landscape in Greek and South Italian Vase Painting." Ph.D. diss., State University of New York, Binghamton.

"Nemo." 1891. Review of *Mythology and Monuments of Ancient Athens, being a translation of a portion of the "Attica" of Pausanias by M. de G. Verrall, with introductory essay and archaeological commentary by J. E. Harrison* (London and New York, 1890). *REG* 4: 410–11.

Neudecker, R. 1988. *Die Skulpturenausstattung römischer Villen in Italien.* Mainz.

Newton, C. 1880. "On the study of archaeology" (Oxford lecture, 1850). In *Essays on Art and Archaeology,* 1–38. London.

Nicolet, C. 1991. *Space, Geography, and Politics in the Early Roman Empire* (Jerome Lectures 19). Ann Arbor.

Nock, A. D. 1928. "Oracles théologiques." *REA* 30: 280–90. Reprinted in *Essays on Religion and the Ancient World,* vol. 1, ed. Z. Stewart, 160–68 (Oxford, 1972).

————. 1934. "A vision of Mandulis Aion." *Harvard Theological Review* 27: 53–104.

Reprinted in *Essays on Religion and the Ancient World*, vol. 1, ed. Z. Stewart, 357–400 (Oxford 1972).

Nora, P., ed. 1984–1992. *Les lieux de mémoire*. 3 vols. Paris.

Nörenberg, H. W. 1973. "Untersuchungen zum Schluß der *Periegesis tes Hellados* des Pausanias." *Hermes* 101: 235–52.

Noukhakis, I. E. 1901. *Elliniki Khorografia*. Athens.

Nutton, V. 1971. "Two notes on immunities: *Digest* 27, 1, 6, 10 and 11." *JRS* 61: 52–63.

Oakley, J. H., and R. H. Sinos. 1993. *The Wedding in Ancient Athens*. Madison.

Oberleitner, W. 1994. *Das Heroon von Trysa: Ein Lykisches Fürstengrab des 4. Jahrhunderts v. Chr.* Mainz. Also published in *Antike Welt, Zeitschrift für Archäologie und Kulturgeschichte* 25, Sondernummer.

Oliver, J. H. 1950. *The Athenian Expounders of the Sacred and Ancestral Law*. Baltimore.

Orlandos, A. K. 1976. "Neoterai erevnai en Messene (1957–73)." In *Neue Forschungen in griechischen Heiligtümern*, ed. U. Jantzen, 9–38. Tübingen.

Ousterhout, R., ed. 1990. *The Blessings of Pilgrimage* (Illinois Byzantine Studies 1). Urbana.

Pacifico, P. A. 1704. *Breve descrizzione Corografia del Peloponneso O' Morea*. Venice.

Packer, J. 1998. "*Mire exaedificavit:* Three recent books on Hadrian's Tiburtine villa." *Journal of Roman Archaeology* 11: 583–96.

Paganelis, S. 1891. *Peran tou Isthmou: Peloponnisiakai Entiposeis kai Anamniseis*. Athens.

Palagia, O. 1994. "Tyche at Sparta." *YaleBull*, 65–75.

Paley (Marshall), M. 1947. *What I Remember*. Cambridge.

Panayides, A. M. 1994. "Überlegungen zum Nilmosaik von Praeneste." *Hefte des archäologischen Seminars der Universität Bern* 15: 31–47.

Panayiotopoulos, V. 1985. *Plithismos kai Oikismoi tis Peloponnisou 13os–18os Aionas*. Athens.

Pandiri, T. A. 1985. "*Daphnis and Chloe*: The art of pastoral play." *Ramus* 14: 116–41.

Parke, H. W. 1985. *The Oracles of Apollo in Asia Minor*. London.

———. 1988. *Sibyls and Sibylline Prophecy in Classical Antiquity*. London and New York.

Parker, R. 1989. "Spartan religion." In Powell 1989: 142–72.

Pasquali, G. 1913. "Die schriftstellerische Form des Pausanias." *Hermes* 48: 161–223.

Paton, J. M. 1951. *Medieval and Renaissance Visitors to Greek Lands* (Gennadeion Monographs 3). Princeton.

Peacock, S. J. 1988. *Jane Ellen Harrison: The Mask and the Self*. New Haven and London.

Pearson, L. 1962. "The pseudo-history of Messenia and its authors." *Historia* 11: 397–426.

Perdrizet, P., and G. Lefebvre. 1919. *Les graffites grecs du Memnonion d'Abydos*. Nancy.

Perrin, E. 1994. "Héracleidès le Crétois à Athènes: Les plaisirs du tourisme culturel." *REG* 107: 192–202.

Peters, W. J. T. 1963. *Landscape in Romano-Campanian Mural Painting*. Assen.

Petrakos, V. C. 1968. *Ho Oropos kai to hieron tou Amphiaraou*. Athens.

Petrie, Sir C. 1960. *The Victorians*. London.

Pettersson, M. 1992. *Cults of Apollo in Sparta: The Hyakinthia, the Gymnopaidiai and the Karneia*. Stockholm.

Pfister, F., ed. 1951. *Die Reisebilder des Herakleides*. Vienna.

Philippson, A. 1892. *Der Peloponnes*. Berlin.

Phillips, K. M. 1968. "Perseus and Andromeda." *AJA* 72: 1–23.

Phinney, E., Jr. 1967. "Hellenistic painting and the poetic style of Apollonius." *Classical Journal* 62: 145–49.

Picard, C. 1922. *Éphèse et Clare: Recherches sur les sanctuaires et les cultes de l'Ionie du nord*. Paris.

Piccirillo, M. 1989. *Madaba: Le chiese e i mosaici*. Milan.

———. 1993. *The Mosaics of Jordan*. Amman.

Pirenne-Delforge, V. 1998a. "La notion de 'panthéon' dans la *Périégèse* de Pausanias." In Pirenne-Delforge 1998b: 129–48.

———, ed. 1998b. *Les panthéons des cités des origines à la "Périégèse" de Pausanias* (*Kernos* Supplément 8). Liège.

Pirenne-Delforge, V., and G. Purnelle. 1997. *Pausanias, "Periegesis": index verborum, liste de fréquence, index nominum*, 2 vols. (*Kernos* Supplément 5). Liège.

Plommer, H. 1955. Review of I. T. Hill, *The Ancient City of Athens: Its Topography and Monuments* (London, 1953). *JHS* 75: 186–87.

Pollitt, J. J. 1974. *The Ancient View of Greek Art: Criticism, History, and Terminology*. New Haven.

———. 1986. *Art in the Hellenistic Age*. Cambridge and New York.

Porter, D. 1991. *Haunted Journeys: Desire and Transgression in European Travel Writing*. Princeton.

Porter, J. I. 1992. "Hermeneutic lines and circles: Aristarchus and Crates on Homeric exegesis." In *Homer's Ancient Readers: The Greek Epic's Earliest Exegetes*, ed. R. Lamberton and J. J. Keaney, 67–114. Princeton.

———. 2000. *Nietzsche and the Philology of the Future*. Stanford.

———. 2001. "Des sons qu'on ne peut entendre: Cicéron, les 'κριτικοί,' et la tradition du sublime dans la critique littéraire." In *Cicéron et Philodème: La polémique en philosophie*, ed. C. Auvray-Assayas and D. Delattre, 315–41. Paris.

Pouqueville, F. C. H. L. 1826. *Voyage dans la Grece*. 2d ed. Paris.

Powell, A. 1988. *Athens and Sparta: Constructing Greek Political and Social History from 478 B.C*. London.

———. ed. 1989. *Classical Sparta: Techniques behind Her Success*. Norman.

Pozzi, E., ed. 1991. *Il Toro Farnese: La "montagna di marmo" tra Roma e Napoli*. Naples.

Pratt, M. L. 1992. *Imperial Eyes: Travel Writing and Transculturation*. London.

Preller, L. 1838. *Polemonis Periegetae Fragmenta*. Leipzig.

Pritchett, W. K. 1980. *Studies in Ancient Greek Topography*, vol. 3. Berkeley and London.

———. 1982. *Studies in Ancient Greek Topography*, vol. 4. Berkeley and London.

———. 1989. *Studies in Ancient Greek Topography*, vol. 6. Berkeley and London.

———. 1998. *Pausanias Periegetes*, vol. 1. Amsterdam.

———. 1999. *Pausanias Periegetes*, vol. 2. Amsterdam.

Prontera, F. 1985. "Pittura e cartografia." In *Ricerce di pittura ellenistica: Lettura e interpretazione della produzione pittorica dal IV secolo A.C. all' ellenismo. Quaderni dei Dialoghi di Archaeologia* 1: 137–38.

Puech, B. 1992. "Prosopographie des amis de Plutarque." *ANRW* II Principat, 33.6: 4831–93.

Pugliese Caratelli, G., ed. 1990. *Pompei: Pitture e mosaici*. Vol. 1, Regio I, Parte Prima. Rome.

Quadlbauer, F. 1958. "Die genera dicendi bis Plinius d. J." *Wiener Studien* 71: 55–111.

"R." 1890. Review of *Mythology and Monuments of Ancient Athens, being a translation of a portion of the "Attica" of Pausanias by M. de G. Verrall, with introductory essay and archaeological commentary by J. E. Harrison* (London and New York, 1890). *Oxford Magazine* 8: 393–94.

Raban, J. 1987. *For Love and Money: Writing, Reading, Travelling, 1969–1987*. London.

Rabe, H. 1913. *Hermogenis Opera*. Leipzig.

———. 1926. *Apthonii Progymnasmata*. Leipzig.

Ragkavis, I. P. 1853. *Ta Ellinika*. Athens.

Rapp, G. R., Jr., and S. E. Aschenbrenner, eds. 1978. *Excavations in Nichoria in Southwest Greece*, Vol. I: *Site, Environs, and Techniques*. Minneapolis.

Rawson, E. 1969. *The Spartan Tradition in European Thought*. Oxford. Reprinted Oxford, 1991.

Reade, J. E. 1980. "Space, scale, and significance in Assyrian art." *Baghdader Mitteilungen* 11: 71–74.

Reardon, B. P. 1971. *Courants littéraires grecs des IIe et IIIe siècles après J.-C.* Paris.

Regenbogen, O. 1956. "Pausanias." *RE Suppl.* 8: 1008–1097.

Reinach, S. 1892. "Exegetae." In *Dictionnaire des antiquités grecques et romaines*, vol. 2.1, ed. C. Daremberg and E. Saglio, 883–86. Paris.

R[ichards], G. C. 1890. Review of *Mythology and Monuments of Ancient Athens, being a translation of a portion of the "Attica" of Pausanias by M. de G. Verrall, with introductory essay and archaeological commentary by J. E. Harrison* (London and New York, 1890). *JHS* 11: 218–20.

Ridgway, B. S. 1971. "The setting of Greek sculpture." *Hesperia* 40: 336–56.

Riedweg, C. 1987. *Mysterienterminologie bei Plato, Philo and Klemens von Alexandria*. Berlin.

Robert, C. 1888. "Olympische Glossen." *Hermes* 23: 424–53.

———. 1890. *Homerische Becher* (Programm zum Winckelmannsfeste der Archaeologischen Gesellschaft zu Berlin, no. 50). Berlin.

———. 1909. *Pausanias als Schriftsteller: Studien und Beobachtungen*. Berlin.

Robert, J., and L. Robert. 1970. "Bulletin épigraphique." *REG* 83: 362–488.

Robert, L. 1955. "Inscriptions de Dardanelles." *Hellenica* 10: 266–82.

———. 1960. "Recherches épigraphiques." *REA* 62: 276–361.

———. 1969a. "Inscriptions." In *Laodicée du Lycos: Le nymphée. Campagnes 1961–1963 (Relevés et plans de Holger Schmidt, avec des études de Louis Robert et Xavier de Planhol)*, ed. J. Des Gagniers et al., 247–389. Quebec.

———. 1969b. "Recherches épigraphiques." In *Opera Minora Selecta*, vol. 2, 792–877. Amsterdam. Reprint of Robert 1960.

———. 1977. "Documents d'Asie Mineure." *BCH* 101: 43–132.

———. 1987. *Documents d'Asie Mineure*. Athens.

Robert, L., and J. Robert. 1954. *La Carie. Histoire et géographie historique avec le receuil des inscriptions antiques*. Vol. 2, *Le plateau de Tabai et ses environs*. Paris.

———. 1989. *Claros I: Décrets hellénistiques*. Paris.

Roberts, A., trans. 1994. *Knopf Guides: Greece*. New York.

Roberts, C. H., and T. C. Skeat. 1983. *The Birth of the Codex*. London.

Roberts, W. R. 1899. *Longinus on the Sublime*. Cambridge.

Robertson, G., M. Mash, L. Tickner, J. Bird, B. Curtis, and T. Putnam, eds. 1994. *Travellers' Tales: Narratives of Home and Displacement*. London.

Robinson, J. 1990. *Wayward Women: A Guide to Women Travellers*. Oxford.

Rocha-Pereira, M. H. 1989. *Pausaniae Graeciae Descriptio*. Teubner ed., 3 vols. Leipzig.

Roebuck, C. A. 1941. *A History of Messenia from 369 to 146 B.C.* Chicago.

Rogl, C. 1997. "Homerische Becher aus der Stadt Ellis." In *Δ'Επιστημονική Συνάντηση για την Ελληνιστική Κεραμική, Μυτιλήνη, Μάρτιος 1994*, 317–28. Athens.

Roobaert, A. 1977. "Le danger hilote?" *Ktema* 2: 141–55.

Rosaldo, R. 1989. *Culture and Truth: The Remaking of Social Analysis.* Boston.

Rose, H. J. 1934. "Obituary of L. R. Farnell." *CR* 48: 117.

———. 1941. "Obituary of J. G. Frazer." *CR* 55: 57–58.

Ross, L. 1851. *Wanderungen in Griechenland.* Halle.

Ross Holloway, R. 1967. "Panhellenism and the sculptures of the Zeus Temple at Olympia." *GRBS* 8: 93–101.

Roth, M., with C. Lyons and C. Merewether. 1997. *Irresistible Decay: Ruins Reclaimed* (Getty Research Institute for the History of Art and the Humanities, Bibliographies and Dossiers Series). Los Angeles.

Rotroff, S. I. 1982. *Hellenistic Pottery: Athenian and Imported Moldmade Bowls* (*The Athenian Agora* 22). Princeton.

Rougé, J. 1969. "'Ο Θειότατος Αὔγουστο." *Revue de philologie, de littérature et d'histoire anciennes* 71: 83–92.

Rouveret, A. 1989. *Histoire et imaginaire de la peinture ancienne* (*V siècle av. J.-C.– I siècle ap. J.-C.*). (Bibliothèque des Écoles Françaises d'Athènes et de Rome 274). Paris and Rome.

Roux, G. 1958. *Pausanias en Corinthie.* Paris.

Rubinstein, L. 1995. "Pausanias as a source for the Classical Greek polis." In Hansen and Raaflaub 1995: 211–19.

Russell, D. A. 1995. Introduction to *Longinus: "On the Sublime."* In *Aristotle: "Poetics,"* ed. and trans. S. Halliwell; *Longinus: "On the Sublime,"* trans. W. H. Fyfe, rev. D. A. Russell; *Demetrius: "On Style",* ed. and trans. D. C. Innes (Loeb Classical Library), 145–58. Cambridge, Mass.

———, ed. 1964. *Longinus, "On the Sublime."* Oxford.

———. 1992. *Dio Chrysostom: Orations vii, xii and xxxvi.* Cambridge.

Russell, D. A., and M. Winterbottom. 1989. *Classical Literary Criticism.* Oxford.

Ruston, A. R. 1984. *The Hibbert Trust: A History.* London.

Rutherford, I. 1998a. "Island of the extremity: Space, language, and power in the pilgrimage traditions of Philae." In *Pilgrimage and Holy-Space in Late Antique Egypt,* ed. D. Frankfurter, 229–56. Leiden.

———. 1998b. "*Theoria* as theatre: The pilgrimage theme in Greek literature." *Proceedings of the Leeds International Latin Seminar* 10: 131–56.

———. 2000. "*Theoria* and *Darshan*: Pilgrimage as gaze in Greece and India." *CQ* 50: 133–46.

———. Forthcoming. "To the land of Zeus: Patterns of pilgrimage in Aelius Aristides." *Aevum Antiquum.*

Said, E. 1983. *The World, the Text, and the Critic.* Cambridge, Mass.

Sandby, W. 1822. *The History of the Royal Academy of Arts.* Vol. 1. London.

Sanders, J. M., ed. 1992. *ΦΙΛΟΛΑΚΩΝ: Lakonian Studies in Honour of Hector Catling.* Oxford and Athens.

Sandys, J. E. 1887. *An Eastern Vacation in Greece.* London.

Saunders-Forster, C. G. 1887. *Beneath Parnassian Clouds and Olympian Sunshine.* London.

Schapiro, M. 1973. *Words and Pictures: On the Literal and the Symbolic in the Illustration of a Text.* The Hague.

Schefold, K. 1960. "Origins of Roman landscape painting." *Art Bulletin* 42: 87–96.

————. 1964. *Frühgriechische Sagenbilder*. Munich. English translation: *Myth and Legend in Early Greek Art* (London 1966).

————. 1978. *Götter- und Heldensagen der Griechen in der spätarchaischen Kunst.* Munich. English translation: *Gods and Heroes in Late Archaic Greek Art* (Cambridge 1992).

————. 1981. *Die Göttersage in der klassischen und hellenistischen Kunst*. Munich.

————. 1989. *Die Sagen von den Argonauten, von Theben und Troia in der klassischen und hellenistischen Kunst*. Munich.

————. 1993. *Götter- und Heldensagen der Griechen in der früh- und hoch- archaischen Kunst* (new ed. of Schefold 1964). Munich.

Schefold, K., and F. Jung. 1988. *Die Urkönige: Perseus, Bellerophon, Herakles und Theseus in der klassischen und hellenistischen Kunst*. Munich.

Schissel von Fleschenberg, O. 1913. "Die Technik des Bildeinsatzes." *Philologus* 72: 83–114.

Schlesier, R. 1991. "Prolegomena to Jane Harrison's interpretation of ancient Greek religion." In Calder 1991a: 185–226.

Schmidt, O. E. 1899. *Ciceros Villen* (Neue Jahrbucher für das klassische Altertum, Geschichte und deutsche Literatur). Leipzig. Reprinted Darmstadt, 1972.

Schmitz, T. 1997. *Bildung und Macht* (Zetemata 97). Munich.

Schneider, C. 1967. *Kulturgeschichte des Hellenismus*. Munich.

Schneider, W. J. 1997. "Ein kryptisches Denkmal in Zentrum des Pausanias-Perihegese." *Hermes* 125: 492–505.

Schuchhardt, C. 1891. *Schliemann's Excavations: An Archaeological and Historical Study, Translated by E. Sellers, with an Appendix on the Recent Discoveries at Hissarlik by Dr Schliemann and Dr Dörpfeld, and an Introduction by W. Leaf, Litt. D.* London. Reprinted Chicago, 1974.

Scott, J. C. 1985. *Weapons of the Weak: Everyday Forms of Peasant Resistance*. New Haven.

Scranton, R. L. 1951. *Corinth.* Vol. 1.3, *Monuments of the Lower Agora and North of the Archaic Temple*. Princeton.

Segal, C. 1959. "ὕψος and the problem of cultural decline in the *De Sublimitate*." *Harvard Studies in Classical Philology* 64: 121–46.

————. 1981. *Poetry and Myth in Ancient Pastoral*. Princeton.

————. 1987. "Writer as hero: The heroic ethos in Longinus, *On the Sublime*." In *Stemmata: Hommages à J. Labarbe*, ed. J. Servais, T. Hackens, and B. Servais-Soyez, 207–229. Brussels.

————. 1994. "Classical criticism and the canon, or, Why read the ancient critics?" In *Reading World Literature: Theory, History, Practice*, ed. S. Lawall, 87–112. Austin.

Selden, D. L. 1998. "Alibis." *Classical Antiquity* 17(2): 289–412.

Settis, S. 1968. "Il ninfeo di Erode Attico a Olimpia e il problema della composizione della "Periegesi" di Pausania." *Annali della Scuola Normale Superiore di Pisa* (ser. II) 37: 1–63.

————, ed. 1988. *La Colonna Traiana*. Turin.

Shanks, M. 1996. *Classical Archaeology of Greece: Experiences of the Discipline*. London.

Shapiro, A. 1992. "The marriage of Theseus and Helen." In *Kotinos: Festschrift für Erika Simon*, ed. H. Froning, T. Hölscher, and H. Mielsch, 232–36. Mainz.

Shaw, P. J. 1997. "Message to Sparta: The route of Pheidippides before Marathon." *Geographia Antiqua* 6: 53–75.

Shero, L. R. 1938. "Aristomenes the Messenian." *TAPA* 69: 500–531.

Shilleto, A. R. 1886. *Pausanias's "Description of Greece," Translated into English with Notes and Index*. London.

Shipley, G. 1992. "Perioikos: The discovery of classical Lakonia." in Sanders 1992: 211–26.

———. 1997. " 'The Other Lakedaimonians': The dependent Perioikic poleis of Laconia and Messenia." In Hansen 1997: 189–281.

Sidebottom, H. 1996. "Dio of Prusa and the Flavian dynasty." *CQ* 46.2: 447–56.

Sinn, U. 1979. *Die homerischen Becher: Hellenistische Reliefkeramik aus Makedonien* Mitteilungen des Deutschen Archäologischen Instituts, Athenische Abteilung, Beiheft 7). Berlin.

Small, J. P. 1997. *Wax Tablets of the Mind: Cognitive Studies in Memory and Literacy in Classical Antiquity*. London.

Smith, A. C. 1994. "Queens and empresses as goddesses: The public role of the personal tyche in the Graeco-Roman world." *YaleBull* 1994: 87–105.

Smith, R. R. R. 1981. "Greeks, foreigners, and Roman republican portraits." *JRS* 71: 24–38.

Snodgrass, A. M. 1980. *Archaic Greece: The Age of Experiment*. Berkeley.

———. 1986. "Interaction by design: The Greek city-state." In *Peer Polity Interaction and Sociopolitical Change*, ed. C. Renfrew and J. F. Cherry, 47–58. Cambridge.

———. 1987. *An Archaeology of Greece: The Present State and Future Scope of a Discipline*. Berkeley and Los Angeles.

———. 1988. "The archaeology of the hero." *Annali del Seminario di Studi del Mondo Classico, Sezione di Archeologia e Storia Antica, Napoli* 10: 19–26.

———. 1998. *Homer and the Artists: Text and Picture in Early Greek Art*. Cambridge.

Sourvinou-Inwood, C. 1990. "What is *polis* religion?" In *The Greek City from Homer to Alexander*, ed. O. Murray and S. Price, 295–322. Oxford.

Spawforth, A. J. S. 1989. "Agonistic festivals in Roman Greece." In *The Greek Renaissance in the Roman Empire: Papers from the Tenth British Museum Colloquium* (*BICS* Supplement 55), ed. S. Walker and A. Cameron, 193–97. London.

———. 1994. "Symbol of unity? The Persian-Wars tradition in the Roman empire." In Hornblower 1994: 233–47.

Spencer, A. J. 1993. *Early Egypt*. Norman.

Spencer, N. 1998. "The history of archaeological investigations in Messenia." In *Sandy Pylos: An Archaeological History from Nestor to Navarino*, ed. J. L. Davis, 23–41. Austin.

Spencer, T. 1954. *Fair Greece, Sad Relic: Literary Philhellenism from Shakespeare to Byron*. London.

Spengel, L. 1853–56. *Rhetores Graeci*. 3 vols. Leipzig.

Spier, J. 1989. "A group of Ptolemaic engraved garnets." *JWalt* 47: 21–38.

Stadter, P. 1995. " 'Subject to the erotic': Male sexual behaviour in Plutarch." In Innes, Hine, and Pelling 1995: 221–36.

Stanley, A. P. 1844. "Greek topography. Colonel Leake's *Topography of Athens* . . . Second edition, London 1841." *Classical Museum* 1: 41–81.

Starr, C. G. 1965. "The credibility of early Spartan history." *Historia* 14: 257–72. Reprinted in C. G. Starr, *Essays on Ancient History: A Selection of Articles and Reviews*, ed. A. Ferrill and T. Kelly (Leiden, 1979).

Steinmeyer-Schareika, A. 1978. *Das Nilmosaik von Palestrina und eine ptolemäische Expedition nach Äthiopien* (Habelts Dissertationsdrucke, Reihe klassische Archäologie 10). Bonn.

Stephanus, H. 1831–63. *Thesaurus Linguae Graecae*. Rev. ed. 8 vols. Paris.

Stewart, A. 1993. *Faces of Power: Alexander's Image and Hellenistic Politics.* Berkeley.

———. 1996a. "A hero's quest: Narrative and the Telephos Frieze." In Dreyfus and Schraudolph 1996–97, vol. 1: 39–52.

———. 1996b. "Reflections." In *Sexuality in Ancient Art,* ed. N. B. Kampen, 135–54. Cambridge and New York.

Stewart, J. G. 1959. *Jane Ellen Harrison: A Portrait from Letters.* London.

Stewart, S. 1984. *On Longing: Narratives of the Miniature, the Gigantic, the Souvenir, the Collection.* Durham, N.C. Reprinted Baltimore, 1993.

Stibbe, C. M. 1989. "Beobachtungen zur Topographie des antiken Spartas." *BABesch* 64: 61–94.

Stone, D. L., and A. Kampke. 1998. "Dialiskari: A Late Roman villa on the Messenian coast." In *Sandy Pylos: An Archaeological History from Nestor to Navarino,* ed. J. L. Davis, 192–98. Austin.

Stoneman, R. 1987. *Land of Lost Gods: The Search for Classical Greece.* Norman

Strasburger, H. 1966. *Die Wesensbestimmung der Geschichte durch die antike Geschichtsschreibung.* Wiesbaden.

Stray, C. 1998. *Classics Transformed: Schools, Universities, and Society in England, 1830–1960.* Oxford.

Strid, O. 1976. *Über Sprache und Stil des "Periegeten" Pausanias* (Acta Universitatis Upsaliensis, Studia Graeca Upsaliensia 9). Uppsala.

Stuart, J., and N. Revett. 1762–1816. *The Antiquities of Athens.* 4 vols. London.

Stuart Jones, H. 1894. "The Chest of Kypselos." *JHS* 14: 30–80.

Summerson, J. N. 1963. "The vision of J. M. Gandy." In *Heavenly Mansions and Other Essays on Architecture,* by J. N. Summerson, 111–34. New York.

Sutton, S. B. 1988. "What is a 'village' in a nation of migrants?" *Journal of Modern Greek Studies* 6: 187–215.

———. 1994. "Settlement patterns, settlement perceptions: Rethinking the Greek village." In *Beyond the Site: Regional Studies in the Aegean Area,* ed. N. P. Kardulias, 313–35. Lanham, Md.

———. 1995a. "Crumbling walls and bare foundations: The process of housing in Greece." In *Constructed Meanings: Form and Process in Greek Architecture,* ed. E. Pavlides and S. B. Sutton. *Modern Greek Studies Yearbook* 11: 319–44.

———. 1995b. "The perception and making of an ancient site: The accounts of travellers, farmers, and archaeologists in nineteenth-century Nemea." *Simeion Anaforas (Point of Reference)* 3: 14–21.

———. 1997. "Disconnected landscapes: Ancient sites, travel guides, and local identity in modern Greece." *Anthropology of Eastern Europe Review* 15: 27–34.

Swain, S. 1991. "Plutarch, Hadrian, and Delphi." *Historia* 40.3: 318–30.

———. 1996. *Hellenism and Empire: Language, Classicism, and Power in the Greek World,* A.D. *50–250.* Oxford.

Swift, E. H. 1951. *Roman Sources of Christian Art.* New York.

Symeonoglou, S. 1985. *The Topography of Thebes from the Bronze Age to Modern Times.* Princeton.

Symonds, R. 1986. *Oxford and Empire.* Basingstoke.

Szelest, H. 1953. *De Pausaniae Clausulis* (Auctarium Maeandreum 3). Warsaw.

Tait, A. A. 1993. *Robert Adam: Drawings and Imagination.* Cambridge.

Talbert, R. 1989. "The role of the helots in the class struggle at Sparta." *Historia* 38: 22–40.

Tarbell, F. B. 1890. Review of *Mythology and Monuments of Ancient Athens, being a translation of a portion of the "Attica" of Pausanias by M. de G. Verrall, with introductory essay and archaeological commentary by J. E. Harrison* (London and New York, 1890). *CR* 4: 430–32.

Taylor, T., trans. 1794. *The "Description of Greece" by Pausanias*. London.

Televantou, C. 1994. Ακρωτήρι Θήρας · Οι Τοιχογραφίες της Δυτικής Οικίας. Athens.

Themelis, P. G. 1993. "Damophon von Messene: Sein Werk im Lichte der neuen Ausgrabungen." *Antike Kunst* 36: 24–40.

———. 1994a. "Artemis Ortheia at Messene: The epigraphical and archaeological evience." In *Ancient Greek Cult Practice from the Epigraphical Evidence*, ed. R. Hägg, 101–122. Stockholm.

———. 1994b. "Damophon of Messene: New evidence." In *Archaeology in the Peloponnese: New Excavations and Research*, ed. K. A. Sheedy, 1–37. Oxford.

Théodoridès, A. 1989. "Pèlerinage au Colosse de Memnon." *Chronique d'Égypte* 64: 267–82.

Thompson, H. A., and R. E. Wycherley. 1972. *The Agora of Athens: The History, Shape, and Uses of an Ancient City Center* (Agora 14). Princeton.

Thrower, N. J. W. 1996. *Maps and Civilization: Cartography in Culture and Society*. Rev. ed. Chicago.

Tobin, J. 1997. *Herodes Attikos and the City of Athens: Patronage and Conflict under the Antonines*. Amsterdam.

Tod, M. N. 1957. "Sidelights on Greek philosophers." *JHS* 77: 132–41.

Torelli, M. 1982. *Typology and Structure of Roman Historical Reliefs*. Ann Arbor.

———. Forthcoming. "Pausania a Corinto." In Aupert and Knoepfler, forthcoming.

Torelli, M., and D. Musti. 1991a. "Commento." In Musti and Torelli 1991b: 203–72.

———. 1991b. "Nota introduttiva al Libro IV." In Musti and Torelli 1991b: ix–xxviii.

Totti, M. 1985. *Ausgewählte Texte der Isis- und Sarapis-Religion*. Hildesheim.

Tozer, Rev. H. F. 1887. [Review] Two Books on Pausanias: *Pausanias' Description of Greece*, translated into English, with Notes and Index, by Arthur Richard Shilleto. Two Vols. George Bell and Sons. 1886. 10 shillings; *Pausanias der Perieget;* Untersuchungen über seine Schriftstellerei und seine Quellen, von Dr. A. Kalkmann. Berlin, Reimer. 1886. 8 Mk. *CR* 1:101–103.

Travlos, J. 1971. *Pictorial Dictionary of Ancient Athens*. London.

Trendelenburg, A. 1914. *Pausanias in Olympia*. Berlin.

Tresp, A. 1914. *Die Fragmente der griechischen Kultschriftsteller*. Giessen.

Treves, P. 1944. "The problem of a history of Messenia." *JHS* 64: 102–106.

Tsigakou, F.-M. 1981. *The Rediscovery of Greece: Travellers and Painters of the Romantic Era*. London and New Rochelle, N.Y.

Turner, F. M. 1984. *The Greek Heritage in Victorian Britain*. New Haven.

Tybout, R. A. 1989. *Aedificiorum Figurae: Untersuchungen zu den Architekturdarstellungen des frühen zweiten Stils*. Amsterdam.

Valmin, M. N. 1930. *Études topographiques sur la Messénie ancienne*. Lund.

———. 1938. *The Swedish Messenia Expedition*. Lund.

van Bremen, R. 1996. *The Limits of Participation: Women and Civic Life in the Greek East in the Hellenistic and Roman Periods*. Amsterdam.

Van den Abbeele, G. 1992. *Travel as Metaphor: From Montaigne to Rousseau*. Minneapolis.

Vanderpool, E. 1949. "The route of Pausanias in the Athenian Agora." *Hesperia* 18: 128–37.

van Dommelen, P. 1998. *On Colonial Grounds: A Comparative Study of Colonialism and Rural Settlement in First Millennium B.C. West Central Sardinia*. Leiden.

van Nortwick, T. 1992. *Somewhere I Have Never Travelled*. New York and Oxford.

van Paassen, C. 1957. *The Classical Tradition of Geography*. Groningen.

Vatin, C. 1981. "Monuments votifs de Delphes." *BCH* 105: 429–59.

Vermeule, C. C. 1995. "Neon Ilion and Ilium Novum: Kings, soldiers, citizens and tourists at Classical Troy." In *The Ages of Homer: A Tribute to Emily Townsend Vermeule*, ed. J. B. Carter and S. P. Morris, 467–82. Austin.

Vernant, J.-P. 1969. "Hestia-Hermes: The religious expression of space and movement among the Greeks." *Social Science Information* 8.4: 131–68.

———. 1991. *Mortals and Immortals: Collected Essays*. Ed. F. I. Zeitlin. Princeton.

Versakis, F. 1916. "To ieron tou Korynthou Apollonos." *Archaiologikon Deltion* 2: 65–118.

Veyne, P. 1983. *Les Grecs ont-ils cru à leurs mythes? Essai sur l'imagination constituante*. Paris.

———. 1988a. "Conduct without belief and works of art without viewers." *Diogenes* 143: 1–22.

———. 1988b. *Did the Greeks Believe in Their Myths? An Essay on the Constitutive Imagination*. Trans. P. Wissing. Chicago and London.

———. 1991. *La société romaine*. Paris.

von Blanckenhagen, P. H. 1957. "Narration in Hellenistic and Roman art." *AJA* 61: 78–83.

———. 1963. "The Odyssey Frieze." *RM* 70: 106–43.

———. 1968. "Daedalus and Icarus on Pompeian walls." *RM* 75: 106–43.

von Hartel, W. R., and F. Wickhoff, eds. 1895. *Die Wiener Genesis*. Vienna.

von Hesberg, H. 1988. "Bildsyntax und Erzählweise in der hellenistischen Flächenkunst." *JdI* 103: 309–365.

von Massow, W. 1916. "Die Kypseloslade." *AM* 41: 1–117.

von Steuben, H. 1968. *Frühe Sagendarstellungen in Korinth und Athen*. Berlin.

Wagner, A. 1967. *Heralds of England*. London.

Wagstaff, J. M. 1992. "Colonel Leake in Laconia." In Sanders 1992: 277–83.

Walbank, F. W. 1948. "The geography of Polybius." *Classica et mediaevalia: Revue danoise de philologie et d'histoire* 9: 155–82.

Walker, H. J. 1995. *Theseus and Athens*. New York.

Wallace-Hadrill, A. 1994. *Houses and Society in Pompeii and Herculaneum*. Princeton.

Waugh, E. 1946. *When the Going Was Good*. London.

Waywell, G., and J. Wilkes. 1995. "Excavations at the ancient theatre of Sparta 1992–4: Preliminary report." *BSA* 90: 435–60.

Waywell, G., J. Wilkes, and S. Walker. 1999. "The ancient theatre at Sparta." In Cavanagh and Walker 1999: 97–111.

Webb, R. 1997. "Mémoire et imagination: Les limites de l'*enargeia* dans la théorie rhétorique grecque." In *Dire l'évidence (philosophie et rhétorique antiques)*, ed. C. Lévy and L. Pernot, 229–48. Paris.

Wegener, S. 1985. *Funktion und Bedeutung landschaftlicher Elemente in der griechischen Reliefkunst archaischer bis hellenistischer Zeit*. Frankfurt, Bern, and New York.

Wegner, M. 1931. "Die Kunstgeschichtliche Stellung der Marcussäule." *JdI* 46: 61–174.

Weitzmann, K. 1947. *Illustrations in Roll and Codex: A Study of the Origin and Method of Text Illustration*. Princeton.

———. 1948. *The Joshua Roll: A Work of the Macedonian Renaissance*. Princeton.

———. 1959. *Ancient Book Illumination* (Martin Classical Lectures 16). Cambridge, Mass.

West, F. 1984. *Gilbert Murray: A Life*. London.

West, M. 1995. " 'Longinus' and the grandeur of God." In Innes, Hine, and Pelling 1995: 335–42.

Whitby, M. 1994. "Two shadows: Images of Spartans and helots." In *The Shadow of Sparta*, ed. A. Powell and S. Hodkinson, 87–126.

Whitmer, P. O. 1993. *When the Going Gets Weird: The Twisted Life and Times of Hunter S. Thompson*. New York.

Whittaker, H. 1991. "Pausanias and his use of inscriptions." *Symbolae Osloenses* 66: 171–86.

Wickhoff, F. 1900. *Roman Art: Some of Its Principles and Their Application to Early Christian Art*. Trans. and ed. E. Strong. London and New York.

Wilamowitz, U. von. 1877. "Die Thucydideslegende." *Hermes* 12: 326–67.

Wilkins, W. 1816. *Atheniensia or Remarks on the Topography and Buildings of Athens*. London.

Williams, M. F. 1991. *Landscape in the "Argonautica" of Apollonius Rhodius* (Studien zur klassischen Philologie 63). Frankfurt, Bern, and New York.

Wilson, D. 1987. *Gilbert Murray O.M., 1866–1957*. Oxford.

Wilson, J. B. 1979. *Pylos 425 B.C.: A Historical and Topographical Study of Thucydides' Account of the Campaign*. Warminster.

Winter, F. E. 1971. *Greek Fortifications* (*Phoenix* Supplement 9). Toronto.

Winterbottom, M. W., ed. 1971. *Seneca, Controversiae and Suasoriae*. Cambridge, Mass., and London.

Wirth, T. 1983. "Zum Bildprogramm der Räume n und p in der Casa dei Vettii." *RM* 90: 449–55.

Wiseman, J. R. 1978. *The Land of the Ancient Corinthians* (Studies in Mediterranean Archaeology 50). Göteborg.

Wolf, F. A. 1985. *Prolegomena to Homer, 1795*. Trans. A. Grafton, G. W. Most, and J. E. G. Zetzel. Princeton.

Wood, R. 1753. *The Ruins of Palmyra, Otherwise Tedmor, in the Desert*. London.

———. 1758. *The Ruins of Baalbec, Otherwise Heliopolis in Coelosyria*. London.

Woolf, G. 1994. "Becoming Roman, staying Greek: Culture, identity and the civilizing process in the Roman East." *PCPS* 40: 116–43.

Wordsworth, C. 1836. *Athens and Attica: Journal of a Residence There*. London.

———. 1839. *Greece, A Descriptive, Historical and Pictorial Account*. London. Rev. ed. by H. F. Tozer, 1882.

Wright, J. C., J. F. Cherry, J. L. Davis, E. Mantzourani, S. B. Sutton, and R. F. Sutton Jr. 1990. "The Nemea Valley Archaeological Project: A preliminary report." *Hesperia* 59: 579–659.

Wycherley, R. E. 1935. *Pausanias, "Description of Greece": Companion Volume to the Loeb Edition*. Vol. 5. Cambridge, Mass. Rev. ed., Cambridge, Mass. 1955.

———. 1959. "Pausanias in the Agora of Athens." *GRBS* 2: 23–44.

———. 1978. *The Stones of Athens*. Princeton.

Yates, F. 1966. *The Art of Memory*. London.

Young, J. E. 1993. *The Texture of Memory: Holocaust Memorials and Meaning*. New Haven.

Zacharakis, C. G. 1992. *A Catalogue of Printed Maps of Greece, 1477–1800*. 2d ed. Athens.

Zanker, P. 1979. "Die Villa als Vorbild des späten pompejanischen Wohngeschmacks." *JdI* 94: 460–523.

———. 1998. *Pompeii: Public and Private Life*. Trans. D. L. Schneider. Cambridge, Mass.

Zecchini, G. 1991. "Teoria e prassi del viaggio in Polibio." In *Idea e realtà del viaggio: Il viaggio nel mondo antico*, ed. G. Camassa and S. Fasce, 111–41. Genoa.

Zeitlin, F. I. 1994. "The artful gaze: Vision, ekphrasis and spectacle in Euripidean theatre." In *Art and Text in Ancient Greek Culture*, ed. S. Goldhill and R. Osborne, 138–96. Cambridge.

Žižek, S. 1989. *The Sublime Object of Ideology*. London.

———. 1991. "Grimaces of the real, or When the phallus appears." *October* 58: 45–68.

Contributors

SUSAN E. ALCOCK is Associate Professor of Classical Archaeology and Classics, and Arthur F. Thurnau Professor at the University of Michigan. She is the author of *Graecia Capta: The Landscapes of Roman Greece* (1993) and the editor or co-editor of *Placing the Gods: Sanctuaries and Sacred Space in Ancient Greece* (1994), *The Early Roman Empire in the East* (1997), and *Empires* (2001). Her current work includes a book entitled *A Matrix for Memory: Landscape, Monuments, and the Greek Past*, articles on landscape archaeology and the early imperial east, and publication of fieldwork in Messenia.

STEPHEN BANN has recently moved from the University of Kent to take up a new chair of History of Art at the University of Bristol. He is the author of *The Clothing of Clio* (1984), *The True Vine* (1989), *The Inventions of History* (1990), *Under the Sign: John Bargrave as Collector, Traveler and Witness* (1994), and *Romanticism and the Rise of History* (1995). His most recent work has been on French nineteenth-century painting and visual culture, including *Paul Delaroche: History Painted* (1997) and a forthcoming study of the relationship between printmaking, painting and photography entitled *Parallel Lines*.

MARY BEARD teaches Classics at Cambridge (U.K.), and is a Fellow of Newnham College. She is co-author of *Classics: A Very Short Introduction* (1995), *Religions of Rome* (1998), and author of *The Invention of Jane Harrison* (2000).

BETTINA BERGMANN, Associate Professor of Art at Mount Holyoke College, teaches ancient art and environmental studies. Her research sheds light on the enhancement of domestic space through scenes painted on the walls of Roman houses, and the role that women (both real and mythological) played in that domestic space. She has written several articles on Roman landscape, co-edited *The Art of Ancient Spectacle* (1999), and guest curated an exhibition on the "visual afterlife" of the empress Faustina the Elder (1999).

EWEN BOWIE is E. P. Warren Praelector in Classics at Corpus Christi College, Oxford, and Reader in Classical Languages and Literature in the University of Oxford. He has made a number of contributions to the study of early Greek elegiac and iambic poetry, Attic comedy, and Hellenistic poetry, but the majority of his work has been on the Greek literature and society of the high Roman empire. His articles in this field have discussed the writings of many central authors (among them Pausanias, Philostratus, and Heliodorus) and addressed the place of sophistic rhetoric, prose writing, and poetry in Imperial Greek society as a whole. He is currently completing a commentary on Longus, *Daphnis and Chloe*.

PAUL CARTLEDGE is Professor of Greek History in the University of Cambridge and a Fellow of Clare College. He is the author, co-author, editor, or co-editor of nine books, including three on Spartan history. The most recent are *The Cambridge Illustrated History of Ancient Greece* (1998) and *Democritus and Atomistic Politics* (1998). He is currently preparing for publication a collection of his Spartan essays and a history of Greek political thought.

JOHN F. CHERRY is Professor of Classical Archaeology and Greek at the University of Michigan, where he directs the Interdepartmental Program in Classical Art and Archaeology. He co-edits the *Journal of Mediterranean Archaeology* and is co-author or co-editor of eight books, including *Peer Polity Interaction and Sociopolitical Change* (1986), *Landscape Archaeology as Long-Term History* (1991), and *Provenance Studies and Bronze Age Cyprus* (1994). Pausanias links several of his interests, including Greek prehistory, regional archaeological survey, landscape archaeology, and travel writing, past and present.

ADA COHEN is Associate Professor of Art History at Dartmouth College. She is the author of *The Alexander Mosaic: Stories of Victory and Defeat* (1997) and has published articles on Greek art of the Classical and Hellenistic periods. She is currently completing a book on the imagery of battle, hunt, and abduction in late Classical and Hellenistic art and culture.

JAŚ ELSNER is Humfry Payne Senior Research Fellow in Classical Art and Archaeology at Corpus Christi College, Oxford, and was previously Lecturer and then Reader in the History of Art at the Courtauld Institute, University of London. He is the author of *Art and the Roman Viewer* (1995) and *Imperial Rome and Christian Triumph* (1998), co-author of *Pilgrimage Past and Present in the World Religions* (1995), editor of *Art and Text in Roman Culture* (1996), and co-editor of *Reflections of Nero* (1994), *The Cultures of Collecting* (1994), and *Voyages and Visions: Towards a Cultural History of Travel* (1999). Many of his various interests—ancient writing about art, the ancient viewing of images, the history of travel writing and of pilgrimage—intersect in the *Periegesis* of Pausanias.

JOHN HENDERSON is Reader in Latin Literature, University of Cambridge, and Fellow of King's College. His books include *Figuring out Roman Nobility:*

Juvenal's Eighth Satire (1997), *Fighting for Rome* (1998), *A Roman Life: Rutilius Gallicus on Paper and in Stone* (1998), *Juvenal's Mayor: The Professor Who Lived on 2ᴰ a Day* (1998), and *Writing Down Rome* (1999). He is co-author of *Classics: A Very Short Introduction* (1995) and *Classical Art: Greece through Rome* (forthcoming).

C. P. JONES is George Martin Lane Professor of Classics and History at Harvard University. He is the translator of Philostratus, *Life of Apollonius of Tyana* (1971) and the author of *Plutarch and Rome* (1971), *The Roman World of Dio Chrysostom* (1978), *Culture and Society in Lucian* (1986), and *Kinship Diplomacy in the Ancient World* (1999). He is the co-editor of Louis Robert, *Le martyre de Pionios, prêtre de Smyrne* (1994).

DAVID KONSTAN is the John Rowe Workman Distinguished Professor of the Classics and Professor of Comparative Literature at Brown University. He has published *Roman Comedy* (1983), *Greek Comedy and Ideology* (1994), *Sexual Symmetry: Love in the Ancient Novel and Related Genres* (1995), and *Friendship in the Classical World* (1997). He has also translated Simplicius's commentary on Book 6 of Aristotle's *Physics* (1989) and, along with other colleagues, Philodemus's essay *On Frank Criticism* (1998). He is currently working on a book on pity and compassion in the Classical world.

JAMES I. PORTER is Associate Professor of Greek, Latin, and Comparative Literature at the University of Michigan. He is the author of *Nietzsche and the Philology of the Future* (2000) and *The Invention of Dionysus: An Essay on The Birth of Tragedy* (2000), editor of *Constructions of the Classical Body* (1999), and co-editor of Philodemus, *On Poems, Book 5* (in progress). He has written on Classical and modern literature, philosophy, and literary theory. His current projects include *The Material Sublime,* a book on noncanonical aesthetic theory in ancient Greece and Rome and *What Is "Classical" about Classical Antiquity?* a study on the problem of classicism.

IAN RUTHERFORD is Professor of Greek at Reading University. His major research interests are Greek lyric poetry, papyrology, the religions of the ancient world, especially pilgrimage, the demotic literature of Egypt, and the cultures and religions of ancient Anatolia. He is the author of *Pindar's Paeans: A Reading of the Fragments with a Survey of the Genre* (forthcoming) and of numerous articles on Greek poetry and religion.

A. M. SNODGRASS studied classics, ancient history, and philosophy at Oxford and taught for fifteen years at the University of Edinburgh. Since 1976 he has been Laurence Professor of Classical Archaeology at the University of Cambridge. His books include *Early Greek Armour and Weapons* (1964), *The Dark Age of Greece* (1971), *Archaic Greece* (1980), *An Archaeology of Greece: The Present State and Future Scope of a Discipline* (1987), and *Homer and the Artists* (1998). He has been active in intensive archaeological survey in Greece, co-directing a long-term project in Boeotia.

SUSAN BUCK SUTTON is Professor of Anthropology at Indiana University—Purdue University at Indianapolis. She is the editor of the *Journal of Modern Greek Studies* and publishes on migration, settlement, and the construction of community in modern Greek life. She is co-author or co-editor of *Landscape and People of the Franchthi Region* (1987), *Constructed Meaning: Form and Process in Greek Architecture* (1995), and *Contingent Countryside: Settlement, Economy and Land Use in the Southern Argolid since 1700* (2000).

MARIO TORELLI is Professor of Archaeology and History of Greek and Roman Art in the University of Perugia (Italy). He is the author of a number of articles and books on Roman and Etruscan art and civilization, on the romanization of Italy, and on the *Periegesis* of Pausanias, including *Typology and Structure of Roman Historical Reliefs* (1982), *Studies on the Romanization of Italy* (1995), and *Tota Italia: Essays in the Cultural Formation of Roman Italy* (1999).

J. M. WAGSTAFF is Professor Emeritus and Visiting Professor in the Department of Geography, University of Southampton. He is the author of *The Evolution of Middle Eastern Landscapes* (1985) and co-editor of *An Island Polity: The Archaeology of Exploitation in Melos* (1982). His *Atlas of Modern Greece: Boundaries and Sovereignty, 1820–1994* is with the publisher. He is currently completing his biography of Colonel Leake (1777–1860), the topographer of Classical Greece, and researching the geography of the Morea/Peloponnese during the Venetian occupation of ca. 1684–1715.

Index of Cited Passages in Pausanias

General Index